Equity and Full Participation for Individuals with Severe Disabilities

Equity and Full Participation for Individuals with Severe Disabilities

A Vision for the Future

edited by

Martin Agran, Ph.D.
University of Wyoming, Laramie

Fredda Brown, Ph.D.
Queens College, City University of New York, Queens

Carolyn Hughes, Ph.D.
Queens College, City University of New York, Queens

Carol Quirk, Ed.D.
Maryland Coalition for Inclusive Education, Hanover

and

Diane Ryndak, Ph.D.
University of Florida, Gainesville

·P A U L·H·
BROOKES
PUBLISHING CO.®

Baltimore • London • Sydney

Paul H. Brookes Publishing Co.
Post Office Box 10624
Baltimore, Maryland 21285-0624

www.brookespublishing.com

Typeset by Auburn Associates, Inc., Baltimore, Maryland.
Manufactured in the United States of America by
Sheridan Books, Inc., Chelsea, Michigan.

All royalties from the sale of this book will be donated to TASH.

Individuals described in this book are real people or composites based on
the authors' experiences. Real names and identifying details used by permission.

Library of Congress Cataloging-in-Publication Data

Equity and full participation for individuals with severe disabilities: a vision for the future / edited
   by Martin Agran, Ph.D., Fredda Brown, Ph.D., Carolyn Hughes, Ph.D., Carol Quirk, Ed.D., and
   Diane Ryndak, Ph.D.
      pages   cm
   Includes bibliographical references and index.
   ISBN-13: 978-1-59857-270-4 (pbk.)
   ISBN-10: 1-59857-270-9 (pbk.)
   1. People with disabilities.   2. People with disabilities—Education.   3. People with disabilities—
   Services for.   I. Agran, Martin.
   HV1568.A135 2014
   362.4—dc23   2013022917

British Library Cataloguing in Publication data are available from the British Library.

2018   2017   2016   2015   2014   2014

10   9   8   7   6   5   4   3   2   1

Contents

About the Online Companion Materials

Attention instructors! PowerPoints are available to help you teach a course using *Equity and Full Participation for Individuals with Severe Disabilities*. Please visit http://www.brookespublishing.com/agran to access customizable PowerPoint presentations for Chapters 1–18, totaling more than 300 slides.

About the Editors

Martin Agran, Ph.D., Professor, Department of Professional Studies (Special Education Program), University of Wyoming, Department 3374, 1000 East University Avenue, Laramie, Wyoming 82071

Dr. Agran received his Ph.D. from the University of Illinois at Urbana-Champaign. He has published numerous articles or chapters and has authored or edited 13 books. Dr. Agran served as a Fulbright Scholar in the Czech Republic and has guest lectured in Australia, Russia, and South Korea. His research interests include self-determination, secondary-level education for students with severe disabilities, and personnel preparation. He was the recipient of numerous awards, including Outstanding Research and Scholarship Award (University of Wyoming), Outstanding Research Award (Council for Exceptional Children, Division on Developmental Disabilities), Donald McKay Outstanding Faculty Research Award (University of Northern Iowa), Thomas Haring Research Award (TASH), and *JASH* Distinguished Reviewer (TASH). He is Editor-in-Chief of *Research and Practice for Persons with Severe Disabilities* and is a member of the TASH National Board of Directors.

Fredda Brown, Ph.D., Professor of Special Education, Educational and Community Programs, Queens College, City University of New York, 65-30 Kissena Boulevard, Queens, New York 11367

Dr. Brown received her Ph.D. from the University of Kansas. She is Director of the Queens College Regional Center for Autism Spectrum Disorders. Dr. Brown is the editor of five books and the author of numerous journal articles and book chapters relating to education of individuals with severe disabilities. She is past Editor-in-Chief of *Research and Practice for Persons with Severe Disabilities (RPSD)* and currently serves on several editorial boards, including the *Journal of Positive Behavior Interventions* and *RPSD*. She has sat on the National Board of Directors of the Association for Positive Behavior Supports and TASH. She presents her work and ideas nationwide to professionals and families, advocating for positive, dignified, and effective methods of addressing the learning and behavioral needs of individuals with disabilities.

Carolyn Hughes, Ph.D., Visiting Professor, Queens College, City University of New York, 65-30 Kissena Boulevard, Queens, New York 11367

Dr. Hughes is Project Director of the Supports Intensity Scale–Children at the Research Foundation and Queens College of the City University of New York (CUNY). Before joining CUNY in the fall of 2012, Dr. Hughes was Professor of Special Education at Vanderbilt University. She received her Ph.D. from the University of Illinois at Urbana-Champaign. Dr. Hughes has published numerous books, chapters, and articles addressing social interaction and self-directed learning skills among high school students with disabilities and their peers and improving outcomes for youth from high-poverty backgrounds. She is an editorial board member of many journals in the developmental disabilities field, including the *American Journal on Intellectual and Developmental Disabilities,* and is Associate Editor of *Research and Practice for Persons with Severe Disabilities.* In 2012, she received the Education Award from the American Association on Intellectual and Developmental Disabilities (AAIDD) and was designated as a Fellow of AAIDD in 2013.

Carol Quirk, Ed.D., Co-executive Director, Maryland Coalition for Inclusive Education, 7484 Candlewood Road, Suite R, Hanover, Maryland 20176

Dr. Quirk directs the professional development services of the Maryland Coalition for Inclusive Education (MCIE). Before founding MCIE, she was Executive Director of a supported employment agency for adults with developmental disabilities, Adjunct Faculty at The Johns Hopkins University, Director of a North Carolina Technical Assistance Project for early intervention services, a psychologist at a regional residential center, and teacher of students with severe disabilities in Connecticut. She received her Ed.D. from The Johns Hopkins University. Dr. Quirk was a member of the National Board of Directors and Past President of TASH and is currently a member of the President's Committee for People with Intellectual Disabilities. She has provided consultation to Russia, Vietnam, and Trinidad and Tobago related to including students with disabilities and transition planning; she serves as an expert witness on issues related to inclusive education and positive behavioral supports; and she has provided consultation and strategic planning for other nonprofit organizations. Dr. Quirk was a winner of the Top 100 Minority/Women Business Entrepreneurs in 2008 for the mid-Atlantic region and was recognized by the National Academy of Public Administration Standing Panel of Social Equity for her community service. In 2012, she received the Distinguished Alumna Award from The Johns Hopkins University.

Diane Ryndak, Ph.D., Professor, School of Special Education, School Psychology, and Early Childhood Studies, University of Florida, 618 S.W. 12th Street, Post Office Box 117050, 1403 Norman Hall, Gainesville, Florida 32611

Dr. Ryndak received her Ph.D. from the University of Illinois at Urbana-Champaign. She is the author or coauthor of numerous articles, chapters, and books and co-editor of two compendia of TASH articles most frequently used by institutions of higher education. Several of her articles have been republished in the compendia and in international journals, and one of her books has been republished in Japan. Dr. Ryndak served as a Fulbright Research Scholar in Poland, where she returns frequently to work with colleagues at The Maria Grzegorzewska Academy for Special Education in Warsaw and across Poland. She has represented the U.S. Department of State with efforts related to the inclusion of citizens with disabilities in all aspects of life in the Ukraine; conducted over 30 international presentations; and guest lectured in Turkey, Peru, Sweden, and the United Kingdom. Her body of work focuses on inclusive education and access to the general curriculum for students with extensive support needs, student outcomes achieved by inclusive services, pre-service teacher preparation, and technical assistance for sustainable school reform efforts related to inclusive education. Dr. Ryndak has served multiple terms as a member of and Secretary for the TASH National Board of Directors and as the chair of the TASH Publications Committee, National Agenda Committee on Inclusive Education, Conference Committee, International Issues Committee, and Personnel Preparation Committee. She has served as Associate Editor for *Research and Practice for Persons with Severe Disabilities (RPSD)* and as a member of the editorial or review board for seven peer-reviewed professional journals, including *RPSD, American Journal on Intellectual and Developmental Disabilities, Journal of Ethnographic and Qualitative Research,* and *Teacher Education and Special Education.*

Contributors

Linda M. Bambara, Ph.D.
Professor of Special Education
College of Education
Lehigh University
111 Research Drive
Bethlehem, PA 18015

Christine Bigby, Ph.D.
Research Program Leader
Living with Disability Research Group
School of Allied Health
LaTrobe University
Bundoora
Victoria, Australia 3086

Jane Boone, B.A.
Employment Partnership Manager,
    Retired
Division of Developmental Disabilities
Washington State Department of
    Social and Health Services
Post Office Box 45310
Olympia, WA 98504

Kristen Bottema-Beutel, Ph.D.
Postdoctoral Fellow
Department of Special Education
PMB 228, Peabody College
Vanderbilt University
Nashville, TN 37203

Matthew E. Brock, M.A.
Department of Special Education
PMB 228, Peabody College
Vanderbilt University
Nashville, TN 37203

Diane M. Browder, Ph.D.
Snyder Distinguished Professor of
    Special Education
University of North Carolina at
    Charlotte
9201 University City Boulevard
Charlotte, NC 28223

John Butterworth, Ph.D.
Director of Employment Systems
    Change and Evaluation Senior
    Research Fellow
Institute for Community Inclusion
University of Massachusetts, Boston
100 Morrissey Boulevard
Boston, MA 02125

Michael Callahan, M.Ed.
President
Marc Gold & Associates
4101 Gautier-Vancleave Road,
    Suite 102
Gautier, MS 39553

Erik W. Carter, Ph.D.
Associate Professor
Department of Special Education
PMB 228, Peabody College
Vanderbilt University
Nashville, TN 37203

Ellen Condon, M.Ed.
Transition Projects Director
Rural Institute on Disabilities
University of Montana
700 S.W. Higgins Avenue, Suite 250
Missoula, MT 59803

Susan Copeland, Ph.D.
Associate Professor
Special Education Program
Department of Educational Specialties
MSCO5 3040
1 University of New Mexico
Albuquerque, NM 87131

J.S. de Valenzuela, Ph.D.
Associate Professor
Special Education Program
Department of Educational
  Specialties
MSCO5 3040
1 University of New Mexico
Albuquerque, NM 87131

Latanya L. Fanion, Ed.D.
Research Assistant
Department of Educational
  Leadership
School of Education
Clark Atlanta University
223 James P. Brawley Drive SW
Atlanta, GA 30314

Lise Fox, Ph.D.
Professor
Department of Child and Family Studies
University of South Florida
4202 E. Fowler Avenue
Tampa, FL 33620

Wei Gao, Ph.D.
Director of Special Education
Half The Sky Foundation
Unit 4-2-142
Jainguomenwai Diplomatic Compound
Chaoyang District, Beijing 100600

Meg Grigal, Ph.D.
Senior Research Fellow and
  Co-principal Investigator
Think College
Institute for Community Inclusion
University of Massachusetts, Boston
100 Morrissey Boulevard
Boston, MA 02125

Mary Frances Hanline, Ph.D.
Professor
Early Childhood Special Education
School of Teacher Education
Florida State University
Tallahassee, FL 32306

Debra Hart, Ph.D.
Educational Coordinator and Principal
  Investigator
Think College
Institute for Community Inclusion
University of Massachusetts, Boston
100 Morrissey Boulevard
Boston, MA 02125

Mike Head, M.S.W.
Former Director
Office of Long Term Care Supports
  and Services
Michigan Office of Services to the
  Aging
Post Office Box 30676
Lansing, MI 48909

Melissa E. Hudson, Ph.D.
Alternate Assessment Specialist
American Institutes for Research,
  #5280
1000 Thomas Jefferson Street NW
Washington, DC 20007

Pam Hunt, Ph.D.
Professor
Department of Special Education
San Francisco State University
Burk Hall 501
1600 Holloway Avenue
San Francisco, CA 94132

Elizabeth Keefe, Ph.D.
Professor
Special Education Program
Department of Educational Specialties
MSCO5 3040
1 University of New Mexico
Albuquerque, NM 87131

Donna Lehr, Ph.D.
Associate Professor of Special
    Education
Boston University School of Education
Two Silber Way
Boston, MA 02215

Richard Luecking, Ed.D.
President
TransCen
401 N. Washington Street, Suite 450
Rockville, MD 20850

Julie Marron, M.B.A.
President
Institute for Health Quality and Ethics
75 Sprague Hill Road
Chepachet, RI 02814

Philip McCallion, Ph.D.
Professor and Co-director
Center for Excellence in Aging &
    Community Wellness
University at Albany, State University
    of New York
Albany, NY 12222

Mary McCarron, Ph.D.
Dean of the Faculty of Health Sciences
University of Dublin Trinity College
College Green
Dublin 2, Ireland

John McDonnell, Ph.D.
Professor
Department of Special Education
College of Education
University of Utah
1705 E. Campus Center Drive,
    Room 221
Salt Lake City, UT 84112

Bethany R. McKissick, Ph.D.
Assistant Professor
Department of Curriculum,
    Instruction, and Special Education
College of Education, Allen Hall 310
Mississippi State University
Mississippi State, MS 39762

Ann Mickelson, Ph.D.
A.J. Pappanikou Center for
    Developmental Disabilities
University of Connecticut
263 Farmington Avenue
Farmington, CT 06030

Tom Nerney, M.A.
Executive Director
Institute for Health Policy and Ethics
75 Sprague Hill Road
Chepachet, RI 02814

John O'Brien
58 Willowick Drive
Lithonia, GA 30038

**Ann-Marie Orlando, Ph.D.,
    CCC-SLP**
Assistant Scholar
University of Florida
School of Special Education, School
    Psychology, & Early Childhood
    Studies
Post Office Box 117050
Gainesville, FL 32611

Deborah S. Reed, Ed.D.
Assistant Professor
Department of Exceptional, Deaf and
    Interpreter Education
College of Education
University of North Florida
1 UNF Drive, Building 57, Room 3504
Jacksonville, FL 32225

Lyle T. Romer, Ph.D.
Executive Director
Total Living Concept
1132 West James Street
Kent, WA 98032

Joanna Smogorzewska, Ph.D.
Unit of Special Education
Department of Education
Maria Grzegorzewska Academy of
    Special Education
ul 40 Szczesliwicka
02-792 Warsaw, Poland

Martha E. Snell, Ph.D.
Professor of Special Education, Retired
University of Virginia
Room 234 Ruffner Hall
Post Office Box 400273
405 Emmet Street
Charlottesville, VA 22904

David Sommerstein, M.Ed.
Associate News Director
North Country Public Radio
St. Lawrence University
Canton, NY 13617

Lynne Sommerstein, M.Ed.
Lecturer
Exceptional Education Department
Buffalo State College—KH 204
1300 Elmwood Avenue
Buffalo, NY 14222

**Michelle Sommerstein,
   IEP Diploma**
122 N. Cayuga Road
Williamsville, NY 14221

Robert Sommerstein. J.D.
69 Delaware Avenue, Suite 1010
Buffalo, NY 14202

Fred Spooner, Ph.D.
Professor
Department of Special Education and
   Child Development
University of North Carolina at
   Charlotte
9201 University City Boulevard
Charlotte, NC 28223

Grzegorz Szumski, Ph.D.
Professor
Unit of Special Education
Department of Education
Maria Grzegorzewska Academy of
   Special Education
ul 40 Szczesliwicka
02-792 Warsaw, Poland

Pamela Walker, Ph.D.
Research Project Director II
Center on Human Policy
Syracuse University
805 South Crouse Avenue
Syracuse, NY 13244

Virginia L. Walker, Ph.D.
Graduate Student
Department of Special Education
University of Virginia
Room 234 Ruffner Hall
Post Office Box 400273
405 Emmet Street
Charlottesville, VA 22904

Michael Wehmeyer, Ph.D.
Professor of Special Education
Director
Kansas University Center on
   Developmental Disabilities
University of Kansas
1200 Sunnyside Avenue, Room 3136
Lawrence, KS 66045

Cate Weir, Pd.D.
Project Coordinator
Center on Postsecondary Education
   Options for Students with
   Intellectual Disabilities
Consortium on Postsecondary
   Education for Individuals with
   Developmental Disabilities
Institute for Community Inclusion
University of Massachusetts, Boston
100 Morrissey Boulevard
Boston, MA 02125

Juliann Woods, Ph.D., CCC-SLP
Professor
School of Communication Science and
   Disorders
Florida State University
201 Bloxham Street, Room 411
Tallahassee, FL 32306

Foreword

For almost 40 years, TASH has been a leader in fighting for equity, opportunity, and inclusion for individuals with disabilities, especially those with the most significant disabilities. The membership of TASH started primarily with teacher educators and researchers who saw that those with more severe disabilities were not getting adequate attention in the traditional academic journals and books in the field of special education and related areas. Inspired and reinforced by federal legislation, which at that time was called the Education for All Handicapped Children Act of 1975 (PL 94-142) and today called the Individuals with Disabilities Education Improvement Act (IDEA) of 2004 (PL 108-446), these professors came together and began to promote just causes like quality education and a full life for individuals with severe disabilities. Besides being professionals, they were advocates, and, as such, they reached out not only to other professionals but also to families and individuals with disabilities so they could build a robust, diverse organization that would argue and lobby on behalf of their target constituency for a fair and typical life.

As much as anything, however, the founders of TASH (known originally as the American Association for the Education of the Severely and Profoundly Handicapped, then as The Association for the Severely Handicapped, then later as The Association for Persons with Severe Handicaps, and now simply as TASH) were educators. They knew that, if the organization really was to do anything meaningful, there was a need to teach others. TASH was a source of information about many things, from how to teach someone to eat with a spoon, to how to replace challenging behavior with an appropriate alternative, to how to involve family members in their child's school, to how to help someone find a meaningful job in his or her community.

There was so much to teach and so much to learn! This was true in the mid-1970s, and it remains true today. There are so many people—professionals, families, policy makers, and many members of society—who are unaware of the values of TASH, unaware that this movement has been underway for nearly 40 years, and, most sadly, unaware of the potential of people with severe disabilities to learn, to live, and to be happy in their own homes and communities. There are so many people, many of whom are well intentioned, who think special schools, segregated sheltered workshops, and communal living facilities are satisfactory answers and are arrangements of which a modern society can be proud.

So above all, as was recognized by TASH founders, there remains a critical need for TASH to teach. And so TASH does. TASH teaches by providing reports in its online newsletter, *TASH In Action*; through its online, reader-friendly magazine, *Connections*; and through its reputable, widely respected, refereed journal, *Research and Practice for Persons with Severe Disabilities*. TASH works with its many state chapters to offer regional training and workshops designed to respond to the needs of its members in their own communities. TASH offers online training to provide up-to-date practical information that helps professionals and nonprofessionals learn how to implement practices in the real world that are based on TASH values. And of course, every year since its founding, TASH has offered an annual international conference that brings together people from all over the world to learn from each other, to teach each other, and to communicate with each other how to make better lives for individuals with significant disabilities and their families. For those encountering this text, we encourage you to consider becoming a member of TASH, as a contributor to a vibrant community, and as a recipient of the wealth of knowledge other members have contributed over the years.

In 1991, under the leadership of TASH members Luanna H. Meyers, Charles A. Peck, and Lou Brown, Paul H. Brookes Publishing Co. published *Critical Issues in the Lives of People with Severe Disabilities*. In this publication, which remains recognized as a classic work, more than 80 individuals, as either writers or editors, contributed to a greater understanding of issues relevant to the lives of individuals with severe disabilities. The issues addressed were extensive, ranging from deinstitutionalization, to inclusive schooling, to the rejection of using aversive interventions as a way to control behavior. The book was necessary because it helped TASH teach about these issues, about the positive directions in which we were moving, and the negative conditions that we had to reject. Those who were professionals benefited greatly from the efforts of their colleagues, and the impact of this work on individuals and families, while incalculable, was no doubt profound and long lasting.

Now we are fortunate to have this new work, *Equity and Full Participation for Individuals with Severe Disabilities: A Vision for the Future*, again by Brookes Publishing. Once more, some of the most prolific and respected researchers, writers, and educators, who have for many years been TASH members and supporters, have come together to teach us about TASH values and how these values can be applied to improve outcomes for individuals with severe disabilities and their families. As you read this book, you will recognize that some of the same battles must continue to be waged. You will see that there remains a need to address issues like social justice, school inclusion, community integration, and health care. But happily, we see new frontiers coming into view—perhaps new barriers to confront—but nevertheless areas that we did not consider nearly 25 years ago in the predecessor to this edition. In this iteration, we learn about the importance and potential of literacy instruction, of access to the general curriculum in the regular classroom, of postsecondary education for young adults, about customized employment for individuals perceived as the most challenging to employ, and about respectfully supporting people with challenging behaviors. We also learn that there is a need to look internally at issues like poverty and disability and responsiveness to people of diverse cultures and backgrounds—and externally at international relationships. Clearly the message is that what we value should be available to more people so they may realize the benefits of justice and equality. Once again, through this comprehensive product, we see TASH working as a teacher as well as an advocate and promoter of better lives for more people.

We are unlike any other organization in what we believe, in our tenacity, and in who comprises our membership. We see us as parents and families and advocates; as teachers, administrators, professors, researchers, service providers, policy makers, and other professionals; as an amalgam of people with many different hats who, with the exception of where our values intersect, may have little opportunity to know each other, to understand each other, or to appreciate the needs of each other. No matter who we are, TASH members are united in our belief that the least dangerous assumption is to presume competence and that no one should need to "earn" their way in. TASH envisions communities in which no one is segregated and everyone belongs. This vision will be realized when all individuals have a home of their choosing, have a meaningful job, are included in their neighborhood schools and colleges, have a way to communicate, enjoy individualized supports and a quality of life similar to that available to all people, and have tools and opportunities to advocate for themselves. TASH truly is a unique organization. Sometimes we feel that its not easy being TASH, but it is necessary for us to be who we are and do what we do.

Once again, with this new book, we are teachers. Thanks to the efforts of our colleagues and thanks to Brookes Publishing, once more TASH is taking the lead through another venue to let the world know who we are, what we stand for, and, most important, how we can make it happen. We believe you will find this book to be an informative and inspiring, yet practical, guide to our continuing movement forward, and like the first *Critical Issues* book, we believe this work will have an immediate and lasting impact on people's lives.

David L. Westling
TASH President

Barbara Trader
TASH Executive Director

Preface

In 1991, *Critical Issues in the Lives of People with Severe Disabilities*, co-edited by Luanna H. Meyer, Charles A. Peck, and Lou Brown, was published by Paul H. Brookes Publishing Co. The book was officially sponsored by TASH and, at the time, represented the most comprehensive collection of papers, policy statements, and resolutions regarding values, research, and practices that affect the lives of people with severe disabilities. As the co-editors noted, the book served in effect as a history of TASH and provided compelling evidence of the positive social, educational, and philosophical changes that have occurred to advance the equality, independence, and competence of people with severe disabilities. There is no question that the information shared in this text benefited and improved the quality of lives, directly or indirectly, for untold numbers of individuals with extensive support needs. *But times change*, as the saying goes, and much has changed since *Critical Issues* was published. Many additional issues and concerns have emerged and challenged the field in continued efforts to promote and support the full inclusion and quality of life for people with severe disabilities.

Since TASH was founded in 1974, so much has been accomplished in achieving the mission but there is much more that needs to be done. We felt that a current text with state-of-the-art information was critically needed because, as noted previously, much has changed since the publication of the first edition. We are paying far more attention to promoting students' access to the general curriculum; we are committed to reducing racial disparities, as well as enhancing cultural competence; we are endeavoring to fully ensure person-centered planning and self-advocacy; we are seeking to minimize the high-poverty status that many individuals with severe disabilities experience; we are ensuring that the health needs and well-being of individuals with extensive support needs are fully promoted; and we are expanding our mission to learn about and address the needs of individuals with severe disabilities globally. Our intent for this book is not to just update the information presented in *Critical Issues* and present a second edition, although in a sense the book does that by serving as a compendium of information about recommended practices, skills, and current knowledge about severe disabilities, but to continue the dialogue *Critical Issues* initiated so we can become better informed about how we can ultimately achieve the goals TASH seeks.

This book has particular relevance at this time, given the many economic and political challenges facing the disability community. Efforts to fully include students in general education have been thwarted by school district preoccupation with standardized examinations. Furthermore, students from culturally diverse backgrounds continue to disproportionately receive special education services in separate settings that incorporate few recommended practices. Few secondary-level students or adults with extensive support needs are either being encouraged to participate in postsecondary programs or are receiving support to do so. Adult services and supports have been reduced. The extent to which inclusive practices are being followed has stalemated, if not decreased, and the majority of school-age children with severe disabilities remain in segregated, self-contained settings. Although the value of supported and customized employment has been lauded, there has been a reduction in the number of individuals receiving customized employment or supported living services, and the majority of "working" adults participate in segregated or sheltered employment. The state of supported living services is similar, with a decrease in funding and a decrease in the number of adults with severe disabilities in customized community living options. Decisions about educational and community services continue to be made for, instead of by, people with support needs. Medical interventions, as well as related services or therapies, are often discounted if it is felt that they will not make much of a difference, given the severity of the individual's disability. And the number of individuals with extensive support needs who live in poverty remains disturbingly high. For those committed to ensuring that people with severe disabilities receive a full array of equitable, valued, and effective services, this is a time of great concern. This book is designed to provide clarity to professionals, students, parents, and practitioners about current issues and conflicts, and to suggest potential solutions to these problems. We hope this book will also be read by politicians and policy makers who are concerned about the issues and conflicts discussed, and inspired by the ideas and solutions presented, and we trust they will make decisions and take actions that will make positive differences in the lives of the people we (and they) support.

The issues addressed in the book are complex and demand examination from different viewpoints. Although all TASH members are guided by the same mission—to promote full inclusion and participation in every aspect of education, community living, and citizenship—TASH's membership is composed of people from varied and diverse backgrounds and professions—teachers, direct service providers, academicians, parents, students, self-advocates, and support personnel, among others. We have made an attempt to represent this diversity in the contributors to this book. Our contributors include researchers, parents, and self-advocates; members who are of color and from different countries, both first world and developing; students; and policy makers. We believe that having authors with differing cultural backgrounds, perspectives, and experiences adds greater depth and richness to our discussion.

As was done in *Critical Issues*, the book aims to address the full array of services and supports available across the life span to enhance and enrich lives. Many of the values and principles discussed in the book resist simple categorization. For example, all individuals, regardless of age, should enjoy full participation and inclusion in their communities; all individuals should be provided opportunities to make choices that affect their lives; all individuals deserve medical and therapeutic interventions to promote their health and well-being; and so forth. But for matters of organization, we decided to assign the chapters to the following sections: *Foundations, Children and Youth, Adult Outcomes*, and *A Look Around and Ahead*.

Foundations provides an underlying basis for many of the key issues addressed in the book. In Chapter 1, Michael Wehmeyer examines existing inequities in our educational and social services system. In Chapter 2, Carolyn Hughes and Latanya L. Fanion discuss the devastating effects of poverty on individuals with severe disabilities and their families—a problem that has long been ignored. In Chapter 3, Michelle Sommerstein (self-advocate) and her family share their reflections of being a "service recipient" and its impact on their family. In Chapter 4, John O'Brien discusses the value of person-centered planning and the organizational and systemic challenges faced when providing it. In Chapter 5, Martin Agran and Carolyn Hughes examine the need to promote the self-determination of people with severe disabilities and ways in which it can be realized. In Chapter 6, Fredda Brown and Linda M. Bambara examine how to provide meaningful and effective positive behavior support to those with challenging behaviors.

Children and Youth includes chapters that address the wide variety of challenges facing early intervention services and schools in providing state-of-the-art educational services to students with severe disabilities. In Chapter 7, Lise Fox, Mary Frances Hanline, Juliann Woods, and Ann Mickelson discuss the value of early intervention and education, the family issues that need to be addressed, and how to best prepare early childhood educators. In Chapter 8, John McDonnell and Pamela Hunt advocate for inclusive education and examine the many curricular and programmatic decisions that need to be made to realize it. In Chapter 9, Susan Copeland, Elizabeth Keefe, and J.S. de Valenzuela discuss how literacy instruction can best be provided and the challenges that need to be addressed when providing such instruction to students with significant disabilities. In Chapter 10, Erik W. Carter, Kristen Bottema-Beutel, and Matthew E. Brock discuss the importance of developing friendships and social relationships for students with severe disabilities, the barriers that may exist in establishing them, and several recommended strategies to overcome these barriers. In Chapter 11, Fred Spooner, Bethany R. McKissick, Melissa E. Hudson, and Diane M. Browder discuss the need to provide students with access to the general curriculum and suggest ways in which academic instruction can be delivered in the general education classroom. Last, in Chapter 12, Donna Lehr examines the challenges of supporting students with health care needs in general education, the teacher's role and responsibilities in serving these students, and the difficulties in meeting both the students' health care and educational needs.

Adult Outcomes includes chapters that examine the array of educational, employment, and community living services available for adults with significant disabilities. In Chapter 13, Michael Callahan, John Butterworth, Jane Boone, Ellen Condon, and Richard Luecking describe strategies to facilitate transition services and promote customized employment. In Chapter 14, Meg Grigal, Debra Hart, and Cate Weir discuss ways in which students with severe disabilities can gain access to postsecondary education. In Chapter 15, Lyle T. Romer and Pamela Walker discuss the value of supported living, its relationship to person-centered living, and how the latter can be used to achieve the former. In Chapter 16, Christine Bigby, Philip McCallion, and Mary McCarron discuss the need to provide appropriate medical and social services to elderly individuals with severe disabilities. They examine the approaches used to serve this population across several English-speaking countries. In Chapter 17, Tom Nerney, Julie Marron, and Mike Head examine Medicaid—what its values are, how its costs are allocated, and how its dollars can best be spent.

The last section, *A Look Around and Ahead*, includes two chapters. In Chapter 18, Diane Ryndak, Deborah S. Reed, Grzegorz Szumski, Ann-Marie Orlando, Joanna Smogorzewska, and Wei Gao discuss various ways developing countries have tried to achieve equity and social inclusion for all citizens and some of the barriers they face to achieve these outcomes. Last, in Chapter 19, Martha E. Snell and Virginia L. Walker identify discrepancies in service provision and how reform is needed in public awareness, policy development, legislature, and the kind of research that should be conducted. They note that these discrepancies continue to exist despite a network of supportive laws that have been put in place since the mid-1970s and recommend ways to have an impact on public opinion and create supportive societal conditions.

In 2010, TASH developed a National Agenda. This agenda established major goals believed to be essential in our committed efforts to achieve full recognition, respect, and equality for individuals with severe disabilities. Items in the National Agenda included the following: promoting inclusive education, enhancing community living, providing customized employment, ensuring diversity and cultural competency, and guaranteeing human rights for all. We trust that the book will have an impact on informing parents, students, self-advocates, and the professional community about services needed to support people with severe disabilities in every aspect of life in their home communities and, in doing so, help achieve the goals set in TASH's National Agenda.

Acknowledgments

TASH has been fortunate to have many heroes, champions, and leaders who have inspired us and shown us ways to achieve the outcomes we seek—equality, opportunity, and inclusion for all people; who have persuaded us to think outside the box and not be restricted by "old" ways of thinking and reacting; and who have allowed us to better understand the true value and meaning of the actions and expressions of the individuals we serve, support, and respect. It is with these thoughts that we also dedicate this book to Edward Carr, June Downing, Doug Guess, and John Nietupski for their contributions, insight, and wisdom.

To Kristle and Hailey and my parents, as always

—MA

To my family, who have taught me about love, diversity, and optimism

—FB

*To Brook and Meghan, who share my commitment to
social justice, and Baby Delilah of the next generation*

—CH

*To Jon, Chris, and Liza, who understand
my passion and are the lights of my life*

—CQ

*To Michael, my family, and the many individuals
who have taught me the value of diversity and advocacy*

—DR

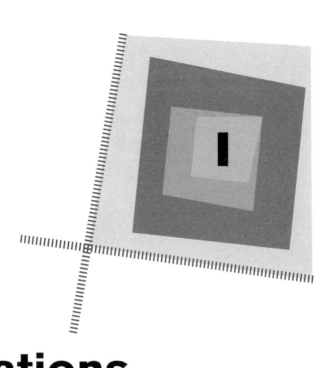

Foundations

Disability in the 21st Century

Seeking a Future of Equity and Full Participation

Michael Wehmeyer

This book's purpose is to address contemporary issues in supporting people with severe disabilities to live rich, full, and high-quality lives in their communities. It will be difficult to achieve the vision established in this book until there is a fundamental change in the way in which disability itself is understood. A new and different way to understand disability in the 21st century does exist. This chapter describes that new paradigm and discusses the implications of its adoption for a future of equity and full participation.

HISTORICAL UNDERSTANDINGS OF DISABILITY

I coedited a book titled *Mental Retardation in the 21st Century* (Wehmeyer & Patton, 2000). Use of the stigmatizing term *mental retardation* has been discontinued for reasons subsequently discussed. I coauthored a chapter in that text with Hank Bersani, Jr., and Raymond Gagne, two leaders of the self-advocacy movement, that characterized the current era as representing the third wave of the disability movement. Our formulations were guided by issues pertaining to civil rights and social justice emerging through the field's growing acceptance of the self-advocacy movement and focus on self-determination. Significant progress in elaborating better ways of understanding disability has provided a theoretical and scientific foundation to bolster the philosophical and moral issues that propelled our proposal of a new wave of the disability movement. The oft-cited adage that "what is past is prologue" is apropos in considering how to ensure a future of equity and full participation.

The First Wave of the Disability Movement: The Professional Era

Professionals dominated the first wave of the disability movement, which spanned through the latter half of the 19th and first half of the 20th centuries. At the height of this first wave, professionals defined the issues and created the then new discipline of disability as a subdiscipline within the fields of medicine, psychology, and education (Dybwad & Bersani, 1996). These professionals made decisions on their own or in consultation with one another. Parents and the public assumed that these professionals knew what was best because of their education and social status. Emphasis was on diagnosing and determining who would benefit from treatment. The images associated with disability were often universally negative. People with disabilities were stereotyped as menaces to society or responsible for many societal problems (see Figure 1.1) (Trent, 1994; Wehmeyer, 2013).

How disability itself was understood during this era was an extension of the medical model adopted by these early professionals. Disability historically was understood as an extension of a medical model that conceived health as an interiorized state of functioning and health problems as an individual pathology; that is, as a problem within the person. Disability within such a context was understood to be medical in nature and a characteristic of a person, as residing with that person. The person was viewed as broken in some way. The language of the professions that emerged to support people with disabilities reflects that conceptualization; people with disabilities were described as diseased, pathological, atypical, or aberrant, depending on the profession (Wehmeyer et al., 2008).

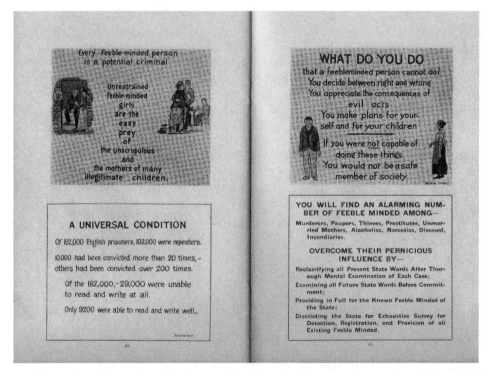

Figure 1.1. The menace of the feebleminded from undated report from the New Jersey Institution for Feebleminded Women (author's collection).

The way in which disability is understood drives how people with disabilities are treated in both the sense of the nature and structure of services and supports provided to them and in the sense of how others, including the public, respond to them. The earliest efforts on behalf of people with disabilities were habilitative in nature and driven by tenets of social justice and social welfare. Thus, schools were established beginning in the 1830s and into the 1870s to educate children who were deaf or blind or who had an intellectual disability. People with severe disabilities were not included in these early efforts, however. For example, early schools for children with intellectual disability included only people who had limited support needs. Such efforts, however, transmogrified over time from habilitative in nature and intended to benefit the person to serving to isolate and segregate people with disabilities from society, eventually for the purposes of protecting society (Smith & Wehmeyer, 2012).

The professionals that built this system were not interested in the rights of people whom they called "retardates" or "mentally deficient." People with severe disabilities were seen as menaces to society; threats to "racial hygiene"; and links to crime, poverty, promiscuity, and the decline of civilization by the first decades of the 20th century. They were seen as subhuman ("a vegetable") or as objects to be feared and dreaded by these professionals and society at large. The U.S. Supreme Court ruled in 1927 that involuntary sterilization of people who were deemed to be feebleminded was constitutional, resulting in the forced sterilization of an estimated 50,000 people with intellectual and developmental disabilities by the 1970s (Smith & Wehmeyer, 2012).

More than 275,000 Americans, including most people with severe disabilities, lived in institutions that had become massive warehouses by the late 1960s. The Willowbrook State School on Staten Island, built to house 4,000 people, had an institution census of more than 6,000 inmates by the mid-1960s. After a tour of Willowbrook in 1965, a visibly distraught Senator Robert Kennedy told reporters,

I think—particularly at Willowbrook—that we have a situation that borders on a snake pit; the children live in filth; many of our fellow citizens are suffering tremendously because of lack of attention, lack of imagination, lack of adequate manpower. (Smith & Wehmeyer, 2012, p. 176)

Disability scholar Burton Blatt was propelled by Kennedy's pronouncements and arranged to tour four institutions in the northeast, none of which were named but one of which was almost certainly Willowbrook, and brought with him photographer Fred Kaplan, who surreptitiously snapped photographs of the horrific conditions in the facilities. The resulting photo essay showed the stark black-and-white photographs of naked and apparently starving "inmates" with severe disabilities and rows of iron beds with children confined to them, juxtaposed with poetry verses and essays selected by Blatt. "There is hell on earth," began *Christmas in Purgatory,* "and in America there is a special inferno. We were visitors there during Christmas, 1965" (Blatt & Kaplan, 1969, p. 1).

The Second Wave of the Disability Movement: The Parent Era

The parent era was the second wave of the disability movement and occurred during the middle of the 20th century. Advances in science and medicine greatly increased the life expectancy of people with disabilities. A growing worldwide emphasis on rehabilitation and training emerged, catapulted forward by the large number of veterans disabled in World War II. Successes in developing vaccines for diseases such as polio and tuberculosis gave hope to greater cures for disabling conditions. The earlier stereotypes of disability were replaced with more humane ones, though this change was still problematic. People with disabilities were viewed as objects to be fixed, cured, rehabilitated, and, at the same time, pitied. They were viewed as victims of their disabling condition, worthy of charity. Shapiro described this when discussing the emergence of the poster child as a fundraising tool:

> The poster child is a surefire tug at our hearts. The children picked to represent charity fund-raising drives are brave, determined, and inspirations, the most innocent victims of the cruelest whims of life and health. Yet they smile through their unlucky fates. No other symbol of disability is more beloved by Americans than the cute and courageous poster child. (1993, p. 12)

People with severe disabilities were viewed as holy innocents within this stereotype (e.g., special messengers, children of God) and, thus, incapable of sin and not responsible for their own actions. People with severe disabilities came also to be perceived as eternal children, partially based on the prevalent use of mental age calculated from intelligence scores. Although no longer feared and blamed for all social ills, people with intellectual and developmental disabilities were perceived as children that needed protection, pity, and care.

The advances in science and changes in societal perceptions emboldened parents to demand to participate in decisions that affected their children and to reject the pessimistic forecasts of professionals as well as the treatment regimens associated with those forecasts, most notably institutionalization. Parents and family members began to advocate for services that would enable their children to remain at home, attend school, and live and work in their communities. Professionals slowly joined in the parent rebellion and recognized the importance of parents in the decision-making process. The movement eventually gained political clout and radically and unalterably changed the face of disability services during the 1950s, 1960s, and 1970s (Abeson & Davis, 2000).

The parent era ushered in the community era. Inclusion in communities and schools became the focus. Deinstitutionalization, spearheaded by pioneers such as Burton Blatt and nurtured by the wide adoption of the Normalization Principle (Nirje, 1969) and the emergence of the independent living movement, resulted in the shift from large congregate settings to community-based, although still congregate, living and educational settings. Nevertheless, this second wave did not alter the understanding of disability. Disability was still seen as aberrant, atypical, or pathological; as residing outside the normative experience and as a characteristic, quality, or condition of the person. People with disabilities were seen as broken or diseased. Terms such as *invalid, cripple,* and *handicapped,* which were prevalent during this era, spoke to this understanding. People with disabilities were treated as victims to be pitied and helped (see Figure 1.2). Beyond the hope for a cure engendered by scientific advances, not much else changed about the way disability was understood.

The Third Wave of the Disability Movement: The Self-Advocacy Era

The self-advocacy or self-determination movement emerged in the 1970s and 1980s (Wehmeyer, Bersani, & Gagne, 2000). Parents and family members told profession-

Figure 1.2. Retarded children can be helped campaign from the National Association for Retarded Children (author's collection).

als during the second wave of the disability movement that they were the consumers of services and they were the ones who speak for their children. This emphasis changed as their children aged and the movement matured. Parents, family members, and professionals began to recognize that people with intellectual and developmental disabilities could speak for themselves (Abeson & Davies, 2000). The self-advocacy or self-determination movement emerged as people with disabilities, increasingly referred to as self-advocates, began to claim their own voices. This movement emphasized empowerment, self-determination, and community inclusion.

Several factors contributed to the emergence of the third wave. The progress achieved by parents in establishing community-based programs (e.g., education, community living, employment settings) created a climate that led to further protections and higher expectations. Several other movements also contributed to the emergence of the third wave.

The first movement was adopting the Normalization Principle as an organizing basis for service delivery in the 1970s. Bengt Nirje explained that the Normalization Principle had its basis in "Scandanavian experiences from the field" (1969, p. 180) and emerged, in essence, from a Swedish law on mental retardation passed in 1968. In its original conceptualization, the Normalization Principle provided guidance for creating services that "let the mentally retarded obtain an existence as close to the normal as possible" (p. 181). Nirje stated, "As I see it, the normalization principle means making available to the mentally retarded patterns and conditions of everyday life which are as close as possible to the norms and patterns of the mainstream of society" (p. 181). Nirje identified eight facets and implications of the Normalization Principle.

1. Normalization means a normal rhythm of day;
2. Normalization implies a normal routine of life;
3. Normalization means to experience the normal rhythm of the year;

4. Normalization means the opportunity to undergo normal developmental experiences of the life cycle;
5. Normalization means that the choices, wishes and desires [of the mentally retarded themselves] have to be taken into consideration as nearly as possible, and respected;
6. Normalization also means living in a bisexual world;
7. Normalization means normal economic standards [for the mentally retarded];
8. Normalization means that the standards of the physical facility should be the same as those regularly applied in society to the same kind of facilities for ordinary citizens. (1969, pp. 181–182)

Scheerenberger noted that "at this stage in its development, the normalization principle basically reflected a lifestyle, one diametrically opposed to many prevailing institutional practices" (1987, p. 117) and suggested that "no single categorical principle has ever had a greater impact on services [for people with mental retardation] than that of normalization" (p. 117).

Second, the independent living and disability rights movements were critical to the emergence of the new wave of the disability movement. The independent living movement began in the 1960s and was strongly influenced by the social and political consciousness of other civil rights movements occurring in the United States at that time (Ward, 1996). This civil rights perspective and the recognition of the lack of power held by and value held for people with disabilities at that time led many people with disabilities to equate their experiences and marginality with members of racial and ethnic minority groups and to begin to respond to societal barriers to social, economic, and political inclusion within an empowerment framework. *Empowerment* is a term usually associated with social movements and typically is used in reference to actions that enhance the possibilities for people to govern their own lives (Rappaport, 1981). The concepts of right to integration and meaningful equality of opportunity stressed by other civil rights groups, as well as the methods and tactics utilized by these groups, was adopted by the disability rights movement.

Ed Roberts, a leader in the independent living and disability rights movement, emphasized the connection between the struggle of other minorities for equality and the marginal status of people with disabilities. Roberts defined *independence* in terms of the control people with disabilities had over their lives and argued that it should be measured not by the tasks one can perform without assistance, but by the quality of one's life with adequate support.

A third factor of note was the emergence of the self-advocacy or people-first movement. The origins of the self-advocacy movement in the United States are usually attributed to a small group of people with intellectual disability in Salem, Oregon, who were credited with formulating the phrase, "We are people first" (Edwards, 1982). The roots of that movement lie in Sweden in the late 1960s and 1970s. Beginning in 1965 in Sweden, Bengt Nirje described the use of social clubs called *flamslattsklubben* to promote training in Sweden for adolescents with intellectual disabilities. This training was embedded within Nirje's (1969) development of the Normalization Principle. Within just a few years, training for the social groups included instruction in parliamentary procedures.

The self-advocacy movement rapidly gained ground both in the United States and internationally. There were 1,000 members in Oregon alone, with sister groups in 3 states and requests from 42 states for assistance in starting similar organizations, within 5 years of forming the Oregon self-advocacy group (Edwards, 1982). The first self-advocacy conference took place in October of 1974 in Otter Crest, Oregon. Edwards described one moment from that historic meeting: "The earth moved just a bit when Valerie Schaaf, first president of People First, stepped onto the podium and spoke clearly into the microphone: 'This, the first People First convention, is officially called to order'" (p. 4).

It was increasingly evident by the 1990s that there was a need for new ways of conceptualizing disability. Historic models that focused on impairment, pathology, and incapacity were inconsistent with the empowerment focus of the independent living and disability rights movements. People with disabilities became unwilling to accept conceptualizations of disability that focused on personal incapacity and incompetence.

A 21st-CENTURY UNDERSTANDING OF DISABILITY

Traditional conceptualizations began to be replaced toward the end of the 20th century by ways of thinking about disability that focused more on the interaction between personal capacity and the context in which people with disabilities lived, learned, worked, and played. The most notable of these were the World Health Organization's (WHO) International Classification of Functioning, Disability, and Health (ICF) and the American Association on Mental Retardation's (AAMR) 1992/2002 classification system. The ICF and AAMR (now American Association on Intellectual and Developmental Disabilities [AAIDD]) frameworks are functional classification systems because disability is seen as an outcome of the interaction between a person's limitations and the environmental context in which that person must function.

The WHO's ICF is forwarded as a biopsychosocial model in which disability and functioning are viewed as outcomes of interactions between health conditions (diseases, disorders, and injuries) and contextual factors, which include environmental and personal factors. The ICF proposes three levels of human functioning on which these health conditions and contextual factors act.

1. *Body functions and structures:* The physiological functions of body systems and the anatomical parts of bodies, including organs and limbs

2. *Activities:* The execution of tasks or actions by the person

3. *Participation:* Pertaining to involvement in life situations

The effect of health conditions and contextual factors on body functions and structures might result in *impairments,* defined as problems in body function or structure, whereas the impact on activity and participation factors may result in activity limitations or participation restrictions. The notion that disability is a function of the relationship between the person, his or her health condition, and the social context is the key element of the ICF.

The AAMR's 1992 definition and classification system followed the lead of the WHO ICF by proposing a functional definition of "mental retardation." Disability within this definitional framework is not something that a person has or something that is a characteristic of the person but is instead a state of functioning in which limitations in functional capacity and adaptive skills must be considered within the context of environments and supports. The manual's authors proposed that "mental retardation is a *state* in which functioning is impaired in certain specific ways"

(Luckasson et al., 1992, p. 10). A *functional limitation* is defined as the "effect of specific impairments on the performance or performance capability of the person," whereas *disability* is described as the "expression of such a limitation in a social context" (p. 10). Luckasson and colleagues noted that "mental retardation is a disability *only* as a result of this interaction" (p. 10); that is, only as a result of the interaction between the functional limitation and the social context, in this case the environments and communities in which people with intellectual disability live, learn, work, and play. This functional model suggests that intellectual disability is not something a person has, such as a disease, nor is it something someone is, but is instead a state of functioning that exists based on the interaction between the person's functional limitations and the social or environmental context in which that person functions.

By defining the disability as a function of the reciprocal interaction between the environment and the person's functional limitations, the focus of the problem shifts from being a deficit within the person to being the relationship between the person's functioning and the environment and, subsequently, to identifying and designing supports to address the person's functioning within that context. Historic models of disability services created programs that provide services that were largely designed to meet the needs of people within largely homogeneous groupings based on indicators of personal incompetence.

From Programs and Services to Personalized Supports

It is important to understand what is intended by the use of the term *supports* because the idea of supports, the process of providing supports, and the categorization of levels of supports are at the heart of the new paradigm. The 1992 AAMR manual defined *supports* as

> Resources and strategies that promote the interests and causes of individuals with or without disabilities; that enable them to access resources, information and relationships inherent within integrated work and living environments; and that result in their enhanced interdependence, productivity, community integration, and satisfaction. (Luckasson et al., 1992, p. 101)

What characteristics of providing supports differentiate this intervention approach from traditional models of service delivery? First, three key aspects of supports are identified in the AAMR manual: 1) they pertain to resources and strategies; 2) they enable individuals to gain access to other resources, information, and relationships within integrated environments; and 3) their use results in increased integration and enhanced personal growth and development. In other words, supports have the unambiguous intent to enhance community integration and inclusion by enabling people to gain access to a wide array of resources, information, and relationships. Second, supports are individually designed and determined with the active involvement of key stakeholders in the process, particularly the person benefiting from that support. Traditional service delivery models have too often been designed primarily in a top-down process; that is, beginning with purported homogenous characteristics of a given population and designing one-size-fits-all programs. Finally, Luckasson and Spitalnik suggested that "supports refer to an array, not a continuum, of services, individuals, and settings that match the person's needs" (1994, p. 88). Luckasson and Spitalnik referred to a constellation of supports needed by people with intellectual disabilities in which the person is in the center and the types of supports range from self-directed and self-mediated supports (e.g., the person, his or her family and friends, nonpaid co-workers or neighbors), to generic supports (those that everyone uses) and specialized supports (e.g., those provided in a disability service system).

In summary, the new paradigm in disability supports abandons old notions of disability as residing within or being a characteristic of a person. It instead focuses on the interaction between the individual; his or her personal characteristics, including competencies; and the environment or context in which that person must function. This emphasis on functioning requires that interventions focus less on fixing or curing the individual and more on designing and implementing supports that address the fit between the person and the context in which he or she must function. Second, the array of supports needed must be provided in the community, which culminated with the independent living, deinstitutionalization, and normalization movements. Third, the independent living and civil rights movements have resulted in a focus on legislative and civil protections and assurances of equal opportunity and access and the emergence of a new disability movement (i.e., self-advocacy or self-determination movement). This movement focuses on natural supports, consumer controlled and directed services, and empowerment.

This shift in understanding disability has implications for supporting people with severe disabilities across the life span. The following sections examine the effect of this shift on education and life span practices and supports.

BEYOND DISABILITY IN EDUCATION:
THIRD-GENERATION INCLUSIVE PRACTICES

Numerous educational practices show evidence of the effect of functional models of disability and focus on a supports model. These practices emphasize enhancing personal capacity and modifying the context in which the student learns, including modifications to the curriculum itself, which reduces the gap between the student's capabilities and the demands of the environment. These practices include applying universal design for learning (UDL), using educational and assistive technology, applying positive behavior interventions and supports (PBIS), and promoting access to the general education curriculum, the latter of which is a central theme in the third generation of inclusive practices. These are briefly described by illustrating how the educational process may differ as a function of the changing ways of thinking about disability.

Turnbull, Turnbull, Wehmeyer, and Shogren (2013) suggested that this new paradigm of disability and the design of supports to enable people with disabilities to be successful, along with school reform efforts, led the field of education into a third generation of inclusive practices. The first generation of inclusive practices focused on changing prevailing educational settings for students with disabilities from separate, self-contained settings to the regular education classroom. First-generation inclusion was additive in nature; that is, resources and students were added to the general education classroom. The second generation of inclusive practices was more generative in nature because they focused on improving practice in the general education classroom instead of moving students from separate settings to regular classroom settings. Research and practice during this phase emphasized aspects of instructional practices that promoted inclusion, such as collaborative teaming and team teaching; differentiated instruction; developing family, school, and community partnerships; and so forth.

The most salient characteristic of the third generation of inclusion is that the focal point for such efforts switched from advocacy and supports with regard primarily to where a student receives his or her educational program, which Turnbull et al. (2013) suggested was the focus of the first two generations of inclusive practices, to a focus on what the student is taught. The third generation of inclusion presumes a student's presence in the general education classroom and emphasizes the quality of the educational program in that setting instead of focusing on integrating into the classroom. Nothing about the first or second generations of inclusion is either obsolete or unimportant. In fact, both remain critical to ensure high-quality educational programs for students with disabilities. The need to consider issues pertaining to third-generation inclusive practices is an outcome of the success of efforts during these first two generations. The expectations for students have become higher as more students with disabilities are educated and successfully supported in the general education classroom. At this point in the evolution of inclusive practices, educators need to consider how to maximize participation in the general education classroom and progress in the general education curriculum. Fortunately, most educators believe that ensuring access to the general education curriculum for students with disabilities is important, as is raising expectations held for students (Agran, Alper, & Wehmeyer, 2002).

The shift toward promoting access to the general education curriculum for students with disabilities has been the most visible change in educational practice since the mid-2000s. The Individuals with Disabilities Education Improvement Act (IDEA) of 2004 (PL 108-446) required schools to ensure that students are involved with and make progress in the general education classroom by providing modifications to the curriculum and supplementary aids and services to ensure that students are educated with their typically developing peers to the maximum extent. Emerging practices related to new ways of thinking about disability enable us to meet the challenge presented by third-generation inclusive education demands and promote access to the general education curriculum.

Universal Design for Learning

Content information, particularly in core academic areas, historically has been presented through print-based formats (e.g., textbooks, worksheets) and lectures. Students who cannot read well or who have difficulty with memory or attention do not have access to the content exclusively presented through these mediums and, thus, will not have the opportunity to learn that content. Applying principles of UDL to curriculum development by providing multiple means for presenting information and for students to respond to that information is an example of these functional models' emphasis on modifying the context to ensure a better fit between the student's capacities and that context. Orkwis and McLane defined UDL as "the design of instructional materials and activities that allows learning goals to be achievable by individuals with wide differences in their abilities to see, hear, speak, move, read, write, understand English, attend, organize, engage, and remember" (1998, p. 9).

UDL promotes flexibility in representing content (how instructional materials present the content), presenting content (how educators and materials deliver content), and demonstrating content mastery (how students provide evidence of their learning). Flexibility in the presentation and representation of content information can be achieved by providing information in a variety of formats, including text, graphics or pictures, digital and other media formats (audio or video, movies), or performance formats (plays, skits). Developing curricular materials in digital (electronic text) formats allows computers to provide multiple output formats. For example, electronic text can be converted to multiple output formats using specially designed media players, including electronic braille, digital talking book format, and sign language avatars, as well as allowing for output in multiple languages and letting the user modify features of the presentation, including font size and color and background color. Students can provide evidence of their learning in multiple ways, including written reports, exams, portfolios, drawings, performances, oral reports, videotaped reports, and other alternative means (Wehmeyer, 2011).

Pedagogical or instructional modifications can provide greater access to content information. For example, using graphic or advance organizers improves the comprehension of students with and without disabilities. Both graphic and advance organizers are flexible ways of presenting content information to students.

Using UDL to drive curriculum design is a perfect example of the effect of functional models of disability on education. These modifications alter the context to enable learners with a wide array of abilities and experiences to have access to content information. They improve the fit between the student with a disability and the curriculum through which content information is presented.

Educational and Assistive Technology

Providing supports to promote a better fit between a student's capacities and the educational context places a greater emphasis on using educational and assistive technologies. The role of technology in special education traditionally has been narrowly prescribed as benefiting only students with more severe impairments who need some assistive technology device, such as an augmentative and alternative communication (AAC) device, to accommodate for their impairments. This was consistent with an understanding of disability that focused on fixing the person. The role of technology, including information, electronic, and assistive technologies, within a functional model and supports system, however, becomes critical to addressing not only the student's capacities but also the educational context. Computer-assisted instruction (CAI), for example, involves using computer-based technologies to perform a variety of instructional roles, from initial delivery of content information to drill-and-practice activities. Research supports the efficacy of CAI with students with and without disabilities, including students with more severe disabilities (Wehmeyer, Smith, Palmer, Davies, & Stock, 2004).

Finally, technology can play a meaningful role in promoting the inclusion of students with disabilities in general education classrooms. Assistive technologies, such as AAC devices, provide alternative means for students with disabilities to interact with their peers without disabilities as well as participate in classroom learning activities. Many devices can promote peer interactions by providing a topic of conversation between the student with a disability and a peer. Technology devices such as tablet PCs and smartphones are socially desirable and can facilitate social interactions as well as provide needed supports.

Positive Behavior Interventions and Supports

Implementing schoolwide PBIS is a final example of applying functional models and support paradigms to education. Managing the classroom to ensure a nondisruptive learning environment for all students and dealing with challenging behavior problems exhibited by a few students is an ongoing concern for many teachers working with students with disabilities. PBIS is an area of intervention and treatment that has moved from emphasizing the person with a disability as the problem to be fixed to recognizing that treatment and intervention must focus on the social and environmental context and the interaction between that context and the individual's limitations. PBIS changes the environment to make the exhibition of problem behaviors irrelevant or counterproductive for the person. PBIS focuses on two primary modes of intervention—altering the environment before a problem behavior occurs and teaching appropriate behaviors as a strategy for eliminating the need for problem behaviors to be exhibited (Carr et al., 1999).

PBIS has focused attention on addressing problem behaviors in school settings and school violence by providing interventions at an individual, classroom, or whole-school level (Carr et al., 1999). PBIS has reduced office referrals in schools, created classroom environments more conducive to learning, and assisted students with chronic behavior problems to improve their behavior. PBIS applies behaviorally based approaches to enhance the capacity of schools, families, and communities to design effective environments that improve the fit or link between the students and the environments in which teaching and learning occurs. Attention is focused on creating and sustaining school environments that improve lifestyle results (e.g., personal, health, social, family, work, recreation) for all children and youth by making problem behavior less effective, efficient, and relevant and desired behavior more functional.

Turnbull, Turnbull, Erwin, and Soodak (2006) discussed the effect of PBIS at several levels of activity. First, the approach recognizes that "a student's behavior is affected by the philosophies, policies, procedures, practices, personnel, organization and funding of education agencies and other human service agencies involved in the student's education" (p. 185). The first level of intervention will necessarily focus on systems change, that being the process of changing features of the agency or agencies that may contribute to problem behavior. Included in such systemic efforts are service integration efforts that bring together a wide array of supports in a unified and easily accessible manner.

Second, PBIS emphasizes altering the environment. Turnbull et al. noted that such environments are altered by

a. Making different life arrangements by building on student strengths and preferences, identifying student and family priorities, building social and friendship networks and promoting health and wellness;

b. Improving the quality of the student's physical environment, including increasing the predictability and stability of events in school building, minimizing noise and other irritants;

c. Making personal accommodations for students;

d. Making instructional accommodations for students (2006, p. 185)

Focusing on skill instruction to enhance the possibility that students will act appropriately is a third level of action for PBIS. Such activities can extend from teaching specific behavior patterns or routines (e.g., how to behave in school hallways between classes) to promoting general problem-solving and self-management skills.

Once again, PBIS attempts to modify the context in which students learn, in this case school and classroom settings, to ensure a better fit for the student. Capacity building and context modification activities are involved.

Self-Determination

Promoting self-determination and student-directed learning is the main aspect of third-generation inclusive practices (Turnbull et al., 2013). Functional models of disability are strength based and focus on promoting students to become their own support to the greatest degree possible.

The international literature in special needs education documents that an effective education for students with disabilities must include instruction to promote student self-determination. Research has linked higher levels of self-determination to positive adult outcomes, including employment and independent living, for youth with special educational needs (Shogren, Palmer, Wehmeyer, Williams-Diehm, & Little, 2012; Wehmeyer & Palmer 2003; Wehmeyer & Schwartz, 1997), as well as to a higher quality of life (Lachapelle et al., 2005; Nota, Ferrari, Soresi, & Wehmeyer, 2007; Wehmeyer & Schwartz, 1998). Furthermore, most school standards for all students include a focus on skills leading to enhanced self-determination (e.g., goal setting, problem solving, decision making, self-advocacy, self-management), and all students benefit when instruction is available schoolwide to address these component elements (Wehmeyer, Field, Doren, Jones, & Mason, 2004). Finally, there is evidence that students with special educational needs can acquire the knowledge and skills to become more self-determined if provided such instruction (Algozzine, Browder, Karvonen, Test, & Wood, 2001; Wehmeyer, Palmer, Shogren, Williams-Diehm, & Soukup, 2013; Wehmeyer et al., 2012).

What Is Self-Determination? Numerous frameworks serve as a basis for instructional design to promote self-determination (Wehmeyer, Abery, Mithaug, & Stancliffe, 2003) as well as specially designed instructional methods, materials, strategies, and assessments to promote and measure self-determination (Wehmeyer et al., 2007; Wehmeyer & Field, 2007). Wehmeyer proposed a functional model of self-determination in which *self-determined behavior* refers to "volitional actions that enable one to act as the primary causal agent in one's life and to maintain or improve one's quality of life" (2005, p. 117). An act or event is self-determined if the individual's action reflects four essential characteristics: 1) the individual acted autonomously, 2) the behaviors were self-regulated, 3) the person initiated and responded to event(s) in a psychologically empowered manner, and 4) the person acted in a self-realizing manner. *Self-determination* refers to self-caused (versus other) action; that is, to people acting volitionally, based on their own wills. The word *volitional* is defined as the act or instance of making a conscious choice or decision. *Conscious* means intentionally conceived or done; that is, deliberate. Volitional behavior, then, implies that one acts consciously and with intent. Self-determined behavior is volitional and intentional, not simply random and nonpurposeful.

The concept of causal agency is central to this perspective. Broadly defined, *causal agency* implies that it is the person who makes or causes things to happen in his or her life. "Doing it yourself" is one frequent misinterpretation of self-determination. An obvious problem exists for most students with special educational needs when self-determination is interpreted this way because they frequently have limits to the number and types of activities they can independently perform. The capacity to perform specific behaviors, however, is secondary in importance to whether one is the causal agent (e.g., caused in some way to happen) over outcomes those specific behaviors are implemented to achieve. Students who may not be able to independently make a complex decision or solve a difficult problem may be able to participate in the decision-making process with support and, thus, have the opportunity to be the causal agent in the decision-making process and consequently act in a self-determined manner.

Wehmeyer et al. (2003) argued that self-determination emerges across the life span as children and adolescents learn skills and develop attitudes and beliefs that enable them to be causal agents in their lives. These skills and attitudes are referred to in this model as component elements of self-determined behavior and include choice-making, problem-solving, decision-making, goal-setting and attainment, self-advocacy, and self-management skills.

Self-Determination and Access to the General Education Curriculum

There are two ways that promoting self-determination provides access to and promotes progress in the general education curriculum. First, educational standards frequently include goals and objectives that pertain to component elements of self-determined behavior, including educational emphasis on teaching goal-setting, problem-solving, and decision-making skills. Students are expected to learn and apply effective problem-solving, decision-making, and goal-setting processes in virtually every set of school standards. Teachers can promote self-determination and promote progress in the general education curriculum by identifying where in the general education curriculum all students are expected to learn skills and knowledge related to the component elements of self-determined behavior.

Second, teaching young people with and without disabilities self-regulation, self-management, problem-solving, goal-setting, and decision-making skills provides an effective means to enable students to more effectively engage with and progress through activities in the general education curriculum.

Raising Expectations for Students with Severe Disabilities

Changing expectations of people with disabilities is at the heart of the shifting understanding of disability and of third-generation inclusive practices. This is very important for people with severe disabilities. Functional models of disability begin with the student's strengths and focus on enhancing capacity or modifying the learning context so that students can be successful. It is important to point out that in this regard the IDEA 2004 regulations do not require that the educational programs of students with severe disabilities be exclusively determined by the general education curriculum. Indeed, these regulations stipulate that the educational programs of students with disabilities should include a focus on the general education curriculum to the maximum degree appropriate. IDEA 2004 continues to require that the educational programs of students with disabilities address other educational needs that are not part of the general education curriculum. IDEA 2004 also clearly expects students to receive instruction to promote both academic achievement and enhanced functional performance. The individualized education program team determines what proportion of the student's educational program reflects instruction derived from the general education curriculum versus functional content, and factors such as age, grade level, and severity of disability will all factor into that decision (Turnbull et al., 2013). Still, the social, functional, and nonacademic content that students with severe disabilities need is equally affected by practices such as PBIS or UDL. The proliferation of tablet PC-based programs and cloud computing programs focused on social issues illustrates the relevance.

BEYOND DISABILITY IN ADULTHOOD: COMMUNITY INCLUSION AND QUALITY LIVES

Functional models of disability present as much of a challenge to traditional ways of supporting adults with severe disabilities as they do to the education system. First, these models emphasize the role of assessing support needs to ensure that people with disabilities are best enabled to succeed in typical environments. Thompson and colleagues (2009) differentiated between supports and support needs as such:

- Supports are resources and strategies that aim to promote the development, education, interests, and personal well-being of a person and enhance individual functioning (Luckasson et al., 1992).

- Support needs is a psychological construct referring to the pattern and intensity of supports necessary for a person to participate in activities linked with normative human functioning.

- Support needs do not intend to reflect a disturbance of human capacity; rather, the person's support needs reflect a limitation in human functioning as a result of either personal capacity or the context in which the person is functioning.

Addressing the person–environment mismatch is a major implication of conceptualizing disability as a state of functioning instead of an inherent trait. The focus is not solely on fixing the person, as historically has been the case. Figure 1.3

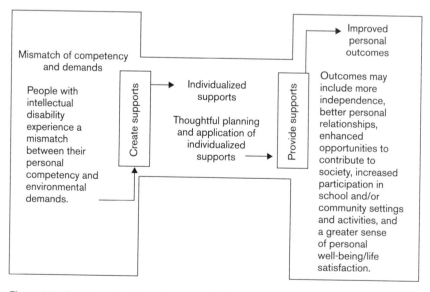

Figure 1.3. Supports model. (From Thompson, J.R., Bradley, V., Buntinx, W., Schalock, R.L., Shogren, K.A., Snell, M.E.,...Yeager, M.H. [2009]. Conceptualizing supports and the support needs of people with intellectual disability. *Intellectual and Developmental Disabilities, 47*[2], 135–146; reprinted by permission. Copyright 2009 by the American Association on Intellectual and Developmental Disabilities.)

shows a mismatch between personal competency and environmental demands that results in support needs that necessitate particular types and intensities of individualized supports. Second, it is more likely that individualized supports based on thoughtful planning and application will lead to improved human functioning and personally valued outcomes (Thompson et al., 2009).

Supports are a universe of resources and strategies that enhance human functioning. No person will need all of the types of supports available. And there must be few people who do not need any supports, regardless of ability or disability. People's support needs differ both quantitatively (in number) and qualitatively (in nature) (Thompson et al., 2009). Planning to enable adults with severe disabilities to live better quality lives should incorporate a supports plan (see Figure 1.4). The process depicted in this figure is fairly self-explanatory, and although it is not feasible to discuss the process in detail in this chapter, it is important to observe that supports assessment, using instruments such as the Supports Intensity Scale (Thompson et al., 2003), must become more prevalent if educators are to achieve the potential envisioned by the new disability paradigm, and such assessments must contribute information to planning teams for designing personalized supports.

Self-Determination as a Gateway to a Better Life

Promoting self-determination becomes central in supporting adults with disabilities to achieve more positive outcomes. Walker and colleagues (2011) proposed a social-ecological model to promote self-determination that 1) adopts the person–environment fit model of disability, emphasizing both capacity enhancement and modifications to environments and contexts; 2) proposes that efforts to achieve meaningful adult outcomes (e.g., employment, community inclusion, independent

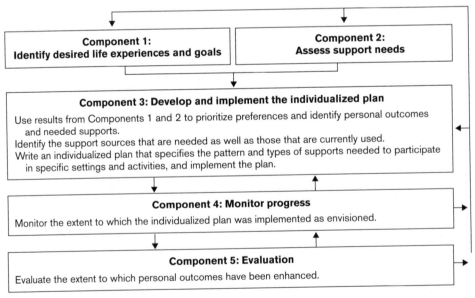

Figure 1.4.   Incorporating supports planning into person-centered planning. (From Thompson, J.R., Bradley, V., Buntinx, W., Schalock, R.L., Shogren, K.A., Snell, M.E.,…Yeager, M.H. [2009]. Conceptualizing supports and the support needs of people with intellectual disability. *Intellectual and Developmental Disabilities, 47*[2], 135–146; reprinted by permission. Copyright 2009 by the American Association on Intellectual and Developmental Disabilities.)

living) for adults with disabilities must recognize principles of adult learning, particularly that adults learn in more self-directed, self-guided fashions; and 3) uses efforts to promote self-determination as a gateway to achieving meaningful adult outcomes. A thorough description of this model is beyond the scope of this chapter, but the model recognizes that learning in adulthood is complex and involves mediating and moderating factors, such as gender or cultural contexts, that must be taken into account when supporting people with severe disabilities to achieve outcomes such as employment or independent living. The social-ecological model emphasizes the importance of social networks and social capital on achieving meaningful outcomes for adults with disabilities.

Supported Employment and the Promise of Technology

Practices that abide by the principles proposed in the Walker et al. (2011) model and reflect new ways of thinking about disability are already in place. Supported employment is the most obvious practice. It has been known for decades that people with severe disabilities can competitively work through strategies used in supported employment, such as job carving or job sharing, as well as in innovative employment models, such as customized employment or self-employment. These outcomes are achieved by supports that enable the worker to gain as many skills needed for the job as possible, and modifications to the job description, job tasks, or workplace environment further reduce the gap between the person's capacities and his or her success on the job (Wehman, 2011).

In addition, the potential for technology to reduce the gap between personal capacity and the demands of the environment for adults with severe disabilities and enable them to live, learn, work, and play in their communities is significant. Technology advances are already making better lives available to people with cognitive impairments. Scanning and computer technologies in most stores make it possible for someone who does not know how to calculate totals or count change to work in retail settings; tablet and smartphone technologies can provide audio and video prompting that enable people with cognitive disabilities to successfully complete multistep, complex tasks without another person prompting them (Davies, Stock, & Wehmeyer, 2003). Those same smartphones can use global positioning satellite data to enable a person to navigate a transit system or walk to a destination (Davies, Stock, Holloway, & Wehmeyer, 2010). The potential for technology to support successful functioning across multiple domains is promising, to say the least (Stock, Davies, Wehmeyer, & Lachapelle, 2011).

CONCLUSION: SEEKING A FUTURE OF EQUITY AND FULL PARTICIPATION

Society is at a tipping point for achieving a future of equity and full participation for people with severe disabilities. Gladwell (2000) described a *tipping point* as that moment of critical mass at which a phenomenon goes from obscurity to popularity, the threshold right before some idea or practice becomes widely adopted. All of the ingredients are present to achieve a future of equity and full participation. Recognizing and adopting the idea that disability is not a problem within a person but the gap between personal capacity and the demands of the context that can be closed with adequate supports is the final and critical element to achieve society's goals and the goals and dreams of people with disabilities and their families.

Questions for Study and Reflection

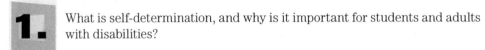

1. What is self-determination, and why is it important for students and adults with disabilities?

2. Describe how people with more severe disabilities can be supported to become more self-determined.

3. How does a functional/social-ecological model of disability differ from historic understandings of disability?

4. What implications exist for education and adult supports as a result of a new paradigm for disability?

5. What are supports and support needs, and why are they important?

RESOURCES

Agran, M., King-Sears, M., Wehmeyer, M.L., & Copeland, S.R. (2003). *Teachers' guides to inclusive practices: Student-directed learning strategies.* Baltimore, MD: Paul H. Brookes Publishing Co.

National Gateway to Self-Determination *http://www.ngsd.org*

Shogren, K.A. (2013). *Self-determination and transition planning.* Baltimore, MD: Paul H. Brookes Publishing Co.

University of Kansas Beach Center on Disability *http://www.beachcenter.org/*

University of North Carolina–Charlotte Self-Determination/Self-Advocacy Synthesis Project *http://www.uncc.edu/SDSP/*

University of Oklahoma Zarrow Center for Learning Enrichment *http://education.ou.edu/zarrow/*

Wehmeyer, M.L., Agran, M., Hughes, C., Martin, J., Mithaug, D.E., & Palmer, S. (2007). *Promoting self-determination in students with intellectual and developmental disabilities.* New York, NY: Guilford Press.

Wehmeyer, M.L., & Field, S. (2007). *Self-determination: Instructional and assessment strategies.* Thousand Oaks, CA: Corwin Press.

REFERENCES

Abeson, A., & Davis, S. (2000). The parent movement in mental retardation. In M.L. Wehmeyer & J.R. Patton (Eds.), *Mental retardation in the 21st century* (pp. 19–34). Austin, TX: PRO-ED.

Agran, M., Alper, S., & Wehmeyer, M. (2002). Access to the general curriculum for students with significant disabilities: What it means to teachers. *Education and Training in Mental Retardation and Developmental Disabilities, 37,* 123–133.

Algozzine, B., Browder, D., Karvonen, M., Test, D.W., & Wood, W.M. (2001). Effects of interventions to promote self-determination for individuals with disabilities. *Review of Educational Research, 71,* 219–277.

Blatt, B., & Kaplan, F. (1969). *Christmas in purgatory: A photographic essay on mental retardation.* Boston, MA: Allyn & Bacon.

Carr, E.G., Horner, R.H., Turnbull, A.P., Marquis, J., Magito-McLaughlin, D., McAtee, M.L., ... Doolabh, A. (1999). *Positive behavior support for people with developmental disabilities: A research synthesis.* Washington, DC: American Association on Mental Retardation.

Davies, D.K., Stock, S.E., Holloway, S., & Wehmeyer, M.L. (2010). Evaluating a GPS-based transportation device to support independent bus travel by people with intellectual disability. *Intellectual and Developmental Disabilities, 48,* 454–463.

Davies, D., Stock, S., & Wehmeyer, M. (2003). A palmtop computer-based intelligent aid for individuals with intellectual disabilities to increase independent decision making. *Research and Practice for Persons with Severe Disabilities, 28,* 182–193.

Dybwad, G., & Bersani, H. (1996). *New voices: Self-advocacy by people with disabilities.* Brookline, MA: Brookline Books.

Edwards, J. (1982). *We are people first: Our handicaps are secondary.* Portland, OR: Ednick.

Gladwell, M. (2000). *The tipping point: How little things can make a big difference.* New York, NY: Little, Brown.

Individuals with Disabilities Education Improvement Act (IDEA) of 2004, PL 108-446, 20 U.S.C. §§ 1400 *et seq.*

Lachapelle, Y., Wehmeyer, M.L., Haelewyck, M.C., Courbois, Y., Keith, K.D., Schalock, R., ... Walsh, P.N. (2005). The relationship between quality of life and self-determi-nation: An international study. *Journal of Intellectual Disability Research, 49,* 740–744.

Luckasson, R., Coulter, D.L., Polloway, E.A., Reiss, S., Schalock, R.L., Snell, M.E., ... Stark, J.A. (1992). *Mental retardation: Definition, classification, and systems of supports* (9th ed.). Washington, DC: American Association on Mental Retardation.

Luckasson, R., & Spitalnik, D.M. (1994). Political and programmatic shifts of the 1992 AAMR definition of mental retardation. In V.J. Bradley, J.W. Ashbaugh, & B.C. Blaney (Eds.), *Creating individual supports for people with developmental disabilities: A mandate for change at many levels* (pp. 81–96). Baltimore, MD: Paul H. Brookes Publishing Co.

Nirje, B. (1969). The normalization principle and its human management implications. In R.B. Kugel & W. Wolfensberger (Eds.), *Changing patterns in residential services for the mentally retarded* (pp. 179–195). Washington, DC: President's Committee on Mental Retardation.

Nota, L., Ferrari, L., Soresi, S., & Wehmeyer, M.L. (2007). Self-determination, social abilities, and the quality of life of people with intellectual disabilities. *Journal of Intellectual Disability Research, 51,* 850–865.

Orkwis, R., & McLane, K. (1998). *A curriculum every student can use: Design principles for student access.* Reston, VA: Council for Exceptional Children.

Rappaport, J. (1981). In praise of a paradox: A social policy of empowerment over prevention. *American Journal of Community Psychology, 9,* 1–25.

Scheerenberger, R.C. (1987). *A history of mental retardation: A quarter century of promise.* Baltimore, MD: Paul H. Brookes Publishing Co.

Shapiro, J.P. (1993). *No pity: People with disabilities forging a new civil rights movement.* New York, NY: Times Books.

Shogren, K., Palmer, S., Wehmeyer, M.L., Williams-Diehm, K., & Little, T. (2012). Effect of intervention with the Self-Determined Learning Model of Instruction on access and goal attainment. *Remedial and Special Education, 33,* 150–161.

Smith, J.D., & Wehmeyer, M.L. (2012). *Good blood, bad blood: Science, nature, and the myth of the Kallikaks.* Washington, DC: American Association on Intellectual and Developmental Disabilities.

Stock, S.E., Davies, D.K., Wehmeyer, M.L., & Lachapelle, Y. (2011). Emerging new practices in technology to support independent community access for people with intellectual and cognitive disabilities. *Neurorehabilitation, 28,* 1–9.

Thompson, J.R., Bradley, V., Buntinx, W., Schalock, R.L., Shogren, K.A., Snell, M.E.,… Yeager, M.H. (2009). Conceptualizing supports and the support needs of people with intellectual disability. *Intellectual and Developmental Disabilities, 47*(2), 135–146. doi:10.1352/1934-9556-47.2.135

Thompson, J.R., Bryant, B., Campbell, E.M., Craig, E.M., Hughes, C., Rotholz, D., … Wehmeyer, M.L. (2003). *Supports Intensity Scale.* Washington, DC: American Association on Mental Retardation.

Trent, J.W. (1994). *Inventing the feeble mind: A history of mental retardation in the United States.* Berkeley: University of California Press.

Turnbull, A.P., Turnbull, H.R., Erwin, E.J., & Soodak, L.C. (2006). *Families, professionals, and exceptionality: Positive outcomes through partnerships and trust* (5th ed.). Upper Saddle River, NJ: Merrill/Prentice Hall.

Turnbull, A.P., Turnbull, H.R., Wehmeyer, M.L., & Shogren, K.A. (2013). *Exceptional lives: Special education in today's schools* (7th ed.). Upper Saddle River, NJ: Merrill/Prentice Hall.

Walker, H.M., Calkins, C., Wehmeyer, M., Walker, L., Bacon, A., Palmer, S., … Johnson, D. (2011). A social-ecological approach to promote self-determination. *Exceptionality, 19,* 6–18.

Ward, M.J. (1996). Coming of age in the age of self-determination: An historical and personal perspective. In D.J. Sands & M.L. Wehmeyer (Eds.), *Self-determination across the life span: Independence and choice for people with disabilities* (pp. 3–16). Baltimore, MD: Paul H. Brookes Publishing Co.

Wehman, P. (2011). JVR 20th anniversary: Editor's introduction. *Journal of Vocational Rehabilitation, 35,* 143.

Wehmeyer, M.L. (2005). Self-determination and individuals with severe disabilities: Reexamining meanings and misinterpretations. *Research and Practice for Persons with Severe Disabilities, 30,* 113–120.

Wehmeyer, M.L. (2011). Access to the general education curriculum for students with significant cognitive disabilities. In J.M. Kauffman & D.P. Hallahan (Eds.), *Handbook of Special Education* (pp. 544–556). New York, NY: Routledge.

Wehmeyer, M.L. (Ed.). (2013). *The story of intellectual disability: An evolution of meaning, understanding, and public perception.* Baltimore, MD: Paul H. Brookes Publishing Co.

Wehmeyer, M.L., Abery, B., Mithaug, D.E., & Stancliffe, R.J. (2003). *Theory in self-determination: Foundations for educational practice.* Springfield, IL: Charles C. Thomas Publisher.

Wehmeyer, M.L., Agran, M., Hughes, C., Martin, J., Mithaug, D.E., & Palmer, S. (2007). *Promoting self-determination in students with intellectual and developmental disabilities.* New York, NY: Guilford Press.

Wehmeyer, M.L., Bersani, H., & Gagne, R. (2000). Riding the third wave: Self-determination and self-advocacy in the 21st century. In M.L. Wehmeyer & J.R. Patton (Eds.), *Mental retardation in the 21st century* (pp. 315–333). Austin, TX: PRO-ED.

Wehmeyer, M.L., Buntinx, W.E., Lachapelle, Y., Luckasson, R., Schalock, R., Verdugo-Alonzo, M., … Yeager, M. (2008). The intellectual disability construct and its relationship to human functioning. *Intellectual and Developmental Disabilities, 46,* 311–318.

Wehmeyer, M.L., & Field, S. (2007). *Self-determination: Instructional and assessment strategies.* Thousand Oaks, CA: Corwin Press.

Wehmeyer, M.L., Field, S., Doren, B., Jones, B., & Mason, C. (2004). Self-determination and student involvement in standards-based reform. *Exceptional Children, 70,* 413–425.

Wehmeyer, M.L., & Palmer, S.B. (2003). Adult outcomes from students with cognitive disabilities three years after high school: The impact of self-determination. *Education and Training in Developmental Disabilities, 38,* 131–144.

Wehmeyer, M.L., Palmer, S., Shogren, K., Williams-Diehm, K., & Soukup, J. (2013). Establishing a causal relationship between interventions to promote self-determination and enhanced student self-determination. *Journal of Special Education, 46,* 195–210.

Wehmeyer, M.L., & Patton, J.R. (2000). *Mental retardation in the 21st century.* Austin, TX: PRO-ED.

Wehmeyer, M.L., & Schwartz, M. (1997). Self-determination and positive adult outcomes: A follow up study of youth with mental retardation or learning disabilities. *Exceptional Children, 63,* 245–255.

Wehmeyer, M.L., & Schwartz, M. (1998). The relationship between self-determination and quality of life for adults with mental retardation. *Education and Training in Mental Retardation and Developmental Disabilities, 33,* 3–12.

Wehmeyer, M.L., Shogren, K., Palmer, S., Williams-Diehm, K., Little, T., & Boulton, A. (2012). The impact of the Self-Determined Learning Model of Instruction on student self-determination. *Exceptional Children, 78,* 135–153.

Wehmeyer, M.L., Smith, S.J., Palmer, S.B., Davies, D.K., & Stock, S. (2004). Technology use and people with mental retardation. In L.M. Glidden (Ed.), *International review of research in mental retardation* (Vol. 29, pp. 293–337). San Diego, CA: Academic Press.

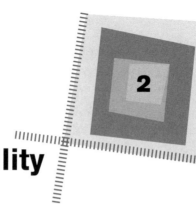

Poverty and Disability

Addressing the Ties that Bind

Carolyn Hughes and Latanya L. Fanion

"There is no reason why individuals with significant disabilities should not contribute to the nation's productivity and gross national product. There is no reason to exclude these persons from the opportunity to participate in the American dream of greater wealth and economic independence because of a label of severe disability."

—Wehman (2006, p. 123)

Vast numbers of people with severe disabilities continue to live in poverty despite years of legislation and advocacy efforts to improve outcomes for individuals with disabilities. Many have limited access to adequate health care, housing, transportation, or educational opportunities and report less satisfaction with life than do their counterparts without disabilities (National Organization on Disability, 2010). Unemployment and underemployment rates have stagnated at 80% for more than 30 years for adults with disabilities (U.S. Department of Labor, 2012), a fact in itself ensuring the financial dependence of a growing proportion of the population. This chapter argues that the persistence of poverty is partially due to the failure of public policy, the literature, and the field to acknowledge and address the interrelation of poverty and disability (She & Livermore, 2009).

This chapter's objectives are to 1) describe the extent and effects of poverty in the United States, particularly in relation to individuals with severe disabilities and their families and those from culturally diverse backgrounds; 2) discuss disability as both a cause and effect of poverty; and 3) propose strategies to address the challenges caused by the intersection of poverty and disability to improve the lives of people with severe disabilities. The content of this chapter aligns well with TASH's (2010) national agenda to address the full participation, equal opportunity, and quality of life of all people, including those of diverse ethnic, racial, and cultural backgrounds. Although the chapter's main focus is people with severe disabilities—those who "are most likely to need ongoing, individualized supports to participate in inclusive communities and enjoy a quality of life similar to that available to all people" (TASH, 2013)—it also addresses the issues of poverty and disability in general.

POVERTY IN THE UNITED STATES: PERVASIVE AND UNDERESTIMATED

The number of people living in poverty in the United States has significantly increased for the fourth consecutive year to reach 46.2 million (15.1% of the population) as reported by the U.S. Census Bureau (DeNavas-Walt, Proctor, & Smith, 2011). Poverty differentially affects children and racial and ethnic groups. Among children under 18 years old, 22.0% (16.4 million) live in poverty versus 13.7% of people ages 18–64. The rate of Blacks (27.4%) and Hispanics (26.6%) living in poverty is more than twice that of Whites (9.9%) and Asians (12.1%). Having health insurance coverage varies by race and ethnic group as well, with 30.7% (Hispanics), 20.8% (Blacks), 18.1% (Asians), and 11.7% (Whites) without coverage. Coverage also varies by household income, with 26.9% of members of households with less than $25,000 annual income without coverage versus 8.0% of household members with $75,000 or more annual household incomes. The uninsured rate for children in poverty (15.4%) is one third more than all children in the United States (9.8%) (DeNavas-Walt et al., 2011).

In addition, increasing numbers of public school students are being identified as low income or living in poverty as determined by their eligibility for free or reduced-price lunch. In 2007, the South became the first region in the United States in which low-income students were the majority of the public school population, increasing from 37% in 1989 to 54% (Suitts, 2007). California, New Mexico, and Oregon also serve a majority of low-income public school students, whereas the nation as a whole is approaching this threshold at 46% of the public school population (Suitts, 2007). In addition, students from racially and ethnically diverse groups make up an increasing proportion of the school population. White students are now in the minority in the South and several western states (National Center for Education Statistics, 2007; Orfield, 2009; Suitts, 2010). The majority of U.S. public school students is expected to be of color and low income by 2020 (Ball, 2009; National Center for Education Statistics, 2006; Suitts, 2010).

Unfortunately, these findings likely underrepresent actual poverty rates. Federal guidelines have long been criticized for underestimating numbers of people living in poverty (e.g., Fremstad, 2009; O'Brien, & Pedulla, 2010; She & Livermore, 2009). One problem is that the federal definition of poverty is outmoded at its current level of $17,057 household income for a family of three. The official poverty measure was developed in the 1960s and based on food expenses representing one third of a household budget. The formula remains at three times the annual cost of food; however, food now accounts for only one seventh of a typical family budget. In addition, the poverty formula excludes expenses for child care, health insurance, transportation, and other family needs as well as noncash benefits, such as housing assistance or food stamps (Annie E. Casey Foundation, 2009). The National Academy of Sciences and others have proposed new poverty measures, but resistance to identifying more individuals in need of social services and, thereby, challenging the status quo of wealth distribution in the United States persists (Cassidy, 2006).

Poverty and Disability

Poverty is also more prevalent among individuals with disabilities. More than twice the percentage of people with a disability ages 18–64 (27.9%) live in poverty as compared with those without a disability (12.5%) (DeNavas-Walt et al., 2011). Likewise, median income of householders with a disability ages 18–64 ($25,550) is half of that of their counterparts without a disability ($58,736). The majority of working-age adults living in chronic poverty has one or more disabilities (65%) (She & Livermore, 2009). In addition, more than one fourth of children with disabilities are living in families with earnings below the poverty level (Parish, Rose, & Andrews, 2010). Children with disabilities are also more likely to be from single-parent families and families of racially and ethnically diverse backgrounds (Parish, Rose, Grinstein-Weiss, Richman, & Andrews, 2008). These children may face additional obstacles, such as racism or prejudice, along with the educational, employment, and social challenges associated with poverty (Hughes & Avoke, 2010; McDonald, Keys, & Balcazar, 2007; She & Livermore, 2009).

Moreover, older students with disabilities and those from some racially and ethnically diverse groups and low-income backgrounds are more likely to be identified for special education services and placed in more restrictive educational settings outside general education classes (Hehir, Grindal, & Eidelman, 2012; U.S. Department of Education, 2010). More than half of students identified with intellectual disability—of which Black students are three times more likely than their White peers to be identified—spend the majority of their school day outside the general education classroom (U.S. Department of Education, 2010). Hehir et al. (2012) found that in Massachusetts both general and special education students on average score exceptionally well on national tests as compared with their counterparts in other states. These researchers, however, attributed poorer test performance of low-income special education students who are Black or Hispanic to their disproportionate placement outside general education. Further compounded with the disproportionate representation in some special education programs of Blacks and other racially and ethnically diverse groups is the fact that these students overwhelmingly attend underresourced, high-poverty schools (Balfanz & Legters, 2004; Orfield, 2009) and have parents who report insufficient access to special education services to meet their children's needs due to unavailability or financial hardship (Levine, Marder, & Wagner, 2004).

Effects of Poverty: It Is Not Just Not Enough Money

The effects of poverty are more than simply a lack of money. Growing up in an impoverished home or blighted neighborhood can have profound influences on children and their families, including unemployment, underemployment, and job instability; school dropout; substance abuse; and incarceration (e.g., Annie E. Casey Foundation, 2009; Sharkey, 2009; She & Livermore, 2009). Stressors associated with living in poverty, such as increased crime, persistent joblessness, limited health care and transportation, and inadequate housing can affect children's and family members' overall mental and physical health, producing high levels of anxiety, hypertension, fear, or depression (Wodtke, Harding, & Elwert, 2011). Chronic poverty and material hardship (e.g., poor nutrition, inadequate housing, limited health care) may contribute to disability and debilitating health conditions (She & Livermore, 2009). Youth exposed to long-term poverty may have less opportunity to volunteer; be actively involved in their communities; or participate in organized sports, extracurricular activities, or community groups (Hughes et al., 2004; Rothwell, 2012).

Students from low-income neighborhoods are also more likely to attend schools that are racially and ethnically segregated and have limited resources, less experienced teachers, poor standardized test scores, and low graduation rates (Orfield, 2009; Rothwell, 2012). These schools—typically located in communities with low property tax revenues to finance education—are historically underfunded and understaffed and have the highest dropout rates nationally reported. Almost 50% of Black and 40% of Hispanic students, as compared with only 11% of White students, attend high schools with dropout rates that average 50% or more (Balfanz & Legters, 2004; Rothwell, 2012). Furthermore, the average Black or Hispanic student attends a school where 60% of students live below the poverty line (Orfield, 2009).

Research investigating the gap in academic achievement among students from different racial, ethnic, and economic groups indicates that the schools these students attend vary substantially with respect to factors such as rigor of curriculum, teacher preparation and experience, teacher expectations, use of technology, safety on campus, and parent participation (e.g., Barton, 2003; Somers & Piliawsky, 2004). Unfortunately, living in a high-poverty neighborhood practically ensures that a student will attend an underresourced, underfunded, underperforming school with poor postschool outcomes: 60% of high school dropouts and only 5% of students enrolled in elite universities are from high-poverty neighborhoods and public schools (Kahlenberg, 2010). Research shows that high-performing schools are overwhelmingly located in or near more affluent communities, thereby segregating school populations and disproportionately concentrating low-income and racially and ethnically diverse students in low-performing schools by virtue of family income and housing patterns alone (Rothwell, 2012). Unfortunately, widespread and exclusionary residential zoning laws serve to maintain residential segregation of neighborhoods by differential housing costs (Boustan, 2012).

Limited Opportunity in School   Few studies have investigated the effects that attending a high-poverty, underresourced school has on students with more severe disabilities. Hughes, Cosgriff, Agran, and Washington (2013) found that students identified with severe disabilities (e.g., having extensive support needs and substantial delays in cognitive functioning, adaptive behavior, and verbal skills) attending a high-poverty urban high school spent significantly less time per week attending general education classes, participating in school-based job training, and receiving community-based instruction than their counterparts attending two more affluent schools. Students attending the high-poverty school also scored significantly lower than their counterparts when asked to report their use of self-determination skills, including self-advocating, self-monitoring, choice making, and problem solving. They were also significantly less likely to agree with the statement "If I have the ability, I will be able to get the job I want" than were students from higher income schools. Findings suggested that some high-poverty schools may provide limited educational experiences outside separate special education classrooms for students with more severe disabilities. These students likely are not making it into the pipeline leading to adult employment and economic mobility, in part because of the limits of their schools and neighborhoods (Sharkey, 2009), underscoring the need to provide access to inclusive environments with a range of opportunities to high-poverty youth with severe disabilities (Hughes & Avoke, 2010). Unfortunately, limited opportunity conspires to further hinder chances to emerge from poverty. A widespread assumption is that students with severe disabilities will not be able to work, despite many examples to the contrary, resulting in possible reluctance of providers to invest in these students' "human capital" (e.g., skills, knowledge, education)—a standard approach to poverty alleviation (She & Livermore, 2009).

Postschool Outcomes   The co-occurrence of disability—including severe disabilities—and poverty is associated with poor postschool outcomes, such as low graduation and postsecondary enrollment rates and increased unengagement, unemployment, and underemployment (Newman, Wagner, Cameto, & Knokey, 2009). Although there is no severe disabilities category in the Individuals with Disabilities Education Improvement Act (IDEA) of 2004 (PL 108-446) legislation, Newman et al. (2009) reported that only 31% of youth with intellectual disability are employed after leaving high school (primarily part time), only 7% attend postsecondary school as a sole postschool activity, only 14% live independently or semi-independently, only 26% have a checking account, and only 11% participate in a community group, such as a sports team or church club. These percentages are considerably lower than those of most other disability categories (e.g., learning disabilities). Students with disabilities from low-income households also fare more poorly across these same postschool indicators than do their counterparts from higher income homes. In addition, White youth are more likely to be employed than Blacks (63% versus 35%) or Hispanics (54%), to hold a skilled labor job, or to have a checking account (Newman et al., 2009).

Adult Outcomes   The 54 million Americans (19%) reported to have some type of disability represent one of the largest and fastest growing minority groups in the nation (Brault, 2008). *Disability*, typically defined in the adult literature as "a physical or mental impairment that substantially limits one or more major life activities" or "being regarded as having such an impairment" (Americans with Disabilities Amendments Act [ADA] of 2008 [PL 110-325]; § 12102), occurs more frequently across different racial and ethnic groups. Disability rates in the United States in 2007 for adults ages 21–64 years were 6% (Asian), 13% (White), 11% (Hispanic), 17% (Black), and 23% (Native American) (Erickson, Lee, & von Schrader, 2010). Adults with disabilities are more likely than the general population to experience the effects of poverty and material hardship, including food insecurity, inadequate housing and medical care, and difficulty paying bills (Fremstad, 2009; Parish et al., 2008, 2010; Yamaki & Fujiura, 2002). These outcomes are particularly salient for the two thirds (35 million) of the population with disabilities identified as having a disability substantial enough to interfere with everyday activities (Fremstad, 2009). The definition of a *severe disability* used by the U.S. Census Bureau is notably much broader than that of TASH (2013) and includes physical limitations, such as the inability to climb stairs or prepare a meal, without the presence of an intellectual disability. At the same time, 27% of adults ages 25–64 years identified with a severe disability by the U.S. Census Bureau in 2005 were reported to be living in poverty compared with 12% of adults with a less severe disability and 9% without a disability (Brault, 2008).

Employment Outcomes   Only 18% of individuals with disabilities age 16 years and over (excluding institutionalized populations) are reported to be employed versus 64% of individuals without disabilities (U.S. Department of Labor, 2012). Adults with intellectual, developmental, or severe disabilities are even less likely to be employed, although reported rates differ across studies due to varying definitions of *employment* and *severe disabilities* and sources of support services (e.g., vocational rehabilitation). For example, Erickson et al. (2010) reported that only 14% of adults with cognitive disabilities (i.e., having serious difficulty concentrating, remembering, or making decisions) and 9% with independent living disabilities (i.e., difficulty doing errands alone such as visiting a doctor's office or shopping), respectively, were employed full time. Nationally, employees with intellectual and developmental disabilities experience limited work hours and few wage increases or are restricted to working in segregated facility-based settings earning considerably less than minimum wage (Butterworth, Smith, Cohen Hall, Migliore, & Winsor, 2008; Metzel, Boeltzig, Butterworth, Sulewski, & Gilmore, 2007). It is these workers in entry-level jobs who are unfortunately often the first to be laid off or have their hours further cut in times of economic hardship, such as a recession (Bureau of Labor Statistics, 2009; Kaye, 2009). These deplorable findings explain in part the prevalence of poverty among people of working age with disabilities, especially those with more substantial disabilities—few are working, and those who are working are underemployed and working for wages below the poverty level.

Well-Being and Quality of Life   The repercussions of mass unemployment or underemployment and poverty-level wages on the daily lives and well-being of adults with severe disabilities are not trivial. The sixth National Organization on Disability *Survey of Americans with Disabilities* (2010) conducted by telephone with almost 2,000 respondents with and without disabilities ages 18 years and over or their proxies (10% of respondents were by proxy) revealed disturbing findings regarding the quality of life of adults with disabilities and, in particular, a subset of respondents identified with severe disabilities. *Disability* is broadly defined in the survey (e.g., a physical, health, cognitive, or emotional condition that prevents full participation in daily activities) and includes a wider population than intellectual or developmental disabilities. In the 2010 survey, 57% of participants with disabilities also identified their disability as severe (no definition provided). These individuals reported that they were less likely to socialize with friends or family, attend religious services, or go to a restaurant or entertainment event than did respondents without disabilities or respondents identifying themselves as having less intensive disabilities.

For example, only 37% of respondents self-identifying with a severe disability reported eating at a restaurant at least twice a month compared with 63% of adults with a mild disability and 75% without a disability. In addition, 41% of respondents with a self-reported severe disability considered access to transportation to be a problem (versus 24% with mild disabilities and 16% without disabilities), 23% reported having gone without needed health care during the past year (versus 13% with mild disabilities and 10% without disabilities), and only 27% reported feeling very satisfied with life (versus 44% with mild disabilities and 61% without disabilities). Furthermore, participants with disabilities who responded to the National Organization on Disability (2004) survey reported being 1) more worried about their future health and well-being (e.g., being unable to take care of self, losing health insurance, becoming disconnected from family or friends) and 2) more likely to feel that their lives would get worse rather than better over the next 4 years than did respondents without disabilities.

Prevailing Legislation and Policy

Compounding the limited experiences, opportunities, resources, and levels of satisfaction reported by people who identified as having more substantial disabilities in the National Organization on Disability surveys is the lack of affordable housing for the great majority of adults with disabilities who are unemployed or underemployed and receiving federal Supplemental Security Income (SSI) payments. The latest yearly housing report conducted by the Technical Assistance Collaborative and the Consortium for Citizens with Disabilities Housing Task Force concluded that "there is not one state or community in the nation where a person with a disability receiving SSI payments can afford to rent a modest—not luxurious—one-bedroom or efficiency housing unit" (Cooper, Korman, O'Hara, & Zovistoski, 2009, p. 1). People with disabilities in general must pay on average nationally 112% of monthly income to rent a modest one-bedroom unit (range = 100% of income in Vermont to 178% in Washington, D.C.). Cooper and colleagues cited 1) the failure of SSI payments (average monthly SSI income is $688) to match the increasing cost of basic human needs; 2) inadequate funding, support, and implementation of federal housing programs for people with disabilities (e.g., public housing, Section 8 programs); and 3) limited community supports as partial causes of the chronic lack of affordable housing for people with disabilities, resulting in unsafe and unhealthy residential situations, unnecessary institutionalization, and homelessness.

Having a safe and comfortable home environment is fundamental to quality of life; the failure to provide access to adequate subsidized housing for large numbers of people with disabilities, including intellectual and developmental disabilities, is deplorable. Barney Frank, Chairman of the Committee on Financial Service in the U.S. House of Representatives, which has jurisdiction over federal housing programs, argued, "A lack of adequate housing is a serious obstacle to a decent life for anyone. It can be particularly troublesome for people dealing with disabilities, for whom the physical and emotional stresses of a lack of decent shelter are added burdens" (2009, p. ii).

In fact, the percentage of adults with disabilities living in poverty is increasing despite increasing public expenditures for support (Stapleton, O'Day, Livermore, & Imparato, 2005). This seeming contradiction is partly due to what Stapleton and colleagues referred to as the "poverty trap" in which income supports (e.g., SSI) and other benefits (e.g., health care) are reduced or lost if an employee earns over a federally determined threshold, which itself is set below a living wage. Piecemeal efforts to decrease disincentives for workers to earn more (e.g., Ticket to Work) fail to address the complexity of the challenges that working and living in poverty present (e.g., lack of health care, few neighborhood resources, increased stressors associated with daily living) or the increased expenses of having a disability (e.g., home health aide, ongoing therapy, accessible transportation). The effect of such federal disability programs (e.g., Ticket to Work, SSI, housing) is to relegate adults with disabilities to a life of poverty and limited opportunity for advancement.

CHALLENGES AND CONTROVERSIES: FAILURE TO ADDRESS THE INTERACTION OF POVERTY AND DISABILITY

The overlap of poverty and disability has resulted in a call for viewing disability as both a cause and a consequence of poverty (e.g., Blanchett, 2008; Emerson, 2007;

Fremstad, 2009). For example, higher rates of poverty are experienced by families with children or other family members with a disability due in part to the extra costs of having a disability (e.g., home health care, assistive technology, transportation). In addition, having a disability, particularly an intellectual disability, can limit one's employability and wages earned (Brault, 2008; Emerson, 2007; Sinclair & Yeargin-Allsopp, 2007). For example, job training programs for people with intellectual disabilities often target low-paying, part-time, entry-level jobs that offer few benefits or opportunities for promotion or advancement (Metzel et al., 2007).

Yet, growing up in poverty increases the likelihood of having a disability due to a gamut of factors, such as exposure to environmental hazards (e.g., lead poisoning, unsanitary drinking water, preterm births), environmental stress (e.g., unsafe neighborhood, lack of transportation), or lack of material needs (e.g., inadequate food, housing, or medical care) (e.g., Duncan & Brooks-Gunn, 2000; Shipler, 2004). In addition, poverty likely exacerbates an already existing disability. Research indicates that the increased risk of poorer physical and mental health and well-being among some children and youth with intellectual disability may be attributed to exposure to poverty and related inequalities and exclusion (e.g., Emerson & Hatton, 2007). Although rarely acknowledged or discussed in the poverty literature, current findings indicate that almost half (47%) of all adults who experience income poverty for a period of at least 12 months and nearly two thirds (65%) of those experiencing long-term poverty have one or more disabilities (Fremstad, 2009).

Rarely do the disability and poverty literatures acknowledge or learn from each other (e.g., Blanchett, 2008; Fremstad, 2009; She & Livermore, 2009). Fremstad argued that any attempt to reduce poverty must take disability into account, and if the costs of having a disability are not considered, then the income needs of individuals with disabilities or their families will be underestimated. The poverty literature largely fails to acknowledge or consider the prevalence and impact of disability, however. Conversely, others have argued that the disability literature fails to acknowledge the vast number of people with disabilities who are living in poverty and experiencing material hardship; until the literature does, inequities in experiencing quality of life (e.g., good health, safe and comfortable home, community participation) by individuals with disabilities will persist (e.g., Blanchett, 2008; Emerson, 2007; Gerber, 2009). Furthermore, the effects of poverty and interrelation of poverty and disability are generally unknown by the public. She and Livermore (2009) argued that although the recent recession has focused attention on increasing rates of poverty both in the United States and globally, practically no attention is paid to the intersection of poverty and disability.

Recommended Policy, Research, and Practice

Challenges must be addressed on multiple fronts when the third largest minority group in the United States—people with disabilities and, in particular, those with intellectual and developmental disabilities—is experiencing mass unemployment and underemployment; lack of affordable housing; food scarcity and material hardship; limited health care and transportation; few education or job training opportunities; and limited socializing, community participation, and satisfaction with life. Educators, policy makers, adult services providers, parents, and advocates need to ensure that providing quality employment with health care and other benefits, suf-

ficient community and residential supports, and appropriate education and employment training opportunities for people with severe disabilities—and disabilities, in
general—are in the national spotlight and on the national agenda as legislative and
funding priorities. We propose a number of recommendations in order to address
the intersection of poverty and disability in future policy, research, and practice.

First, the disability and poverty literatures need to recognize and learn from
each other (Fremstad, 2009; She & Livermore, 2009). Disability research needs to
systematically address the socioeconomic status of participants with disabilities,
whereas poverty studies must incorporate the effects of disability (e.g., increased
expenses and support needs) into research designs. Poverty researchers and anti-
poverty advocates must take disability into account as both a cause and a consequence of poverty because two thirds of adults experiencing chronic poverty have a
disability (Fremstad, 2009). Furthermore, the current literature must acknowledge
the inadequacy of the federal measure of poverty, which sorely underestimates prevalence and fails to address the multidimensional aspects of poverty. An expanded
definition of poverty beyond a simple lack of income and one that incorporates the
added expenses of a disability needs to be proposed and adopted by both the poverty and disability literatures.

Second, the persistence of poverty and related lack of opportunity must
be addressed at its root—home, school, and community. Many low-income students, including those with disabilities, are denied the opportunity to attend well-
resourced, high-performing schools because widespread discriminatory zoning laws
deny the construction or use of inexpensive housing or rental property in affluent
neighborhoods where these schools overwhelmingly are located (Rothwell, 2012).
In particular, students who are Black or Hispanic and low income and their families
are priced out and zoned out of living in more affluent communities with abundant
resources such as recreational facilities, employment opportunities, transportation
options, and entertainment choices, as well as schools that offer a range of educational opportunities, supports, and services. Instead, these students likely are living
in neighborhoods and attending schools that limit rather than nurture students'
opportunities to acquire essential life skills associated with successful adulthood.
Rothwell (2012) called for exclusionary zoning alternatives and revised housing
policies to promote affordable housing and more integrated neighborhoods racially,
ethnically, and economically, thus providing access to resources and opportunities
related to well-being and quality of life for all neighborhood residents.

Third, the U.S. Department of Justice and the U.S. Department of Education
(2011) jointly issued new guidelines for considering race when assigning students to
K–12 schools to increase diversity and reduce racial isolation. The guidelines provide
clarification for how school districts may legally consider race to promote diversity in
the wake of recent Supreme Court decisions (e.g., *Parents Involved in Community
Schools v. Seattle School District No. 1*, 2007). They also represent a revolution-
ary change by reversing the race-neutral guidelines governing student enrollment
policy issued by the previous presidential administration following the Supreme
Court cases. The current document argues that racially isolated schools fail to provide the full benefits that public schools can offer, hampering student achievement
due to high teacher turnover, less rigorous curricula (e.g., few college preparatory
courses), and inferior facilities and educational resources (U.S. Department of Justice & U.S. Department of Education, 2011). School districts now have guidance in

drawing attendance boundaries and transferring students to legally achieve greater student diversity, taking into account students' race as well as the socioeconomic status of families and neighborhoods and proximity of subsidized housing. Proactive adherence by school districts in implementing the new guidelines will be a powerful first step in achieving educational equality for students, including those with disabilities, attending racially isolated, high-poverty schools—a major impetus toward improving student performance and postschool outcomes.

Fourth, the much-awaited reauthorization of the Elementary and Secondary Education Act (ESEA) of 1965 (PL 89-10) is being considered by Congress. Darling-Hammond (2012) argued that disparities in school funding must be addressed if we expect low-performing schools (i.e., those that are underresourced and serve low-income, racially and ethnically isolated students) to achieve adequate yearly progress on state exams (e.g., U.S. Department of Education, 2011). She suggested establishing common resource standards across schools and incentives to achieve them, including well-qualified teachers, high-quality curricula, and equitable instructional resources. Darling-Hammond also argued,

> The ESEA should tie standards for equal educational opportunity to standards for learning: indicators of learning opportunities—the availability of qualified teachers, appropriate courses, materials and equipment, and necessary services—should be published alongside test results, and states should be expected to show evidence of progress toward resource equalization along with evidence of learning. (2012, p. 8)

The reauthorization of the ESEA and IDEA 2004 should resurrect the early goals of the 1965 ESEA and Education for All Handicapped Children Act of 1975 (PL 94-142) to compensate for the effects of poverty and disability, particularly among racial, ethnic, and other minority and disenfranchised groups that experience the highest rates of unemployment, such as the near 50% unemployment rates of Black urban male high school dropouts (Mincy, 2006). Critics of the charter school and teacher accountability movements (e.g., Darling-Hammond, 2012; Ladd & Fiske, 2011; Ravitch, 2010; Rothstein, 2011) argued these reform movements fail to address the root of the problem—poverty. They argued that the many out-of-school factors that influence student performance, including the socioeconomic conditions experienced by increasing numbers of public school students, must be taken into account in current legislation revision and school reform efforts, rather than focusing on ineffective teachers as the primary source of poor student outcomes. Special educators must be informed of and actively participate in these movements to ensure that students with severe disabilities are included.

Fifth, recommended standards for students with disabilities who are transition age should include transition services as mandated by the IDEA 2004, such as experiences in the community and instruction in employment and daily living skills. If we intend to improve postschool outcomes for students with disabilities as they enter their adult lives, then including employment, postsecondary education, independent living, economic self-sufficiency, community participation, social engagement, and quality of life in existing federal transition mandates must increase, and the responsibility of schools for achieving students' postschool outcomes must be expanded (Rusch, Hughes, Agran, Martin, & Johnson, 2009). Rusch and colleagues recommended that high schools should have primary responsibility and be held accountable for 1) ensuring that students have identified a desired postschool placement—postsecondary education or employment—prior to school exit, 2) assisting students and their families in making the transition to this placement, and 3) coordinating postschool services and supports to ensure placement and outcome success (Hughes & Avoke, 2010). In addition, opportunities to participate in stimulating environments outside of the special education classroom in which students can make choices, problem-solve, and learn self-determination skills as well as develop career interests through job sampling, job training, or internship opportunities must be provided, particularly in low-income schools where these opportunities may be less likely to occur (Washington, Hughes, & Cosgriff, 2012).

Sixth, teachers must be educated about the effects of poverty on children and families. Teachers are confronted daily by the symptoms of poverty—a high school student receiving cell phone calls from her mother during class telling the student that she needs to get a second job because the family is not reporting enough income to qualify for a rental apartment. Or a young man having difficulty staying awake in class because he takes three buses to and from his after-school job, returns home at midnight to do his homework, and wakes up at 5:00 a.m. to catch the bus to school. Teachers who are not aware of the effects of poverty may interpret students' behavior as disrespect or disinterest in learning. Teacher preparation programs need to educate preservice teachers about the effects of poverty and help them identify and respond in a caring and empathetic way to its symptoms (Ravitch, 2010). Teachers can learn to engage and support students from high-poverty homes, as well as learn when to seek outside support, such as from a social worker or health services provider (Rothstein, 2011). Viewing disability, especially intellectual disability, as the fit between the environment and the individual (Thompson, Wehmeyer, & Hughes, 2010) and education as providing the supports needed to optimize the fit may help teachers incorporate needed supports related not only to the disability itself but also to challenges associated with poverty conditions experienced by students (She & Livermore, 2009).

Seventh, advocacy efforts should focus on policy reforms to expand disability support programs, such as SSI benefits, job-training programs, and supported employment to allow individuals to achieve maximum economic self-sufficiency. At the same time, disability advocates need to publicize "illustrations of competence" that highlight examples of the many people with severe disabilities who are gainfully, skillfully, and successfully employed (e.g., Brown, Shiraga, & Kessler, 2006; Certo et al., 2008) in order to educate the public and raise expectations for what people with disabilities can do. The presumption held by the public should be that individuals with severe disabilities *can* work with appropriate supports (Stapleton et al., 2005). Disability policy must be amended to allow people with severe disabilities to emerge from poverty and experience the benefits of a living wage, health care, and access to transportation and employment advancement.

Finally, we faced two challenges in writing this chapter. One is that there is no universal definition of *severe disabilities;* in fact, such a category does not exist in special education legislation. The adult literature, however, has a range of definitions of the term, typically much broader than the TASH (2013) definition. Some readers may argue for a more standard definition of *severe disabilities*, although such definitions are often value based or lack universal acceptance (e.g., level of required support versus personal deficits) (see Thompson et al., 2010). Because a universal definition of severe disabilities currently does not exist, we sought to clarify definitions of the populations addressed across studies in order to incorporate findings from disparate sources. Readers should be aware as they read the literature, however, that similar terminology across studies may not indicate similar populations.

Second, we discussed issues in this chapter that we believe apply to both the narrower population of individuals with severe disabilities and those with disabilities in general. We caution against having a restricted view of the interconnections between disability and poverty. We argue that there are many contemporary issues relevant to both populations, such as expanding the role of schools in addressing students' postschool outcomes and ensuring that the intersection of poverty and disability is on the national agenda. These issues apply to people with disabilities, in general, as well as people with severe disabilities. There are, of course, issues that are more disability specific, such as assuring accessibility in the community for people with physical or sensory impairments. At the same time, we suggest that there are benefits to placing some of the challenges of severe disability in the larger context of disability and poverty.

CONCLUSION

People with severe disabilities should not be relegated to living a life of poverty. Wehman (2006) argued that there is no reason to deny these individuals the opportunity to experience the expectations we all have for a full, safe, satisfying, and, even sometimes, exciting life. We need to loosen the binds that keep a large proportion of the severe disabilities population tethered to a life of poverty and unfulfilled hopes and dreams. We can work together to make a concerted effort to address the interrelation of poverty and disability to ensure that all people have the opportunity to experience well-being and quality of life.

Questions for Study and Reflection

1. Describe how poverty differentially affects groups of people in the United States, including racial and ethnic groups, children, and people with disabilities.

2. What are some factors that might account for the persistence of poverty among people with disabilities?

3. Describe the effects of poverty on an individual's well-being and quality of life.

4. How do poverty and disability affect each other?

5. What is the relation between poverty and opportunity?

6. Evaluate and prioritize the suggestions in this chapter for alleviating poverty among people with disabilities, especially those with severe disabilities.

7. Suggest additional strategies for alleviating poverty and improving well-being and quality of life of people with severe disabilities.

RESOURCES

Annie E. Casey Foundation *http://www.aecf.org/*

The Civil Rights Project/Proyecto Derechos Civiles at the University of California, Los Angeles (UCLA) *http://civilrightsproject.ucla.edu/*

Institute for Community Inclusion *http://www.communityinclusion.org/*

National Organization on Disability *http://www.nod.org/*

Southern Education Foundation *http://www.southerneducation.org/*

REFERENCES

Americans with Disabilities Amendments Act (ADA) of 2008, PL 110-325, 42 U.S.C. §§ 12101 *et seq.*

Annie E. Casey Foundation. (2009). *Counting what counts: Taking results seriously for vulnerable children and families.* Baltimore, MD: Author. Retrieved from http://datacenter.kidscount.org/Databook/2009/OnlineBooks/AEC186_essay_FINAL.pdf

Balfanz, R., & Legters, N.E. (2004). Locating the dropout crisis: Which high schools produce the nation's dropouts? In G. Orfield (Ed.), *Dropouts in America: Confronting the graduation crisis* (pp. 57–84). Cambridge, MA: Harvard University Press.

Ball, A.F. (2009). Toward a theory of generative change in culturally and linguistically complex classrooms. *American Educational Research Journal, 46,* 45–72.

Barton, P.E. (2003). *Parsing the achievement gap: Baselines for tracking progress.* Princeton, NJ: Educational Testing Service. Retrieved from http://www.ets.org/Media/Research/pdf/PICPARSING.pdf

Blanchett, W.J. (2008). We've come a long way but we're not there yet: The impact of research and policy on racially/ethnically and culturally diverse individuals with disabilities and/or those affected by poverty. *TASH Connections, 34,* 11–13, 20.

Boustan, L.P. (2012). School desegregation and urban change: Evidence from city boundaries. *American Economic Journal: Applied Economics, 4,* 85–108.

Brault, M.W. (2008). *Current population reports. Americans with Disabilities: 2005. Household economic studies.* Washington, DC: U.S. Census Bureau.

Brown, L., Shiraga, B., & Kessler, K. (2006). The quest for ordinary lives: The integrated post-school vocational functioning of fifty workers with significant disabilities. *Research and Practice for Persons with Severe Disabilities, 31,* 93–121.

Bureau of Labor Statistics. (2009). *Economic news release: Mass layoffs summary.* Washington, DC: U.S. Department of Labor. Retrieved from http://www.bls.gov/news.release/mslo.nr0.htm

Butterworth, J., Smith, F.A., Cohen Hall, A., Migliore, A., & Winsor, J. (2008). *StateData: The national report on employment services and outcomes.* Boston, MA: Institute for Community Inclusion. Retrieved from http://www.communityinclusion.org/pdf/statedatabook_F.pdf

Cassidy, J. (2006, April 3). Relatively deprived: How poor is poor? *The New Yorker,* 42–47.

Certo, N.J., Luecking, R.G., Murphy, S., Brown, L., Courey, S., & Belanger, D. (2008). Seamless transition and long-term support for individuals with severe intellectual disabilities. *Research and Practice for Persons with Severe Disabilities, 33,* 85–95.

Cooper, E., Korman, H., O'Hara, A., & Zovistoski, A. (2009). *Priced out in 2008: The housing crisis for people with disabilities.* Boston, MA: Technical Assistance Collaborative. Retrieved from http://www.tacinc.org

Darling-Hammond, L. (2012, January 17). *Why is Congress redlining our schools?*

Retrieved from http://www.washington post.com

DeNavas-Walt, C., Proctor, B.D., & Smith, J.C. (2011). *Income, poverty, and health insurance coverage in the United States: 2010.* Washington, DC: U.S. Department of Commerce, U.S. Census Bureau. Retrieved from http://www.census.gov/prod/2011pubs/p60-239.pdf

Duncan, G.J., & Brooks-Gunn, J. (2000). Family poverty, welfare reform, and child development. *Child Development, 71,* 188–196. doi:10.1111/1467-8624.00133

Education for All Handicapped Children Act of 1975, PL 94-142, 20 U.S.C. §§ 1400 *et seq.*

Elementary and Secondary Education Act of 1965, PL 89-10, 20 U.S.C. §§ 241 *et seq.*

Emerson, E. (2007). Poverty and people with intellectual disabilities. *Mental Retardation and Developmental Disabilities Research Reviews, 13,* 107–113. doi:10.1002/mrdd.20144

Emerson, E., & Hatton, C. (2007). Contribution of socioeconomic position to health inequalities of British children and adolescents with intellectual disabilities. *American Journal on Mental Retardation, 112,* 140–150. doi:10.1352/0895-8017(2007)112[140:COSPTH]2.0.CO;2

Erickson, W., Lee, C., & von Schrader, S. (2010). *2008 Disability Status Report: United States.* Ithaca, NY: Cornell University Rehabilitation Research and Training Center on Disability Demographics and Statistics.

Frank, B. (2009). Foreword. In E. Cooper, H. Korman, A. O'Hara, & A. Zovistoski (Eds.), *Priced out in 2008: The housing crisis for people with disabilities* (pp. i–ii). Boston, MA: Technical Assistance Collaborative. Retrieved from http://www.tacinc.org

Fremstad, S. (2009). *Half in ten: Why taking disability into account is essential to reducing poverty and expanding economic inclusion.* Washington, DC: Center for Economic and Policy Research. Retrieved from http://www.cepr.net/documents/publications/poverty-disability-2009-09.pdf

Gerber, M. (2009, July). *Special education: Our future role and needed policy supports.* Keynote session presented at the 2009 OSEP Project Directors' Conference, Washington, DC.

Hehir, T., Grindal, T., & Eidelman, H. (2012). *Review of special education in the commonwealth of Massachusetts.* Boston, MA: Thomas Hehir and Associates. Retrieved from http://www.doe.mass.edu/sped/2012/0412sped.pdf

Hughes, C., & Avoke, S.K. (2010). The elephant in the room: Poverty, disability, and employment. *Research and Practice for Persons with Severe Disabilities, 35,* 5–14.

Hughes, C., Cosgriff, J., Agran, M., & Washington, B. (2013). Student self-determination: A preliminary investigation of the role of participation in inclusive settings. *Education and Training in Autism and Developmental Disabilities, 48,* 3–17.

Hughes, C., Wehby, J.H., Carter, E.W., Plank, D., Wilson, L., Johnson, S., & Barton-Arwood, S. (2004). Summer activities of youth with high-incidence disabilities from high-poverty backgrounds. *Career Development for Exceptional Individuals, 27,* 27–42. doi:10.1177/088572880402700103

Individuals with Disabilities Education Improvement Act (IDEA) of 2004, PL 108-446, 20 U.S.C. §§ 1400 *et seq.*

Kahlenberg, R. (Ed.). (2010). *Rewarding strivers: Helping low-income students succeed in college.* New York, NY: The Century Foundation.

Kaye, H.S. (2009). Stuck at the bottom rung: Occupational characteristics of workers with disabilities. *Journal of Occupational Rehabilitation, 19,* 115–128. doi:10.1007/s10926-009-9175-2

Ladd, H.F., & Fiske, E.B. (2011, December 11). *Class matters. Why won't we admit it?* Retrieved from http://www.nytimes.com

Levine, P., Marder, C., & Wagner, M. (2004). *Services and supports for secondary school students with disabilities. A special topic report of findings from the National Longitudinal Transition Study–2 (NLTS–2).* Menlo Park, CA: SRI International. Retrieved from http://www.nlts2.org/reports/2004_05/nlts2_report_2004_05_complete.pdf

McDonald, K.E., Keys, C.B., & Balcazar, F.E. (2007). Disability, race/ethnicity, and gender: Themes of cultural oppression, acts of individual resistance. *American Journal of Community Psychology, 39,* 145–161. doi:10.1007/s10464-007-9094-3

Metzel, D.S., Boeltzig, H., Butterworth, J., Sulewski, J.S., & Gilmore, D.S. (2007).

Achieving community membership through community rehabilitation provider services: Are we there yet? *Intellectual and Developmental Disabilities, 45,* 149–160. doi:10.1352/1934-9556 (2007)45[149:ACMTCR]2.0.CO;2

Mincy, R.B. (Ed.). (2006). *Black males left behind.* Washington, DC: Urban Institute.

National Center for Education Statistics. (2006). *Characteristics of the 100 largest public elementary and secondary school districts in the United States: 2003–04 statistical analysis report.* Washington, DC: U.S. Department of Education. Retrieved from http://nces.ed.gov/pubs2006/2006329.pdf

National Center for Education Statistics. (2007). *Status and trends in the education of racial and ethnic minorities.* Washington, DC: U.S. Department of Education. Retrieved from http://nces.ed.gov/pubs2007/minoritytrends/tables/table_7_2.asp?referrer=report

National Organization on Disability. (2004). *NOD/Harris 2004 survey of Americans with disabilities.* Washington, DC: Author.

National Organization on Disability. (2010). *Kessler Foundation/NOD 2010 survey of Americans with disabilities.* Washington, DC: Author.

Newman, L., Wagner, M., Cameto, R., & Knokey, A.M. (2009). *The post-high school outcomes of youth with disabilities up to 4 years after high school. A report from the National Longitudinal Transition Study–2 (NLTS–2).* Menlo Park, CA: SRI International. Retrieved from http://www.nlts2.org/reports/2009_04/nlts2_report_2009_04_complete.pdf

O'Brien, R.L., & Pedulla, D.S. (2010, Fall). *Beyond the poverty line.* Retrieved from http://www.ssireview.org/articles/entry/beyond_the_poverty_line

Orfield, G. (2009). *Reviving the goal of an integrated society: A 21st century challenge.* Los Angeles: University of California, Los Angeles (UCLA), The Civil Rights Project/Proyecto Derechos Civiles. Retrieved from http://www.civilrightsproject.ucla.edu/

Parents Involved in Community Schools v. Seattle School District No. 1, 551 U.S. 701 (U.S. 2007).

Parish, S.L., Rose, R.A., & Andrews, M.E. (2010). TANF's impact on low-income mothers raising children with disabilities. *Exceptional Children, 76,* 234–253.

Parish, S.L., Rose, R.A., Grinstein-Weiss, M., Richman, E.L., & Andrews, M.E. (2008). Material hardship in U.S. families raising children with disabilities. *Exceptional Children, 75,* 71–92.

Ravitch, D. (2010, December). *PISA: It's poverty, not stupid.* Retrieved from http://nasspblogs.org

Rothstein, R. (2011, September 1). Grading the education reformers: Steven Brill gives them much too easy a ride. *Education Review, 14,* 1–10.

Rothwell, J. (2012). *Housing costs, zoning, and access to high-scoring schools.* Washington, DC: Brookings Institution. Retrieved from http://www.brookings.edu/research/papers/2012/04/19-school-inequality-rothwell

Rusch, F.R., Hughes, C., Agran, M., Martin, J.E., & Johnson, J.R. (2009). Toward self-directed learning, post-high school placement, and coordinated support: Constructing new transition bridges to adult life. *Career Development for Exceptional Individuals, 32,* 53–59.

Sharkey, P. (2009). *Neighborhoods and the black–white mobility gap.* Washington, DC: Economic Mobility Project, The Pew Charitable Trusts. Retrieved from http://www.economicmobility.org/assets/pdfs/PEW_NEIGHBORHOODS.pdf

She, P., & Livermore, G.A. (2009). Long-term poverty and disability among working-age adults. *Journal of Disability Policy Studies, 19,* 244–256.

Shipler, D.K. (2004). *The working poor: Invisible in America.* New York, NY: Alfred A. Knopf.

Sinclair, L.B., & Yeargin-Allsopp, M. (2007). Racial and ethnic minorities with intellectual disabilities: A public health perspective. *TASH Connections, 33,* 20–23, 37.

Somers, C.L., & Piliawsky, M. (2004). Dropout prevention among urban, African American adolescents: Program evaluation and practical implications. *Preventing School Failure, 48,* 17–22.

Stapleton, D.C., O'Day, B., Livermore, G.A., & Imparato, A.J. (2005). *Dismantling the poverty trap: Disability policy for the 21st century.* Ithaca, NY: Rehabilitation Research and Training Center for Economic Research on Employment Policy for Persons with Disabilities. Retrieved from

http://digitalcommons.ilr.cornell.edu/edi
collect/124

Suitts, S.T. (2007). *A new majority: Low income students in the South's public schools.* Atlanta, GA: Southern Education Foundation. Available at http://www.southerneducation.org

Suitts, S.T. (2010). *A new diverse majority: Students of color in the South's public schools.* Atlanta, GA: Southern Education Foundation. Available at http://www.southerneducation.org

TASH. (2010). *2010 TASH national agenda.* Retrieved from http://tash.org/about/initiatives/

TASH. (2013). *TASH mission and vision.* Retrieved from http://tash.org/about/mission/

Thompson, J.R., Wehmeyer, M.L., & Hughes, C. (2010). Mind the gap! Implications of a person–environment fit model of intellectual disability for students, teachers, and schools. *Exceptionality, 18,* 168–181. doi:10.1080/09362835.2010.513919

U.S. Department of Education. (2010). *29th annual report to Congress on the implementation of the Individuals with Disabilities Education Act, 2007.* Washington, DC: Author.

U.S. Department of Education. (2011). *Comparability of state and local expenditures among schools within districts: A report from the study of school-level expenditures.* Washington, DC: Office of Planning, Evaluation and Policy Development, Policy and Program Studies Service.

U.S. Department of Justice & U.S. Department of Education. (2011, December 2). *Guidance on the voluntary use of race to achieve diversity in postsecondary education.* Washington, DC: Author. Retrieved from http://www.justice.gov/crt/about/edu/documents/guidancepost.pdf

U.S. Department of Labor. (2012, June 8). *Persons with a disability: Labor force characteristics—2011.* Washington, DC: Author. Retrieved from http://www.bls.gov/news.release/pdf/disabl.pdf

Washington, B.H., Hughes, C., & Cosgriff, J.C. (2012). High-poverty youth: Self-determination and involvement in educational planning. *Career Development and Transition for Exceptional Individuals, 35,* 14–28. doi:10.1177/0885728811420135

Wehman, P. (2006). Integrated employment: If not now, when? If not us, who? *Research and Practice for Persons with Severe Disabilities, 31,* 122–126.

Wodtke, G.T., Harding, D.J., & Elwert, F. (2011). Neighborhood effects in temporal perspective: The impact of long-term exposure to concentrated disadvantage on high school graduation. *American Sociological Review, 76,* 713–736. doi:10.1177/0003122411420816

Yamaki, K., & Fujiura, G.T. (2002). Employment and income status of adults with developmental disabilities living in the community. *Mental Retardation, 40,* 132–141. doi:10.1352/0047-6765(2002)040<0132: EAISOA>2.0.CO;2

Forty Years of Living and Thriving with Disabilities

Perceptions of a Self-Advocate and Her Family

Michelle Sommerstein, Lynne Sommerstein,
Robert Sommerstein, David Sommerstein, and Diane Ryndak

Valentine's Day 40 years ago was the beginning of our family's venture into the world of disabilities. As parents, we had had little experience with individuals with disabilities, having gone to school at a time in which there were no classmates with disabilities evident in our schools. Michelle was the second child in our family, and we quickly realized that her development would not be similar to that of her brother, David. This realization necessitated that we become educated about disability-related legislation, service delivery options, advocacy, and self-advocacy. This also eventually led to assisting other families and self-advocates in their quest for effective and meaningful services as well as instructing in the preservice preparation of special and general educators. This chapter discusses several issues that we have encountered during this 40-year experience with services related to education, community living and participation, and customized employment (Ryndak, Morrison, & Sommerstein, 1999; Ryndak, Ward, Alper, Montgomery, & Storch, 2010). It also discusses the effect of our experiences on our family. We believe that these issues continue to be critical for individuals with severe disabilities and their families. We have provided two sections for each issue identified. The first section provides Michelle's perspective that exemplifies the issue, and the second section provides the family's perspective about the issue. In addition, we used an assisted-writing process that Michelle described in the following way: "What I have written are my own ideas. I said my ideas and used a word bank of words I said to help me write my thoughts down. I had help to use good English."

CRITICAL ISSUE 1 (ACROSS SERVICE DELIVERY SYSTEMS): THE NEGATIVE EFFECT OF LABELS REQUIRES ALTERNATIVE MEANS OF DETERMINING ELIGIBILITY THAT RESULTS IN A PRESUMPTION OF COMPETENCE, RATHER THAN INCOMPETENCE

Michelle's Perspective

"About my disability, people think that I can't do a lot, but I really can. I just need to be given a chance. I like being treated like an adult person even though I sometimes talk a little weird. I understand everything you say. It just takes me longer to answer. I know what I want to say, but sometimes my brain messes up the words when they come out."

Family's Perspective

The impact of labeling individuals with disabilities underlies all of the issues we will discuss. When Michelle was 1 year old she was evaluated by a psychologist who gave her the task of stacking six white cubes. She was pronounced "mentally retarded with cerebral palsy" because she was unable to accomplish the task. We have been upset with this term because of the limitations it placed on her; Michelle continues to be upset and offended by this term because of its negative connotations. We were told she would never talk or walk, and it was recommended that we "put her in a special place." Even though we really did not know what that meant, we said we would keep her in our home. This was the first time we disagreed with the experts and the first of many times we were referred for professional counseling.

In truth, Michelle has had many disability labels over the years, none of which were positive, yet she has amazed us for 40 years with her abilities, resilience, and achievements beyond the assumptions of labels and beliefs of professionals. Michelle's standardized testing placed self-fulfilling prophecies on her from the time of diagnosis, through her educational years, and into adult life. We have found that service providers (e.g., medical, education, and adult services providers) consistently have had low expectations for Michelle based on their assessments, labels, and expertise, although their expectations of Michelle were higher once she was included in general education contexts when she was 15 years old. We are sure she is not the only student to have this experience. As lay advocates for individuals with disabilities and as faculty in teacher preparation, we find that service providers usually use the labels placed on individuals with disabilities to drive their expectations and services. For example, a student's labels drive the curriculum content to which he or she has access, the contexts in which services are delivered, and the outcomes that are deemed expected.

We understand that the Individuals with Disabilities Education Improvement Act (IDEA) of 2004 (PL 108-446) requires the identification of a specific disability beyond the age of 9 for eligibility for special education and related services, but this practice of labeling and differentiating by type of disability leads to segregation, low expectations, and self-fulfilling prophecies, especially for students with severe disabilities. Downing discussed the danger in the low expectations associated with labeling in the following way:

Since we can never be sure of what students can learn, assuming competence is the least dangerous assumption. When students are assumed to be competent, they gain access to age-level experiences and information. If assumed to not be competent, those around them can limit their access to materials, information, am experiences. The tendency may be to restrict activities to those that teachers feel students can understand and demonstrate that understanding. The danger of such an approach is that students can be denied access to a number of learning and social activities and environments, which in turn limits their ability to learn. (2010, p. 10)

It makes more sense just to identify a student as having a disability and, therefore, eligible for services under IDEA 2004, but not identify a specific classification for that student. This would eliminate the need for disability classification and could allow educational personnel to focus on the individualized needs of each student with a disability without the preconceived beliefs about the limits that are associated with some classifications.

CRITICAL ISSUE 2 (EARLY INTERVENTION AND PRESCHOOL SERVICES): LIMITED ACCESS TO INCLUSIVE EARLY INTERVENTION AND INCLUSIVE PRESCHOOL SETTINGS REQUIRES RENEWED EMPHASIS ON DEVELOPING INCLUSIVE SERVICES

Michelle's Perspective

"I went to the same preschool as my older brother and my friends on my street. I liked being with them because they let me play with them at school and home."

Family's Perspective

Early intervention services were not mandated or provided in 1975 when Michelle was 2 years old, but a newspaper article about the importance of early services for young children with developmental delays led us to think about systematically stimulating her language development and coordination, both of which were significantly delayed. We visited an agency for "retarded children" in Buffalo, New York, and observed a class for toddlers and preschoolers with disabilities. Although all of these children were certainly adorable, it did not make sense to us to have her participate in a class comprising children whose language was as delayed as hers. We were concerned about the lack of children who would be modeling age-appropriate language with every interaction across all activities.

Without knowing anything about the least restrictive environment (LRE) mandate of the Education for All Handicapped Children Act of 1975 (PL 94-142) or inclusive education, we began our search for services that kept Michelle with her neighborhood friends and other typically developing children. Fortunately for us, we are a financially secure and educated family. We approached our son's preschool teachers about having Michelle attend preschool with her brother if a parent came along to assist. Their agreement allowed Michelle to participate in one of the first programs providing early intervention services for children with disabilities along with typically developing children. Because she was younger than the preschool children, we euphemistically called it "advanced placement preschool" with the hope that she would remain there for her preschool years. Michelle had comprehensive and inclusive early intervention services, including privately paid speech-language therapy. She received these services, however, because we sought and paid for services we believed would be most effective for her development, and we were able to participate in coordinating and providing those services. All of this was possible because we are an educated, empowered, and financially secure family.

Early intervention services today have had a significant positive effect on the development of many young children with disabilities. Although the natural context for early intervention services is in the home, many young children receive services in child care, resulting in integrated early intervention services. These integrated early intervention services are limited, and they are more difficult to gain access to than segregated services. Unless a parent is knowledgeable, has the financial resources to pay for child care services, and can locate an integrated child care that has the expertise needed to serve young children with disabilities, it is most likely that his or her child would receive early intervention services in a segregated program. Although some service providers recognize the need for inclusive early intervention, many still follow traditional service delivery models that group young children with disabilities together. In addition, such traditional segregated programs most often are provided at no cost to a parent, whereas inclusive child care most often requires a parent to pay tuition. This is a significant, natural disincentive for parents to send their children with severe disabilities to inclusive settings (see Chapter 7).

Many of the same issues pertain to preschool services. Although mandates for preschool services for students with disabilities vary from state to state, all parents of children with severe disabilities should have the option to select preschool services in inclusive settings for their child. These options unfortunately are not consistently or broadly available across states. Similarly, universal preschool initiatives for children who do not have disabilities also are not available across states, although in some states they have added an inclusive option for children with severe disabilities (see Chapter 7).

CRITICAL ISSUE: 3 (EDUCATIONAL SERVICES): SCHOOLS' PRESUMPTION THAT THE NEEDS OF STUDENTS WITH SEVERE DISABILITIES SHOULD BE MET IN SEGREGATED CONTEXTS REQUIRES SYSTEMIC CHANGES IN EDUCATIONAL SERVICES AND TEACHER PREPARATION FOR INCREASED USE OF INCLUSIVE EDUCATION PRACTICES

Michelle's Perspective

"When I started school, I went to a special class far away from home. I rode the little bus a long time, and I used to fall asleep. It was very hot on the bus. I went to five different schools by the time I was 11. I didn't like going to school so far away. I didn't know anyone. I wanted to go to school with my brother and the kids on my street.

"I stayed in a special class until I was 15. I felt stupid there. I was very angry. I used to put my head down on the desk and look out the door and see the kids there. I wanted to be with the kids and do what they did. I wanted to have a locker, eat lunch with my friends from Girl Scouts and soccer, and walk in the halls with them.

"I knew I could do more than I was doing. I got into lots of trouble because I sometimes didn't do what the teacher told me. I was very angry. I knew I was smart, but I didn't feel smart. I felt stupid. Having a teacher aide made me feel different from the other kids."

Family's Perspective

Special classes were the norm for students with severe disabilities when Michelle entered school in 1978, the second year the Education for All Handicapped Children Act was implemented. We believed at that time that school personnel were the experts, that they knew best when they told us that Michelle needed to be with other children who had disabilities to receive the services she needed. We allowed them to place her in a neighboring school district in what was called the "severe" class, comprised of six students with severe disabilities, one special education teacher, and one paraprofessional. We were told it would be a good placement for her because the teacher used similar strategies to those we used to support Michelle at home. What we had not considered was what her psychologist had documented in an evaluation he conducted when she was 1 year old: "Michelle is an incredible mimic." Michelle learned to bite her wrist and rock back and forth that first year in a self-contained class; we are not aware of what the other children learned from her. What we learned that year was that they could not replace the benefit of having Michelle with children without disabilities to be role models for her, regardless of the intensity of the educational practices in segregated settings. Yet, each year the school personnel continued to recommend that she be placed in a self-contained class, and we continued to believe that they knew best.

Michelle's behavior gradually deteriorated over the next 10 years while school personnel continued to recommend she be placed in self-contained classes. Up until this point, Michelle was segregated from typically developing peers only while at school; the remainder of her life was spent with her family, neighbors, and friends in the community. It took us those 10 years to realize that she was not learning commensurate with even the most pessimistic results of standardized tests. An independent evaluation when Michelle was 14 years old determined that her behavior was inappropriate when she was in the self-contained class, but her behavior was appropriate and consistent with her typically developing peers during the few non-academic times they were together (e.g., chorus, lunch). She was the same mimic she had been when she was 1 year old. Michelle's uncooperative behaviors diminished and her engagement in instruction dramatically increased when she finally was allowed to attend general education classes with her typically developing peers. We hypothesize that this was a result of an increased motivation to learn. She unfortunately had lost 10 years of learning.

It is clear to us as we reflect on practices we see in schools that placing students with severe disabilities in general education classes and settings with supports as the first option (and sometimes as any option) is still the exception rather than the rule. Furthermore, placement in general education classes and settings is almost always a result of extensive efforts by parents who 1) are educated, 2) are economically situated to have the time and financial resources to advocate, and 3) have a connection to experts in inclusive education. Current practice still assumes that intense services require segregation, which is consistent with Taylor's (1988) criticism of the LRE concept.

CRITICAL ISSUE 4 (EDUCATIONAL SERVICES): THE PRESUMPTION THAT SCHOOL PERSONNEL KNOW WHAT IS BEST FOR A STUDENT REQUIRES MORE RESPECTFUL AND MEANINGFUL COLLABORATION AMONG TEACHERS, SELF-ADVOCATES, AND PARENTS

Michelle's Perspective

"I learned better in a regular class. I had lots of friends. I watched my friends and did what they did. I had a locker, too. My friends once decorated it for my birthday. My special education teacher, my speech teacher, and my OT [occupational therapist] helped me, too. I liked working with my speech teacher because she let me bring friends with me to speech. I was happy doing work like what the other kids did. My work wasn't the same, but I was OK with that because the kids knew I didn't do exactly the same work. I learned a lot more. I knew I could learn and do more than they thought I could."

Family's Perspective

Our request in 1988 for supports and services in inclusive general education contexts for Michelle was met with strong resistance from our school district. It was somewhat understandable in the context of the time because the practice of including students with severe disabilities was just beginning; in fact, the term *inclusive education* had not yet emerged in the field, and the focus was on teaching functional activities in naturally occurring settings. The bigger issue, however, was the insistence by the school district personnel that they knew what was best for Michelle and that they implement their plan over the services requested by us. Taylor described this practice as "the primacy of professional decision-making" (1988, p. 224). There was, and still is, the presumption that school personnel know what is best for each student, including those with severe disabilities; this presumption minimizes and, in many cases, eliminates meaningful input from the student and family members.

In spite of all the rhetoric and funding related to unified teacher preparation and school reform facilitating inclusive services for all students, in most states, general and special educators with initial licensures do not have the skills, knowledge, and supervised experiences that are critical to meeting the needs of students with severe disabilities in general education contexts. Educational decisions should not be determined solely by school personnel because the student and family are left with the results of decisions made related to educational placement, curriculum, and assessment long after the student has aged out of school and the school personnel are no longer in their lives. School personnel should yield to parents' requests related to where their child should receive services, regardless of the settings they request, unless a student is either a danger to him- or herself or others or an ongoing disruption to classmates in spite of appropriate supports and services. Family values should trump school values because family members are the individuals who will be living with the outcomes of services when the student exits school services.

Lack of education for parents on inclusive education and inclusive practices is also a significant contributing factor to the proliferation of students with severe disabilities being placed in restrictive settings. Parents need to understand how and why inclusive education will benefit their children while not having a negative effect on typically developing students and that services in inclusive classes do not mean their child will receive fewer or less intense supports and instruction. We believe that more respectful and meaningful collaboration needs to occur among teachers, self-advocates, and parents.

CRITICAL ISSUE 5 (EDUCATIONAL SERVICES): THE PRESUMPTION THAT LEARNING ENDS AT 21 YEARS OLD REQUIRES A RECONCEPTUALIZATION OF TRANSITION SERVICES, FUNCTIONAL CURRICULUM, AND COMMUNITY-BASED INSTRUCTION

Michelle's Perspective

"I was glad I got to be with my friends in regular classes. I wanted to work on the same things they did. I didn't like going to school after my friends graduated. I liked trying out jobs and learning to take the bus after my friends graduated. There was a lot I didn't learn in school because I wasn't given a chance. I can do more than they thought I could. I want to take classes now and learn more. I want to read and write better and take acting and sign language classes. I took computer classes at the library, but they are too easy for me now."

Family's Perspective

Michelle's middle and high school personnel repeatedly suggested community-based instruction so she could learn independent living, vocational training, and community participation. Our family, however, valued access to modified academics and students without disabilities more than immediate instruction on skills that could be taught by staff in adult services. The extensive practice of trying to teach in 13 years of school services the skills students with severe disabilities will need over a lifetime seems ludicrous and limiting. Estimating early on what skills they will need as adults and, therefore, estimating their capabilities far into the future seems like a dangerous practice that limits students' access to both the general curriculum and peers without disabilities, as well as age-appropriate experiences. We believed as a family that we needed to maximize the opportunities that Michelle would have in school but would not have once her peers without disabilities graduated. What seemed to help school personnel understand this was our frequent statement, "We could always hire a coach to teach her how to access the community and perform well on a job, but we will never be able to hire a school full of typically developing peers. We also can figure out how Michelle can participate in activities in the community, but we will never be able to duplicate the middle and high school experiences that she would miss if she were removed from inclusive general education contexts."

Schools need to reconceptualize the practice of making families choose between instruction in life skills and academics. This should not be an either/or proposition. The years that typically developing students are in school (ages 5–18 years) can be used to teach school-based content infused with instruction on individual needs (e.g., communication, life skills, functional activities), whereas the additional special education years (ages 18–21 years) can be used to assist students in making the transition to adult life by teaching community-based activities, vocational skills, and skills to participate in the community. Adult services agencies can be used beyond the age of 21 to teach the remaining skills needed for community living and meaningful participation in adult life.

CRITICAL ISSUE 6 (EDUCATIONAL SERVICES AND TRANSITION): A RECONCEPTUALIZATION OF TRANSITION SERVICES REQUIRES AN EXPANSION OF SUPPORTED EDUCATIONAL OPPORTUNITIES IN POSTSECONDARY EDUCATION AND ADULT EDUCATION

Michelle's Perspective

"After high school, I knew exactly what I wanted to do. I wanted to go to college just like my brother, David. I wanted to be on my own, make new friends, learn more, work, and make money. I wanted to be like the other kids in my family. I got a lot out of college. I learned to cook, clean my room, take buses and taxis, and travel by plane alone. I also learned to go to bars safely. Best of all, I learned to be me."

Family's Perspective

We were determined to find inclusive postsecondary education for Michelle after she graduated from high school. Whether it was the context of the time in which self-determination services were just coming into their own or if it was our own lack of confidence in professionals after our experiences with educational services, we decided to take the lead in developing postsecondary services, with forced participation from the school district. We found a small out-of-state college in Burlington, Vermont, where she could continue her learning in an age-appropriate environment without meeting the requirements of a college degree program. We found sufficient supports to keep her safe and productive while away from home and family, but, again, all of this was possible because we are an educated, empowered, and financially secure family.

Our experience with postsecondary education in the early 1990s was one of the first initiatives in the nation for young adults with severe disabilities. Our experience has fortunately been followed by many other families through the development of postsecondary education services for individuals with severe disabilities in colleges nationwide. Most of these services, however, are designed for young adults in their early to mid-20s. Now that Michelle is ready to learn phonics (i.e., she understands the importance of it for her life in a literate world), there are limited inclusive opportunities with supports to assist her as an adult. In addition, she recently discovered her own ability and interest in computers through free introductory and intermediate computer classes at the local library. Although Michelle would like to enroll in additional courses on using computers, the courses that are offered through the library now are too easy for her. If Michelle were to register for computer courses at the local college or adult continuing education program, then she would need support to participate and benefit from the instruction. Her Medicaid waiver plan could pay for such support, but the waiver dollar amount would remain the same and would require a reallocation of the plan's current funding; thus, Michelle would need to eliminate some support that she currently requires and is receiving.

We believe that the current focus of postsecondary programs on young adults limits inclusive lifelong learning opportunities for adults with severe disabilities. We believe that a future initiative for self-advocates and their families will be advocacy for extending inclusive postsecondary education services and inclusive continuing education for older adults with severe disabilities.

CRITICAL ISSUE 7 (ADULT LIVING): UNDERSTANDING AND ADDRESSING THE COMPLEX ISSUES RELATED TO SUPPORTED ADULT LIVING REQUIRES A RECONCEPTUALIZATION OF ADULT SERVICES AND GOVERNMENT BENEFITS TO SUPPORT AND MAINTAIN INCREASED INDEPENDENCE, MOBILITY, AND FAMILY NEEDS

Michelle's Perspective

"I don't want to live someplace that someone makes the rules. I want to make my own rules and do what I want. I want to hire my own staff and fire them if I don't like them. I love the people who work for me now."

Family's Perspective

When Michelle aged out of educational services, we again decided to take the lead in establishing an independent living option for her and finding her customized employment. Our experiences with educational services resulted in a lack of confidence in professionals overall, so we decided to take the lead in developing her adult services, with little input from adult agencies.

After Michelle successfully completed her college experience with a certificate of continuing education, she returned home with a strong desire to continue to live on her own. Again, as with postsecondary education, we decided to go it alone. We rented an apartment on a bus line and hired a roommate to live with Michelle. It was a disaster, not only for the roommate who was unprepared for Michelle's needs, but also for her family, who provided daily intensive involvement.

The Medicaid waiver was fortunately being developed nationwide and in New York, and Michelle enrolled in it, using assistance from an adult services agency to provide financial management and to identify potential personnel for Michelle to hire. Although this has proven to be a successful vehicle for individualization, these services are based on Medicaid eligibility. Medicaid eligibility requirements, however, have not yet grasped or reflected the complexities of life faced by adults with severe disabilities. For example, in 2011, Michelle had been employed part time for 16 years by the state of New York in the court system, and she received the full benefits of a state employee, including medical insurance, regular pay increases, vacation and sick days, and unemployment insurance. As her pay increased over the years, her reliance on Supplemental Security Income (SSI) decreased, but her Medicaid eligibility was not in question. SSI regulations fortunately encouraged the employment of people with disabilities. As a family that tried to minimize Michelle's dependence on government assistance, we thought this process was appropriate and that her support needs would be met for the long term. Life was finally becoming easier for all of us because of her employment income, benefits, and Medicaid-funded supports.

With the recent national economic crisis, numerous positions were eliminated in the New York State court system in 2011, and people were laid off. These changes included Michelle's position, and she was laid off, despite her supervisor's fight against it. Along with position elimination and tears came unemployment payments, normally a positive outcome of losing a job. For Michelle, however, unemployment payments are considered unearned income by SSI and Medicaid, which upset the balance of Michelle's income and her Medicaid eligibility, which were required to fund the supports she needed to maintain her independence in the community. The same issue arose when Michelle was required by SSI to apply for Social Security Disability Insurance (SSDI) benefits. It is ironic that we hoped Michelle would not qualify for SSDI, but she did. Unemployment and SSDI are still considered unearned income even though she had earned her unemployment and SSDI benefits by being employed part time at a job that provided appropriate wages and benefits. Because this income was unearned instead of earned, it resulted in computations that worked against her in qualifying for the Medicaid funding required to maintain her supports.

Complicated and exhausting advocacy by our family ensued to keep Michelle eligible for Medicaid for health insurance and, more important, for home, community, and job-development support. Although our adult services agency is a forward-thinking organization and was supportive of our advocacy efforts, they simply did not have answers to the eligibility issues and did not have contacts with government personnel who could address these collective administrative problems. The complexity of issues resulting from Medicaid rules not being adjusted for the increased productivity of people with disabilities left them relying on us to figure out how to maintain Michelle's eligibility for the services on which she relies to maintain her independence. Again, we are an educated, empowered, and financially secure family with a law degree, access to networks, and the ability to take the initiative to solve a problem. The only difference now is that we are older and more exhausted. Regardless of Michelle's remarkable progress in developing the skills to become as independent as possible, our concerns for the future continue because of issues with regulations and benefit management.

The lack of portability for Medicaid waiver services from state to state and, in some cases, from county to county, is an even more glaring critical issue with regard to benefits. Individuals with severe disabilities who wish to relocate to another state to be with relatives or friends must be recertified in their new location and go to the end of the waiting list for Medicaid waiver services in their new location. This also becomes a problem for parents who wish to retire to another state and take their adult child with severe disabilities with them. The choice is to leave their adult child with severe disabilities behind or stay put. We cannot help but worry about what will happen to Michelle's Medicaid waiver if and when she decides to live near her brother in another city. Families with members who have severe disabilities need portability for Medicaid waivers, at least for the federal portion of the funding.

CRITICAL ISSUE 8 (ADULT LIVING): UNDERSTANDING AND ADDRESSING THE COMPLEX ISSUES OF COMMUNITY LIVING REQUIRES AN IMPROVED STRUCTURE FOR EMBEDDING SUPPORT FOR THE DEVELOPMENT OF SOCIAL RELATIONSHIPS, NATURAL SUPPORTS, AND IMPROVED QUALITY OF LIFE

Michelle's Perspective

"I don't like it when people think I have to go to special stuff for people with disabilities. I like to be with all different people. I want to pick my own friends. I want more friends. I want a girlfriend like me (with disabilities) to be my best friend to go to bingo and bowling with my other friends."

Family's Perspective

Beyond issues related to maintaining the supports needed for Michelle's independence as life unfolds, Michelle runs the risk of her independence leading to isolation and loneliness, like many adults with severe disabilities who do not have spouses or families of their own. Although this is consistent with the risk of any single adult, most single adults are not dependent on others for daily support (e.g., transportation). Perhaps the fully inclusive life Michelle has chosen is more isolating than it need be; that is, we wonder whether our collective insistence on Michelle having a fully inclusive life has added a challenge to her life. In retrospect, we wonder whether having some experiences in inclusive contexts with peers who had disabilities would have allowed her to develop more friendships that could have lasted into adult life. Opportunities for such experiences did not exist at the time, however, because she often has been the first person with severe disabilities to have inclusive services at various stages of her life (e.g., high school, postsecondary education, community living). We cannot help being a bit wistful when we see friendships among adults with disabilities who live together, while Michelle still struggles to have a best friend. She needs consistent opportunities to develop friendships and relationships with adults both with and without disabilities in inclusive contexts.

Perhaps society is not quite ready to embrace the vision of Robert Perske's *Circles of Friends* (Perske & Perske, 1988), which, in our experience, is still an unattainable or at least difficult-to-attain dream. Perhaps those connections will be easier to establish in adulthood when more typically developing children are educated next to children who have severe disabilities. Currently, though, we have to wonder if different living arrangements for Michelle (e.g., having roommates who also have disabilities, having live-in staff) would facilitate greater sociability and interdependence in her life.

It is important to note, as Michelle's independence in adult life increases, the independence of her parents decreases. She currently relies on her parents for frequent interactions that enrich her adult life. She has not been successful at developing an ongoing connection with many other adults to fill this role. We believe an organized entity is necessary in society to address this need. For example, the social structure that supports interactions among members of a religious community or interest group (e.g., book club, theater lovers) could expand outreach and support to individuals with severe disabilities in a way that is individualized, inclusive, and meaningful. Perhaps siblings of individuals with severe disabilities who live away from their family could locate and join such organized entities in their new communities and reach out to adults with disabilities in their town. This would require an awareness of the issue and a structure that supports establishing meaningful and ongoing interpersonal connections. This might reduce the dependence that many adults with disabilities have on their parents by expanding their natural support networks.

CRITICAL ISSUE 9 (CUSTOMIZED EMPLOYMENT): THE EARLY PROMISE OF SUPPORTED EMPLOYMENT THAT HAS BYPASSED THE MAJORITY OF ADULTS WITH SEVERE DISABILITIES NEEDS TO BE REFOCUSED ON CUSTOMIZED COMPETITIVE EMPLOYMENT AND JOB RESTRUCTURING FOR INCREASED PRODUCTIVITY AND IMPROVED QUALITY OF LIFE

Michelle's Perspective

"I could do more than they let me do at my job at the courthouse. I knew I could learn the new computer program, but they wouldn't let me. I felt frustrated about that. I was very sad when I got laid off. My job was very important to me. I want to get a new job and work and make money and see friends."

Family's Perspective

Michelle found her part-time job as a clerk at the county court because of her parents' connections and initiative. Although our local agency that supports job development for adults with disabilities looked around for existing jobs that people with disabilities traditionally have filled (e.g., positions in food service, cleaning and building maintenance), Michelle expressed an interest in working in an office. While the agency looked for a job for Michelle, we decided to write a letter of inquiry on Michelle's behalf to everyone we knew in our personal, professional, and religious networks. The letter described Michelle's desire for employment in an office, her skills, and the supports she would have from a job coach. A year later, the administrator of the court called about a position. He was someone we knew in the legal community, and he was familiar with Michelle. He had kept the letter in his drawer until a position became available. Michelle applied for this position, was hired, and remained with the county court for 16 years.

We have discovered that not much has changed in terms of job development for people with disabilities since Michelle last looked for a job 16 years ago. The selection of jobs seems to be similar to what was available then, except that the barriers for employment of people with disabilities in those jobs are not quite as significant. The expansion of employment in diverse settings seems to have been painfully slow and based on the same preconceived ideas of what individuals with severe disabilities are capable of doing, rather than customized job development. Now, after almost 2 years of Michelle's unemployment, we find that job development still consists primarily of locating existing jobs with openings, rather than restructuring jobs in competitive inclusive settings to match her interests and abilities. It is frustrating for Michelle and us to look around our community and see large corporations in big buildings that might need a clerk to sort, file, shred, or enter data. It would be inappropriate, however, for us to approach such businesses and, to date, her job support agency does not seem inclined to do so. The bigger question is, "What are our federal and state governments doing to promote the employment of individuals with disabilities?" We believe they would say they are doing a lot, but they are not doing enough if their efforts do not positively affect the people and businesses in our own community.

CRITICAL ISSUE 10 (SELF-DETERMINATION AND GUARDIANSHIP): ALTHOUGH SELF-DETERMINATION AND GUARDIANSHIP SOMETIMES ARE PERCEIVED AS MUTUALLY EXCLUSIVE, THIS CONFLICT MUST BE RECONCILED TO PROMOTE THE INDEPENDENCE, SAFETY, AND WELFARE OF ADULTS WITH SEVERE DISABILITIES

Michelle's Perspective

"I don't like it when people tell me what to do. I like to decide things on my own. My parents help me sometimes, but sometimes I want to decide by myself. Sometimes I make mistakes with money or other decisions, and my family helps me to get out of trouble. I like that, and I learn from that."

Family's Perspective

As groundbreakers, our family has pushed for Michelle's maximum independence in an inclusive life. That is what most parents want for their children. We decided that guardianship was not necessary when Michelle left for her college experience in Vermont. We could teach her the skills she would need to make reliable judgments. It soon became evident that we were being naïve, not about her ability to learn the skills, but about others in the community who might want to take advantage of her. After she went to Montreal with a young man that we did not know, we realized that she could be at great risk for manipulation, not unlike many other young women. We felt that she was at greater risk than most women who do not have disabilities, however, and applied for guardianship with Michelle's knowledge and participation in the process.

Some advocates maintain that guardianship is an infringement on the rights of individuals with disabilities, but we strongly feel that guardianship can be a necessary protection when sparingly and respectfully used. We believe that the issue is not whether parents should apply for guardianship of their adult children, but rather it is an issue of determining which individual with disabilities needs the protections of it, as well as when and how to apply it. We firmly believe that guardianship should not be an automatic process, but the necessity of it should be carefully considered among the individual and the people who know him or her best and who share a mutual trust. Given Michelle's extensive and varied experiences in the community, we all are grateful that we collectively decided to have the safety net of guardianship for Michelle. We never make decisions without her involvement, and those decisions are made only when issues of safety or financial difficulties arise. It is comforting for both Michelle and her family that we chose to have this safety net.

We believe that the decision to obtain guardianship is based on the needs of an individual and his or her family's values. Obtaining guardianship was the right decision for Michelle and her family. How guardianship is used is of key importance. Parents need training in sparingly using guardianship without infringing on their adult child's rights. For example, Michelle needed a nonurgent medical procedure that we at first were inclined to consent to without consulting her because it was easier and more expeditious. However, after much consideration and input from her brother, we recognized the need for Michelle to make the decision with our input. The decision-making process took longer and involved the counseling of her service coordinator and psychologist, but Michelle came to the same conclusion that we did. We learned and continue to learn to reconcile Michelle's need for the protection provided through guardianship with respect for her rights as an adult. We believe that to some the transition process unnecessarily sets up an either/or situation related to guardianship instead of promoting an individualized process and solution. This situation needs to be reconciled to promote the independence, safety, and welfare of adults with severe disabilities.

CONCLUSION

Some of the critical issues we have experienced are the result of being at the forefront of the movement to include individuals with severe disabilities throughout Michelle's life. What we have tried to highlight here are those issues that we believe continue to be significant in the lives of other people with severe disabilities today. We feel that special attention needs to be paid to the unique and highly codependent relationship frequently found between the fully included individual with severe disabilities and his or her lifelong advocates, parents, and siblings. Although this relationship is often beautiful and successful, it sometimes can be a little suffocating for all parties. The adult with disabilities might feel that his or her parents or supports can be too protective or controlling. Parents and siblings might feel the needs of the adult with disabilities can significantly affect their combined and individual lives, both financially and socially. For example, most parents return to couple status after raising children into adulthood and frequently socialize with other couples. Parents of adults with disabilities often must consider whether their adult child with disabilities will join them at social events, making their couple a threesome. Likewise, other couples must consider whether they are inviting a couple or a threesome and what accommodations would be needed and appropriate.

Again, in trying to maintain Michelle's fully inclusive life, her parents' independence decreased as her independence increased. We need to find ways to alleviate the intensity derived from this codependence without giving up fully inclusive living. It is essential that we develop structures that support participation in inclusive contexts for all individuals with severe disabilities without relying on families alone. Like other community members, at times of difficulty adults with disabilities will struggle to make sense of their situations in life. Although they will need the support of family and friends, adults with disabilities benefit from serious reflection on and initiatives related to the supports and services to assist them in finding their place in an unstructured adult world and in finding meaning and value for each day as fully participating adults. This goal should be not only for families that are educated, empowered, and financially secure, but also for every family.

Questions for Study and Reflection

1. How does labeling to determine eligibility for special education and related services affect self-advocates and their families? If you were rewriting special education legislation, how might you describe the process for determining a student's eligibility for services to avoid the negative implications?

2. How do early intervention and preschool services assist families of young children with developmental delays?

3. What are the presumptions used to justify the placement of students with severe disabilities in self-contained classes and segregated special schools?

4. How can school personnel involve families in prioritizing goals and reinforcing instruction in inclusive general education contexts? Why would this be important to self-advocates and families?

5. Why is it important to develop meaningful collaboration with self-advocates and parents of students with severe disabilities? What can teachers, parents, and self-advocates jointly do to develop meaningful collaboration?

6. What services (e.g., supported living in own apartment, support during customized employment) are available to self-advocates beyond the age of 21 years? How can collaborative teams use this information to avoid duplication of services and maximize each student's participation in inclusive contexts with educational supports between 15 and 21 years of age? Why would this be important to self-advocates and families?

7. How do collaborative teams promote developing natural supports in schools and in the community? Why would this be important to self-advocates and families?

8. How does guardianship affect self-advocates and families? What role does self-determination play in considering and using guardianship?

RESOURCES

Council of Parent Attorneys and Advocates is an independent nonprofit organization that works to protect special education rights. *http://www.copaa.org/*

National Dissemination Center for Children with Disabilities provides information on disabilities and disability-related issues for children and youth birth to age 22 years. *http://www.NICHCY.org*

Parent Training and Information Centers are federally funded and provide training and information to parents of infants, toddlers, children, and youth with disabilities. *http://wdcrobcolp01.ed.gov/Programs/EROD/org_list.cfm?category_ID=SPT*

Self-Advocates Becoming Empowered works for the full inclusion of people with developmental disabilities. *http://www.sabeusa.org/*

REFERENCES

Downing, J.E. (2010). *Academic instruction for students with moderate and severe intellectual disabilities in inclusive classrooms.* Thousand Oaks, CA: Corwin Press.

Education for All Handicapped Children Act of 1975, PL 94-142, 20 U.S.C. §§ 1400 *et seq.*

Individuals with Disabilities Education Improvement Act (IDEA) of 2004, PL 108-446, 20 U.S.C. §§ 1400 *et seq.*

Perske, R., & Perske, M. (1988). *Circles of friends.* Nashville, TN: Abingdon Press.

Ryndak, D.L., Morrison, A.P., & Sommerstein, L. (1999). Literacy prior to and after inclusion in general education settings. *Journal of The Association for Persons with Severe Handicaps, 24,* 5–22.

Ryndak, D.L., Ward, T., Alper, S., Montgomery, J., & Storch, J.F. (2010). Long-term outcomes of services for two persons with significant disabilities with differing educational experiences: A qualitative consideration of the impact of educational experiences. *Education and Training in Autism and Developmental Disabilities, 45,* 323–338.

Taylor, S.J. (1988). Caught in the continuum: A critical analysis of the principle of the least restrictive environment. *Journal of The Association for Persons with Severe Handicaps, 13,* 45–53.

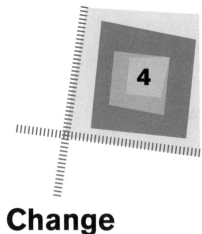

Person-Centered Planning and the Quest for Systems Change

John O'Brien

TASH advocates deep change in typical service practice in its position statements on community living (TASH, 2011) and integrated employment (TASH, 2009). These statements, which are the most recent expressions of positions that reach back to the organization's early history, converge with Article 19 (living independently and being included in the community) and Article 27 (work and employment) of the United Nations (2006) Convention on the Rights of Persons with Disabilities, which adds the moral force of a worldwide consensus of advocates, experts, and politicians to the weight of international law in those nations who are party to the convention. Article 19 provides the right to choose where and with whom one lives with the personal assistance necessary to support inclusion and prevent isolation or segregation from the community. Article 27 provides the right to an opportunity to gain a living by work freely chosen in a labor market that is open, inclusive, and accessible. The United States has signed but not ratified the convention as of this writing; however, these two articles are largely consistent with long-standing U.S. policy. *TASH values* in this chapter is shorthand for these two results—people live included in community life as occupants of their own homes and workers in integrated jobs.

Progress toward realizing these rights can be marked by steadily growing numbers of people with severe disabilities securely inhabiting their own homes and filling contributing roles in the life of communities, especially by holding jobs in integrated settings. Available measures of the performance of services to adults with developmental disabilities show how far there is to go to make TASH values real. Fewer than 30% of people with developmental disabilities receiving residential support in the United States in 2010 lived in a place they or another person with developmental disabilities owned or rented (states report a range from 2% to 85%) (Larson, Ryan, Salmi, Smith, & Wuorio, 2012), and 20% of all adults funded by developmental disability services were in integrated employment (states report a range from 5% to 88%) (data gathered August 2, 2012, from http://StateData.info). In addition, the Council on Quality and Leadership (CQL; 2010) reported that only about one third of 7,800 interviewed as part of their accreditation process perform the social roles they desire in their communities. None of these accounts specifically spoke to the experience of people with severe disabilities or about the quality of people's home or work life, but they indicated the distance that services must travel in order to approach TASH values (see Chapter 15).

The term *system* in this chapter refers to the network of policies and practices concerned with assisting people with severe disabilities. This network is reproduced and changed by the interaction of people with disabilities and their families and allies, advocacy groups, service providers, administrators charged with managing the availability and quality of services, and legislators and courts as they take an interest in policy and resources for people with disabilities. The U.S. Centers for Medicare & Medicaid Services has promoted person-centered planning in initiatives to shift the system's balance of long-term care from institutions to community services since at least 2001(National Health Policy Forum, 2008). It has been central to policies aimed at transforming the system in England since 2000 (Routledge, Sanderson, & Greig, 2002). This chapter reflects on the functions person-centered planning has been assigned in system change efforts, the effect it has had, and lessons some of its practitioners have learned. The chapter first reviews approaches and contexts for person-centered planning and then discusses what the implementation of person-centered planning reveals about the work of deep change when it is deployed as a part of three different change strategies.

APPROACHES AND CONTEXTS

Person-centered planning is involved in many efforts to reform systems from New York to New South Wales. The effectiveness of person-centered planning depends on the competence of facilitators, the adequacy of the match of a planning approach to the situation, and the context in which planning is done.

Approaches

Table 4.1 identifies nine of the most frequently used approaches to person-centered planning. Although each approach has continually refined its practices over time, none is new (Lyle O'Brien & O'Brien, 2002b). TASH's 1991 account of critical issues included a chapter that drew on 10 years of experience of person-centered planning, understood as the shared construction of stories that led to action for inclusion through an organized search for capacity and connection, engaging people with developmental disabilities, their families and allies, and their communities (O'Brien & Mount, 1991). Services and systems have adapted some of these practices and incorporated them into their reform efforts over time and to varying degrees, often labeling the result person-centered plans. Some practitioners throughout this history have facilitated person-centered plans outside formally organized services

Table 4.1. Common approaches to person-centered planning

Approach	Defining features
Personal futures planning	An individual and his or her allies generate powerful images of a rich life in the community that will guide a search for opportunities for the person to take up valued social roles and guide the development of service arrangements to support him or her in those roles. They collect and organize information that describes, for example, the individual's relationships, important places, things that energize him or her, the person's gifts and capacities, and his or her ideas and dreams of a desirable future (Mount, 2000).
Pathfinders: Group person-centered planning	Groups (individuals with their families and allies) support one another to make, implement, and revise individual personal futures plans. Emphasis is on taking action toward a desirable future in a community setting before seeking services. Mutual support grows with shared discoveries, questions, and resources. A large group meets once to plan and then quarterly for at least 1 year to share learning and revise plans. Groups do their own facilitating and recording with guidance from a large-group facilitator. This approach is commonly used when people share a life transition, such as moving from school to adult life (Lyle O'Brien & O'Brien, 2002a; Mount & Lyle O'Brien, 2002).
Make a difference	This approach applies personal futures planning as a way to build organizational capacity by developing learning partnerships between a staff member and an individual. It is aimed at developing a contributing community role for the individual (O'Brien & Mount, 2005).
PATH	This group process helps discover a way to move toward a positive and possible goal, which is rooted in life purpose, by enrolling others, building strength, and finding a workable strategy (O'Brien, Pearpoint, & Kahn, 2010).
MAPS	This group process helps clarify gifts, identify meaningful contributions, specify the necessary conditions for contribution, and make agreements that will develop opportunities for contribution (O'Brien, Pearpoint, & Kahn, 2010).
Support plans	This approach is a way to mobilize all available resources to support a person's citizenship. It is based on six keys to citizenship—self-determination, direction, money, home, support, and community life (Duffy, 2004).
Essential lifestyle planning (ELP)	This approach asks what is important to and for a person in everyday life. It specifies the support the person requires and person-specific ways to address issues of health or safety that balance what is important *to* the person and what is important *for* the person. The approach clearly identifies opportunities for improved assistance and guides continuing learning about the person's supports in a way that is easily understood by those who assist the person (Smull & Sanderson, 2005).
Person-centered thinking tools	This approach is a set of tools deconstructed from ELP and adopted through whole-organization training that develops the skills and behaviors necessary to think and work in a way that delivers person-centered support at the direct support, agency management, and system management levels (Sanderson & Lewis, 2012).
Facilitated discovery	This systematic process of answering, "Who is this person?" generates a rich background for negotiating a customized employment role and focuses particularly on people failed by typical methods for supporting employment (Callahan, Shumpert, & Condon, 2011).

Key: MAPS, Making Action Plans; PATH, Planning Alternative Tomorrows with Hope.

to assist people and families who want something different from what the system offers. Sometimes these efforts at the edge of the system have opened better ways to realize TASH values.

Contexts

Two distinctions are important for understanding the differing contributions that person-centered planning can make to people living in their own homes and working in real jobs—the difference between working in a system and working on a system (Deming, 2000) and the difference between technical problem solving and meeting adaptive challenges (Heifetz, 1998). In some contexts, person-centered planning is a way to work in a system, implementing and improving procedures to perform system-defined and regulated functions according to its rules. In other contexts, person-centered planning is a way to work on the system, revealing, testing, and reshaping rules and typical patterns of practice to suit new purposes. Working in the system makes sense when the system reliably produces assistance to people in their own homes and jobs. Working on the system makes sense when the system needs to embrace new purposes and innovate in order to realize TASH values. A technical change occurs when it is necessary to support new purposes and correctly apply expert knowledge to a clearly defined, if complicated and demanding, problem. For example, deciding on new criteria and procedures for allocating self-directed individual budgets is a technical change. Necessary change can be called meeting an adaptive challenge when new ways must be found to navigate uncertain territory and when a common understanding of purpose and ways of proceeding must be negotiated among people and organizations with different interests who face real losses. For example, successfully closing a sheltered workshop and finding integrated work for its participants is an adaptive challenge because it departs from the familiar and demands creating new patterns of relationship and practice.

Person-centered planning in practice is a means to identify important future possibilities for a person and coordinate action that moves toward that future. The horizon of possibilities people identify and the extent of social learning they mobilize to move toward those possibilities varies with the context for planning. Table 4.2 outlines six contexts for person-centered planning in terms of the function person-centered planning is expected to perform, the main actors who are intended to productively meet when the process performs its function, the initiator and owner of the process, and its intended benefits.

Given the gap between what TASH values and what most people who receive services currently experience, person-centered planning will make its greatest contribution when those involved are working on the system to generate adaptive change. The difficulty of working this way means that the contribution of person-centered planning is profoundly contingent on the values, purposes, commitments, relationships, and creativity of those who practice it.

Most person-centered plans happen as a matter of routine when people join the developmental disabilities service system, make a transition that calls for a change of services, or meet requirements for an annual individual service plan. Context 1 (service planning) and Context 2 (support planning) modify or replace procedures for producing individual service plans. Both of these contexts are owned by the service system, at least to the extent that the terms of people's participation are governed by system rules and routines. Plans that result in the entry of new or modified goals in a plan maintained by a service coordinator are typical of these two contexts.

Table 4.2. Contexts and functions for person-centered planning

Function	Actors	Initiator	Intended benefit
Context 1: Service planning Define outcomes Choose service provider (or self-management) Work in system Technical change	System management engages person (person can include family members, in many cases)	System service coordination	Best fit between person and available service options and providers Best available service option at points of life transition (e.g., leaving school, leaving family home, moving from institution or nursing home) Good mix of paid and unpaid (natural) assistance Agreed-on, individually referenced measure of outcomes
Context 2: Support planning Identify goals and specify service offerings Work in system Technical change	System management and person engage service provider	System service coordination typically part of an individualized service plan	Mutually agreed-on goals, roles, procedures, and schedules that reflect individual choice as much as possible within existing service offerings Regular, required update of goals and service offerings Provider appreciation of personal history and preferences
Context 3: Service improvement Improve quality of existing service offerings by adjusting the service provided to changing conditions and opportunities Work in system Technical change	Service provider engages person	Service provider or system reform process	Best fit between person and day-to-day routines Effective framework for identifying and pursuing opportunities for improvement Assistants and their managers are better informed about the person, which provides greater potential for good relationships
Context 4: Customized employment Discover the basis for negotiating employment Work in system Technical change	Employment facilitator engages person and network	Employment facilitator	Identifying interests and capacities that are of economic value to an employer as an integral part of negotiating customized employment
Context 5: Innovation through partnership Generate innovation in service offerings—new roles supported in new ways Work on system Adaptive change	Service innovator engages person	Service innovators seeking partners in learning through action Person negotiating a new service arrangement	Learning that produces more individualized supports fit to what could be for the person and community Pathways to new and valued social roles Coproduction of new service capacities through strong and sustainable relationships
Context 6: Person- and family-generated action learning Pursue a good life in contributing community roles Work on system Adaptive change	Person and allies engage community settings and, when necessary, support providers with the assistance of independent facilitation	Person and allies	Action arising from deeper understanding of a person's emergent future Pathways to contributing community roles Establishing desired partnership with service system and providers (best use of individual budget)

Context 3 (service improvement) includes intentional efforts to improve the quality of existing services by discovering more about how each person would want to live and adjusting services and policies to offer a better fit. Adjustments to group home schedules and the addition of new activities that better reflect residents' interests are common results of planning in this context. Participants in person-centered planning are working in the system in these first three contexts, aiming to negotiate the best possible fit between people's ideas about the way they want to live and whatever flexibility is available in existing service offerings and policies.

Context 4 (customized employment) aims to negotiate a personalized job role that matches what a person can contribute to a need with cash value to an employer. The discovery process described in Table 4.1 is the essential first stage in customized employment. Practitioners are working in the system where this service is developed and funded. This is an important support offering for systems to develop, given the importance of customized employment to assuring people with severe disabilities access to employment (Callahan & Condon, 2007).

In Context 5 (innovation through partnership), people in the system consciously choose to work on the system, forming coproductive partnerships with people, family members, and community members and their associations, surfacing conflicting values and devising challenges to the assumptions that limit possibilities and inventing new ways to support people in their own homes and valued community roles, especially inclusive education and employment. Listening to the educational aspirations of some of the people they support led Onondaga Community Living into partnership with Syracuse University to create ACCESS, an opportunity for inclusive university study (Onondaga Community Living, 2012).

Context 6 (person- and family-generated action learning) is created by people and family members with their allies and is often supported by skilled facilitators who act independently of any service (Lord, Leavitt, & Dingwall, 2012). It can exist at the edge of the system, outside publicly funded disability services, or it can mobilize a partnership with service providers and system managers committed to innovation. Self-directed individual budgets multiply the resources available. Person-centered planning in this context can open new pathways to valued community roles. Skilled facilitation can create a deeper understanding of a person's identity and capacities, extend resourcefulness, and initiate the creation of new forms of assistance.

Resources matter in all six contexts. There must be adequate investment in those who facilitate plans in order to expect good results. Facilitators need well-designed opportunities to learn whatever processes they use and improve their practice by systematically reflecting on their experience. They need adequate time and space to develop and maintain the sort of relationship with people and families that matches the task they are assigned. The richness and reach of plans depends on the resources those engaged in planning can steer. Levels of energy, good ideas about what is possible, connections and networks, skills, good character, and good will in those who offer assistance make a difference, as does the accessibility of mainstream resources, the adequacy of public funds and the flexibility with which they can be configured, and the capacity of available services to offer personalized assistance. Person-centered planning can assist people to build strength of common purpose when resources are sufficient and guide and motivate learning by connecting with new people, trying new things, and building on what works.

WHAT PERSON-CENTERED
PLANNING REVEALS ABOUT SYSTEM CHANGE

Person-centered planning offers a perspective on change that reveals some of the ways the system responds to different change strategies and clarifies what it takes to make TASH values real.

Change Strategy 1: Adopt New Rules
and Procedures for Individual Planning

This strategy for system change affects the largest number of people. The logic is straightforward: a new approach to planning specifies goals and objectives and mobilizes resources that drive change by specifying the outcomes that people want from the service system and instructing service providers to deliver it. There are at least four reasons that this strategy makes sense to managers and advocates who want change. First, practices associated with person-centered planning do improve people's experience of service when capably done. A chart that identifies a person's important relationships, a helpful format for discussion of what is important to a person and what is important for a person, and a one-page profile that serves as a summary introduction of the person to support workers all carry face validity as components of a good individual plan, and each draws attention to potential improvements in assistance. Second, person-centered planning enacts important values. The participation, voice, and choice of people with disabilities and their families are central to most contemporary accounts of good practice. When an established approach to person-centered planning is ably performed, many people and families find the experience an accessible and engaging way to have their say about what they want from services. Understanding and responding to the whole person is valued. Capable person-centered planning allows the construction of accounts of the person that include expressions of the person's strengths, capacities, desires, preferences, relationships, and cultural identity. An evidence base for practice is valued. There is modest evidence that associates person-centered planning with an increased number and variety of community activities, greater choice of activities, expanded social networks, increased contact with family and friends with disabilities, decreases in challenging behavior, and satisfaction with life and services—meaningful results even though they may not include the results TASH values (Claes, Van Hove, Vandevelde, van Loon, & Schalock, 2010; Holburn, Jacobson, Schwartz, Flory, & Vietze, 2004; Robertson et al., 2006). Quality is valued. *Person-centered* is sticky, signaling aspiration to quality in everything from nursing home regimens to self-managed individualized supports for a rich community life. Third, most people who experience well-designed opportunities to learn about person-centered planning report enthusiasm for applying what they have learned, and many identify specific positive changes in people's lives that have resulted from their training (Amado & McBride, 2002; Dinora, 2011; Lunt & Hinz, 2011). Fourth, since the human service reforms of the 1960s, there has been a powerful but seldom questioned assumption that service behavior is controlled by individual plans. On this mechanistic assumption, changing a plan issues new instructions that service providers convert into outcomes that embody quality as defined by the system's mission.

These are good reasons to implement changes in the way individual plans are constructed and whose voice is heard in the planning process. It seems that changing the individual planning process is not sufficient to increase the number of people with disabilities who are supported in their own homes to live an engaged and contributing community life and gain at least part of their living from integrated employment. The usual results of a system modifying its planning process by adopting person-centered planning discloses three challenges to realizing TASH's values—many systems simply lack the capacity to support people in their own homes and jobs, and existing offerings tend to overpower new possibilities; competing values limit the practice of person-centered planning; and person-centered planning tends to slide from a relational process to a transactional procedure.

Most instances of person-centered planning are powerfully influenced by the state of available local services, and most local service systems have not reached a tipping point that routinely offers personalized supports to valued social roles rather than assistance based on pessimism about people's employability and grouping people on the basis of disability for daytime and residential services. A system with wide competence in customized employment will radiate a far different sense of possibility than one that is only familiar with less individualized and less powerful approaches to employment support. A system that organizes its residential support to people with severe disabilities around group homes will typically develop person-centered plans that select and refine what is offered in group settings. There is nothing nefarious here, though there is a danger. Most people plan within the horizon they can see, and most planning conversations are powerfully shaped by what their owners take for granted. Most people interpret visions of possibility in terms of their current reality—group homes will be celebrated as people's own homes; group-based community experience programs and sheltered workshops will be unchallenged as the outer limit of meaningful occupation for all but the exceptionally capable or connected person. The danger is that person-centered planning will mask the work necessary to overcome system-defined and controlled housing and unemployment behind the belief that people have chosen these conditions through person-centered plans.

Even reforms that employ person-centered planning to guide expenditure of individual budgets struggle to overcome the inertia of "stick with what is most commonly available." Substantial numbers of people and families choose to invest their individual budgets in whatever available local services they can afford; others pool individual budgets and set up group living arrangements or day programs that differ little from typical services that underperform on TASH values; others individualize assistance but do not seek contributing community roles. This may happen because self-managing supports to a person's own home or integrated job is too difficult, the allocation of funds is too small or rules governing expenditure discourage people, or those involved do not know what is possible. The highly desirable policy of granting people discretion to direct their service funding is not a sufficient link between person-centered planning and the results that TASH values.

Person-centered planning can play a part in developing new opportunities for people to be at home and work, but its practice is constrained by competing system values. Accountability for establishing and maintaining the flow of funds for services often means that those charged with facilitating person-centered plans are also responsible for compliance with rules that, for example, set the timing of person-centered planning meetings and reviews and meeting requirements for documentation that can take considerable time and attention to system-determined and audited detail. Those who facilitate may also be expected to enforce system or organizational policies that limit what can be offered or purchased (e.g., "The system cannot pay for that") or implement an organizational risk management plan (e.g., "We cannot allow that"). Ensuring that everyone in a system has equal access to a person-centered plan means that a proportion of planning meetings will happen with people who are not interested in change at the time their plan is due. Responsibility to make the most of scarce public funds often means that those responsible for facilitation have large and growing numbers of people to plan with and are charged to represent the system's strategies for rationing in the planning process (e.g., "We only fund needs, not wants, and the cost-effective way to meet your need is a group home and a group-based community experience program"). Growing numbers multiplied by compliance with increasing detail complexity means less time to build relationships and less time to join people in learning from action that springs from planning. This can undermine job satisfaction for those who facilitate and lead to increased turnover, which leads to a lack or loss of personal knowledge and makes building trust with people and their families more difficult. Although the ways that systems serve the values of accountability, equity, and economy badly need redesign, these competing values are legitimate and, maybe more important, sanctions for failure to comply shape not only the behavior but also the consciousness of many staff assigned to do person-centered planning.

Capacity-expanding person-centered planning arises from people's free choice to work for change they care about. It is personal and relational. It generates knowledge that leads to positive action when people with developmental disabilities and their families trust those facilitating their plans with at least a glimpse of what really matters to them. This trust unlocks an energy that animates any effective person-centered planning process, a sense of identification with the person's human desires for an ordinary life—greater control of daily routine, friends, an intimate relationship, a real home of their own, a job, and other roles that fit their interests and desires to develop and contribute. This trust personalizes and animates the planning process in ways that more detached discussions cannot. It calls participants in planning to step into the gap between deep desire and current reality and act together to move toward what matters most. Absorption of person-centered planning into the routine and required, professionally distanced bureaucratic functions of selecting, specifying, and monitoring services substitutes transaction and compliance for relationship and shared purpose.

Change Strategy 2: Use Person-Centered Planning in Service Reform

Person-centered planning has been assigned an important part in deinstitutionalization and whole system reform. The most careful studies of its effects, described next, report on its effect in these environments.

Deinstitutionalization The Willowbrook Futures Project involved 40 people who remained in state institutions because the extent of their challenging behavior exceeded the willingness of service providers to provide the supports they required, despite their membership in a class entitled by court order to community placement. The study divided the group in half to contrast the effects of person-centered planning with traditional interdisciplinary team planning and assessed participants' quality of life at 8-month intervals for almost 3 years (Holburn et al., 2004). Compared with those receiving traditional individualized service plans (ISPs), person-centered planning participants were significantly more likely to move into a community living arrangement specifically designed for them; their teams were more strongly mobilized to identify opportunities and solve problems than the ISP planning teams were; and measures of autonomy, choice making, daily activities, and satisfaction showed greater improvement.

A second narrative account of the Willowbrook Futures Project documents the perspective of those planning with Hal, one of its participants. Those involved in person-centered planning with Hal had to go far beyond making a good plan to deliver on the desired results of a home chosen by Hal's parents and taking steps toward community employment (Holburn & Vietze, 2002). Power shifted as Hal's parents were actively engaged in problem solving and decision making about where and with whom he would live and from whom he would receive assistance. Risks grew and subsided as safe ways for Hal to be individually present in family and community life were tested in action. An understanding of Hal's identity, interests, and relationships provided a frame for applying technical expertise in behavior analysis to supporting activities and relationships that mattered to Hal. Innovations emerged—a community bridge builder, selected by Hal's parents, assisted him to try out a number of community roles in his new neighborhood before he moved from the institution; personalized funding for day services allowed him to escape long-term placement in a disability group space and routine that did not suit him when he tried it in favor of community activities that reflected his interests and engaged his competencies. This took persistence and sustained commitment to values-guided problem solving and skillful advocacy. There were delays despite legal advocacy for the move, a high level of flexibility and cooperation from system authorities, additional funding to support innovation, and an unusually high level of competence in team members and consultants. It took 2 years from the time Hal's father located a suitable house until the house satisfied administrative requirements and Hal could move in. There were strong pulls away from the more individualized, person-directed supports identified through person-centered planning into the typical facility-based services. Hal gained access to a community life because his allies chose to use their power and competencies to move from working in the deinstitutionalization process to working on the process to personalize supports for him. They joined to assert and defend family responsibility for selecting a house and staff. The professionals involved persisted in creating the conditions that allowed them to deploy their expertise in behavior analysis in service of the arrangements identified as desirable for Hal through person-centered planning.

Whole System Reform   In 2001, the English government adopted Valuing People, a policy that called for national transformational change in service delivery, after consulting with people with intellectual and developmental disabilities, family members, service providers, and professional experts (Routledge et al., 2002). The policy goal is to assure that people exercise their rights, experience independence, have the power of choice in the services and supports they receive, and are included as active participants in their communities. The change effort included new governance structures that provided people with disabilities and their families a key role in planning and decision making, carefully developed and authoritative guidance, a cadre of change agents and trainers, funds dedicated to the change, and research and evaluation. Person-centered planning plays a central role in the transformation process.

The initiative to implement person-centered planning to guide and energize the implementation of Valuing People included a longitudinal study that followed 93 people from four diverse areas that demonstrated a common approach to person-centered planning in a way that allowed an assessment of the effect of person-centered planning on their lives (Robertson et al., 2006). Large-scale training exposed a broad cross section of people in each locality to the values and purposes of person-centered planning. Expert external consultants supported local organizations over 2 years to develop policies, procedures, and practices necessary to implement person-centered planning and provided intensive training (85–100 hours) and support to local person-centered planning facilitators and local managers. The impact was meaningful but modest, despite top-down requirements, local commitment, and extensive investment in training. Person-centered planning demonstrated positive impact on measures of contact with friends and family, choice, and an increase in the number, variety, and extent of community activities. Negative outcomes included greater staff-perceived risk, more identified health needs, and more identified emotional and behavioral needs. These negative outcomes are likely the result of greater attention to health and mental health needs and greater presence in community being seen as potentially risky. Evidence of a significant effect on inclusive social relationships or paid employment was lacking. Since the study's conclusion, the policy has been revitalized, person-centered planning remains an important element of the reform, and people's use of personal budgets has significantly grown, but delivery on TASH values remains modest. Approximately 15% of people in funded residential services lived in their own home in 2010, and about 7% of adults with any degree of intellectual and developmental disability regularly worked in either paid or unpaid jobs (the range across 152 local authorities is from 1% to 30% employment among people served) (Emerson et al., 2012).

Valuing People has created many positive changes, but the tipping point to people's widespread access to their own homes and jobs is yet to come. The reform aimed at a significant shift in power toward people with disabilities and their families, which poses a substantial adaptive challenge. Those in management face growing uncertainty about how to be accountable for prudent use of increasingly scarce funds, compliance with multiple agendas and standards set by central government, labor agreements and contractual relationships, and conflicting demands from those who see the move away from congregate, staff-controlled services as a serious threat and those who see it as a moral imperative. Those people and families who are expected to take up power and make and manage support plans that meld system assistance with mainstream services and natural supports face new roles and responsibilities, often while practical supports to these responsibilities are either lacking or in their early stages of development and mainstream services remain inaccessible. A centralized change effort pushed from the top of government has the advantage of some authority to drive the change, but its medium is technical change through rules, monitoring, guidance, and expert technical assistance and training. Transformation can only happen to the extent that local people are willing and able to do the work of moving together through adaptive challenges. Overemphasis on technical change and transactional strategies severely limits the effect of person-centered planning on TASH values.

Change Strategy 3: Person-Centered Planning Guides Purposeful Innovation

The first two change strategies assume that the capacity to support people in their own homes and jobs exists, either in the system as it is (Change Strategy 1) or as a best-practice technology that can be assimilated as part of a reform through detailed requirements, training, and technical assistance (Change Strategy 2). It is as if person-centered planning is assumed to work by assisting a consumer to place an order that directs available resources to deliver what is agreed in the plan. The person-centered planning facilitator mediates between consumer and provider like a good waiter who advises on the menu, accurately transcribes what a diner wants, and negotiates special requests with the kitchen.

The third change strategy suspends the assumption that existing resources can do what is necessary and reframes the task as generating innovations that emerge in particular individual circumstances. Innovation guided by TASH values detects new possibilities, crosses boundaries, and mobilizes diverse resources in order to open and sustain new opportunities for people to be at home and work. This process of person-by-person innovation differs in both process and content from routinely placing people in group homes or placing a person on a predeveloped job. People, families, and service providers join their resources and organize themselves as innovation generators (Meissner, 2013). Innovations grow through a process of social learning in partnership with people and their families and allies and those community members who offer housing, jobs, and other opportunities for membership, engagement, and contribution. Partnerships design, negotiate, acquire, update, and improve the means to create and sustain people in contributing roles at work and home as their life circumstances change.

The whole system's task is to generate an ecology of social innovation that makes it easier to form partnerships and act resourcefully. Person-centered planning in this environment provides a forum to negotiate and renew the partnership and the highest purposes of the partners, hold the knowledge created as partners try new things, and support the design of next steps. Things almost never work out as anticipated and experience often modifies people's interests, so planning is a record of intentions and designs and a source of prototypes—good tries to be improved through further learning in community settings—not a blueprint that guarantees attainment of preset individual goals. Tying people to measurable goals a year away is unnecessary because the process of innovation involves multiple adjustments (Kay, 2010). Accountability is oriented toward higher purpose, and outcomes can be tracked on a population base in an ecology of social innovation. What proportion of people receiving public support are secure in their own homes with individualized supports? What proportion of people are earning in integrated jobs? What is the trend and distribution of their earnings?

People and their families, allies, and partners are capable of generating and self-managing the innovations necessary to pursue a good community life when they have sufficient capabilities—good connections to a diverse network of relationships, working links to local resources and associations, opportunities to develop knowledge and skills (including knowledge of what is possible for people with severe disabilities), assets (greatly aided by control of a flexible individual budget of public money to pay for assistance and accommodation), and a sense of self-efficacy. Independent facilitation that supports planning, opening opportunities, and organizing assistance multiplies the number of people and families that can self-manage their assistance (Lord et al., 2012) and helps family groups to support one another to plan and develop individual opportunities and learn together from their efforts (Mount & Lyle O'Brien, 2002). Educational opportunities for people and families to deepen their understanding of and desire to experience what TASH values and learn about how others realize these values positively influences demand and advocacy. Reflection on organizational journeys to partnership with people and their families identifies some of the adaptive challenges that are likely to arise (Inclusion Press, 2008; Meissner, 2013; Mount & VanEck, 2011).

Systems in most places invest most of their resources in operating and attempting to control the quality of group living arrangements and congregate alternatives to real employment. Significant costs are sunk in buildings. There is attachment to approaches to services and enabling administrative policies and procedures that are irreconcilably at odds with TASH values. The loyalty and advocacy of many people, families, and service providers when these insufficient forms of service are threatened complicates the adaptive challenge. More people and families will be able to form productive partnerships with service providers and redesign their offerings as more service providers choose to make the journey from serving groups of people with developmental disabilities camped out at the margin of community life to supporting people in their own homes and jobs as engaged and contributing citizens.

The results that TASH values cannot be delivered to consumers. Real homes and real jobs must be cocreated by active citizens working in partnership to make good use of system and community resources. A powerful assumption that responsibility for a good life can be fully delegated to service providers is embedded in the administration of system funds and the expectations of many families. This expectation needs to be renegotiated in recognition of the need for partnership.

A large number of people with severe disabilities live with the daily practical support of their families, and family investments have been critical in generating many innovative living arrangements. An understanding of person-centered planning that ignores the person-in-family, perhaps from a desire to respect the person's autonomy, risks distorting the realities of interdependency in every person's life. Missing the opportunity to provide a space in which all of those who are interdependent with a person can search for what they want to cocreate robs the person of powerful emotional and practical resources. Holding the inevitable conflicts among people as they search for their next steps forward is an essential contribution of person-centered planning facilitators.

Tension continues between demands for stability and demands for innovation. Stability requires maintaining financial viability, complying with system requirements, improving quality within the limits of existing group-based services, and satisfying those who choose not to enter partnerships to seek real homes and real jobs. Innovation requires investing time in building partnerships by operating from a place of generative awareness; deepening understanding of values; designing, learning from, and redesigning multiple individualized forms of support; growing new methods of appreciating and safeguarding quality; creating new roles in organizational structures and alliances to support innovation; dealing fairly with staff's conditions of employment; redirecting funds and negotiating money and regulatory room for innovations from funders and monitors; and developing access to additional community and mainstream resources. The organization must find a form that allows it to be ambidextrous, dealing creatively with competing commitments and attending to both the necessities of stability and the desire for innovation (Meissner, 2013).

There are real losses; not everything can be win-win. Familiar routines, procedures, expectations, and assumptions must change. Buildings become redundant. Uncertainties grow, and predictability declines, at least for the time of transition. Ways of exercising power that may have been taken for granted need to shift. Managers and growing numbers of staff, family members, and people with disabilities need to develop their leadership capacities and act as instruments of change. This means developing the ability to engage self and others in sensing possibilities, mobilizing action, learning from action, and sustaining what works. The commitment to operate from a generative level of awareness animates both person-centered planning and the organization's strategic and tactical plans.

It is not enough to exclusively focus on individual strategies to assist a person to take up the roles characteristic of secure and valued citizens by addressing the question, "How can this person's interests and capacities make a positive difference in this community?" It is also necessary to play a constructive role in building inclusive communities by addressing the complementary question, "How can we design our social arrangements so that everyone is welcomed as a contributor?"

Stronger contexts for person-centered planning emerge as more organizations choose to move into the gap between their current structures and the ecology of innovation necessary to move toward TASH values. Good efforts can be threatened, even crushed, because governments under economic or political pressure retain the power to cut or constrain necessary resources in ways that may overwhelm a social innovator's adaptive capacity. Even as the rights of people with severe disabilities gain greater recognition, to the degree that they rely on public resources, the force of these rights remains contingent on administrative structures that continue to (unconsciously) reproduce devaluing assumptions about the capacities of people with severe disabilities and even the worth of public investment in their lives. This is why a diverse network of strong and personally committed allies guided by a person-centered planning process and holding the search for the valued roles of worker and neighbor remain a person's best safeguards.

CONCLUSION

Competent person-centered planning can make a positive contribution to what people with severe disabilities experience in any context and under any change strategy described in this chapter. The depth of systemic and societal change necessary to create wide and reliable pathways to homes of people's choice and integrated jobs means that person-centered planning will only serve those valued outcomes when people are willing to partner to create new strategies and structures to act together. The work of articulating broad values, enshrining them in law and policy, and demonstrating their feasibility at a small scale is mostly done, though these victories remain vulnerable to regression. The adaptive work of creating new roles and relationships for significantly more people with severe disabilities remains a critical field for innovation.

Questions for Study and Reflection

As you consider Questions 1–3, think of yourself as a strategist for the whole system that must function differently if people are to have their own homes and integrated jobs (e.g., people with disabilities; family members; employers and co-workers; real estate agents, landlords, and neighbors; direct service workers; service managers; people responsible for administering the system; the public officials responsible for funding and governing available services). Give yourself great powers of persuasion so that you will be able to strongly influence people to try your strategy. Your powers unfortunately do not include the ability to increase the flow of public money for services.

1. What do you think are the most critical issues the system must address in order to make significant progress on supporting people with severe disabilities to live in their own homes and work in integrated jobs?

2. Which critical issue do you think offers the greatest leverage—making real progress on this issue would open the way to real homes and real jobs? Consider this issue and define the technical problems that need to be solved, distinguish and define the adaptive challenges involved in making progress, and outline a strategy to move the system forward.

3. What contribution do you think person-centered planning could make to your strategy? Describe in some detail and identify the resources you would need to invest in order to get the results you want from person-centered planning.

4. This question is for you personally, not for the master strategist who answered the previous questions. What questions worth pursuing has your reading of this chapter brought into focus for you, and what steps might you take to pursue them?

RESOURCES

TASH Values Person-Centered Planning Services

TASH. (2009). *TASH resolution on integrated employment.* Retrieved from http://tash.org/advocacy-issues/community-living/

TASH. (2011). *TASH resolution on choice and community living.* Retrieved from http://tash.org/advocacy-issues/community-living/

United Nations Convention on the Rights of Persons with Disabilities *http://www.un.org/disabilities/convention/conventionfull.shtml*

Background Materials from Developers and Practitioners of Person-Centered Planning

Holburn, S., & Vietze, P.M. (Eds.). (2002). *Person-centered planning: Research, practice, and future directions.* Baltimore, MD: Paul H. Brookes Publishing Co.

O'Brien, J., & Lyle O'Brien, C. (Eds.). (1998). *A little book about person-centered planning.* Toronto, Canada: Inclusion Press. Available at http://www.inclusion.com/bklittlebook.html

O'Brien, J., & Lyle O'Brien, C. (Eds.). (2002). *Implementing person-centered planning: Voices of experience.* Toronto, Canada: Inclusion Press. Available at http://www.inclusion.com/bkimplementingpcp.html

Approaches to Person-Centered Planning

Person-Centered Thinking and Essential Lifestyle Planning

Helen Sanderson Associates *http://www.helensandersonassociates.co.uk*

Learning Community for Person Centered Practices *http://www.learningcommunity.us*

New Paths to Inclusion *http://www.personcentredplanning.eu*

Personal Futures Planning

Mount, B., & VanEck, S. (2011). *Keys to life: Creating customized homes for people with disabilities using individualized supports.* Troy, NY: The ARC of Rensselaer County.

O'Brien, J., & Mount, B. (2005). *Make a difference: A guidebook for person-centered direct support.* Toronto, Canada: Inclusion Press. Available at http://www.inclusion.com/bkmakeadifference.html

PATH and MAPS

Facilitation for inclusion with PATH and MAPS [DVD]. Toronto, Canada: Inclusion Press. Available at http://www.inclusion.com/dvdfacilitation.html

O'Brien, J., Pearpoint, J., & Kahn, L. (2010). *The PATH and MAPS handbook: Person-centered ways to build community.* Toronto, Canada: Inclusion Press. Available at http://www.inclusion.com/bkpathmapshandbook.html

Person-Centered Planning and Other Efforts to Strengthen Citizenship and Build Community

The Centre for Welfare Reform *http://www.centreforwelfarereform.org*

Citizen-Centered Leadership Resource and Learning Center *http://www.cclds.org*

O'Brien, J., & Blessing, C. (2011). *Conversations on citizenship and person-centered work.* Toronto, Canada: Inclusion Press. Available at http://www.inclusion.com/bkcitizenship.html

Person-Centered Planning and Self-Directed Support and Individual Budgeting

In Control *http://www.in-control.org.uk*

Inclusion Press (Producer). (2008). *My life, my choice: Stories, struggles and successes with person-directed living* [DVD]. Toronto, Canada: Author. Available at http://www.inclusion.com/dvdmylife.html

Lord, J., Leavitt, B., & Dingwall, C. (2012). *Facilitating an everyday life: Independent facilitation and what really matters in a new story.* Toronto, Canada: Inclusion Press. Available at http://www.inclusion.com/bkfacilitating.html

REFERENCES

Amado, A., & McBride, M. (2002). Realizing individual, organizational and systems change: Lessons learned in 15 years of training about person-centered planning and principles. In S. Holburn & P.M. Vietze (Eds.), *Person-centered planning: Research, practice and future directions* (pp. 361–378). Baltimore, MD: Paul H. Brookes Publishing Co.

Callahan, M., & Condon, E. (2007). Discovery: The foundation of job development. In C. Griffin, D. Hammis, & T. Geary (Eds.), *The job developer's handbook: Practical tactics for customized employment* (pp. 23–33). Baltimore, MD: Paul H. Brookes Publishing Co.

Callahan, M., Shumpert, N., & Condon, E. (2011). *Discovery: Charting the course for employment.* Gautier, MS: Marc Gold and Associates.

Claes, C., Van Hove, G., Vandevelde, S., van Loon, J., & Schalock, R. (2010). Person-centered planning: Analysis of research and effectiveness. *Intellectual and Developmental Disabilities, 48,* 422–453.

Council on Quality and Leadership. (2010). Measuring what really matters. *Data Quarterly, 11.*

Deming, W.E. (2000). *Out of the crisis.* Cambridge, MA: The MIT Press.

Dinora, P. (2011). *Becoming a person-centered organization: Evaluation results 2009–2010.* Richmond: Virginia Commonwealth University, Partnership for People with Disabilities.

Do, H. (2007). *Valuing people now: From progress to transformation.* London, England: Department of Health.

Duffy, S. (2004). *Keys to citizenship: A guide to getting good support services for people with learning difficulties.* Birkenhead, England: Paradigm.

Emerson, E., Hatton, C., Robertson, J., Roberts, H., Baines, S., Evison, F., & Glover, G. (2012). *People with learning disabilities in England 2011: Services and supports.* Lancaster, United Kingdom: Improving Health and Lives: Learning Disability Observatory.

Heifetz, R. (1998). *Leadership without easy answers.* Cambridge, MA: Harvard University Press.

Holburn, S., Jacobson, J., Schwartz, A., Flory, M., & Vietze, P. (2004). The Willowbrook Futures Project: A longitudinal analysis of person-centered planning. *American Journal on Mental Retardation, 109,* 63–76.

Holburn, S., & Vietze, P. (2002). A better life for Hal: Five years of person-centered planning and applied behavior analysis. In S. Holburn & P.M. Vietze (Eds.), *Person-centered planning: Research, practice, and future directions* (pp. 291–314). Baltimore, MD: Paul H. Brookes Publishing Co.

Inclusion Press (Producer). (2008). *My life, my choice: Stories, struggles and successes with person-directed living* [DVD]. Toronto, Canada: Author.

Kay, J. (2010). *Obliquity: Why our goals are best achieved indirectly.* London, England: Profile Books.

Larson, S., Ryan, A., Salmi, P., Smith, P.D., & Wuorio, A. (2012). *Residential services for persons with developmental disabilities: Status and trends through 2010.* Minneapolis: University of Minnesota Institute on Community Integration.

Lord, J., Leavitt, B., & Dingwall, C. (2012). *Facilitating an everyday life: Independent facilitation and what really matters in a new story.* Toronto, Canada: Inclusion Press.

Lunt, J., & Hinz, A. (Eds.). (2011). *Training and practice in person centred planning: A European perspective.* Retrieved from http://tinyurl.com/7tbvet8

Lyle O'Brien, C., & O'Brien, J. (2002a). Large group process for person-centered planning. In J. O'Brien & C. Lyle O'Brien (Eds.), *Implementing person-centered planning: Voices of experience* (pp. 275–284). Toronto, Canada: Inclusion Press.

Lyle O'Brien, C., & O'Brien, J. (2002b). The origins of person-centered planning. In J. O'Brien & C. Lyle O'Brien (Eds.), *Implementing person-centered planning: Voices of experience* (pp. 25–57). Toronto, Canada: Inclusion Press.

Meissner, H. (2013). *Creating blue space: Fostering innovative support practices for people with developmental disabilities.* Toronto, Canada: Inclusion Press.

Mount, B. (2000). *Person-centered planning: Finding directions for change using personal futures planning.* Amenia, NY: Capacity Works.

Mount, B., & Lyle O'Brien, C. (2002). *Building new worlds: A sourcebook for students with disabilities in transition from high school to adult life.* Amenia, NY: Capacity Works.

Mount, B., & VanEck, S. (2011). *Keys to life: Creating customized homes for people with disabilities using individualized supports.* Troy, NY: The ARC of Rensselaer County.

National Health Policy Forum. (2008). *CMS programs for self-directed services: Independence plus and the DRA: Historical reference.* Washington, DC: Author.

O'Brien, J., & Mount, B. (1991). Telling new stories: The search for capacity among people with severe handicaps. In L.H. Meyer, C.A. Peck, & L. Brown (Eds.), *Critical issues in the lives of people with severe disabilities* (pp. 89–92). Baltimore, MD: Paul H. Brookes Publishing Co.

O'Brien, J., & Mount, B. (2005). *Make a difference: A guidebook for person-centered direct support.* Toronto, Canada: Inclusion Press.

O'Brien, J., Pearpoint, J., & Kahn, L. (2010.) *The PATH and MAPS handbook: Person-centered ways to build community.* Toronto, Canada: Inclusion Press.

Onondaga Community Living. (2012). *ACCESS.* Retrieved from http://www.oclinc.org/college/college_index.htm

Robertson, J., Emerson, E., Hatton, C., Elliott, J., Macintosh, B., Romeo, R., & Knapp, M. (2006). Longitudinal analysis of the impact and cost of person-centered planning for people with intellectual disabilities in England. *American Journal on Mental Retardation, 111,* 400–416.

Routledge, M., Sanderson, H., & Greig, R. (2002). Planning with people: The development of guidance on person-centered planning from the English Department of Health. In J. O'Brien & C. Lyle O'Brien (Eds.), *Implementing person-centered planning: Voices of experience* (pp. 373–396). Toronto, Canada: Inclusion Press.

Sanderson, H., & Lewis, J. (2012). *A practical guide to delivering personalization: Person-centred practice in health and social care.* London, England: Jessica Kingsley Publishers.

Smull, M., & Sanderson, H. (2005). *Essential lifestyle planning for everyone.* Stockport, United Kingdom: HSA Press.

TASH. (2009). *TASH resolution on integrated employment.* Retrieved from http://tash.org/advocacy-issues/employment

TASH. (2011). *TASH resolution on choice and community living.* Retrieved from http://tash.org/advocacy-issues/community-living.

United Nations. (2006) *UN Convention on the Rights of Persons with Disabilities.* Retrieved from http://www.un.org/disabilities/convention/conventionfull.shtml

Promoting Self-Determination and Self-Directed Learning

Martin Agran and Carolyn Hughes

Promoting self-determination, especially choice making, is a recommended practice. Failure to offer such opportunities (and related instruction) is considered neither in the best interests of the individuals served nor the individuals who support them (Agran & Hughes, 2005). Although the extent to which people with severe disabilities are taught to become more self-determined varies considerably (if they are taught at all), promoting self-determination has been recognized as an important need since educational services for students with severe disabilities were mandated in the 1970s. This chapter discusses the importance of promoting self-determination for individuals with severe disabilities. Self-determination is considered both a process to apply and an outcome for individuals to achieve, which provides them with a means to identify their preferences and desires and become more active in managing and directing their own behavior. A brief historical overview is presented and is followed by a review of self-determination practices and concerns—in particular, self-determination as an evidence-based practice and the value of self-determination in gaining access to the general curriculum. Next, there is a discussion of the alignment of self-determination with TASH's national agenda, as well as an examination of relevant legislation, mandates, and policies pertaining to self-determination. This chapter also addresses supporting self-determination in inclusive education, supporting the ongoing relationship between self-determination and opportunity, and promoting self-determination among youth from culturally diverse backgrounds.

HISTORICAL ANTECEDENTS

Self-determination has been valued and advocated since the early 1970s, even though there is current interest in self-determination and educators are making committed efforts to enhance active student involvement in educational planning and decision making. Nirje (1972) indicated that individuals with intellectual disabilities have the right to self-determination. They are citizens with the same rights as all other citizens, and service providers need to respect the choices, wishes, and desires of the people they serve.

In the first issue of the *American Association for the Education of the Severely/Profoundly Handicapped Review* (the original name of *Research and Practice for Persons with Severe Disabilities*), Williams, Brown, and Certo (1975) argued that the strategies used with students with severe disabilities resulted in students who were too externally controlled and cue dependent. Consequently, students are unable to appropriately respond, generalize, and transfer behaviors without external agents (i.e., teachers, paraprofessionals) present to deliver cues and consequences to them. Williams et al. suggested that students need to be taught how to provide their own cues, evaluate the quality of their responses, and self-correct inappropriate responding.

Mithaug and Hanawalt (1978) asked three adults to select the work tasks they preferred in one of the first investigations to systematically determine if individuals with severe intellectual disabilities have preferences. The findings suggested that individuals with extensive support needs do indeed have preferences and can consistently express them. Mithaug and Hanawalt suggested that such choice making enhances motivation and increases productivity and task accuracy. Guess and Siegel-Causey (1985) advanced the self-determination initiative by indicating that students with severe disabilities are given few, if any, opportunities to make choices and decisions in their best interests. Educators decide what they think is best for these students based on how they perceive the students' roles—in effect, educators decide what students learn and how they behave. Students fail to recognize that they are "self-directing and purposeful human beings" with their own agendas. Their failure to achieve desired outcomes should be seen as a failure in behavioral and educational technologies rather than an inability or opposition to making choices.

This early research provoked stakeholders (e.g., educators, advocates) to rethink their traditional approach to educational and service delivery. Educators and service providers began to explore ways for individuals with varying support needs to become contributing members regarding decisions and actions that directly affect their lives, rather than continue to believe that individuals with severe disabilities cannot determine or regulate their own behavior.

REALIZING SELF-DETERMINATION

Although there is general consensus regarding the value of self-determination (Agran & Hughes, 2005), there are varying definitions as to what it is and how it is manifested (Powers, 2006; Wehmeyer, 1998). Self-determination is a complex construct involving the interplay of several components. For some professionals, it is a desired outcome and similarly defined to outcomes relating to independence or success. For others, it is a number of selected strategies that allow students to exert increased control over their learning experiences. Such strategies allow individuals

SD is...
1 outcome

2 set of strategies to direct behavior + learning

t ... ndent of control by others (e.g.,
t ... participants in their own learn-
in ... become self-directed learners to
a ... Fisher, Sax, & Jorgensen, 1998).
T ... to problem-solve; retrieve, pro-
ce ... direct their own behavior and
lea ...

wh ... elf-determination is created in
de ... provided so that students can
env ... influence or manipulate their
act ... eyer, 2010). Students need to
beh ... they perform self-determined
enc ... vironments in which they are
... consequences of those choices.

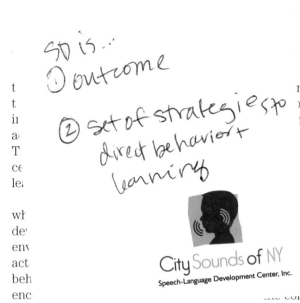

City Sounds of NY
Speech-Language Development Center, Inc.

CURRENT PRACTICE, CONCERNS, AND CHALLENGES

Self-determination as a psychological construct is related to successful individual performance and personal volition, particularly with respect to people with disabilities (Walker et al., 2011; Wehmeyer, Agran, et al., 2007). Self-determination is associated with positive academic, social, and adult outcomes for youth with a range of disabilities (Fowler, Konrad, Walker, Test, & Wood, 2007; Lachapelle et al., 2005; Wehmeyer & Palmer, 2003). Self-determination or student-directed learning strategies have demonstrated educational efficacy across a wide range of learning and adaptive skills and students with a variety of disabilities and have been well validated and supported in the literature (see Agran, King-Sears, Wehmeyer, & Copeland, 2003; Agran & Wehmeyer, 1999; Wehmeyer, Agran, et al., 2007). These strategies aim to teach students to set appropriate goals for themselves, monitor their performance, identify solutions to current or future problems, verbally direct their own behavior, reinforce themselves, or evaluate their own performance. Individuals are seen as causal agents in affecting their own outcomes (e.g., making and acting on personal decisions, choosing to advocate for themselves), which is consistent with a model of self-determination. Although proponents of self-determination theory acknowledge that individuals do not have direct control over many aspects of their social or economic conditions, it is assumed that people who are self-determined can gain access to resources or expertise through others in order to achieve desired outcomes (Bandura, 2001; Walker et al., 2011). Achieving personal outcomes by gaining access to the support or influence of others is particularly relevant to people with severe disabilities, who typically require extensive support in order to fully participate in everyday life activities (Thompson, Wehmeyer, & Hughes, 2010). The following sections discuss self-determination as an evidence-based practice and its value in gaining access to the general curriculum.

Evidence-Based Practice

The importance placed on students' involvement in their own educational decision making was established in the Individuals with Disabilities Education Act (IDEA) Amendments of 1997 (PL 105-17), which mandated including students in their individualized education program (IEP) meetings when planning for the transition from

school to adult life and requiring educa
ests and preferences. Active involvemen
valued as a means to promote students'
tive postschool outcomes and provides
learning (Martin, Van Dycke, Christens
Palmer, Soukup, Garner, & Lawrence, 2
has suggested that the role of student-d
motes positive academic, social, and ac
and developmental disabilities (e.g., Fov
torell, Gutierrez-Recacha, Perda, & Ayus
Lachapelle and colleagues reported that
to quality of life for adults with intellect
positive relation between self-determina
ment, independent living) for students v

As noted previously, self-determination has demonstrated educational efficacy across a wide range of learning and adaptive skills and students with a variety of disabilities and has been well validated and supported in the literature (see Agran et al., 2003; Agran & Wehmeyer, 1999; Wehmeyer, Agran, et al., 2007). A growing body of research literature suggests that student-directed learning strategies may greatly enhance a student's participation in general education for students with intellectual and developmental disabilities. Gilbert, Agran, Hughes, and Wehmeyer (2001) taught five middle school students with cognitive disabilities to self-monitor a set of classroom survival skills in their general education classrooms (e.g., Spanish, reading, history). Target behaviors included greeting teachers and students, using a day planner, and asking and answering questions. All target behaviors increased, and all students reported that they felt a greater membership in their classes. Copeland, Hughes, Agran, Wehmeyer, and Fowler (2002) taught four high school students with intellectual disabilities a set of self-regulation strategies (i.e., goal setting, self-monitoring, goal evaluation) to increase their level of performance of specified study skills (e.g., responding to worksheets, reading comprehension). The instruction produced immediate effects and increased the students' report card grades to satisfactory levels. Agran, Blanchard, Wehmeyer, and Hughes (2001) taught six secondary-level students with varying disabilities to use several student-directed learning strategies (i.e., goal setting, self-monitoring, problem solving) to modify selected academic, study, and social skills (e.g., scheduling time to complete assignments, completing assignments, initiating conversation with peers). All students dramatically increased their performance levels to 100%. Agran et al. (2005) taught six adolescents with mild to moderate disabilities to self-monitor their instruction-following skills in their content classes. All achieved rapid gains. Wehmeyer, Palmer, Agran, Mithaug, and Martin (2000) conducted a field test of a self-determination model (i.e., Self-Determined Learning Model of Instruction) with teachers responsible for the instruction of 40 adolescents with intellectual disabilities, learning disabilities, or emotional or behavior disorders. Students identified a total of 43 goals they wanted to achieve. Fifty-five percent of the students achieved their goals, and 30% exceeded their goals.

Researchers have demonstrated the effects of published curricula in promoting self-determination (e.g., Cross, Cooke, Wood, & Test, 1999; Hoffman & Field, 1995; Powers et al., 2001; Zhang, 2001b). For example, Cross et al. (1999) found that introducing the *ChoiceMaker* curriculum (Martin & Marshall, 1995) to teach students with intellectual disability choice-making and goal-setting skills resulted in increased scores on The Arc's Self-Determination Scale (Wehmeyer & Kelchner, 1995). The effects of instructional packages on increasing students' active involvement in transition planning and the IEP process have also been demonstrated (e.g., Allen, Smith, Test, Flowers, & Wood, 2001; Martin, Van Dycke, Christensen, et al., 2006; Mason, McGahee-Kovac, Johnson, & Stillerman, 2002). For example, Martin, Van Dycke, Christensen, et al. (2006) used the *Self-Directed IEP* curriculum (Martin, Marshall, Maxson, & Jerman, 1997) to teach secondary special education students to increase their speaking, goal-setting, and leadership roles in their IEP meetings.

Access to the General Curriculum

An emerging evidence base is documenting that students with severe disabilities can gain access to and become actively engaged in the general education curriculum. Spooner, Dymond, Smith, and Kennedy (2006) suggested that there are four general approaches to promote access to the general education curriculum for students with severe cognitive disabilities—peer supports, universal design for learning, teaching and assessing content standards, and self-determination. Self-determination, in particular, serves as a curriculum augmentation strategy (self-initiated instructional practice) that allows students to provide their own cues and consequences and employ a problem-solving approach that will allow them to process information (Copeland & Cosbey, 2009; Wehmeyer, Field, Doren, & Mason, 2004). Wehmeyer (2005) noted that self-determination strategies serve as an entry point to the curriculum and a useful instructional strategy that will allow students to self-regulate their learning and become more self-determined. For example, Agran, Wehmeyer, Cavin, and Palmer (2010) taught three high school students with intellectual disability to use a self-regulated problem-solving strategy to improve a variety of academic and communication skills across a variety of general education classrooms. The students were taught to set goals, plan courses of action to achieve their goals, evaluate their progress, and modify their goals or plans as needed. The students learned to generate and respond to a series of questions (e.g., "What do I want to learn?" "What can I do to make this happen?"). Dramatic improvements were reported for all students. Wehmeyer et al. noted that self-determination strategies produce two major benefits. First, they allow students to meet state standards that require that students learn how to set goals, problem-solve, and make decisions. Second, students are better prepared to enhance their overall academic performance as these skills have utility across all content areas.

Concerns and Challenges

Studies show, however, that few students are actively involved in the IEP process or consistently regulate or manage their own behavior without instruction and support. Martin, Van Dycke, Greene, et al. (2006) reported that secondary students who did not have any training generally talk only 3% of the time at IEP meetings. Secondary students in Hughes, Cosgriff, Agran, and Washington's (2013) study likewise self-reported having received little instruction and assumed only a minimal role at their IEP meetings. In addition, Agran and Hughes (2008) reported that the majority of students in their sample (high school and junior high school) stated that they had not been taught to either lead their IEP meetings (80% at the high school level, 96% at the junior high school level) or how to conduct their IEP meetings. Unfortunately, in virtually all studies in which instruction was provided to increase self-determination or active involvement in educational planning, participants were students with high-incidence disabilities or mild intellectual disability. Self-determination curricula investigated, such as the *Self-Directed IEP* (Martin et al., 1997) and *ChoiceMaker* (Martin & Marshall, 1995), require considerable content reading, necessitating modifications to allow access by students with more severe disabilities and limited reading skills. Teachers of students with severe disabilities, however, overwhelmingly reported not knowing how to teach self-determination skills to these students (Wehmeyer, Agran, & Hughes, 2000).

Recommendations for Change

Addressing self-determination among people with severe disabilities requires teachers and other providers to adopt two fundamental conceptual approaches: 1) realize that people with severe disabilities, including those with limited verbal repertoires, do have preferences and can make choices (Cannella, O'Reilly, & Lancioni, 2005); and 2) be aware that the skills that compose self-determination, such as problem solving, goal setting, and choice making, typically must be taught to people with severe disabilities and opportunities to practice these skills must be provided (Wehmeyer, Agran, et al., 2007). Assumptions are too often made with respect to the capacity of people with severe disabilities to act autonomously. Teachers, providers, and caregivers must learn to be attentive and responsive to individuals' unique communication modes; some individuals may express preferences via facial expressions or body language or by approaching or reaching for an object or person, whereas others may whine, scream, grab or strike at an object, or hit themselves or others to communicate a choice or preference (Machalicek et al., 2010). Effective communication skills must be taught to people with severe disabilities and limited verbal repertoires, and people must learn to recognize and respect these individuals' preferences and choices as an example of self-determination and self-advocacy.

A substantial body of research indicates that people with severe disabilities, limited language skills, and intellectual disability can learn to perform the strategies that compose self-determination and self-directed learning (e.g., self-monitoring, self-evaluating, goal setting; see Wehmeyer, Agran, et al., 2007). For example, Copeland and Hughes (2000) taught two high school students with severe disabilities to use picture prompts to increase their independent performance of job task sequences. Acquisition of the picture prompt strategy was associated with decreased prompting by an adult trainer. Hughes et al. (2011) taught five high school students with intellectual disability and autism to use communication books to prompt themselves to initiate conversation with general education peers. Self-prompted communication book use by participants generalized across peers and settings. Gilbert et al. (2001) taught five middle school students with severe intellectual disability to self-monitor their performance of a set of classroom survival skills, such as having appropriate materials and acknowledging teacher comments. Self-monitoring was associated with increases in target skills for all participants. User-friendly guides for teaching such self-directed learning strategies are available in several publications (e.g., Agran et al., 2003; Wehmeyer, Agran, et al., 2007).

ALIGNMENT WITH TASH NATIONAL AGENDA

All TASH national agenda items are predicated on the assumption that service, placement, and support decisions are based on an individual's preferences, choices, and wishes. The revised TASH Resolution on Choices (TASH, 2000) strongly advocated that all individuals have the right to freedom of choice. Professionals and parents have assumed that people with severe intellectual disability are not capable of making choices in their own best interests. Expectations need to change regarding the capability of individuals to express their preferences and make choices, especially with the continuing recognition that individuals with severe disabilities can learn to be self-determined. Self-determination provides access to the general curriculum and thus enhances inclusive education. Community living is based on person-centered planning and individual preference. Decisions regarding employment, such as community living, are based on person-centered planning. Committed efforts are being made to develop culturally responsive and informed self-determination curricula. Choice making and self-directed behavioral interventions have become integral components in positive behavior interventions and supports. In all, the national agenda is advanced by the self-determination initiative.

Related Legislation, Mandates, Practices, and Policies

Researchers have suggested that self-determination is a right and entitlement, even though it is not legally mandated per se (Mithaug, 2005; United Nations [2006] *UN Convention on the Rights of Persons with Disabilities* [CRPD]). This is evident at international and national levels. Relating to the CRPD mandates:

> In order, however, to demolish the spells of the past in discriminating children with disabilities, states and societies must first and foremost respect the principle of non-discrimination, uphold the idea that the best interests of the child must prevail in all actions affecting him/her, and must give generous opportunity and possibility for children with disabilities to voice their opinion and to have their views heard and respected. The marginalization of children with disabilities will not be solved unless it is recognized that these children must be included in the overall decision-making process. (2006, pp. 3–4)

In addition, in 2011 the World Health Organization emphasized the importance of child- and adult-centered educational and health programs and indicated that self-determination is a civil right.

The Individuals with Disabilities Education Improvement Act (IDEA) of 2004 (PL 108-446) mandated that students' preferences and interests must be considered when developing IEPs and individualized transition plans. Concentrated efforts must be made to ensure that students have an active role in educational planning. IEP teams must endeavor to obtain input from students on their preferences and wishes and ensure educational and service and support goals are based on these preferences; optimally, the value of teaching students to lead their own IEP meetings has been promoted. The Rehabilitation Act Amendments of 1992 (PL 102-569) and the Workforce Investment Act of 1998 (PL 105-220) emphasized the importance of self-determination for adults regarding the services and supports they desire.

The need to promote self-determination has been both nationally and internationally recognized across age levels. But the question remains as to whether this recognition has been translated into systematic instruction in which students' and consumers' choices are indeed secured, implemented, and supported. The next section addresses this issue.

EFFECT OF PRACTICE AND POLICY ON RECOMMENDED PRACTICES, INTEGRATED SERVICES, AND QUALITY OF SERVICES AND SUPPORTS

Self-determination has had a dramatic effect on the extent to which individuals with severe disabilities have been taught to advocate for their needs and determine the services and supports they desire. Choice making is considered an essential component of practically all educational and program planning. Consequently, choice making is regarded as the central element of self-determination (Wehmeyer, Agran, et al., 2007). Choice making initiates the self-determination process and prompts action (Deci & Ryan, 1985; Schloss, Alper, & Jayne, 1993). Choices allow individuals to make educational and service decisions that best match their wishes, interests, and capabilities and, in doing so, promote greater engagement and motivation on their part (Mithaug, 2005). Self-determination is largely understood in terms of personal choice. Promoting choice making has become an important focus of disability services and supports, is a basic component in service delivery (Wehmeyer, 2001), and serves as the foundational credo for many educational and human services (Bambara, 2004). It provokes self-determination and self-regulation by allowing individuals with intellectual disabilities to express their preferences, make choices based on those preferences, and, subsequently, act on those choices. Choice making has been a focal point in the self-determination movement (Agran & Wehmeyer, 2003). A mistaken belief may exist, however, that the act of choosing is sufficient in promoting self-determination; in other words, choice making in and of itself produces self-determination (Agran, Wehmeyer, & Krupp, 2010). Consequently, individuals may not be taught other self-directed learning strategies. Choice making is an important component of self-determination, but it is only one of several components (e.g., problem solving, goal setting, self-evaluation). Wehmeyer (2005) suggested that the intent is not only to teach individuals to choose but also to take control over their lives. Expressing preferences and making choices based on these preferences is a critical first step, but it is just that. Choice making has a vital and integral role in promoting self-determination, but it does not necessarily ensure it. The immediate benefit of choice making is that it allows individuals to select a preferred stimulus or condition to one that is least preferred. Choice making is beneficial in that it provides a means to express a preference, but it does not teach individuals how to evaluate the relative weight or value of the choices they make (Agran et al., 2010). Individuals will need to learn to assess the consequences of their actions—in other words, problem-solve. Although choice making and problem solving are typically not associated, competency in problem solving can only be developed if individuals are given the opportunity to experience the consequences of their actions and determine if they are meeting their expectations. Individuals can begin to take more ownership and control over their lives when they understand the need to practice choice making and problem solving. Self-determined individuals are aware of their needs and make decisions to meet those needs by setting goals, taking action, and adjusting through ongoing self-evaluation. Individuals will continue to be dependent on others if they do not have opportunities to make meaningful choices and practice problem solving.

Current Research and Practice: Self-Determination, Environment, and Opportunity

Research suggests that exercising self-determination skills (e.g., choice making, problem solving, self-advocating) and being actively involved in educational planning relate to relevant skill instruction received, environmental factors, and opportunity to practice skills (e.g., Shogren et al., 2007). Early studies in residential settings for adults with intellectual disabilities revealed that residents had little opportunity for making choices or decisions or advocating for themselves in their daily lives (e.g., Kishi, Teelucksingh, Zollers, Park-Lee, & Meyer, 1988; Wehmeyer & Meltzer, 1995). Subsequent studies examined the type of residential environment in relation to opportunities to practice self-determination. Less restrictive settings that provided supports and accommodations were associated with greater opportunities for choice making, decision making, and promoting self-determination for adults with intellectual disability (e.g., Robertson et al., 2001; Wehmeyer & Bolding, 2001; Wehmeyer & Garner, 2003).

Investigating Instruction versus Opportunity   The extent to which individuals are taught to be self-determined largely depends on the setting and the opportunities presented in that setting. Both the quality and frequency of self-determined responses are contingent on the opportunities for individuals to demonstrate (and be reinforced) for these behaviors. Although residential settings provide many opportunities for residents to demonstrate their self-determination, only one published study was found in which self-determination skills were taught to adults in a residential setting. Specifically, Hughes (1992) taught four adults with severe intellectual disability and limited verbal skills living in a group home to solve problems related to completing daily living skills (e.g., cleaning room) by using self-instruction to guide their performance. Participants learned to use their verbal behavior to solve problems (e.g., cord in the way when vacuuming) and apply their self-instructions to novel problems not involved in training (e.g., spray can missing when dusting). Although the gains reported were noteworthy, there was no discussion of opportunities to be self-determined in such settings. Although numerous studies investigated self-determination and involvement in educational planning in school settings, the primary focus has been on outcomes of instruction; consequently, little is known about how opportunity or environmental factors influence performance of self-determination skills at school (Carter, Owens, Trainor, Sun, & Swedeen, 2009; Chambers et al., 2007; Shogren et al., 2007).

Zhang (2001a) asked general and special education teachers to rate how often students with mild intellectual disabilities demonstrated 13 self-determination behaviors (e.g., making choices, setting goals, self-advocating) in their respective classrooms. Special versus general education teachers reported higher rates of self-determination behavior, suggesting that special education settings are more conducive to self-determination than general education environments. Zhang suggested, however, that teacher bias or expectations may have influenced results because special education teachers are more likely to be aware of the IDEA 2004 mandate to address students' interests, preferences, and choices in educational programming. Zhang did not report environmental features or actual opportunities or activities that may have related to exercising self-determination in either setting. Furthermore, student perspective on opportunity to exercise self-determination (e.g., making choices) across settings was not sought.

Carter et al. (2009) asked special education teachers of high school students with severe intellectual and developmental disabilities to use the AIR (American Institutes for Research) Self-Determination Scale (Wolman, Campeau, DuBois, Mithaug, & Stolarski, 1994) to rate opportunities for students to engage in and demonstrate self-determination behaviors at school. The AIR scale provides examples of opportunities for self-determination for each of six questionnaire items; however, the focus of this instrument is only on the teachers' provision of opportunities and not environmental factors or activities that could influence self-determination (e.g., IEP meetings). The example for the goal-setting item is, "Troy's teachers let him know that he is responsible for setting his own goals to get his needs and wants met." The AIR scale asks teachers to rate their own actions in providing opportunities for students to practice self-determination but not the outcome of their actions. Teachers in Carter et al.'s study found that opportunities for self-determination were *sometimes* to *almost always* available at school, although they reported that students *almost never* to *sometimes* demonstrated self-determined behaviors. No evidence was provided by the authors to corroborate teacher report, however; therefore, it is not known to what extent opportunities actually existed across the school day. Shogren et al. (2007) suggested that the opportunities that teachers perceive themselves as creating, as indicated on the AIR scale, may not actually affect students' level of self-determination—a notion that may relate to the fact that special education teachers overwhelmingly report not knowing how to teach self-determination (Wehmeyer, Agran, et al., 2000). In addition, Carter et al. did not provide student input on opportunities to practice self-determination skills because of concerns with the validity of responses of students with severe intellectual disabilities. Therefore, it is not known if students' perspectives would have matched those of their teachers.

Inclusion as an Environmental Factor   Few investigations in schools have examined inclusiveness of setting in relation to self-determination skills (Shogren et al., 2010); that is, what is the relationship of school inclusion to self-determination for students with severe disabilities. Hughes et al. (2013) investigated the association of level of participation in inclusive activities in school and community and students' reported self-determination skill use. Forty-seven students with severe intellectual disability from three high schools participated. Findings revealed significant differences across schools in student participation in general education and school- and community-based transition activities, which were associated with level of self-determination skill use. Students attending schools offering more inclusive activities reported significantly more frequent use of six of nine self-determination skills: self-advocacy (How often do you speak up for yourself?), choice making (How often do you make choices by yourself?), self-reinforcing (How often do you tell or reward yourself that you did well when you finish a task?), self-monitoring (How often do you count the number of times you perform a task?), self-evaluating (How often do you compare how well you are doing now with how well you did in the past?), and problem solving (How often do you solve problems by yourself at school, work, or home?). Inclusive activities and self-determination were positively associated.

Walker et al. found that "the degree to which one is socially included affects one's opportunities to engage in self-determined actions; it also affects the experiences in which one learns about individual preferences, interests, wants, needs, and desires" (2011, p. 15). Walker and colleagues further argued that research clearly shows inclusion in community and school provides greater opportunities to make choices, express preferences, set goals, and become more self-determined when compared with more restrictive settings and experiences. This viewpoint is corroborated by findings of Hughes et al. (2013), who showed that students participating significantly less in inclusive classes and school- and community-based transition instruction reported significantly less frequent use of self-determination skills than did students in more inclusive settings.

Numerous studies have demonstrated the positive effects of both inclusive school environments and community-based training on postschool outcomes such as employment, postsecondary education, and independent living (e.g., Cimera, 2010; Test et al., 2009). Attending school exclusively in separate special education classrooms and having very limited or no community-based instruction provides students with little opportunity to independently make choices, solve problems, or speak up for themselves. Wehmeyer and Metzler (1995) suggested that educational environments that are highly structured, restrictive, or protective typically do not provide opportunities for independent problem solving or decision making. Students do not have the opportunity to develop the skills to independently respond to the ever-changing, unpredictable events and vicissitudes that comprise everyday life in inclusive school and community settings when daily activities are more predictable.

Inclusive environments may present frequent challenges for the individual that can prompt independent performance and self-determination skills. For example, the bus route that a student takes to a community-based jobsite may unexpectedly change, causing the student to have to problem-solve options to get to work. Or, a student must learn to prompt and reinforce herself to get to class on time when walking in the hall to her inclusive class without a teacher. The students in Hughes et al. (2013) who were already at a disadvantage because of limited access to inclusive school and community instructional environments reported significantly less use of self-determination skills than did their counterparts experiencing more inclusive educational environments, suggesting that segregated settings can hinder self-determination. Hughes and colleagues' findings suggested that the degree to which students are included in school and community may affect their opportunities to make choices, set personal goals, express preferences, and develop other self-determination skills, as argued by others (e.g., Walker et al., 2011; Wehmeyer, Palmer, et al., 2007). Further investigation of the effects of participation in inclusive settings and activities in relation to self-determination in school and community settings appears warranted at this point.

RESEARCH AND PRACTICE:
SELF-DETERMINATION AND CULTURALLY DIVERSE POPULATIONS

The majority of public school students are expected to be of color and from low-income families by 2020 (Ball, 2009; National Center for Education Statistics, 2006; Suitts, 2010). Students from low-income families now comprise the majority of the public school population in the South and in California, New Mexico, and Oregon, and 46% of the national public school population is low income (Suitts, 2007). In addition, White public school students are now in the minority in the South and several western states (National Center for Education Statistics, 2007; Orfield, 2009; Suitts, 2010). Students from high-poverty or culturally diverse backgrounds rarely have been included as participants in investigations of self-determination or self-directed learning, despite the changing demography of the school population (Carter et al., 2009; Shogren et al., 2007). It is alarming that students of color do not appear to be receiving such instruction, given the critical need for self-determination instruction by students with cognitive disabilities. Few of those who are receiving such instruction are getting it from culturally responsive interventions. Ironically, no self-determination curricula have endeavored to synthesize culturally responsive practices and self-determination instruction, which underscores the importance of developing such culturally responsive instructional materials.

Self-Determination and Poverty

Self-determination rarely has been investigated in relation to overcoming the adverse effects associated with high-poverty communities or schools, although several researchers have suggested doing so (e.g., Chambers et al., 2007; Wehmeyer et al., 2011). People who are self-determined are characterized as skilled in obtaining resources and supports and speaking up for their own needs. It is more likely that individuals who assert themselves will be successful in gaining access to these limited opportunities, considering that limited resources, such as few jobs in a community or minimal college counselor availability at school, are typical of a high-poverty environment. Therefore, skills that comprise self-determination, such as setting goals, problem solving, and self-advocating, may be instrumental in addressing the challenges of underresourced, high-poverty schools and neighborhoods. Yet, underresourced environments may hinder the development of self-determination skills because of scarce opportunities to make choices, exercise preferences, and experience stimulating and varied educational events on a consistent basis. Wehmeyer and colleagues (2011) suggested that oppression, segregation, and discrimination—often associated with high-poverty environments—inhibit the development of self-determination skills, especially when coexisting with disability.

Washington, Hughes, and Cosgriff (2012) compared involvement in educational planning and use of self-determination strategies reported by two groups of students attending a high-poverty, predominately Black high school: 19 students with severe intellectual disabilities and 20 general education seniors identified as successful students. The school enrolled 1,070 students, of which 81% were Black, 16% White, and 3% Hispanic or Asian; 74% qualified for free or reduced-price lunch. The high school was being taken over by the state at the time of the study because of its 53% dropout rate and failure to make annual yearly progress on state exit examinations. In addition, it had been identified as a segregated, high-need "dropout factory"

(Balfanz & Legters, 2007). Most (56%) households in the community were single parent, and 42% had an income of less than $25,000.

Findings revealed that special education students participated in few activities (e.g., general or career education classes, transition activities, employment) on a daily basis outside their self-contained special education classes. In contrast, more than half of general education students attended both career and general education classes as well as worked part time in the community. Special education students were significantly less likely to report involvement in seven of eight educational planning activities (e.g., evaluating progress on school goals). Few were aware of their IEP goals, and none had led (or actively participated in) their IEP meetings. Special education students also reported significantly less use of eight of nine self-determination strategies (e.g., independently solving problems). Examples were primarily limited to home environments, such as solving a dispute with a sibling, versus examples across school, home, and community as cited by general education students.

Implications of Findings

Important implications for research and practice can be drawn from Washington et al. (2012) and Hughes et al. (2013). First, participants with severe intellectual disability spent the overwhelming majority of their day in self-contained special education classrooms where they likely had few opportunities to choose, independently solve problems, or learn self-determination skills. Restrictiveness of setting must be considered in relation to any investigation of self-determination. For example, limited self-advocacy may simply represent a lack of instruction and opportunity rather than a student's capacity to learn to self-advocate. Second, poverty in itself is a moderating factor that must be considered when designing any program to promote self-determination (Wehmeyer et al., 2011). Limited resources, high student and teacher mobility, and blighted neighborhoods severely restrict opportunities for community-based experiences and learning and practicing self-advocacy skills for youth with severe disabilities in high-poverty schools. Students are likely to develop a restricted repertoire of choices, preferences, and bases for making decisions without out a range of experiences across varied settings (Robertson et al., 2001). Not only must instruction to learn to problem-solve or independently make decisions be provided to students with severe intellectual disabilities, but Washington et al.'s (2012) study suggested that opportunity must also be addressed, particularly in relation to high-poverty environments.

Third, it is critical to know the extent to which individuals who are successful in adverse conditions practice self-determination and self-directed learning strategies. Washington et al. (2012) established a normative standard for general education students' involvement in educational planning and use of self-determination skills as demonstrated by a group of 20 second-semester seniors identified as successful within the high-poverty high school environment (i.e., low absences, having passed all state exit exams, sufficient credits to graduate, enrollment in at least one advanced placement [AP] or honors class, good grades, having applied to at least one college). Findings indicated that this group of successful seniors frequently exercised most of the self-determination skills queried (e.g., solving problems themselves, setting their own goals, speaking up for themselves, making their own choices, instructing themselves to do a job or task). A normative standard emerges of frequent use of self-advocacy and self-determination skills by general education students who were successful within a high-poverty environment.

Findings are encouraging that a group of general education students identified as successful in the environment did take an active and self-determined role in their high school education. They represented only 20 of 400 students in their freshman class cohort, however, and 20 of 114 members of that cohort who were graduating 4 years later. Their persistence in achieving expectations for completing high school and preparing for college (e.g., having few absences, enrolling in AP and honors classes, applying to college) when few other students did so may have related to their resilience and self-determination (Morales, 2010). These students cited multiple examples of how they monitored themselves to maintain good attendance, pass their classes, graduate on time, and maintain positive relationships with others (e.g., "I try to improve every 6 weeks, set high personal standards, and evaluate mistakes")—all of which are factors associated with high school completion in at-risk environments (Floyd, 1996). Self-determination may have been what separated these students from their many counterparts who did not demonstrate a similar level of academic achievement and may serve as a standard to seek when designing educational opportunities and instruction for students with severe disabilities.

Recommendations for Research and Practice

Washington et al.'s (2012) findings suggested that traditionally disenfranchised and underserved populations, such as children and youth with severe intellectual disability from culturally diverse backgrounds who are attending high-poverty schools, may be missing out on learning and exercising critical self-determination skills and actively participating in their educational planning. Findings underscored the need to teach self-advocacy and self-determination skills and provide opportunities to apply these skills in daily activities in inclusive school and community settings outside the self-contained special education classroom. Because teachers report not knowing how to teach such skills to students with more severe needs (Wehmeyer, Agran, et al., 2000), support should be provided to teachers in order to incorporate self-determination instruction in inclusive settings into curricula for students with severe intellectual disabilities attending high-poverty schools serving culturally diverse populations.

Furthermore, only a small number of general education students in the same environment were found to be achieving the benchmarks typically associated with successful high school completion. Their achievement may have related to their resilience and self-determination. It is important to address factors, such as promoting resilience and self-determination, associated with increasing the odds that more students will succeed in at-risk environments, especially in an era when few students of color, particularly Black males, from high-poverty backgrounds are graduating from high school and going on to college (Barton & Coley, 2010; Holzman, 2010). Education as a field holds equity, opportunity, and achievement as values for all students (Duncan, 2011). Self-determination is associated with academic achievement and positive postschool outcomes for students with disabilities (Fowler et al., 2007; Wehmeyer & Palmer, 2003). Research and practice designed to increase self-determination must begin to include all students, particularly those who have been left out of previous efforts (Walker et al., 2011; Wehmeyer et al., 2011).

RECOMMENDED PRACTICES

Wehmeyer (2005) suggested that self-determination is not just a set of skills. Teaching individuals self-directed strategies will have little effect if their decisions and actions are not supported by educators, service providers, parents, and other stakeholders. Also, the number and types of opportunities individuals are given to exercise their self-determination are most important. Although the teaching sequence varies across strategies, the following steps are recommended.

First, it is critical that individuals are provided a rationale on why teaching them to determine their own behavior, problem-solve, or self-evaluate is advantageous. Individuals need to be taught that self-directed behavior change is to their advantage and will produce many benefits and that self-determination strategies provide a useful set of tools that will allow them to decide how best to learn, adapt to a variety of situations, and seek to achieve self-selected goals.

Second, Agran, Storey, and Krupp (2010) reported that consumers with extensive support needs valued opportunities to make choices. Among the choices they valued were who they would like to work with, which task they wanted to do first, and what they wanted to do after work. Many individuals with extensive support needs do not know how to make choices because of limited opportunities and need to be taught using systematic instructional procedures (Cannella et al., 2005; Martin, Woods, Sylvester, & Gardner, 2005). The belief by many teachers and service providers that there are no instructional materials available to teach choice making or other self-determination strategies is one of the major obstacles to promoting consumer self-determination. Suffice it to say that such materials are available (see Agran & Martin, 2008; Wehmeyer, Palmer, et al., 2000; Wehmeyer, Agran, et al., 2007). Educators and service providers need to infuse choice-making opportunities into the ongoing routines of the school or work settings because it will allow students and consumers to have a major say about and investment in their learning and performance. Also, informed choices become meaningless without providing appropriate supports and options. Individuals need to experience and see the consequences of their choices, and, thus, these choices need to be respected and followed even though the provider may not agree with the choice made.

Third, it is important to consider the degree to which individuals are supported to make decisions based on their interests, select actions to achieve desired outcomes, and evaluate how well they have performed. Will such self-determination be actively encouraged and respected? Will sufficient opportunities be provided for individuals to engage in these actions? It is critical that such support is available for self-determination to be realized.

Fourth, a decision needs to be made regarding which self-determination strategy is most appropriate, given the target behavior and the nature of the environment and task. Three variables need to be considered: 1) which strategy best fits into the environment (e.g., self-instruction may not be the best strategy in a quiet classroom); 2) which strategy is acceptable to all stakeholders (e.g., some teachers may object to self-reinforcement); and 3) which strategy is preferred by the student and his or her family.

Fifth, identify each of the responses when teaching the strategies. A sequence needs to be developed that involves both the task steps and steps in the strategy chosen. Needless to say, the latter (e.g., referring to picture cues) needs to be sequenced to facilitate task completion. Next, the strategy is taught using levels of assistance and prompting appropriate to the student's needs.

Last, the student's task performance as well as execution of the strategy needs to be monitored and evaluated. Among the questions to address are "Is the student consistently applying the strategy?" and "Does it appear to have a positive effect on his or her performance?"

FUTURE RESEARCH AND POLICY DEVELOPMENT

Although self-determination has been recognized as a critical component of instructional programming and service delivery planning, the number of individuals with severe disabilities who are systematically taught to use one or more self-determination strategies—other than being provided choice-making opportunities—remains few. Furthermore, many students with severe disabilities have limited knowledge about self-determination and have reported few opportunities to learn and practice these skills (Carter et al., 2009). Many educators have indicated that they do not know how to teach self-determination skills to their students, which compounds the problem (Wehmeyer, Agran, et al., 2000). Carter, Sisco, and Lane (2011) asked a sample of professionals their knowledge about self-determination and the extent to which they teach these skills. Although the majority indicated that they taught choice making, fewer than 50% taught any other forms of self-determination. A review of the self-determination literature reveals that most self-determination applications are conducted with students with mild disabilities. Furthermore, relatively few students with severe disabilities have been taught to lead their IEPs and have a more active voice in educational decision making (Agran & Hughes, 2008). Last, there have been relatively few investigations of adults using self-determination strategies in work, residential, and other community environments. Most investigations have been conducted in classroom settings. The need for further investigations of the effects of self-determination across diverse ages and settings is needed.

Numerous researchers have suggested that if children are to be self-determined, then this outcome should be promoted as early as possible (Erwin & Brown, 2003; Lee, Palmer, Turnbull, & Wehmeyer, 2006). Cook, Brotherson, Weigel-Garrey, and Mize (1996) noted that home offers children the earliest opportunity to make choices, exercise control, and exhibit competence—factors strongly associated with self-determination. The home clearly is the setting where children first learn to express their preferences, set goals, and make decisions (Lee et al., 2006). The home environment provides children with the opportunity to practice the early behavior characteristics of self-determination (Brotherson, Cook, & Parette, 1996; Wehmeyer & Palmer, 2000). Strategies to promote the development of self-determination in early childhood environments (e.g., home, preschool) are receiving increased attention (Erwin & Brown, 2003) and warrant further investigation.

Choice making (and other forms of self-determination) is contingent on the assumption that an individual's expression of a choice or wish is understood by service providers or support personnel. Accordingly, communication competence is synonymous with self-determination (Brown, Gothelf, Guess, & Lehr, 1998). Brown et al. indicated, however, that consumers who have severe communication challenges may employ nonsymbolic, idiosyncratic, or self-selected modes of communication to express their choices. Consequently, self-determination for these individuals presumes that the communication receivers (e.g., caregivers, support people) can interpret such communication. The preferences and choices of consumers who have communication challenges often need to be inferred through such responses as time engaged (e.g., the more preferred the task, the more time will be engaged), facial expressions (e.g., frown may suggest a nonpreferred task), or sound production (e.g., a hum may suggest a preferred task). The responsiveness of partners then becomes a factor critical in choice making and is a reminder that choice making is not a single, isolated behavior but one that involves reciprocal exchanges and environmental support (Bambara, 2004). Further research is warranted on practices service providers can employ to best understand self-determined expressions by individuals to ensure that programs are indeed driven by their preferences, needs, and interests.

CONCLUSION

Self-determination theory proposes that human beings have three essential needs: *autonomy, competence,* and *relatedness,* all of which contribute to human well-being (Deci & Ryan, 2000; Véronneau, Koestner, & Abela, 2005). Self-determination meets this need of autonomy by teaching individuals with severe disabilities to make choices and decisions based on their own wishes and preferences and to employ one or more self-determined strategies that allow them to monitor, evaluate, and adjust their performance. *Competence* refers to an individual's capacity to achieve mastery in his or her environments—a primary goal of self-determination. Relatedness addresses feelings of connection and closeness to significant others that can be achieved as individuals become more self-regulated and self-determined. Self-determination and related instructional and behavior change strategies represent a forceful and promising way for students and adults to achieve successful learning outcomes. Failure to provide such instruction will only perpetuate dependency and helplessness.

Questions for Study and Reflection

1. It has been suggested that students who engage in challenging behaviors are expressing their self-determination. Discuss why this might be so.

2. What is the relative value of the self-determination strategies discussed in the chapter? If you were to select one strategy, which one would you choose? On what basis would you make this decision?

3. In what way might teaching students to use self-determination strategies change their relationships with teachers or service providers? How might this change the roles of these professionals?

4. Researchers have suggested that self-determination should be taught in the same way you would teach any other behavior. How would you go about teaching a self-determination strategy?

5. What indicators would you use to determine if an individual has mastered self-determination at some level? What information would you want to obtain?

RESOURCES

American Association on Intellectual and Developmental Disabilities *http://www
.aaidd.org*

The Arc *http://www.thearc.org/*

Autism Society of America *http://www.autism-society.org*

National Council on Independent Living *http://www.ncil.org*

National Down Syndrome Congress *http://www.ndsccenter.org*

The Pacer Center *http://www.pacer.org/tatra/resources/self.asp*

Zarrow Center for Learning Enrichment at the University of Oklahoma *zarrowcenter
@ou.edu*

REFERENCES

Agran, M., Blanchard, C., Wehmeyer, M., & Hughes, C. (2001). Teaching students to self-regulate their behavior: The differential effects of student- versus teacher-delivered reinforcement. *Research in Developmental Disabilities, 22,* 319–332.

Agran, M., & Hughes, C. (2005). Introduction to special issue: Self-determination: How far have we come? *Research and Practice for Persons with Severe Disabilities, 30,* 105–107.

Agran, M., & Hughes, C. (2008). Asking student input: Students' opinions regarding their individualized education program involvement. *Career Development for Exceptional Individuals, 31,* 69–76.

Agran, M., King-Sears, M., Wehmeyer, M., & Copeland, S. (2003). *Teachers' guides to inclusive practices: Student-directed learning.* Baltimore, MD: Paul H. Brookes Publishing Co.

Agran, M., & Krupp, M. (2011). Providing choice making in employment programs: The beginning or end of self-determination? *Education and Training in Autism and Developmental Disabilities, 45,* 565–575.

Agran, M., & Martin, J.E. (2008). Self-determination: Enhancing competence and independence. In K. Storey & P. Bates (Eds.), *The road ahead: Transition to adult life for persons with disabilities* (pp. 189–214). St. Augustine, FL: Training Resource Network.

Agran, M., Sinclair, T., Alper, S., Cavin, M., Wehmeyer, M., & Hughes, C. (2005). Using self-monitoring to increase following-direction skills of students with moderate to severe disabilities in general education. *Education and Training in Developmental Disabilities, 40,* 3–13.

Agran, M., Storey, K., & Krupp, M. (2010). Choosing and choice making are not the same: Asking "what do you want for lunch?" is not self-determination. *Journal of Vocational Rehabilitation, 33,* 77–88.

Agran, M., & Wehmeyer, M. (1999*). Teaching problem solving to students with mental retardation.* Washington, DC: American Association on Mental Retardation. (Italian translation, *Insegnare a risolvere I problem,* published by Vannini Editoria Scientifica.)

Agran, M., & Wehmeyer, M. (2003). Self-determination. In D. Ryndak & S. Alper (Eds.), *Curriculum and instruction for students with significant disabilities in inclusive settings* (pp. 259–276). Needham Heights, MA: Allyn and Bacon.

Agran, M., Wehmeyer, M.L., Cavin, M., & Palmer, S.B. (2010). Promoting active engagement in the general education classroom and access to the general education curriculum for students with cognitive disabilities. *Education and Training in Autism and Developmental Disabilities, 45,* 163–174.

Agran, M., Wehmeyer, M., & Krupp, M. (2010). Promoting self-regulated learning. In A. Mourad & J. de la Fuente Arias (Eds.), *International perspectives on applying self-regulated learning in different settings.* New York, NY: Peter Lang.

Allen, S.K., Smith, A.C., Test, D.W., Flowers, C., & Wood, W.M. (2001). The effects of Self-Directed IEP on student participation in IEP meetings. *Career Development for Exceptional Individuals, 4,* 107–120.

Balfanz, R., & Legters, N.E. (2007). Locating the dropout crisis: Which high schools produce the nation's dropouts? In G. Orfield, (Ed.), *Dropouts in America: Confronting the graduation crisis* (pp. 57–84). Cambridge, MA: Harvard University Press.

Ball, A.F. (2009). Toward a theory of generative change in culturally and linguistically complex classrooms. *American Educational Research Journal, 46,* 45–72. doi: 10.3102/0002831208323277

Bambara, L.M. (2004). Fostering choice-making skills: We've come a long way but still have a long way to go. *Research and Practice for Persons with Severe Disabilities, 29,* 169–171.

Bandura, A. (2001). Social cognitive theory: An agentic perspective. *Annual Review of Psychology, 52,* 1–26. doi: 10.1146/annurev.psych.52.1.1

Barton, P.E., & Coley, R.J. (2010). *The black–white achievement gap: When progress stopped.* Princeton, NJ: Educational Testing Service. Retrieved from http://www.ets.org/Media/Research/pdf/PICBWGAP.pdf

Brotherson, M.J., Cook, C.C., & Parette, H.P. (1996). A home-centered approach to assistive technology provision for young children with disabilities. *Focus on Autism and Other Developmental Disabilities, 11,* 86–95.

Brown, F., Gothelf, C., Guess, D., & Lehr, D. (1998). Self-determination for individuals with the most severe disabilities: Moving beyond chimera. *JASH, 25,* 17–26.

Cannella, H.I., O'Reilly, M.F., & Lancioni, G.E. (2005). Choice and preference assessment research with people with severe to profound developmental disabilities: A review of the literature. *Research in Developmental Disabilities, 26,* 1–15.

Carter, E.W., Owens, L., Trainor, A.A., Sun, Y., & Swedeen, B. (2009). Self-determination skills and opportunities of adolescents with severe intellectual and developmental disabilities. *American Journal on Intellectual and Developmental Disabilities, 114,* 179–192. doi: 10.1352/1944-7558-114.3.179

Carter, E.W., Sisco, L.G., & Lane, K.L. (2011). Paraprofessional perspectives on promoting self-determination among elementary and secondary students with severe disabilities. *Research and Practice for Persons with Severe Disabilities, 36,* 1–10.

Chambers, C.R., Wehmeyer, M.L., Saito, Y., Lida, K.M., Lee, Y., & Singh, V. (2007). Self-determination: What do we know? Where do we go? *Exceptionality, 15,* 3–15. doi: 10.1080/09362830709336922

Cimera, R.E. (2010). Can community-based high school transition programs improve the cost-efficiency of supported employment? *Career Development for Exceptional Individuals, 33,* 4–12. doi: 10.1177/0885728809346959

Cook, C., Brotherson, M.J., Weigel-Garrey, C., & Mize, I. (1996). Homes to support the self-determination of children. In D.J. Sands & M.L. Wehmeyer (Eds.), *Self-determination across the lifespan: Independence and choice for people with disabilities* (pp. 91–110). Baltimore, MD: Paul H. Brookes Publishing Co.

Copeland, S.R., & Cosbey, J. (2009). Making progress in the general curriculum: Rethinking effective instructional practices. *Research and Practice for Persons with Severe Disabilities, 33,* 214–227.

Copeland, S., & Hughes, C. (2000). Acquisition of a picture prompt strategy to increase independent performance. *Education and Training in Mental Retardation and Developmental Disabilities, 35,* 294–305.

Copeland, S.R., Hughes, C., Agran, M., Wehmeyer, M.L., & Fowler, S.E. (2002). An intervention package to support high school students with mental retardation in general education classrooms. *American Journal on Mental Retardation, 107,* 32–45.

Cross, T., Cooke, N.L., Wood, W.M., & Test, D.W. (1999). Comparison of the effects of MAPS and ChoiceMaker on students' self-determination skills. *Education and Training in Mental Retardation and Developmental Disabilities, 34,* 499–510.

Deci, E.L., & Ryan, R.M. (1985). *Intrinsic motivation and self-determination in human behavior.* New York, NY: Plenum.

Deci, E.L., & Ryan, R.M. (2000). The "what" and "why" of goal pursuits: Human needs and the self-determination of behavior. *Psychological Inquiry, 11,* 227–268.

Duncan, A. (2011, April 26). *Secretary Arne Duncan's remarks at the release of the National Institute for Early Education Research Report, "The State of Preschool 2010."* Retrieved from http://www.ed.gov/

news/speeches/secretary-arne-duncans-remarks-release-national-institute-early-education-research-rep

Erwin, E.J., & Brown, F. (2003). From theory to practice: A contextual framework for understanding self-determination in early childhood environments. *Infants & Young Children, 16,* 77–87.

Fisher, D., Sax, C., & Jorgensen, C.M. (1998). Philosophical foundations of inclusive, restructuring schools. In C.M. Jorgensen (Ed.), *Restructuring high schools for all students* (pp. 29–47). Baltimore, MD: Paul H. Brookes Publishing Co.

Floyd, C. (1996). Achieving despite the odds: A study of resilience among a group of African American high school seniors. *Journal of Negro Education, 65,* 181–189. doi: 10.2307/2967312

Fowler, C.H., Konrad, M., Walker, A.R., Test, D.W., & Wood, W.M. (2007). Self-determination interventions' effects on the academic performance of students with developmental disabilities. *Education and Training in Developmental Disabilities, 42,* 270–285.

Gilbert, G., Agran, M., Hughes, C., & Wehmeyer, M. (2001). The effects of peer-delivered self-monitoring strategies on the participation of students with severe disabilities in general education classrooms. *Journal of The Association for Persons with Severe Handicaps, 26,* 25–36.

Guess, D., & Siegel-Causey, E. (1985). Behavioral control and education of severely handicapped students: Who's doing what to whom? And why? In D. Bricker & J. Filler (Eds.), *Severe mental retardation: From theory to practice* (pp. 230–244). Reston, VA: Council for Exceptional Children, Division of Mental Retardation.

Hoffman, A., & Field, S. (1995). Promoting self-determination through effective curriculum development. *Intervention in School and Clinic, 30,* 134–141.

Holzman, M. (2010). *Yes we can: The Schott 50 state report on public education and black males: 2010.* Cambridge, MA: Schott Foundation for Public Education.

Hughes, C. (1992). Teaching self-instruction utilizing multiple exemplars to produce generalized problem-solving by individuals with severe mental retardation. *American Journal on Mental Retardation, 97,* 302–314.

Hughes, C., Cosgriff, J.C., Agran, M., & Washington, B.H. (2013). Student self-determination: A preliminary investigation of the role of participation in inclusive settings. *Education and Training in Autism and Developmental Disabilities, 48,* 3–17.

Hughes, C., Golas, M., Cosgriff, J., Brigham, N., Edwards, C., & Cashen, K. (2011). Effects of a social skills intervention among high school students with intellectual disabilities and autism and their general education peers. *Research and Practice for Persons with Severe Disabilities, 36,* 46–61.

Individuals with Disabilities Education Act Amendments (IDEA) of 1997, PL 105-17, 20 U.S.C. §§ 1400 *et seq.*

Individuals with Disabilities Education Improvement Act (IDEA) of 2004, PL 108-446, 20 U.S.C. §§ 1400 *et seq.*

Kishi, G., Teelucksingh, B., Zollers, N., Park-Lee, S., & Meyer, L. (1988). Daily decision-making in community residences: A social comparison of adults with and without mental retardation. *American Journal on Mental Retardation, 92,* 430–435.

Lachapelle, Y., Wehmeyer, M.L., Haelewyck, M.C., Curbois, Y., Keith, K.D., Schalock, R., & Walsh, P.N. (2005). The relationship between quality of life and self-determination: An international study. *Journal of Intellectual Disability Research, 49,* 740–744. doi: 10.1111/j.1365-2788.2005.00743.x

Lee, S., Palmer, S., Turnbull, A., & Wehmeyer, M.L. (2006). A model for parent–teacher collaboration to promote self-determination in young children with disabilities. *Teaching Exceptional Children, 38,* 36–41.

Machalicek, W., O'Reilly, M.F., Rispoli, M., Davis, T., Lang, R., Hetlinger Franco, J., & Chan, J.M. (2010). Training teachers to assess the challenging behaviors of students with autism using video teleconferencing. *Education and Training in Autism and Developmental Disabilities, 45,* 203–215.

Martin, J.E., & Marshall, L.H. (1995). Choice-Maker: A comprehensive self-determination transition program. *Intervention in School and Clinic, 30,* 147–156.

Martin, J.E., Marshall, L.H., Maxson, L.M., & Jerman, P.L. (1997). *The Self-Directed IEP.* Longmont, CO: Sopris West Educational Services.

Martin, J.E., Van Dycke, J.L., Christensen, W.R., Greene, B.A., Gardner, J.E., & Lovett, D.L. (2006). Increasing student participation in IEP meetings: Establishing the Self-Directed IEP as an evidence-based practice. *Exceptional Children, 72,* 299–316.

Martin, J.E., Van Dycke, J.L., Greene, B.A., Gardner, J.E., Christensen, W.R., Woods, L.L., & Lovett, D.L. (2006). Direct observation of teacher-directed IEP meetings: Establishing the need for student IEP meeting instruction. *Exceptional Children, 72,* 187–200.

Martin, J.E., Woods, L.L., Sylvester, L., & Gardner, J.E. (2005). A challenge to self-determination: Disagreement between the vocational choices made by individuals with severe disabilities and their caregivers. *Research and Practice for Persons with Severe Disabilities 30,* 147–153.

Martorell, A., Gutierrez-Recacha, P., Perda, A., & Ayuso-Mateos, J.L. (2008). Identification of personal factors that determine work outcome for adults with intellectual disability. *Journal of Intellectual Disability Research, 52,* 1091–1101.

Mason, C.Y., McGahee-Kovac, M., Johnson, L., & Stillerman, S. (2002). Implementing student-led IEPs: Student participation and teacher reactions. *Career Development for Exceptional Individuals, 25,* 171–192.

Mithaug, D.E. (2005). In pursuit of self-interest. *Research and Practice for Persons with Severe Disabilities, 30,* 163–167.

Mithaug, D.E., & Hanawalt, D.A. (1978). The validation of procedures to assess prevocational task preferences in retarded adults. *Journal of Applied Behavior Analysis, 11,* 153–162.

Morales, E.E. (2010). Linking strengths: Identifying and exploring protective factor clusters in academically resilient low-socioeconomic urban students of color. *Roeper Review, 32,* 164–175. doi: 10.1080/02783193.2010.485302

National Center for Education Statistics. (2006). *Characteristics of the 100 largest public elementary and secondary school districts in the United States: 2003–04 statistical analysis report.* Washington, DC: U.S. Department of Education. Retrieved from http://nces.ed.gov/pubs2006/2006329.pdf

National Center for Education Statistics. (2007). *Status and trends in the education of racial and ethnic minorities.* Washington, DC: U.S. Department of Education. Retrieved from http://nces.ed.gov/pubs2007/minoritytrends/tables/table_7_2.asp?referrer=report

Nirje, B. (1972). The right to self-determination. In W. Wolfensberger, (Ed.), *Normalization: The principle of normalization in human services* (pp. 176–200). Toronto, Canada: National Institute on Mental Retardation.

Orfield, G. (2009). *Reviving the goal of an integrated society: A 21st century challenge.* Los Angeles: The Civil Rights Project/Proyecto Derechos Civiles at the University of California, Los Angeles (UCLA). Retrieved from http://www.civilrightsproject.ucla.edu/

Powers, L.E. (2006). Self-determination by individuals with severe disabilities: Limitations or excuses. *Research and Practice for Persons with Severe Disabilities, 30,* 168–172.

Powers, L.E., Turner, A., Westwood, D., Matuszewski, J., Wilson, R., & Phillips, A. (2001). Take charge for the future: A controlled field-test of a model to promote student involvement in transition planning. *Career Development for Exceptional Individuals, 24,* 89–104.

Rehabilitation Act Amendments of 1992, PL 102-569, 29 U.S.C. §§ 701 *et seq.*

Robertson, J., Emerson, E., Hatton, C., Gregory, N., Kessissoglou, S., Hallam, A., & Walsh, P.N. (2001). Environmental opportunities and supports for exercising self-determination in community-based residential settings. *Research in Developmental Disabilities, 22,* 487–502. doi: 10.1016/S0891-4222(01)00085-3

Schloss, P.J., Alper, S., & Jayne, D. (1993). Self-determination for persons with disabilities: Choice, risk, and dignity. *Exceptional Children, 60,* 215–225.

Shogren, K.A., Bovaird, J.A., Palmer, S.B., & Wehmeyer, M.L. (2010). Locus of control orientations in students with intellectual disability, learning disabilities, and no disabilities: A latent growth curve analysis. *Research and Practice for Persons with Severe Disabilities, 35,* 80–92.

Shogren, K.A., Wehmeyer, M.L., Palmer, S.B., Soukup, J.H., Little, T.D., Garner, N., & Lawrence, M. (2007). Examining individual and ecological predictors of the self-determination of students with disabilities. *Exceptional Children, 73,* 488–509.

Spooner, F., Dymond, S.K., Smith, A., & Kennedy, C.H. (2006). What we know and need to know about accessing the general curriculum for students with significant cognitive disabilities. *Research and Practice for Persons with Severe Disabilities, 31,* 277–283.

Suitts, S.T. (2007). *A new majority: Low income students in the South's public schools.* Atlanta, GA: Southern Education Foundation.

Suitts, S.T. (2010). *A new diverse majority: Students of color in the South's public schools.* Atlanta, GA: Southern Education Foundation.

TASH. (2000). *TASH Resolution on Choices.* (2000). Washington, DC: Author.

Test, D.W., Mason, C., Hughes, C., Konrad, M., Neale, M., & Wood, W.M. (2004). Student involvement in individualized education program meetings. *Exceptional Children, 70,* 391–412.

Test, D.W., Mazzotti, V.L., Mustain, A.L., Fowler, C.H., Kortering, L., & Kohler, P. (2009). Evidence-based secondary transition predictors for improving post-school outcomes for students with disabilities. *Career Development for Exceptional Individuals, 32,* 160–181. doi: 10.1177/0885728809346960

Thompson, J.R., Wehmeyer, M.L., & Hughes, C. (2010). Mind the gap! Implications of a person-environment fit model of intellectual disability for students, educators, and schools. *Exceptionality, 18,* 168–181. doi: 10.1080/09362835.2010.513919

United Nations. (2006). *UN convention on the rights of persons with disabilities.* (2006). New York, NY: Author.

Véronneau, M.H., Koestner, R.F., & Abela, J.R.Z. (2005). Intrinsic need satisfaction and well-being in children and adolescents: An application of the self-determination theory. *Journal of Social and Clinical Psychology, 24,* 280–292.

Walker, H.M., Calkins, C., Wehmeyer, M.L., Walker, L., Bacon, A., Palmer, S.B., & Johnson, D.R. (2011). A social-ecological approach to promote self-determination. *Exceptionality, 19,* 6–18. doi: 10.1080/09362835.2011.537220

Washington, B.H., Hughes, C., & Cosgriff, J.C. (2012). High-poverty youth: Self-determination and involvement in educational planning. *Career Development and Transition for Exceptional Individuals, 35,* 14–28.

Wehmeyer, M.L. (1998). Self-determination and individuals with significant disabilities: Examining meanings and misinterpreta-tions. *Journal of The Association for Persons with Severe Handicaps, 23,* 5–16.

Wehmeyer, M.L. (2001). Self-determination and mental retardation. In L.M. Glidden (Ed.), *International review of research in mental retardation* (Vol. 24, pp. 1–48). Hillsdale, NJ: Lawrence Erlbaum Associates.

Wehmeyer, M.L. (2005). Self-determination and individuals with severe disabilities: Reexamining meanings and misinterpretations. *Research and Practice for Per-sons with Severe Disabilities, 30,* 113–120.

Wehmeyer, M.L., Abery, B.H., Zhang, D., Ward, K., Willis, D., Hossain, W.A., & Walker, H.M. (2011). Personal self-determination and moderating variables that impact efforts to promote self-determination. *Exceptionality, 19,* 19–30. doi: 10.1080/09362835.2011.537225

Wehmeyer, M.L., Agran, M., & Hughes, C. (2000). A national survey of teachers' promotion of self-determination and student-directed learning. *Journal of Special Education, 34,* 58–68. doi: 10.1177/002246690003400201

Wehmeyer, M.L., Agran, M., Hughes, C., Martin, J.E., Mithaug, D.E., & Palmer, S.B. (2007). *Promoting self-determination in students with developmental disabilities.* New York, NY: Guilford Press.

Wehmeyer, M.L., & Bolding, N. (2001). Enhanced self-determination of adults with intellectual disability as an outcome of moving to community-based work or living environments. *Journal of Intellectual Disability Research, 45,* 371–383. doi: 10.1046/j.1365-2788.2001.00342.x

Wehmeyer, M.L., Field, S., Doren, B., & Mason, C. (2004). Self-determination and student involvement in standards-based reform. *Exceptional Children, 70,* 413–425.

Wehmeyer, M.L., & Garner, N.W. (2003). The impact of personal characteristics of people with intellectual and developmental disability on self-determination and autonomous functioning. *Journal of Applied Research in Intellectual Disabilities, 16,* 255–265. doi: 10.1046/j.1468-3148.2003.00161.x

Wehmeyer, M.L., & Kelchner, K. (1995). *The Arc's Self-Determination Scale: Procedural guidelines.* Arlington, TX: The Arc.

Wehmeyer, M.L., Kelchner, K., & Richards, S. (1996). Essential characteristics of self-determined behavior of individuals with mental retardation. *American Journal on Mental Retardation, 100,* 632–642.

Wehmeyer, M.L., & Metzler, C.A. (1995). How self-determined are people with mental retardation: The National Consumer Survey. *Mental Retardation, 33,* 111–119.

Wehmeyer, M.L., & Palmer, S. (2000). Promoting the acquisition and development of self-determination in young children with disabilities. *Early Education and Development, 11,* 465–481.

Wehmeyer, M.L., & Palmer, S.B. (2003). Adult outcomes for students with cognitive disabilities three years after high school: The impact of self-determination. *Education and Training in Developmental Disabilities, 38,* 131–144.

Wehmeyer, M.L., Palmer, S.B., Agran, M., Mithaug, D.E., & Martin, J. (2000). Teaching students to become causal agents in their lives: The self-determining learning model of instruction. *Exceptional Children, 66,* 439–453.

Wehmeyer, M.L., Palmer, S.B., Soukup, J.H., Garner, N.W., & Lawrence, M. (2007). Self-determination and student transition planning knowledge and skills: Predicting involvement. *Exceptionality, 15,* 31–44. doi: 10.1080/09362830709336924

Williams, W., Brown, L., & Certo, N. (1975). Basic components of instructional programs for severely handicapped students. *AAESPH, 1,* 1–39.

Wolman, J.M., Campeau, P.L., DuBois, P.A., Mithaug, D.E., & Stolarski, V.S. (1994). *AIR Self-Determination Scale and user guide.* Palo Alto, CA: American Institutes for Research.

Workforce Investment Act (WIA) of 1998, PL 105-220, 29 U.S.C. §§ 2801 *et seq.*

Zhang, D. (2001a). Self-determination and inclusion: Are students with mild mental retardation more self-determined in regular classrooms? *Education and Training in Mental Retardation and Developmental Disabilities, 36,* 357–362.

Zhang, D. (2001b). The effect of Next S.T.E.P. instruction on the self-determination skills of high school students with learning disabilities. *Career Development for Exceptional Individuals, 24,* 121–132.

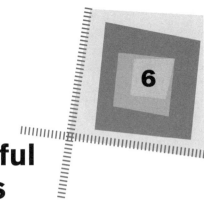

Providing Respectful Behavior Supports

Fredda Brown and Linda M. Bambara

hildren and adults who have severe developmental or intellectual disabilities are at high risk for developing problem behaviors, perhaps more than any other disability group (Dunlap & Carr, 2007). Deficiencies in social-communication and other adaptive behaviors coupled with problematic contexts that are poorly matched to individuals' needs and preferences often manifest in a host of problem behaviors displayed by this population. Problem behaviors, such as aggression, property destruction, self-injury, excessive tantrums, stereotypic or repetitive behaviors, unresponsiveness, and extreme withdrawal can greatly interfere with individuals' learning, social relationships, inclusion in integrated environments, and overall quality of life. Persistent problem behaviors unfortunately are all too often met with punitive or restrictive interventions, which can further exacerbate individuals' problem behaviors and lead to segregation from normative experiences in inclusive settings.

We wish we could report that the negative cycle that perpetuates problem behaviors and the exclusion of individuals with severe disabilities from inclusive settings has ceased. It has not. We are optimistic in transforming this cycle thanks to the tremendous advances in behavior intervention since the mid-20th century, especially the discipline of positive behavior supports (PBS). PBS emerged during the mid-1980s as an alternative to the then more common-place restrictive interventions aimed at managing problem behaviors and revolutionized the way practitioners think about and approach behavior challenges. Furthermore, what started out as an intervention approach primarily targeted at individuals with severe disabilities has evolved into a systems-change approach that can be applied to entire schools and community settings. A considerable body of research has documented the efficacy of PBS across diverse populations at the individual and the schoolwide level (Carr et al., 1999; Goh & Bambara, 2012; Horner et al., 2009; Safran & Oswald, 2003). PBS has gained national recognition in a few short decades, greatly influencing policy and practice related to behavior interventions in schools as well as in home and community settings for individuals with developmental disabilities.

This rapid development and expansion of PBS is the good news. The bad news is that considerable work needs to be done, as is the case with all evolving applications of recommended and evidence-based practices. Numerous challenges exist that impede the full adoption of PBS for individuals with severe disabilities. Although PBS first emerged as an approach for individuals with severe and other developmental disabilities, the expansion of PBS across populations and systems has caused some to question if those with severe disabilities are once again being overlooked (Bambara & Lohrmann, 2006; Brown & Michaels, 2006; Crimmins & Farrell, 2006; Hawken & O'Neill, 2006). This chapter's purpose is not to reiterate the research and methods of PBS for addressing the unique problems of individuals with severe disabilities, which has been reviewed elsewhere (e.g., Dunlap & Carr, 2007), but rather to raise some unresolved challenges and controversies surrounding the implementation of positive, respectful supports for those with the most intense needs. The goal of raising these challenges is to stimulate discussion and future action that will move society closer to strengthening effective practice for its most vulnerable citizens. The chapter begins by providing a brief overview of the definition and history of PBS, followed by a description of the core elements of PBS. Next, challenges surrounding treatment acceptability, legal issues, and implementation of individualized interventions in school settings are discussed. Finally, the chapter reviews various positions on the use of PBS by professional and advocacy organizations and concludes by making recommendations for research and practice.

DEFINITION AND BRIEF HISTORY
OF POSITIVE BEHAVIOR SUPPORTS

Many authors have offered various definitions to capture the developing framework of PBS as it has evolved (e.g., Bambara, 2005; Carr et al., 2002; Dunlap & Carr, 2007; Knoster, Anderson, Carr, Dunlap, & Horner, 2003; Sugai & Horner, 2006). PBS can be described as an approach to intervention and prevention that blends research-based strategies derived from applied sciences along with philosophical values about the rights of people with and without disabilities to enhance individuals' quality of life, minimize and prevent problem behaviors, and produce valued outcomes for relevant stakeholders. The overriding goal is to produce sustained quality of life changes for individuals within typical school, home, and community settings (Carr, 2007). PBS emphasizes using research-based strategies to teach individuals new skills that will increase their likelihood of success and redesign environments to support the display of positive behaviors, minimize the need for problem behaviors, and produce valued outcomes, whether it is applied at the individual or systems level (Carr et al., 2002). Although the predominate strategies of PBS are rooted in the behavioral sciences, PBS is open to using innovations derived from other disciplines, such as biomedical and social sciences, positive and community psychology, and systems-change theory, in order to produce positive change (Carr et al., 2002; Carr, 2007).

Furthermore, PBS clearly espouses person- and family-centered values when evaluating the appropriateness and acceptability of targeted goals, intervention strategies, and outcomes (Dunlap & Carr, 2007).

In short, PBS is the marriage between values and scientific technology for behavior, environmental, and system change. The importance of this marriage and the impetus for PBS can be traced to the early 1980s when numerous disability advocates, researchers, and leaders, many of whom led the TASH organization, loudly protested against using restrictive and aversive interventions to treat severe problem behaviors among individuals with developmental and severe disabilities (e.g., Durand & Kishi, 1987; Evans & Meyer, 1985; LaVigna & Donnellan, 1986; McGee, Menolascino, Hobbs, & Menousek, 1987). The TASH *Resolution on the Cessation of Intrusive Interventions* (Meyer, Peck, & Brown, 1991) and the TASH monograph *Use of Aversive Procedures with Persons Who Are Disabled: An Historical Review and Critical Analysis* (Guess, Helmstetter, Turnbull, & Knowlton, 1987), which presented a critical review of research using punishment (e.g., contingent restraint, contingent electric shock, application of noxious stimuli), negative reinforcement (e.g., removal of finger/thumb pressure to the neck), and overcorrection procedures (e.g., forced body movement, contingent exercise, restitution) to reduce problem behaviors, are two works that were especially seminal in advancing what became known as the nonaversive movement. Protesters argued that using these procedures was cruel and inhuman, largely ineffective (e.g., merely suppressing problem behavior for the short term at best), and inconsistent with goals of helping individuals achieve a quality of life in integrated community settings.

Beginning around the same time, and as a context for the nonaversive moment, the fields associated with special education and developmental disabilities in general were undergoing an important transformation in the conceptualization of services and acceptable interventions for individuals with developmental disabilities (Bambara, 2005; Carr et al., 2002; Dunlap & Carr, 2007; Spooner & Brown 2011). Increasing emphasis was placed on the full participation of individuals with developmental disabilities in inclusive community and school settings (e.g., Hunt & McDonnell, 2007; Smull & Bellamy, 1991) and using procedures that were supportive of an inclusive lifestyle. Person-centered planning (e.g., O'Brien, O'Brien, & Mount, 1997), a process that invites family members, friends, and the individual to design and create a better life for an individual with developmental disabilities, gave way to person-centered values, which has guided the field to define quality-of-life outcomes in terms of what individuals with disabilities want for themselves, based on their personal preferences and interests. Moreover, person-centered values gave voice to individuals with disabilities and their families in terms of defining valued outcomes. The construct of self-determination (e.g., Stancliffe, 2001; Wehmeyer & Schalock, 2001) similarly encouraged practitioners to teach specific skills and create opportunities that enabled individuals to express their preferences and exert greater control over the direction of their lives. The movements that spurred inclusion, person-centered values, and self-determination made it virtually impossible to accept that the use of aversive interventions was morally correct and a choice that people with developmental disabilities would select for themselves.

Partially fueled by the increasing social demands for respectful interventions, researchers in applied behavior analysis (ABA) during the late 1970s and early 1980s began developing and testing nonaversive alternatives for treating the most challenging problem behaviors. These new advances in technology provided practitioners with a systematic, conceptual framework for understanding human behavior and the tools for more sophisticated behavior change. Research in functional analysis (e.g., Carr, Newsom, & Binkoff, 1980; Iwata, Dorsey, Slifer, Baumann, & Richman, 1982) and functional assessment (e.g., Dunlap, Kern-Dunlap, Clarke, & Robbins, 1991; Lennox & Miltenberger, 1989) provided a pivotal contribution to advancing this new technology, which gave way to functional communication training (e.g., Carr & Durand, 1985; Durand & Carr, 1991) and a host of antecedent interventions (e.g., Kern, Chouka, & Sokol, 2002) that focused on modifying environmental conditions not only as a means of intervention but also the prevention of problem behaviors.

The values advanced by disability advocates and the emergent nonaversive technology of ABA joined forces in the early 1990s to create PBS (Evans & Meyer, 1985; Horner et al., 1990, Lavigna & Donnellan, 1986). Early iterations of PBS focused primarily on the needs of individuals with severe developmental disabilities and emphasized individualized, comprehensive interventions that were driven by functional assessment data, applied across multiple settings throughout the day, consisted of multiple interventions (e.g., teaching alternative skills, environmental modification), and were matched to the skills, values, and resources of practitioners and families who implemented the intervention (Bambara, Mitchell-Kvacky, & Iacobelli, 1994; Horner & Carr, 1997).

The Individuals with Disabilities Education Act (IDEA) Amendments of 1997 (PL 105-17) demonstrated that PBS was becoming an established technology by introducing PBS concepts such as functional assessment and positive interventions to schools. The language used in the amendments extended the application of PBS to all students with disabilities, not only those with developmental disabilities. PBS underwent another important development soon after its concepts were operationalized for schools. Schoolwide positive behavior supports (SWPBS) merged PBS constructs with a public health prevention model (e.g., Walker et al., 1996) and emerged as a systemic approach to address whole-school contexts as a means of prevention and intervention of problem behavior for all students following a tiered intervention approach (Horner, Sugai, & Anderson, 2010; Sugai & Horner, 2006). The tiers consist of primary prevention (i.e., universal strategies applied to all students), secondary prevention (i.e., more intense, group-based interventions for students who are not responsive to universal strategies but not in need of more intensive intervention), and tertiary prevention (i.e., individualized, comprehensive, and function-based interventions for students who present intensive or chronic problem behaviors).

KEY FEATURES OF POSITIVE BEHAVIOR SUPPORTS

The evolutionary development of PBS has led to defined features that distinguish PBS from more traditional forms of behavior interventions. The key features of PBS have been described in a variety of ways by a variety of organizations (e.g., Association for Positive Behavior Supports [APBS], Office of Special Education Programs Technical Assistance Center on Positive Behavior Interventions and Supports) and authors (e.g., Bambara & Kern, 2005; Carr et al., 2002; Dunlap, Carr, Horner, Zarcone, & Schwartz, 2008). Certain elements, however, are common across all descriptions. The APBS Standards of Practice: Individual Level (SPI), adopted by the APBS board of directors in March 2007, is one document that combines key features found in many of the PBS documents. The SPI was developed by members of APBS to better define what is meant by PBS practice at the individual level of intervention. If a professional used positive reinforcement, then is it considered PBS? If a functional assessment was conducted, then is it considered PBS? The organization recognized that standards of practice were critical to further define the practice of PBS. The intent of the SPI is to respond to the widespread use of PBS, the multiple disciplines that utilize PBS procedures, and the various theoretical perspectives that professionals bring to their respective PBS practices.

The APBS standards include many competencies that reflect the foundations of ABA because it is an integral part of PBS, as well as those concepts and methods that define the uniqueness of PBS. The SPI is composed of six major sections: 1) foundations, 2) collaboration and teaming, 3) basic principles of behavior, 4) data-based decision making, 5) comprehensive person-centered and functional behavioral assessments (FBAs), and 6) development and implementation of comprehensive multi-element behavior support plans. Each of these sections further identifies the specific skill components that are considered foundational to implementing PBS (see the appendix at the end of this chapter).

In addition to the foundational concepts related to implementing ABA and PBS, SPI specifically includes a variety of standards that must be met in order for an intervention plan to be considered a PBS plan. The following foundational assumptions quoted from the SPI (APBS, 2007) are examples of critical elements that underscore the practice of PBS:

- "Positive strategies are effective in addressing the most challenging behavior"

- "When positive behavior intervention strategies fail, additional functional assessment strategies are required to develop more effective PBS strategies"

- "Techniques that do not cause pain or humiliation or deprive the individual of basic needs"

- "Seek out collaboration, support and/or assistance when intended outcomes are not achieved in a timely manner"

- "Reduction of problem behavior is an important, but not the sole, outcome of successful intervention; effective PBS results in improvements in quality of life, acquisition of valued skills, and access to valued activities"

- "Identification of outcomes that enhance quality of life and are valued by the individual, their families and the community"

- "Sharing data with team members for team-based, person-centered, decision-making"

- "Behavior support plans facilitate the individual's preferred lifestyle"

- "Strategies that are acceptable in inclusive community settings"

- "Constructive and respectful multi-component intervention plans that emphasize antecedent interventions, instruction in prosocial behaviors, and environmental modification"

- "Build opportunities for choice/control throughout the day that are age-appropriate and contextually appropriate"

CHALLENGES AND CONTROVERSIES

Although the field of PBS has become established with an increasing evidence base, many challenges and controversies remain, especially with regard to applying PBS for individuals with severe disabilities. Important questions remain. Is there ever any justification for using intrusive interventions? What policies, regulations, and laws support or hinder the implementation and progress of PBS? How can schools best implement and maintain PBS practices? The following sections explore these challenges.

Treatment Acceptability

Using aversive interventions, including restraint and seclusion, remains a heated debate among some professionals and families. Although there may be some gray areas that even those who consider themselves supportive of PBS may debate (e.g., use of extinction, observation time-out, reprimands), several procedures have no place in the delivery of PBS, including the use of (nonemergency) restraint, seclusion, and other aversive interventions. Reports have described the devastation that restraint, seclusion, and other aversive interventions cause to individuals and their families. Westling, Trader, Smith, and Marshall (2010) discussed several national level reports that have been issued specifically regarding the use of restraint, seclusion, and other aversive interventions (e.g., Council of Parent Attorneys and Advocates, 2009; National Disability Rights Network, 2009; U.S. Government Accountability Office, 2009). These reports speak to the lack of oversight of these types of practices, the lack of data available on the incidence of such practices, and the lack of appropriate educational and behavior support that contributes to the use of such practices. Although the exact incidence of death due to such practices may not be exact, it has been firmly established that children and adults are dying as a result of such procedures (U.S. Government Accountability Office, 2009).

Focusing on respectful and nonaversive interventions to address even the most challenging behaviors is one of the distinguishing features common across descriptions and definitions of PBS. Opposition to using aversive interventions has been at the heart of many controversies in the clinical and academic worlds, beginning in the late 1980s (e.g., Butterfield, 1990; Guess et al., 1987; Horner et al., 1990; Luiselli & Cameron, 1998; Repp & Singh, 1990; Spreat & Walsh, 1994) and continuing today (Spooner & Brown, 2011). Questions that have been posed include the following: Is there ever justification for using aversive interventions? Are there some behaviors that are so severe or dangerous that only using aversive interventions would be effective? The social acceptability, or treatment acceptability, of a behavior intervention is considered to be one of the most important factors when deciding whether to implement a particular procedure (Foxx, Bremer, Shultz, Valdez, & Johndrow, 1996). Treatment acceptability ratings are critical as legal and ethical issues have increased regarding the use of behavior interventions with individuals with disabilities (Cross Calvert & Johnston, 1990; Foxx et al., 1996).

Early discussions of treatment acceptability, although without the use of the term, began in the 1970s. Wolfensberger's (1972) principle of normalization includes reference to the "utilization of means which are as culturally normative as possible in order to establish and/or maintain personal behaviors and characteristics which are as culturally normative as possible" (1972, p. 28). The "utilization of means which are as culturally normative as possible" refers to the standard that strategies for behavior change should reflect those that are acceptable in the general community and with individuals who do not have a disability. Woolf (1978) described social validity as consisting of three standards that must be acceptable to consumers: the goals of the treatment, the treatment procedures, and the results of the intervention. These early discussions helped move the focus from looking at behavior change as a sole outcome and encouraged practitioners to include the acceptability of the strategies as a critical factor in evaluating behavioral efforts.

Kazdin, French, and Sherick defined *treatment acceptability* as the "judgments of lay persons, clients, and others of whether the procedures proposed for treatment are appropriate, fair and reasonable for the problem or client" (1981, p. 900). The definitions of "appropriate, fair and reasonable," however, are not operationalized and have led to much discussion. For example, if a strategy has been experimentally demonstrated to be effective with other students (i.e., there is an evidence base), but that strategy is considered unacceptable to parents or to a teacher, then is it appropriate? Deciding when it is time to move on to more intrusive procedures has been a divisive issue for many parents and professionals. Spooner and Brown pointed out,

> What works is only one part of the equation. Scientific evidence for an intervention must be balanced with its social validity, that is, the treatment acceptability, of the intervention. Both standards must be met for our field to incorporate it into our menu of best practices (2011, p. 512)

Much of the research regarding treatment acceptability focuses on using decelerative strategies to reduce severe behavior problems. Researchers studied judgments of parents, teachers, and other school personnel (Elliott, Witt, Galvin, & Peterson, 1984; Fairbanks & Stinnett, 1997; Jones, Eyberg, Adams, & Boggs, 1998; Pickering & Morgan, 1985); psychologists and professional organization members (Keyes, Creekmore, Karst, Crow, & Dayan, 1988; Spreat & Walsh, 1994); direct care staff (Miltenberger & Lumley, 1997; Tarnowski, Mulick, & Rasnake, 1990); residential administrators (Lindeman, Miltenberger, & Lennox, 1992); supported employment supervisors and job coaches (Helms & Moore, 1993); pediatric nurses (Tarnowski, Kelly, & Mendlowitz, 1987); and undergraduate and graduate students (Kazdin, 1980; Smith & Linscheid, 1994). Some of these studies focused on the characteristics of the individual with the disability and the behavior intervention and how these affect perceptions of treatment acceptability; other studies explored contextual variables that might influence judgments on treatment acceptability.

Student and Program Characteristics   Research findings in general and across audiences demonstrated that strategies that focus on increasing appropriate behaviors are deemed to be more acceptable than strategies to reduce behaviors. Some researchers demonstrated that acceptability of treatments vary as a function of the severity of the problem behavior (Cross Calvert & Johnston, 1990; Kazdin, 1980; Lindeman et al., 1992; Smith & Linscheid, 1994; Tarnowski, Rasnake, Mulick, & Kelly, 1989). That is, although aversive interventions are generally less acceptable than nonaversive interventions, the more severe or frequent the problem behavior, the more likely that an aversive or restrictive procedure would be considered acceptable (Smith & Linscheid, 1994). Furthermore, aversive interventions are considered more acceptable when the level of the disorder is more severe (Miltenberger, 1990;

Tarnowski et al., 1989). Tarnowski et al. (1989) did not find any significant difference in treatment acceptability regarding interventions for children and adults. The level of complexity and effort of an intervention, however, was related to treatment acceptability; that is, the more complex the intervention, the less acceptable it was thought to be (Elliott et al., 1984).

Spreat and Walsh (1994) found that the respondents' predictions of treatment success was the strongest predictor of treatment acceptability. If an intervention was deemed likely to be effective, then it was considered more acceptable. They also found that their respondents were more accepting of intrusive interventions if less restrictive procedures had first been attempted. These findings supported the position of the Association for Behavior Analysis position statement on Right to Effective Treatment where it is stated that

> Consistent with the philosophy of least restrictive yet effective treatment, exposure of an individual to restrictive procedures is unacceptable unless it can be shown that such procedures are necessary to produce safe and clinically significant behavior change. It is equally unacceptable to expose an individual to a nonrestrictive intervention (or a series of such interventions) if assessment results or available research indicate that other procedures would be more effective. Indeed, a slow-acting but nonrestrictive procedure could be considered highly restrictive if prolonged treatment increases risk, significantly inhibits or prevents participation in needed training programs, delays entry into a more optimal social or living environment, or leads to adaptation and the eventual use of a more restrictive procedure. Thus, in some cases, a client's right to effective treatment may dictate the immediate use of quicker acting, but temporarily more restrictive, procedures. (1989, p. 383)

The least restrictiveness doctrine also calls for using nonaversive interventions before more restrictive interventions are considered (Lennox & Miltenberger, 1989; Repp & Singh, 1990).

Not all professionals and parents support this concept. The idea of developing criteria (e.g., initial use of positive procedures) that must be met before using aversive interventions has caused significant division in the field of behavior analysis. Although some professionals and families believe that the failing of a less intrusive intervention provides justification for using more restrictive interventions, others believe that such a failure requires additional analysis to design a better intervention, not a more restrictive one. The APBS SPI (2007) includes the following three related standards. PBS interventions assume the following:

1. "Techniques that do not cause pain or humiliation or deprive the individual of basic needs"

2. "Positive strategies are effective in addressing the most challenging behavior"

3. "When positive behavior intervention strategies fail, additional functional assessment strategies are required to develop more effective PBS strategies"

Contextual Variables   Several other factors have been found to influence treatment acceptability. Miller and Kelley (1992) examined marital distress and found that parents experiencing this form of distress rated positive reinforcement as less acceptable than parents who were not distressed; they also judged time-out in a room to be more acceptable than parents who were not distressed. Miller and Kelley also found that fathers had significantly higher acceptability ratings for spanking and medication than did mothers, who preferred less punitive interventions.

Much of the research on treatment acceptability has been with middle class, American families, with little focus on cultural and socioeconomic factors (Njardvik & Kelley, 2008). Researchers are only more recently reaching out to study these variables. For example, researchers studied the difference in perceptions of treatment acceptability between different cultures, including Dominican and Puerto Rican immigrant mothers in the United States (Calzada & Eyberg, 2002), European Canadian families and South Asian Canadian families (Ho, Bluestein, & Jenkins, 2008), and parents in Iceland and the United States (Njardvik & Kelley, 2008). These studies demonstrated that cultural beliefs, especially regarding child-rearing practices, influence family perceptions of treatment acceptability of various interventions. In general, these studies suggested that promoting various intervention strategies to families must be culturally sensitive; that is, some behavior interventions used to treat problem behaviors in American families may be unacceptable to parents of other cultures (Njardvik & Kelley, 2008). Tarnowski, Simonian, Park, and Bekeny (1992), however, found that treatment acceptability ratings of various single-component and multiple-component treatments did not vary as a function of race or socioeconomic status. Rasnake, Martin, Tarnowski, and Mulick (1993) found that knowing behavioral principles in a group of institutional direct care providers did not influence treatment acceptability.

Treatment Acceptability: Future Directions   National policy and state regulations are either restricting or banning the use of interventions that are considered unacceptable for individuals without disabilities (Spooner & Brown, 2011). At the same time, there is a need to focus on using evidence-based strategies. The field of severe disabilities and the work of professional organizations such as TASH need to promote a focus on both quality-of-life and evidence-based practices (Horner & Dunlap, 2012). Spooner and Brown pointed out, "We project that in time, and with the support of research and advocacy that demonstrates the power of positive interventions, that restrictions will be a thing of the past and total banning of these strategies will be the practice" (2011, p. 512). It will take significant shifts in thinking about using various consequence-based strategies for real change to take place (Brown, Michaels, Oliva, & Woolf, 2008; Spooner & Brown, 2011). An increased need exists to continue to reexamine treatment acceptability because of the increased availability of less intrusive treatments and changes in educational law (Carter, 2008), and we expect that fewer professionals will look toward punitive and aversive interventions to address severe problem behaviors (Spooner & Brown, 2011).

Legal Issues Regarding Positive Behavior Supports

Although the evidence base for PBS strategies continues to grow and the ethical justification for such strategies is strong, a gap exists between research and practice (McDonnell & O'Neill, 2003; Spooner & Browder, 2003). Questions remain: What are the factors that lead to more widespread implementation of PBS? What are the factors that inhibit the growth of implementing PBS? Brown et al. (2008) found that professionals who have differing opinions on treatment acceptability essentially use the same reasons to determine a strategy as acceptable or unacceptable. That is, most professionals report that they look at the literature and consider their own values and what they have found to be successful in the past. One conclusion that can be inferred from these findings is that it may not be the influence of research (i.e., there is literature to support any of the professionals' perceptions) that influences perceptions of treatment acceptability. What the law mandates is one aspect that will necessarily influence the growth or the nongrowth of PBS.

Zirkel (2011b) discussed the difference between the *should* of professional norms and the *must* of the legal requirement in the Individuals with Disabilities Education Improvement Act (IDEA) of 2004 (PL 108-446). He delineated two issues that legally must be addressed when a student exhibits problem behavior: 1) whether the student is entitled to an FBA or a behavior intervention plan and 2) whether its contents and implementation are appropriate under IDEA 2004 and any relevant state special education laws (Zirkel, 2011b).

The issue of student behavior was addressed for the first time in IDEA 1997 (Gartin & Murdick, 2001). IDEA did not contain any local education agency requirements pertaining to FBAs or behavior intervention plans until this time. Zirkel summarized the history of inclusion of the language of PBS by explaining that IDEA 1997 initially included the following: "In the case of a child whose behavior impedes his or her learning or that of others, consider, when appropriate, strategies, including positive behavior interventions, strategies, and supports" (2011a, pp. 185–186). The language used in this amendment suggests using PBS for students with problem behaviors, although what exactly PBS is and under what conditions it should be used is vague and insufficiently defined. IDEA 2004 strengthened this language by requiring the IEP team to specifically consider using PBS and other strategies to address the problem behavior of students whose behavior impedes their learning or the learning of others. Furthermore, IDEA 1997 required that any changes in placement because of behavior be accompanied by an FBA and a behavior intervention plan when the behavior was determined to be a manifestation of a disability. Although there is now a legal mandate requiring an FBA and a behavior intervention plan, the issue of lacking a definition and criteria for these procedures remains (Zirkel, 2011b). A significant implication of this lack of clarity is that parents have less hope of winning if they make a complaint about the process or quality of the FBA and behavior intervention plan (Zirkel, 2011b).

State statutes, policies, and regulations may be more or less rigorous regarding behavior support than the IDEA 2004 requirements. Zirkel (2011a) analyzed state statutes and regulations regarding FBA and behavior intervention plans and found that no state special education law requires both an FBA and a behavior intervention plan; 31 states had requirements in addition to IDEA 2004, but these were limited in scope and specificity, and only 17 states provided definitions of FBAs and/or behavior intervention plans, which were not comprehensive in scope).

A further definition of an FBA and a behavior intervention plan is the legal challenge that must be addressed. Few specifics are available at this point in time that will hold the states accountable (Zirkel, 2011a). It has been recognized, however, that if staff are not adequately prepared to competently conduct the necessary FBAs and develop PBS strategies and schools are not willing or able to make changes in their culture (Gartin & Murdick, 2001), then enforcing the law will continue to be a challenge.

Support for Positive Behavior Supports
for Students with Severe Disabilities in Schools

The rapid nationwide expansion of SWPBS has raised a number of thorny issues around whether the behavioral needs of students with severe disabilities are being adequately supported and addressed in public schools. The crux of the issue is whether the current emphasis on the majority of students, those most likely without disabilities and served by universal and group supports, is somehow trumping the needs of the minority, those individuals with severe disabilities who are most likely to require individualized supports to successfully participate in inclusive school settings (Carr, 2006). Two central concerns arise. First, are the needs of students with severe disabilities being fully addressed within the schoolwide applications of PBS? Second, is there sufficient support for individualized interventions in schools?

Addressing the Needs of Students with Severe Disabilities   The intention of SWPBS is to build a system of prevention and intervention to address the needs of all students through increasingly intensive tiers of intervention. Staff training at the primary prevention tier involves all school staff and emphasizes universal supports for all students with the goal of building a coherent social culture that is immediately responsive to problem behaviors and students' needs (Horner, Sugai, Todd, & Lewis-Palmer, 2005). The foundational principles of PBS imparted through schoolwide primary prevention trainings can potentially foster an inclusive school environment where school staff share a common language of behavior support and are prepared to receive training in group or individual interventions should they be needed by students (Freeman et al., 2006; Horner et al., 2010). Theoretically, applying the primary (universal) and secondary (group) tiers should reduce the need for the most intensive and individualized intervention at the tertiary tier; however, whether a culture of support is indeed being established in schools to address the unique needs of students with severe disabilities has been questioned. In a survey of 51 state SWPBS coordinators (Landers, Courtade, & Ryndak, 2012), 41% reported that students with severe disabilities were not discussed during schoolwide trainings, and only 12% indicated that initial trainings included specific strategies to address these students' unique needs. Furthermore, open-ended survey questions raised considerable doubt about the extent to which Tier 3 (individualized interventions) was introduced to the schoolwide community. Some respondents indicated that initial trainings in SWPBS had only focused on Tiers 1 and 2, with the intent that Tier 3 training would be introduced at an unspecified later date once strategies for the first two tiers were in place. Others indicated that Tier 3 trainings were introduced within school districts but limited to a group of personnel (e.g., special educators), during professional development activities by trainers who were not affiliated with SWPBS.

The findings of this survey support the concern raised by others (Brown & Michaels, 2006; Crimmins & Farrell, 2006; Sailor et al., 2006) that in practice SWPBS runs the risk of bifurcation, in which universal and group interventions become the sole concern of general education and individualized supports the concern of special education, especially when applied in educational systems in which school inclusion is not the overarching framework. The chief reliance on office discipline referrals, the primary outcome measure used by researchers to evaluate the effectiveness of SWPBS and by schoolwide teams to make critical decisions about school improvement (e.g., Bradshaw, Mitchell, & Leaf, 2010; Horner et al., 2009), seems to support this divide. Discipline referral data captures an important outcome for the greatest number of students, but, as a global measure, it does not address more specific outcomes that would be most relevant to students with severe or other disabilities (e.g., emotional behavior disorders) who are at highest risk for or may simply require more intensive, individualized interventions. The omission to measure outcomes such as reductions in segregation, school exclusion, use of restraint, and aversive interventions makes it entirely possible for these practices to coexist with SWPBS within a separate educational system that is relegated for students with severe and other disabilities. What does not get measured does not get counted, and what is not counted does not factor into a school's priority for change.

The intended outcome of creating a schoolwide culture of social support will not be realized for students with severe disabilities unless stronger efforts are made to ensure that these students are involved in SWPBS, whether intervention is provided at the universal, group, or individual level. The absence of a supportive school culture in which all school personnel share a foundational understanding of PBS and how it relates to students with severe disabilities can create a significant impediment to implementation, even when a core group of staff are highly trained to provide intervention for these students. For example, school team members in a qualitative study who trained in individualized PBS interventions reported that the lack of schoolwide understanding of their work caused them to feel isolated from the general school community and generated misinterpretations by other school staff about the effectiveness and appropriateness of individualized PBS interventions (Bambara, Nonnemacher, & Kern, 2009). They reported that school staff in the general school community viewed individualized interventions as being unfair to other students and too soft on problem behaviors, creating significant barriers to implementation. Bambara, Goh, Kern, and Caskie (2012) asked 293 professionals with experience in implementing individualized PBS interventions in schools across five states to rate factors perceived to be most problematic or helpful to implementing individualized supports. Results indicated that among the 10 most problematic and frequently experienced barriers, 5 pertained to the School Culture: Practices and Beliefs domain. Chief among the five was the perception that individualized PBS interventions were not well understood by the entire school staff. Other perceived barriers in this domain were beliefs that problem behaviors should be punished, students with problem behaviors are better served in segregated settings, and behavior interventions should result in rapid reductions in problem behaviors. The results of these two studies strongly suggested that the core beliefs or mindset of the general school community is one of the greatest impediments to implementing PBS. Thus, if schoolwide training does not adequately address the needs of individuals with severe disabilities or introduce individualized or tertiary PBS interventions to the general school community, then efforts to address and prevent problem behaviors of these students through positive and respectful supports will be thwarted. Brown and Michaels (2006) suggested that rather than initially focusing on universal supports, the application of PBS strategies could simultaneously occur across all three tiers of the school. Other authors made concrete recommendations for how students with severe disabilities can be included in primary and secondary prevention efforts (Boden, Ennis, & Jolievette, 2012; Hawken & O'Neill, 2006); however, efforts to include students with severe disabilities in the entire schoolwide system of supports is in its infancy.

Is There Sufficient Support for Individualized Interventions in Schools?

Whether school personnel implementing individualized PBS are provided with sufficient resources, in the form of time, training, and expertise, to implement and sustain recommended practice standards is a closely related concern to including students with severe disabilities in schoolwide initiatives. Individualized interventions are complex compared with universal and group supports; they require a highly specialized skill set in FBA and the design of multicomponent and ecologically valid behavior support plans. Individualized interventions also require a sustained commitment of all team members to participate on problem-solving teams throughout all phases of the individualized support process, from assessment to the evaluation and modification of the support plan (Bambara & Kern, 2005). Such commitment requires ongoing support from fellow team members and the general school community as well as excellent collaboration and negotiation skills to effectively resolve divergent opinions regarding problem behaviors and competing resource demands.

Unlike schoolwide applications of PBS that have been increasingly adapted to match typical school practices and priorities, experts (e.g., Crimmins & Farrell, 2006; Scott & Kamps, 2007) have raised numerous concerns about the fit and support of individualized interventions in schools. In addition to concerns about school culture reported in the Bambara et al. (2012) survey previously described, school professionals identified issues of time and training as chief barriers to implementation. Insufficient time to implement an individualized approach, lack of time to meet and plan with others, and the time required to develop and implement individualized support plans were the most problematic barriers. They also reported insufficient training in terms of adequacy and number of personnel trained as key issues. Factors related to ongoing professional development and practice, such as teaming and collaborating with professionals and families and ongoing supports to team members as they implement PBS practices, were identified as key in supporting sustained individualized PBS practices in school. Yet, the perceived barriers suggest a conflict between these supportive and recommended practices and fit with school priorities, organization, and resources.

These findings echoed the concerns raised by others (Brown & Michaels, 2006; Crimmins & Farrell, 2006; Snell, 2006). It is critical to also simultaneously promote ongoing support for individualized interventions in schools in the current zeitgeist of promoting universal PBS practices. Although all levels of PBS interventions share common philosophical roots, the standards of practice for individualized interventions substantially differ from universal and group procedures, with the former being more technological and complex. Furthermore, no evidence currently documents that universal and group interventions do reduce the need for individualized interventions for students with disabilities. Ongoing support for individualized PBS seems to require two forms of attention—modifying existing school practice to better accommodate individualized interventions (e.g., create time for teams to meet, increase training efforts, expand school priorities to include individualized interventions) while also considering ways to modify individualized PBS practices, especially with regard to efficiency, to better fit typical school demands.

RELATED POSITIONS OF
PROFESSIONAL AND DISABILITY ORGANIZATIONS

This chapter has described the expanding use of PBS within school and community settings as well as the challenges in implementing PBS. Treatment acceptability is a significant divisive issue among professionals. Numerous disability organizations and self-advocates have strongly opposed the use of aversive interventions and have been powerful and persistent in their opposition to aversive interventions, especially in the area of nonemergency restraint and seclusion. Two types of organizational responses have been used to support the provision of respectful behavioral approaches—position statements that promote using PBS (i.e., what we should do) and position statements that oppose aversive interventions (i.e., what we should not do). There is surprising continuity and agreement across the various position statements that have been proffered:

- Alliance to Prevent Restraint, Aversive Interventions and Seclusion (http://tash .org/advocacy-issues/restraint-and-seclusion-aprais)

- Council for Exceptional Children (http://www.cec.sped.org/~/media/Files/Policy/ CEC%20Professional%20Policies%20and%20Positions/restraint%20and%20 seclusion.pdf)

- National Down Syndrome Society (http://www.ndss.org/About-NDSS/Media-Kit/ Position-Papers/The-Use-of-Restraints-Aversive-Interventions-and-Seclusion)

- Self-Advocates Becoming Empowered (http://www.sabeusa.org/user_storage/ File/sabeusa/Position%20Statements/Policy%20Statement-Aversives.pdf)

- TASH: Position on Positive Alternatives (http://tash.org/advocacy-issues/ restraint-and-seclusion-aprais/positive-alternatives)

- The ARC of the United States (http://www.thearc.org/page.aspx?pid=2368)

The power of these positions is diminished, however, without laws to support implementation and enforcement.

The U.S. Department of Education has identified 15 principles for state, district, and school staff; parents; and other stakeholders to consider when developing written policies on using restraint and seclusion. This document stated,

> We believe states, local school districts, preschool, elementary, and secondary schools, parents, and other stakeholders should consider as the framework for when states, localities, and districts develop and implement policies and procedures that should be in writing related to restraint and seclusion to ensure that any use of restraint or seclusion in schools does not occur except when there is a threat of imminent danger of serious physical harm to the student or others, and occurs in a manner that protects the safety of all children and adults at school. (2012, p. 11)

These 15 principles are as follows:

1. Every effort should be made to prevent the need for the use of restraint and for the use of seclusion.
2. Schools should never use mechanical restraints to restrict a child's freedom of movement, and schools should never use a drug or medication to control behavior or restrict freedom of movement (except as authorized by a licensed physician or other qualified health professional).

3. Physical restraint or seclusion should not be used except in situations where the child's behavior poses imminent danger of serious physical harm to self or others and other interventions are ineffective and should be discontinued as soon as imminent danger of serious physical harm to self or others has dissipated.

4. Policies restricting the use of restraint and seclusion should apply to all children, not just children with disabilities.

5. Any behavioral intervention must be consistent with the child's rights to be treated with dignity and to be free from abuse.

6. Restraint or seclusion should never be used as punishment or discipline (e.g., placing in seclusion for out-of-seat behavior), as a means of coercion or retaliation, or as a convenience.

7. Restraint or seclusion should never be used in a manner that restricts a child's breathing or harms the child.

8. The use of restraint or seclusion, particularly when there is repeated use for an individual child, multiple uses within the same classroom, or multiple uses by the same individual, should trigger a review and, if appropriate, revision of strategies currently in place to address dangerous behavior; if positive behavioral strategies are not in place, staff should consider developing them.

9. Behavioral strategies to address dangerous behavior that results in the use of restraint or seclusion should address the underlying cause or purpose of the dangerous behavior.

10. Teachers and other personnel should be regularly trained on the appropriate use of effective alternatives to physical restraint and seclusion, such as positive behavioral interventions and supports, and only for cases involving imminent danger of serious physical harm.

11. Every instance in which restraint or seclusion is used should be carefully and continuously and visually monitored to ensure the appropriateness of its use and safety of the child, other children, teachers, and other personnel.

12. Parents should be informed of the policies on restraint and seclusion at their child's school or other educational setting as well as applicable Federal, State, or local laws.

13. Parents should be notified as soon as possible following each instance in which restraint or seclusion is used with their child.

14. Policies regarding the use of restraint and seclusion should be regularly reviewed and updated as appropriate.

15. Policies regarding the use of restraint and seclusion should provide that each incident involving the use of restraint or seclusion should be documented in writing and provide for the collection of specific data that would enable teachers, staff, and other personnel to understand and implement the preceding principles. (U.S. Department of Education, 2012, pp. 12–13)

These documents and position statements are a small sample of the reactions of professional and disability organizations to using restraint, seclusion, and other aversive strategies. They reflect not only their support for the continued development and implementation of positive supports for individuals with problem behaviors, but also the outrage at using aversive strategies on individuals with disabilities.

CONCLUSIONS: TOWARD THE ENCULTURATION OF POSITIVE BEHAVIOR SUPPORTS

Just as PBS is a multicomponent approach to supporting individuals with problem behaviors, a multicomponent approach is needed to have PBS become the foundation and presumption of supports for people with disabilities. We envision a four-component package of action to work toward the enculturation of PBS in human services, which is based on the growth of PBS since the 1990s and the challenges faced by professionals (see Figure 6.1). We believe that all four of the components are critical and will work together to create an environment where PBS will become the norm.

Legal Ban on Using Aversive Interventions

Many attempts have been made by self-advocates and their families and professionals to ban the use of aversive interventions, especially in the areas of contingent electric shock and restraint and seclusion. Progress has been made, but often the progress is quelled by limitations. For example, contingent electric shock is no longer allowed for new students entering the Judge Rotenberg Center (a facility where aversive interventions are used) but continues for students already receiving this aversive intervention. This is progress, but it is not enough. Many states are now working on policies regarding aversive interventions, but some are choosing to restrict and improve monitoring of the aversive interventions, rather than totally banning their use. We believe that unless there is a total ban on using such strategies, rather than improved monitoring of aversive interventions, there will be little impetus to address the most challenging problem behaviors in other than aversive ways.

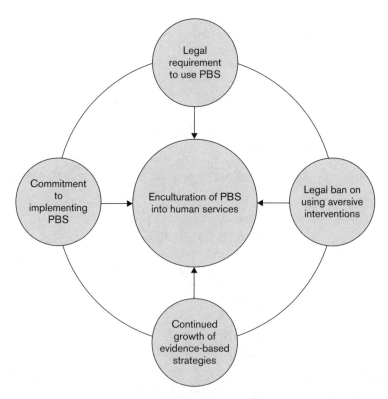

Figure 6.1.   Four component approach to enculturation of positive behavior supports (PBS) into human services.

Legal Requirement to Use Positive Behavior Supports

Banning aversive interventions is a strategy that lets those in the field know what not to do, but if there is no mandate on what they should do instead, then there may be a variety of other strategies that may take its place. There appears to be a trend in supporting the use of PBS, as evidenced in IDEA 2004 and the movement on the part of many states to design policies in support of this strategy. We believe that both of these legal requirements are necessary to establish PBS as the mainstay of education of individuals with disabilities.

Continued Growth of Evidence-Based Strategies

We have seen an increasing research base supporting the use of PBS for individuals with severe disabilities since the late 1990s. This research has focused on areas such as antecedent interventions, functional assessment strategies, functional communication, the effect of lifestyle changes and self-determination on problem behavior, treatment fidelity, and staff training issues. Research efforts must continue to respond to the current challenges and the new challenges that will arise as PBS becomes more standard practice. To what extent does the extant research address the use of PBS with those with the most severe behavior problems in inclusive settings? How do we best work with individuals who have dual diagnosis (e.g., intellectual disability and mental illness)? How do we best collaborate with families from other cultures? What are the most effective strategies to reduce using restraints and seclusion and replace these strategies with alternate positive strategies? How do we refine the process for developing individualized behavior supports so that practitioners can implement plans with fidelity and sustain practice over time? What will it take to enhance the treatment acceptability of PBS and shift belief away from restrictive interventions to proactive and function-based interventions even when facing initial treatment failure?

Commitment to Implementing Positive Behavior Supports

Commitment is the final component to have PBS acculturated into human services. If the environments in which individuals are participating (e.g., school, home, community) are not committed to using PBS, then success is unlikely. We must be mindful of developing strategies that are a contextual fit for the environments in which we want them to be used; this will increase the probability of their use. PBS will become the standard of practice for individuals with disabilities through the convergence of legal support, continued research, and commitment.

Questions for Study and Reflection

1. What were some of the movements in the field that spurred our interest in a nonaversive technology of behavior support?

2. Reducing problem behaviors is just one component of a successful intervention. What other variables must be considered to evaluate the effect of a behavior support plan?

Discuss how and why the following two items from the APBS SPI may affect program monitoring, evaluation, and modification.
- Add functional assessment strategies to develop more effective PBS when positive behavior intervention strategies fail.
- Use techniques that do not cause pain or humiliation or deprive the individual of basic needs.

4. Various studies have concluded that the core beliefs or mindset of the school community is one of the greatest impediments to implementing PBS. If you were in a context (e.g., school, residential program) that did not have a PBS mindset, what might you do to try to change their perspectives?

RESOURCES

Web Sites

Association for Positive Behavior Support *http://www.APBS.org*

U.S. Office of Special Education Programs (OSEP) Technical Assistance Center on Positive Behavioral Interventions and Supports *http://www.pbis.org/*

Journals

Journal of Positive Behavior Interventions (http://pbi.sagepub.com)

Research and Practice for Persons with Severe Disabilities

Books

Bambara, L., Dunlap, G., & Schwartz, I. (Eds.). (2004). *Positive behavior support: Critical articles on improving practice for individuals with severe disabilities*. Austin, TX: PRO-ED.

Bambara, L.M., & Kern, L. (2005). *Individualized supports for students with problem behaviors: Designing positive behavior plans*. New York, NY: Guilford Press.

Crone, D.A., & Horner, R.H. (2003). *Building positive behavior support systems in schools: Functional behavioral assessment*. New York, NY: Guilford Press.

Crone, D.A., Horner, R.H., & Hawken, L.S. (2004). *Responding to problem behavior in schools: The behavior education program*. New York, NY: Guilford Press.

Dunlap, G., Iovannone, R., Kincaid, D., Wilson, K., Christiansen, K., Strain, P.S., & English, C. (2010). *Prevent-teach-reinforce: The school-based model of individualized positive behavior support*. Baltimore, MD: Paul H. Brookes Publishing Co.

Hieneman, M., Childs, K., & Sergay, J. (2006). *Parenting with positive behavior support: A practical guide to resolving your child's difficult behavior*. Baltimore, MD: Paul H. Brookes Publishing Co.

Janney, R., & Snell, M.E. (2008). *Teacher's guides to inclusive practices: Behavioral support* (2nd ed.). Baltimore, MD: Paul H. Brookes Publishing Co.

Lucyshyn, J.M., Dunlap, G., & Albin, R.W. (Eds.). (2002). *Families and positive behavior support: Addressing problem behaviors in family contexts.* Baltimore, MD: Paul H. Brookes Publishing Co.

Luiselli, J.K., & Cameron, M.J. (Eds.). (1998). *Antecedent control: Innovative approaches to behavioral support.* Baltimore, MD: Paul H. Brookes Publishing Co.

O'Neill, R., Horner, R., Albin, R., Sprague, J., Storey, R., & Newton, J. (1997). *Functional assessment and program development for problem behavior: A practical handbook.* Pacific Grove, CA: Brooks/Cole.

Sailor, W., Dunlap, G., Sugai, G., & Horner, R. (Eds.). (2009). *Handbook of positive behavior support (Issues in clinical child psychology).* New York, NY: Springer

REFERENCES

Association for Behavior Analysis. (1989). *The right to effective treatment.* Retrieved from http://www.abainternational.org/abai/policies-and-positions/right-to-effective-behavioral-treatment,-1989.aspx

Association for Positive Behavior Support. (2007). *PBS standards of practice: Individual level.* Retrieved from http://www.apbs.org/files/apbs_standards_of_practice.pdf

Bambara, L.M. (2005). Evolution of positive behavior support. In L.M. Bambara & L. Kern (Eds.), *Individualized supports for students with problem behaviors: Designing positive behavior plans* (pp. 1–24). New York, NY: Guilford Press.

Bambara, L.M., Goh, A., Kern, L., & Caskie, G. (2012). Perceived barriers and enablers to implementing individualized positive behavior interventions and supports in school settings. *Journal of Positive Behavior Interventions.* [Advanced online publication.] doi:10.1177/1098300712437219

Bambara, L.M., & Kern, L. (2005). *Individualized supports for students with problem behaviors: Designing positive behavior plans.* New York, NY: Guilford Press.

Bambara, L.M., & Lohrmann, S. (2006). Introduction to special issue on severe disabilities and school-wide positive behavior support. *Research and Practice for Persons with Severe Disabilities, 31,* 1–3.

Bambara, L.M., Mitchell-Kvacky, N., & Iacobelli, S. (1994). Positive behavioral support for students with severe disabilities: An emerging multicomponent approach for addressing challenging behaviors. *School Psychology Review, 23,* 263–278.

Bambara, L.M., Nonnemacher, S., & Kern, L. (2009). Sustaining school-based individualized positive behavior support: Perceived barriers and enablers. *Journal of Positive Behavior Interventions, 11,* 161–176. doi:10.1177/1098300708330878

Boden, L.J., Ennis, R.P., & Jolievette, K. (2012). Implementing check in/check out for students with intellectual disability in self-contained classrooms. *Teaching Exceptional Children, 45,* 32–40.

Bradshaw, P., Mitchell, M.M., & Leaf, P.J. (2010). Examining the effects of school-wide positive behavioral interventions and supports on student outcomes. *Journal of Positive Behavior Interventions, 12,* 133–148.

Brown, F., & Michaels, C.A. (2006). School-wide positive behavior support initiatives and students with severe disabilities: A time for reflection. *Research and Practice for Persons with Severe Disabilities, 31,* 57–61.

Brown, F., Michaels, C.A., Oliva, C., & Woolf, S. (2008). Personal paradigm shifts in ABA and PBS experts. *Journal of Positive Behavior Interventions, 10,* 212–228.

Butterfield, E.C. (1990). The compassion of distinguishing punishing behavioral treatment from aversive treatment. *American Journal on Mental Retardation, 95,* 137–141.

Calzada, E.J., & Eyberg, S.M. (2002). Normative parenting in a sample of Dominican and Puerto Rican mothers of young children. *Journal of Clinical Child and Adolescent Psychology, 31,* 354–363.

Carr, E.G. (2006). SWPBS: The greatest good for the greatest number, or the needs of the majority trump the needs of the minority? *Research and Practice for Persons with Severe Disabilities, 31,* 54–56.

Carr, E.G. (2007). The expanding vision of positive behavior support: Research perspectives on happiness, helpfulness, hopefulness. *Journal of Positive Behavior Interventions, 9,* 3–14.

Carr, E.G., Dunlap, G., Horner, R.H., Koegel, R.L., Turnbull, A.P., Sailor, W.,...Fox, L.(2002). Positive behavior support: Evolution of an applied science. *Journal of Positive Behavior Interventions, 4,* 4–16.

Carr, E.G., & Durand, V.M. (1985). Reducing behavior problems through functional communication training. *Journal of Applied Behavior Analysis, 18,* 111–126.

Carr, E.G., Horner, R.H., Turnbull, A.P., Marquis, J.G., Magito-McLaughlin, D., McAtee, M.L.,...Doolabh, A.(1999). *Positive behavior support for people with developmental disabilities: A research synthesis.* Washington, DC: American Association on Mental Retardation.

Carr, E.G., Newsom, C.D., & Binkoff, J.A. (1980). Escape as a factor in the aggressive behavior of two retarded children. *Journal of Applied Behavior Analysis, 13,* 101–117.

Carter, S. (2008). Further conceptualization of treatment acceptability. *Education and Training in Developmental Disabilities, 43,* 135–143.

Council of Parent Attorneys and Advocates. (2009). *Unsafe in the schoolhouse: Abuse of children with disabilities.* Retrieved from http://c.ymcdn.com/sites/www.copaa.org/resource/collection/662B1866-952D-41FA-B7F3-D3CF68639918/UnsafeCOPAAMay_27_2009.pdf

Crimmins, D., & Farrell, A.F. (2006). Individualized behavioral supports at 15 years: It's still lonely at the top. *Research and Practice for Persons with Severe Disabilities, 31,* 31–35. doi:10.2511/rpsd.31.1.31

Cross Calvert, S., & Johnston, C. (1990). Acceptability of treatments for child behavior problems: Issue and implications for future research. *Journal of Clinical Child Psychology, 19,* 61–74.

Dunlap, G., & Carr, E.G. (2007). Positive behavior support and developmental disabilities. In S.L. Odom, R.H. Horner, M.E. Snell, & J. Blacher (Eds.), *Handbook of developmental disabilities* (pp. 469–482). New York, NY: Guilford Press.

Dunlap, G., Carr, E.G., Horner, R.H., Zarcone, J.R., & Schwartz, I. (2008). Positive behavior support and applied behavior analysis: A familial alliance. *Behavior Modification, 32,* 682–698.

Dunlap, G., Kern-Dunlap, L., Clarke, S., & Robbins, F.R. (1991). Functional assessment, curricular revision, and severe behavior problems. *Journal of Applied Behavior Analysis, 24,* 387–397.

Durand, V.M., & Carr, E.G. (1991). Functional communication training to reduce challenging behavior: Maintenance and application in new settings. *Journal of Applied Behavior Analysis, 24,* 251–264.

Durand, V.M., & Kishi, G. (1987). Reducing severe behavior problems among persons with dual sensory impairments: An evaluation of a technical assistance model. *Journal of The Association for Persons with Severe Handicaps, 12,* 2–10.

Elliott, S.N., Witt, J.C., Galvin, G.A., & Peterson, R. (1984). Acceptability of positive and reductive behavioral interventions: Factors that influence teachers' decisions. *Journal of School Psychology, 22,* 353–360.

Evans, I.M., & Meyer, L.H. (1985). *An educative approach to behavior problems: A practical decision model for interventions with severely handicapped learners.* Baltimore, MD: Paul H. Brookes Publishing Co.

Fairbanks, L.D., & Stinnett, T.A. (1997). Effects of professional group membership, intervention type, and diagnostic label on treatment acceptability. *Psychology in the Schools, 34,* 329–335.

Foxx, R.M., Bremer, B.A., Shultz, C., Valdez, J., & Johndrow, C. (1996). Increasing treatment acceptability through video. *Behavioral Interventions, 11,* 171–180.

Freeman, R., Eber, L., Anderson, C., Irvin, L., Horner, R., Bounds, M., & Dunlap, G. (2006). Building inclusive school cultures using school-wide positive behavior support: Designing effective individual support systems for students with significant disabilities. *Research and Practice for Persons with Severe Disabilities, 31,* 4–17.

Gartin, B.C., & Murdick, N.L. (2001). A new IDEA mandate: The use of functional assessment of behavior and positive behavior supports. *Remedial and Special Education, 22,* 344–349.

Goh, A., & Bambara, L.M. (2012). Individualized positive behavior support in school settings: A meta-analysis. *Remedial and Special Education.* [Advanced online publication.] doi:10.1177/0741932510383990

Guess, D., Helmstetter, E., Turnbull, R.H., & Knowlton, S. (1987). *Use of aversive procedures with persons who are disabled: An historical review and critical analysis.* Seattle, WA: The Association for Persons with Severe Handicaps.

Hawken, L.S., & O'Neill, R.E. (2006). Including students with severe disabilities in all levels of school-wide positive behavior support. *Research and Practice for Persons with Severe Disabilities, 31,* 46–53.

Helms, B.J., & Moore, S.C. (1993). Perceptions of aversiveness by supported employment supervisors and job coaches. *Education and Training in Mental Retardation, 28,* 212–219.

Ho, C., Bluestein, D.N., & Jenkins, J.M. (2008). Cultural differences in the relationship between parenting and children's behavior. *Developmental Psychology, 44,* 507–522.

Horner, R.H., & Carr, E.G. (1997). Behavioral support for students with severe disabilities: Functional assessment and comprehensive intervention. *Journal of Special Education, 1,* 84–104.

Horner, R.H., & Dunlap, G. (2012). Future directions for TASH: Combining values and science. *Research and Practice for Persons with Severe Disabilities, 37,* 111–115.

Horner, R.H., Dunlap, G., Koegel, R.L., Carr, E.G., Sailor, W., Anderson, J.,...O'Neill, R. (1990). Toward a technology of "nonaversive" behavioral support. *Journal of The Association for Persons with Severe Handicaps, 15,* 125–134.

Horner, R.H., Sugai, G., & Anderson, C.M. (2010). Examining the evidence base for school-wide positive behavior support. *Focus on Exceptional Children, 42,* 1–14.

Horner, R.H., Sugai, G., Smolkowski, K., Eber, L., Nakasato, J., Todd, A.W., & Esperanza, J. (2009). A randomized, wait-list controlled effectiveness trial assessing school-wide positive behavior support in elementary schools. *Journal of Positive Behavior Interventions, 11,* 134–144. doi: 1098300709332067v1

Horner, R.H., Sugai, G., Todd, A.W., & Lewis-Palmer, T. (2005). Schoolwide positive behavior support. In L.M. Bambara & L. Kern (Eds.), *Individualized supports for students with problem behaviors: Designing positive behavior plans* (pp. 359–390). New York, NY: Guilford Press.

Hunt, P., & McDonnell, J. (2007). Inclusive education. In S.L. Odom, R.H., Horner, M. Snell, & J. Blacher (Eds.), *Handbook on developmental disabilities* (pp. 269–291). New York, NY: Guilford Press.

Individuals with Disabilities Education Act Amendments (IDEA) of 1997, PL 105-17, 20 U.S.C. §§ 1400 *et seq.*

Individuals with Disabilities Education Improvement Act (IDEA) of 2004, PL 108-446, 20 U.S.C. §§ 1400 *et seq.*

Iwata, B.A., Dorsey, M.F., Slifer, K.J., Baumann, K.E., & Richman, G.S. (1982). Toward a functional analysis of self-injury. *Analysis and Intervention in Developmental Disabilities, 2,* 3–20.

Jones, M.L., Eyberg, S.M., Adams, C.D., & Boggs, S.R. (1998). Treatment acceptability of behavioral interventions for children: An assessment by mothers of children with disruptive behavior disorders. *Child and Family Therapy, 20,* 15–26.

Kazdin, A.E. (1980). Acceptability of alternative treatments for deviant child behavior. *Journal of Applied Behavior Analysis, 13,* 259–273.

Kazdin, A.E., French, N., & Sherick, R. (1981). Acceptability of alternative treatments for children: Evaluations by inpatient children, parents, and staff. *Journal of Consulting and Clinical Psychology, 49,* 900–907.

Kern, L., Chouka, C., & Sokol, N.G. (2002). Assessment-based antecedent interventions used in natural settings to reduce challenging behavior: An analysis of the literature. *Education and Treatment of Children, 25,* 113–130.

Keyes, J., Creekmore, W., Karst, R., Crow, R., & Dayan, M. (1988). The AAMR position statement on aversive therapy: The controversy. *Mental Retardation, 26,* 314–318.

Knoster, T., Anderson, J., Carr, E.G., Dunlap, G., & Horner, R.H. (2003). Challenges and opportunities: Introducing the Association for Positive Behavior Support. *Journal of Positive Behavior Interventions, 5,* 183–186. doi: 10.1177/10983007030050030801

Landers, E., Courtade, G., & Ryndak, D. (2012). Including students with severe disabilities in school-wide positive behavioral interventions and supports: Perceptions of state coordinators. *Research and Prac-*

tice for Persons with Severe Disabilities, 37, 1–8.

LaVigna, G.W., & Donnellan, A.M. (1986). *Alternatives to punishment: Solving behavior problems with non-aversive strategies.* New York, NY: Irvington.

Lennox, D.B., & Miltenberger, R.G. (1989). Conducting a functional assessment of problem behavior in applied settings. *Journal of The Association for Persons with Severe Handicaps, 14,* 304–311.

Lindeman, D.P., Miltenberger, R.G., & Lennox, D.B. (1992). Acceptability of behavioral interventions: Perceptions of superintendents of public residential facilities. *Behavioral Interventions, 7,* 35–44.

Luiselli, J.K., & Cameron, M.J. (Eds.). (1998). Conclusions and future directions. In J.K. Luiselli & M.J. Cameron (Eds.), *Antecedent control: Innovative approaches to behavioral support* (pp. 373–379). Baltimore, MD: Paul H. Brookes Publishing Co.

McDonnell, J.J., & O'Neill, R. (2003). A perspective on single/within subject research methods and "scientifically based research." *Research and Practice for Persons with Severe Disabilities, 28,* 138–142.

McGee, J.J., Menolascino, F.J., Hobbs, D.C., & Menousek, P.E. (1987). *Gentle teaching: A nonaversive approach to helping persons with mental retardation.* New York, NY: Human Sciences Press.

Meyer, L.H., Peck, C.A., & Brown, L. (Eds.). (1991). *Critical issues in the lives of people with severe disabilities.* Baltimore, MD: Paul H. Brookes Publishing Co.

Miller, D.L., & Kelley, M.L. (1992). Treatment acceptability: The effects of parent gender, marital adjustment, and child behavior. *Child & Family Behavior Therapy, 14,* 11–23.

Miltenberger, R. (1990). Assessment of treatment acceptability: A review of the literature. *Topics in Early Childhood Special Education, 10,* 24–38.

Miltenberger, R.G., & Lumley, V.A. (1997). Evaluating the influence of problem function on treatment acceptability. *Behavioral Interventions, 12,* 105–111.

National Disability Rights Network. (2009). *School is not supposed to hurt.* Retrieved from http://www.ndrn.org/images/Documents/Resources/Publications/Reports/SR-Report2009.pdf

Njardvik, U., & Kelley, M.L. (2008). Cultural effects on treatment acceptability: A comparison of the acceptability of behavioral interventions between Icelandic and American parents. *Nordic Psychology, 60,* 283–294.

O'Brien, C.L., O'Brien, J., & Mount, B. (1997). Person-centered planning has arrived, or has it? *Mental Retardation, 35,* 480–483.

Pickering, D.M., & Morgan, S.B. (1985). Parental ratings of treatments of self-injurious behavior. *Journal of Autism and Developmental Disorders, 15,* 303–314.

Rasnake, L.K., Martin, J, Tarnowski, K.J., & Mulick, J.A. (1993). Acceptability of behavioral treatments: Influence of knowledge of behavioral principles. *Mental Retardation, 31,* 247–251.

Repp, A.C., & Singh, N.N. (1990). *Perspectives on the use of nonaversive and aversive interventions for persons with developmental disabilities.* Sycamore, IL: Sycamore.

Safran, S.P., & Oswald, K. (2003). Positive behavior supports: Can schools reshape disciplinary practices? *Exceptional Children, 69,* 361–373.

Sailor, W., Zuna, N., Choi, J., Thomas, J., McCart, A., & Blair, R. (2006). Anchoring schoolwide positive behavior support in structural school reform. *Research and Practice for Persons with Severe Disabilities, 31,* 18–30. doi:10.2511/rpsd .31.1.18

Scott, T.M., & Kamps, D.M. (2007). The future of functional behavioral assessment in school settings. *Behavioral Disorders, 32,* 146–157.

Smith, F.A., & Linscheid, T.R. (1994). Effect of parental acceptance or rejection of a proposed aversive intervention on treatment acceptability. *American Journal on Mental Retardation, 99,* 262–269.

Smull, M.W., & Bellamy, T.G. (1991). Community services for adults with disabilities: Policy challenges in the emerging supports paradigm. In L.H. Meyer, C.A. Peck, & L. Brown (Eds.), *Critical issues in the lives of people with severe disabilities* (pp. 527–541). Baltimore, MD: Paul. H. Brookes Publishing Co.

Snell, M.E. (2006). What's the verdict: Are students with severe disabilities included in school-wide positive behavior support? *Research and Practice for Persons with Severe Disabilities, 31,* 62–65.

Spooner, F., & Browder, D.M. (2003). Scientifically based research in education and students with low incidence disabilities. *Research and Practice for Persons with Severe Disabilities, 28,* 117–125.

Spooner, F., & Brown, F. (2011). Educating students with significant cognitive disabilities: Historical overview and future projections. In J.M. Kauffman & D.P. Hallahan (Eds.), *Handbook of special education* (pp. 503–515). New York, NY: Routledge.

Spreat, S., & Walsh, D.E. (1994). Impact of treatment efficacy and professional affiliation on ratings of treatment acceptability. *Mental Retardation, 32,* 227–233.

Stancliffe, R.J. (2001). Living with support in the community: Predictors of choice and self-determination. *Mental Retardation and Developmental Disabilities Research Reviews, 7,* 91–98.

Sugai, G., & Horner, R.H. (2006). A promising approach for expanding and sustaining school-wide positive behavior support. *School Psychology Review, 35,* 245–259.

Sugai, G., Horner, R.H., Dunlap, G., Hieneman, M., Lewis, T.J., Nelson, C.M.,...Ruef, M. (2000). Applying positive behavior support and functional behavioral assessment in schools. *Journal of Positive Behavior Interventions, 2,* 131–143.

Tarnowski, K.J., Kelly, P.A., & Mendlowitz, D.R. (1987). Acceptability of behavioral pediatric interventions. *Journal of Consulting and Clinical Psychology, 55,* 435–436.

Tarnowski, K.J., Mulick, J.A., & Rasnake, L.K. (1990). Acceptability of behavioral interventions for self-injurious behavior: Replication and interinstitutional comparison. *American Journal on Mental Retardation, 95,* 182–187.

Tarnowski, K.J., Rasnake, L.K., Mulick, J.A., & Kelly, P.A. (1989). Acceptability of behavioral interventions for self-injurious behavior. *American Journal on Mental Retardation, 93,* 575–580.

Tarnowski, K.J., Simonian, S., Park A., & Bekeny, P. (1992). Acceptability of treatments for child behavioral disturbance: Race, socioeconomic status, and multicomponent treatment effect. *Child and Family Behavior Therapy, 14,* 25–37.

U.S. Department of Education. (2012). *Restraint and seclusion: Resource document.* Retrieved from http://www2.ed.gov/policy/seclusion/index.html

U.S. Government Accountability Office. (2009). *Seclusion and restraints: Selected cases of death and abuse at public and private schools and treatment centers.* Testimony before the committee on Education and Labor, House of Representatives, Washington, DC.

Van Houten, R., Axelrod, S., Bailey, J.S., Favell, J.E., Fox, R.M., Iwata, B.A., & Lovaas, O.I. (1988). The right to effective treatment. *Journal of Applied Behavior Analysis, 4,* 381–384.

Walker, H.M., Horner, R.H., Sugai, G., Bullis, M., Sprague, J.R., Bricker, D., & Kaufman, M.J. (1996). Integrated approaches to preventing antisocial behavior patterns among school-age children and youth. *Journal of Emotional and Behavior Disorders, 4,* 194–209.

Wehmeyer, M.L., & Schalock, R.L. (2001). Self-determination and quality of life: Implications for special education services and supports. *Focus on Exceptional Children, 33,* 1–16.

Westling, D.L., Trader, B.R., Smith, C.A., & Marshall, D. (2010). Use of restraints, seclusion and aversive procedures on students with disabilities. *Research and Practice for Persons with Severe Disabilities, 35,* 116–127.

Wolfensberger, W. (1972). *The principle of normalization in human services.* Toronto, Canada: National Institute on Mental Retardation.

Woolf, M.M. (1978). Social validity: The case for subjective measurement or how applied behavior analysis is finding its heart. *Journal of Applied Behavior Analysis, 11,* 203–214.

Zirkel, P.A. (2011a). Case law for functional behavior assessments and behavior intervention plans: An empirical analysis. *Seattle University Law Review, 35,* 175–212.

Zirkel, P.A. (2011b). What does the law say? *Teaching Exceptional Children, 43,* 65–67.

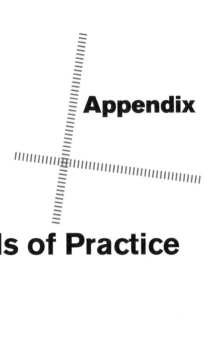

Appendix

Association for Positive Behavior Supports Standards of Practice

Individual Level

I. Foundations of PBS

    A. Practitioners of PBS have an historical perspective on the evolution of PBS and its relationship to ABA and movements in the disability field

        1. History of applied behavior analysis and the relationship to PBS

        2. Similarities and unique features of PBS and ABA

        3. Movements in the field of serving persons with disabilities that influenced the emergence of PBS practices

            a. Deinstitutionalization

            b. Normalization and social role valorization

            c. Community participation

            d. Supported employment

            e. Least restrictive environment and inclusive schooling

            f. Self-determination

    B. Practitioners applying PBS with individuals adhere to a number of basic assumptions about behavior

        1. Problem behavior serves a function

        2. Positive strategies are effective in addressing the most challenging behavior

        3. When positive behavior intervention strategies fail, additional functional assessment strategies are required to develop more effective PBS strategies

        4. Features of the environmental context affect behavior

        5. Reduction of problem behavior is an important, but not the sole, outcome of successful intervention; effective PBS results in improvements in quality of life, acquisition of valued skills, and access to valued activities

    C. Practitioners applying PBS with individuals include at least 11 key elements in the development of PBS supports

        1. Collaborative team-based decision-making

        2. Person-centered decision-making

        3. Self-determination

From the Association for Positive Behavior Support (www.apbs.org)

4. Functional assessment of behavior and functionally derived interventions

5. Identification of outcomes that enhance quality of life and are valued by the individual, their families and the community

6. Strategies that are acceptable in inclusive community settings

7. Strategies that teach useful and valued skills

8. Strategies that are evidence-based, and socially and empirically valid to achieve desired outcomes that are at least as effective and efficient as the problem behavior

9. Techniques that do not cause pain or humiliation or deprive the individual of basic needs

10. Constructive and respectful multi-component intervention plans that emphasize antecedent interventions, instruction in prosocial behaviors, and environmental modification

11. Ongoing measurement of impact

D. Practitioners applying PBS with individuals commit themselves to ongoing and rigorous professional development

1. Pursue continuing education and inservice training as well as consulting peer-reviewed journals and current publications to stay abreast of emerging research, trends and national models of support

2. Attend national, regional, state and local conferences

3. Seek out collaboration, support and/or assistance when faced with challenges outside of one's expertise

4. Seek out collaboration, support and/or assistance when intended outcomes are not achieved in a timely [manner]

5. Seek out knowledge from a variety of empirically-based fields relevant to the people whom they serve. These fields include education, behavioral and social sciences, and the biomedical sciences

E. Practitioners of PBS understand the legal and regulatory requirements related to assessment and intervention regarding challenging behavior and behavior change strategies.

1. Requirements of IDEA with respect to PBS

2. The purpose of human rights and other oversight committees regarding behavior change

3. Works within state/school/agency regulations and requirements

II. Collaboration and Team Building

A. Practitioners of PBS understand the importance of and use strategies to work collaboratively with other professionals, individuals with disabilities, and their families

1. Understands and respects the importance of collaboration in providing effective PBS services

2. Uses skills needed for successful collaboration, including the ability to:

a. Communicate clearly

b. Establish rapport

c. Be flexible and open

d. Support the viewpoints of others

e. Learn from others

f. Incorporate new ideas within personal framework

g. Manage conflict

B. Practitioners of PBS understand the importance of and use strategies to support development and effectiveness of collaborative teams

1. Includes the critical members of a PBS team for the individual considering the age, setting, and types of abilities and disabilities of the individual
2. Evaluates team composition considering the needs of the individual and assists the team in recruiting additional team members to address needed areas of expertise
3. Uses essential team skills, including:
   a. Facilitation
   b. Coaching
   c. Mediation
   d. Consensus building
   e. Meeting management
   f. Team roles and responsibilities
4. Uses strategies and processes to demonstrate sensitivity to and respect for all team members, and diverse opinions and perspectives
5. Facilitates the inclusion of and respect for the values and priorities of families and all team members
6. Supports and participates in advocacy necessary to access supports to carry out team decisions

III. Basic Principles of Behavior
   A. Practitioners of PBS utilize behavioral assessment and support methods that are based on operant learning
      1. The antecedent/behavior/consequence model as the basis for all voluntary behavior
      2. Operational definitions of behavior
      3. Stimulus control, including discriminative stimuli and S-deltas
      4. The influence of setting events (or establishing operations), on behavior
      5. Antecedent influences on behavior
      6. Precursor behaviors
      7. Consequences to increase or decrease behavior
   B. Practitioners of PBS understand and use antecedent manipulations to influence behavior, such as:
      1. Curricular modifications
      2. Instructional modifications
      3. Behavioral precursors as signals
      4. Modification of routines
      5. Opportunities for choice/control throughout the day
      6. Clear expectations
      7. Pre-correction
      8. Errorless learning
   C. Practitioners of PBS understand and use consequence manipulations to increase behavior
      1. Primary reinforcers, and conditions under which primary reinforcers are used
      2. Types of secondary reinforcers and their use
      3. Approaches to identify effective reinforcers, including:
         a. Functional assessment data
         b. Observation

        c. Reinforcer surveys

        d. Reinforcer sampling

    4. Premack principle

    5. Positive reinforcement

    6. Negative reinforcement

    7. Ratio, interval, and natural schedules of reinforcement

    8. Pairing of reinforcers

D. Practitioners of PBS understand consequence manipulations to decrease behavior

    1. The use of punishment, including characteristics, ethical use of punishment, and potential side effects of punishment procedures. *(Any use of punishment, including strategies that are found within integrated natural settings, must be within the parameters of the 11 key elements identified above in IC, with particular attention to IC9 "techniques that do not cause pain or humiliation or deprive the individual of basic needs")*

    2. Differential reinforcement, including:

        a. Differential reinforcement of alternative behavior

        b. Differential reinforcement of incompatible behavior

        c. Differential reinforcement of zero rates of behavior

        d. Differential reinforcement of lower rates of behavior

    3. Extinction, including:

        a. Characteristics of extinction interventions

        b. How to use extinction

        c. Using extinction in combination with interventions to develop replacement behaviors

    4. Response cost, including:

        a. Cautions associated with use of response cost.

        b. Using response cost with interventions to develop replacement behaviors.

    5. Timeout, including:

        a. Types of timeout applications

        b. How to implement

        c. Cautions associated with use of timeout

        d. Using timeout with interventions to develop replacement behaviors

E. Practitioners of PBS understand and use methods for facilitating generalization and maintenance of skills

    1. Forms of generalization, including:

        a. Stimulus generalization

        b. Response generalization

        c. Generalization across subjects

    2. Maintenance of behaviors across time.

IV. Data-Based Decision-Making

A. Practitioners of PBS understand that data-based decision-making is a fundamental element of PBS, and that behavioral assessment and support planning begins with defining behavior.

    1. Using operational definitions to describe target behaviors

    2. Writing behavioral objectives that include:

        a. Conditions under which the behavior should occur

  b. Operational definition of behavior

  c. Criteria for achieving the objective

B. Practitioners of PBS understand that data-based decision-making is a fundamental element of PBS, and that measuring behavior is a critical component of behavioral assessment and support

 1. Using data systems that are appropriate for target behaviors, including:

  a. Frequency

  b. Duration

  c. Latency

  d. Interval recording

  e. Time sampling

  f. Permanent product recording

 2. Developing data collection plans that include:

  a. The measurement system to be used

  b. Schedule for measuring behavior during relevant times and contexts, including baseline data

  c. Manageable strategies for sampling behavior for measurement purposes

  d. How, when, and if the inter-observer agreement checks will be conducted

  e. How and when procedural integrity checks will be conducted

  f. Data collection recording forms

  g. How raw data will be converted to a standardized format (e.g., rate, percent)

  h. Use of criterion to determine when to make changes in the instructional phase

C. Practitioners of PBS use graphic displays of data to support decision making during the assessment, program development, and evaluation stages of behavior support.

 1. Converting raw data in standardized format

 2. Following graphing conventions, including:

  a. Clearly labeled axes

  b. Increment scales that allow for meaningful and accurate [presentation]

 3. Representation of the data

  a. Phase change lines

  b. Clearly labeled phase change descriptions

  c. Criterion lines

D. Practitioners of PBS use data-based strategies to monitor progress

 1. Using graphed data to identify trends and intervention effects

 2. Evaluating data regularly and frequently

 3. Sharing data with team members for team-based, person-centered, decision-making

 4. Using data to make decisions regarding program revisions to maintain or improve behavioral progress, including decisions relating to maintaining, modifying, or terminating interventions

 5. Using data to determine if additional collaborations, support and/or assistance is needed to achieve intended outcomes

V. Comprehensive Person Centered and Functional Behavior Assessments

A. Practitioners understand the importance of multi-element assessments including:

 1. Person Centered Planning

      2. Quality of Life

      3. Environmental/ecology

      4. Setting events

      5. Antecedents and consequences

      6. Social Skills/Communication/Social Networks

      7. Curricular/instructional needs (e.g., learning style)

      8. Health/biophysical

B. Comprehensive assessments result in information about the focus individual in at least the following areas:

      1. Lifestyle

      2. Preferences and interests

      3. Communication/social abilities & needs

      4. Ecology

      5. Health and safety

      6. Problem routines

      7. Variables promoting and reinforcing problem behavior:

         a. Preferences/reinforcers

         b. Antecedents

         c. Setting events

         d. Potential replacement behavior

      8. Function(s) of behavior

      9. Potential replacement behaviors

C. Practitioners who apply PBS conduct Person Centered Assessments that provide a picture of the life of the individual including:

      1. Indicators of quality of life comparable to same age individuals without disabilities (e.g., self-determination, inclusion, friends, fun, variety, access to belongings)

      2. The strengths and gifts of the individual

      3. The variety and roles of persons with whom they interact (e.g., family, friends, neighbors, support providers) and the nature, frequency and duration of such interactions

      4. The environments & activities in which they spend time including the level of acceptance and meaningful participation, problematic and successful routines, preferred settings/activities, the rate of reinforcement and/or corrective feedback, and the age appropriateness of settings, activities & materials

      5. The level of independence and support needs of the individual including workplace, curricular and instructional modifications, augmentative communication and other assistive technology supports, and assistance with personal management and hygiene

      6. The health and medical/biophysical needs of the individual

      7. The dreams and goals of the individual and their circle of support

      8. Barriers to achieving the dreams and goals

      9. The influence of the above information on problem behavior.

D. PBS practitioners conduct Functional Behavioral Assessments that result in:

      1. Operationally defined problem behavior

      2. The context in which problem behavior occurs most often

      3. Identification of setting events that promote the potential for problem behavior

       4. Identification of antecedents that set the occasion for problem behavior

       5. Identification of consequences maintaining problem behavior

       6. A thorough description of the antecedent/behavior/consequence relationship

       7. An interpretation of the function(s) of behavior

       8. Identification of potential replacement behavior

    E. PBS practitioners conduct indirect and direct assessment strategies

       1. Indirect assessments include file reviews, structured interviews (e.g., person centered planning), checklists, and rating scales (e.g., MAS)

       2. Direct assessments include such strategies as scatterplots, anecdotal recording, ABC data, and time/activity analyses

       3. Summarize data in graphic and narrative formats

    F. PBS practitioners work collaboratively with the team to develop hypotheses that are supported by assessment data

       1. All assessment information is synthesized and analyzed to determine the possible influence of the following on the occurrence or nonoccurrence of problem behavior:

         a. Setting events (or establishing operations)

         b. Antecedents/triggers

         c. Consequences for both desired and challenging behaviors

         d. Ecological variables

         e. Lifestyle issues

         f. Medical/biophysical problems

       2. Hypotheses statements are developed that address:

         a. Setting events

         b. Antecedents

         c. Consequences for both desired and challenging behaviors

         d. Function(s) problem behavior serves for the individual

    G. PBS practitioners utilize Functional Analysis of Behavior as necessary on the basis of an understanding of:

       1. The differences between functional assessment and functional analysis

       2. The advantages & disadvantages of functional analysis

       3. The conditions under which each approach may be conducted

VI. Development and Implementation of Comprehensive, Multi-Element Behavior Support Plans

    A. PBS practitioners apply the following considerations/foundations across all elements of a PBS plan

       1. Behavior support plans are developed in collaboration with the individual and his or her team

       2. Behavior support plans are driven by the results of person centered and functional behavior assessments

       3. Behavior support plans facilitate the individual's preferred lifestyle

       4. Behavior support plans are designed for contextual fit, specifically in relation to:

         a. The values and goals of the team

         b. The current and desired routines within the various settings in which the individual participates

         c. The skills and buy-in of those who will be implementing the plan

      d.   Administrative support

   5. Behavior support plans include strategies for evaluating each component plan of the plan

B. Behavior Support Plans include interventions to improve/support Quality of Life in at least the following areas:

   1. Achieving the individual's dreams

   2. The individual's health and physiological needs

   3. Promote all aspects of self determination

   4. Improvement in individual's active, successful participation in inclusive school, work, home and community settings

   5. Promotion of social interactions, relationships, and enhanced social networks

   6. Increased fun and success in the individual's life

   7. Improved leisure, relaxation, and recreational activities for the individual throughout the day

C. PBS practitioners develop behavior support plans that include antecedent interventions to prevent the need for problem behavior using the following strategies:

   1. Alter or eliminate setting events to preclude the need for problem behavior

   2. Modify specific antecedent triggers/circumstances based on the FBA

   3. Identify and address behaviors using precursors (i.e., individual's signal that a problem behavior is likely to occur)

   4. Make the individual's environment/routines predictable (e.g., personal schedule in format the individual can understand)

   5. Build opportunities for choice/control throughout the day that are age appropriate and contextually appropriate

   6. Create clear expectations

   7. Modify curriculum/job demands so the individual can successfully complete tasks

D. PBS plans address effective instructional intervention strategies that may include the following:

   1. Match instructional strategies to the individual's learning style

   2. Provide instruction in the context in which the problem behaviors occur and the use of alternative skills, including instruction in skills such as:

      a.   Communication skills

      b.   Social skills

      c.   Self-management/monitoring skills

      d.   Other adaptive behaviors as indicated by the FBA and continued evaluation of progress data (e.g., relaxation techniques)

   3. Teach replacement behavior(s) based on competing behavior analysis

   4. Select and teach replacement behaviors that can be as or more effective than the problem behavior

   5. Utilize instructional methods of addressing a problem behavior proactively (including pre-instruction; modeling; rehearsal; social stories; incidental teaching; use of peer buddies; meeting sensory needs; direct instruction; verbal, physical, and/or visual prompting)

E. PBS practitioners employ consequence intervention strategies that consider the following:

   1. Reinforcement strategies are function based and rely on naturally occurring reinforcers as much as possible.

2. Use the least intrusive behavior reduction strategy (e.g., error correction, extinction, differential reinforcement).

3. Emergency intervention strategies are used only where safety of the individual or others must be assured.

4. Plans for avoiding power struggles and provocation.

5. Plan for potential natural consequences. Consider when these should happen and when there should be attempts to avoid them. Although some natural consequences are helpful to the individual (e.g., losing money, missing a bus), others can be detrimental and provide no meaningful experience (e.g., being hit by a car, admission to psychiatric unit).

F. PBS practitioners develop plans for successful implementation of positive behavior support plans that include:

1. Action plans for implementation of all components of the intervention including:

   a. Activities, dates and documentation describing who is responsible for completing each task

   b. Materials, training and support needed for those doing intervention

   c. How data will be collected and analyzed to address both impact and fidelity of intervention

   d. Timelines for meetings, data analysis and targeted outcomes

   e. Training, supports and time needed for plan implementation

   f. Criteria for team meetings for immediate modification of PBS plan

   g. Plans for review of contextual fit, function based interventions, and lifestyle enhancements

2. Strategies to address systems change needed for implementation of PBS plans that may include:

   a. Modifying policies/regulations

   b. Support and training for personnel & families

   c. Accessing needed resources (financial & personnel)

   d. Increasing flexibility in routines, & staffing schedules

   e. Recruiting additional individuals to be team members (e.g., bus driver, peers, neighbors, extended family

   f. Interagency collaboration

G. PBS Practitioners evaluate plan implementation and use data to make needed modifications

1. Implement plan, evaluate and monitor progress according to timelines

2. Collect data identified for each component of PBS plan

3. Analyze data on regular basis to determine needed adjustments

4. Evaluate progress on Person Centered Plans (e.g., quality of life, social networks, personal preferences, upcoming transitions)

5. Modify each element of the PBS plan as indicated by evaluation data

Standards Committee Chairs:

Jacki Anderson, Fredda Brown, Brenda Scheurmann

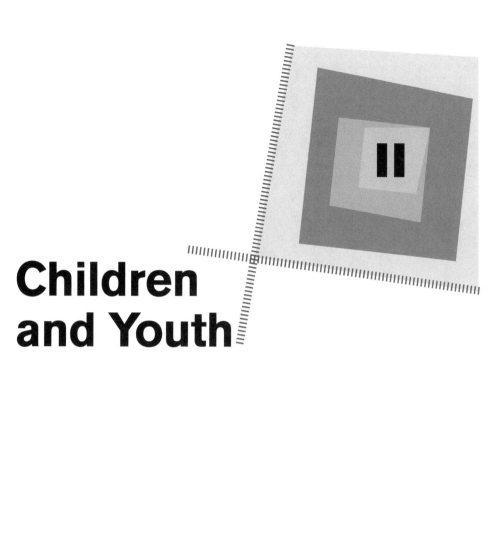

Children
and Youth

7

Early Intervention and Early Education

Lise Fox, Mary Frances Hanline, Juliann Woods, and Ann Mickelson

The provision of early intervention and early education to young children with severe disabilities is extremely important to children's potential trajectory of learning and community inclusion. The early years of development are a critical period for all young children and are marked by rapid development of the neural connections needed for all subsequent learning and development (Shonkoff, 2010). This makes the experiences children have during this time period, including supports and services relating to special needs, of utmost importance. In our discussion here, we refer to the provision of supports and services to young children ages birth to 3 years and their families as early intervention and refer to early education programs as those programs serving children younger than 5 years of age. More than 50 years of research support the importance of early intervention and early education. In general, the outcomes linked to the provision of early intervention/ early childhood services include maximizing child developmental outcomes, family stability and support, and better adult outcomes for the child with disabilities (Bruder, 2010; Dunst, 2012; Guralnick, 2005). This chapter describes many of the critical issues and needs that must be considered in the design and delivery of supports and services to very young children with severe disabilities and their families. Although early intervention and early education services and supports are essential for all children who might be at risk for or have a developmental delay, the needs of children with severe disabilities for effective early intervention are particularly urgent because the consequences for not providing early intervention can include compounded delays in a child's cognitive, social, and communication development and deleterious effects on physical growth and development and general health status (Guralnick, 2005). In addition, the lack of effective services might increase family stress and negatively affect family functioning.

Early intervention and early education services have been included as a part of the Individuals with Disabilities Education Improvement Act (IDEA) of 2004 (PL 108-446) services since the Education of the Handicapped Act Amendments of 1986 (PL 99-457) that mandated preschool services for children with disabilities and provided an opportunity for states to develop systems to provide early intervention to children from birth to age 3. Unlike special education services for school-age children, the provision of special education services and supports for infants, toddlers, and preschoolers occurs within a variety of natural contexts, as school enrollment is not an expectation for very young children. Thus, services might be provided in the home, early education programs, community settings, preschool programs, Head Start programs, or other settings that provide supports to young children and their families. The focus for the delivery of services to infants and toddlers is also slightly different than that for preschoolers and school-age children due to the mandate of natural environments for the delivery of services and the acknowledgment that the family context, rather than a school setting, is often the natural environment for very young children. In addition, family systems theory plays an influential role in the philosophy of early intervention and informs the perspective by considering that the child develops within the family system with the family or primary caregivers being the most influential change agent for the very young child. Because the family is pivotal in promoting their child's development, they are partners in the design and delivery of early intervention services. Intervention, as outlined in the individualized family service plan (IFSP), is family centered as opposed to the more child-centered services and supports seen in the individualized education program (IEP), which is used in preschool and school-age situations. IFSPs focus on family priorities and needs and consider both the developmental intervention needs of the child and the needs of the family in their caregiving role. Preschool services often occur in more academic settings such as community early childhood programs, Head Start classrooms, or school-based early childhood programs. Recommended practice asserts, however, that services and implementation should remain attuned to family priorities and needs.

It is important to understand some of the unique challenges and circumstances that must be considered when providing supports and services to young children with severe disabilities and their families. These unique aspects exist in tandem with challenges and circumstances faced across all of early care and education. A major concern for all early intervention and education is the delivery of effective services to children who live in poverty. The developmental status of children in poverty is a growing concern as the numbers of children in poverty increases nationally. The proportion of young children under age 6 living in poverty is on the rise; it has grown from 44% in 2005 to 48% in 2010 (Addy & White, 2012a). Children in poverty are at an increased risk for poor developmental outcomes, are more likely to have low birth weight and suffer hunger or abuse, and are less likely to have adequate medical care (Addy & White, 2012b). Children with disabilities are more likely to live with families who are poor (Fujiura & Yamaki, 2000) and families of children with disabilities experience significantly greater hardship than other families in poverty (Parish, Rose, Grinstein-Weiss, Richman, & Andrews, 2008). Data from the 10-year National Early Intervention Longitudinal Study (NEILS) indicate that families participating in early intervention are more likely than families in the general population to have challenges (Hebbeler et al., 2007). Those challenges include foster care placement (i.e., one in seven children in early intervention are in foster care), multiple children with special needs (i.e., one in five households include more than one child with a special need), multiple demographic risk factors (i.e., more than half of the families possessed two or more risk factors), and poverty (i.e., 43% of families receiving early intervention services had incomes of $25,000 or less). Service systems are clearly challenged by these complex factors in their efforts to provide services in a manner that can support families whose life circumstances might place them at a disadvantage to address their child's intervention needs.

These factors increase the vulnerability of families whose children have intensive support needs and might be medically vulnerable. The following sections discuss challenges and considerations for family support, the design and delivery of early intervention and early education programs, and the implications for personnel preparation.

FAMILY SUPPORT

The birth of a child uniquely affects each family. For families with a child with significant medical, developmental, and/or social needs, the effect has profound lifetime implications. It is not a question of a positive or negative effect; rather, the questions are "How adequate are the resources?" and "How effective are the supports and services that wrap around the child and family?"

Family Issues and Challenges

Studies of families with young children with severe disabilities in early intervention generally report early identification and initiation of services related to the type of disability and fairly high satisfaction with both the services provided and the service providers on the team, with a few notable exceptions. Despite reports of satisfaction with services and providers, nearly 20% of families served in early intervention reported they are not aware of or familiar with their IFSP (Bailey, Hebbeler, Scarborough, Spiker, & Mallik, 2004). This is a major concern as the IFSP documents the child's and family's strengths, concerns, and priorities and guides the intervention that is to occur. Gaps between the concept of family centeredness and actual practice were most evident in the finding that professionals, rather than family members, were serving in the role of decision makers. This is exacerbated for families of lower socioeconomic status or cultural diversity. In addition, families have described having little input regarding the services their family receives (Bailey et al., 2004).

The role of the early intervention provider is to "enhance the family's capacity to meet the developmental needs of the infant/toddler" (IDEA 2004, Section 1436). The familial caregiver in this approach is the intervention agent who promotes child learning, and the provider supports and enhances the caregiver's consistency and effectiveness to implement early learning opportunities with fidelity in natural environments. There is an expectation that early intervention services will produce positive outcomes for both the child and caregiver through the capacity-promoting interactions of the caregiver and child in their everyday routines and activities. The focus of the early interventionist is to coach the caregiver to embed meaningful interventions to support functional outcomes, increase the child's participation in everyday routines, and promote positive interactions between the caregiver and child. Through these coaching supports, the frequency and consistency of learning opportunities for the child might be increased. However, in spite of the legal emphasis and the logic behind the approach, remarkably little Part C research with caregivers as implementers of their children's interventions has been reported (Hebbeler, Spiker, & Kahn, 2012; McWilliam, 2012; Peterson, Luze, Eshbaugh, Jeon, & Kantz, 2007), and even less research has been conducted that is focused to the unique learning needs of infants/toddlers with severe disabilities. More disconcerting for this unique population is that no research on the effect to the familial caregiver responsible for delivering intervention has been reported, although it is likely that this responsibility could increase the challenges of already overburdened caregivers. With families of children with severe disabilities reporting increased stress, exhaustion, and a sense of isolation (Miodrag & Hodapp, 2010), fewer visits from an early intervention provider or the shift from professionally delivered to parent-implemented interventions might be perceived as a loss of support and service.

Navigating Services and Supports

Community-based options that provide reliable and flexible services are not available, despite the recognition of the physical and emotional demands of caring for a child with intensive support needs and its subsequent effect on the family's ability to provide adequate care. Such services include early intervention and education services, comprehensive medical and therapeutic care, respite services, resources, and advocacy. Understanding how the community and social networks affect parents' abilities to gain access to services for their children with severe disabilities is essential in order to design more effective interventions for families.

The home is the traditional site for caregiving. Early intervention is predominantly a home-based service. Nursing or respite services are most frequently provided in the home. Nursing and respite services, however, are limited by eligibility, availability, accessibility, and affordability. There is simply no funding for many families. If payment is available, then adequately trained personnel frequently are in limited supply. Health care is also a major challenge. Because of greater access to Medicaid or private insurance, children from very low or very high socioeconomic status backgrounds are more likely than others to utilize formal health services. Families with middle incomes often are stressed the most. Utilization decreases when insurance copayments are increased or coverage is reduced (Patrick, Padgett, Burns, Schlesinger, & Cohen, 1993). In addition, insurance companies often create barriers to efficient treatment. Prior approvals, waiting periods, and treatment limitations necessitate the caregivers' full attention simply to navigate the system, let alone successfully obtain services for their children.

Factors other than economics are well known as having the potential to facilitate or inhibit service utilization. Parents cite many reasons for not following through with recommendations or referrals for services, including scheduling conflicts, susceptibility to infection or illness, inability to support the child without assistance for travel, and the child's unique behavioral needs. Although scheduling and transportation are common barriers to services that can be overcome with service planning and financial assistance, closer examination is needed to understand the decision-making processes associated with parents' difficulties, inability, or refusal to obtain services necessary for their children's treatment. A shift from the stereotypical portrayal of children with severe disabilities as burdens and their parents as overwhelmed is a good first step. Yet, the importance of providing supports and services for children and families in ways that emphasize their inclusion in the community is a necessity. Caregivers express interest in options for services in the community and their own home that permit scheduled rest times or part-time employment. This particularly is the case for consistent respite services. Assurance that the personnel caring for their child are competent and nurturing also is integral to achieving positive outcomes for the child and family.

DESIGN AND DELIVERY OF EARLY INTERVENTION AND EARLY EDUCATION PROGRAMS

The TASH *Resolution on Educating Young Children with Significant Disabilities* stated,

> All young children are entitled to high quality early childhood education and care. Educating young children with significant disabilities is built on the idea that all children need meaningful opportunities within natural settings and with typical developing peers. All children, therefore, deserve to have age appropriate and positive learning experiences. (1999, p. 1)

Other aspects of early intervention and education valued by TASH are 1) responding to individual priorities and choices; 2) maintaining a healthy partnership between families and professionals; 3) utilizing technology to ensure young children are able to interact with their world; and 4) providing supports that are integrated, coordinated, and embedded into naturally occurring routines and activities. Outcomes such as peer relationships, competence, and self-esteem are considered important. Thus, the education and intervention for young children with severe disabilities should center on developing skills, membership, and relationships (Snell & Brown, 2011). Several issues of importance to this vision are discussed in the following sections.

Inclusion

Inclusion is the foundation for the intervention and education of young children with severe disabilities because within the context of inclusive settings membership and relationships with peers without disabilities develop (Buysse, Goldman, & Skinner, 2002; Odom, Zercher, Li, Marquart, & Sandall, 2006; TASH, 2010). In 2006, 85.5% of infants and toddlers served under Part C of IDEA 2004 received services in their homes, 5.3% received services in community-based settings (i.e., those settings in which children without disabilities are usually found), and 9.2% received services in "other" settings (i.e., hospitals, residential facilities, clinics, early intervention centers for children with disabilities) (U.S. Department of Education, 2008). A regular early childhood program was the setting in which the largest percentage of 3- to 5-year-olds (i.e., 44.5%) received Part B services at least 80% of the time. More than half of the preschoolers receiving services were more isolated, however. That is, 7.4% of preschoolers spent only 40%–79% of their time in regular early childhood programs, and 11.3% spent less than 40% of their time in regular early childhood programs. Of the remaining preschoolers, 24.2% received services in separate special education classes; 7.8% by a service provider without attendance at a special education or early childhood program; and 4.8% in a separate school, in a residential facility, or at home (U.S. Department of Education, 2008).

These data indicate that although the majority of infants and toddlers were receiving services in natural environments (i.e., 85.5% in home; 5.3% in community settings), few (i.e., 5.3%) did so in inclusive early care and education settings. In addition, the majority of preschoolers were isolated from peers without disabilities for the majority of time. The National Professional Development Center on Inclusion, a center funded by the Office of Special Education Programs (OSEP), concluded that "universal access to inclusive programs is not yet a reality for all children from birth to age 5 with disabilities" (2009, p. 2). The lack of progress in increasing opportunities for inclusion since the mid-2000s is surprising because research has documented the ability of teachers to include children with severe disabilities in all aspects of early childhood programs (e.g., Hanline & Correa-Torres, 2012; Kliewer et al., 2004), as well as increases in language, social, cognitive, and literacy development for all children, including those with severe disabilities, in inclusive settings (e.g., Buysse et al., 2002; Holahan & Costenbader, 2000; Rafferty, Piscitelli, & Boettcher, 2003).

These studies demonstrated that inclusive programming is a viable and productive educational reality. However, for inclusion to be successful, early care and education programs must be of high quality. Program quality is the foundation on which the supports and services to meet the individual needs of young children with severe disabilities are built (Sandall, Schwartz, & Joseph, 2001). Although the field does not have exact standards or one agreed-on approach to evaluate early childhood programs, two dimensions typically are included in program evaluation efforts. The first, process quality, includes such factors as interactions, activities, materials, learning opportunities, and health and safety routines. The second dimension, structural quality, includes the size of each group of children, the adult–child ratio, and the education and training of the teachers and staff (Espinosa, 2002).

These factors are critical to the educational outcomes of all children and to the successful inclusion of children with severe disabilities. The National Association for the Education of Young Children (NAEYC; 2009), however, estimates that as many as 40% of infant and toddler care settings potentially might be harmful to children's healthy development. Furthermore, the National Institute for Early Childhood Research (NIEER) concluded in its annual report on the state of preschools in the country that only 12 states could be verified as providing enough per-child funding to state-funded prekindergarten (pre-K) programs to meet all 10 NIEER benchmarks for quality standards (Barnett, Carolan, Fitzgerald, & Squires, 2011). The lack of consistent quality in early care and education programs, attributed in part to a continual decline in federal and state funding along with the struggle to maintain a well-qualified early childhood caregiving and teaching force, presents challenges to the inclusion of young children with severe disabilities.

Systematic and Individualized Instruction

Although the overall quality of early care and education programs facilitates inclusion that results in forming relationships and membership, inclusion alone will not necessarily result in children with severe disabilities learning critical functional and developmental skills in the areas of communication, social interactions, and self-determination (Dunst, 2012; Horn, Chambers, & Saito, 2009; Horn & Kang, 2012; Odom, Buysse, & Soukakou, 2011). Attaining these skills, however, can be supported within the context of early intervention services provided in the home, as well as inclusive early care and education settings, when systematic intervention strategies are embedded within daily routines and activities. Intentional instruction related to responsive parent–child interactions can be embedded in everyday family routines and activities in home-based early intervention (Smith, Romski, Sevcik, Adamson, & Bakeman, 2011). Systematic instruction can be embedded in the routines and activities of the center-based program in early care and education settings (Horn, Lieber, Li, Sandall, & Schwartz, 2000).

Using embedded instruction is a recommended practice in early intervention (Sandall, Hemmeter, Smith, & McLean, 2005) as well as in inclusive preschool programs (Horn et al., 2000). Emerging research documents its effectiveness for young children who evidence a range of disabilities (Wolery, 2005). Instruction embedded in daily routines and activities affords the opportunity to distribute practice across time, materials, and settings. These practices have been shown to be effective for teaching young children a variety of functional language, social, and literacy skills (e.g., Kaiser & Roberts, 2013) and to enhance generalization of learning (Strain, Schwartz, & Barton, 2012; Wolery & Hemmeter, 2011). Horn et al. (2009) suggested that the effectiveness of the embedded instruction might be enhanced by using modifications, including environmental support; adapting materials; providing special equipment; using children's preferences; simplifying the activity; providing adult support; providing peer support; and rearranging naturally occurring activities to support the child's participation (i.e., invisible supports).

Valued outcomes can be achieved by using embedded instruction and other modifications. For instance, young children with severe disabilities can learn self-determination through instruction that teaches them to make choices, make their choices known to others, and have those choices honored. The ability to demonstrate self-determination comes, in part, by being able to communicate one's wants and needs. The ability to communicate often is delayed, idiosyncratic, and contextualized in young children with severe disabilities (Carter & Iacono, 2002), so targeted communication skills often include gestures, prelinguistic vocalizations, and eye gaze. Augmentative and alternative communication (AAC) (Schlosser & Sigafoos, 2006) and other assistive technology may be used to promote communication and self-determination. Young children with severe disabilities have learned basic signaling skills, choice making, and independent power mobility through AAC and assistive technology. Yet, research identifying effective teaching strategies and use of the technology to promote engagement in everyday activities and routines is lacking (Campbell, Milbourne, Dugan, & Wilcox, 2006).

Challenging behavior is an additional area of concern that can cause the child's placement within an inclusive early education program to be in jeopardy. Researchers indicated that early educators lack the skills and resources to effectively intervene with challenging behavior, and data on preschool expulsions indicate that young children who have persistent challenging behavior often are expelled from programs (Gilliam, 2005). Although there has been substantial progress with implementing positive behavior interventions and supports within early childhood programs, the implementation is not widespread. The lack of effective intervention when young children have challenging behavior is a critical concern because substantial research indicates that without intervention, those behavior challenges will continue to intensify and compromise the child's future outcomes (Dunlap & Fox, 2011).

Service Delivery Transitions

The early childhood years involve numerous service delivery transitions for children with severe disabilities and their families. These transitions include taking the child home from the hospital or birth center, entering the early intervention service delivery system, and making the transition from early intervention to preschool and then from preschool to kindergarten (Rous & Hallam, 2011). Effective and supportive services during these times are related to more positive child and family outcomes (e.g., Lo Casale-Crouch, Mashburn, Downer, & Pianta, 2008) and should be included in the delivery of early intervention and education services.

Children with severe disabilities generally are identified prenatally, at birth, or shortly thereafter because the disabilities are often the result of chromosomal/ genetic differences or neurobiological causes resulting in disabilities that are visibly evident (Batshaw, Roizen, & Lotrecchiano, 2013). This early identification necessitates a transition to home that is different from what the families anticipated. Families might make the transition to home with early intervention services already in place, or they might enter the early intervention system earlier than families whose children have more mild disabilities (Hebbeler et al., 2007). No research regarding this transition has been conducted for children specifically identified as having severe disabilities, although research in the 1990s indicated that families taking premature infants home from the neonatal intensive care unit required extensive support, such as parent-to-parent contact, assistance in obtaining family-centered community services, and the use of discharge procedures that facilitate continued parent–professional communication (e.g., Bruder & Cole, 1991; Hanline & Deppe, 1990). Families also might need individualized services to respond to the health needs (e.g., seizure medication, tracheostomies, feeding tubes) that often accompany severe disabilities. This transition of entering the early intervention service delivery system is not anticipated by most parents and significantly adds to the stress of adapting to parenthood (Bernheimer & Weisner, 2007; Nelson, 2002).

Children make the transition to preschool at age 3 (i.e., Part B services). Although approximately one third of children receiving early intervention no longer receive IDEA 2004 services at age 3 (U.S. Department of Education, 2008), it is highly likely that children with severe disabilities will continue to need specialized services to develop skills, form relationships, and establish and maintain membership in a community. As most children receive early intervention in the home, this transition often begins the process of receiving services outside of the home. In addition, this transition involves a change from family-centered services to school-focused services. Furthermore, most preschoolers with severe disabilities receive their early education services in segregated settings, often highlighting the child's differences. These changes bring a myriad of challenges to children, families, and professionals. Effective transition supports and services during the transition to preschool focus on clearly articulated interagency agreements and transition policies, effective communication and collaboration among individuals in the different agencies, and collaboration from the provision of supports to the children and their families (Rous, Myers, & Stricklin, 2007).

Effective supports provided to children and families during the transition to kindergarten are similar to those needed during the transition from early intervention to preschool. Recommended family services include talking with families about the transition process, arranging visits to placement options, providing opportunities for parent-to-parent contact, and establishing personal contact between the parents and new teacher. Recommended supports for children include visits to the new school to learn about the physical and social environments and providing a curriculum that teaches skills needed in the new educational setting. Making a transition to a new educational setting might be more challenging for children with severe disabilities than for other children because skill generalization and learning a new environment can be more challenging for them. It is not likely that children with severe disabilities will have established relationships with children who will be attending their preschool programs because they receive early intervention in the home. In addition, if they do not make the transition from their preschool to kindergarten with friends, then establishing new relationships and becoming a member of the new school community might be difficult. Therefore, close attention must be paid to the child's engagement in the physical and social environments of the new setting, as well as adaptation to the classroom culture (Rous et al., 2007), so the goals of relationship formation and membership are reached.

Collaboration

The medical, education, and physical needs of children with severe disabilities cannot be met by one professional or by one agency (Snell & Brown, 2011); therefore, collaboration among professionals from diverse disciplines is required. Effective collaboration requires the sharing of knowledge and expertise among team members and the meaningful participation of family members and other caregivers (Giangreco, 2011). The quality of services and supports that actually are delivered to the child and family are ultimately reliant on the effectiveness of the collaboration and the ability of the early intervention and early childhood education professionals to ensure consistent delivery of high-quality instruction and support.

Barriers that make teaming a challenge exist, despite the critical importance of collaboration and teaming. Many providers in early intervention are independent contractors (i.e., do not work directly for an agency that provides services), and funding models often do not compensate contractors for the time devoted to collaborative teaming activities. Early educators are not granted time out of the classroom in early education programs, and there is minimal support for the release time required to consult with an early childhood special educator to either receive additional training or collaboratively plan individualized supports and instruction. These barriers present such formidable challenges that actual collaboration is minimal, resulting in services that are fragmented or poorly implemented.

IMPLICATIONS FOR PERSONNEL PREPARATION

Children with severe disabilities and their families face unique and compounded challenges, beyond those shared by all children and families, related to securing support across need areas. Rapidly diversifying demographic features of families and communities further complicate the context in which services to these families are implemented. Understandably, the personnel who work with this population should initially and continually be prepared for this reality. Yet, professional development in early childhood education, early childhood special education, and related services often is not reflective of these needs, and persistent shortages of qualified personnel endure at both state and national levels (Able-Boone, Crais, & Downing, 2003).

The preservice preparation of teachers and related services personnel historically has been comprised of discrete, segregated preparation programs marked by disjointed experiences, often only loosely connected to authentic family and community needs and contexts. This issue is further compounded by the need to procure discipline-specific licenses, and the historic fact that different philosophies of service delivery drive the various disciplines (Bruder & Dunst, 2005). In-service professional development also is documented as being disconnected from the needs essential to effective early intervention and early childhood services for children with severe disabilities (Bruder, Mogro-Wilson, Stayton, & Dietrich, 2009). Although in-service training across the early childhood landscape now exists in most states, the content and format often are marked by the absence of recommended practices (Bruder et al., 2009).

Yet, the reality of work in early intervention or early childhood requires practitioners to respond to growing diversity in the population of children and families served with a larger and more flexible skill set (Bruder et al., 2009; Horn & Kang, 2012; Ryndak, Clark, Conroy, & Holthaus-Stuart, 2001), including a focus on implementing evidence-based practices (Dunst, 2009; Odom, 2009; Odom & Wolery, 2003). This is compounded by the presence of a severe disability. Indeed, just as families are faced with both typical challenges and challenges related to their child's severe disability, professionals working with them must be armed with the specialized knowledge and skills particular to specific severe disabilities, in addition to the competencies required for effective services for all young children with disabilities (Able-Boone et al., 2003; Horn & Kang, 2012). The following section describes a few of the critical issues that greatly affect the preparation of professionals involved in early intervention and early childhood special education.

Context of Preparation

Early intervention and early childhood education services and supports were designed to be delivered in a manner that was family centered, interdisciplinary, and collaborative (Klein & Gilkerson, 2000; Sandall et al., 2005). With that framework came recommendations for personnel preparation for the highly variable cadre of professionals who would encompass the early childhood professional community. The breadth of the professional work force involved is certainly wide and includes not only professionals with special education or child development training, but also occupational therapists, physical therapists, nurses, speech-language pathologists (SLPs), paraprofessionals, audiologists, nutritionists, social workers, counselors, psychologists, and service coordinators (Sopko, 2010).

Professionals who are trained to provide early childhood services must be prepared for the diverse settings in which their services might be provided. In Part C early intervention services, professionals typically work in home or community early childhood program settings (i.e., family child care, early care and education, early Head Start). For professionals delivering preschool services (ages 3–5 years), those service settings might include private child care centers, home-based centers, Head Start, state-funded pre-K, and public school early childhood programs (Kagan, Kauerz, & Tarrant, 2008).

In addition to the presence of numerous professional roles and service settings, requirements for working in early childhood education contexts vary. States were asked in a survey to identify the requirements for professionals to serve as Part C service providers. Examination of results for early interventionists (i.e., early childhood special educators or the equivalent of instructional personnel) illustrated that a majority of states (73.2%) require a bachelor's degree (Sopko, 2010). Only 39%, however, require state certification, and 9.8% report no requirement at all (Sopko, 2010). A similar issue is the requirement for early education teachers. Although state teaching certification is a common requirement for early childhood special educators and early educators working in the public schools, the preparation requirements for community early care and education personnel can be minimal. Numerous early childhood settings across the states do not require staff to have either college degrees or specific certification (Stayton et al., 2009). The National Child Care Information and Technical Assistance Center (2011) reported that the preservice education requirement for a teacher in a child care program was zero hours of training in 27 states. In Head Start settings, less than half the teachers have a bachelor's degree (Government Accountability Office [GAO], 2012).

Recommendations for Personnel Preparation

TASH (2002) published a resolution pertaining to teacher education that confirmed the crucial contribution of university programs to ensuring quality and inclusive education for children with severe disabilities. Coming from TASH's *Resolution on Quality Inclusive Education,* which provides the foundational moral imperative for the education of students with disabilities in inclusive general education classes with same-age peers, the teacher education resolution asserted that

Teacher education programs must be inclusive and collaborative, so that (a) special and general educators are prepared to meet the needs of all students through collaboration and effective teaching, and (b) the expertise required to meet the individualized needs of each student is easily accessible on education teams. (2002, p. 1)

Furthermore, TASH (2002) emphasized that teachers should be prepared at two levels—the initial entry level, with teachers possessing a broad base of knowledge in general and special education and an advanced level, with specialists having additional expertise in either general education or special education. The expertise for working with students with the most severe disabilities would occur at the advanced level. This is not to say that initial teacher education programs would not address severe disabilities. It is vital that initial teacher preparation programs prepare all teachers to create inclusive communities of learners and acquire basic expertise related to serving students with severe disabilities in such settings (TASH, 2002). Advanced training would provide teachers with in-depth knowledge and skills related to specialization for meeting the educational needs of students with severe disabilities, such as using current effective practices, and the ability to blend research and theory into all aspects of educational environments (TASH, 2002).

Much of what has been discussed here pertains to education professionals trained in the context of undergraduate and graduate programs. Early care and education professionals, however, represent another substantial teacher population in the early childhood arena and are integral members of collaborative teams who work with children and families. Training for such professionals gradually is improving but remains marked by severe limitations fueled by the fact that this sector of the early childhood work force faces low wages and related minimal education requirements. The average income for community-based early education and care workers was documented in a federal report on the status of the early childhood and education work force as ranging from $11,500 to $18,000 per year for various positions (GAO, 2012). The combination of minimal requirements pertaining to professional credentials and low wages led to an early care and education work force with limited educational preparation for working with children, nonetheless children with severe disabilities. Yet, if inclusive opportunities are to be realized for young children with severe disabilities, then these important professionals need professional development that prepares them to create and sustain meaningful inclusive educational contexts.

Preparation of Medical Personnel and Related Services Professionals

Many different professional roles are involved in providing early intervention and early childhood education, and this group is not limited to educators. Related services personnel (e.g., occupational and physical therapists, SLPs) and medical professionals are integral members of support networks and providers of services for children with severe disabilities. Furthermore, the contexts in which early childhood services should be provided are conceptualized with principles rooted in family-centered, interdisciplinary, and collaborative services (Klein & Gilkerson, 2000). All personnel working with young children and their families must be prepared to work as members of interdisciplinary teams to realize this vision.

Medical personnel are involved in all children's lives, but they often are even more central in the lives of children with severe disabilities. The American Medical Association (AMA) recognized that medical professionals are prepared to fulfill a primary role of diagnostician and identify appropriate interventions with the intent to cure, or at least ameliorate, a patient's disorder (Kohrman, 2006). Patients with chronic disease or disability, therefore, can be confounding to physicians. Kohrman noted in the AMA *Journal of Ethics,*

> For [patients with chronic conditions and/or disability], improvement may be unlikely or incremental at best, and maintenance of the status quo is often the best to be hoped for. When the patient with the chronic condition is a child, the frustrations seem even greater; we see in childhood the promise of growth and attainment of new skills leading to competent adulthood, a state that many chronically disabled children will never achieve. To add to our confusion and frustration, many of these children's lives are dependent upon complicated technologies that require sophisticated medical skills to initiate and immense vigilance and dedication by the child's caretakers to sustain. We are rarely prepared, however, to help in the organization of the myriad services that families of disabled children must count on when the child is at home, especially those in nonmedical realms, such as school, transportation and respite services. (2006, p. 685)

Medical professionals are faced with the philosophical notion of fixing problems and are challenged when faced with aspects of diversity and disability that do not lend themselves to such an approach. Kohrman (2006) illuminated that doctors and other medical professionals simply are not prepared for the complex support children with severe disabilities and their families require.

This complex support system includes a myriad of other professionals as well. Almost half of the children receiving early intervention services received related services from occupational and physical therapists as well as SLPs (Campbell, Chiarello, Wilcox, & Milbourne, 2009). These professionals traditionally have been trained in preparation programs that are separate not only from education but also from each other. Each professional organization has developed professional standards and has adopted recommended practices for early intervention and early childhood contexts (Campbell et al., 2009). However, likely due to the breadth of content required of licensure, which usually is across the life span, most related services providers receive little training specific to early intervention and early childhood or pertaining to young children with severe disabilities (Campbell et al., 2009). This creates a significant conundrum, given the vision for early intervention and childhood services, and represents an additional barrier to implementing interdisciplinary, family-centered services for any child.

Bruder and Dunst (2005) also examined the emphasis on recommended early intervention practice found across the disciplines of early childhood special education, occupational and physical therapy, speech-language pathology, and multidisciplinary programs. Their findings indicated that the major recommended practices (e.g., family-centered services, IFSPs, natural environments, teaming, service coordination) are not fully embedded in professional preservice programs. Effective services for children with severe disabilities and their families require a high level of collaboration and interdisciplinary practice. In-service professional development around these recommended practices for early intervention also is seen to be lacking for professionals (Campbell et al., 2009).

Clearly, if general recommended practice for early intervention and early childhood services is not well established in preparatory and in-service professional development requirements and programs, then the programs are not likely to fully prepare graduates as effective, collaborative, and interdisciplinary professionals who work most effectively with children and families. It is of no surprise that many therapists express a lack of competence for working with young children and their families (Campbell et al., 2009). This is an echoed sentiment in education, as well, in which many traditionally prepared general educators continue to express reservations regarding their ability to practice inclusively (Blanton, Pugach, & Florian, 2011). The increased complexity and level of need presented by children with severe disabilities and their families, coupled with the characteristics of preparation for educators and related services providers, leads to a significant disconnect between recommended practice and the programs charged with preparing professionals to implement them.

Response and Capacity of Institutes of Higher Education

Institutes of higher education have reacted in several ways in response to desires to prepare early childhood teachers for working with ever diversifying groups of children in inclusive settings (Ryndak et al., 2001). Some have maintained discrete early childhood education and early childhood special education preparatory programs, whereas others have engaged in variations of collaborative approaches to personnel preparation. This primarily is seen in teacher education across early childhood education and early childhood special education with the creation of blended (i.e., unified) personnel preparation programs. Blended programs entail "the purposeful integration of general and special education at the preservice level, and [are] increasingly characterized by graduates earning two (or more) teaching licenses either

simultaneously or sequentially, [and are] an unmistakable trend in the initial preparation of teachers today" (Pugach, Blanton, & Correa, 2011, p. 183). The NAEYC
and the Division for Early Childhood (DEC) developed standards and accreditation
criteria specific to blended early childhood teacher education programs. A blended
early childhood professional preparation program combines all the elements called
for in NAEYC's early childhood standards and those in the Council for Exceptional
Children's (CEC) early childhood special education standards in a curriculum that
is planned, implemented, and evaluated by an interdisciplinary group of faculty and
other individuals (Hyson, 2003). Licensure in some states also has been observed
to have evolved in response to the emergence of blended teacher licensure (Piper,
2007; Stayton & McCollum, 2002; Stayton & Miller, 1993).

A strong case has been made in favor of collaboration and unification of early
childhood and early childhood special education for decades (Piper, 2007). In fact,
the vast majority of the literature on the topic is conceptual and descriptive in nature
and seeks specifically to justify the practice and philosophy. The literature includes
discussions of the social, moral, legal, and educational benefits of inclusive services
for all children (e.g., Bailey, McWilliam, Buysse, & Wesley, 1998; Kilgo & Bruder,
1997; Odom et al., 2011), as well as specific calls for inclusive services for young
children with disabilities (e.g., Gargiulo, Sluder, & Streitenberger, 1997). Indeed,
some have argued that separate personnel preparation is "immoral and inefficient"
(Miller, 1992, p. 39). Lim and Able-Boone (2005) argued that the need to infuse
diversity into all aspects of teacher education further supports the notion of blended
preparation programs, and Xu, Gelfer, and Filler (2003) called for alternative models
for preparing early childhood teachers, based on similar views regarding diversity.

The argument for blended preparation programs appears centered on a social
justice perspective for inclusive education services (Piper, 2007) and the well-
documented inadequacy in general early childhood education programs to prepare
teachers for diverse inclusive education contexts (Stayton & McCollum, 2002). Some
argue, however, that specific aspects of special education preparation could be lost
with fully blended preparation programs. For example, Clifford, Macy, Albi, Bricker,
and Rahn (2005) stated that early intervention and early childhood special education comprise a legitimate professional field whose personnel require specialized
preparation and licensure. They further stressed the need for early childhood special education personnel to experience authentic field experiences to acquire clinical intervention skills. Many also argue that the emphasis on blending or merging
regular and special education has afforded less time and opportunity to cover particular content focused on disabilities, especially low-incidence disabilities (Able-
Boone et al., 2003).

Winton (2000) suggested a process of backward mapping when designing
and conducting personnel preparation. The field has identified the components of
high-quality services for children with disabilities and their families, and the preceding sections of this chapter illuminate the unique contexts and needs of children with severe disabilities and their families. Taken together, the components of
high-quality services and the particulars of working with this population can aid in
identifying personnel preparation needs for professionals who will work with young
children with severe disabilities and their families. Most notably, personnel must
be well prepared to understand and empower families who are striving to navigate complex systems. In addition, personnel must work as members of collabora-

tive interdisciplinary teams and successfully navigate the multifarious landscape of roles and responsibilities involved in providing early intervention and early childhood services. The nature of the preservice preparation of professionals and ensuring competency in the critical skill sets needed to work collaboratively to ensure the inclusion and active participation of very young children and their families within their communities are the critical issues that continue to challenge the vision of providing high-quality early intervention and early education services.

SUMMARY

This chapter described the issues and challenges for providing effective early intervention and early education services to young children with severe disabilities and their families. The early years are pivotal to a child's future access to inclusive education, community living, and employment for several reasons. First, this is the entry point for children and families into a service system. Thus, the system must be supported by policy and funding to provide effective intervention that can maximize the abilities of the child and support the family in ensuring that their child experiences equity, diversity, and quality of life. Second, the notion of inclusion begins with early care and education settings where children and parents can realize that typically developing children and children with disabilities are more alike than different and where young children with severe disabilities can experience their first friendships. The quality of that experience, however, can have a significant impact on a family's perspective about the importance of a child's inclusion with peers who do not have disabilities. Inclusive early care and education must provide high-quality programs and effective interventions so that families are confident about the value of inclusion both for their children with disabilities and for society. Finally, the early years of development are critical to a child's overall learning trajectory. This is the time in which the foundation of all academic learning occurs. Children must receive effective supports during these years to develop the communication, mobility, and preacademic skills that will be vital to their future learning. Intervention and assistive technology cannot wait for a more optimal time or sufficient resources during the early years. The ultimate goal of early intervention and early education is to support the child's self-determination, ability to be independent, engagement in learning, communication, and development of meaningful social relationships with peers and adults.

Questions for Study and Reflection

1. Early intervention and early education services are provided in natural settings versus school programs. How does this diverse context for the delivery of services and supports create issues for ensuring that optimal services and supports are provided? How might the diversity of settings offer opportunities to strengthen the supports that are provided to the child and family and the child and family's access to community inclusion?

2. The role of the early interventionist and early educator is to build the capacity of the family to support their child's development and to ensure that a quality education program is provided to children with disabilities. What is the implication of this role for the importance of collaboration with family members and other professionals? What skills might be needed by the early intervention and early childhood special education professional to fill this role?

3. The goal for early intervention and early childhood special education is to promote the child's progress toward meaningful outcomes. Although inclusive employment, community living, and full participation might seem like a future concern for a parent of a toddler or preschooler, the foundation for those goals begins in the early childhood years. What can professionals do to support families in understanding the critical importance of eliminating the physical and social obstacles that prevent equality, diversity, and quality of life for their children?

4. The importance of voice and self-determination is a critical issue for individuals with severe disabilities. How might families and professionals ensure that very young children receive opportunities to express their feelings and preferences, make decisions, and establish independence? What supports might be necessary for the family and child? What experiences should be offered to the child in the early years to begin the path of self-determination?

RESOURCES

The following resources provide more information related to early intervention and early childhood programs.

The Center for Evidence-Based Practices is an applied research center of the Orelena Hawks Puckett Institute. The major aim of its activities and initiatives is to bridge the research-to-practice gap in early intervention, early childhood education, parent and family support, and family-centered practices by conducting research, preparing practice-based research syntheses, and producing evidence-based products. *http://www.evidencebasedpractices.org/index.php*

The DEC of the CEC is a nonprofit organization advocating for individuals who work with or on behalf of children with special needs, birth through age 8, and their families. The DEC was founded in 1971 and is dedicated to promoting policies and practices that support families and enhance the optimal development of children. *http://www.dec-sped.org/index.aspx*

The Early Childhood Technical Assistance Center is funded by the Office of Special Education Programs to improve state early intervention and early childhood special education service systems, increase the implementation of effective practices, and enhance the outcomes of these programs for young children and their families. *http:// ectacenter.org*

The Early Intervention Family Alliance is a national group of family leaders dedicated to improving outcomes for infants and toddlers with disabilities and their families. It works to assure meaningful family involvement in developing Part C policies and implementing them at community, state, and federal levels. *http:// www.eifamilyalliance.org*

The NAEYC is the leading membership association for those working with and on behalf of children from birth through age 8. NAEYC convenes thought leaders, teachers and other practitioners, researchers, and other stakeholders and sets standards of excellence for programs and teachers in early childhood education. NAEYC members include teachers, paraeducators, center directors, trainers, college educators, families of young children, and the public at large. *http://www .naeyc.org*

The Technical Assistance Center on Social Emotional Intervention for Young Children takes the research that shows which practices improve the social-emotional outcomes for young children with, or at risk for, delays or disabilities and creates free products and resources to help decision makers, caregivers, and service providers apply these recommended practices in the work they do every day. *http:// www.challengingbehavior.org*

REFERENCES

Able-Boone, H., Crais, E., & Downing, K. (2003). Preparation of early intervention practitioners for working with young children with low incidence disabilities. *Teacher Education and Special Education, 26,* 79–82.

Addy, S., & White, V.R. (2012a). *Basic facts about low-income children, 2010: Children under age 6.* New York, NY: National Center for Children in Poverty. Retrieved from http://www.nccp.org

Addy, S., & White, V.R. (2012b). *Basic facts about low-income children, 2010. Children under age 3.* New York, NY: National Center for Children in Poverty. Retrieved from http://www.nccp.org

Bailey, D.B., Hebbeler, K., Scarborough, A., Spiker, D., & Mallik, S. (2004). First experiences with early intervention: A national perspective. *Pediatrics, 113,* 887–896.

Bailey, D.B., McWilliam, R.A., Buysse, V., & Wesley, P.W. (1998). Inclusion in the context of competing values in early childhood education. *Early Childhood Research Quarterly, 13,* 27–47.

Barnett, W.S., Carolan, M.E., Fitzgerald, J., & Squires, J.H. (2011). *The state of preschool 2011: State preschool yearbook.* New Brunswick, NJ: National Institute for Early Education Research.

Batshaw, M.L., Roizen, N.J., & Lotrecchiano, G.R. (Eds.). (2013). *Children with disabilities* (7th ed.). Baltimore, MD: Paul H. Brookes Publishing Co.

Bernheimer, L.P., & Weisner, T.S. (2007). "Let me just tell you what I do all day:" The family story at the center of intervention research and practice. *Infants and Young Children, 20,* 192–201.

Blanton, L.P., Pugach, M.C., & Florian, L. (2011). *Preparing general education teachers to improve outcomes for students with disabilities.* Washington, DC: American Association of Colleges for Teacher Education & National Center for Learning Disabilities.

Bruder, M.B. (2010). Early childhood intervention: A promise to children and families for their future. *Exceptional Children, 76,* 339–356.

Bruder, M.B., & Cole, M. (1991). Critical elements of transition from NICU to home and follow-up. *Children's Health Care, 20,* 40–49.

Bruder, M., & Dunst, C. (2005). Personnel preparation in recommended early intervention practices: Degree of emphasis across disciplines. *Topics in Early Childhood Special Education, 25,* 25–33.

Bruder, M., Mogro-Wilson, C., Stayton, V., & Dietrich, S. (2009). The national status of in-service professional development systems for early intervention and early childhood special education practitioners. *Infants and Young Children, 22,* 13–20.

Buysse, V., Goldman, B.D., & Skinner, M.L. (2002). Setting effects on friendship formation among young children with and without disabilities. *Exceptional Children, 68,* 503–517.

Campbell, P., Chiarello, L., Wilcox, M.J., & Milbourne, S. (2009). Preparing therapists as effective practitioners in early intervention. *Infants and Young Children, 22,* 21–31.

Campbell, P.H., Milbourne, S., Dugan, L.M., & Wilcox, M.J.(2006). A review of the evidence on practices for teaching young children to use assistive technology devices. *Topics in Early Childhood Special Education, 26,* 3–13.

Carter, M., & Iacono, T. (2002). Professional judgments of the intentionality of communicative acts. *Augmentative and Alternative Communication, 19,* 155–169.

Clifford, J.R., Macy, M.G., Albi, L.D., Bricker, D.D., & Rahn, N.L. (2005). A model of clinical supervision for preservice professionals in early intervention and early childhood special education. *Topics in Early Childhood Special Education, 25,* 167–176.

Dunlap, G., & Fox, L. (2011). Function-based interventions for children with challenging behavior. *Journal of Early Intervention, 33,* 333–343.

Dunst, C. (2009). Implications of evidence-based practices for personnel preparation development in early childhood intervention. *Infants and Young Children, 22,* 44–53.

Dunst, C. (2012). Parapatric speciation in the evolution of early intervention for infants and toddlers with disabilities and their families. *Topics in Early Childhood Special Education, 31,* 208–215.

Education of the Handicapped Act Amendments of 1986, PL 99-457, 20 U.S.C. §§ 1400 *et seq.*

Espinosa, L.M. (2002). *High quality preschool: Why we need it and what it looks like.* New Brunswick, NJ: National Institute for Early Education Research.

Fujiura, G.L., & Yamaki, K. (2000). Trends in demography of childhood poverty and disability. *Exceptional Children, 66,* 187–200.

Gargiulo, R.M., Sluder, L.C., & Streitenberger, D. (1997). Preparing early childhood educators for inclusive programs: A call for professional unification. *Early Childhood Education Journal, 25,* 137–139.

Giangreco, M. (2011). Foundational concepts and practices for educating students with severe disabilities. In M.E. Snell & F. Brown (Eds.), *Instruction of students with severe disabilities* (7th ed., pp. 1–30). Upper Saddle River, NJ: Merrill-Pearson.

Gilliam, W.S. (2005). *Prekindergarteners left behind: Expulsion rates in state prekindergarten systems.* Unpublished manuscript, Yale University, New Haven, CT.

Government Accountability Office. (2012). *Early childhood education: HHS and education are taking steps to improve workforce data and enhance worker quality.* Washington, DC: U.S. Government Printing Office.

Guralnick, M.J. (2005). Early intervention for children with intellectual disabilities: Current knowledge and future prospects. *Journal of Applied Research in Intellectual Disabilities, 18,* 313–324.

Hanline, M.F., & Correa-Torres, S.M. (2012). Social experiences of preschoolers with severe disabilities in an inclusive early education setting: A qualitative study. *Education and Training in Autism and Developmental Disabilities, 47,* 109–121.

Hanline, M.F., & Deppe, J. (1990). Discharging the premature infant: Family issues and implications for intervention. *Topics in Early Childhood Special Education, 9,* 15–25.

Hebbeler, K., Spiker, D., Bailey, D.B., Scarborough, A., Mallik, S., Simeonsson, R., ... Nelson, L. (2007). *Early intervention for infants and toddlers with disabilities and their families: Participants, services, and outcomes.* Menlo Park, CA: SRI International.

Hebbeler, K., Spiker, D., & Kahn, L. (2012). Individuals with Disabilities Education Act's early childhood programs: Powerful vision and pesky details. *Topics in Early Childhood Special Education, 31,* 199–207.

Holahan, A., & Costenbader, V. (2000). A comparison of developmental gains for preschool children with disabilities in inclusive and self-contained classrooms. *Topics in Early Childhood Special Education, 20,* 224–235.

Horn, E., Chambers, C., & Saito, Y. (2009). Techniques for teaching young children with moderate/severe or multiple disabilities. In S. Raver (Ed.), *Early childhood special education: 0 to 8 years: Strategies for positive outcomes* (pp. 255–278). Upper Saddle River, NJ: Merrill-Pearson.

Horn, E., & Kang, J. (2012). Supporting young children with multiple disabilities: What do we know and what do we still need to learn? *Topics in Early Childhood Special Education, 31,* 241–248.

Horn, E., Lieber, J., Li, S., Sandall, S., & Schwartz, I. (2000). Supporting young children's IEP goals in inclusive settings through embedded learning opportunities. *Topics in Early Childhood Special Education, 20,* 208–223.

Hyson, M. (Ed.). (2003). *Preparing early childhood professionals: NAEYC's standards for programs.* Washington, DC: National Association for the Education of Young Children.

Individuals with Disabilities Education Improvement Act (IDEA) of 2004, PL 108-446, 20 U.S.C. §§ 1400 *et seq.*

Kagan, S.L., Kauerz, K., & Tarrant, K. (2008). *The early care and education teaching workforce at the fulcrum: An agenda for reform.* New York, NY: Teachers College Press.

Kaiser, A.P., & Roberts, M.Y. (2013). Parent-implemented enhanced milieu teaching with preschool children with intellectual disabilities. *Journal of Speech, Language, and Hearing Research, 56,* 295–309.

Kilgo, J., & Bruder, M.B. (1997). Creating new visions in institutions of higher education: Interdisciplinary approaches to personnel preparation in early intervention. In P.J. Winton, J.A. McCollum, & C. Catlett (Eds.), *Reforming personnel preparation in early intervention: Issues, models, and practical strategies* (pp. 81–101). Baltimore, MD: Paul H. Brookes Publishing Co.

Klein, N.K., & Gilkerson, L. (2000). Personnel preparation for early childhood intervention programs. In J.P. Shonkoff & S.J. Meisels (Eds.), *The handbook of early childhood intervention* (2nd ed., pp. 454–486). New York, NY: Cambridge University Press.

Kliewer, C., Fitzgerald, L.M., Meyer-Mork, J., Hartman, P., English-Sand, P., & Raschke, D. (2004). Citizenship for all in the literate community: An ethnography of young children with significant disabilities in inclusive early childhood settings. *Harvard Educational Review, 74,* 373–403.

Kohrman, A. (2006). Medicine and society: Talking with families about severely disabled children. *American Medical Association Journal of Ethics, 8,* 685–688.

Lim, C.I., & Able-Boone, H. (2005). Diversity competencies within early childhood teacher preparation: Innovative practices and future directions. *Journal of Early Childhood Teacher Education, 26,* 225–238.

Lo Casale-Crouch, J., Mashburn, A.J., Downer, J.T., & Pianta, R.C. (2008). Pre-kindergarten teachers' use of transition practices and children's adjustment to kindergarten. *Early Childhood Research Quarterly, 23,* 124–139.

McWilliam, R.A. (2012). Implementing and preparing for home visits. *Topics in Early Childhood Special Education, 31,* 224–231.

Miller, P. (1992). Segregated programs of teacher education in early childhood: Immoral and inefficient practice. *Topics in Early Childhood Special Education, 11,* 39–53.

Miodrag, N., & Hodapp, R.M. (2010). Chronic stress and health among parents of children with intellectual and developmental disabilities. *Current Opinion in Psychiatry, 23,* 407–411.

National Association for the Education of Young Children. (2009). *When babies and toddlers are in child care: Accreditation is a key to quality.* Retrieved from https://www.naeyc.org/resources/research/when+babies

National Child Care Information and Technical Assistance Center. (2011, July). *Minimum requirements for preservice qualifications and annual ongoing training hours for center teaching roles in 2011.* Retrieved from http://occ-archive.org/pubs/cclicensingreq/cclr-teachers.html

National Professional Development Center on Inclusion. (2009). *Research synthesis points on early childhood inclusion.* Chapel Hill: University of North Carolina, FPG Child Development Institute. Retrieved from http://npdci.fpg.unc.edu

Nelson, A.M. (2002). A metasynthesis: Mothering other-than-normal children. *Qualitative Health Research, 12,* 515–530.

Odom, S. (2009). The tie that binds: Evidence-based practice, implementation science, and outcomes for children. *Topics in Early Childhood Special Education, 29,* 53–61.

Odom, S.L., Buysse, V., & Soukakou, E. (2011). Inclusion for young children with disabilities: A quarter century of research perspectives. *Journal of Early Intervention, 33,* 344–356.

Odom, S.L., & Wolery, M. (2003). A unified theory of practice in early intervention/early childhood special education: Evidence-based practice. *Journal of Special Education, 37,* 164–173.

Odom, S.L., Zercher, C., Li, S., Marquart, J., & Sandall, S. (2006). Social acceptance and social rejection of young children with disabilities in inclusive classes. *Journal of Educational Psychology, 98,* 807–823.

Parish, S.L., Rose, R.A., Grinstein-Weiss, M., Richman, E.L., & Andrews, M.E. (2008). Material hardship in U.S. families raising children with disabilities. *Exceptional Children, 75,* 71–92.

Patrick, C., Padgett, D.K., Burns, B.J., Schlesinger, H.J., & Cohen, J. (1993). Use of inpatient services by a national population: Do benefits make a difference? *Journal of the American Academy of Child and Adolescent Psychiatry, 32,* 144–152.

Peterson, C.A., Luze, G.J., Eshbaugh, E.M., Jeon, H.J., & Kantz, K.R. (2007). Enhancing parent-child interactions through home visiting: Promising practice or unfulfilled promise? *Journal of Early Intervention, 29,* 119–140.

Piper, A.W. (2007). What we know about integrating early childhood education and early childhood special education teacher preparation programs: A review, a reminder, and a request. *Journal of Early Childhood Teacher Education, 28,* 163–180.

Pugach, M.C., Blanton, L.P., & Correa, V.I. (2011). A historical perspective on the role of collaboration in teacher education reform: Making good on the promise of teaching all students. *Teacher Education and Special Education, 34,* 183–200.

Rafferty, Y., Piscitelli, V., & Boettcher, C. (2003). The impact of inclusion on language development and social competence among preschoolers with disabilities. *Exceptional Children, 69,* 467–479.

Rous, B.S., & Hallam, R.A. (2011). Transition services for young children with disabilities: Research and future directions. *Topics in Early Childhood Special Education, 31,* 232–240.

Rous, B., Myers, C.T., & Stricklin, S.B. (2007). Strategies for supporting transitions of young children with special needs and their families. *Journal of Early Intervention, 30,* 1–18.

Ryndak, D.L., Clark, D., Conroy, M., & Holthaus-Stuart, C. (2001). Preparing teachers to meet the needs of students with severe disabilities: Program configuration and expertise. *Journal of The Association for Persons with Severe Handicaps, 26,* 96–105.

Sandall, S.R., Hemmeter, M.L., Smith, B.J., & McLean, M.E. (2005). *DEC recommended practices: A comprehensive guide for practical application in early intervention/early childhood special education.* Missoula, MT: Division for Early Childhood, Council for Exceptional Children.

Sandall, S., Schwartz, I., & Joseph, G. (2001). A building blocks model for effective instruction in inclusive early childhood settings. *Young Exceptional Children, 4,* 3–9.

Schlosser, R.W., & Sigafoos, J. (2006). AAC interventions for persons with developmental disabilities: Narrative review of comparative single subject experimental studies. *Research in Developmental Disabilities, 27,* 1–29.

Shonkoff, J.P. (2010). Building a new biodevelopmental framework to guide the future of early childhood policy. *Child Development, 81,* 357–367

Smith, A., Romski, M., Sevcik, A., Adamson, L.B., & Bakeman, R. (2011). Parent stress and its relation to parent perceptions of communication following parent-coached language intervention. *Journal of Early Intervention, 33,* 135–150.

Snell, M.E., & Brown, F. (2011). *Instruction of students with severe disabilities* (7th ed.). Upper Saddle River, NJ: Pearson.

Sopko, K.M. (2010). *Workforce preparation to serve children who receive Part C services.* Retrieved from http://www.projectforum.org/docs/WorkforcePreparationtoServeChildrenWhoReceivePartCSvcs.pdf

Stayton, V.D., & McCollum, J. (2002). Unifying general and special education: What does the research tell us? *Teacher Education and Special Education, 25,* 211–218.

Stayton, V.D., & Miller, P. (1993). Combining general and special education standards in personnel preparation programs: Experiences from two states. *Topics in Early Childhood Special Education, 13,* 372–387.

Stayton, V.D., Sylvia, L., Smith, B.J., Bruder, M.B., Mogro-Wilson, C., & Swigart, A. (2009). State certification requirements for early childhood special educators. *Infants and Young Children, 22,* 4–12.

Strain, P.S., Schwartz, I.S., & Barton, E.E. (2012). Providing interventions for young children with autism spectrum disorders: What we still need to accomplish. *Journal of Early Intervention, 33,* 321–332.

TASH. (1999). *Resolution on educating young children with significant disabilities.* Available at http://www.tash.org

TASH. (2000). *Resolution on quality inclusive education.* Available at http://www.tash.org

TASH. (2002). *TASH resolution on teacher education.* Available at http://www.tash.org

TASH. (2010). *TASH national agenda.* Available at http://www.tash.org

U.S. Department of Education. (2008). *30th annual report to Congress on the implementation of IDEA.* Washington, DC: Author.

Winton, P. (2000). Early childhood intervention personnel preparation. *Topics in Early Childhood Special Education, 20,* 87–94.

Wolery, M. (2005). DEC recommended practices: Child-focused practices. In S. Sandall, M.L. Hemmeter, B.J. Smith, & M.E. McLean (Eds.), *DEC recommended practices: A comprehensive guide for practical application in early intervention/early childhood special education* (pp. 71–106). Longmont, CO: Sopris West Educational Services.

Wolery, M., & Hemmeter, M.L. (2011). Classroom instruction: Background, assumptions, and challenges. *Journal of Early Intervention, 33,* 371–380.

Xu, Y., Gelfer J., & Filler, J. (2003). An alternative undergraduate teacher preparation program in early childhood education. *Early Child Development and Care, 173,* 489–497.

Inclusive Education and Meaningful School Outcomes

John McDonnell and Pam Hunt

Inclusive education for students with severe disabilities has been embraced as a recommended practice by advocacy groups, such as the American Association on Intellectual and Developmental Disabilities/The ARC, (2008), the National Down Syndrome Congress (2005), and TASH (2010), and professionals (Snell & Brown, 2011; Westling & Fox, 2009). Although the ultimate goal of inclusive education has always been to achieve students' equal access to the community and full participation in society, the strategies used to realize these goals have substantially changed since the mid-1990s. Consequently, the definition of inclusive education and what educational and social outcomes it should produce for students has also evolved (Hunt & McDonnell, 2007).

This chapter's purpose is to summarize what is currently known about inclusive education for students with severe disabilities and explore the issues that will affect the expansion and quality of these programs in the future. Specifically, it 1) provides a definition of inclusive education based on current knowledge, 2) reviews the most recent research on the effect of inclusive education on student achievement and growth, 3) discusses what educational and social outcomes should drive the design and implementation of inclusive education, 4) provides recommendations on strategies that may increase the ability of practitioners and individualized education program (IEP) teams to achieve meaningful outcomes for students in inclusive classes, and 5) discusses areas for future research.

INCLUSIVE EDUCATION:
COMMUNITY, DIVERSITY, AND COLLABORATION

The term *inclusion* began to appear in the literature around 1990 (e.g., Gartner & Lipsky, 1987; Sailor, 1991; Stainback & Stainback, 1990). The definitions of inclusive education and the description of inclusion models were focused almost wholly on the full-time placement of students with disabilities in general education classrooms (Sailor & Skrtic, 1995). Although the definitions of *inclusion* varied, there were a number of widely accepted programmatic features that included first, and foremost, the delivery of educational services to students with disabilities through full-time placement in chronologically age-appropriate general education classes, within the context of the core curriculum and general class activities, and in integrated community settings. In addition, students with disabilities attend schools that they would attend if they did not have an identified disability, their representation in schools and classrooms is in natural proportion to their representation in the district at large, and there is a zero-rejection district policy so that no student is excluded on the basis of type or extent of disability (Gartner & Lipsky, 1987; Sailor, 1991; Stainback & Stainback, 1990).

Contemporary discussions, however, often move beyond considering inclusive education as a special education service delivery model and focus on whole-school restructuring to create inclusive school communities in which all students are valued members. Emphasis is placed on educational policies and practices that ensure that all students have an equitable share of educational resources and can achieve their highest potential (Ainscow, Howes, Farrell, & Frankham, 2003; Ferguson, Kozleski, & Smith, 2005; Hunt & McDonnell, 2007; Sailor & Roger, 2005; Sailor & Skrtic, 1995; TASH, 2000); thus, the focus has shifted from inclusive education as special education policy and practice to designing educational arrangements to promote membership and achievement of all children, regardless of their differences in culture, gender, language, ability, class, and ethnicity (Ainscow et al., 2003; Ferguson et al., 2005; Saldana & Waxman, 1997; TASH, 2000). In addition, emphasis is placed on unifying school resources and integrating categorical programs in ways that benefit all students in general education classrooms (Ferguson et al., 2005; Miles & Darling-Hammond, 1998; Sailor & Roger, 2005).

All students in a successful inclusive school are presumed competent and able to benefit from the general education curriculum. Educators not only have high expectations for all students, but they also believe that they (the educators) can gain the knowledge and skills they need to effectively teach all students by engaging in collaborative working arrangements with other educators and family members (Ainscow et al., 2003; Ferguson et al., 2005; Hunt, Hirose-Hatae, Doering, Karasoff & Goetz, 2000; Sailor & Roger, 2005; Snell & Janney, 2005; TASH, 2000). Collaborative teaming provides the vehicle for blurring the lines between general, special, and bilingual education and other categorical programs to create a unified school system that "anchors its work in curriculum content, students' performance, and learning assessment strategies, all of which reflect learning outcomes that are valued by local communities and families and informed by national and state standards, curriculum frameworks, and assessment strategies" (Ferguson et al., 2005, p. 7). Fiscal and staff resources are allocated to promote the academic achievement and social development of all students in the school, and educational services are planned and delivered by qualified general and special education teachers and paraprofessional staff (Miles & Darling-Hammond, 1998; Sailor & Roger, 2005).

The collaborative teaming process provides opportunities for general and special educators and family members to share their knowledge, skills, and experience to identify strategies to individualize learning, increase students' engagement in educational activities, and support the development of positive social relationships (Giangreco, Cloninger, Dennis, & Edelman, 2002; Hunt, Soto, Maier, & Doering, 2003; Udvari-Solner & Thousand, 1995). Support plans generated through collaborative processes are based in real-life (local) knowledge and a shared repertoire of experiences with the child, and implementing the individualized supports requires joint enterprise and shared responsibility and accountability (Giangrego et al., 2002; Hunt et al., 2003; Mortier, Hunt, Leroy, De Schauwer, & Van Hove, 2010).

Faculty and staff in inclusive classrooms strive to create communities in which all students are valued members, and emphasis is placed on the value of diversity, multiculturalism, social justice, and belonging for everyone (Hunt et al., 2000; Kohn, 2006; Sapon-Shevin, 1990; TASH, 2000). Teachers promote community building by employing strategies to increase individual students' sense of identity and self-worth while, at the same time, increasing the students' capacity for cooperation, interdependence, and respect for cultural, language, and ability differences. Priority is given to implementing facilitation strategies and social supports to develop positive social relationships and friendships between classmates with and without disabilities. Students are given ongoing and structured opportunities to recognize each other's accomplishments. Literature is used to teach lessons addressing equity, cultural and ability diversity, and social justice, and regularly scheduled class meetings may be used for problem solving and conflict resolution (Gibbs, 1994; Hunt et al., 2000; Kohn, 2006; Sapon-Shevin, 1990).

Designing curriculum and employing instructional practices and technologies that make the core curriculum accessible and meaningful to all students is a final key dimension of inclusive schools. Universal Design for Learning principles guide curriculum development to ensure that 1) content is presented in different ways to increase accessibility, 2) students are given the opportunity to express what they know through multiple means, and 3) attention is given to engaging students in learning activities by stimulating their interest and motivation (Center for Applied Special Technology [CAST], 2012; Curry, 2003). In addition, differentiated instruction is used to develop and implement curricular and instructional adaptations and modifications needed to increase accessibility and engagement for all students, align IEP goals of students with disabilities with the general education curriculum, and support student progress in achieving those goals (Janney & Snell, 1997; Wehmeyer, 2006).

RESEARCH ON THE EFFECT OF INCLUSIVE EDUCATION

Research on the effect of inclusive education has examined a number of different outcomes for students and can be categorized into two broad groups. The first and largest group of studies examined the immediate effect of inclusive education on student educational achievement and social connectedness. The second group focused on the effect of inclusive education on students' postschool outcomes. This area of research has received surprisingly little attention in spite of the obvious importance of understanding how inclusive education affects the quality of students' lives after they leave school (Hunt & McDonnell, 2007; Ryndak, Alper, Hughes, & McDonnell, 2012). The following section summarizes the research on the short- and long-term outcomes of inclusive education.

Short-Term Outcomes of Inclusive Education

Research on inclusive education addressed a number of issues, including its effect on student achievement and learning, social connectedness, the characteristics and contexts of the instruction that students receive, and the validation of curriculum and instructional strategies that support students in general education classes (Hunt & McDonnell, 2007). A full review of this literature is beyond the scope of the present chapter, so we focus on selected studies examining the relative effectiveness of inclusive education on student achievement, friendships and social connections, and quality of instruction that students receive in inclusive education classes.

Academic Achievement and Student Learning   Several studies directly compared the academic achievement of students in inclusive and separate educational programs (Cole, Waldron, & Majd, 2004; Fisher & Meyer, 2002; Peetsma, Vergeer, Roeleveld, & Karsten, 2001). For example, Fisher and Meyer compared the development of adaptive behavior and the social competence of two matched groups of students with moderate to profound disabilities who were educated in general education classes for the majority of the school day or in self-contained special education classrooms. They found that only the students served in inclusive educational programs made significant gains in adaptive behavior and social competence. Comparisons between the groups showed that gains in adaptive behavior were significantly higher for students in inclusive classes than those in self-contained classes, and no significant differences in gains were found in social competence.

A common criticism of inclusive education is that placing students with disabilities in general education classrooms will negatively affect the achievement of peers without disabilities (Kauffman & Hallahan, 1995). Studies that have directly examined this issue, however, found that there is no effect on the academic performance of students without disabilities when students with severe disabilities are included in general education classes (Cole et al., 2004; McDonnell et al., 2003; Sharpe, York, & Knight, 1994).

For example, McDonnell et al. (2003) examined the educational achievement of 14 students with severe disabilities served in general education classes and 545 of their peers without disabilities enrolled in five elementary schools. The achievement of students with severe disabilities was measured using a standardized assessment of adaptive behavior in a pre–post design. The academic performance of students without disabilities was measured using scores from a state-mandated, criterion-referenced test in reading/language arts and mathematics. A posttest-only control group design was used to compare scores of students without disabilities enrolled in classes with one of the students with severe disabilities to students enrolled in classes that did not include students with severe disabilities. The authors found that 13 of the 14 students with developmental disabilities made significant gains in adaptive behavior, and no differences were found between the two groups of students without disabilities in either reading or math performance.

Friendships and Social Connections Numerous studies examined how inclusive education affects the development of friendships and the social connections between students with and without disabilities (Boutot & Bryant, 2005; Cole & Meyer, 1991; Fryxell & Kennedy, 1995; Hunt, Farron-Davis, Beckstead, Curtis, & Goetz, 1994; Kennedy & Itkonen, 1994; Kennedy, Shukla, & Fryxell, 1997). These studies suggested that there are numerous social benefits of inclusive education when practitioners take active steps to promote social interactions between peers with and without disabilities.

Fryxell and Kennedy (1995) compared the social interactions of two matched groups of students enrolled full time in general education classes or in self-contained special education classrooms. They found that students served in general education classes had significantly more social contacts with peers without disabilities than students enrolled in self-contained classrooms. Students served in general education classes on average had more than seven times the number of contacts per day with peers without disabilities than students served in self-contained special education classes. Students enrolled in general education classes also received significantly more social support from others during the school day and provided more social support to their peers without disabilities than students in self-contained classes. Finally, the mean number of peers without disabilities identified by students with severe disabilities as members of their social networks was 17 times higher for students served in the general education classes than those served in self-contained classes.

Hunt et al. (1994) conducted a program evaluation examining the effects of placement in inclusive and separate special education programs on a number of variables including the extent to which students with severe disabilities initiated and engaged in social interactions with peers. The researchers conducted six observations with randomly selected stratified samples of students based on severity of disability. These observations were conducted with two students in each of eight full inclusion and eight special education classes. They found students in inclusive education programs had higher rates of initiating social interactions with peers. These social interactions were significantly more social than task oriented for students less affected by intellectual disability. Both groups of students with severe disabilities enrolled in inclusive education programs had significantly higher rates of reciprocal interactions with peers without disabilities.

Quality of Instruction The nature and quality of instruction that students with severe disabilities receive in general education classes is another area of research that has received a substantial amount of attention (Foreman, Arthur-Kelly, & Pascoe, 2004; Hunt et al., 1994; Logan & Keefe, 1997; McDonnell, Thorson, McQuivey, & Kiefer-O'Donnell, 1997; Soukup, Wehmeyer, Bashinski, & Bovaird, 2007). These studies found that the instruction provided to students in inclusive educational settings is comparable with or superior to the instruction provided to students in separate educational settings. Furthermore, the more time students spend in general education classes, the more likely it is that they will participate in instruction that is aligned with the general education curriculum.

Logan and Keefe (1997) conducted an observational study examining the instructional context, teacher behavior, and engaged behavior of 30 elementary students with developmental disabilities enrolled in general education and self-contained special education classrooms. Their analysis showed that students enrolled in general education classes received a greater proportion of their instruction through academic rather than functional daily living activities as compared with students served in special education classes. In addition, they found that students in general education classes received more one-to-one instruction and more attention from the classroom teacher than students in self-contained classrooms. Finally, no differences were found between the two groups on their level of task engagement.

Soukup et al. (2007) examined the extent to which 19 students with severe disabilities gained access to the general education curriculum in various educational placements. Students were divided into three groups: students ($n = 6$) who spent between 75% and 100% in general education classes, students ($n = 7$) who spent between 51% and 74% of the school day in general education classes, and students ($n = 6$) who spent less than 50% of the school day in general education classes. Students were observed using the Access Code for Instructional Structure and Student Response (Access CISSAR) during science and social studies classes. The authors found that students who spent more than 75% of the school day in general education classes were working on core curriculum standards during 98% of the day; students who spent between 51% and 75% of the school day in general education classes were working on core curriculum standards during 93% of the observation intervals; and students who spent less than 50% of the school day in general education classes worked on core curriculum standards during 46% of the observation intervals.

Effect of Inclusive Education on Postschool Outcomes

Although there is a substantial base of research examining the immediate effect of inclusive education on students' learning and quality of instruction, the amount of research examining the effects of these programs on students' postschool quality of life is surprisingly limited (Ryndak et al., 2012). Several studies reported improved adjustment to employment for students enrolled in general education classes, especially if they had taken general vocational education classes (Baer et al., 2003; Benz, Lindstrom, & Yovanoff, 2000; Benz, Yovanoff, & Doren, 1997; Blackorby, Hancock, & Siegel, 1993; Heal, Khoju, & Rusch, 1997; Ryndak, Ward, Alper, Montgomery, & Storch, 2010; Wagner, Blackorby, Cameto, & Newman, 1993; Wagner, Newman, Cameto, Levine, & Garza, 2006; White & Weiner, 2004). For example, White and Weiner (2004) conducted a correlational study examining the relationship between educational placement and community-based instruction on employment outcomes for 104 young adults with severe disabilities. One of the strongest predictors of paid, community employment for these students following school was the degree to which they were included in general education contexts with age-appropriate peers prior to graduation.

Inclusive education also appears to have a positive effect on students' adjustment to community living (Blackorby et al., 1993; Heal & Rusch, 1995; Heal et al., 1997, Ryndak et al., 2010). Ryndak et al. conducted a retrospective qualitative study that examined the effect of inclusive education on two individuals with severe disabilities who attended the same self-contained class when they were 15 years of age. Data sources included 1) observations at age 15 and 25; 2) interviews with the individuals with severe disabilities, family members, friends, and adult services providers; and 3) educational and adult services records. One of these individuals was identified as the student in his or her class less affected by intellectual disability, and the other was identified as the student most affected by disability. The first student remained in self-contained classes in subsequent school years, whereas the second student received services in general education classes. Three years after exiting the educational system, the student more affected by disability, yet educated in general education classes, consistently had been employed as a judicial system government employee, living in an apartment with weekly support for budgeting and independent functioning, and participating within an extensive social support network. In contrast, the other student had lost numerous jobs and at the time was working at a sheltered workshop, living with family members, and had no social support network beyond family members.

WHAT OUTCOMES SHOULD DRIVE INCLUSIVE EDUCATION?

It is perhaps not surprising that the expected outcomes for students in inclusive educational programs and the curriculum models used to drive educational planning have changed as the number of students served in general education classes has grown and the amount of time they spend in these settings has increased. Students with severe disabilities were served most often in special schools or separate classes located in typical schools in the 1980s and 1990s. The predominate curriculum approaches were person-centered ecological curricular frameworks (see Brown et al., 1979; Ford et al., 1989; Neel & Billingsley, 1989; Sailor et al., 1986; Wilcox & Bellamy, 1987). The underlying assumptions of these frameworks were that educational programs should enhance students' ability to use community resources, live where and with whom they chose, have paid employment in typical businesses and industries, and be independent and have autonomy in making their own lifestyle choices. Emphasis was placed on increasing students' presence and competence in community rather than school settings. These frameworks typically resulted in identifying functional IEP goals and objectives that targeted teaching routines, activities, and key academic and developmental skills that would have a tangible effect on students' immediate and future quality of life.

It soon became clear, however, that simply making students more competent in community settings was insufficient to achieve students' full acceptance and membership in the community. As a result, the expected outcomes of these curricular frameworks were expanded from increasing students' presence and participation in the community to developing age-appropriate social relationships and friendships (Giangreco, Dennis, Cloninger, Edelman, & Schattman, 1993; Giangreco & Putnam, 1991). Social connectedness became as important in defining students' quality of life as having satisfying work and a comfortable home, being able to use community resources, and having control over one's life.

Advocates and researchers began to emphasize the need for students to attend their neighborhood schools, participate in the instructional and extracurricular activities of general education classes and the school, and develop meaningful friendships with peers without disabilities. This led to efforts to validate instructional approaches and strategies that would allow students to learn content in the general education curriculum. Indeed, the body of research showing that if students with severe disabilities were provided systematic instruction, curricular adaptations and modifications, and adequate support, then these students could successfully participate in the instructional activities of general education classes and learn complex curriculum content expanded rapidly (Fisher & Frey, 2001; Gilberts, Agran, Hughes, & Wehmeyer, 2001; Hughes et al., 2002; Janney & Snell, 1997; King-Sears, 1999; Koegel, Harrower, & Koegel, 1999; McDonnell, Mathot-Buckner, Thorson, & Fister, 2001; Ryndak, Morrison, & Sommerstein, 1999).

The passage of the No Child Left Behind Act (NCLB) of 2001 (PL 107-110) and the Individuals with Disabilities Education Improvement Act (IDEA) of 2004 (PL 108-446) was a watershed in how the field thought about educational outcomes and curriculum for students with severe disabilities. These laws created a new set of expectations for teachers, schools, and school districts. These two statutes established the requirement that IEP teams identify how students with disabilities, including those with severe disabilities, will be involved and progress in the general education curriculum in reading and language arts, mathematics, and science (Yell, Shriner, & Katsiyannis, 2006). NCLB mandated that states establish rigorous academic content and academic achievement standards for all students in the areas of reading and language arts, mathematics, and science. Academic achievement standards must be aligned with the academic content standards and be incorporated into a comprehensive assessment system that is used to assess students' adequate yearly progress toward mastering the academic content standards. IDEA 2004 requires that students with disabilities participate in the statewide assessment system or an alternate assessment that is linked to grade-level academic content standards. State and local education agencies must use these assessment data to determine if students with disabilities are making adequate yearly progress in mastering the academic content standards.

The enactment of these mandates has generated concern and sparked discussion among advocates and researchers given the broad support in the field for an ecological approach to curriculum development with a focus on quality of life outcomes for students with severe disabilities. Some researchers suggested that the IDEA 2004 mandate for all students to be involved and progress in the general education curriculum has forced a reexamination of expectations for individuals with severe disabilities. Wehmeyer wrote,

> We are now asked to think about the potential that students with severe disabilities could learn to read, do math, and engage in science. It may be hard to imagine now, but I am guessing that in 10 years from now we will wonder how we could not see the potential. (2006, p. 325)

A growing body of research provides evidence that students with severe disabilities can learn complex academic skills when provided with explicit and systematic instruction (Bradford, Shippen, Alberto, Houchins, & Flores, 2006; Browder, Ahlgrim-Delzell, Courtade, Gibbs, & Flowers, 2008; Browder, Mims, Spooner, Ahlgrim-Delzell, & Lee, 2008; McDonnell, Johnson, Polychronis, & Riesen, 2002; Ryndak et al., 1999). It has also been argued that students with severe disabilities have the right to full access to the general education curriculum and that "to deny someone an opportunity that all other members of a society are afforded should require a compelling rationale" (Courtade, Spooner, Browder, & Jimenez, 2012, p. 5).

Other researchers, however, expressed concern that the emphasis on academic content, standards-based academic goals, and high-stakes testing will result in the abandonment of an ecological approach as the basis for selecting IEP goals and designing curriculum and instruction for students with severe disabilities. They envisioned a shift in the focus of educational programs from teaching functional routines and skills that are necessary to live, work, and participate in the community to the instruction of isolated language arts, mathematics, and science concepts and skills that have little application and potential to generalize to students' everyday lives (Ayres, Douglas, Lowrey, & Sievers, 2011; Lowrey, Drasgow, Renzaglia, & Chezan, 2007; Ryndak et al., 2012). There is concern that instruction on grade-level academic content takes time away from instruction of functional skills needed for adult life (Ayres et al., 2011).

We have suggested recently that the potential outcomes of inclusive education could be improved by reconciling these two curricular approaches through a process that allows IEP teams to work within an ecological curricular framework to develop standards-based goals that reflect meaningful knowledge and skills that are tailored to students' individual needs and applicable to their everyday lives (Hunt, McDonnell, & Crockett, 2012). This process must begin with a clear vision of the high-priority, quality-of-life goal areas identified for students through person-centered planning processes. These valued life goals should serve as the primary consideration throughout the process of selecting core content standards and designing the extensions of those standards to address students' current levels of symbol understanding and use and academic progress. In addition, we have proposed that in order to reconcile an ecological curricular framework with a standards-based academic curriculum, the traditional quality-of-life domains should be broadened beyond home, friendships, community participation, and work to include acquiring academic knowledge and skills that 1) enrich students' lives because they enhance their understanding of the arts, literature, science, history, and culture; 2) affect students' roles as citizens in the community; 3) promote students' ability to become lifelong learners; or 4) support students' personal growth and development.

This kind of approach would provide several advantages to developing educational goals. First, an educational planning approach driven by valued life goals would ensure an appropriate balance in students' IEPs of standards-based academic and functional goals that address, for example, developing communicative and social competence and positive peer relationships; increasing independence within school, community, and vocational routines; and teaching self-determination and problem-solving skills. Second, because IEP teams would approach state standards frameworks with a clear vision of students' valued life goals to guide them in prioritizing and selecting content standards, the decisions that IEP teams make would be more meaningful to students and would not be based on team member preferences or arbitrary guidelines. Third, IEP teams would be encouraged to examine subject area domains in standards frameworks beyond literacy, math, and science to identify other domains that might contribute to achieving students' valued life goals. It would allow IEP teams to think broadly about how students could more fully participate in all instructional contexts in general education classes.

IMPLICATIONS FOR PRACTICE

An educational planning process based on valued life outcomes that are linked to standards-based academic content challenges practitioners to expand their thinking about how instruction and social supports are used to achieve students' IEP goals and objectives in inclusive education programs. The solutions to improving educational effectiveness for students with severe disabilities require that professionals think more broadly about how they would improve the effectiveness of instructional and social supports for all students in a class. Although technology is still emerging, at least three strategies appear to be especially critical in improving the effectiveness of instruction in inclusive education, including using approaches that enhance generalization, establishing and sustaining social interactions between students and their peers, and promoting collaboration and data-based problem solving by faculty and staff.

Enhance Generalization

Research demonstrated that instruction can be organized and delivered in general education classes in ways that will promote students' acquisition of a wide array of complex concepts and skills (Gilberts et al., 2001; McDonnell et al., 2002; McDonnell, Thorson, Allen, & Mathot-Buckner, 2000; Neef, Nelles, Iwata, & Page, 2003). These studies also showed that students can generalize these skills to other stimulus materials, tasks, and settings in the school, but no studies have specifically examined the generalization of skills learned in general education classes to typical performance settings. The existing literature on promoting generalization by students with severe disabilities, however, suggests that several strategies can improve the likelihood that this will occur (Horner, McDonnell, & Bellamy, 1986; Rosenthal-Malek & Bloom, 1998).

The first strategy is to teach instructional targets in multiple ways during the school day. This means using different strategies and teaching formats such as embedded instruction (McDonnell et al., 2002), cooperative learning (Dugan et al., 1995), peer-mediated learning (McDonnell et al., 2000), and heterogeneous small groups (Rankin et al., 1999) to teach the same skill to students throughout the day. Using multiple strategies and formats provides the practitioner with opportunities to present learning tasks that vary stimulus materials, response options, and irrelevant contextual variables. Systematically varying these factors during instruction has been shown to substantially increase the likelihood that students will generalize knowledge and skills to nontrained tasks and settings (Cooper, Heron, & Heward, 2007).

Second, practitioners should infuse authentic tasks into instruction. Students should be required to complete real-world problems that reflect the actual demands of their daily lives during instruction on academic content. Extending instructional activities to include authentic learning activities creates opportunities for students to use knowledge and skills across a variety of contexts and to use materials and responses that more closely reflect typical performance conditions. Anchoring instruction to activities that are important to students may also increase motivation by allowing them to see the link between instruction and their day-to-day activities.

Third, practitioners should design instruction to help students to control their own learning and to work as part of a team to independently solve problems. The ability to generalize concepts, operations, and processes to new problems and situations is inherent in the independent use of knowledge and skills. Furthermore, these abilities also provide the basis for students to become self-directed, lifelong learners and to continue to use their knowledge and skills to increase their independence and autonomy. This includes using strategies such as the Self-Determined Learning Model of Instruction (Agran, Cavin, Wehmeyer, & Palmer, 2006) and cooperative learning (Cushing, Kennedy, Shukla, Davis, & Meyer, 1997; Hunt et al., 1994).

Finally, practitioners should embed instruction on academic knowledge and skills into daily school routines and activities (McDonnell, Johnson, & McQuivey, 2008; Snell & Brown, 2011). Providing embedded instruction to students within the ongoing routines and activities of the general education classroom and school is also an important way to support the mastery and generalization of academic knowledge and skills. It presents opportunities for practitioners to offer a wide range of stimulus materials and require students to adjust their responses to specific stimulus conditions that are known to promote the development of generalized performance (Horner at al., 1986; Rosenthal-Malek & Bloom, 1998).

Establish and Sustain Social Interactions

Developing positive social relationships and friendships with peers is a valued life goal for all students and a high-priority educational outcome. Abundant evidence shows that students' developmental and emotional well-being are significantly affected by the quality of their social relationships. Positive peer relationships provide nurturance, support, membership, and companionship and promote self-esteem and self-confidence (Bukowski, Newcomb, & Hartup, 1996; Janney & Snell, 2006; Ladd, 1990; Schwartz, Staub, Peck, & Gallucci, 2006). In addition, evidence shows that children who have positive peer relationships develop more positive attitudes toward school and actively engage in academic activities in ways that promote learning (Ladd & Kochenderfer, 1996). Finally, child development theorists with varying theoretical backgrounds (e.g., Bruner, Flavel, Piaget, and Vygotsky) suggested that positive peer relationships provide a context and a mechanism for developing social, communication, and cognitive abilities.

Establishing inclusive school and classroom communities in which all students are valued members and diversity is celebrated provides the context for developing positive social relationships and friendships between students with disabilities and their peers; however, it is likely that these positive relationships will not evolve unless they are actively encouraged and systematically facilitated by educational team members who consider positive peer relationships to be a high-priority educational outcome (Carter & Hughes, 2007; Hunt, Doering, Maier, & Mintz, 2009; Janney & Snell, 2006). Numerous conditions have been identified that are essential to developing positive social relationships for students with disabilities, including 1) opportunities to be with peers with diverse abilities, backgrounds, and interests; 2) motivation to interact with schoolmates and having an effective means to do so; 3) availability of informed and motivated peers; and 4) social supports to facilitate positive social interactions and the development and sustainment of friendships (Carter & Hughes, 2007; Hunt, Farron-Davis, Wrenn, Hirose-Hatae, & Goetz, 1997; Janney & Snell, 2006; Kennedy, 2002). A comprehensive package of social supports is necessary to ensure that each of these conditions is addressed.

Hunt and her colleagues (Hunt et al., 2009) suggested that there are at least three major building blocks for establishing and maintaining positive relationships. The first building block is information provided to peers that will assist them in developing positive social relationships with their schoolmates with disabilities. Multiple formats have been used to share information with peers, including class lessons that explore concepts related to cultural and ability diversity, equity and democracy, and cooperation and independence (Gibbs, 1994; Hunt et al., 1997; Janney & Snell, 2006). In addition, schoolwide or grade-level events have been used to increase awareness of the experiences of schoolmates with disabilities and the accommodations, equipment, and assistive technology that facilitate their educational and social participation in the school community. Finally, friendship clubs have been established for students with and without disabilities that are facilitated by an adult and structured to allow all members to share their concerns or problems and receive feedback and support from their peers.

The second building block is identifying and using a variety of interactive media that serve as the basis for reciprocal social interactions. Interactive media provide a means—or both a means and a context—for supporting sustained interactions between students with disabilities and their peers (Hunt et al., 1997, 2009). These connectors include, for example, nonverbal communicative behaviors, low- and high-tech communication systems, and conversation books, as well as interactive educational activities, interactive toy play, and games and other leisure activities that allow the participants to focus on each other and require turn taking and reciprocity.

The final building block is the arrangement of interactive activities and implementation of facilitation strategies to promote positive social interactions across activities and settings (Causton-Theoharis & Malmgren, 2005; Hunt et al., 1997; Janney & Snell, 2006; Merges, Durand, & Youngblade, 2005). Peer partner activities and interactive, small-group educational and leisure activities offer multiple opportunities for social exchanges, turn taking, and interdependent participation to complete a task and to share materials and information. Social facilitators structure the activities, prepare augmentative and alternative communication (AAC) devices, and provide the adaptations and peer supports necessary to ensure that students with disabilities are actively engaged and interacting with other students. They also give information to both students with disabilities and their peers on how to interdependently participate to accomplish a task or play a game. Social facilitators provide information to peers at naturally occurring opportunities during interactive activities about the communication system, assistive technology, equipment, and adaptations that the students with disabilities may be using. In addition, information or modeling is provided that helps peers to interpret the nonsymbolic communicative behaviors of their classmates with disabilities or the comments made by them using an AAC device so that the peers can be responsive and effective communication partners. Finally, an effective adult facilitator knows when to facilitate and when to step back; that is, facilitators fade their physical presence in order to avoid creating adult dependency and interfering with student-to-student social interactions. They do this by initially providing support using strategies such as those previously described and then fading their support and physical presence once it is clear that social interactions between students are spontaneously occurring and students with disabilities are independently participating or are receiving adequate support from peers.

All three components of the social support package are implemented through the collaborative efforts of members of the educational team, and regularly scheduled team meetings can serve as the vehicle for tailoring the intervention to meet the needs of individual students and for coordinating team member activities.

Promote Collaboration and Data-Based Problem Solving

Learning and other educational resources are organized to meet the needs of all students in general education classrooms to provide an effective, quality education for a heterogeneous student body in an inclusive school. Team processes are used by teachers, principals, and other educational personnel to examine how best to organize people and time to deliver educational services to students and engage in data-based problem solving (Ferguson et al., 2005; Hunt et al., 2000; Iano, 2004; Miles & Darling-Hammond, 1998; Sailor & Roger, 2005).

The benefits of a collaborative, team-planning approach are significant. Teachers no longer have to face the challenges of meeting the range of student needs presented by an ever changing and diverse student population alone. In addition, collaborative planning and problem solving "synergistically increase the powers and capabilities of all teachers as their diverse ideas are brought together and combined" (Iano, 2004, p. 337). The collaborative teaming process at the classroom level offers ongoing opportunities for general and special educators and parents to share knowledge and skills to generate novel methods for individualizing learning. Collaborative planning meetings and activities might focus on developing and implementing individualized academic and social supports for any students in inclusive classrooms who need them, creating classroom curricula and activities through the combined efforts of general and special educators that incorporate the principles of universal design for learning, and designing and implementing a variety of cooperative teaching models that incorporate the expertise and interests of each of the general and special educators (Hunt et al., 2003; Snell & Janney, 2005; Thousand & Villa, 2000).

Collaborative teaming activities are informed by both educational process and student outcome data. An effective collaborative teaming process requires not only a structure for addressing the issues but also a system for monitoring individual accountability for agreed-on responsibilities (Nevin, Thousand, Paolucci-Whitcomb, & Villa, 1990; Salisbury, Evans, & Palombaro, 1997). Student progress data guide the selection of curricula, the design of educational activities, and the allocation of educational resources. In addition, student progress data can serve as a powerful motivator when it provides evidence that the actions of educators have had a positive effect on student learning and engagement in the learning process (Ainscow et al., 2003).

FUTURE RESEARCH

Although the accumulated evidence suggests that inclusive educational programs have a positive effect on students' education and social outcomes, significant expansion of inclusive educational programs will require that a number of curriculum, instruction, school organization, and policy challenges be addressed. The future research agenda on inclusive education must address a number of interrelated components that affect the immediate and long-term outcomes achieved by students, including the following.

- *Developing and validating schoolwide models of inclusive education.* Although there is general agreement that staff and resources in inclusive educational programs need to be organized in ways that meet the needs of all students (Ferguson et al., 2005; Miles & Darling-Hammond, 1998; Sailor & Roger, 2005), the effect of these structures on the educational and social outcomes for students with severe disabilities have not been closely examined. Practitioners also need to understand how these structural changes affect the contexts of instruction for students, such as where instruction is delivered, who provides instruction, and what instructional formats are used to promote student learning.

- *Restructuring fiscal policies to support expansion of inclusive education.* Current fiscal policy at both the state and federal levels presents significant challenges to establishing the kind of schoolwide models that can meet the needs of all students, including those with severe disabilities. These include 1) regulations that govern fiscal accountability, 2) a lack of understanding of what is and is not required by the law, and 3) a lack of a cohesive state and federal policy framework (McLaughlin & Verstegen, 1998). Not only does the current fiscal policy structure limit the ability of practitioners and administrators to use all available resources in schools, but some funding models may also create disincentives for developing inclusive educational programs and incentivize school districts to serve students with the most severe disabilities in separate educational settings.

- *Further development of person-centered educational planning systems that align ecological curricular frameworks and academic content standards.* Practitioners need to examine issues such as whether these planning systems have an observable effect on the balance of functional and standards-based goals within IEPs, how IEP teams extend academic content standards for students who currently do not use symbols to communicate, and the social validity of such systems in enhancing students' quality of life (Hunt et al., 2012; Ryndak et al., 2012).

- *Continued refinement of and research on the effect of universally designed curriculum and instruction.* The active participation of students with severe disabilities in the general education curriculum means that both special and general education teachers have access to curriculum materials and teaching resources that can be quickly and easily adjusted to the specific learning needs of all students in a class.

- *Development and validation of strategies that lead to the generalization of knowledge and skills acquired in general education classes to typical performance settings.* This may include approaches such as integrated computer and web-based technologies and service learning.

- *Evaluation of preservice and in-service teacher education models that prepare teachers to work in inclusive educational settings.* Although a number of approaches to preparing teachers to work in inclusive programs have been described in the literature (Paul, Epanchin, Rosselli, Duchnowski, & Cranston-Gingras, 2002; Sindelar, Pugach, Griffin, & Seidl, 1995), there has been no comprehensive evaluation of whether these programs lead to documented improved teacher practice or student outcomes. A close examination of the preparation practices that result in improved teacher effectiveness in inclusive educational programs is warranted given the current political environment and questions about the value of preparation for teachers nationally.

- *Conduct longitudinal studies that examine the effect of inclusive education on students' quality of life and the unique and combined contribution that key programmatic features of inclusive education have on these outcomes.* Although the available evidence suggests that there is some association between inclusive education and improved postschool outcomes (Ryndak et al., 2012), it seems clear that the expansion of these programs in the future will require additional research that assesses their impact on students' quality of life after exiting school.

CONCLUSION

The expected outcomes of inclusive education are that all students become full members of the community and have the educational opportunities necessary to realize their dreams and aspirations. The significant progress that has been made in achieving these outcomes since the mid-1990s is rooted in the field's commitment to social justice, strong advocacy, and research focused on developing and validating practical approaches to meeting students' needs. The current challenge is moving inclusive education from recommended practice to common practice.

Inclusive education is and should be about maximizing student learning in all areas of life and creating classroom and school environments that promote students' full acceptance. As practitioners have become more successful in supporting students in these settings, it is only logical that they ask whether students can do and learn more. These questions should prod them to challenge their conventional ways of thinking about curriculum and instruction and to continuously reassess the expected outcomes of inclusive education. It is clear that students have exceeded what was thought possible in the mid-1990s, and it seems likely that they will continue to exceed expectations if given the opportunity.

Creating those opportunities, however, necessitates maintaining a continued focus on research and development. New methods, strategies, and approaches for supporting students in inclusive classrooms that are built on validated practices that reflect common values and beliefs need to be vigorously pursued. This chapter offered a number of recommendations for how the continued development and expansion of inclusive education for students with severe disabilities can be sustained.

Questions for Study and Reflection

1. Contemporary discussions of inclusive education often move beyond inclusion as a special education service delivery model and focus on whole-school restructuring to create inclusive schools where all students are valued members. Describe the roles of general and special educators, the principal, and families in such a school.

2. What does the research say about the characteristics of general education classrooms that may contribute to educational outcomes and social connectedness for students with severe disabilities? What are priority questions for future research in this area?

3. What did IDEA 2004 and NCLB require related to access, student outcomes, and accountability for students with disabilities? How might the emphasis on standards-based academic goals and instruction be reconciled with an ecological approach to curriculum development with a focus on quality-of-life outcomes?

4. What strategies can be used to increase the likelihood that students with severe disabilities will generalize academic knowledge and skills from classroom instructional contexts to their everyday lives? What social supports and facilitation strategies can educational team members put into place to facilitate the development of positive peer relationships?

5. How do collaborative planning and problem solving by general and special educators increase the capabilities of all the teachers?

RESOURCES

Center for Applied Special Technology *http://www.cast.org*

LeadScape *http://www.niusileadscape.org*

Maryland Coalition for Inclusive Education *http://www.mcie.org*

The Schoolwide Integrated Framework for Transformation *http://swiftschools.org*

REFERENCES

Agran, M., Cavin, M., Wehmeyer, M., & Palmer, S. (2006). Participation of students with moderate to severe disabilities in the general education curriculum: The effects of the Self-Determined Learning Model of Instruction. *Research and Practice for Persons with Severe Disabilities, 31,* 230–241.

Ainscow, M., Howes, A., Farrell, P., & Frankham, J. (2003). Making sense of the development of inclusive practices. *European Journal of Special Needs Education, 18,* 227–242.

American Association on Intellectual and Developmental Disabilities/ARC. (2008, May 18). *Education: A joint statement by AAIDD and ARC.* Retrieved from http://www.aaidd.org/content_147.cfm?navID=34

Ayres, K.M., Douglas, K.H., Lowrey, K.A., & Sievers, C. (2011). I can identify Saturn, but I can't brush my teeth: What happens when the curricular focus for students with severe disabilities shifts. *Education and Training in Autism and Developmental Disabilities, 46,* 11–21.

Baer, R., Flexer, R., Beck, S., Amstutz, N., Hoffmon, L., Brothers, J., & Zechman, C. (2003). A collaborative follow-up study on transition. *Career Development for Exceptional Individuals, 26,* 7–25.

Benz, M., Lindstrom, L., & Yovanoff, P. (2000). Improving graduation and employment outcomes of students with disabilities: Predictive factors and student perspectives. *Exceptional Children, 66,* 509–529.

Benz, M.R., Yovanoff, P., & Doren, B. (1997). School-to-work components that predict postschool success for students with and without disabilities. *Exceptional Children, 63,* 151–165.

Blackorby, J., Hancock, G.R., & Siegel, S. (1993). *Human capital and structural explanations of post-school success for youth with disabilities: A latent variable exploration of the National Longitudinal Transition Study.* Menlo Park, CA: SRI International.

Boutot, E.A., & Bryant, D.P. (2005). Social integration of students with autism in inclusive settings. *Education and Training in Developmental Disabilities, 40,* 14–23.

Bradford, S., Shippen, M.E., Alberto, P., Houchins, D.E., & Flores, M. (2006). Using systematic instruction to teach decoding skills to middle school students with moderate intellectual disabilities. *Education and Training in Developmental Disabilities, 41,* 333–343.

Browder, D., Ahlgrim-Delzell, L., Courtade, G., Gibbs, S., & Flowers, C. (2008). Evaluation of the effectiveness of an early literacy program for students with significant developmental disabilities. *Exceptional Children, 75,* 33–52.

Browder, D., Mims, P.J., Spooner, F., Ahlgrim-Delzell, L., & Lee, A. (2008). Teaching elementary students with multiple disabilities to participate in shared stories. *Research and Practice for Persons with Severe Disabilities, 33,* 3–12.

Browder, D.M., Wakeman, S.Y., Flowers, C., Rickelmann, R.J., Pugalee, D., & Karvonen, M. (2007). Creating access to the general education curriculum with links to grade-level content for students with significant cognitive disabilities: An explication of the concept. *Journal of Special Education, 41,* 2–16.

Brown, L., Branston, M.B., Hamre-Nietupski, S., Pumpian, I., Certo, N., & Gruenewald, L. (1979). A strategy for developing chronological-age-appropriate and functional curricular content for severely handicapped adolescents and young adults. *Journal of Special Education, 13,* 81–90.

Bukowski, W.M., Newcomb, A.F., & Hartup, W.W. (1996). Friendship and its significance in childhood and adolescence: Introduction and comment. In W.M. Bukowski, A.F. Newcomb, & W.W. Hartup (Eds.), *The company they keep: Friendship in childhood and adolescence* (pp. 1–15). Cambridge, NY: Cambridge University Press.

Carter, E.W., & Hughes, C. (2007). Social interaction interventions: Promoting socially supported environments and teaching new skills. In S.L. Odom, R.H. Horner, M.E. Snell, & J. Blacher (Eds.), *Handbook of developmental disabilities* (pp. 310–329). New York, NY: Guilford Press.

Carter, E.W., & Kennedy, C.H. (2006). Promoting access to the general curriculum using peer support strategies. *Research and Practice for Persons with Severe Disabilities, 31,* 284–292.

Causton-Theoharis, J., & Malmgren, K. (2005). Increasing peer interactions for students with severe disabilities via paraprofessional training. *Teaching Exceptional Children, 72,* 431–444.

Center for Applied Special Technology (CAST). (2012). *Universal design for learning guidelines version 2.0.* Retrieved from http://www.udlcenter.org/aboutudl/udlguidelines

Claes, C., Van Hove, G., Vandevelde, S., Van Loon, J., & Schalock, R.L. (2010). Person-centered planning: Analysis of research and effectiveness. *Intellectual and Developmental Disabilities, 48,* 432–453.

Cole, C.M., Waldron, N., & Majd, M. (2004). Academic progress of students across inclusive and traditional settings. *Mental Retardation, 42,* 136–144.

Cole, D.A., & Meyer, L.H. (1991). Social integration and severe disabilities: A longitudinal analysis of child outcomes. *Journal of Special Education, 25,* 340–351.

Cooper, J.O., Heron, T.E., & Heward, W.L. (2007). *Applied behavior analysis* (2nd ed.). Upper Saddle River, NJ: Pearson.

Courtade, G., Spooner, F., Browder, D., & Jimenez, B. (2012). Seven reasons to promote standards-based instruction for students with severe disabilities: A reply to Ayres, Lowrey, Douglas, and Sievers (2011). *Education and Training in Autism and Developmental Disabilities, 47,* 3–13.

Curry, C. (2003). Universal design: Accessibility for all learners. *Educational Leadership, 61*(2), 55–60.

Cushing, L.S., & Kennedy, C.H. (1997). Academic effects of providing peer support in general education classrooms on students without disabilities. *Journal of Applied Behavior Analysis, 30,* 139–152.

Cushing, L.S., Kennedy, C.H., Shukla, S., Davis, J., & Meyer, K.A. (1997). Disentangling the effects of curricular revision and social grouping within cooperative learning arrangements. *Focus on Autism and Other Developmental Disabilities, 12,* 231–240.

Dugan, E., Kamps, D., Leonard, B., Watkins, N., Rheinberger, A., & Stackhaus, J. (1995). Effects of cooperative learning groups during social studies for students with autism and fourth-grade peers. *Journal of Applied Behavior Analysis, 28,* 175–188.

Ferguson, D.L., Kozleski, E.B., & Smith, A. (2005). *Transformed, inclusive schools: A framework to guide fundamental change in urban schools.* Retrieved from the National Institute for Urban School Improvement web site: http://www.niusileadscape.org/lc/Record/618?search_query=Transformed%20Inclusive%20Schools

Fisher, D., & Frey, N. (2001). Access to the core curriculum: Critical ingredients for student success. *Remedial and Special Education, 22,* 148–157.

Fisher, M., & Meyer, L.H. (2002). Development and social competence after two years for students enrolled in inclusive and self-contained educational programs. *Research and Practice for Persons with Severe Disabilities, 27,* 165–174.

Ford, A., Schnorr, R., Meyer, L.H., Davern, L.A., Black, J., & Dempsey, P. (1989). *The Syracuse community-referenced curriculum guide for students with moderate and severe disabilities.* Baltimore, MD: Paul H. Brookes Publishing Co.

Foreman, P., Arthur-Kelly, M., & Pascoe, S. (2004). Evaluating the educational experiences of students with profound and multiple disabilities in inclusion and segregated classroom settings: An Australian perspective. *Research and Practice for Persons with Severe Disabilities, 29,* 183–193.

Fryxell, D., & Kennedy, C.H. (1995). Placement along the continuum of services and its impact on students' social relationships. *Journal of The Association for Persons with Severe Handicaps, 20,* 259–269.

Gartner, A., & Lipsky, D.K. (1987). Beyond special education: Toward a quality education system for all students. *Harvard Educational Review, 57,* 367–395.

Giangreco, M.F., Cloninger, C.J., Dennis, R.E., & Edelman, S.W. (2002). Problem-solving methods to facilitate inclusive education. In J.S. Thousand, R.A. Villa, & A.I. Nevin (Eds.), *Creativity and collaborative learning: The practical guide to empowering students and teachers* (2nd ed., pp. 111–134). Baltimore, MD: Paul H. Brookes Publishing Co.

Giangreco, M.F., Dennis, R., Cloninger, C., Edelman, S., & Schattman, R. (1993). "I've counted Jon:" Transformational experiences of teachers in the education of students with disabilities. *Exceptional Children, 59,* 359–371.

Giangreco, M.F., & Putnam, J.W. (1991). Supporting the education of students with severe disabilities in regular education environments. In L.H. Meyer, C.A. Peck, & L. Brown (Eds.), *Critical issues in the lives of people with severe disabilities* (pp. 245–270). Baltimore, MD: Paul H. Brookes Publishing Co.

Gibbs, J. (1994). *Tribes: A new way of learning together.* Santa Rosa, CA: Center Source Publications.

Gilberts, G.H., Agran, M., Hughes, C., & Wehmeyer, M. (2001). The effects of peer delivered self-monitoring strategies on the participation of students with severe disabilities in general education classrooms.

Journal of The Association for Persons with Severe Handicaps, 26, 25–36.

Heal, L.W., Khoju, M., & Rusch, F.R. (1997). Predicting quality of life of youths after they leave special education high school programs. *Journal of Special Education, 31,* 279–299.

Heal, L.W., & Rusch, F.R. (1995). Predicting employment for students who leave special education high school programs. *Exceptional Children, 61,* 472–487.

Horner, R.H., McDonnell, J., & Bellamy, G.T. (1986). Efficient instruction of generalized behaviors: General case programming in simulation and community settings. In R.H. Horner, L.H. Meyer, & H.D. Fredericks (Eds.), *Educating learners with severe handicaps: Exemplary service strategies* (pp. 289–314). Baltimore, MD: Paul H. Brookes Publishing Co.

Hughes, C., Copeland, S.R., Agran, M., Wehmeyer, M.L., Rodi, M.S., & Presley, J.A. (2002). Using self-monitoring to improve performance in general education high school classes. *Education and Training in Mental Retardation and Developmental Disabilities, 37,* 262–272.

Hunt, P., Doering, K., Maier, J., & Mintz, E. (2009). Strategies to support the development of positive social relationships and friendships for students who use AAC. In G. Soto & C. Zangari (Eds.), *Practically speaking: Language, literacy, and academic development for students with AAC needs* (pp. 247–264). Baltimore, MD: Paul H. Brookes Publishing Co.

Hunt, P., Farron-Davis, F., Beckstead, S., Curtis, D., & Goetz, L. (1994). Evaluating the effects of placement of students with severe disabilities in regular education versus special classes. *Journal of The Association for Persons with Severe Handicaps, 19,* 200–214.

Hunt, P., Farron-Davis, F., Wrenn, M., Hirose-Hatae, A., & Goetz, L. (1997). Promoting interactive partnerships in inclusive educational settings. *Journal of The Association for Persons with Severe Handicaps, 22,* 127–137.

Hunt, P., Hirose-Hatae, A., Doering, K., Karasoff, P., & Goetz, L. (2000). "'Community' is what I think everyone is talking about." *Remedial and Special Education, 21,* 305–317.

Hunt, P., & McDonnell, J. (2007). Inclusive education. In S.L. Odom, R.H. Horner, M. Snell, & J. Blacher (Eds.), *Handbook on developmental disabilities* (pp. 269–291). New York, NY: Guilford Press.

Hunt, P., McDonnell, J., & Crockett, M.A. (2012). Reconciling an ecological curriculum framework focusing on quality of life outcomes with the development and instruction of standards-based academic goals. *Research and Practice for Persons with Severe Disabilities, 37,* 139–152.

Hunt, P., Soto, G., Maier, J., & Doering, K. (2003). Collaborative teaming to support students at risk and students with severe disabilities in general education classrooms. *Exceptional Children, 69,* 315–332.

Iano, R.P. (2004). Inside the schools: Special education and inclusion reform. In D. Gallagher, L. Heshusius, R.P. Iano, & T.M. Skrtic (Eds.), *Challenging orthodoxy in special education: Dissenting voices* (pp. 311–352). Denver, CO: Love Publishing.

Individuals with Disabilities Education Improvement Act (IDEA) of 2004, PL 108-446, 20 U.S.C. §§ 1400 *et seq.*

Janney, R.E., & Snell, M.E. (1997). How teachers include students with moderate and severe disabilities in elementary classes: The means and meaning of inclusion. *Journal of The Association for Persons with Severe Handicaps, 22,* 159–169.

Janney, R., & Snell, M.E. (2006). *Teachers' guides to inclusive practices: Social relationships and peer support* (2nd ed.). Baltimore, MD: Paul H. Brookes Publishing Co.

Kauffman, J.M., & Hallahan, D. (1995). *The illusion of inclusion.* Austin, TX: PRO-ED.

Kennedy, C.H. (2002). Promoting social-communicative interactions in adolescents. In H. Goldstein, L.A. Kaczmarek, & K.M. English (Eds.), *Promoting social communication: Children with developmental disabilities from birth to adolescence* (pp. 307–329). Baltimore, MD: Paul H. Brookes Publishing Co.

Kennedy, C.H., & Itkonen, T. (1994). Some effects of regular class participation on the social contacts and social networks of high school students with severe disabilities. *Journal of The Association for Persons with Severe Handicaps, 19,* 1–10.

Kennedy, C.H., Shukla, S., & Fryxell, D. (1997). Comparing the effects of educational placement on the social relationships of intermediate school students with severe disabilities. *Exceptional Children, 64,* 31–47.

King-Sears, M.E. (1999). Teacher and researcher co-design self-management content for an inclusive setting: Research training, intervention, and generalization effects on student performance. *Education and Training in Mental Retardation and Developmental Disabilities, 34,* 134–156.

Koegel, L.K., Harrower, J.K., & Koegel, R.L. (1999). Support for children with developmental disabilities in full inclusion classrooms through self-management. *Journal of Positive Behavioral Interventions, 1,* 26–34.

Kohn, A. (2006). *Beyond discipline: From compliance to community* (10th anniversary ed.). Alexandria, VA: Association for Supervision and Curriculum Development.

Ladd, G.W. (1990). Having friends, keeping friends, making friends, and being liked by peers in the classroom: Predictors of children's early school adjustment? *Child Development, 61,* 1081–1100.

Ladd, G.W., & Kochenderfer, B.J. (1996). Linkages between friendship and adjustment during early school transitions. In W.M. Bukowski, A.F. Newcomb, & W.W. Hartup (Eds.), *The company they keep: Friendship in childhood and adolescence* (pp. 322–345). Cambridge, NY: Cambridge University Press.

Logan, K.R., & Keefe, E.B. (1997). A comparison of instructional context, teacher behavior, and engaged behavior for students with severe disabilities in general education and self-contained elementary classrooms. *Journal of The Association for Persons with Severe Handicaps, 22,* 16–27.

Lowrey, K.A., Drasgow, E., Renzaglia, A., & Chezan, L. (2007). Impact of alternate assessments on curricula for students with severe disabilities: Purpose driven or process driven. *Assessment for Effective Intervention, 32,* 244–253.

McDonnell, J., & Hardman, M.L. (2010). *Successful transition programs: Pathways for students with intellectual and developmental disabilities.* Thousand Oaks, CA: Sage Publishing.

McDonnell, J., Johnson, J.W., & McQuivey, C. (2008). *Embedded instruction for students with developmental disabilities in general education classes.* Alexandria,

VA: Division of Developmental Disabilities, Council for Exceptional Children.

McDonnell, J., Johnson, J.W., Polychronis, S., & Riesen, T. (2002). The effects of embedded instruction on students with moderate disabilities enrolled in general education classes. *Education and Training in Mental Retardation and Developmental Disabilities, 37,* 363–377.

McDonnell, J., Mathot-Buckner, C., Thorson, N., & Fister, S. (2001). Supporting the inclusion of students with severe disabilities in typical junior high school classes: The effects of class wide peer tutoring, multi-element curriculum, and accommodations. *Education and Treatment of Children, 24,* 141–160.

McDonnell, J., Thorson, N., Allen, C., & Mathot-Buckner, C. (2000). The effects of partner learning during spelling for students with severe disabilities and their peers. *Journal of Behavioral Education, 10,* 107–122.

McDonnell, J., Thorson, N., Disher, S., Mathot-Buckner, C., Mendel, J., & Ray, L. (2003). The achievement of students with developmental disabilities and their peers without disabilities in inclusive settings: An exploratory study. *Education and Treatment of Children, 26,* 224–236.

McDonnell, J., Thorson, N., McQuivey, C., & Kiefer-O'Donnell, R. (1997). The academic engaged time of students with low incidence disabilities in general education classes. *Mental Retardation, 35,* 18–26.

McLaughlin, M.J., & Verstegen, D. (1998). Increasing regulatory flexibility of special education programs: Problems and promising strategies. *Exceptional Children, 64,* 371–384.

Merges, E.M., Durand, V.M., & Youngblade, L.M. (2005). The role of communicative partners. In J.E. Downing (Ed.), *Teaching communication skills to students with severe disabilities* (2nd ed., pp. 175–199). Baltimore, MD: Paul H. Brookes Publishing Co.

Miles, K.H., & Darling-Hammond, L. (1998). Rethinking the allocation of teaching resources: Some lessons from high-performing schools. *Educational Evaluation and Policy Analysis, 20,* 9–29.

Mortier, K., Hunt, P., Leroy, M., De Schauwer, E., & Van Hove, G. (2010). Communities of practice in inclusive education. *Educational Studies, 36*(3), 345–355.

National Down Syndrome Congress. (2005, May). *Inclusive education.* Retrieved from http://ndsccenter.org/about-ndsc/position-statements/

Neef, N.A., Nelles, D.F., Iwata, B.A., & Page, T.J. (2003). Analysis of precurrent skills in solving mathematic semantics story problems. *Journal of Applied Behavior Analysis, 36,* 21–34.

Neel, R.S., & Billingsley, F.F. (1989). *Impact: A functional curriculum handbook for students with moderate to severe disabilities.* Baltimore, MD: Paul H. Brookes Publishing Co.

Nevin, A.I., Thousand, J.S., Paolucci-Whitcomb, P., & Villa, R.A. (1990). Collaborative consultation: Empowering public school personnel to provide heterogeneous school for all. *Journal of Educational and Psychological Consultation, 1,* 41–67.

No Child Left Behind Act of 2001, PL 107-110, 115 Stat. 1425, 20 U.S.C. §§ 6301 *et seq.* (2006).

Paul, J., Epanchin, B., Rosselli, H., Duchnowski, A., & Cranston-Gingras, A. (2002). Developing and nurturing a collaborative culture for change: Implications for higher education. In W. Sailor (Ed.), *Whole-school success and inclusive education: Building partnerships for learning, achievement, and accountability* (pp. 228–245). New York, NY: Teachers College Press.

Peetsma, T., Vergeer, M., Roeleveld, J., & Karsten, S. (2001). Inclusion in education: Comparing pupils' development in special and regular education. *Educational Review, 53,* 125–135.

Phelps, L.A., & Hanley-Maxwell, C. (1997). School-to-work transitions for youth with disabilities: A review of outcomes and practices. *Review of Educational Research, 67,* 197–226.

Rankin, D.H., Logan, K.R., Adcock, J., Angelica, J., Pittman, C., Sexton, A., & Straight, S. (1999). Small group learning: Effects of including a student with intellectual disabilities. *Journal of Developmental and Physical Disabilities, 11,* 159–177.

Rosenthal-Malek, A., & Bloom, A. (1998). Beyond acquisition: Teaching generalization for students with developmental disabilities. In A. Hilton & R. Ringlaben (Eds.), *Best and promising practices in developmental disabilities* (pp. 139–155). Austin, TX: PRO-ED.

Ryndak, D.L., Alper, S., Hughes, C., & McDonnell, J. (2012). Documenting the impact of educational contexts on long-term outcomes for students with significant disabilities. *Education and Training in Autism and Developmental Disabilities, 47,* 127–138.

Ryndak, D.L., Morrison, A.P., & Sommerstein, L. (1999). Literacy before and after inclusion in general education settings: A case study. *Journal of The Association for Persons with Severe Handicaps, 24,* 5–22.

Ryndak, D.L., Ward, T., Alper, S., Montgomery, J., & Storch, J.F. (2010). Long-term outcomes of services for two persons with significant disabilities with differing educational experiences: A qualitative consideration of the impact of education experiences. *Education and Training in Autism and Developmental Disabilities, 45,* 323–338.

Sailor, W. (1991). Special education in the restructured school. *Remedial and Special Education, 12*(6), 8–22.

Sailor, W., Halvorsen, A., Anderson, J., Goetz, L., Gee, K., Doering, K., & Hunt, P. (1986). Community intensive instruction. In R.H. Horner, L.H. Meyer, & H.D. Bud Fredericks (Eds.), *Education of learners with severe handicaps: Exemplary service strategies* (pp. 251–288). Baltimore, MD: Paul H. Brookes Publishing Co.

Sailor, W., & Roger, B. (2005). Rethinking inclusion: Schoolwide applications. *Phi Delta Kappan, 86,* 503–509.

Sailor, W., & Skrtic, T. (1995). Modern and postmodern agendas in special education: Implications for teacher education, research, and policy development. In J. Paul, H. Roselli, & D. Evans (Eds.), *Integrating school restructuring and special education reform* (pp. 418–433). New York, NY: Harcourt Brace.

Saldana, D.C., & Waxman, H.C. (1997). An observational study of multicultural education in urban elementary schools. *Equity and Excellence in Education, 30,* 40–46.

Salisbury, C.L., Evans, I.M., & Palombaro, M.M. (1997). Collaborative problem-solving to promote the inclusion of young children with significant disabilities in primary grades. *Exceptional Children, 63,* 195–209.

Sands, D.J., & Wehmeyer, M.L. (1996). *Self-determination across the life span: Independence and choice for people with disabilities.* Baltimore, MD: Paul H. Brookes Publishing Co.

Sapon-Shevin, M. (1990). Student support through cooperative learning. In W. Stainback & S. Stainback (Eds.), *Support networks for inclusive schooling: Interdependent integrated education.* (pp. 65–79). Baltimore, MD: Paul H. Brookes Publishing Co.

Schwartz, I.S., Staub, D., Peck, C.H., & Gallucci, C. (2006). Peer relationships. In M.E. Snell & F. Brown (Eds.), *Instruction of students with severe disabilities* (6th ed., pp. 375–404). Upper Saddle River, NJ: Pearson.

Sharpe, M., York, J.L., & Knight, J. (1994). Effects of inclusion on the academic performance of classmates without disabilities: A preliminary study. *Remedial and Special Education, 15,* 281–287.

Sindelar, P., Pugach, M., Griffin, C., & Seidl, B. (1995). Reforming teacher education: Challenging the philosophy and practices of educating regular and special educators. In J. Paul, H. Roselli, & D. Evans (Eds.), *Integrating school restructuring and special education reform* (pp. 140–166). New York, NY: Harcourt Brace.

Snell, M.E., & Brown, F. (2011). *Instruction of students with severe disabilities* (7th ed.). Upper Saddle River, NJ: Pearson.

Snell, M.E., & Janney, R.E. (2005). *Teachers' guides to inclusive practices: Collaborative teaming* (2nd ed.). Baltimore, MD: Paul H. Brookes Publishing Co.

Soukup, J.H., Wehmeyer, M.L., Bashinski, S.M., & Bovaird, J.A. (2007). Classroom variables and access to the general curriculum for students with disabilities. *Exceptional Children, 75,* 101–120.

Stainback, W., & Stainback, S. (Eds.). (1990). *Support networks for inclusive schooling: Interdependent integrated education.* Baltimore, MD: Paul H. Brookes Publishing Co.

TASH. (2000). *TASH resolution on quality inclusive education* (3rd ed.). Retrieved from http://tash.org/advocacy-issues/inclusive-education

TASH. (2010). *2010 national agenda: Inclusive education.* Retrieved from http://tash.org/advocacy-issues/inclusive-education

Thousand, J.S., & Villa, R.A. (2000). Collaborative teaming: A powerful tool in school restructuring. In R. Villa & J. Thousand (Eds.), *Restructuring for caring and effective education: Piecing the puzzle together* (2nd ed., pp. 254–291). Baltimore, MD: Paul H. Brookes Publishing Co.

Turnbull, R., Turnbull, A., Shank, M., Smith, S.J., & Leal, D. (2004). *Exceptional lives: Special education in today's schools* (4th ed.). Upper Saddle River, NJ: Merrill Prentice Hall.

Udvari-Solner, A., & Thousand, J. (1995). Promising practices that foster inclusive education. In R. Villa & J. Thousand (Eds.), *Creating an inclusive school* (pp. 87–109). Alexandria, VA: Association for Supervision and Curriculum Development.

Wagner, M., Blackorby, J., Cameto, R., & Newman, L. (1993). *What makes a difference? Influences on postschool outcomes of youth with disabilities. The third comprehensive report from the National Longitudinal Transition Study of Special Education Students.* Menlo Park, CA: SRI International.

Wagner, M., Newman, L., Cameto, R., Levine, P., & Garza, N. (2006). *An overview of findings from Wave 2 of the National Longitudinal Transition Study–2.* Menlo Park, CA: SRI International. Retrieved from http://www.nlts2.org/reports/2006_08/ nlts2_report_2006_08_complete.pdf

Wagner, M., Newman, L., Cameto, R., Levine, P., & Marder, C. (2003, November). *Going to school: Instructional contexts, programs, and participation of secondary school students with disabilities.* Menlo Park, CA: SRI International.

Wehmeyer, M. (2006). Beyond access: Ensuring progress in the general education curriculum for students with severe disabilities. *Research and Practice for Persons with Severe Disabilities, 31,* 322–326.

Westling, D.L., & Fox, L. (2009). *Teaching students with severe disabilities* (4th ed.). Upper Saddle River, NJ: Merrill Prentice Hall.

White, J., & Weiner, J.S. (2004). Influence of least restrictive environment and community based training on integrated employment outcomes for transitioning students with severe disabilities. *Journal of Vocational Rehabilitation, 21,* 149–156.

Wilcox, B., & Bellamy, G.T. (1987). *The activities catalog: An alternative curriculum for youth and adults with severe disabilities.* Baltimore, MD: Paul H. Brookes Publishing Co.

Yell, M.L., Shriner, J.G., & Katsiyannis, A. (2006). Individuals with Disabilities Education Improvement Act of 2004 and IDEA Regulations of 2006: Implications for educators, administrators, and teacher trainers. *Focus on Exceptional Children, 39,* 1–24.

Literacy and Communication

Susan Copeland, Elizabeth Keefe, and J.S. de Valenzuela

The United Nations Convention on the Rights of Persons with Disabilities (2006) stated that education is a human right for everyone, regardless of disability status. It also stated that the purpose of education is to facilitate "effective participation in a free society" (Article 24: 1-c). Literacy, a critical component of education, empowers active involvement in home, school, community, and employment settings (Conners, 2003). This perspective of literacy aligns with TASH's vision calling for individuals with severe disabilities of all ages to live lives that demonstrate "equity, diversity, and quality of life" (TASH, 2010a, para 4).

Individuals with severe disabilities have not always received literacy instruction, nor has it always been provided in the most effective manner, despite the importance of literacy as a means of participation in one's society (Copeland & Keefe, 2007). Browder, Wakeman, Spooner, Ahlgrim-Delzell, and Algozzine (2006) reported that instruction for this group of learners most often has focused on teaching single words in isolation with a primary focus on functional reading (i.e., using words or symbols to participate in daily activities). Providing a balanced and comprehensive instruction that creates opportunities to acquire conventional literacy skills that might increase authentic participation across one's life is a more empowering approach. Research shows that an individual's disability label or IQ score does not reliably predict what stage of literacy he or she can achieve. It is crucial, therefore, for all children to receive high-quality literacy instruction beginning early in their lives (e.g., Allor, Mathes, Roberts, Cheatham, & Champlin, 2010; Conners, 2003).

Several converging phenomena have contributed to a renewed interest in examining effective literacy instruction for individuals with severe disabilities, including

1) legislative mandates (e.g., No Child Left Behind Act [NCLB] of 2001 [PL 107-110]; Individuals with Disabilities Education Act Amendments [IDEA] of 1997 [PL 105-17]; Individuals with Disabilities Education Improvement Act [IDEA] of 2004 [PL 108-446]) that have created increased accountability for the teaching and learning of students with severe disabilities (Copeland & Cosbey, 2008–2009); 2) the IDEA 2004 mandate to provide authentic access to the general curriculum; 3) calls from people with disabilities and other advocates for the right of people with disabilities to receive a challenging and effective education (Jackson, Ryndak, & Wehmeyer, 2008–2009); and 4) findings from literacy intervention research that have created a deeper understanding of how to conceptualize literacy for individuals with severe disabilities and how to design more effective instruction (e.g., Erickson, Hatch, & Clendon, 2010).

This chapter begins by describing key challenges to literacy instruction for people with severe disabilities, embedding legislative and policy issues that affect this instruction. Next, it describes how high-quality literacy instruction aligns with TASH's (2010b) national agenda. Then, it reviews the research examining effective literacy instruction for individuals with severe disabilities across the age span and makes recommendations for effective practices based on this review. The chapter ends by considering where future research and policy initiatives should focus in advancing effective literacy instruction for people with severe disabilities.

KEY CHALLENGES

Five basic challenges faced in literacy instruction for people with severe disabilities are discussed next, including 1) the definition of literacy for people with severe disabilities, 2) incorporation of assistive technology, 3) the initial preparation and ongoing professional development of teachers, 4) legislative mandates and the challenges and opportunities they created for people with severe disabilities, and 5) the frequently unmet needs of people with severe disabilities from culturally and linguistically diverse backgrounds.

Defining Literacy

Literacy opportunities historically have been denied to many groups of people over time based on gender, ethnicity, language, and socioeconomic characteristics that bore no relation to the ability of these groups to achieve literacy (Lumsford, Moglen, & Slevin, 1990). Knoblauch noted that "literacy is one of those mischievous concepts, like virtuousness and craftsmanship, that appear to denote capacities but that actually convey value judgments" (1990, p. 74). How we define literacy has been one of the biggest hurdles for people with severe disabilities who are presumed to be incapable of achieving literacy skills. Kliewer, Biklen, and Kasa-Hendrickson noted that much of the history of literacy instruction for students with severe disabilities can be characterized as a "narrative of pessimism" (2006, p. 75). Consider the circular logic described by Kliewer and Biklen (2007) that occurs when students with severe disabilities are placed in segregated educational settings and denied access to literacy instruction. When these students fail to develop literacy skills in these settings, this acts as confirmation that they indeed are incapable of developing literacy skills and, thus, a justification for further denying opportunities to obtain literacy instruction.

People with severe disabilities "represent the last group of people routinely denied opportunities for literacy instruction" (Keefe & Copeland, 2011, p. 92). Educators, service providers, families, and self-advocates must explicitly address this challenge if opportunities for high-quality literacy instruction in school, community, and home settings are to become available.

Rather than spend time debating the definition of literacy, certain core definitional elements should be agreed on, allowing an expansion of the vision of what literacy is for all students. Keefe and Copeland proposed the following elements to guide our approach to defining literacy and providing instructional opportunities in any setting.

1. All people are capable of acquiring literacy.
2. Literacy is a human right and is a fundamental part of the human experience.
3. Literacy is not a trait that resides solely in the individual person. It requires and creates a connection (relationship) with others.
4. Literacy includes communication, contact, and the expectation that interaction is possible for all individuals; literacy has the potential to lead to empowerment.
5. Literacy is the collective responsibility of every individual in the community; that is, to develop meaning making with all human modes of communication in order to transmit and receive information. (2011, p. 97)

Incorporating these elements expands on, rather than replaces, conventional approaches to defining literacy. The research discussed later in this chapter makes it clear that people with severe disabilities are capable of acquiring both conventional and expanded literacy abilities.

Incorporating Assistive Technology

Our expanded definition of literacy makes it clear that communication is a foundational element of literacy. We also believe all models of communication must be encouraged and recognized when working with students with severe disabilities. In this respect, assistive technology and augmentative and alternative communication (AAC) play a major role in the lives of many people with nontraditional modes of communication, both in the classroom and beyond (Downing, 2005). Literacy instruction is of particular importance for individuals who use assistive technology and AAC because "the ability to interpret symbols and symbolic language and translate those symbols into expressive language is fundamental to the ability of students who use AAC to communicate" (Ruppar, Dymond, & Gaffney, 2011, p. 101). In turn, implementing effective assistive technology and AAC is fundamental to the ability to gain access to and demonstrate literacy.

The right to assistive technology and its services is governed by IDEA 2004, which defined an *assistive technology device* as "any item, piece of equipment, or product system, whether acquired commercially off the shelf, modified, or customized, that is used to increase, maintain, or improve functional capabilities of a child with a disability" (§ 1412). Acquiring literacy skills is central to improving the functional capabilities of any student with a severe disability. It is critical that individuals with disabilities, educators, families, and advocates are aware of the right to assistive technology in order to ensure that students with severe disabilities are able to gain access to assistive technology and AAC consistent with the IDEA 2004 mandates. Training for using assistive technology is provided for in IDEA 2004. We have worked with schools and often have seen that training emphasizes the technical use of assistive technology devices, rather than the design and use of assistive technology to promote literacy and other academic and social skills. For example, Luckasson and Schalock (2012) described a multidimensional model whereby assistive technology can be thoughtfully integrated as a component of a system of supports for individuals with intellectual disability. The purpose of such systems is to reduce "the mismatch between a person's capabilities and the demands of the environment" (Luckasson & Schalock, 2012, p. 3). We propose that assistive technology and AAC should be viewed as a component of a system of supports in the classroom to ensure students can meaningfully participate in literacy instruction. Although each individual is different, some examples of how this can be achieved include 1) AAC devices to enhance social and linguistic interactions; 2) low and high assistive technology adaptations to materials, such as books and other curriculum materials, to provide access; 3) use of assistive technology to motivate and engage learners; and 4) use of assistive technology to provide alternative ways for students to respond and demonstrate understanding.

Effective Teacher Preparation

There is a lack of consensus and research regarding the content and configuration of teacher preparation programs for teachers of students with severe disabilities (Ryndak, Clark, Conroy, & Stuart, 2001). In general, "programs that prepare teachers to work with students with extensive support needs face additional, unique challenges in preparing professionals to facilitate the development of functional skills and to ensure access to the general education curriculum" (Delano, Keefe, & Perner, 2008–2009, p. 232). Teacher preparation programs are influenced and affected by contextual factors, such as philosophy, federal mandates, state certification requirements, and research (Delano et al., 2008–2009). In particular, Delano et al. noted the variability in state certification requirements for teachers of students with severe disabilities, depending on whether a state's certification is generic or disability specific. They further suggested that the effect of NCLB and IDEA 2004, the mandates related to accountability, definitions of a highly qualified teacher, and evidence-based practices have implications for the content and implementation of teacher preparation programs (see Delano et al. [2008–2009] for a more in-depth discussion of these areas).

Another challenge arises from the fact that there are not enough special education teachers in the United States. Special education has been an area of critical teacher shortages in all of the states from 1990 to 2012 (U.S. Department of Education Office of Postsecondary Education, 2012). Vermont was the only state not reporting a shortage of special education teachers in 2012–2103. Many states specifically have indicated shortages of teachers for students with severe disabilities. NCLB and IDEA 2004 allow teachers in shortage areas to be considered highly qualified through alternative certification and portfolio pathways. This unfortunately results in individuals with little or no formal preparation being hired to teach students with severe disabilities (Delano et al., 2008–2009).

NCLB and IDEA 2004 created additional requirements for teachers to have specific knowledge of reading instruction in the areas of phonemic awareness, phonics, vocabulary, fluency, and comprehension. Little research exists on the effect of these requirements on teacher preparation programs for teachers of students with severe disabilities. Copeland, Calhoon, and de Valenzuela (2008) reported results of a survey in which they found only 3 out of 28 institutions of higher education offered coursework in the area of reading instruction for students with severe disabilities. Copeland, Keefe, Calhoon, Tanner, and Park (2011) reported the results of a study using interviews to explore faculty experiences and perceptions related to preparing teachers to address literacy for students with severe disabilities. Participants reported a number of challenges with teacher candidates, including 1) lack of background knowledge and experience about the reading process, 2) very low expectations for students with severe disabilities, and 3) difficulty designing individualized literacy instruction consistent with the individualized education program. One consistent theme is related to finding sufficient time to address all the competencies needed for teacher candidates to teach literacy to students with severe disabilities. Some faculty were required to make time within courses designed to address literacy instruction for all students with disabilities. Other faculty described the tension they perceived between deciding how much time to spend on preparing teacher candidates to address literacy skills versus more traditional functional skills. Finding classroom settings where teacher candidates could observe and experience exemplary literacy instruction for students with severe disabilities was another consistent challenge.

Copeland et al. (2011) suggested implications for practice that emerged from their research. They reported the importance of having high expectations for students with severe disabilities in the area of literacy and broadening how literacy is conceptualized. Teacher preparation programs must acknowledge the importance of including a variety of evidence-based instructional practices that will help teacher candidates design appropriate literacy instruction for the unique and diverse needs of students with severe disabilities. Copeland et al. felt that creating a dichotomy between functional and academic approaches to literacy instruction is neither justified nor useful because "after all, literacy is a functional skill" (2011, p. 138).

Research in preparing general education teachers reports a relationship between the number of reading methods courses and fieldwork hours with teacher effectiveness on teaching reading (Hoffman et al., 2005; Maloch et al., 2003). Initial preparation of teacher candidates must provide them the skills and experiences they need to ensure students with severe disabilities realize their literacy potential. Effective teacher preparation remains one of the greatest challenges for literacy instruction for students with severe disabilities.

The importance of ongoing professional development for teachers is closely related to the challenge of initial teacher preparation. As research demonstrates more about effective strategies for teaching reading for students with severe disabilities, teachers must have opportunities to learn how to implement these strategies with their students.

Legislative Mandates

The context within which services for students with severe disabilities are educated has been affected in major ways by NCLB and IDEA 2004. These federal mandates represent a double-edged sword for students with disabilities in the areas of accountability, highly qualified teachers, and evidence-based practices. Delano et al. (2008–2009) noted that it is positive that schools are held accountable for the progress of students with disabilities. Labeling schools as failing based on these scores, however, can lead to the narrowing of curriculum as well as increased blame and segregation of students with disabilities. Similarly, the requirement in NCLB and IDEA 2004 that all general and special education teachers must be highly qualified in their teaching area and content seems at first glance to be a positive development for students with disabilities. Teachers going through alternative routes to certification are considered highly qualified, however, resulting in unprepared or underprepared teachers working with students with severe disabilities.

NCLB and IDEA 2004 require that teachers implement evidence-based practices. Delano et al. (2008–2009) noted that what constitutes evidence-based practice for students with severe disabilities is complex. NCLB and IDEA 2004 defined evidence-based practice very narrowly and in ways that might be difficult to meet in various educational settings (Berliner, 2002), particularly to a very diverse group such as students with severe disabilities (Emmons et al., 2009). NCLB further defined evidence-based reading instruction through the work of the National Reading Panel (NRP; 2000). The research used to identify evidence-based reading practices did not include or reference students with severe disabilities, and there is no guarantee that a program considered evidence based for students without disabilities is equally evidence based for students with severe disabilities. The research base on effective literacy instruction for students with severe disabilities has grown since the mid-2000s, and an overview of this research referenced to the areas of reading instruction identified by the NRP is provided later in this chapter. Identifying evidence-based practices for literacy instruction for students with severe disabilities remains an area of significant challenge for the future.

Cultural and Linguistic Diversity

The effect of differences between home and school languages on cognitive, linguistic, and academic development has been the subject of considerable debate. Although this issue has been examined in reference to typically developing students and students with mild disabilities, little is known about the multilingual potential of individuals with intellectual disability (Kay-Raining Bird et al., 2005). The available research suggests that bilingualism is possible in this population; however, the effect of bilingualism on their development is a still emerging area of research (Kay-Raining Bird at al., 2005). Yet, according to de Valenzuela and Niccolai, "Virtually no attention has been paid, either in the schools or in the professional literature, to the language needs of CLD [culturally and linguistically diverse] students with mental retardation and severe disabilities" (2004, p. 149).

There appears to be a virtually unchallenged assumption that bilingualism is neither possible nor important for individuals with intellectual disability. This situation is problematic for a number of reasons, including 1) the potentially large population of English language learners (ELLs) with intellectual disability or severe disabilities; 2) legal requirements affecting ELLs in public K–12 schools, including students with disabilities; and 3) historical and continuing concerns about the inaccurate identification of students with intellectual disability or severe disabilities who are culturally and linguistically diverse. No data are available showing the number of students who are both ELLs and identified with intellectual disability; however, this number can be estimated from counts of ELLs and percentage of individuals with intellectual disability in the student population. According to the National Center for Education Statistics (NCES; 2003), 3,768,653 students received English language development services in 2001–2002, and 1.2 % of all students were identified with intellectual disability in 2003–2004 (NCES, 2006). These data suggest there are approximately 45,224 ELLs with intellectual disability in K–12 schools.

Several studies have examined the effect of the language of instruction on ELLs with intellectual disability. None of these studies demonstrated an advantage to using English with ELLs with intellectual disability, even when the students had been educated only in English and the task was to acquire sight words in English (Rohena, Jitendra, & Browder, 2002). Indeed, several studies found Spanish language instruction more effective than either instruction in English alone or instruction in a combination of English and Spanish (Durán, 1991; Durán & Heiry, 1986).

The relative effectiveness of instruction in students' home language versus the language of the dominant culture has not been well established in the area of literacy instruction for students with intellectual disability. Although research has established the importance of home literacy experiences on later literacy development of children without disabilities, less is known about the influence of home literacy experiences on literacy development of children with severe disabilities (Weikle & Hadadian, 2004). Many of the studies available have found that parents of these children might have lower expectations for their children's literacy learning or might not see literacy as a priority for their children, given the numerous other areas of difficulty their child might experience (e.g., Marvin, 1994). Children with severe disabilities might also have physical or sensory issues that make access to literacy experiences more difficult (Martin, 1994). None of the studies examining home literacy have looked at children with severe disabilities whose home language is not English. In fact, there is little research examining literacy acquisition of children with severe disabilities from diverse linguistic backgrounds in general (Verhoeven & Vermeer, 2006).

We believe that the language education needs of students with intellectual disability who are culturally and linguistically diverse must become a priority for teaching and research. This includes developing methods to accurately assess the relative proficiency of ELLs with intellectual disability in both the home and school languages. Also needed is an awareness that special education services cannot replace bilingual and English as a second language instruction and educational planning must take a student's home language and cultural background into account. Finally, because oral language is the foundation on which literacy is developed, it is critical that a student's home language and current primary language be taken into account when developing literacy programs. It is the responsibility of educators and school systems to ensure that the home languages of ELLs with intellectual disability are taken into account when developing educational programs and determining placement. We believe that failure to do so is a social injustice as well as an egregious violation of the equal educational opportunities assured by the Civil Rights Act of 1964 (PL 88-352).

LITERACY IN RELATION TO THE TASH NATIONAL AGENDA

The area of literacy is of critical importance to all aspects of the TASH (2010b) national agenda. Access to high-quality literacy instruction is a human right and based on social justice principles (Keefe & Copeland, 2011). The design of effective literacy instruction across the life span cannot ignore issues of diversity and cultural competence. This approach to literacy is founded on the assumption that individuals with severe disabilities are capable of acquiring literacy and should be full members of the "literate community" (Kliewer, 2008, p. 23).

It is only through the presumption of competence and access to high-quality literacy instruction that individuals with severe disabilities will be welcomed and valued as members of their schools and communities across the life span. The presumption of competence, together with an expanded definition of literacy, will increase access to inclusive school and community environments. Effective literacy instruction for individuals with severe disabilities will lead to improved employment outcomes for them. Finally, defining literacy for people with severe disabilities to emphasize the importance of reciprocal social relationships and effective communication as critical elements of literacy has the potential to improve outcomes in all areas identified in the TASH (2010b) national agenda.

REVIEW OF RESEARCH AND RECOMMENDED PRACTICES FOR LITERACY INSTRUCTION

Many ways exist to frame a discussion of the existing research in literacy instruction, given the diversity of literacy skills demonstrated by people with severe disabilities. We have organized a brief review of the related research and recommended practices around the core components of a balanced and comprehensive literacy instructional program. A comprehensive instructional program that includes teaching language, word recognition, vocabulary and text comprehension, fluency, and writing (i.e., composing a message using symbols) is more likely to enhance meaning-making and lead to successful outcomes. Research findings increasingly support providing literacy instruction in a cohesive, integrated manner to maximize positive outcomes (e.g., Allor et al., 2010). Perhaps most important, research across each of these instructional areas supports holding high expectations for the literacy development of individuals with severe disabilities. Holding high expectations makes providing quality instruction more likely and increases opportunities to use literacy skills to fully participate in all aspects of life.

Language and Communication

Language forms the basis for literacy (Sturm & Clendon, 2004). Impairment in one or more areas of language has a detrimental effect on literacy development (Clarke, Snowling, Truelove, & Hulme, 2010). Although individuals with severe disabilities as a group have a broad range of language abilities (Van der Schuit, Segers, Van Balkom, Stoep, & Verhoeven, 2010), they typically experience difficulty with many aspects of language and communication (Snell et al., 2010). Nonetheless, research demonstrates that appropriate language intervention provided early facilitates language and communication development for people with severe disabilities, regardless of skill level (e.g., Van der Schuit et al., 2010).

Building language and communication skill begins with the expectation that a child is capable of communicating. It also requires that the communication partners of people with severe disabilities consistently "recognize, respond to, and value the expressive communication that the individual already produces" (de Valenzuela & Tracey, 2007, p. 26). Frequent, engaging, and meaningful communication opportunities, combined with a literacy-rich environment and high expectations, are critical to building the language and communication foundation on which later literacy skills will grow (Downing, 2011). Given the strength of research evidence supporting language and communication intervention (e.g., Snell et al., 2010), there is no reason that any person with severe disabilities should be denied access to instruction focused on building language through a reliable and consistent means of communication.

Tied to the importance of supporting communication and language development is the importance of rich home literacy environments (e.g., Ricci, 2011). Research has shown positive effects on attitudes of typically developing young children toward reading and emergent literacy skills when caregivers have regularly read to them, modeled interest in literacy activities, and provided a wide range of literacy materials and activities (Ricci, 2011). A small but growing number of studies indicate that early literacy experiences in the home can positively affect early reading skills of children with severe disabilities (e.g., Ricci, 2011).

Word Recognition

Skilled readers use two processes in identifying words—sight recognition and decoding. They typically recognize most words visually and use decoding skills only when they encounter a novel word. Research supports teaching people with severe disabilities both sight recognition and decoding skills (e.g., Browder, Ahlgrim-Delzell, Courtade, Gibbs, & Flowers, 2008). High-quality instruction on both word recognition approaches maximizes a person's opportunities to acquire literacy skills.

The strong link between vocabulary and word reading is another important finding from research examining word recognition (e.g., Allor, Mathes, Champlin, & Cheatham, 2009; Burgyone et al., 2012). Strong oral language abilities underlie all aspects of literacy development. Any comprehensive instructional program must include components to build these critical language skills.

Sight Word Instruction In addition to the potentially functional value of sight words, research suggests that building a base of sight words can facilitate acquisition of decoding skills (e.g., Lemons & Fuchs, 2010). Instructional methods to teach sight words have included response prompting and fading (Browder et al., 2006), embedded instruction (e.g., Jameson, McDonnell, Johnson, Riesen, & Polychronis, 2007), stimulus prompts (e.g., Walsh & Lamberts, 1979), and stimulus shaping (e.g., The Edmark Reading Program). It is critical to teach for comprehension from the beginning of word recognition instruction by incorporating newly acquired words immediately into connected text and then into meaning-making activities (Allor et al., 2009). Careful consideration of which words to teach is also critical. Words targeted for instruction should be meaningful to the student with severe disabilities and include words that will increase opportunities for genuine participation in his or her home, school, community, and employment settings.

Decoding Instruction Research findings demonstrate that people with severe disabilities can benefit from instruction in phonemic and phonological awareness and phonics (e.g., Browder, Ahlgrim-Delzell, Flowers, & Baker, 2012). Researchers have taught these skills using a wide variety of instructional approaches (e.g., picture cues, response prompts, modeling, computer programs, the Nonverbal Reading approach, published reading programs) (e.g., Browder et al., 2008; Heller & Alberto, 2010; Light, McNaughton, Weyer, & Karg, 2008).

The few but accumulating research studies examining decoding instruction point to some crucial considerations when designing instruction for students with severe disabilities. First, beginning instruction when students are young helps foster their literacy development (e.g., Burgoyne et al., 2012). This does not mean that older individuals should be excluded from instruction (e.g., see Moni, Jobling, Morgan, & Lloyd, 2011). Rather, it points to the importance of beginning high-quality comprehensive literacy instruction early to improve literacy outcomes. Second, instruction on decoding must be structured and explicit (e.g., Allor et al., 2010). It should build on what students already know and include well-paced instruction with clear directions and feedback (e.g., Allor et al., 2009). Third, people with severe disabilities benefit from intensive and sustained instruction to demonstrate meaningful growth (Allor et al., 2010; Burgoyne et al., 2012) (e.g., participants in the Allor et al. study received 40–50 minutes of intensive instruction per day across 2–3 years). Finally, decoding instruction must be provided within meaningful and engaging activities, using texts that are appropriate and engaging (e.g., Moni et al., 2011).

Vocabulary and Text Comprehension

Tompkins cited Judith Irwin's (1991) definition of *reading comprehension* as the "reader's process of using prior experiences and the author's text to construct meaning that is useful to that reader for a specific purpose" (2007, p. 198). This definition implies an active process with the following multiple component skills: 1) adequate decoding skill; 2) vocabulary knowledge; 3) knowledge of grammar, syntax, and pragmatics; and 4) the ability to relate general knowledge on a topic to the text being read (Conners, Moore, Loveall, & Merrill, 2011). Successful comprehension requires that these skill areas concurrently and smoothly work together. Many individuals with severe disabilities have difficulties in one or more of these areas, particularly those that are a part of oral (versus phonological) language (Erickson, Hanser, Hatch, & Sanders, 2009).

Vocabulary knowledge has a unique relationship with comprehension that merits specific attention. Restricted vocabulary knowledge limits reading comprehension. Reading widely is one of the most important ways in which new vocabulary is learned. Individuals who struggle to comprehend tend to read less, resulting in acquiring fewer new word meanings. This in turn affects their comprehension, which then makes them less motivated to read, and so forth (Cunningham & Stanovich, 1991). Just knowing standard word meanings is not sufficient for understanding connected text (Nation, 2009). To make meaning of connected text, the reader must understand how word meanings change depending on how a word is being used. They must also quickly and efficiently gain access to the meaning of words as they read the text (Nation, 2009). Erickson et al. noted, "Words that beginning readers are learning to read must already exist in their oral vocabulary" (2009, p. 92). Individuals with severe disabilities often have limited vocabularies and difficulty processing semantic memory (Conners et al., 2011). Their reading comprehension is affected when they encounter new words in a text and are unable to map them onto words in their listening or speaking vocabularies (Erickson et al., 2010) or take longer to locate the word meaning and assimilate it into the overall understanding of the text being read (Conners et al., 2011).

Vocabulary instruction for people with severe disabilities can be indirect (e.g., read alouds, independent reading) but also should include systematic and explicit instruction. Zangari and Van Tatenhove (2009) stressed that instruction should focus on helping individuals relate word meanings to their current understanding of a concept as well as include multiple examples of how a word can be used. Students then should use the new words in speaking, writing, reading, and listening tasks. Strategies such as using graphic organizers and semantic maps and sorting words related to meaning or use are examples of ways to provide this type of strong vocabulary instruction.

Although few studies directly examine reading comprehension instruction for people with severe disabilities, the existing research does provide some useful direction. Several authors have noted the positive relationship between using engaging texts and meaningful activities and developing reading comprehension of people with severe disabilities (e.g., Allor et al., 2010; Erickson et al., 2010). This requires that teachers pay close attention to the individual interests and skill levels of students and provide adapted texts and technology as needed to create access to interesting and motivating texts. It is also important to provide experiences with a range of types of texts (Allor et al., 2009; Erickson et al., 2010).

Research suggests considering three sets of variables during teacher-led instruction. First, Erickson et al. (2010) highlighted the importance of activating students' background knowledge on a topic they are reading about, setting a clear goal for reading a particular text, and revisiting that purpose to help students make sense of what they are reading. Second, Koppenhaver (2010) suggested teaching specific reading comprehension strategies with explicit instruction that includes both how and when to use the strategy. Third, Morgan, Moni, and Jobling (2009) recommended teaching students to generate questions about a text and demonstrate an understanding of the story grammar of a text.

In addition to teacher-led instruction, a small but growing group of studies supports using cooperative learning activities to build reading comprehension. This has taken the form of small groups of students with and without disabilities (e.g., Whalon & Hanline, 2008) as well as small groups of peers with similar disabilities (Alfassi, Weiss, & Lifshitz, 2009). Findings from these studies suggest that all group members, including those without disabilities, strengthen their comprehension through these activities.

Fluency

Fluency (i.e., accurately and quickly reading a text with appropriate phrasing and intonation) is linked to the ability to make meaning from a text (Keefe, 2007). Lack of sufficient decoding skills, other language skills (e.g., vocabulary), and sensory or physical challenges experienced by many people with severe disabilities all can affect fluency (Allor & Chard, 2011; Keefe, 2007). Few researchers have examined reading fluency of people with intellectual disability or other severe disabilities, and none have examined reading fluency of people with severe intellectual disability (Erickson et al., 2009).

The scant research that examines fluency of students with severe disabilities suggests that sustained and intensive instruction is needed for students to make progress (Allor et al., 2010; Coleman & Heller, 2010). Based on research with students with learning disabilities and those with intellectual disability, however, Allor and Chard (2011) provided several recommendations for fluency instruction. First, they suggested that effective literacy instruction must concurrently teach both word-level and meaning-level skills for literacy skills, including fluency, to progress. Second, they recommended having students practice with a wide variety of texts written at an appropriate level (i.e., students should be able to read the passage with at least 90% accuracy) on topics of interest to the students. Third, they highlighted the importance of making fluency instruction engaging and motivating because research supports frequent and intensive practice. Finally, they recommended modeling fluent reading (e.g., through read-alouds) with a variety of text genres and providing explicit feedback on students' performance. Researchers also suggest that repeated readings of a text, done in varied ways, should be an integral part of fluency instruction (e.g., Coleman and Heller, 2010).

Writing

Because of the wide variation in literacy levels among people with severe disabilities, we prefer the definition of *writing* provided by van Kraayenoord, Moni, Jobling, Koppenhaver, and Elkins: "[It] involves constructing meanings by choosing and arranging symbols and understanding how these meanings change as a result of audience, context, and purpose" (2004, p. 36). This definition recognizes that written communication can include text but might also include pictures, graphics, and/or symbols. Writing is an important part of a comprehensive literacy instruction program, whatever form it takes. Sturm and Koppenhaver (2000) suggested that it might be especially helpful for individuals with severe disabilities to acquire the ability to compose written messages because writing is a permanent form of language that can be revisited multiple times for multiple purposes.

Instruction on writing often is not provided in schools, especially for students who have complex communication needs (Williams, Koppenhaver, & Wollak, 2007). Indeed, few researchers have examined writing instruction for individuals with severe disabilities; the majority of these studies have included participants with mild or moderate intellectual disability (Joseph & Konrad, 2009). Instructional methods examined in the extant research include strategy instruction (e.g., Konrad & Test, 2007), use of Four-Blocks (Hedrick, Katims, & Carr, 1999), teaching composition of a text using print and symbols (Foley & Staples, 2003), and use of computer programs (e.g., Williams et al., 2007).

Instruction on writing for people with severe disabilities begins with the expectation that a student has a message to communicate. Next is providing appropriate instruction and support to facilitate that message being conveyed through print, pictures, symbols, or graphics. Because there is such a small research base from which to draw recommendations, experts indicate that instruction on writing for students with disabilities should follow the same general guidelines as instruction for typically developing students, with appropriate modifications and accommodations (Graham et al., 2012). Most important, students should be provided with opportunities to write every day, for a range of meaningful purposes, using a variety of strategies (Graham et al., 2012).

DIRECTIONS FOR FUTURE RESEARCH AND POLICY

The growing research base that examines literacy instruction for people with severe disabilities consistently demonstrates the benefit of comprehensive literacy instruction for all children. Many teacher preparation programs are not yet preparing preservice and practicing teachers to utilize what is known about literacy instruction for students with severe disabilities in their teaching practice, despite the promising research findings in this area (Copeland et al., 2011; Ruppar et al., 2011). If comprehensive literacy instruction for students with severe disabilities is to become a reality, then teacher educators must make room in their preparation programs for coursework and practice that provide the knowledge and skills practitioners need to create effective literacy instruction for these learners.

It is in the best interests of all students for them to be educated together across subject areas (TASH, 2010b). Literacy is no exception. Little of the current research on literacy instruction, however, has been conducted within inclusive settings. There is a critical need to examine literacy instructional practices for children with severe disabilities, including students with extensive support needs, within the educational settings of their typically developing peers. It is also time to recognize that the number of students with severe disabilities in the nation's schools who are culturally and linguistically diverse is growing. Very little attention has been given to the language or literacy instructional needs of these learners, either through research or in policy. It is also not an area typically addressed in teacher preparation programs. Given the increasing diversity of schools, this must become a priority for teacher educators, policy makers, and researchers.

Finally, although the national educational mandates have many flaws, they do require that schools be accountable for the educational progress of all students, including those with severe disabilities (e.g., NCLB). Despite the many difficulties with the manner in which this mandate has been implemented, it has positively influenced academic instruction for students with severe disabilities. Practitioners must not lose the focus on accountability for the academic instruction of students with severe disabilities. Needed changes in instruction will not be supported or sustained unless school districts recognize and value the academic progress of these learners.

CONCLUSION

Creating high-quality, effective literacy instruction for students with severe disabilities requires the students and their parents, educational practitioners, researchers, and policy makers to work together. The current amount of information is heartening when considering the paucity of information on effective, comprehensive instructional programs and approaches available in the mid-2000s. It is essential, however, that practitioners sustain these efforts so that the goal of "literate citizenship" for all becomes a reality (Kliewer, 2008, p. 20).

Questions for Study and Reflection

1. What are some of the implications of how literacy is defined? How might literacy be defined so that it includes all children?

2. Describe the rationale and supporting research base for providing comprehensive literacy instruction for all students.

3. What are the key legislative mandates that have spurred interest in developing more effective literacy instruction for students with severe disabilities?

4. Discuss the potential effect of cultural and linguistic diversity on literacy for students with severe disability.

RESOURCES

Books

Carnahan, C., & Williamson, P. (Eds.). (2010). *Quality literacy instruction for students with autism spectrum disorders.* Shawnee Mission, KS: AAPC Textbooks.

Copeland, S.R., & Keefe, E.B. (2007). *Effective literacy instruction for students with moderate or severe disabilities.* Baltimore, MD: Paul H. Brookes Publishing Co.

Downing, J.E. (2005). *Teaching literacy to students with significant disabilities: Strategies for the K–12 inclusive classroom.* Thousand Oaks, CA: Corwin Press.

Erickson, K., & Koppenhaver, D. (2007). *Children with disabilities: Reading and writing the Four-Blocks way.* Greensboro, NC: Carson-Dellosa.

Kluth, P., & Chandler-Olcott, K. (2008). *A land we can share: Teaching literacy to students with autism.* Baltimore, MD: Paul H. Brookes Publishing Co.

Soto, G., & Zangari, C. (2009). *Practically speaking: Language, literacy, and academic development for students with AAC needs.* Baltimore, MD: Paul H. Brookes Publishing Co.

Web Sites

Cast UDL Book Builder (*http://bookbuilder.cast.org*)—This site includes accessible fiction and nonfiction books on a range of topics for readers of all ages. It also allows creation of accessible books using the principles of universal design for learning.

Center for Literacy and Disability Studies (*http://www.med.unc.edu/ahs/clds*)—This site contains a wealth of resources, ideas, videos, and information on literacy instruction for individuals with severe disabilities.

Literacy for Children with Combined Vision and Hearing Loss (*http://www.nationaldb.org/literacy*)—This site contains numerous resources for literacy instruction for individuals with severe disabilities.

Tar Heel Reader (*http://tarheelreader.org*)—This site has free accessible books on a range of topics for readers of all ages. It also allows individuals to easily create their own books.

REFERENCES

Alfassi, M., Weiss, I., & Lifshitz, H. (2009). The efficacy of reciprocal teaching in fostering the reading literacy of students with intellectual disabilities. *European Journal of Special Needs Education, 24,* 291–305. doi: 10.1080/08856350903016854

Allor, J.A., & Chard, D.J. (2011). A comprehensive approach to improving reading fluency for students with disabilities. *Focus on Exceptional Children, 43,* 1–12.

Allor, J.H., Mathes, P.G., Champlin, T., & Cheatham, J.P. (2009). Research-based techniques for teaching early reading skills to students with intellectual disabilities. *Education and Training in Developmental Disabilities, 44,* 356–366.

Allor, J.H., Mathes, P.G., Roberts, J.K., Cheatham, J.P., & Champlin, T.M. (2010). Comprehensive reading instruction for students with intellectual disabilities: Findings from the first three years of a longitudinal study. *Psychology in the Schools, 47,* 445–466. doi: 10.1002/pits.20482

Berliner, D.C. (2002). Educational research: The hardest science of all. *Educational Researcher, 31,* 21–24.

Browder, D.M., Ahlgrim-Delzell, L., Courtade, G., Gibbs, S.L., & Flowers, C. (2008). Evaluation of the effectiveness of an early literacy program for students with significant developmental disabilities. *Exceptional Children, 75,* 33–52.

Browder, D., Ahlgrim-Delzell, L., Flowers, C., & Baker, J. (2012). An evaluation of a multicomponent early literacy program for students with severe developmental disabilities. *Remedial and Special Education, 33,* 237–246.

Browder, D.M., Wakeman, S.Y., Spooner, F., Ahlgrim-Delzell, L., & Algozzine, B. (2006). Research on reading instruction for individuals with significant cognitive disabilities. *Exceptional Children, 72,* 392–408.

Burgoyne, K., Duff, F.J., Clarke, P.J., Buckley, S., Snowling, M.J., & Hume, C. (2012, April 26). Efficacy of a reading and language intervention for children with Down syndrome: A randomized controlled trial. *Journal of Child Psychology and Psychiatry, 53,* 1044–1053.

Civil Rights Act of 1964, PL 88-352, 20 U.S.C. §§ 241 *et seq.*

Clarke, P.J., Snowling, M.J., Truelove, E., & Hulme, C. (2010). Ameliorating children's reading-comprehension difficulties: A randomized controlled trial. *Psychological Science, 21,* 1106–1116. doi: 101177/0956797610375449

Coleman, M.B., & Heller, K.W. (2010). The use of repeated reading with computer modeling to promote reading fluency with students who have physical disabilities. *Journal of Special Education Technology, 25,* 29–41.

Conners, F.A. (2003). Reading skills and cognitive abilities of individuals with mental retardation. *International Review of Research in Mental Retardation, 27,* 191–229.

Conners, F.A., Moore, M.S., Loveall, S.J., & Merrill, E.C. (2011). Memory profiles of Down, Williams, and Fragile X syndromes: Implications for reading development. *Journal of Developmental and Behavioral Pediatrics, 32,* 405–417.

Copeland, S.R., Calhoon, J.A., & de Valenzuela, J.S. (2008). *What are we teaching teachers about literacy instruction for students with intellectual or severe disabilities? A survey of teacher preparation programs.* Unpublished manuscript.

Copeland, S.R., & Cosbey, J. (2008–2009). Making progress in the general curriculum: Rethinking effective instructional practices. *Research and Practice for Persons with Severe Disabilities, 33,* 214–227.

Copeland, S.R., & Keefe, E.B. (2007). *Effective literacy instruction for students with moderate or severe disabilities.* Baltimore, MD: Paul H. Brookes Publishing Co.

Copeland, S.R., Keefe, E.B., Calhoon, A.J., Tanner, W., & Park, S. (2011). Preparing teachers to provide literacy instruction to all students: Faculty experiences and perceptions. *Research and Practice for Persons with Severe Disabilities, 36,* 126–141.

Cunningham, A.E., & Stanovich, K.E. (1991). Tracking the unique effects of print exposure in children: Associations with vocabulary, general knowledge, and spelling. *Journal of Educational Psychology, 83,* 264–274.

de Valenzuela, J.S., & Niccolai, S.L. (2004). Language development in culturally and linguistically diverse students with special education needs. In L. Baca & H. Cervantes (Eds.), *The bilingual special education interface* (4th ed., pp. 125–161). Upper Saddle River, NJ: Merrill.

de Valenzuela, J.S., & Tracey, M. (2007). The role of language and communication as the basis for literacy. In S.R. Copeland & E.B. Keefe (Eds.), *Effective literacy instruction for students with moderate or severe disabilities* (pp. 23–40). Baltimore, MD: Paul H. Brookes Publishing Co.

Delano, M.E., Keefe, L., & Perner, D. (2008–2009). Personnel preparation: Recurring challenges and the need for action to ensure access to general education. *Research and Practice for Persons with Severe Disabilities, 33,* 232–240.

Downing, J.E. (2005). *Teaching literacy to students with significant disabilities: Strategies for the K–12 inclusive classroom.* Thousand Oaks, CA: Corwin Press.

Downing, J.E. (2011). Teaching communication skills. In M.E. Snell & F. Brown (Eds.), *Instruction of students with severe disabilities* (7th ed., pp. 461–491). Boston, MA: Pearson.

Durán, E. (1991). Effects of using Spanish only, Spanish and English, and English only cues with students of limited English proficiency who have moderate to severe disabilities. *OSERS News in Print, 3,* 24–27.

Durán, E., & Heiry, T.J. (1986). Comparison of Spanish only, Spanish and English, and English only cues with handicapped students. *Reading Improvement, 23,* 138–141.

Emmons, M., Keefe, E.B., Moore, V.M., Sanchez, R.M., Mals, M.M., & Neely, T.Y. (2009). Teaching information literacy skills to prepare teachers who can bridge the research-to-practice gap. *Reference and User Services Quarterly, 49,* 140–150.

Erickson, K., Hanser, G., Hatch, P., & Sanders, E. (2009). *Research-based practices for creating access to the general curriculum in reading and literacy for students with significant intellectual disabilities.* (Final report to the Council of Chief State School Officers, Assessing Special Education Students, State Collaborative on Assessment and Student Standards). Chapel Hill, NC: Center for Literacy and Disabilities Studies. Retrieved from http://www.ksde.org/LinkClick.aspx?fileticket=y8Ms1dYL4Ps%3D&tabid=2384

Erickson, K.A., Hatch, P., & Clendon, S. (2010). Literacy, assistive technology, and students with significant disabilities. *Focus on Exceptional Children, 42,* 1–16.

Foley, B., & Staples, A. (2003). Developing augmentative and alternative communication and literacy interventions for adults with autism in a supported employment setting. *Topics in Language Disorders, 23,* 325–343.

Graham, S., Bollinger, A., Booth Olson, C., D'Aoust, C., MacArthur, C., McCutchen, D., & Olinghouse, N. (2012). *Teaching elementary school students to be effective writers: A practice guide* (NCEE 2012-4058). Washington, DC: U.S. Department of Education, Institute of Education Sciences, National Center for Education Evaluation and Regional Assistance.

Hedrick, W.B., Katims, D.S., & Carr, N.J. (1999). Implementing a multimethod, multilevel literacy program for students with mental retardation. *Focus on Autism and Other Developmental Disabilities, 14,* 231–239.

Heller, K.W., & Alberto, P.A. (2010). Reading instruction and adaptations. In S. Best, K.W. Heller, & J. Bigge (Eds.), *Teaching individuals with physical, health, or multiple disabilities* (6th ed., pp. 375–406). Upper Saddle River, NJ: Merrill/Prentice Hall.

Hoffman, J.V., Roller, C., Maloch, B., Sailors, M., Duffy, G., & Beretvas, S.N. (2005). Teachers' preparation to teach reading and their experiences and practices in the first three years of teaching. *Elementary School Journal, 105,* 267–287.

Individuals with Disabilities Education Act Amendments (IDEA) of 1997, PL 105-17, 20 U.S.C. §§ 1400 *et seq.*

Individuals with Disabilities Education Improvement Act (IDEA) of 2004, PL 108-446, 20 U.S.C. §§ 1400 *et seq.*

Irwin, J.W. (1991). *Teaching reading comprehension processes* (2nd ed.). Boston, MA: Allyn & Bacon.

Jackson, L.B., Ryndak, D.L., & Wehmeyer, M.L. (2008–2009). The dynamic relationship between context, curriculum, and student learning: A case for inclusive education as a research-based practice. *Research and Practice for Persons with Severe Disabilities, 33,* 175–195.

Jameson, J.M., McDonnell, J., Johnson, J.W., Riesen, T., & Polychronis, S. (2007). A comparison of one-to-one embedded instruction in the general education classroom and one-to-one massed practice instruction in the special education classroom. *Education and Treatment of Children, 30,* 23–44.

Joseph, L.M., & Konrad, M. (2009). Teaching students with intellectual or developmental disabilities to write: A review of the literature. *Research in Developmental Disabilities, 30,* 1–19.

Kay-Raining Bird, E., Cleave, P.L., Trudeau, N., Thordardottir, E., Sutton, A., & Thorpe, A. (2005). The language abilities of bilingual children with Down syndrome. *American Journal of Speech-Language Pathology, 14,* 187–199.

Keefe, E.B. (2007). Fluency. In S.R. Copeland & E.B. Keefe, *Effective literacy instruction for students with moderate or severe disabilities* (pp. 63–77). Baltimore, MD: Paul H. Brookes Publishing Co.

Keefe, E.B., & Copeland, S.R. (2011). What is literacy? The power of a definition. *Research and Practice for Persons with Severe Disabilities, 36,* 92–99.

Kliewer, C. (2008). *Seeing all kids as readers: A new vision for literacy in the inclusive early childhood classroom.* Baltimore, MD: Paul H. Brookes Publishing Co.

Kliewer, C., & Biklen, D. (2007). Enacting literacy: Local understanding, significant disability, and a new frame for educational opportunity. *Teachers College Record, 109,* 2579–2600.

Kliewer, C., Biklen, D., & Kasa-Hendrickson, C. (2006). Who may be literate? Disability and resistance to the cultural denial of competence. *American Educational Research Journal, 2,* 163–192.

Knoblauch, C.H. (1990). Literacy and the politics of education. In A.A. Lumsford, H. Moglen, & J. Slevin (Eds.), *The right to literacy* (pp. 74–80). New York, NY: The Modern Language Association of America.

Konrad, M., & Test, D.W. (2007). Effects of GO 4 IT NOW! Strategy instruction on the written IEP goal articulation and paragraph-writing skills of middle school students with disabilities. *Remedial and Special Education, 28,* 277–291.

Koppenhaver, D., (2010). Reading comprehension. In C. Carnahan & P. Williamson (Eds.), *Quality literacy instruction for students with autism spectrum disorders* (pp. 355–385). Shawnee, Mission, KS: AAPC Textbooks.

Lemons, C.J., & Fuchs, D. (2010). Modeling response to reading intervention in children with Down syndrome: An examination of predictors of differential growth. *Reading Research Quarterly, 45,* 134–168. dx.doi.org/10.1598?RRQ.45.2.1

Light, J., McNaughton, D., Weyer, M., & Karg, L. (2008). Evidence-based literacy instruction for individuals who require augmentative and alternative communication: A case study of a student with multiple disabilities. *Seminars in Speech and Language, 29,* 120–132. doi: 10.1055/s-2008-1079126

Luckasson, R., & Schalock, R.L. (2012). Human functioning supports, assistive technology and evidence–based practices in the field of intellectual disability. *Journal of Special Education Technology, 27,* 3–10.

Lumsford, A.A., Moglen, H., & Slevin, J. (1990). *The right to literacy.* New York, NY: The Modern Language Association of America.

Maloch, B., Flint, A.S., Eldridge, D., Harmon, J., Loven, R., Fine, J.C.,…Martinez, M. (2003). Understandings, beliefs, and reported decision-making of first-year teachers from different reading teacher preparation programs. *Elementary School Journal, 103,* 431–457.

Martin, J.R. (1994). Reading positions/positioning readers: Judgment in English. *Prospect, 10,* 27–37.

Marvin, C. (1994). Home literacy experiences of preschool children with single and multiple disabilities. *Topics in Early Childhood Special Education, 14,* 436–454.

Moni, K.B., Jobling, A., Morgan, M., & Lloyd, J. (2011). Promoting literacy for adults with intellectual disabilities in a community-based service organization. *Australian Journal of Adult Learning, 51,* 456–478.

Morgan, M., Moni, K.B., & Jobling, A. (2009). Who? Where? What? When? Why? How? Question words: What do they mean? *British Journal of Learning Disabilities, 37,* 178–185. doi: 10.1111/j.1468-3156.2008.00539.x

Nation, K. (2009). Reading comprehension and vocabulary: What's the connection?

In R.K. Wagner, C. Schatschneider, & C. Phythian-Sence (Eds.), *Beyond decoding: The behavioral and biological foundations of reading comprehension* (pp. 176–194). New York, NY: Guilford Press.

National Center for Education Statistics. (2003). *Common Core of Data (CCD): Public Elementary/Secondary School Universe Survey, 2001–2002 and Local Education Agency Universe Survey, 2001–2002.* Retrieved from http://www .nces.ed.gov/pubs2003/Overview03/tables/ table_10.asp

National Center for Education Statistics. (2006). *Digest of Education Statistics, 2005 (NCES 2006-030).* Retrieved from http://www.nces.ed.gov/fastfacts/display .asp?id=64

National Reading Panel. (2000). *Teaching children to read* (NIH Pub. No. 00-4754). Washington, DC: National Institute of Health and Human Performance.

No Child Left Behind Act of 2001, PL 107-110, 115 Stat. 1425, 20 U.S.C. §§ 6301 *et seq.* (2006).

Ricci, L. (2011). Home literacy environments, interest in reading and emergent literacy skills of children with Down syndrome versus typical children. *Journal of Intellectual Disability Research, 55,* 596–609. doi: 10.1111/j.1365-2788.2011/01 415.x

Rohena, E.I., Jitendra, A.K., & Browder, D.M. (2002). Comparison of the effects of Spanish and English constant time delay instruction on sight word reading by Hispanic learners with mental retardation. *Journal of Special Education, 36,* 169–184.

Ruppar, A.L., Dymond, S.K., & Gaffney, J.S. (2011). Teachers' perspectives on literacy instruction for students with severe disabilities who use augmentative and alternate communication. *Research and Practice for Persons with Severe Disabilities, 36,* 100–111.

Ryndak, D.L., Clark, D., Conroy, M., & Stuart, C.H. (2001). Preparing teachers to meet the needs of students with severe disabilities: Program configuration and expertise. *Journal of The Association for Persons with Severe Handicaps, 26,* 96–105.

Snell, M.E., Brady, N., McLean, L., Ogletree, B.T., Siegel, E., Sylvester, L.,...Sevick, R. (2010). Twenty years of communication intervention research with individuals who have severe intellectual and developmental disabilities. *American Journal on Intellectual and Developmental Disabilities, 115,* 364–380.

Sturm, J.M., & Clendon, S.A. (2004). Augmentative and alternative communication, language, and literacy. Fostering the relationship. *Topics in Language Disorders, 24,* 76–91.

Sturm, J.M., & Koppenhaver, D.A. (2000). Supporting writing development in adolescents with developmental disabilities. *Topics in Language Disorders, 20,* 73–92.

TASH. (2010a). *Mission and vision.* Retrieved from http://tash.org/about/ mission

TASH. (2010b). *National agenda.* Retrieved from http://tash.org/about/initiatives

Tompkins, G.E. (2007). *Literacy for the 21st century* (2nd ed.). Upper Saddle River, NJ: Pearson.

United Nations. (2006). *Convention on the rights of persons with disabilities.* Retrieved from http://www.un.org/ disabilities

U.S. Department of Education Office of Postsecondary Education. (2012). *Teacher shortage areas nationwide listing 1990–1991 through 2012–2013.* Retrieved from http://www.ed.gov/about/offices/list/ ope/pol/tsa.doc

Van der Schuit, M., Segers, E., Van Balkom, H., Stoep, J., & Verhoeven, L. (2010). Immersive communication intervention for speaking and non-speaking children with intellectual disabilities. *Augmentative and Alternative Communication, 26,* 203–220. doi: 10.3190/07434618.2010.505696

van Kraayenoord, C.E., Moni, K., Jobling, A., Koppenhaver, D., & Elkins, J. (2004). Developing the writing of middle school students with developmental disabilities: The WriteIdeas Model of Writing. *Literacy Learning: The Middle Years, 12,* 36–46.

Verhoeven, L., & Vermeer, A. (2006). Literacy achievement of children with intellectual disabilities and differing linguistic background. *Journal of Intellectual Disability Research, 50,* 725–738.

Walsh, B.F., & Lamberts, F. (1979). Errorless discrimination and picture fading as techniques for teaching sight words to TMR students. *American Journal of Mental Deficiency, 83,* 473–479.

Weikle, B., & Hadadian, A. (2004). Literacy, development and disabilities: Are we moving in the right direction? *Early Child Development and Care, 174,* 651–666.

Whalon, K., & Hanline, M.F. (2008). Effects of reciprocal questioning intervention on the question generation and responding of children with autism spectrum disorder. *Education and Training in Developmental Disabilities, 43,* 267–287.

Williams, A.R., Koppenhaver, D.A., & Wollak, B. (2007). Email interactions of preservice teachers and adolescents with special needs. *American Reading Forum Online Yearbook, 27.* Retrieved from http://americanreadingforum.org/yearbook/ yearbooks /07_yearbook/html/arf_07_Williams.htm

Zangari, C., & Van Tatenhove, G. (2009). Supporting more advanced linguistic communicators in the classroom. In G. Soto & C. Zangari (Eds.), *Practically speaking: Language, literacy, and academic development for students with AAC needs* (pp. 173–193). Baltimore, MD: Paul H. Brookes Publishing Co.

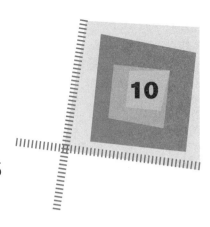

10

Social Interactions and Friendships

Erik W. Carter, Kristen Bottema-Beutel, and Matthew E. Brock

elationships are at the core of a good life. Although findings from decades of research have consistently converged on this simple point (Rubin, Bukowski, & Laursen, 2009), your own personal experiences likely affirm the importance of relationships to human flourishing. Interactions and affiliations with friends, classmates, family members, co-workers, neighbors, and many others in schools and communities help shape a person and the quality of life he or she experiences. It is not surprising, therefore, that the extent to which children and youth encounter supportive relationships with peers and adults can have a profound effect on their success in school and overall well-being (Ryan & Ladd, 2012). Relationships clearly matter in the lives of young people.

The diverse array of relationships adults identify as essential to their own thriving are just as important for children and youth with severe disabilities. Relationships assume a variety of forms throughout childhood and adolescence, ranging from casual and occasional to intimate and durable. Relationships with family members are the most prominent for many young people with disabilities. Relationships with same-age peers assume increasing importance, however, as children enter and progress through school. For example, interactions with classmates, clubmates, and teammates typically become more frequent and can evolve into close friendships or affiliations with networks of peers (e.g., cliques, crowds). Romantic relationships often emerge during adolescence, and interactions with co-workers and community members might increase as youth spend more of their school day off campus. Within the context of schools, the extensive interactions students have with general and special educators, related services providers, and other support staff are especially noteworthy. Each of these relationships can take on different forms and functions in the lives of students at different points in their development. And each might require a somewhat distinct set of skills, attitudes, and opportunities to successfully navigate. Yet, this constellation of relationships collectively provides students with a rich context for learning an array of social, communication, and related skills; enhancing their sense of belonging and contribution; making personal connections that build social capital; promoting engagement in school and community activities; learning peer norms and values; obtaining support; and raising personal aspirations for adulthood (Carter, 2011; Rubin et al., 2009).

Supporting individuals with severe disabilities to enjoy meaningful relationships has long been central to the mission of TASH (Brown et al., 1979), and this focus has relevance to all five pillars of its national agenda (TASH, 2010). A fundamental premise of inclusive education is that students without disabilities learn best alongside their peers with disabilities, and fostering supportive relationships enhances, rather than detracts from, academic rigor and relevance (Carter, Asmus, & Moss, in press; Ryndak, Moore, Orlando, & Delano, 2008/2009). The social-related skills students possess can also influence the success with which they are able to find and maintain employment (Carter, Austin, & Trainor, 2012), and the relationships established in the workplace can determine whether a particular job is one actually worth keeping. Supporting community living is not merely about the location where someone resides but also involves establishing connections within a network of supportive relationships within a community. Being culturally competent requires understanding the importance and place of relationships in the lives of individuals with severe disabilities and actively supporting those relationships. Finally, having the opportunities and supports to maintain personally valued relationships is widely considered a fundamental human right and is at the heart of what makes humans flourish (National Joint Committee for the Communicative Needs of Persons with Severe Disabilities, 1992; Nussbaum, 2006).

THE IMPORTANCE OF BEING INTENTIONAL

Yet, the relationships considered so central to healthy development and well-being are few or fleeting for too many children and youth with severe disabilities, especially with the interactions and relationships students have with their peers within school and community settings. Findings from numerous descriptive, intervention, and longitudinal studies focused on the social lives of students with severe disabilities and suggested a similar conclusion—peer relationships are likely to remain elusive unless adults take active steps to support their development (Carter, Sisco, Chung, & Stanton-Chapman, 2010).

Regular interaction opportunities and shared activities usually provide the context for peer relationships to develop and deepen. Yet, inclusive learning opportunities are inconsistently available for students with severe disabilities from one school, district, or state to the next (see Chapter 8). Nationally, only 17% of students with intellectual disability, 39% of students with autism, and 13% of students with multiple disabilities spend most or all of their school day (i.e., 80% or more) in classes with their peers without disabilities (U.S. Department of Education, 2010). Social interactions among students with disabilities and their peers might seldom occur even within inclusive classrooms, clubs, cafeterias, and community settings (Hughes et al., 1999; Rehm & Bradley, 2006). For example, Chung, Carter, and Sisco

(2012) found that elementary and middle school students who used augmentative and alternative communication (AAC) systems almost exclusively interacted with support staff in general education classrooms, despite being in close proximity to peers. A similar picture has been described in observational studies carried out in both elementary (Dymond & Russell, 2004; Katz, Miranda, & Auerbach, 2002) and secondary schools (Carter, Sisco, Brown, Brickham, & Al-Khabbaz, 2008), as well as reflected in the baseline and comparison phases of scores of intervention studies (see Carter et al., 2010; Snell et al., 2010).

Infrequent interactions can limit or preclude altogether the formation of peer relationships and lasting friendships. According to a nationally representative sample of parents of adolescents (ages 13–16) participating in the first wave of the National Longitudinal Transition Study–2, only 22% of youth with intellectual disability, 6% of youth with autism, and 14% of youth with multiple disabilities frequently saw friends outside of school (Wagner, Cadwallader, Garza, & Cameto, 2004). According to these parents, nearly 42% of youth with intellectual disability, 84% of youth with autism, and 63% of youth with multiple disabilities rarely or never received telephone calls from friends. Only 54% of youth with intellectual disability, 24% of youth with autism, and 38% of youth with multiple disabilities spent time with friends outside of formal groups at least weekly. The social connections of younger students are similarly disappointing: 17% of children with intellectual disability, 21% of children with multiple disabilities, and 32% of children with autism had never visited with friends during the past 12 months, according to parents of students ages 6–13 who participated in the Special Education Elementary Longitudinal Study (Wagner et al., 2002). As many as 50% of children with intellectual disability, 81% of children with autism, and 64% of children with multiple disabilities never or rarely received telephone calls from friends. Only 80% of children with intellectual disability, 68% of children with autism, and 74% of children with multiple disabilities had been invited to other children's social activities during the previous year. Other studies echo these findings and suggest many students with disabilities are on the peripheries of peer social networks, both within and beyond the classroom (Rotheram-Fuller, Kasari, Chamberlain, & Locke, 2010; Webster & Carter, 2007).

Although peer interactions and friendships might be limited, interactions with special educators, paraprofessionals, and related services providers remain quite prominent in the lives of many students with severe disabilities. For example, many paraprofessionals spend part or all of their assignment providing one-to-one support to students with severe disabilities (Fisher & Pleasants, 2012) and/or spend a substantial proportion of their day in close proximity to the students with whom they work (Giangreco & Broer, 2005). Although one-to-one adult support can be instrumental in addressing some of the educational and support needs of students, it does not always promote academic and social participation in general education settings (Chung et al., 2012).

CHALLENGES TO OVERCOME

Fostering supportive relationships and friendships among students with severe disabilities and their peers can be a challenging endeavor, despite broad affirmation within the field of the need to expand the social contacts and connections of students with severe disabilities (Carter & Pesko, 2008). What barriers sometimes stand in the way of developing meaningful social relationships? This section addresses three factors that can coalesce to limit the availability and quality of opportunities students have to spend time together and forge friendships. Such information can inform the design and delivery of instruction and support to address these student-, peer-, and support-related factors.

Student-Related Factors

Many students with severe disabilities experience complex communication challenges that can make interactions with peers and adults initially more difficult to navigate (Snell et al., 2010). For example, expressive and receptive language difficulties are especially pervasive among children and youth with severe disabilities. Kearns, Towles-Reeves, Kleinert, Kleinert, and Thomas (2011) conducted a multistate study of students participating in alternate assessments based on alternate academic achievement standards and found that approximately 72% of students with severe disabilities used verbal or written words, signs, braille, or AAC systems to expressively communicate. Yet, 17% of students relied primarily on gestures, objects/textures, or pointing to express their intentions, and 10% relied primarily on cries, facial expressions, or changes in muscle tone. Indeed, 11%–23% of students with intellectual disability, autism, or multiple disabilities are reported to use some type of electronic communication aid or AAC system (Blackorby et al., 2002). Although such communication differences do not inherently preclude the development of peer relationships, they can necessitate creative consideration of how to support ongoing conversations and social exchanges among students. Similarly, students with severe disabilities also might struggle to perform age-appropriate social skills that can contribute to high-quality interactions with others (Carter, Owens, Trainor, Sun, & Swedeen, 2009). For example, students might have had limited opportunities to learn skills such as using social amenities, taking turns, establishing eye contact, and appropriately initiating or responding. Such social-related skill deficits can affect the frequency and quality of students' interactions within and beyond the classroom.

Difficulties performing other skills outside of the social-communication domains also can limit interaction opportunities. Students who have not developed skills perceived to be requisite to participation in particular inclusive school and community activities are frequently excluded from those activities, further missing out on opportunities to engage in shared activities alongside their peers. For example, although inclusive activities actually can provide a rich context for learning important skills, educators might believe a student lacks the reading skills to participate in a particular general education class, the motor skills to participate in a recreational activity, or the technological skills to help out with a group presentation. Similarly, the occurrence of challenging behaviors (e.g., aggressive, stereotypic, self-injurious, or inappropriate social behaviors) frequently is cited by educators as a factor that limits a student's participation in inclusive educational opportunities (Carter & Hughes, 2006). Such collateral and behavioral skill deficits can lead educators and family members to limit involvement in particular activities, which correspondingly limits opportunities to meet new peers and spend time with current friends.

Peer-Related Factors

Although providing educational interventions and supports that build students' social competence and other capacities is certainly important, the receptivity of peers to developing and maintaining these relationships is also prudent to consider. Concomitant efforts might be needed to ensure peers are confident and comfortable working alongside and interacting with their classmates with severe disabilities. For example, some peers initially might be hesitant or reluctant to initiate conversations with a student who has extensive support needs, particularly if they have had limited experiences in the past (Carter, Hughes, Copeland, & Breen, 2001; Siperstein, Parker, Bardon, & Widaman, 2007). Other students might be unsure of how to communicate with someone who has limited speech, uses an AAC device, or is unable to talk at all. Although attitudes toward and knowledge about disabilities generally have improved over time (Siperstein, Norins, & Mohler, 2007), peers might still hold inaccurate information or perceptions of people with disabilities that could contribute to a reluctance to seek out or develop relationships with their classmates. Finally, peers might simply not have many opportunities to interact and develop friendships with students with severe disabilities because of the prominence of segregated educational models in the United States and elsewhere.

Support-Related Factors

Even when efforts are made to strengthen students' social competence and equip peers with appropriate information and accepting attitudes, relationships among students with severe disabilities and their peers likely will be limited if adequate interaction opportunities and sufficient supports are not available. Several support-related barriers might inadvertently limit or preclude students with and without severe disabilities from interacting with and getting to know one another. First, the proliferation of one-to-one adult support models in inclusive schools may unintentionally stifle the opportunities students have to work directly with their classmates (Chung et al., 2012; Giangreco, 2010). For example, rather than turning to the classmates for support, students with disabilities might learn to turn to adults; and their classmates might channel interactions through paraprofessionals, rather than interacting directly with the student. Moreover, individually assigned paraprofessionals might support students on the peripheries of a classroom and remain in continuous and close proximity. Second, teachers sometimes rely heavily on instructional approaches (e.g., lectures, whole-group discussion, individual seatwork) that provide students relatively few opportunities to work collaboratively and interact with one another, particularly in secondary schools (Mastropieri & Scruggs, 2001). Third, service delivery models in many schools substantially restrict the extent to which students with and without severe disabilities attend classes in common or participate in extracurricular and school-sponsored activities (Kleinert, Miracle, & Sheppard-Jones, 2007; Wagner et al., 2004). It is of little surprise that relationships remain elusive when students are rarely in the same locations at the same times doing the same activities.

OVERARCHING PRINCIPLES

This section briefly addresses four general considerations guiding our recommendations for educational supports and intervention planning focused on fostering social interactions and peer relationships. First, although researchers and practitioners have learned much about designing and implementing inclusive education since the 1990s, much more is known about facilitating interactions among students with severe disabilities and their peers than about how to ensure these interactions evolve into durable relationships, particularly friendships (Carter et al., 2010). Friendships are based on a mutual choice to enter into and maintain these relationships, irrespective of disability status. This recognition reinforces the importance of creating learning contexts in which students with severe disabilities are more likely to be chosen by their peers as friends. It also demarcates an important limit of intervention efforts—friendships can and should be fostered and nurtured by school staff, but they cannot be forced on students. Childhood and adolescent friendships form and falter for myriad reasons that might not always be apparent to adults. Thus, this area of intervention support might need to be guided by both art and science.

A second consideration relates to the role of adults in the social lives of students with severe disabilities. Although friendships between students without disabilities often develop without adults being in immediate proximity or providing support, students with severe disabilities are regularly in close proximity to adults who provide support. This ongoing adult presence and support might qualitatively change the dynamics of how social relationships form and develop. It is important for practitioners to reflect on their own understanding of their roles in this area of support as well as how their presence and involvement is understood by children and youth. The presence of an adult among younger children might be ubiquitous and not require special explanation. In other words, educators, paraprofessionals, and parents are often prominent in the interactions of most early elementary students. The presence of adults among older children and youth—particularly as they make the transition through middle and high school—might lead students to alter their behaviors and interactions in substantial ways from when they are alone with their peers. For example, adolescent interactions often take place outside of the immediate presence and purview of adults (Rubin et al., 2009). Recognizing these shifting dynamics should inform how school staff and families support and facilitate relationships across the grade span.

Third, the nature of students' relationships with one another naturally changes as they age. Therefore, educators should hold a long-term perspective when planning and evaluating support systems related to social relationships, as they should for other educational domains. Students' interests, preferences, involvement, and roles within their peer networks can evolve over time. Likewise, the various skills and attitudes that shape the formation and maintenance of relationships can change. Although younger children might readily accept a classmate with a severe disability into their peer group, adolescents might have a more complex and codified system for introducing others into their networks. It is important for educators to carefully consider the social practices and dynamics considered relevant and important to the peer group in which they are supporting a particular student with severe disabilities to access and how these practices change over time as students make the transition across grades and schools.

Fourth, it is important to consider the breadth of relationships important to all children and youth and to reflect on whether students with severe disabilities have opportunities to move beyond circumscribed roles and experience the full range of social relationships. Most students have opportunities at various times to both give and receive support, to both teach and learn from others, and to both lead and follow their peers. Such reciprocity and balance of roles might be part of what differentiates friendships from helping relationships (e.g., tutoring, mentoring). Yet, a prominent approach for increasing interactions among students with and without severe disabilities in schools involves permanently positioning students in designated roles of receivers of support, learners, and followers. Although such relationships, characterized primarily as helping, might be beneficial for promoting some outcomes (e.g., academic performance, functional skill acquisition), relationships failing to move beyond this dynamic are less likely to involve reciprocity and shared contributions, which are important elements of friendships.

A FRAMEWORK FOR SUPPORTING INTERACTIONS AND RELATIONSHIPS

Making a substantial and sustained difference in the social lives of students with severe disabilities requires careful consideration of multiple aspects of educational services and supports focusing on 1) individual students and their peers; 2) school policies, practices, and culture; or 3) district, state, and federal policies and resources. Figure 10.1 depicts a framework for considering some of the multiple intervention approaches that might be undertaken within an educational context. At the very center of this framework is the intersection of student, peer, and support factors that can affect relationships. What efforts might educators make to ensure a particular student has the opportunities, skills, and supports he or she needs to make meaningful social connections in school? Educators might consider

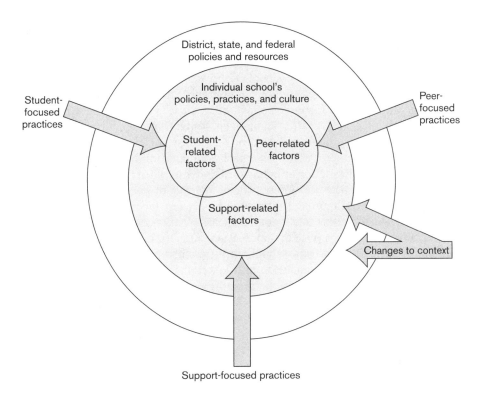

Figure 10.1. Framework for promoting social interactions and relationships for children and youth with severe disabilities.

an array of interventions that build a student's social and communicative competence (i.e., student-focused practices), equip peers to participate in regular interactions (i.e., peer-focused practices), and/or ensure interactions and relationships are actively encouraged and promoted by educational staff (i.e., support-focused practices). Interventions in these areas are designed to address the student-, peer-, and support-related factors described earlier in this chapter.

Although individual students, peers, and ways in which support is provided all represent salient intervention points, it is also prudent to consider broader contextual factors that might enhance or stifle the development of peer relationships. The policies and practices of a given school can shape the opportunities students have to work and spend time with their peers, as well as the extent to which fostering relationships is prioritized by faculty and staff. For example, structural barriers within many schools and districts constrain the opportunities students with and without disabilities have to attend class, spend breaks, eat lunch, and participate in clubs together. Similarly, the culture and commitments of a school might influence whether and how relationships are supported. For example, school leaders might articulate a mission and vision that emphasize the importance of supporting positive relationships alongside—rather than in lieu of—academic excellence and school engagement. Moreover, some schools already focus on supporting diversity and developing a strong sense of belonging among all students—an emphasis that aligns well with goals of expanding the social connections of students with disabilities.

The activities of individual schools also are influenced by the districts, states, and countries within which they are embedded. Policies developed and disseminated at each of these levels directly or indirectly shape how instructional time is allocated within schools and what educational domains are prioritized. For example, accountability efforts can determine how school effectiveness is operationalized, and evolving educational standards can affect what content is ultimately emphasized within classrooms. Similarly, the resources allocated at each of these levels can influence the capacity of schools and staff to implement student-, peer-, and support-focused practices for individual students. For example, professional development opportunities and consultative support addressing social domains might be less available than resources addressing academic or behavioral domains.

Our contention is that the effect of social-focused intervention is maximized by adopting a multifaceted approach addressing all of these factors. Individual students will benefit by learning new social-communication skills, spending time with peers who are confident and effective communication partners, and receiving needed support and social facilitation from school staff. Concurrently, steps should be taken to ensure a commitment to inclusion and belonging permeates the entire school culture so that meaningful interactions and learning opportunities are available throughout the life of a school. Finally, policies and initiatives at district, state, and federal levels should convey clear recognition of the importance of relationships to learning and success in school and beyond. Children and youth with severe disabilities would be most likely to develop relationships that make a noticeable difference in their well-being and quality of life when these multiple factors are addressed in tandem and sustained over time as students progress through elementary, middle, and high school.

RESEARCH-BASED AND RECOMMENDED PRACTICES FOR FOSTERING SOCIAL RELATIONSHIPS

Amidst a rapidly growing evidence base and evolving practices, much is now known about how best to create meaningful opportunities for students with and without severe disabilities to meet, interact, and get to know one another within and beyond the school day. Regular peer interactions and personally valued relationships need not—and we believe must not—be few and far between for children and youth with disabilities in schools and communities. This section highlights three categories of educational practices (i.e., student focused, peer focused, support focused) that can enhance the social lives of students with intellectual disability, multiple disabilities, autism, and other developmental disabilities. These practices are drawn from systematic reviews of the empirical literature (i.e., Carter et al., 2010; Carter, Sisco, & Chung, 2012; Chung et al., 2012; Hughes et al., 2012; Snell et al., 2010) and our own partnerships with inclusive schools. Each category falls within the framework depicted in Figure 10.1 and illustrates avenues through which educators, families, and others can strengthen capacities, confidence, and commitment around supporting rich social lives for students. Our review of student-, peer-, and support-focused practices is not intended to be exhaustive; rather, it is meant to highlight several examples of evidence-based practices within each category. We encourage practitioners and policy makers to remain abreast of new developments and systematic reviews addressing social-related interventions for students with severe disabilities.

Student-Focused Practices

One extensively evaluated approach for improving the quantity and quality of social connections involves providing targeted skill instruction directly to students with severe disabilities. Such student-focused interventions are primarily aimed at building the social and communicative competence of students in order to enhance their contributions when interacting with others or to reduce behaviors that might hinder interaction opportunities. A wide variety of student-focused interventions have been evaluated in the peer-reviewed literature, individually and in combination with other intervention approaches. Such interventions have primarily focused on teaching communication strategies, strengthening social skills, and decreasing or eliminating socially inappropriate behaviors. The quality and frequency of interactions with peers and adults might be more likely to increase by building students' capacity for communication and social interaction.

Building Effective Communication   Many students with severe disabilities experience complex communication challenges. For example, students might have a narrow communication repertoire, communicate in subtle ways understood only by caregivers and close companions, or lack consistent means of functional communication (Ogletree, Bruce, Finch, Fahey, & McLean, 2010). Building social relationships becomes all the more difficult when students are unable to effectively communicate with peers. Several interventions targeting communication skills have evidence of efficacy for students with severe disabilities, including the Picture Exchange Communication System (PECS; Ganz, Davis, Lund, Goodwyn, & Simpson, 2012) and using speech-generating or other AAC devices (Odom, Collet-Klingenberg, Rogers, & Hatton, 2010; Rispoli, Franco, van der Meer, Lang, & Carmargo, 2010).

A student using PECS initially is taught to request a desired item by exchanging a picture symbol for the item. The student is taught in subsequent phases to spontaneously initiate the exchange, discriminate between different picture symbols, build sentence structure by combining picture symbols, and comment and respond to questions (Frost & Bondy, 2002). Systematic instruction also can be used to teach students to use speech-generating devices to communicate by selecting pictures, symbols, words, or letters. These approaches can be drawn on to enable students with severe disabilities to develop functional communication, communicate more clearly, and/or develop wider communicative repertoires. It is important, however, to equip students with specific communication strategies that will enhance participation in shared activities and contribute to enjoyable peer interactions.

Direct Instruction of Social Skills   Although many children and youth learn appropriate social behaviors naturally through observation and incidental instruction, students with severe disabilities usually benefit from receiving more explicit instruction in discrete skills or clusters of social-related skills (Snell et al., 2010). Although intervention efforts should generally be individually tailored for each student, commonly addressed skills include effective attention-getting strategies, appropriate social greetings and conversational initiations, conversational turn taking, or adjusting social behaviors across settings and situations. Intervention strategies such as video modeling, social skills groups, and Social Stories use direct instruction to effectively improve these social skills for students with severe disabilities (Odom et al., 2010; Shukla-Mehta, Miller, & Callahan 2010; Test, Richter, Knight, & Spooner, 2011). Adults, peers, or students using video modeling record themselves as they correctly engage in a targeted social behavior (e.g., appropriately greeting a peer, working collaboratively with a classmate). Students view the video as an example of how to successfully perform the behavior. Social skills groups involve an educator teaching and guiding small groups of students as they role-play and practice specific social skills. Social Stories are written or video-based narratives highlighting specific social cues and describing socially appropriate responses to each cue. These strategies can be drawn on to equip students with severe disabilities to learn social rules and contextually appropriate behaviors they might not acquire naturally on their own.

Reducing Socially Inappropriate Behaviors   Research clearly links problem behavior with more restrictive educational placements, social exclusion, and diminished participation in school and community activities (Horner, Carr, Strain, Todd, & Reed, 2002). Moreover, challenging behaviors can be intimidating to some peers or carry a social stigma. For example, peers might be hesitant to interact with a student who is aggressive toward others or engages in self-injurious behaviors. Reducing or eliminating such behaviors can promote participation in more inclusive settings and remove potential barriers to social interaction. A number of evidence-based practices exist for addressing challenging and socially inappropriate behaviors, including functional communication training, differential reinforcement, and self-management strategies. The starting point for each of these practices involves determining the function of a challenging behavior using functional assessment approaches. When a problem behavior serves a communicative function, functional communication training can be used to replace an inappropriate behavior or subtle communicative attempt with more appropriate and effective forms of communication. Students are taught an appropriate replacement behavior that is easy for them to perform and functionally equivalent to the original behavior (Grey & Hastings, 2005). When the function of a student's challenging behavior is to gain peer or adult attention, differential reinforcement can be used to ignore inappropriate behavior and reinforce desired behaviors. Students engaging in self-stimulatory behavior (e.g., rocking, hand flapping) can be taught self-management strategies to monitor and record the number of times they engage in such behaviors, set goals for reductions, and reward themselves for meeting their goals (e.g., Koegel & Koegel, 1990).

Peer-Focused Practices

Although providing instruction aimed at enhancing the social competence of students with severe disabilities is a frequent focus of educational programming, the occurrence of peer interaction also depends on the receptivity and availability of conversational partners such as classmates, teammates, clubmates, and other students from the same school or neighborhood. Peer-focused intervention strategies are designed to equip these students with the confidence, skills, and opportunities to work alongside, spend time with, and get to know their peers with severe disabilities. The peers are the primary recipients of instructional and support efforts, rather than the student with disabilities. Examples of peer-focused strategies within the research literature have included providing disability- and student-specific information, interaction training, and social-related support to same-age peers who have interests, classes, activities, or other aspects in common with the focus student who has severe disabilities.

Providing Disability-Related Information   Some peers might possess inaccurate information about people with disabilities or be unaware of the social isolation some of their classmates with severe disabilities experience. Providing these peers with accurate information about students with disabilities, potential support needs, and/or effective ways to converse with the students might increase the confidence of peers and the possibility that social overtures will lead to sustained interactions and new relationships. For example, some schools undertake general awareness efforts within a class or across an entire school to foster greater understanding among students about people with disabilities (Lindsay & Edwards, 2013; Siperstein, Pociask, & Collins, 2010; Wolfberg, McCracken, & Tuchel, 2008). Information about disability and diversity can be incorporated into school assemblies, relevant units within academic classes, or other inclusion awareness events sponsored by a school. Awareness activities might include multimedia showings, selected readings, or thoughtful simulations of what it might be like to have a particular support need. Alternatively, informational approaches can focus more directly on the strengths and needs of specific students. For example, circle of friends approaches usually involve holding a classwide discussion, facilitated by an experienced educator, as a context for providing information about a particular student and the ways in which social connections might be fostered (Frederickson & Turner, 2003). Peers discuss the student's strengths and potential difficulties interacting with others, as well as identify possible strategies for supporting increased interactions. Educational teams should thoughtfully implement these interventions and consider how individuals with disabilities might be actively involved in their design and delivery.

Although awareness efforts might be helpful, they often have a limited effect on peer behavior without additional guidance and support. Several approaches provide this support to peers, including peer interaction training, peer support arrangements, and peer networks.

Peer Interaction Training   Peer interaction training involves teaching selected peers specific skills and strategies they can use to converse with students who have complex communication challenges. For example, peers can be taught how to initiate social contacts by identifying students who appear socially isolated and inviting them into play and leisure activities (Kasari, Rotheram-Fuller, Locke, & Gulsrud, 2011). Fellow classmates can be taught conversational skills helpful for sustaining interactions during group activities with a student who is nonverbal or uses an AAC device (Harper, Symon, & Frea, 2008; Hughes et al., 2011). Research clearly confirms that elementary and secondary school students can learn and implement an array of targeted skills that contribute to more frequent and higher quality interactions (Carter et al., 2010). The particular skills taught to peers, however, should be selected based on the individual profiles of the students with whom they will be spending time and the contexts within which social interactions will take place.

Peer Support Arrangements   Peer support arrangements are advocated as an especially promising approach for promoting both social relationships and learning within inclusive classrooms and clubs (Carter, Moss, Hoffman, Chung, & Sisco, 2011; Jimenez, Browder, Spooner, & Dibiase, 2012). These intervention arrangements involve identifying one to three peers without disabilities from the same setting to provide academic- and social-related support to a classmate with severe disabilities. Peers participate in a brief orientation addressing their roles and responsibilities within these arrangements, as well as receive ongoing support from a general educator, special educator, and/or paraprofessional (see strategies for facilitating interactions in the next section). Peers assist with social-related goals through initiating interactions, modeling appropriate social skills, reinforcing communication attempts, and encouraging contributions to group discussions. They support learning by assisting during group activities, sharing materials, reviewing work, explaining key ideas, and offering constructive feedback. Students working with one another throughout the semester discover common interests, learn effective ways to converse with one another, exchange needed support, and introduce one another to their own friends and peer group members.

Peer Network Strategies   Even as increasing numbers of students with severe disabilities attend general education courses, they might have limited social contact outside of the classroom while at lunch, on the playground, in the hallways, or before and after school (Carter, Hughes, Guth, & Copeland, 2005). Peer network strategies offer an avenue for connecting students with and without severe disabilities during these socially rich interaction contexts (Haring & Breen, 1992; Kamps, Potucek, Lopez, Kravits, & Kemmerer, 1997). Peer networks typically involve establishing a structured social group comprised of four to six peers and the focus student with severe disabilities that meets regularly in an effort to increase the student's social contacts and friendships. The network initially is facilitated by an adult (e.g., coach, teacher, guidance counselor) and might gather at lunch, during a study hall or advisory period, or before or after school. As part of each network meeting, students plan additional social contacts that can range from simply saying "hello" in the hallway to more extensive interactions, such as eating lunch together or hanging out after school. The adult facilitator helps students identify times when their schedules align and supports peers in identifying meaningful ways of connecting with the focus student with disabilities. Other schoolmates may join the network over time as they see positive interactions occurring throughout the day.

Support-Focused Practices

Although strengthening the social capacities of students and equipping conversational partners are important elements of social-focused intervention efforts, peer interactions might infrequently occur and be unlikely to lead to relationships if not thoughtfully supported by adults in the setting. Support-focused intervention practices refer to the efforts of educators, parents, and others (e.g., employers, club sponsors, youth group leaders) to proactively create socially supportive environments in which peer interactions are actively prompted and promoted. The effect of student- and peer-focused interventions might be substantially diminished when students lack opportunities, encouragement, and needed assistance to interact with one another. A number of support-focused practices can establish rich contexts within which students can practice and refine their social-related skills and deepen relationships with others.

Facilitating Interactions   Although most school settings offer numerous opportunities for students to interact with one another, such opportunities can sometimes be overlooked by students with disabilities and their peers. Adult facilitation of peer interaction is one approach for promoting sustained social engagement (Causton-Theoharis & Malmgren, 2005; Schaefer & Armentrout, 2002). Facilitation techniques are aimed at encouraging reciprocal interactions among the student with severe disabilities and their peers and often are implemented by special educators or paraprofessionals as small groups of students initially begin working or playing together. Techniques can include highlighting commonalities among students, interpreting behaviors that might be unconventional or difficult to interpret, adapting activities to include a clear role for the student with disabilities, and redirecting conversation away from adults and toward other group members (Carter, 2011; Wolfberg, 2003). As students get to know and gain experience working with one another, peers often begin to naturally interact with students with disabilities without adult support, and adults are able to scale back their direct involvement in ongoing interactions.

In addition to more explicit facilitation strategies, the incidental lessons educators teach to students are also essential to consider. For example, the ways in which special educators, service providers, and paraprofessionals talk about and with students who have severe disabilities serve as primary models for peers, particularly when the peers have had few prior encounters with students with extensive support needs. Peers likely will follow adults who model respectful interactions, use appropriate and affirming language, and convey high expectations for students with severe disabilities.

Arranging Interactive Activities   Both instructional approaches and seating arrangements used in schools can limit or actively discourage interaction opportunities among any students. For example, teacher-led discussions and independent seatwork are prevalent instructional formats in many classrooms. Establishing more interdependent instructional arrangements can increase expectations and opportunities for social interaction without sacrificing important learning outcomes. Cooperative learning groups usually involve organizing students into groups of three to six students, setting shared learning goals for each group, allocating clearly defined roles for each student within their group (e.g., timekeeper, notetaker, reporter), teaching students the social-related skills needed to work collaboratively with one another, and holding all students accountable to meeting these shared goals (Cushing, Kennedy, Shukla, Davis, & Meyer, 1997; Kamps, Lopez, & Golden, 2002). Thus, students gain access to teacher-sanctioned opportunities to work together and interact with one another. Interactive activities beyond the classroom also can be designed around those interests of students with severe disabilities that overlap with interests of their peers (Koegel et al., 2012) or recreational and leisure activities that offer engaging interaction opportunities (e.g., Hughes et al., 2002).

Fading Direct Support   As students approach adolescence, the constant presence of a paraprofessional or special educator could stifle, rather than encourage, interactions among students with and without severe disabilities. Carter et al. (2008) studied inclusive middle and high school classrooms and found that social interactions among students with and without disabilities were least likely to occur when students with severe disabilities were working in close proximity to a paraprofessional or special educator. Yet, individually assigned adult support models remain prevalent within many general education classrooms, workplaces, and other settings (Giangreco, 2010). As students with and without disabilities gain experience and confidence working with one another, educators and paraprofessionals should take steps to fade their direct support and instead encourage students with disabilities to turn to more natural sources of support within a particular school or community setting. Instead of serving as the first line of support, school staff should consider whether students can participate in an activity 1) on their own, 2) if given the right equipment or technology, 3) if given additional skill instruction, 4) if taught self-management strategies, 5) with help from one or more peers, or 6) with help from others in the setting (Carter, Cushing, & Kennedy, 2009).

IMPLICATIONS FOR FUTURE RESEARCH AND POLICY

Although the field has moved toward affirming the importance of fostering relationships and identifying compelling approaches for doing so, much is still to be learned about how best to support meaningful social connections for students with severe disabilities. First, numerous studies demonstrate that discrete interactions among students with severe disabilities and their peers can be increased using a variety of student-, peer-, and support-focused practices (Carter et al., 2010). Much less is known, however, about how to promote sustained interactions in ways that ultimately develop into friendships and long-term relationships (Webster & Carter, 2007). Although social interactions substantially contribute to learning and school satisfaction, it is the absence of friendships and other supportive relationships that most negatively affects quality of life.

Second, new approaches to measurement and data collection will be needed to better understand the factors contributing to the development of peer relationships among students with and without severe disabilities. Documenting the nature and importance of peer affiliations among students with complex communication challenges will require creative combinations of quantitative and qualitative methodologies, including integration of direct observations, self-report measures, and input from educators, family members, peers, and others. Knowing whether students interact with particular peers is one thing, but discerning the importance and effect of those relationships on a student with limited communication is quite another.

Third, romantic relationships become increasingly prominent as students move through adolescence and early adulthood. Yet, discussions about dating, falling in love, marriage, and other intimate relationships are noticeably sparse in the research and practitioner literature (Valenti-Hein & Choinski, 2007). Although such silence might reflect prevailing attitudes about sexuality and people with severe disabilities, it is important that effective approaches for supporting this dimension of young people's lives also are identified and disseminated to schools and families.

Fourth, much of the empirical literature has focused on evaluating student-specific interventions delivered on an individual basis. Although this emphasis reflects the manner in which educational services are designed and delivered for students receiving special education services, concurrent efforts should be undertaken to rigorously evaluate the effect of schoolwide and community programs aimed at fostering friendships among students with and without disabilities. For example, little is known about the most effective ways to design and implement peer partner programs (e.g., peer buddy programs, peer mentoring programs, Best Buddies, recreational programs) or to deliver peer-mediated interventions (e.g., peer support arrangements, peer networks) to multiple students at a particular school at the same time.

Finally, fostering relationships has not received nearly the same attention in local, state, and federal policy as promoting academic rigor and relevance. Although addressing learning and relationships often are viewed as competing priorities, there is good reason to believe that they are complementary. Studies consistently have documented the ways in which students with and without disabilities can acquire myriad social, academic, self-determination, and other life skills when, and because of, working together. Indeed, shared learning experiences foster relationships, and relationships enhance learning (Carter et al., in press). Much more attention should be focused on crafting policies and practices that reflect this dual emphasis.

CONCLUSION

Relationships are at the very heart of what enables people to thrive. The social interactions children and youth with severe disabilities experience, the affiliations they enjoy, and the friendships they encounter as they progress through school can make substantial contributions to their overall quality of life. The absence of such relationships can have disappointing and deleterious effects. Educators, service providers, and parents can play a critical role in ensuring these students have the opportunities, skills, and supports needed to meet, work alongside, and get to know their peers in diverse ways throughout their schooling. Relationships really do matter in the lives of students with severe disabilities. It is essential that policies and practices (i.e., services, supports) reflect this central premise.

Questions for Study and Reflection

1. Which of the potential barriers addressed in this chapter are apparent in the schools and communities with which you are most familiar? Are there additional factors that limit the opportunities students with severe disabilities in these settings have to develop meaningful relationships with peers and others?

2. What might be some indicators that the students with whom you work have (or lack) strong, supportive social connections in their school and community? What data could you collect to help you better answer this question?

3. What are the potential strengths and drawbacks of the three categories of intervention approaches that can promote social interactions and relationships for students with and without severe disabilities?

4. Reflect on a typical school day for students with severe disabilities in the school(s) within which you work. In what ways could peers be more actively engaged in supporting and interacting with students within the classrooms, cafeterias, clubs, and community-based settings in which students spend their time?

5. How might school, district, and state policies shape the extent to which fostering relationships is prioritized by educators, service providers, and families in your community? What changes could be made to elevate the importance of this focus of educational services and supports?

RESOURCES

Bagwell, C.L., & Schmidt, M.E. (2011). *Friendships in childhood and adolescence.* New York, NY: Guilford Press.

Bellini, S. (2006). *Building social relationships: A systematic approach to teaching social interaction skills to children and adolescents with autism spectrum disorders and other social difficulties.* Shawnee Mission, KS: Autism Asperger Publishing.

Beukelman, D.R., & Mirenda, P. (Eds.). (2013). *Augmentative and alternative communication: Supporting children and adults with complex communication needs* (4th ed.). Baltimore, MD: Paul H. Brookes Publishing Co.

Carter, E.W., Cushing, L.S., & Kennedy, C.H. (2009). *Peer support strategies for improving all students' social lives and learning.* Baltimore, MD: Paul H. Brookes Publishing Co.

Carter, E.W., Moss, C.K., Hoffman, A., Chung, Y., & Sisco, L.G. (2011). Efficacy and social validity of peer support arrangements for adolescents with disabilities. *Exceptional Children, 78,* 107–125.

Hughes, C., & Carter, E.W. (2008). *Peer buddy programs for successful secondary school inclusion.* Baltimore, MD: Paul H. Brookes Publishing Co.

Ingersoll, B., & Dvortcsak, A. (2009). *Teaching social communication to children with autism: A manual for parents.* New York, NY: Guilford Press.

Sigafoos, J., Arthur-Kelly, M., & Butterfield, N. (2006). *Enhancing everyday communication for children with disabilities.* Baltimore, MD: Paul H. Brookes Publishing Co.

Taubman, M., Leaf, R., & McEachin, J. (2011). *Crafting connections: Contemporary applied behavior analysis for enriching the social lives of persons with autism spectrum disorders.* New York, NY: DRL Books.

REFERENCES

Blackorby, J., Wagner, M., Cadwallader, T., Cameto, R., Levine, R., Camille, C., & Giacalone, P. (Eds.). (2002). *Behind the label: The functional implications of disability.* Menlo Park, CA: SRI International.

Brown, L., Branston, M., Hamre-Nietupski, S., Johnson, F., Wilcox, B., & Gruenewald, L. (1979). A rationale for comprehensive longitudinal interactions between severely handicapped students and non-handicapped students and other citizens. *AAESPH Review, 4,* 3–14.

Carter, E.W. (2011). Supporting peer relationships. In M.E. Snell & F. Brown (Eds.), *Instruction of students with severe disabilities* (7th ed., pp. 431–460). Upper Saddle River, NJ: Merrill.

Carter, E.W., Asmus, J.M., & Moss, C.K. (in press). Peer support interventions to support inclusive education. In J. McLeskey, N. Waldron, F. Spooner, & B. Algozzine (Eds.), *Handbook of research and practice for effective inclusive schools.* New York, NY: Routledge.

Carter, E.W., Austin, D., & Trainor, A.A. (2012). Predictors of postschool employment outcomes for young adults with severe disabilities. *Journal of Disability Policy Studies, 23,* 50–63.

Carter, E.W., Cushing, L.S., & Kennedy, C.H. (2009). *Peer support strategies for improving all students' social lives and learning.* Baltimore, MD: Paul H. Brookes Publishing Co.

Carter, E.W., & Hughes, C. (2006). Including high school students with severe disabilities in general education classes: Perspectives of general and special educators, paraprofessionals, and administrators. *Research and Practice for Persons with Severe Disabilities, 31,* 174–185.

Carter, E.W., Hughes, C., Copeland, S.R., & Breen, C. (2001). Differences between high school students who do and do not volunteer to participate in peer interaction programs. *Journal of The Association for Persons with Severe Handicaps, 26,* 229–239.

Carter, E.W., Hughes, C., Guth, C., & Copeland, S.R. (2005). Factors influencing social interaction among high school students with intellectual disabilities and their general education peers. *American Journal on Mental Retardation, 110,* 366–377.

Carter, E.W., Moss, C.K., Hoffman, A., Chung, Y., & Sisco, L. (2011). Efficacy and social validity of peer support arrangements for adolescents with disabilities. *Exceptional Children, 78,* 107–125.

Carter, E.W., Owens, L., Trainor, A.A., Sun, Y., & Swedeen, B. (2009). Self-determination skills and opportunities of adolescents with severe intellectual and developmental disabilities. *American Journal on Intellectual and Developmental Disabilities, 114,* 179–192.

Carter, E.W., & Pesko, M.J. (2008). Social validity of peer interaction intervention strategies in high school classrooms: Effectiveness, feasibility, and actual use. *Exceptionality, 16,* 156–173.

Carter, E.W., Sisco, L.G., Brown, L., Brickham, D., & Al-Khabbaz, Z.A. (2008). Peer interactions and academic engagement of youth with developmental disabilities in inclusive middle and high school classrooms. *American Journal on Mental Retardation, 113,* 479–494.

Carter, E.W., Sisco, L.G., & Chung, Y. (2012). Peer-mediated support interventions. In P.A. Prelock & R.J. McCauley (Vol. Eds.), *Communication and language intervention series: Treatment of autism spectrum disorders: Evidence-based intervention strategies for communication and social interactions* (pp. 221–254). Baltimore, MD: Paul H. Brookes Publishing Co.

Carter, E.W., Sisco, L.G., Chung, Y., & Stanton-Chapman, T. (2010). Peer interactions of students with intellectual disabilities and/or autism: A map of the intervention literature. *Research and Practice for Persons with Severe Disabilities, 35,* 63–79.

Causton-Theoharis, J.N., & Malmgren, K.W. (2005). Increasing peer interactions for students with severe disabilities via paraprofessional training. *Exceptional Children, 71,* 431–444.

Chung, Y., Carter, E.W., & Sisco, L.G. (2012). Social interaction of students with severe disabilities who use augmentative and alternative communication in inclusive classrooms. *American Journal on Intellectual and Developmental Disabilities, 117,* 349–367.

Cushing, L.S., Kennedy, C.H., Shukla, S., Davis, J., & Meyer, K.A. (1997). Disentangling the effects of curriculum revision and social grouping within cooperative learning arrangements. *Focus on Autism and Other Developmental Disabilities, 12,* 231–240.

Dymond, S.K., & Russell, D.L. (2004). Impact of grade and disability on the instructional context of inclusive classrooms. *Education and Training in Developmental Disabilities, 39,* 127–140.

Fisher, M., & Pleasants, S. (2012). Roles, responsibilities, and concerns of paraeducators: Findings from a statewide survey. *Remedial and Special Education, 33,* 287–297.

Frederickson, N., & Turner, J. (2003). Utilizing the classroom peer group to address children's social needs: An evaluation of the circle of friends intervention approach. *The Journal of Special Education, 36,* 234–245.

Frost, L.A., & Bondy, A.S. (2002). *The Picture Exchange Communication System training manual* (2nd ed.). Newark, DE: Pyramid Educational Products.

Ganz, J.B., Davis, J.L., Lund, E.M., Goodwyn, F.D., & Simpson, R.L. (2012). Meta-analysis of PECS with individuals with ASD: Investigation of targeted versus non-targeted outcomes, participant characteristics, and implementation phase. *Research in Developmental Disabilities, 33,* 406–418.

Giangreco, M.F. (2010). One-to-one paraprofessionals for students with disabilities in inclusive classrooms: Is conventional wisdom wrong? *Intellectual and Developmental Disabilities, 48,* 1–13.

Giangreco, M.F., & Broer, S.M. (2005). Questionable utilization of paraprofessionals in inclusive schools: Are we addressing symptoms or causes? *Focus on Autism and Other Developmental Disabilities, 20,* 10–26.

Grey, I.M., & Hastings, R.P. (2005). Evidence-based practices in intellectual disability and behaviour disorders. *Current Opinion in Psychiatry, 18,* 469–475.

Haring, T.G., & Breen, C.G. (1992). A peer-mediated social network intervention to enhance the social integration of persons with moderate and severe disabilities. *Journal of Applied Behavior Analysis, 25,* 319–333.

Harper, C.B., Symon, J.B.G., & Frea, W D. (2008). Recess is time-in: Using peers to improve social skills of children with autism. *Journal of Autism and Developmental Disorders, 38,* 815–826.

Horner, R.H., Carr, E.G., Strain, P.S., Todd, A.W., & Reed, K.R. (2002). Problem behavior interventions for young children with autism: A research synthesis. *Journal of Autism and Developmental Disorders, 32,* 423–446.

Hughes, C., Copeland, S.R., Wehmeyer, M.L., Agran, M., Cai, X., & Hwang, B. (2002). Increasing social interaction between general education high school students and their peers with mental retardation. *Journal of Developmental and Physical Disabilities, 14,* 387–402.

Hughes, C., Golas, M., Cosgriff, C., Brigham, N., Edwards, C., & Cashen, K. (2011). Effects of a social skills intervention among high school students with intellectual disabilities and autism and their general education peers. *Research and Practice for Persons with Severe Disabilities, 36,* 46–61.

Hughes, C., Kaplan, L., Bernstein, R., Boykin, M., Reilly, C., Brigham, N.,… & Harvey, M. (2012). Increasing social interaction skills of secondary school students with autism and intellectual disability: A review of interventions. *Research and Practice for Persons with Severe Disabilities, 37,* 288–307.

Hughes, C., Rodi, M.S., Lorden, S.W., Pitkin, S.E., Derer, K.R., Hwang, B., & Cai, X. (1999). Social interactions of high school students with mental retardation and their general education peers. *American Journal on Mental Retardation, 104,* 533–544.

Jimenez, B.A., Browder, D.M., Spooner, F., & DiBiase, W. (2012). Inclusive inquiry science using peer-mediated embedded instruction for students with moderate intellectual disability. *Exceptional Children, 78,* 301–317.

Kamps, D.M., Lopez, A.G., & Golden, C. (2002). School-age children: Putting research into practice. In H. Goldstein, L.A. Kaczmarek, & K.M. English (Vol. Eds.), *Communication and language intervention series: Promoting social communication: Children with developmental disabilities from birth to adolescence* (pp. 279–306). Baltimore, MD: Paul H. Brookes Publishing Co.

Kamps, D.M, Potucek, J., Lopez, A.G., Kravits, T., & Kemmerer, K. (1997). The use of peer networks across multiple settings to improve social interaction for students with autism. *Journal of Behavioral Education, 7,* 335–357.

Kasari, C., Rotheram-Fuller, E., Locke, J., & Gulsrud, A. (2011). Making the connection: Randomized controlled trial of social skills at school for children with autism spectrum disorders. *Journal of Child Psychology and Psychiatry, 53,* 431–439.

Katz, J., Mirenda, P., & Auerbach, S. (2002). Instructional strategies and educational outcomes for students with developmental disabilities in inclusive "multiple intelligences" and typical inclusive classrooms. *Research and Practice for Persons with Severe Disabilities, 27,* 227–238.

Kearns, J.F., Towles-Reeves, E., Kleinert, H.L., Kleinert, J.O., & Thomas, M.K. (2011). Characteristics of and implications for students participating in alternate assessments based on alternate academic achievement standards. *The Journal of Special Education, 45,* 3–14.

Kleinert, H.L., Miracle, S., & Sheppard-Jones, K. (2007). Including students with moderate and severe intellectual disabilities in school extracurricular and community recreation activities. *Intellectual and Developmental Disabilities, 45,* 46–55.

Koegel, R.L., Fredeen, R., Kim, S., Danial, J., Rubinstein, D., & Koegel, L. (2012). Using perseverative interests to improve interactions between adolescents with autism and their typical peers in school settings. *Journal of Positive Behavior Interventions, 14,* 133–141.

Koegel, R.L., & Koegel, L.K. (1990). Extended reductions in stereotypic behavior of students with autism through a self-management treatment package. *Journal of Applied Behavior Analysis, 23,* 119–127.

Lindsay, S., & Edwards, A. (2013). A systematic review of disability awareness interventions for children and youth. *Disability and Rehabilitation, 35,* 623–646.

Mastropieri, M.A., & Scruggs, T.E. (2001). Promoting inclusion in secondary classrooms. *Learning Disability Quarterly, 24,* 265–275.

National Joint Committee for the Communicative Needs of Persons with Severe Disabilities. (1992). Guidelines for meeting the communication needs of persons with severe disabilities. *ASHA, 34,* 2–3.

Nussbaum, M.C. (2006). *Frontiers of justice: Disability, nationality, species membership.* Cambridge, MA: Harvard University Press.

Odom, S.L., Collet-Klingenberg, L., Rogers, S., & Hatton, D. (2010). Evidence-based practices for children and youth with autism spectrum disorders. *Preventing School Failure, 54,* 275–282.

Ogletree, B.T., Bruce, S.M., Finch, A., Fahey, R., & McLean, L. (2010). Recommended communication-based interventions for individuals with severe intellectual disabilities. *Communication Disorders Quarterly, 32,* 164–175.

Rehm, R.S., & Bradley, J.F. (2006). Social interactions at school of children who are medically fragile and developmentally delayed. *Journal of Pediatric Nursing, 21,* 299–307.

Rispoli, M., Franco, J., van der Meer, L., Lang, R., & Carmargo, S. (2010). The use of speech generating devices in communication interventions for individuals with developmental disabilities: A review of the literature. *Developmental Neurorehabilitation, 13,* 276–293.

Rotheram-Fuller, E., Kasari, C., Chamberlain, B., & Locke, J. (2010). Social involvement of children with autism spectrum disorders in elementary school classrooms. *Journal of Child Psychology and Psychiatry, 51,* 1227–1234.

Rubin, K.H., Bukowski, W.M., & Laursen, B. (Eds.). (2009). *Handbook of peer inter-*

actions, relationships, and groups. New York, NY: Guilford Press.

Ryan, A.M., & Ladd, G.W. (Eds.). (2012). *Peer relationships and adjustment*. Charlotte, NC: Information Age Publishing.

Ryndak, D.L., Moore, M.A., Orlando, A., & Delano, M. (2008/2009). Access to the general curriculum: The mandate and role of context in research-based practice for students with extensive support needs. *Research and Practice for Persons with Severe Disabilities, 33–34,* 199–213.

Schaefer, J.E., & Armentrout, J.A. (2002). The effects of peer-buddies on increased initiation of social interaction of a middle school student with Down syndrome and her typical peers. *Down Syndrome Quarterly, 7,* 1–8.

Shukla-Mehta, S., Miller, T., & Callahan, K.J. (2010). Evaluating the effectiveness of video instruction on social and communication skills training for children with autism spectrum disorders: A review of the literature. *Focus on Autism and Other Developmental Disabilities, 25,* 23–36.

Siperstein, G.N., Norins, J., & Mohler, A. (2007). Social acceptance and attitude change: Fifty years of research. In J.W. Jacobson, J.A. Mulick, & J. Rojahn (Eds.), *Handbook of intellectual and developmental disabilities* (pp. 133–154). New York, NY: Springer.

Siperstein, G.N., Parker, R.C., Bardon, J.N., & Widaman, K.F. (2007). A national study of youth attitudes toward the inclusion of students with intellectual disabilities. *Exceptional Children, 73,* 435–455.

Siperstein, G.N., Pociask, S.E., & Collins, M.A. (2010). Sticks, stones, and stigma: A study of students' use of the derogatory term "retard." *Intellectual and Developmental Disabilities, 48,* 126–134.

Snell, M.E., Brady, N., McLean, L., Ogletree, B.T., Siegel, E., Sylvester, L.,...Sevcik, R. (2010). Twenty years of communication intervention research with individuals who have severe intellectual and developmental disabilities. *American Journal on Intellectual and Developmental Disabilities, 115,* 364–380.

TASH. (2010). *TASH national agenda.* Retrieved from http://tash.org/about/initiatives

Test, D.W., Richter, S., Knight, V., & Spooner, F. (2011). A comprehensive review and meta-analysis of the social stories literature. *Focus on Autism and Other Developmental Disabilities, 26,* 49–62.

U.S. Department of Education. (2010). *IDEA data.* Retrieved from https://www.ideadata.org

Valenti-Hein, D., & Choinski, C. (2007). Relationships and sexuality in adolescence and youth adulthood. In A. Carr, G. O'Reilly, P.N. Walsh, & J. McEvoy (Eds.), *The handbook of intellectual disability and clinical psychology practice* (pp. 729–755). New York, NY: Routledge.

Wagner, M., Cadwallader, T.W., Garza, N., & Cameto, R. (2004). Social activities of youth with disabilities. *National Longitudinal Transition Study–2 Data Brief, 3,* 1–4.

Wagner, M., Cadwallader, T.W., Marder, C., Newman, L., Garza, N., & Blackorby, J. (2002). *The other 80% of their time: The experiences of elementary and middle school students with disabilities during their nonschool hours.* Menlo Park, CA: SRI International.

Webster, A.A., & Carter, M. (2007). Social relationships and friendships of children with developmental disabilities: Implications for inclusive settings. A systematic review. *Journal of Intellectual and Developmental Disability, 32,* 200–213.

Wolfberg, P.J. (2003). *Peer play and the autism spectrum: The art of guiding children's socialization and imagination.* Shawnee Mission, KS: Autism Asperger Publishing.

Wolfberg, P.J., McCracken, H., & Tuchel, T. (2008). Fostering peer play and friendships: Creating a culture of inclusion. In K.D. Buron & P.J. Wolfberg (Eds.), *Learners on the autism spectrum: Preparing highly qualified educators* (pp. 182–207). Shawnee Mission, KS: Autism Asperger Publishing.

11

Access to the General Education Curriculum in General Education Classes

Fred Spooner, Bethany R. McKissick, Melissa E. Hudson, and Diane M. Browder

Access to the general curriculum and identification of evidence-based practices that promote learning in this curriculum are two of the most important issues in special education today, especially for individuals with extensive support needs. Evidence-based practices (Cook, Tankersley, & Landrum, 2009) and access to the general curriculum (Jackson, Ryndak, & Wehmeyer, 2008–2009) are complicated concepts. Educators must analyze both the methodological quality and the magnitude of available research on a practice to define an evidence-based practice (Cook et al., 2009; Gersten et al., 2005; Horner et al., 2005). Educators must consider context, curriculum, and student learning to plan for access to the general curriculum (Jackson et al., 2008–2009). The Individuals with Disabilities Education Improvement Act (IDEA) of 2004 (PL 108-446) mandates that students with disabilities have access to and make progress in the general education curriculum. Yet, much progress still needs to be made for all students to be granted access, even with the legal mandate (see Smith, 2007).

This chapter discusses how students with severe disabilities can gain access to the general education curriculum in general education classes and explores the challenges and solutions related to teaching students with severe disabilities so they can gain access to the general education curriculum alongside their peers without disabilities. The chapter specifically addresses 1) legislation, mandates, and policies related to access; 2) teaching students with severe disabilities using evidence-based practices; and 3) future research and policy development.

LEGISLATION, MANDATES, AND POLICIES RELATED TO ACCESS

The Individuals with Disabilities Education Act Amendments (IDEA) of 1997 (PL 105-17) first posited the concept of access to and progress within the general education curriculum by requiring that all students be included in large-scale assessments, including students with the most severe disabilities. This legislation has required states to include students with disabilities in regular assessments since 1997 and alternate assessments since 2000 (U.S. Department of Education, 2005). Alternate assessments allow students with the most severe cognitive disabilities to be included in large-scale assessment systems when participation in regular assessment systems is not possible, even with accommodations or modifications. This mandate for alternate assessments ensures that states, schools, and teachers are held accountable for the learning of all students (Browder & Spooner, 2003; Kleinert & Thurlow, 2001; Thompson & Quenemoen, 2001).

The No Child Left Behind (NCLB) Act of 2001 (PL 107-110) required states to include students with the most severe cognitive disabilities in state accountability systems and provide access to challenging instruction linked to state content standards (U.S. Department of Education, 2005). NCLB specifically mandated that grade-level academic content standards be used for student assessment and that progress toward proficiency in those content standards be judged against grade-level or modified or alternate achievement standards (U.S. Department of Education, 2005, 2007). States can assess the academic progress of students with the most severe cognitive disabilities using an alternate assessment based on alternate achievement standards, but the alternate achievement standards must align with a state's academic content standards, promote access to the general curriculum, and reflect the highest achievement standards possible (Title I, 2003). Alternate assessments also are being developed to align with common core state standards.

IDEA 2004 required that students' individualized education programs (IEPs) reference how the educational program will enable the child to be involved in and make progress in the general education curriculum (§ 300.320[a][2][i][A]). State performance goals for children with disabilities must be the same as the state's definition of adequate yearly progress for all students (§ 300.157[a][2]). Consequently, all students, including those with disabilities, are expected to become proficient on state standards (e.g., common core state standards). Alternate assessments allow for students with severe disabilities to show proficiency through some alternate achievement standards that are based on these same general education state standards but with differences in breadth or depth. The common thread running through all three pieces of legislation is that teachers, schools, and states are accountable for ensuring that each student has the opportunity to achieve at high standards while gaining access to the general education curriculum.

Access and inclusive education should fit well together as access to the general education curriculum takes place in a general education setting (see Chapter 8). Inclusive education is one of TASH's national agenda items and is defined as school communities where all students 1) are valued members of the school community (e.g., general education classrooms, extracurricular activities) who are presumed competent, 2) participate within age- and grade-level classrooms learning alongside peers without disabilities, and 3) create and maintain reciprocal social relationships with a variety of students. *General curriculum access* is defined in this chapter as providing grade-aligned academic instruction for students with disabilities (Browder & Spooner, 2011). Students with disabilities are afforded a right to a full educational opportunity as well as relevancy of a standards-based curriculum. General curriculum access also gives an opportunity for these students to create their own changing expectations through achievements in the general education context (Courtade, Spooner, Browder, & Jimenez, 2012).

TEACHING STUDENTS WITH SEVERE DISABILITIES USING EVIDENCE-BASED PRACTICES IN GENERAL EDUCATION CLASSES

Jackson et al. (2008–2009) advocated that general curriculum access requires thinking about context (general education setting), curriculum, and student learning and cannot be achieved if any one of these components is not addressed. They continued by adding that the purposes of schooling, equity of educational opportunity, and presuming competence are all guiding concepts as to why context, curriculum, and student learning should be located in the general education setting. The social benefits have been well documented for students with disabilities, including increased social interactions with typically developing peers (Brinker, 1985; Carter & Hughes, 2006; Foreman, Arthur-Kelly, Pascoe, & King, 2004; Fryxell & Kennedy, 1995); increased social competence (Fisher & Meyer, 2002); enhanced communication skills (Hunt, Staub, Alwell, & Goetz, 1994); friendship development (Kennedy, Cushing, & Itkonen, 1997); access to social, emotional, and instrumental support systems (Kennedy, Shulka, & Fryxell, 1997); and social acceptance by typically developing peers (Burstein, Sears, Wilcoxen, Cabello, & Spagna, 2004; Carter & Hughes, 2006; Freeman & Alkin, 2000; Peck, Staub, Gallucci, & Schwartz, 2004). There are clearly academic benefits to being taught in the general education classroom, including high levels of active engagement (Hunt, Soto, Maier, & Doering, 2003; Wallace, Anderson, Bartholomay, & Hupp, 2002), improved academic performance (Brinker & Thorpe, 1984; Cole, Waldron, & Majd, 2004; Downing, Spencer, & Cavallaro, 2004; Hawkins, 2011; Hunt, Staub, et al., 1994; Katz & Mirenda, 2002; McDonnell, Mathot-Buckner, Thorson, & Fister, 2001; Teigland, 2009; Westling & Fox, 2009; Wolfe & Hall, 2003), access to the general curriculum (Carter, Cushing, Clark, & Kennedy, 2005), and higher quality IEP goals (Hunt, Farron-Davis, Beckstead, Curtis, & Goetz, 1994). Being educated in an inclusive classroom clearly is a preference for helping students with disabilities to achieve academic goals.

Evidence-Based Practices for Teaching Students with Severe Disabilities

Educators must consider how best to integrate evidence-based practices for interventions and specialized instruction with research-based general education teaching strategies to optimize academic learning for students with severe disabilities in the general education classroom. These considerations should include 1) how to match the instructional strategy with the academic lesson, 2) how special and general education teachers collaborate to embed the specialized instruction into classroom activities and lessons, 3) how to identify the role of the adults (e.g., teachers, paraprofessionals, related services providers) in the delivery of specialized instruction, and 4) how to deliver the instruction in a naturally occurring way while adhering to fidelity of implementation.

Gaining access to the general curriculum has been a major focus of researchers attempting to create more effective instructional systems for students with severe disabilities. The Office of Special Education and Rehabilitative Services (OSERS, Grant Applications Under Part D, 2002) initiated a funding priority to describe and define access to the general curriculum as well as analyze and address how to meet obstructions and challenges in professional development. Spooner, Dymond, Smith, and Kennedy (2006) recapped documented approaches (e.g., peer supports, self-determination, teaching and gaining access to content standards) as well as benefits and pitfalls (e.g., broadening curriculum options, increasing expectations) of providing general curriculum access. A little more is now known regarding evidence-based practices for teaching literacy (Browder, Ahlgrim-Delzell, Spooner, Mims, & Baker, 2009; Browder, Wakeman, Spooner, Ahlgrim-Delzell, & Algozzine, 2006), mathematics (Browder, Spooner, Ahlgrim-Delzell, Harris, & Wakeman, 2008), science (Spooner, Knight, Browder, Jimenez, & DiBiase, 2011), and general academics (Spooner, Knight, Browder, & Smith, 2012).

The educational team should plan individual supports (e.g., communication system, peer supports, target skills, adaptations for English language learners [ELLs]) and then consider how to make academic instruction as effective as possible for the learning targets that have been selected with the general education teacher. The effectiveness of instruction can be enhanced by using the evidence-based practices found in research (e.g., systematic instruction) (Snell, 1983; Spooner et al., 2012; Wolery, Bailey, & Sugai, 1988).

Systematic Instruction   Spooner et al. (2012) defined *systematic instruction* as a set of procedures that 1) teach socially relevant skills, 2) provide observable and measureable definitions of those skills, 3) use data to show functional relationships between introduction of an intervention and acquisition of targeted skills, 4) use components of behavior analysis to promote transfer of stimulus control (e.g., differential reinforcement), and 5) teach skills that can generalize to different settings, people, and/or materials. The researchers found enough evidence to support using systematic instruction as an evidence-based practice for providing academic instruction to students with severe disabilities. They specifically identified the response-prompting procedures of task analytic instruction to teach chained behaviors or tasks (e.g., mathematic calculation) and time delay to teach discrete skills (e.g., vocabulary identification).

Browder et al. (2006) comprehensively reviewed reading literature and found that most of the studies in the review (i.e., 42 out of 54) taught sight words; systematic prompting (e.g., time delay) to teach sight words is an evidence-based practice. Browder et al. (2009) evaluated the efficacy of time delay for teaching literacy to students with severe disabilities and found it to be an evidence-based practice for teaching symbols to students with moderate and severe disabilities.

Professionals know more about teaching literacy and reading to students with severe disabilities than they do about teaching mathematics, based on the number of published investigations that have been documented. Although fewer empirical studies for teaching mathematics to students with severe disabilities exist, a comprehensive literature review and meta-analysis of mathematics studies by Browder,

Spooner, et al. (2008) found that most studies taught number and computation skills (e.g., counting, number matching) or measurement (e.g., money skills) and identified specific prompt fading procedures with feedback to be an evidence-based practice.

Spooner et al. (2011) conducted a comprehensive review of science studies published between 1985 and 2009 in an effort to identify evidence-based practices in science. Systematic instruction was determined to be an evidence-based practice for teaching science skills to students with severe disabilities.

Teaching with Technology   Using technology, specifically computer-assisted instruction (CAI), within an inclusive classroom is an area of research making gains within the field of special education. Panyan (1984) suggested that incorporating CAI within the general education classroom can 1) provide additional benefit for students with severe disabilities, including autism spectrum disorder, due to their differences in attention and motivation from typically developing peers; 2) decrease stereotypic behaviors; 3) provide students with consistent feedback; and 4) increase language.

Pennington (2010) reviewed CAI research from 1997 to 2008 and found that research designed to evaluate its effectiveness in teaching core content-related material is limited. Knight, McKissick, and Saunders (2013) expanded on the work of Pennington by applying both the Horner et al. (2005) and Gersten et al. (2005) criteria for both single-case and group design research to determine whether the published research met criteria for an evidence-based practice in teaching academics to students with severe disabilities. Their analysis determined that although CAI meets moderate levels of evidence for single-case research that has been published since 1993, no studies that used a true group experimental design met criteria for establishing CAI as an evidence-based practice for teaching academics to students with autism spectrum disorder. The researchers noted, however, that CAI programs utilized components of systematic instruction such as differential reinforcement for correct responses, stimulus fading, and error correction in every study that demonstrated experimental control and a successful outcome (i.e., students acquired the targeted academic skills). Furthermore, they suggested that as iPads, iPods, smartphones, and smartboards become standard instructional tools in the classroom, researchers should continue to examine what key feature of these technologies or programs are responsible for acquiring new skills and make decisions to include them in instruction based on individual students and their desired outcomes.

Evidence-Based Practices for Teaching Academic Skills

In the previous section, we laid the groundwork and the rationale for the importance of using evidence-based practices in the instruction of students with severe disabilities in general education settings. We discussed the purpose of schooling and social benefits, as well as the academic benefits of receiving one's education in an inclusive setting. We elaborated on four considerations in integrating evidence-based practices into general education teaching strategies; defined systematic instruction; and alluded to the three overarching reviews for teaching literacy, mathematics, and science to students with severe disabilities, which provide the evidence for teaching academic skills. In this section, we highlight strategies for teaching literacy, mathematics, and science.

Teaching Reading and English Language Arts   There may be no more important outcome from the time students spend in school than that of literacy. Nearly all learning depends on the ability to read and write. Agran (2011) called for meaningful literacy education to be provided and supported for all students, including students with severe disabilities. Yet, literacy instruction for students with severe disabilities has been limited (Browder et al., 2006). Limited reading instruction may be due to a perception that students with severe disabilities will not become independent readers. Kliewer and Biklen (2001) likened this traditional goal of reading to a ladder climbed one rung at a time until the top is reached (e.g., independent reading). Reading instruction is not a priority when students with severe disabilities are not considered able to reach the top of the ladder due to impairments in communication or other aspects of their disability. Although some students with severe disabilities may never learn to read independently, research demonstrated that students can make literacy gains when provided intensive reading instruction (Allor, Mathes, Roberts, Jones, & Champlin, 2010; Browder, Ahlgrim-Delzell, Courtade, Gibbs, & Flowers, 2008).

Beliefs about literacy determine what kind of literacy instruction is taught, who receives it, and for how long (Keefe & Copeland, 2011). Consequently, narrow definitions of literacy (e.g., becoming an independent reader, reading a prescribed set of functional sight words) do not promote literacy instruction for students with severe disabilities. Keefe and Copeland explored the impact of literacy definitions on literacy opportunities and called for educators and researchers to move from traditional skill-centered, functional, and individually focused definitions of literacy, which have often failed students with extensive support needs, to broader definitions of literacy that recognize it as a social phenomenon that occurs in a social milieu.

Ruppar, Dymond, and Gaffney (2011) suggested that literacy instruction can provide opportunities for meaningful, standards-based instruction within a variety of educational settings, including general education classrooms. Two innovations in teaching literacy include strategies for promoting independence in reading through teaching decoding and strategies that promote comprehension. Several experimental studies demonstrated that students with a moderate or severe intellectual disability can acquire phonics skills (e.g., Allor et al., 2010; Al Otaiba & Hosp, 2004; Bradford, Shippen, Alberto, Houchins, & Flores, 2006). The interventionist in most of these studies used direct, explicit instruction. Other studies showed that students can demonstrate comprehension by applying word reading or matching activities (e.g., Browder & Minarovic, 2000; Fiscus, Schuster, Morse, & Collins, 2002; Mechling, Gast, & Langone, 2002). Read alouds can be used for students who do not independently read text, with instruction focusing on using the text to answer comprehension questions (Browder, Lee, & Mims, 2011; Browder, Mims, Spooner, Ahlgrim-Delzell, & Lee, 2008; Mims, Browder, Baker, Lee, & Spooner, 2009; Mims, Hudson, & Browder, 2012).

Teaching Mathematics   Many of the National Council for Teaching Mathematics' (NCTM) six core principles closely align with instructional techniques and philosophies that special education teachers of students with severe disabilities follow and implement in their classrooms. For example, the equity principle suggests that mathematic instruction requires high expectations and strong support that could include practices such as peer tutoring and collaborative learning, which have proven effective in special education classrooms for students with severe disabilities

(Miracle, Collins, Schuster, & Grisham-Brown, 2001). A second principle implies that mathematic instruction should include real-life application across both the educational and home setting. Third, the NCTM principles explain that mathematical learning should build on students' previous knowledge and students should acquire new knowledge from experiences that provide opportunities to learn mathematics with understanding, which promotes teaching for generalization of skills.

The response-prompting procedure, which is a system of least prompts, is one method researchers used to address the instruction of chained mathematical skills to students with severe disabilities. A system of least prompts is a nearly errorless response-prompting procedure that allows the instructor to provide the least intrusive prompt necessary to elicit a correct response from the learner and for students to experience success while acquiring novel skills (Collins, 2007).

For example, system of least prompts could address the NCTM area of data analysis to include students charting and graphing their performance across a variety of skills. Copeland, Hughes, Agran, Wehmeyer, and Fowler (2002) taught four students a self-monitoring strategy and how to graph their performance to address independent worksheet completion in general education settings. Researchers also demonstrated the effectiveness of creating task analytic mathematical lessons that incorporate research-based strategies such as time delay, explicit instruction, and graphic organizers (Browder & Spooner, 2011; Trela, Jimenez, & Browder, 2008).

Using mathematics stories is another strategy researchers used to provide grade-aligned general curriculum access in mathematics. Mathematics stories are similar to word problems. They put a mathematical problem into a real-life context that the student may relate to and that may possibly activate his or her own background knowledge (Browder & Spooner, 2011). For example, instead of a simple subtraction problem, a teacher may create a story about going to the movies, spending some money, and asking the student to determine how much money is left. An algebra teacher may create a story or context about building a fence, highlighting the concept of a pattern within simple linear functions. Applying math concepts to everyday life is an example of authentic instruction in which a connection is made to the larger social context within which students live. This is recognized as an evidence-based general education practice that has applicability for students with severe disabilities (e.g., Newman, King, & Carmichael, 2007).

Teaching Science   Explicit instruction is a growing practice within the field of teaching academic science skills to students with severe disabilities (Flores & Ganz, 2007; Ganz & Flores, 2009; Knight, Smith, Spooner, & Browder, 2011; Smith, Spooner, Jimenez, & Browder, 2013). Explicit instruction is a direct approach to teaching that includes instructional design and delivery procedures. It is considered an active process that emphasizes the learner's role within the learning process (i.e., how he or she processes the instruction provided). Explicit instruction jointly focuses on the information presented and how the learner processes that information and often includes research-based elements such as active engagement, systematic instruction, activation of background knowledge, and use of explicit models to provide instruction (Goeke, 2009). Explicit instruction includes supports in which students are led through the learning process by providing clear expectations and supported by feedback until the student is able to independently perform the skill (Archer & Hughes, 2011).

Knight et al. (2011) examined the effect of explicit instruction to teach science descriptors (e.g., heavy, change, living, dead) to three elementary-age students with severe disabilities. Results of this study demonstrated that explicit instruction was indeed effective in teaching the receptive identification of science descriptors and that all three students maintained these acquired skills over time. Generalization measures implemented following the intervention demonstrated that although students were able to generalize identification of science descriptors to novel materials and within a general education inquiry lesson at high rates, participants were not able to generalize identification of descriptors to pictures representing each descriptor. In addition to suggesting the need for further replication of studies examining explicit instruction for this population, the researchers suggested that future studies examine the use of examples and nonexamples to assess understanding of science descriptors versus sight word reading to increase comprehension for students within this population.

Smith, Spooner, and Wood (2013) evaluated the effectiveness of not only embedded, explicit instruction, but also how to provide that instruction to teach middle school students with autism spectrum disorder and intellectual disability. They targeted science terms and applications of those terms (i.e., a variety of definitions, pictures, video clips, and scenarios) in the context of a general education science classroom. The CAI intervention package used a model-test format implemented on an iPad 2 and PowerPoint software. Not only did the students make the targeted academic gains, but peers without disabilities who were present during trials also shared their eagerness to "do science on an iPad" and said that they liked having students with disabilities in their classroom.

Considerations for Teaching in the General Education Classroom

In the previous section, we discussed the specifics of teaching literacy, mathematics, and science using evidence-based practices. In this section, we delineate considerations for teaching in the general education classroom by using embedded instruction, using peers, focusing on student-directed learning, and teaching students from diverse backgrounds.

Teaching with Embedded Instruction   The specialized instruction provided to students with disabilities in the general education classroom in many of the previous examples was delivered via an embedded approach. Research has suggested using embedded instruction to teach academic skills to students with severe disabilities, including autism spectrum disorders (e.g., Jameson, McDonnell, Johnson, Riesen, & Polychronis, 2007; Jameson, McDonnell, Polychronis, & Riesen, 2008; McDonnell et al., 2006). Using embedded instruction is loosely defined within the literature as providing instruction on skills within ongoing routines or activities within the performance setting versus massed trials in a special education setting (McDonnell, 2011). One example is teaching a student with a disability the concept of change within a science general education class during a lesson about the life cycles and food chains. These embedded trials might occur during a warm-up activity, independent practice, or a hands-on experiment.

Using Peers as Tutors   Empirical research has documented both the effectiveness of teaching academics to students with severe disabilities as well as the effectiveness of peer-mediated instruction within the inclusive classroom (Collins, Branson, Hall, & Rankin, 2001; Hudson, Browder, & Jimenez, in press; Jameson et al.,

2008). Collins et al. (2001) conducted a study in which a general education teacher and three peer tutors taught three students with moderate and severe disabilities to write letters that included the date, greeting, body, and closing in a high school composition class. Jameson et al. (2008) used three peer tutors to teach three students with moderate intellectual disability vocabulary definitions for health (e.g., *lungs*: get less air, can get cancer) and art (e.g., *firing*: heating clay in a special oven) during the general education classes.

Peer tutors have been used to teach comprehension of grade-level adapted text to students with moderate intellectual disability in general education settings. Hudson et al. (in press) used fourth-grade peer tutors to deliver a system of least prompts intervention to teach listening comprehension.

Student-Directed Learning   Teaching students with severe disabilities to direct their own learning is part of the larger construct called self-determination. Agran and Hughes have cogently laid the groundwork for a discussion about self-determination and student-directed learning for individuals with severe disabilities (see Chapter 5). Wehmeyer (1998, 2005) described meanings and misinterpretations about self-determination and suggested that it is neither a set of skills nor is it something that you do. It is not a program, curriculum, model, or process. Spooner et al. (2006) indicated that it was one of the suggested approaches to gaining access to the general curriculum. Agran and Hughes suggest self-determination as a strategy (self-initiated instructional practice) that can enhance the curriculum in that students provide their own cues and consequences and employ a problem-solving approach in processing information (see Chapter 5; Copeland & Cosbey, 2008–2009; Wehmeyer, Field, Doren, Jones, & Mason, 2004).

An increasing body of investigations suggests that student-directed learning strategies may greatly enhance a student's participation in general education for students with intellectual and developmental disabilities (Agran, Blanchard, Wehmeyer, & Hughes 2001; Copeland et al., 2002). The Self-Determined Learning Model of Instruction is one evidence-based curriculum for teaching self-determination (Mithaug, Wehmeyer, Agran, Martin, & Palmer, 1998; Wehmeyer, Palmer, Agran, Mithaug, & Martin, 2000). Educators teach students to set goals, take action on those goals, and adjust their goals and plans as needed. Students pose questions (e.g., What is my goal? What is my plan? What have I learned?) to set and assess progress toward their goals in the Self-Determined Learning Model of Instruction.

Self-determination or student-directed learning strategies have been well validated and supported in the literature (see Agran, King-Sears, Wehmeyer, & Copeland, 2003; Agran & Wehmeyer, 1999; Wehmeyer, Palmer, Soukup, Garner, & Lawrence, 2007) and demonstrated educational efficacy across a wide range of academic and adaptive skills and students with a variety of disabilities. Student-directed learning strategies seek to teach ways for students to monitor their performance, set appropriate goals, deliver their own reinforcers, evaluate their own performance, and identify solutions to current or future problems.

Teaching Students from Diverse Backgrounds   The Office of English Language Acquisition, Language Enhancement, and Academic Achievement for Limited English Proficient Students identified more than 5 million ELLs receiving a public education in the United States in 2008. The U.S. Government Accountability Office (2009) reported that although school population has only grown 3% since the mid-2000s, the number of ELLs has increased 60% in the same time frame. The increasing numbers of ELLs inevitably result in an increase in ELLs who also have disabilities, including students with severe disabilities. This increase has left many special educators wondering how to appropriately serve these students and what practices are most effective. Few studies have focused on providing academic instruction to this population of students (e.g., Duran & Heiry, 1986; Rivera, Wood, & Spooner, 2012; Rohena, Jitendra, & Browder, 2002; Spooner, Rivera, Browder, Baker, & Salas, 2009). The emergence of some studies, specifically in the content area of literacy, has suggested research-based practices that have been effective for students in this population (Spooner et al., 2009). For example, Spooner et al. increased the emergent literacy skills (e.g., book awareness, vocabulary, listening comprehension) of a culturally and linguistically diverse student with moderate intellectual disability through culturally contextual instruction that included books relevant to the student's heritage in the student's native language and gradually increasing instruction in English.

Rivera, Hicks, and Cuero (2012) suggested that systematic instruction procedures that have been deemed an evidence-based practice for students with severe disabilities in teaching literacy (Browder et al., 2006, 2009) also may be effective for students who are ELLs and have severe disabilities. These researchers suggested that practices such as shared stories, explicit vocabulary instruction, multiple exemplars, and technology or visually based instruction can help educators provide quality literacy instruction for these students.

FUTURE RESEARCH AND POLICY DEVELOPMENT

Although there are more than 100 studies on teaching mathematics, science, and English and language arts to students with moderate and severe disabilities, only a small percentage were actually conducted in general education settings. Many of the practices demonstrated for academic learning in self-contained settings may be adaptable to inclusive contexts, and more research is needed to demonstrate what adaptations are essential to produce successful academic learning. For example, in adapting time delay to inclusive settings, teaching trials typically have been embedded in the milieu of a general education teacher's lesson or a small-group activity (e.g., Jameson et al., 2007, 2008; McDonnell et al., 2006). When least intrusive prompts have been adapted for applications to a read-aloud by peers, the prompts focused more on the text itself rather than making a motoric response (e.g., Hudson, 2012). More academic research is needed that focuses on more complex concepts and learning targets. Although it is important for students to gain vocabulary terms to be able to communicate about learning, it also may be feasible for students to learn generalized concepts through strategies such as using graphic organizers (e.g., Knight, Spooner, Browder, Smith, & Wood, 2013). Research also is needed that considers the optimal supports for inclusive contexts. We identified a few in this chapter (e.g., communication, individualized learning targets, peer supports), but there likely are many more that practitioners are effectively using that could be more broadly evaluated and disseminated by researchers who collaborate with practitioners in research.

Consideration needs to be given to what this research suggests about selecting appropriate goals from content standards in addition to how much and how quickly students with severe disabilities learn academic content to meet the increased expectations set by state accountability systems that are linked to grade-level academic content standards. Expecting students with severe disabilities to learn academic content is supported by the numerous studies in the reviews cited in this chapter on literacy, mathematics, and science. Some studies also suggested that this content can be adapted from grade-level content. Targeting attainment of all grade-level standards is not the goal for students with severe disabilities who are taking the alternate assessment, and it has not been demonstrated in research. Teachers, however, will need to know how to identify appropriate content goals from the standard curriculum and work with general educators to make adaptations and modifications so that students with severe disabilities can participate in meaningful ways and receive quality and effective instruction on their individualized goals within the curriculum. Students with severe disabilities also will have additional IEP priorities that educators must consider (e.g., self-regulation; communication; social, physical, or mobility skills). Alternate achievement targets need to be considered for both the next generation of alternate assessments and for planning what will count in teacher effectiveness measures. Some flexibility is needed in policies for school accountability until more research is available to suggest how to set benchmarks for students with severe disabilities. Research has clearly shown that the targets set in the past (e.g., expecting little or no academic learning) have been far too low.

Teacher Preparation

As the expectations and outcomes for children with severe disabilities are increased, preparation for those who are responsible for ensuring higher expectations and more sustainable postschool outcomes will need to follow suit. Teachers who work with these students in front-line environments will need to have a clearer understanding of these higher expectations, the general education setting, and how to adapt content and modify both environments and instruction to increase the likelihood of delivering better outcomes. Following are two examples that reflect the state of affairs and point to some of the needed changes in personnel preparation.

Ruppar et al. (2011) conducted a survey of 69 special education teachers whose students used augmentative and alternative communication devices and took an alternate assessment because many special education teachers considered general education content to be a barrier to instruction in inclusive settings. The authors concluded that teachers may not understand how to adapt literacy content or how gaining access to literacy instruction in a variety of contexts may be of benefit to their students with severe disabilities. Special education teachers typically are not trained in general education content (Spooner et al., 2006). In addition, schools are not generally structured to allow for the kind of collaborative planning among general and special education teachers to enable quality instruction to be planned. Special education teachers may be assigned to deliver instruction or coordinate with general education teachers but need the skills and time to efficiently plan and effectively deliver instruction. A serious need exists for revising teacher preparation programs, which is a challenge for many institutions of higher education. Copeland, Keefe, Calhoon, Tanner, and Park (2011) conducted telephone interviews with nine teacher educators in university programs across the country that prepare special education teacher candidates and asked about the literacy instruction provided to prepare teacher candidates to teach literacy to students with extensive support needs. Three implications for practice were described from the three broad themes:

1) the importance for teachers to have positive expectations for the literacy learning potential of the students with extensive support needs, 2) the importance of including a variety of instructional practices in teacher preparation courses, and 3) the challenges in determining how many literacy methods courses are needed to adequately prepare teacher candidates. The need to inform teachers about the most up-to-date evidence-based practices for teaching literacy to these students was one overarching theme from the conversations.

CONCLUSION

Building on the foundation laid by prior research while promoting greater access is needed to work toward general curriculum access for students with severe disabilities. Teacher training programs will need to change in order for teachers to impart up-to-date evidence-based practices. Comprehensive literature reviews have shown that students can learn academic content in language arts, mathematics, and science, but educators are encouraged to go beyond the narrow range of academics taught in the past. Studies suggest that students with moderate and severe disabilities can learn content aligned with their grade-level placement (based on chronological age). Educators are encouraged to plan the most meaningful priorities for this grade-aligned content with leadership from general educators who know the content best. Some consideration also should be given to how these skills will build across grades and grade bands. Systematic instruction has provided a strong legacy for effective instruction. The next step is to apply and adapt more of these strategies for inclusive contexts and more varied content (e.g., social studies) (Schenning, Knight, & Spooner, 2013). Educators can promote not only access to the general curriculum but also progress in that curriculum by focusing on more content-rich objectives and using proven instructional strategies.

Questions for Study and Reflection

1. What is the relationship between access to the general education curriculum and inclusion?

2. How does a teacher figure out how to provide evidence-based practices in a classroom setting?

3. What are some of the modifications or changes that will need to be made to teacher preparation programs to more effectively prepare teachers to meet higher expectations to achieve grade-level content standards?

4. Discuss the process of determining and evaluating evidence-based practices.

5. What have professionals learned from the evidence-based practice reviews that have been conducted in the areas of reading, mathematics, and science for students with severe disabilities?

RESOURCES

Browder, D.M., Gibbs, S., Ahlgrim-Delzell, L., Courtade, G., & Lee, A. (2007). *Early literacy skills builder.* Verona, WI: Attainment Company.

Courtade, G., Jimenez, B., Trela, K., & Browder, D.M. (2008). *Teaching to standards: Science.* Verona, WI: Attainment Company.

Jimenez, B., Knight, V., & Browder, D.M. (2012). *Early science.* Verona, WI: Attainment Company.

Lee, A., Mims, P.J., & Browder, D. (2011). *Pathway to literacy.* Verona, WI: Attainment Company.

Trela, K., Jimenez, B., & Browder, D.M. (2008). *Teaching to standards: Math.* Verona, WI: Attainment Company.

Zakas, T., & Schreiber, L. (2010). *Building with stories.* Verona, WI: Attainment Company.

REFERENCES

Agran, M. (2011). Promoting literacy instruction for people with severe disabilities: Achieving and realizing a literate identity. *Research and Practice for Persons with Severe Disabilities, 36,* 89–91.

Agran, M., Blanchard, C., Wehmeyer, M.L., & Hughes, C. (2001). Teaching students to self-regulate their behavior: The differential effects of student- vs. teacher-delivered reinforcement. *Research in Developmental Disabilities, 22,* 319–332.

Agran, M., King-Sears, M.E., Wehmeyer, M.L., & Copeland, S.R. (2003). *Teachers' guides to inclusive practices: Student-directed learning.* Baltimore, MD: Paul H. Brookes Publishing Co.

Agran, M., & Wehmeyer, M. (1999). *Teaching problem solving to students with mental retardation.* Washington, DC: American Association on Mental Retardation.

Al Otaiba, S., & Hosp, M.K. (2004). Providing literacy instruction to students with Down syndrome. *Teaching Exceptional Children, 36,* 28–35.

Allor, J., Mathes, P., Roberts, K., Jones, F., & Champlin, T. (2010). Teaching students with moderate intellectual disabilities to read: An experimental examination of a comprehensive reading intervention. *Education and Training in Autism and Developmental Disabilities, 45,* 3–22.

Archer, A.L., & Hughes, C.A. (2011). *Explicit instruction: Effective and efficient teaching.* New York, NY: Guilford Press.

Bradford, S., Shippen, M.E., Alberto, P., Houchins, D.E., & Flores, M. (2006). Using systematic instruction to teach decoding skills to middle school students with moderate intellectual disabilities. *Education and Training in Developmental Disabilities, 41,* 333–343.

Brinker, R.P. (1985). Interactions between severely mentally retarded students and other students in integrated and segregated public school settings. *American Journal of Mental Deficiency, 89,* 587–594.

Brinker, R., & Thorpe, M.E. (1984). Integration of severely handicapped students and the proportion of IEP objectives achieved. *Exceptional Children, 51,* 168–175.

Browder, D.M., Ahlgrim-Delzell, L., Courtade, G.R., Gibbs, S.L., & Flowers, C. (2008). Evaluation of the effectiveness of an early literacy program for students with significant developmental disabilities using group randomized trial research. *Exceptional Children, 75,* 33–52.

Browder, D.M., Ahlgrim-Delzell, L., Spooner, F., Mims, P.J., & Baker, J.N. (2009). Using time delay to teach picture and word recognition to identify evidence-based practice for students with severe developmental disabilities. *Exceptional Children, 75,* 343–364.

Browder, D.M., Lee, A., & Mims, P.J. (2011). Using shared stories and individual response modes to promote comprehension and engagement in literacy for students with multiple, severe disabilities. *Education and Training in Autism and Developmental Disabilities, 46,* 339–351.

Browder, D.M., Mims, P.J., Spooner, F., Ahl-grim-Delzell, L., & Lee, A. (2008). Teaching elementary school students with multiple disabilities to participate in shared stories. *Research and Practice for Persons with Severe Disabilities, 33,* 3–12.

Browder, D.M., & Minarovic, T.J. (2000). Utilizing sight words in self-instruction training for employees with moderate mental retardation in competitive jobs. *Education and Training in Mental Retardation and Developmental Disabilities, 35,* 78–89.

Browder, D.M., & Spooner, F. (2003). Understanding the purpose and process of alternate assessment. In D. Ryndak & S. Alper (Eds.), *Curriculum and instruction for students with significant disabilities in inclusive settings* (pp. 51–72). Boston, MA: Allyn & Bacon.

Browder, D.M., & Spooner, F. (2011). *Teaching students with moderate and severe disabilities.* New York, NY: Guilford Press.

Browder, D.M., Spooner, F., Ahlgrim-Delzell, L., Harris, A., & Wakeman, S. (2008). A meta-analysis on teaching mathematics to students with significant cognitive disabilities. *Exceptional Children, 74,* 407–432.

Browder, D.M., Wakeman, S.Y., Spooner, F., Ahlgrim-Delzell, L., & Algozzine, B. (2006). Research on reading for students with significant cognitive disabilities. *Exceptional Children, 72,* 392–408.

Burstein, N., Sears, S., Wilcoxen, A., Cabello, B., & Spagna, M. (2004). Moving toward inclusive practices. *Remedial and Special Education, 25,* 104–116.

Carter, E.W., Cushing, L.S., Clark, N.M., & Kennedy, C.H. (2005). Effects of peer support interventions on students' access to the general curriculum and social interactions. *Research and Practice for Persons with Severe Disabilities, 30,* 15–25.

Carter, E.W., & Hughes, C. (2006). Including high school students with severe disabilities in general education classes: Perspectives of general and special educators, paraprofessionals, and administrators. *Research and Practice for Persons with Severe Disabilities, 31,* 174–185.

Cole, C.M., Waldron, N., & Majd, M. (2004). Academic progress of students across inclusive and traditional settings. *Mental Retardation, 42,* 136–144.

Collins, B.C. (2007). *Moderate and severe disabilities: A foundational approach.* Upper Saddle River, NJ: Pearson/Merrill/Prentice Hall.

Collins, B.C., Branson, T.A., Hall, M., & Rankin, S.W. (2001). Teaching secondary students with moderate disabilities in an inclusive academic classroom setting. *Journal of Development and Physical Disabilities, 13,* 41–59.

Cook, B.G., Tankersley, M., & Landrum, T.J. (2009). Determining evidence-based practices in special education. *Exceptional Children, 75,* 365–383.

Copeland, S.R., & Cosbey, J. (2008–2009). Making progress in the general curriculum: Rethinking effective instructional practices. *Research and Practice for Persons with Severe Disabilities, 33–34,* 214–227.

Copeland, S.R., Hughes, C., Agran, M., Wehmeyer, M.L., & Fowler, S.E. (2002). An intervention package to support high school students with mental retardation in general education classrooms. *American Journal on Mental Retardation, 107,* 32–45.

Copeland, S.R., Keefe, E.B., Calhoon, A.J., Tanner, W., & Park, S. (2011). Preparing teachers to provide literacy instruction to all students: Faculty experiences and perceptions. *Research and Practice for Persons with Severe Disabilities, 36,* 126–141.

Courtade, G., Spooner, F., Browder, B., & Jimenez, B. (2012). Seven reasons to promote standards-based instruction for students with severe disabilities: A reply to Ayres, Lowrey, Douglas, & Sievers (2011). *Education and Training in Autism and Developmental Disabilities, 47,* 3–13.

Downing, J.E., Spencer, S., & Cavallaro, C. (2004). The development of an inclusive charter elementary school: Lessons learned. *Research and Practice for Persons with Severe Disabilities, 29,* 11–24.

Duran, E., & Heiry, T.J. (1986). Comparison of Spanish only, Spanish and English and English only cues with handicapped students. *Reading Improvement, 23,* 138–141.

Evidence-based practices for reading, math, writing, and behavior. (2009). [Special Issue]. *Exceptional Children, 75.*

Fiscus, R.S., Schuster, J.W., Morse, T.E., & Collins, B.C. (2002). Teaching elementary students with cognitive disabilities food preparation skills while embedding instructive feedback in the prompt and consequence event. *Education and*

Training in Mental Retardation and Developmental Disabilities, 37, 55–69.

Fisher, M., & Meyer, L.H. (2002). Development and social competence after two years for students enrolled in inclusive and self-contained educational programs. *Research and Practice for Persons with Severe Disabilities, 27,* 165–174.

Flores, M.M., & Ganz, J.B. (2007). Effectiveness of direct instruction for teaching statement inference, use of facts, and analogies to students with developmental disabilities and reading delays. *Focus on Autism and Other Developmental Disabilities, 22,* 244–251.

Foreman, P., Arthur-Kelly, M., Pascoe, S., & King, B.S. (2004). Evaluating the educational experiences of students with profound and multiple disabilities in inclusive and segregated classroom settings: An Australian perspective. *Research and Practice for Persons with Severe Disabilities, 29,* 183–193.

Freeman, S.F.N., & Alkin, M.C. (2000). Academic and social attainments of children with mental retardation in general and special education settings. *Remedial and Special Education, 21,* 3–18.

Fryxell, D., & Kennedy, C.H. (1995). Placement along the continuum of services and its impact on students' social relationships. *Journal of The Association for Persons with Severe Handicaps, 20,* 259–269.

Ganz, J.B., & Flores, M.M. (2009). The effectiveness of direct instruction for teaching language to children with autism spectrum disorders: Identifying materials. *Journal of Autism and Developmental Disorders, 39,* 75–83.

Gersten, R., Fuchs, L., Compton, D., Coyne, M., Greenwood, C., & Innocenti, M.S. (2005). Quality indicators for group experimental and quasi-experimental research in special education. *Exceptional Children, 71,* 149–164.

Goeke, J.L. (2009). *Explicit instruction: A framework for meaningful direct teaching.* Upper Saddle River, NJ: Merrill.

Grant Applications under Part D, 67 Fed. Reg. 118 (proposed June 19, 2002, pp. 41792–41799).

Hawkins, R.C. (2011). *The impact of inclusion on the achievement of middle school students with mild to moderate learning disabilities.* Unpublished doctoral dissertation, Walden University, Minneapolis, MN.

Horner, R.H., Carr, E.G., Halle, J., McGee, G., Odom, S., & Wolery, M. (2005). The use of single-subject research to identify evidence-based practice in special education. *Exceptional Children, 71,* 165–180.

Hudson, M.E. (2012). *Effects of a peer-delivered system of least prompts intervention package and academic read-alouds on listening comprehension for students with moderate intellectual disability* (Doctoral dissertation). Retrieved from ProQuest. (AAT3510205)

Hudson, M.E., Browder, D.M., & Jimenez, B.A. (in press). Effects of a peer-delivered system of least prompts with adapted text read-alouds on listening comprehension for students with moderate intellectual disability. *Education and Training in Autism and Developmental Disabilities.*

Hunt, P., Farron-Davis, F., Beckstead, S., Curtis, D., & Goetz, L. (1994). Evaluating the effects of placement of students with severe disabilities in general education versus special classes. *Journal of The Association for Persons with Severe Handicaps, 19,* 200–214.

Hunt, P., Soto, G., Maier, J., & Doering, K. (2003). Collaborative teaming to support students at risk and students with severe disabilities in general education classrooms. *Exceptional Children, 69,* 315–332.

Hunt, P., Staub, D., Alwell, M., & Goetz, L. (1994). Achievement by all students within the context of cooperative learning groups. *Journal of The Association for Persons with Severe Handicaps, 19,* 290–301.

Individuals with Disabilities Education Act Amendments (IDEA) of 1997, PL 105-17, 20 U.S.C. §§ 1400 *et seq.*

Individuals with Disabilities Education Improvement Act (IDEA) of 2004, PL 108-446, 20 U.S.C. §§ 1400 *et seq.*

Jackson, L.B., Ryndak, D.L., & Wehmeyer, M.L. (2008–2009). The dynamic relationship between context, curriculum, and student learning: A case for inclusive education as a research-based practice. *Research and Practice for Persons with Severe Disabilities, 33–34,* 175–195.

Jameson, J.M., McDonnell, J., Johnson, J.W., Riesen, T., & Polychronis, S. (2007). A comparison of one-to-one embedded instruction in the general education classroom and one-to-one massed practice instruction in the special education classroom. *Education and Treatment of Children, 30,* 23–44.

Jameson, J.M., McDonnell, J., Polychronis, S., & Riesen, T. (2008). Embedded, constant time delay instruction by peers without disabilities in general education classrooms. *Intellectual and Developmental Disabilities, 46,* 346–363.

Katz, J., & Mirenda, P. (2002). Including students with developmental disabilities in general education classrooms: Social benefits. *International Journal of Special Education, 17,* 26–36.

Keefe, E.B., & Copeland, S.R. (2011). What is literacy? The power of a definition. *Research and Practice for Persons with Severe Disabilities, 36,* 92–99.

Kennedy, C.H., Cushing, L.S., & Itkonen, T. (1997). General education participation improves the social contacts and friendship networks of students with severe disabilities. *Journal of Behavioral Education, 7,* 167–189.

Kennedy, C.H., Shulka, S., & Fryxell, D. (1997). Comparing the effects of educational placement on the social relationships of intermediate school students with severe disabilities. *Exceptional Children, 64,* 31–47.

Kleinert, H.L., & Thurlow, M. (2001). An introduction to alternate assessments: Historical foundations and essential parameters. In H.L. Kleinert & J.F. Kearns (Eds.), *Alternate assessment: Measuring outcomes and supports for students with disabilities* (pp. 1–15). Baltimore, MD: Paul H. Brookes Publishing Co.

Kliewer, C., & Biklen, D. (2001) "School's not really a place for reading:" A research synthesis of the literate lives of students with severe disabilities. *Journal of The Association for Persons with Severe Handicaps, 26,* 1–12.

Knight, V.F., McKissick, B.R., & Saunders, A. (2013). A review of technology-based interventions to teach academic skills to students with autism spectrum disorder. *Journal of Autism and Developmental Disorders.* [Advance online publication.] doi: 10.1007/s10803-013-1814-y

Knight, V.F., Smith, B.R, Spooner, F., & Browder, D.M. (2011). Using explicit instruction to teach science descriptors to students with autism spectrum disorders. *Journal of Autism and Developmental Disorders, 43,* 378–389. doi: 10.1007/s10803-011-1258-1

Knight, V.F., Spooner, F., Browder, D.M., Smith, B.R., & Wood, C.L. (2013). Using graphic organizers and systematic instruction to teach science concepts to students with autism spectrum disorder. *Focus on Autism and Other Developmental Disabilities.* Advance online publication. doi: 10.1177/1088357612475301

McDonnell, J. (2011). Instructional contexts. In J.M. Kauffman & D.P. Hallahan (Eds.), *Handbook of special education* (pp. 532–543). New York, NY: Routledge/Taylor & Francis Group.

McDonnell, J., Johnson, J.W., Polychronis, S., Riesen, T., Jameson, M., & Kercher, K. (2006). Comparison of one-to-one embedded instruction in general education classes with small group instruction in special education classes. *Education and Training in Developmental Disabilities, 41,* 125–138.

McDonnell, J., Mathot-Buckner, C., Thorson, N., & Fister, S. (2001). Supporting the inclusion of students with moderate and severe disabilities in junior high school general education classes: The effects of classwide peer tutoring, multi-element curriculum, and accommodations. *Education and Treatment of Children, 24,* 141–160.

Mechling, L.C., Gast, D.L., & Langone, J. (2002). Computer-based video instruction to teach persons with moderate intellectual disabilities to read grocery aisle signs and locate items. *Journal of Special Education, 35,* 224–240.

Mims, P.J., Browder, D., Baker, J., Lee, A., & Spooner, F. (2009). Increasing participation and comprehension of students with significant cognitive disabilities and visual impairments during shared stories. *Education and Training in Developmental Disabilities, 44,* 421–430.

Mims, P.J., Hudson, M.E., & Browder, D.M. (2012). Using read-alouds of grade-level biographies and systematic prompting to promote comprehension for students with moderate and severe developmental disabilities. *Focus on Autism and Other Developmental Disabilities, 27,* 65–78.

Miracle, S.A., Collins, B.C., Schuster, J.W., & Grisham-Brown, J. (2001). Peer- versus teacher-delivered instruction: Effects on acquisition and maintenance. *Education and Training in Mental Retardation and Developmental Disabilities, 36,* 373–385.

Mithaug, D.E., Wehmeyer, M.L., Agran, M., Martin, J.E., & Palmer, S. (1998). The self-determined learning model of instruction: Engaging students to solve their learning problems. In M.L. Wehmeyer & D.J. Sands (Eds.), *Making it happen: Student involvement in educational planning, decision-making and instruction* (pp. 299–328). Baltimore, MD: Paul H. Brookes Publishing Co.

Newman, F.M., King, M.B., & Carmichael, D.L. (2007). *Authentic instruction and assessment: Common standards for rigor and relevance in teaching academic subjects.* Des Moines: Iowa Department of Education.

No Child Left Behind Act of 2001, PL 107-110, 115 Stat. 1425, 20 U.S.C. §§ 6301 *et seq.* (2006).

Panyan, M.V. (1984). Computer technology for autistic students. *Journal of Autism and Developmental Disorders, 14,* 375–382.

Peck, C.A., Staub, D., Gallucci, C., & Schwartz, I. (2004). Parent perception of the impacts of inclusion on their nondisabled child. *Research and Practice for Persons with Severe Disabilities, 29,* 135–143.

Pennington, R.C. (2010). Computer-assisted instruction for teaching academic skills to students with autism spectrum disorders: A review of literature. *Focus on Autism and Other Developmental Disabilities, 25,* 239–248. doi: 10.1177/108835761037 8291

Rivera, C.J., Hicks, S.C., & Cuero, K. (2012). Using culturally responsive shared stories to increase literacy skills for students who are emerging bilingual with disabilities. *Perspectives, 34,* 5–8.

Rivera, C.J., Wood, C.L., & Spooner, F. (2012). Comparative effects of Spanish and English vocabulary instruction for English language learners with moderate intellectual disability. *Multiple Voices for Ethnically Diverse Exceptional Learners, 13,* 42–55.

Rohena, E.I., Jitendra, A.K., & Browder, D.M. (2002). Comparison effects of Spanish and English constant time delay instruction on sight words. *Journal of Special Education, 36,* 169–184.

Ruppar, A.L., Dymond, S.K., & Gaffney, J.S. (2011). Teachers' perspectives on literacy instruction for students with severe disabilities who use augmentative and alternative communication. *Research and Practice for Persons with Severe Disabilities, 36,* 100–111.

Ryndak, D.L. (Ed). (2008–2009). Access to the general curriculum [Special issue]. *Research and Practice for Persons with Severe Disabilities, 33–34.*

Schenning, H., Knight, V., & Spooner, F. (2013). Effects of structured inquiry and graphic organizers on social studies comprehension by students with autism spectrum disorders. *Research in Autism Spectrum Disorders, 7,* 526–540. doi:10.1016/j. rasd.2012.12.007

Smith, B.R., Spooner, F., Jimenez, B., & Browder, D.M. (2013). Using an early science curriculum to teach science vocabulary and concepts to students with severe developmental disabilities. *Education and Treatment of Children, 36,* 1–31. doi: 10.1353/etc.2013.0002

Smith, B.R., Spooner, F., & Wood, C.L. (2013). Using embedded computer-assisted explicit instruction to teach science to students with autism spectrum disorder. *Research in Autism Spectrum Disorders, 7,* 433–443. doi: 10.1016/j. rasd.2012.10.01010

Smith, P. (2007). Have we made any progress? Including students with intellectual disabilities in regular education classrooms. *Intellectual and Developmental Disabilities, 45,* 297–309.

Snell, M.E. (Ed.). (1983). *Systematic instruction of the moderately and severely handicapped* (2nd ed.). Columbus, OH: Charles E. Merrill.

Spooner, F., Dymond, S.K., Smith, A., & Kennedy, C.H. (2006). What we know about accessing the general curriculum for students with significant cognitive disabilities. *Research and Practice for Persons with Severe Disabilities, 31,* 277–283.

Spooner, F., Knight, V., Browder, D.M., Jimenez, B., & DiBiase, W. (2011). Evaluating evidence-based practice in teaching science content to students with severe developmental disabilities. *Research and Practice for Persons with Severe Disabilities, 36,* 62–75.

Spooner, F., Knight, V.F., Browder, D.M., & Smith, B.R. (2012). Evidence-based practices for teaching academic skills to students with severe developmental disabilities. *Remedial and Special Education, 33,* 374–387. doi: 10.1177/0741932511421634

Spooner, F., Rivera, C., Browder, D.M., Baker, J., & Salas, S. (2009). Teaching emergent literacy skills using cultural contextual story-based lessons. *Research and Practice for Persons with Severe Disabilities, 34,* 102–112.

Teigland, C. (2009). What inclusive education means for overall student achievement. *TASH Connections, 35,* 12–14.

Thompson, S., & Quenemoen, R. (2001). Eight steps to effective implementation of alternate assessments. *Assessment for Effective Intervention, 26,* 67–74.

Title 1: Improving the academic achievement of the disadvantaged; Final Rule, 68 Fed. Reg. 236 (December 9, 2003).

Trela, K., Jimenez, B.A., & Browder, D.M. (2008). *Teaching to the standards in mathematics: A literacy-based approach for students with moderate and severe disabilities.* Verona, WI: Attainment Company.

U.S. Department of Education. (2005). *Alternate achievement standards for students with the most significant cognitive disabilities: Non-regulatory guidance.* Washington, DC: Author.

U.S. Department of Education. (2007). *Modified academic achievement standards: Non-regulatory guidance.* Washington, DC: Author.

U.S. Government Accountability Office. (2009). *Report to the chairman, subcommittee on higher education, lifelong learning, and competitiveness, committee on education and labor, house of representatives.* Retrieved from http://www.gao.gov/new.items/d09573.pdf

Wallace, T., Anderson, A.R., Bartholomay, T., & Hupp, S. (2002). An ecobehavioral examination of high school classrooms that include students with disabilities. *Exceptional Children, 68,* 345–359.

Wehmeyer, M.L. (1998). Self-determination and individuals with significant disabilities: Examining meaning and misconceptions. *Journal of The Association for Persons with Severe Handicaps, 23,* 5–16.

Wehmeyer, M.L. (2005). Self-determination and individuals with severe disabilities: Reexamining meanings and misinterpretations. *Research and Practice for Persons with Severe Disabilities, 30,* 113–120.

Wehmeyer, M.L., Field, S., Doren, B., Jones, B., & Mason, C. (2004). Self-determination and student involvement in standards-based reform. *Exceptional Children, 70,* 413–425.

Wehmeyer, M.L., Palmer, S.B., Agran, M., Mithaug, D.E., & Martin, J.E. (2000). Promoting causal agency: The self-determined learning model of instruction. *Exceptional Children, 66,* 439–453.

Wehmeyer, M.L., Palmer, S.B., Soukup, J.H., Garner, N.W., & Lawrence, M. (2007). Self-determination and student transition planning knowledge and skills: Predicting involvement. *Exceptionality, 15,* 31–44. doi: 10.1080/09362830709336924

Westling, D.L., & Fox, L. (2009). *Teaching students with severe disabilities* (4th ed.). Upper Saddle River, NJ: Pearson.

Wolery, M., Bailey, D.B., & Sugai, G.M. (1988). *Effective teaching: Principles and procedure of applied behavior analysis with exceptional students.* Boston, MA: Allyn & Bacon.

Wolfe, P.S., & Hall, T.E. (2003). Making inclusion a reality for students with severe disabilities. *Teaching Exceptional Children, 35,* 56–60.

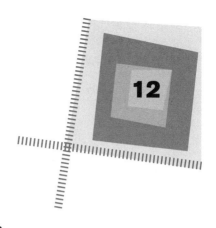

Serving Students with Health Care Needs

Donna Lehr

TASH has long been committed to individuals with severe disabilities who also have complex health care needs. These individuals have faced some unique challenges and discrimination as they seek access to health care and educational services. The purpose of this chapter is to describe some of those challenges and accompanying controversies that have ensued, along with some resolutions and progress that is being made toward meeting these challenges. This purpose is addressed by 1) defining the population of students considered to have severe disabilities with accompanying complex health care needs, 2) describing some of the ways in which they have experienced medical and educational discrimination, and 3) describing educational practices leading to effective inclusion of students with severe disabilities and complex health care needs in educational settings.

DEFINING STUDENTS WITH COMPLEX HEALTH CARE NEEDS

No agreed-on term is used to describe the students who are the focus of this chapter; however, they are often referred to as students with special health care needs or as medically fragile (Lehr, 1990; Muller, 2005). Neither term appropriately captures the essence of these students, nor their needs. The popularization of the term *special health care needs* at the federal level can be traced to former Surgeon General C. Everett Koop in the early 1980s. The term was coined under his leadership and that of Merle McPherson from the Maternal and Child Health Bureau and used as part of an effort to more accurately describe and serve children as their needs shifted over time. Newacheck, Rising, and Kim explained,

As the number and nature of the conditions treated by these programs expanded, the nomenclature used to describe the population shifted from "crippled children" in the 1930s to "handicapped children" in the 1960s and 1970s to CSHCN [Children with Special Health Care Needs] in the late 1980s. (2006, p. 334)

Surgeon General Koop was a pediatrician who brought his expertise and used his platform to develop a campaign focused on the needs of children who have special health care needs. He called on the nation to develop "strategies for comprehensive services needed by children with special health care needs; to address the challenges and burdens of the families of these children; and to stimulate community resources" (Koop, 1988, p. 4).

Although the term was not clearly defined in his campaign, continuing efforts to do so have resulted in the present definition used by the U.S. Department of Health and Human Services as a broad population of children including "those who have one or more chronic physical, developmental, behavioral or emotional conditions for which they require an above routine type or amount of health and related services" (2011, p. 4). Students who have severe asthma are considered to have special health care needs under this definition, as are students who have cancer. Data from the survey of children with special health care needs reveal many such children have comorbidities and "as the number of reported conditions increases, so does the number of reported difficulties. Nearly all of the 16.6% of CSHCN who reported 4 or more conditions also experience 4 or more difficulties" (U.S. Department of Health and Human Services, 2011, p. 4). Although attention to all of these students' needs is important, the challenges in service delivery are different and greater when the children have multiple conditions requiring health care and educational services that are more complex. In addition, some students require the use of medical technology such as ventilators or suctioning equipment for tracheostomy care (Rehm, 2002). The term *medically fragile* is used in an effort to focus attention on students with more complicated needs. Although this term may serve the function of focusing attention on these students, it may not be the type of attention that is conducive to meeting their educational needs. Lehr and McDaid (1993) noted that the term *medically fragile* is both inaccurate and off-putting. The fact that they have survived long enough to become students attests to their resilience, and they may not be as fragile as first thought. Also, describing these students as fragile can cause considerable alarm for school personnel unaccustomed to having such students in school settings. Although it is true that care must be taken to address these students' health care needs, it is best to begin with a point of concern but not panic when the word *fragile* is used to describe a child for whom a school district has responsibility. I prefer to use the term *complex health care needs* instead of the more general and less precise term *special health care needs* or the off-putting term *medically fragile*.

THE CHALLENGE OF GAINING HEALTH CARE, COMMUNITY, AND SCHOOL ACCESS

Although children with complex health care needs have always existed, their challenge to educators is relatively recent. In the past, they either did not live long enough to become students or they were educated in hospitals or at home and not in neighborhood schools (Lehr, 1990). More children are surviving their premature births and, at times, ongoing and complex health care needs because of improvements in lifesaving technology (Woodnorth, 2004). This, along with the movement toward less restrictive residential settings for all individuals with disabilities, has resulted in more students with complex health care needs residing in their home communities and attending their neighborhood schools (Rehm, 2002). These individuals continue to experience medical discrimination, however, and are denied access to the health care that would be provided if they did not have disabilities. In addition, they continue to be provided with education in more restrictive settings than their peers with other types of severe disabilities. The history of medical and education discrimination of children with complex health care needs is traced in the following sections.

Medical Discrimination

There is a history of medical neglect and discrimination for individuals with intellectual impairments, including mandatory sterilization and a lack of quality care provided within institutions (Crossley, 1996). Such decisions seem to be based on presumptions regarding the quality of life of individuals with disabilities as being less than that of those without disabilities and differences related to definitions of medically necessary treatments. The practice of withholding treatment known to be successful with typically developing children but denied to children with known disabilities was brought to the public's attention in the early 1980s (Crossley, 1996). An infant with Down syndrome born in 1982 with a defective esophagus was denied corrective surgery that would have been provided if the infant did not have a disability. The infant was also denied hydration and nutrition and was allowed to die without intervention. Baby Jane Doe was born in 1983 with spina bifida, hydrocephaly, and microencephaly. Her parents made the decision to provide minimum care in the form of antibiotics and bandages rather than allow corrective surgery to close the open spine, which would have been provided if the newborn did not present with a disability. Treatment was denied because the infant had an intellectual impairment due to microencephaly, in addition to the physical impairments from spina bifida. The assumption was that the child would have a poorer quality of life than those with spina bifida alone because of her intellectual impairment. Both decisions were questioned on the basis of the Rehabilitation Act Amendments of 1978 (PL 95-602). The Rehabilitation Act of 1973 (PL 93-112) stated,

> No otherwise qualified individual with a disability in the United States, as defined in section 7(20) shall, solely by reason of her or his disability, be excluded from the participation in, be denied the benefits of, or be subjected to discrimination under any program or activity receiving Federal financial assistance or under any program or activity conducted by any Executive agency or by the United States Postal Service. (§ 504)

It appeared to many that medical discrimination was based on the individuals' anticipated cognitive disabilities. The Baby Doe cases resulted in the so-called Baby Doe Amendment, which was not without controversy. The regulations issued by the U.S. Department of Health and Human Services required hospitals to post notices specifying that failure to provide treatment represented discrimination on the basis of a disability based on Section 504 of the Rehabilitation Act of 1973, and observed instances should be reported. Those regulations were challenged, however, and the

U.S. Supreme Court determined it was the parents who had made the decision to withhold treatment and not the hospital, and absent the parents, infants were not otherwise qualified (*Bowen v. American Hospital Association,* 1986). Crossley pointed out, "Thus the federal government's attempt to attack selective nontreatment as a problem of disability discrimination under section 504 failed" (1996, p. 381). Congress passed the Child Abuse Amendments of 1984 (PL 98-457) as an alternative, and states receiving federal funds had to have procedures in place for reporting instances of medical discrimination and neglect. Those regulations remain in place, although their effectiveness has been questioned (Crossley, 1996).

The controversy regarding Phillip Becker also warrants consideration (Lindsey, 1983). Phillip Becker was a 10-year-old child with Down syndrome who had a congenital heart defect that had become progressively worse and potentially life threatening. He had been institutionalized at birth, although his parents had retained guardianship and refused to grant permission for him to receive the lifesaving corrective surgery for the defect. Several individuals had established a relationship with him through their volunteer work at the residential facility in which he resided, became his advocates, and fought for custody so he could have the surgery. He eventually was adopted, and the surgery was conducted after a long battle that put the issues of parental rights and quality-of-life decisions front and center in the media. The parents' reason for denying treatment was their concern for the quality of Phillip's life as an adult with an intellectual impairment after they died. They preferred that he die rather than live a long life with a disability. The state decided to sever parental rights in this case, making way for the successful surgery for Phillip.

Harvesting organs from infants born with anencephaly is another example of medical discrimination against individuals with disabilities often pointed to in the bioethics and disability literature (American Academy of Pediatrics, 1992; Crossley, 1996; Fost, 1986). This issue was brought to the public's attention in 1987 when an infant with anencephaly was flown from England to a California hospital so that the infant could be used as a live donor for organ transplant. Organ transplants can legally be done when donors are declared brain dead; however, infants with anencephaly have brain stem functioning and are not legally dead. The transplant raised considerable concern about lowering the standards and the different criteria used based on the infant's diagnosis. Some argued the need for donors outweighed the ethical concerns (Crossley, 1996). The ethical discussions that ensued focused on whether the same standards regarding organ donation should be used with those with an intellectual impairment as it would if the individual did not have one, again raising questions of medical discrimination. These discussions continue, although the practice of transplants does not.

Public outcry arose in 2007 when information became known about a controversial treatment for a young child who had encephalopathy and demonstrated little volitional control of body functioning and required tube feeding (Ouellette, 2008). Ashley X (referred to by her parents as the Pillow Angel) demonstrated premature puberty at age 6, which raised concerns about her rapid growth in size and the difficulty of providing the extensive physical care she required. Concern was also raised about the difficulty of menstrual care because she would not be able to care for herself. The parents approved of a hysterectomy, the removal of breast tissue, and estrogen treatment to prevent these challenges. Advocates for individuals with disabilities argued against the intrusive treatments, which would not have been provided if Ashley did not have an intellectual impairment. Some argued that the treatment would result in a better quality of life and that it would enable Ashley's parents to care for her in their home longer than would otherwise be possible. Others argued that the treatment was not the issue, but the problem was society's lack of parental supports for such children, which would enable them to more easily provide home care (Ouellette, 2008).

Medical discrimination controversies center on what is medically necessary for individuals who are viewed as having a low-quality life and not benefiting from some medical procedures, the role of parents in decision making, and the interaction of all stakeholders. What if the procedures are designed to maintain capacity and not improve it, given that "many current definitions of medical necessity require evidence that a service will significantly improve a person's health status" (Ireys, Wehr, & Cooke, 1999, p. 2)? Ireys et al. pointed out,

> Many children and adults with disabilities frequently need health or medical services that will maintain their functional capacity. Defining as medically necessary only services that improve their health status means that they will be denied many services vital to their day-to-day lives. (1999, p. 2)

Aesch argued, "Most bioethics literature and most legal decisions in bioethics cases conclude that the impairment reduces the quality and value to others and to self of the life lived and therefore justifies less effort at preservation or recovery" (2001, p. 302). The challenge for access to necessary medical care continues, as does this debate (Mikochik, 2011).

Gaining Community Access

It is estimated that one million children with disabilities were not receiving any education prior to the Education for All Handicapped Children Act of 1975 (PL 94-142), and many children with complex health care needs were among this group. One of the law's major principles is referred to as zero reject, meaning states were responsible for assuring that all children with disabilities (between the ages of 5 and 18, later extended from 3 to 21) are provided with a free appropriate public education (FAPE). Although the meaning of this provision was challenged in the courts in *Timothy W. v. Rochester, NH,* it was held that the Education for *All* Handicapped Act did mean that school districts could not discriminate against those with severe and multiple disabilities such as those demonstrated by Timothy. The judge decided

> Schools cannot avoid the provisions of EHA [Education of the Handicapped Amendments] by returning to the practices that were widespread prior to the Act's passage unilaterally excluding certain handicapped children from a public education on the ground that they are uneducable. (875 F.2d 954)

Another principle of the law that articulated the congressional preference for education of students in the general education classroom when appropriate has proven more difficult to ensure for this population of students. Their presence in their community schools, and even in segregated schools, has been challenged in several ways.

Few children with disabilities were in their local communities for several reasons. First, the deinstitutionalization movement was still in its infancy when the Education for All Handicapped Children Act of 1975 was passed. Second, children with complex health care needs were among the most likely to still be residing in institutions, traditionally run as medical facilities. Furthermore, there were funding barriers to children receiving the health care services they needed in their family's home, rather than in hospitals; therefore, they were not in their local communities. The health care costs to families for children with special health care needs are estimated to be between "$2,669 to $69,906 compared to $676 to $3,181 for families with non-SHCN children" (Lindley & Mark, 2010, p. 80). These costs can quickly add up and exceed the annual limit and $1,000,000 lifetime cap on private health insurance policies, which may result in relying on Medicaid to cover health care costs. (This cap was recently removed by the Patient Protection and Affordable Care Act of 2010 [PL 111-148].) Payment for many services can be covered only if they are provided in an institution or hospital setting, however, because of the way that Medicaid laws are written. Consider the high profile case of Katie Beckett (Johnson, 2000). Katie contracted encephalitis and went into coma when she was 5 months old (Shapiro, 2010). She required a respirator most of the day to enable her to breathe, and she remained in the hospital for about 3 years. Her parents wanted to return her to their family home when her condition became stable and chronic instead of acute. Katie needed ongoing ventilator access and care, however, and she was not able to return to her home because those costs under Medicaid regulations could be covered if the health care services were provided in a hospital but not at home. Her mother Julie argued that the health care services could be provided at home at a lower cost. Her advocacy attracted the attention of President Ronald Reagan who approved a waiver for Katie, which enabled her to go to her home while continuing to have her health care costs paid through Medicaid. Julie Beckett continued the fight and pushed for reform in regulations so that other children could similarly benefit from this exception. The Tax Equity and Fiscal Responsibility Act (TEFRA) of 1982 (PL 97-248) was passed as a result of Julie Beckett's perseverance. TEFRA allows children to be cared for in their homes instead of remaining in hospitals or institutions so their care costs would be covered by the government. Each state can apply for a waiver to the general rules, which opened the way for children to be in their home communities (Catalyst Center, 2012).

Gaining School Access

Shifting from education delivered in homes to more typical community schools (i.e., from home-based educational services to school-based services) was the next step toward inclusion of children with complex health care needs Considerable controversies arose regarding which health care services would be provided by the schools, who would provide these services, and how safe care should be provided.

Defining Health Care Services Provided   The health care needs of these students (e.g., tube feeding, tracheostomy and ventilator care) were more complex than what traditionally had been provided in schools (Fauteux, 2010). Legal and quality of care and education questions were raised (Lehr, 1990; Lehr, Greene, & Powers, 2003; Lehr & McDaid, 1993).

- Are schools responsible for providing health care services?
- If the schools are responsible for providing the services, then who performs them?

- How can students' safety be ensured?

- How can schools ensure that they will be treated as students and not as patients?

The questions regarding who was responsible to pay for health care services were centered on interpreting related services and medical services as defined in the Education for All Handicapped Children Act of 1975 and clarified through the case of *Irving Independent School District v. Tatro* (1984). Amber Tatro had spina bifida and required clean intermittent catheterization (CIC) while at school. The school district argued it was not their responsibility to provide it because they believed CIC to be a medical service and not a related service. Related services were defined under the law as those which are required to enable a child to benefit from special education services, including transportation and developmental, corrective, and other supportive services (e.g., speech-language pathology and audiology, psychological services, physical and occupational therapy, recreation, medical and counseling services). Medical services were defined as those used "for diagnostic and evaluation purposes only as may be required to assist a handicapped child to benefit from special education" (468 U.S. 883, 890).

The case proceeded through the courts and eventually was heard in the U.S. Supreme Court. A *New York Times* reporter succinctly summarized the argument by saying, "Both sides agree on Amber's need for catheterization. The question facing the Supreme Court is how much of such care Congress intended the public schools to take on" (Maeroff, 1984). It ultimately was decided by the U.S. Supreme Court that CIC was a related service because Amber would not be able to be in school without the provision of care and the care could be provided by someone without extensive medical training.

This case provided clarity for individuals needing CIC, but students began coming to school with even more complicated health care service needs such as ongoing ventilator care and suctioning required for tracheostomy care. What about procedures that cannot be scheduled but have to be provided on an as-needed basis and require constant monitoring for need? School districts responded in a variety of ways. In some cases, students with these health care needs did not come to school but were instead provided educational and health care services in their homes. Other districts hired additional school nurses to provide the care, or children were accompanied to school by a health care worker (i.e., licensed nurse) who provided the services (Lehr, 1999).

Cedar Rapids Community School District v. Garret F. (1999) served to provide further guidance to school districts. Garret, a high school student who sustained spinal cord injuries in a motorcycle accident, was dependent on tracheostomy tube suctioning and ventilator monitoring in addition to CIC. The district argued that these were medical services and not related services because they were more intensive than CIC alone (i.e., they required ongoing monitoring and a greater skill level to perform). It was argued that the services were not diagnostic in nature and therefore did not have to be provided and paid for by the district. This case proceeded through the courts and was decided in favor of the parents. A distinction was made in the decision that helped to define the difference between medical and related services. Tracheostomy and ventilator monitoring and care could be provided by trained individuals and not exclusively by physicians. Garret's mother, who was not a physician, was trained to provide the services; therefore, they were not medical services. The clarification provided by this case was acknowledged in the regulations for the Individuals with Disabilities Education Improvement Act (IDEA) of 2004 (PL 108-446).

> The public agency also is responsible for providing services necessary to the health and safety of a child while the child is in school, with breathing, nutrition, and other bodily functions (e.g., nursing services, suctioning a tracheotomy, urinary catheterization) if these services can be provided by someone who has been trained to provide the service and are not the type of services that can only be provided by a licensed physician. (*Cedar Rapids Community School District v. Garret F.,* 526 U.S. 66 [1999]; Fed. Reg., August 14, 2006, p. 46571)

In addition, the terms *nursing services* and *health care services* were added to the description of related services.

The question of who provides the services was not resolved by the Tatro or Garret case (Lehr, 1990). Can a teacher tube feed a child, or should it be the exclusive responsibility of a nurse who has general training in providing health care services? Should a teacher provide such procedures even though his or her primary role is instructing students? Although it may seem that the school nurse is the simple answer, the following should be considered: 1) there are too few nurses in schools (Bergren & Monsalve, 2012), 2) it would prove costly to add nurses in every school where there are students with complex health care needs, and 3) there could be a tendency to place students with complex health care needs in the settings where there are full-time school nurses and not in their neighborhood schools, thus violating the principle of least restrictive environment (LRE).

Many educational and health care associations and unions addressed this issue in the mid-1980s and weighed in on this question of whose responsibility it was to provide the health care services from the point of view of professional responsibilities, background training, and level of expertise. For example, the American Federation of Teachers, the Council for Exceptional Children (CEC), the National Association of School Nurses, and the National Education Association worked together to develop *Guidelines for the Delineation of Roles and Responsibilities for the Safe Delivery of Specialized Health Care in the Educational Setting*s (CEC, 1990). In addition, all states have nurse practice acts designed to protect recipients from unsafe practices and specify the codes and ethics for this profession, regardless of the setting in which the nurses work. Nurse practice acts include specific statements regarding which procedures can and must be conducted by nurses and which can be delegated to others. If the nurse practice act in a particular state specifies that a health care procedure must be implemented by a nurse, then other professionals who do not hold nursing licenses are prohibited from administering it (Palfrey et al., 1992). Although these guidelines and laws existed, the information was not always known, and there was considerable variability in practice. Regulations for IDEA 2004 included some guidance regarding roles. The terms *school health services* and *school nurse services* were defined as follows.

> School health services and school nurse services means health services that are designed to enable a child with a disability to receive FAPE as described in the child's IEP. School nurse services are services provided by a qualified school nurse. School health services are services that may be provided by either a qualified school nurse or other qualified person. (300/A/300.34/c/13)

Informal observations in the field reveal that there continues to be considerable variability in practice regarding who is actually administering health care procedures in the schools, and more research on this topic is needed.

Provision of Safe Care   Boston Children's Hospital's Project School Care played a dominate role in helping school districts understand the process of welcoming students with complex health care needs and ensuring their safe hygienic care (Palfrey et al., 1992). Initially funded by the federal government,

> The project aims were to define the population of children dependent on medical technology more precisely than previously, to produce guidelines for safe provision of care in schools, and to offer consultation to schools and families around specific procedures (both technical and administrative) thereby enhancing the experience of children assisted by medical technology in schools. (Palfrey et al., 1992, p. 50)

Although the focus initially was on providing such consultative service in Massachusetts' schools, their work quickly gained attention nationwide. States recognized the need to clarify policies and practices for school districts regarding roles, responsibilities, and recommended practices for serving this population of students in schools. The states began to publish guidelines for their school districts, borrowing heavily from the first unpublished documents developed by Project School Care. Their work is now published in *Children and Youth Assisted by Medical Technology in Educational Settings: Guidelines for Care* (Porter, Haynie, Bierle, Caldwell, & Palfrey, 1997). An informal search of the Internet in 2012, along with direct contact with state departments of education, resulted in identifying 27 such state policy and procedure documents. Although it is possible that there are more documents, this reflects a significant difference from the late 1980s when there was no guidance available for schools.

RECOMMENDED PRACTICES IN PROVIDING CARE AND EDUCATION TO CHILDREN

An analysis of these state guidelines and literature reveals some common recommendations for schools providing education for students with complex health care needs. The next section includes descriptions of recommended practices designed to ensure the safe care and education of students with complex health care needs.

Ensuring Safe Care

First and foremost, before addressing the educational needs of all students, attention must be paid to the creation of environments in which students are safe from harm. For students with complex health care needs, this means particular attention to routine care procedures, specialized care procedures, and training of all those charged with providing the care. Careful planning is needed in each of these areas, as described in the following sections.

Providing Hygienic Care   Careful attention has to be paid to meeting the needs of students with complex health care needs, regardless of who is providing the services, in order to ensure that students are safe at school. Practices for providing hygienic care are key. Universal precautions and infection control are important for the care of all children and critical in the care of children with complex health care needs due to their medical vulnerabilities and the intrusive health care procedures some may need to receive. The term *universal precautions* refers to an approach to infection control that results in the treatment of all blood and body secretions and fluids as if they are infectious, not just those known to have infectious diseases (Occupational Safety and Health Administration, 2012). Using universal precautions includes hand washing, wearing protective gear such as gloves whenever touching or being exposed to body fluids, and carefully disposing of waste used in the process. Although attention to such matters is common to health care providers, these are not common procedures used in schools, outside of school nursing offices. Recommendations for attention to such matters are omnipresent in all guidelines reviewed.

Emergency Procedures   Carefully developed and clearly articulated procedures to follow in the case of an emergency are also critical. Although it is common for there to be emergency contact information and plans in place in all schools, the likelihood of needing to follow them increases with the inclusion of students with complex health care needs. In addition, it may be important to add a component to the plan (i.e., notifying emergency medical personnel at the receiving end of an emergency call) because of the increased likelihood that there will be emergency care of a student with complex health care needs. Some programs make arrangements for first responders to visit school programs to learn the likely location of students in school buildings and the health care needs of specific students.

Individualized Health Care Plans   Porter et al. (1997) recommended that individualized health care plans (IHCPs) be developed for all students with special health care needs and include the following.

- A brief health history

- A description of the special health care needs of the child

- A description of the child's current health status

- A description of the medications used at home and school, the person who will be responsible for administering the medications at school, and the possible side effects of the medications

- A description of the special diet and nutritional needs of the student

- Specialized transportation needs

- Specialized equipment needs for administration of the procedures

- Anticipated child-specific problems and responses to the problems

- Child-specific emergency plans

Such plans are typically developed by teams of professionals, including school personnel, the child's physician, and the parents or guardians. Porter et al. (1997) recommended written approvals be secured from the parents or guardians, physician, school nurse, and appropriate school administrator to document agreement by all. The IHCP is included as a part of children's individualized education programs (IEPs) in some school districts.

Health Care Training Three types of training are recommended for schools—general training targeted at all school personnel who are likely to have contact with the student, child-specific training for those who will implement the health care services, and child training designed to teach the student to implement or support the implementation of procedures as is appropriate to meet his or her needs (Porter et al., 1997). The general training should include information designed to increase the awareness of the student's needs, demystify them (Lehr & McDaid, 1993), and explain school emergency plans in general. Although it is possible that some charged with responsibilities for implementing procedures with specific students have had training regarding the protocols to be used for particular health care procedures, child-specific training is aimed at ensuring that the health care provider is competent in administering the particular procedures for each specific child and addressing each child's unique needs. Training is best provided by highly skilled health care educators, but including parents in the training provides an opportunity for the parent to receive a refresher course in procedure administration and for the parent to explain specific techniques found to be effective for the individual child.

One-time training for child-specific procedures is considered insufficient. Ongoing monitoring and supervision of plans and implementation of health care procedures are also considered recommended practices to ensure that procedures are, and continue to be, implemented as planned and modified as necessary.

Additional attention has to be given not only to physical access to buildings and classrooms, but also to electrical access to power the medical technology some students will need (e.g., suctioning machines, ventilators). Plans for emergency generators in the event of power outages are also important as are plans for routine maintenance checks of equipment along with back-up equipment access.

Meeting the Unique Education Needs of Students

Although providing safe care is the first step in addressing the education of students with complex health care needs in the schools, additional consideration must be given to practices that will help to ensure that their educational needs are also met. Make sure that students are treated as students and not as patients in a school setting (Lehr, 1990). Staff concern about the presence of children with complex health care needs in a school setting may interfere with the children being accepted as students, especially if the students are referred to as medically fragile. Their educational needs may be ignored with all the focus being placed on concern for their health care needs. The general and child-specific training approaches previously described, along with the IHCP, can aid in reducing this concern; fear can be reduced when one knows what to do and there is a plan for all.

Curricular adjustments may be necessary to meet the unique needs of students with complex health care needs, particularly when they are educated in inclusive classrooms. Accommodations must be made for both the short- and long-term absences the students may have from their classrooms for specialized health care services or reoccurring illnesses. They may have reduced endurance that could interfere with the learning process. Managing curricular access under these conditions requires the collaboration of many individuals, including general educators, special educators, parents, and school and home health care providers.

There can also be challenges to the nature of the social interactions between students with and without complex health care needs. School personnel are not the only ones who may be put off if the term *medically fragile* is used to describe a student. Consider the different impressions people can have when ongoing care is treated as a medical emergency rather than routine care (Lehr et al., 2003). Lehr et al. contrasted the different impression that might be formed when students are considered to be sick and therefore tube fed, rather than being considered healthy because they are being tube fed. In reality, that might be precisely what is occurring—some children's health greatly improves when they begin to be fed by tube rather than by mouth.

Identifying specific goals and objectives related to the student learning to implement his or her own self-care or self-care management also is important. Lehr and Macurdy (1994) noted that although it is typical to see IEP objectives on skill development related to eating and toileting, it is rare to see goals and objectives related to teaching students to provide or manage their own health care. Teaching these students hand washing and oral and nasal hygiene care skills is a good starting point. More specific goals and objectives may focus on knowledge and skills about the specialized health care procedures the student requires. For example, if a student is fed through a G-tube, then consider some of the following student outcomes (Lehr & Macurdy, 1994).

- Student will explain the reason for the alternative eating method.
- Student will describe the steps necessary to implement the procedure.
- Student will indicate the desire to eat or be fed.
- Student will measure feeding liquid to be placed in feeding bag or syringe.
- Student will pour food into feeding container.
- Student will clean or direct cleaning of feeding equipment.
- Student will feed self through a G-tube.

If the student is unable to provide his or her own care, then directing the care is an alternative step between total dependence and independence. In addition, the principle of partial participation (Baumgart et al., 1982) should be applied to enable program planners to identify the individual steps or parts of steps that the student can perform with adaptations when necessary to facilitate the maximum participation possible.

CONCLUSION

Some of the information in this chapter was presented as a historical chronology, which may have given the impression that society has passed through the phases and can now be confident that all students with complex health care needs receive an FAPE in the LRE. This desired outcome has yet to be achieved. Providing educational services to students with complex health care needs has been and continues to be an elusive and challenging goal. Among the challenges faced are those related to attitudes, training, different perceptions of professional responsibilities, and increasing awareness that there is a knowledge base regarding service provision to this population of students. Many school districts have not had the experience of educating any student with complex health care needs in their community schools because of the low incidence of this population of students. It is possible their experience will be similar to those who began welcoming students with complex health care needs in the early 1980s.

In addition, experienced school personnel are challenged by the arrival of each new student because of his or her unique complex health care needs. Rehm described the process of meeting the needs of students with complex health care needs as "not a singular event, but complex process that involves many people and organizations and that takes place over a long period of time" (2002, p. 71).

This chapter included descriptions of the history and evolution toward more inclusive medical and education practices for students with complex health care needs and descriptions of current recommended practices. Professionals' knowledge is limited to the extant research, policies, and laws that appear in the literature.

Laws aimed at decreasing medical discrimination have been clarified, matters related to rationing of care are still being debated, and the extent that medical discrimination continues for life-sustaining procedures but is not reported is unknown. Also, the question arises about providing access for other types of medical services. For example, I have heard from many parents that their children's physicians have questioned the need for visual examinations and eyeglasses for their children with complex health care needs and severe cognitive impairments as if to say, "Why bother?"

Although the educational needs of students with complex health care needs are not attracting the attention they did in the late 1980s and early 1990s, it would be wrong to believe that it is because everyone has learned all they need to know and has figured out all the answers. For example, the number of students with complex health care needs being educated in schools is unknown because no precise definition of the population exists. There is limited information about the quality of the education and care that they are receiving in schools. Who is providing the health care services in schools—teachers, nurses, or nurses' aides? Last, it is not known to what extent they are being educated in the LRE. Much work is needed to meet TASH's mission to promote the full inclusion and participation of children and adults with significant disabilities in every aspect of their community and to eliminate the social injustices that diminish human rights.

Questions for Study and Reflection

1. What are some activities you think could be done to increase peers' understanding of their classmates with complex health care needs? What would a preschooler want to know? What would a high school student be curious about?

2. What accommodations might need to be made for students with complex health care needs as related to transportation to and from school? What about for participation in after-school activities or on field trips?

3. Assumptions that individuals with disabilities have a poor quality of life were discussed as the basis for medical discrimination. What are some ways that you think these assumptions could be changed?

What may be some ways that schools can help support families of students with complex health care needs?

5. The author presented the notion that it may be hard to treat a student with complex health care needs as a student, rather than a patient, when there is concern about the child's safety. What are ways that this challenge can be addressed?

RESOURCES

American Academy of Pediatrics. (1992) Policy statement: Infants with anencephaly as organ sources: Ethical considerations. *Pediatrics, 89,* 1116–1119.

Heller, K.W. (2004) Integrating health care and educational programs In F.P. Orelove, D. Sobsey, & R.K. Silberman (Eds.), *Educating children with multiple disabilities: A collaborative approach* (4th ed., pp. 379–424). Baltimore, MD: Paul H. Brookes Publishing Co.

Heller, K.W., & Tumlin, J. (2004). Using expanded individualized health care plans to assist teachers of students with complex health care needs. *Journal of School Nursing, 20,* 150–160.

Joiner, T. (2005). When the nurse moves in: The changing dynamics of the medically fragile classroom: A teacher's perspective. *Exceptional Parent, 35,* 30.

Longmore, P.K. (1995). Medical decision making and people with disabilities: A clash of cultures. *Journal of Law, Medicine, and Ethics, 23,* 82–87.

Nagaeswaran, S., Silver, E.J., & Stein, R.W.K. (2008). Association of functional limitation with health care needs and experiences of children with special health care needs. *Pediatrics, 121,* 994–1101.

National Association of School Nurses. (2012). *Do not attempt resuscitation.* Retrieved from http://www.nasn.org/Portals/0/briefs/2012briefdnar.pdf

Raymond, J.A. (2009). The integration of children dependent on medical technology into public schools. *Journal of School Nursing, 25,* 186–194.

Rues, J., Graff, C., & Ault, M. (2011). Understanding special health care procedures. In M. Snell & F. Brown (Eds.), *Instruction of students with severe disabilities* (pp. 304–339). Upper Saddle River, NJ: Pearson.

Sobsey, D., & Thuppal, M. (2004). Children with special health care needs. In F.P. Orelove, D. Sobsey, & R.K. Silberman (Eds.), *Educating children with multiple disabilities: A collaborative approach* (4th ed., 311–378). Baltimore, MD: Paul H. Brookes Publishing Co.

Warfield, M., & Gulley, S. (2006). Unmet need and problems accessing specialty medical and related services among children with special health care needs. *Maternal and Child Health Journal, 10,* 201–216.

REFERENCES

Aesch, A. (2001). Disability, bioethics, and human rights. In G.L. Albrecht, K. Seelman, & M. Bury (Eds.), *Handbook of disability studies* (pp. 297–327). Thousand Oaks, CA: Sage Publications.

American Academy of Pediatrics. (1992). Policy statement: Infants with anencephaly as organ sources: Ethical considerations. *Pediatrics, 89,* 1116–1119.

American Academy of Pediatrics. (1999). Policy statement: Care coordination: Integrating health and related systems of care for children with special health care needs *Pediatrics, 104,* 978–981.

Baumgart, D., Brown, L., Pumpian, I., Nisbet, J., Ford, A., Sweet, M., & Schroeder, J. (1982). Principle of partial participation and individualized adaptations in educational programs for severely handicapped students. *Journal of The Association for the Severely Handicapped, 7,* 17–27.

Bergren, M.D., & Monsalve, L. (2012). The 2011 NASN membership survey: Developing and providing leadership to advance school nursing practice. *NASN School Nurse, 27,* 36–41.

Best, S.J., Heller, K.W., & Bigge, J.L. (2005). *Teaching individuals with physical or multiple disabilities.* Upper Saddle River, NJ: Pearson/Merrill Prentice Hall.

Bowen v. American Hospital Association, 476 U.S. 610 (1986).

Catalyst Center. (2012). *Improving financing of care for children and youth with special health care needs. State at-a-glance chart book on coverage and financing of care for children with special health care needs.* Retrieved from http://www.hdwg.org/catalyst/online-chartbook/

Cedar Rapids Community School District v. Garret F., 526 U.S. 66 (1999).

Child Abuse Amendments of 1984, PL 98-457, 42 U.S.C. §§ 5101 *et seq.*

Council for Exceptional Children. (1990). *Guidelines for the delineation of roles and responsibilities for the safe delivery of specialized health care in the educational settings.* Reston, VA: Council for Exceptional Children.

Crossley, M. (1996). Infants with anencephaly, the ADA, and the Child Abuse Amendments. *Issues in Law and Medicine, 11,* 379.

Education for All Handicapped Children Act of 1975, PL 94-142, 20 U.S.C. §§ 1400 *et seq.*

Fauteux, N. (2010). Keeping children healthy in school, and ready to learn. *Charting Nursing's Future, 14,* 1–8.

Fost, N. (1986). Treatment of seriously ill and handicapped newborns. *Critical Care Clinics, 2,* 149.

Individuals with Disabilities Education Improvement Act (IDEA) of 2004, PL 108-446, 20 U.S.C. §§ 1400 *et seq.*

Ireys, H.T., Wehr, E., & Cooke, R.E. (1999). *Defining medical necessity: Strategies for promoting access to quality care for persons with developmental disabilities, mental retardation, and other special health care needs.* Arlington, VA: National Center for Education in Maternal and Child Health.

Irving Independent School District v. Tatro, 468 U.S. 883 (1984).

Johnson, B.H. (2000). Family-centered care: Four decades of progress. *Families, Systems, and Health, 18,* 137–156.

Koop, C.E. (1988, September 7). *Building community based services systems for children with special health care needs.* Banquet presentation, Surgeon General's Conference, Washington, DC.

Lehr, D.H. (1990). Providing education to students with complex health care needs. *Focus on Exceptional Children, 22,* 1–12.

Lehr, D.H. (1999). U.S. Supreme Court requires school district to pay for nursing services for students with special health care needs. *TASH Newsletter, 25,* 28–30.

Lehr, D.H., Greene, J., & Powers, S. (2003). Managing the needs of students with physical and health challenges in inclusive settings. In D. Ryndak & S. Alper (Eds.), *Inclusion and curriculum for students with significant disabilities* (pp. 432–447). Boston, MA: Allyn & Bacon.

Lehr, D.H., & Macurdy, S. (1994). Special health care needs. In M. Agran, N. Marchand-Martella, & R. Martella (Eds.), *Promoting health and safety for persons with disabilities: Skills for independent living* (pp. 357–383). Baltimore, MD: Paul H. Brookes Publishing Co.

Lehr, D.H., & McDaid, P. (1993). Opening the door further: Integrating students with complex health care needs. *Focus on Exceptional Children, 25,* 1–8.

Lindley, L.C., & Mark, B.A. (2010). Children with special health care needs: Impact of health care expenditures on family financial burden. *Journal of Child and Family Studies, 19,* 79–89.

Lindsey, R. (1983, October 10). Surgery follows pact on custody. *New York Times,* p. A12.

Maeroff, G.I. (1984, May 29). Court asked to limit aid for handicapped. *New York Times.* Retrieved from http://www.nytimes.com/1984/05/29/science/education-court-asked-to-limit-aid-for-handicapped.html

Mikochik, S.L. (2011). Rationing human life: Health care reform and people with disabilities. *Issues in Law and Medicine, 26,* 199–205.

Muller, E. (2005). *Medically fragile: State policies and procedures.* Retrieved from http://www.nasdse.org/portals/0/documents/download%20publications/dfr-0527.pdf

Newacheck, P.W., Rising, J.P., & Kim, S.E. (2006). Children at risk for special health care needs. *Pediatrics, 118,* 334–342.

Occupational Safety and Health Administration. (2012). *Healthwide hazards: (Lack of) universal precautions.* Retrieved from http://www.osha.gov/SLTC/etools/hospital/hazards/univprec/univ.html

Ouellette, A.R. (2008). Growth attenuation, parental choice, and the rights of disabled children: Lessons from the Ashley X case. *Houston Journal of Health Law and Policy, 8,* 207–244.

Palfrey, J.S., Haynie, M., Porter, S., Bierle, T., Cooperman, P., & Lowcock, J. (1992).

Project school care: Integrating children assisted by medical technology into educational settings. *Journal of School Health, 62,* 50–54.

Patient Protection and Affordable Care Act of 2010, PL 111-148, 124 Stat. 119, 318-319 §2702.

Porter, S., Haynie, M., Bierle, T., Caldwell, T.H., & Palfrey, J.S. (Eds.). (1997). *Children and youth assisted by medical technology in educational settings: Guidelines for care* (2nd ed.). Baltimore, MD: Paul H. Brookes Publishing Co.

Rehabilitation Act Amendments of 1978, PL 95-602, 29 U.S.C. §§ 701 *et seq.*

Rehabilitation Act of 1973, PL 93-112, 29 U.S.C. §§ 701 *et seq.*

Rehm, R. (2002, February 28). *Creating a context of safety and achievement at school for children who are medically fragile/technology dependent.* Retrieved from http://www.ncbi.nlm.nih.gov/pubmed/11890196

Shapiro. J. (2010). *Katie Beckett: Patient turned home-care advocate.* Retrieved from http://www.npr.org/templates/story/story.php?storyId=131145687

Tax Equity and Fiscal Responsibility Act (TEFRA) of 1982, PL 97-248, 96 Stat. 324.

Timothy W. v. Rochester, New Hampshire, School District, 875 F.2d 954 (1984).

U.S. Department of Health and Human Services. (2011). *The national survey of children's health: 2007.* Rockville, MD: Author.

Woodnorth, G.H. (2004). Assessing and managing medically fragile children: Tracheostomy and ventilatory support. *Language, Speech, and Hearing Services in Schools, 35,* 363.

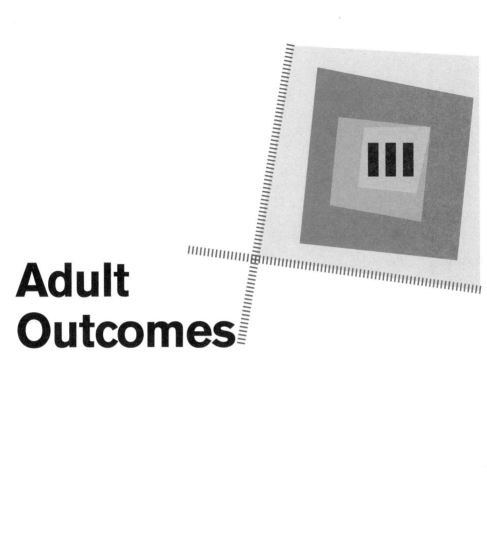

Adult
Outcomes

13

Ensuring Employment Outcomes

Preparing Students for a Working Life

Michael Callahan, John Butterworth, Jane Boone, Ellen Condon, and Richard Luecking

The basic premise of public education is to prepare youth for life. Schooling offers information, skill development, and experiences to youth that are to be applied in their adult life to manage the details of living in one's home and community, raising a family, participating in society, and contributing in one's job. The basic premise of special education, however, has been less clear, especially for students with severe intellectual and developmental disabilities. Since the creation of the individualized education program (IEP), special educators have struggled to come up with a formula that ensures the educational experience effectively connects with a participatory, inclusive, and contributing life when special education students become adults. Adults with intellectual and developmental disabilities continue to experience unacceptable rates of exclusion and segregation after nearly 40 years of access to free and appropriate experiences (National Disability Rights Network, 2011)

Educators and policy makers have theorized since the 1970s that students with intellectual and developmental disabilities would be prepared for an inclusive and participatory life as adults if they were offered access to critical educational skills that were individually determined and provided in a least restrictive environment. Furthermore, it was presumed that the path from school to adult employment would be smooth to ensure a reasonable expectation of a working life when students became adults. But this has not been the case. Most graduating students with intellectual and developmental disabilities make the transition either to a life

Allison Hall, Jean Winsor, Alberto Migliore, and Cady Landa of the Institute for Community Inclusion, University of Massachusetts Boston, developed original source material that was used in parts of this chapter.

of nonwork, languishing on waiting lists for services, or to segregated services that have no requirements for all the investment made during school.

This chapter suggests that even the best, most inclusive transition services in public schools must focus on employment as an outcome of the educational process while students are still in school if there is to be a reasonable expectation of significantly increasing employment for students with intellectual and developmental disabilities. This will not be an easy challenge to meet.

In addition, we view the following features as critical to the success of making the transition to employment: believing that all students can be employed, understanding that employment is a critical aspect of citizenship for all, and using customized and supported employment strategies, when necessary, to avoid the exclusion that competitive, demanding employment often causes. We also recommend using alternative strategies that replace comparative assessments to get to know the strengths, interests, and needs of students by using qualitative approaches, such as discovery (Callahan, Shumpert, & Condon, 2009). Educators and schools need to accept the responsibility of ensuring that all youth with intellectual and developmental disabilities leave school with a paid job.

This chapter's objectives relate to the factors that are necessary to ensure a successful transition from school to employment for youth with intellectual and developmental disabilities. In addition to the general education factors described elsewhere in this book, this chapter addresses the following objectives.

- Establish the case for the importance of paid, individualized employment in the community for youth with intellectual and developmental disabilities.

- Provide details regarding experiential activities for youth with intellectual and developmental disabilities relating to employment.

- Connect emerging recommended practices in the field of employment for adults with the practices used in schools.

- Address the continuing tension between the goal of full inclusion for students with intellectual and developmental disabilities and the need for employment experiences that start early and continue throughout the educational process.

ALIGNMENT WITH TASH'S NATIONAL AGENDA AND RESOLUTIONS

TASH, the national organization advocating for equity, opportunity, and inclusion for people with disabilities, particularly for people with the most severe intellectual and developmental disabilities, has articulated its mission and goals relating to transition and employment since the late 1970s. TASH organized its overall mission in 2009 into five national agenda committees, including inclusive education, community living, employment, diversity/cultural competency, and human rights. The issue of making the transition from school to employment is a component of the employment committee. The TASH Resolution on Integrated Employment is as follows:

STATEMENT OF PURPOSE

TASH recognizes the importance of work in the lives of all people as an element of full participation and inclusion in society. TASH calls for rapid and immediate development of individualized and integrated employment for all people with disabilities and the rapid and permanent replacement of segregated activity centers and sheltered work-shops. TASH affirms the right of all people with severe disabilities to full participation in community life with supports tailored to individual abilities and needs. Integrated employment is a critical element of community living and should contain the following features.

- Integration: Employment of people with significant disabilities must be in regular employment settings where they work alongside people without disabilities. Frequent and ongoing interactions and the development of relationships must be assured.

- Income and benefits: Employment must result in paid compensation of at least the minimum wage, up to prevailing wage, for work performed and should include ben-efits comparable to co-workers performing similar work.

- Customization and choice: Job seekers should be offered access to a customized process that allows for a negotiated relationship with the employer. This process serves to avoid strict competitive employment by focusing on the discrete contribu-tions of the individual in relation to specific needs of the employer. Job selection and the duration of any job must be based on the choice of the individual.

- Control of resources: People with disabilities and those they choose to support them should be given the option of controlling and directing the funding and resources allocated on their behalf for employment.

- Ongoing career advancement: Employment for persons with significant disabilities must be viewed as careers that evolve over time driven by the individual's interests where positive job changes and advancement occur with access to higher pay, greater responsibility and variety, better working conditions that meet personal needs.

- Individualized and natural supports: The assistance and support provided persons with significant disabilities should be individualized according to their conditions for success, and their abilities. The supports provided should maximize natural features of support provided by personnel in the workplace.

- Funding: Funding for "day" services at the federal, state and local levels should be directed towards employment as the first and most important outcome for adults with significant disabilities. Funding for community participation, recre-ation and other non-work outcomes should be designed around the work routines of the individual.

- Education: Employment should be an expected outcome of the educational process for students with significant disabilities of both high school and college settings. Educational settings should provide information, supports and experiences to all students, including students with significant disabilities, on employment and the importance of a working life.

- Business ownership: For those individuals with significant disabilities who wish to own their own business, access to funding, services and supports should be pro-vided in a manner similar to that of wage employment.

- Equal access: People with the greatest support needs must be given high priority for employment.

Adopted December 1989
Revised July 2009

The importance of employment to the full inclusion mandate of TASH is explicit in this resolution. An adult without a job will find it difficult to experience the ben-efits of an inclusive lifestyle. Therefore, teachers and parents must address employ-ment as a central outcome of the role of the educational process.

Related Legislation, Mandates, and Policies

Significant portions of federal policy are designed to support the expectation that youth with disabilities will begin thinking about work, getting good jobs, and beginning careers at an age typical to their peers without disabilities. This requires leadership, knowledge, and intentional partnerships at the state, local, and individual family level to effectively collaborate and make the most of the opportunities identified in federal policy.

The Individuals with Disabilities Education Improvement Act (IDEA) of 2004 (PL 108-446), the Rehabilitation Act of 1973 (PL 93-112), and the Workforce Investment Act (WIA) of 1998 (PL 105-220) all emphasize the importance of employment for young adults with disabilities. IDEA 2004 requires that transition planning be integrated into every student's IEP beginning prior to the first IEP following the student's 16th birthday or younger if determined appropriate. The Rehabilitation Act of 1973 specifies transition services as those services provided to eligible students with disabilities as early as age 14 as "a coordinated set of activities for a student, designed within an outcome-oriented process that promotes movement from school to post school activities including post-secondary education, vocational training, continuing and adult education, adult services, independent living, or community participation" (§ 1401[34]). The WIA promotes a coordinated approach for providing youth services and provides for a wide array of year-round services, including occupational skills training, summer employment opportunities, counseling, internships and job placements, mentoring, tutoring, leadership development, and academic and vocational education.

Legislative, policy, and practice developments support the notion of presumptive employability for all youth making the transition from school to work, including those considered to have severe disabilities. Public policy is increasingly supporting the efficacy of this belief (IDEA, 2004; WIA, 1998). A significant disparity still exists, however, between legislative and policy intent and actual outcomes achieved by youth in transition. It will be necessary to build on practices supported in the transition research literature for all youth to achieve employment outcomes that mirror those promised by the presumption of employability. These findings suggest the importance of activities that will culminate in paid, sustainable employment for all youth with disabilities, regardless of their disability label or their need for support and accommodation to find and keep good jobs.

Related Research

Individuals with intellectual and developmental disabilities have clearly expressed both a desire to be full participants in the typical labor force and an expectation that they would be employed after graduation. Self Advocates Becoming Empowered (2009) issued a policy statement calling for the end of sub–minimum wage or sheltered employment. The research literature documented the desire of individuals with intellectual and developmental disabilities to be employed in the community (Migliore, Mank, Grossi, & Rogan, 2007; Timmons, Hall, Bose, Wolfe, & Winsor, 2011), and 86% of young adults of transition age with an intellectual disability stated that they expect to be employed after graduation (National Longitudinal Transition Study–2 [NLTS–2], n.d.). An increasing number of parents hope that their sons and daughters will go to college. Enrollment in postsecondary education in the general population increased by 38%—from 14.8 million to 20.4 million between 1999 and 2009—and is expected to grow another 14% by 2020 (Snyder & Dillow, 2011). Research similarly shows that parents of students with a range of disabilities cite college as the most desirable outcome. Participation rates, however, remain quite low (Grigal, Neubert, Moon, & Graham, 2003).

Employment is a primary pathway to independence and autonomy for all youth, including youth with disabilities. Yet, there continues to be a great disparity between the employment outcomes of youth with and without disabilities. Data from the American Community Survey showed that the employment rate for young adults age 18–21 years without an identified disability was 37.0% in 2010, compared with 22.3% for young adults who reported any disability and only 8.7% for young adults with a cognitive disability who receive Supplemental Security Income (SSI). For young adults between the ages of 22 and 30, 73.3% without a disability were employed in 2010, compared with 39.5% with any disability and 15.7% with a cognitive disability and SSI (Sulewski, Zalewska, & Butterworth, 2012). Data from the NLTS–2, which documents the secondary and postsecondary experiences of students participating in special education, suggested that employment outcomes for youth with *mental retardation* (the terminology used by the U.S. Department of Education) declined from 46.5% in 1990 to 29.8% in 2005 (Newman, Wagner, Cameto, Knokey, & Shaver, 2010). More recent NLTS–2 data, collected in 2009 when participants were age 21–25, suggest that 37% of youth with an intellectual disability had a paid job outside the home (Migliore & Zalewska, 2012). Employment outcomes of youth with disabilities, and specifically youth with intellectual and developmental disabilities, are still far below their peers without disabilities (Newman et al., 2010).

Grigal, Hart, and Migliore (2011) found that students with intellectual and developmental disabilities were less likely to have competitive employment goals and outcomes and more likely to have sheltered employment goals and outcomes as compared with students with other disabilities. Poor employment outcomes for youth with intellectual and developmental disabilities are a result of a confluence of issues, including lack of emphasis on integrated employment outcomes within state intellectual and developmental disabilities agencies (Butterworth et al., 2011); inadequate collaboration between the adult disability and education systems (Certo et al., 2003; Whelley, Hart, & Zaft, 2004); limited vocational experiences while in school (Carter, Austin, & Trainor, 2011b; Wehman, 2013); and limited efforts to support youth with intellectual and developmental disabilities to directly make the transition to jobs in the community (Certo et al., 2008). The most critical of these issues follow.

Lack of Collaboration Between Key Players Insufficient linkages between the education, rehabilitation, and adult intellectual and developmental disabilities systems are a primary factor in the employment outcomes of youth with intellectual and developmental disabilities, despite mandates for interagency collaboration in legislation such as IDEA 2004 and the Rehabilitation Act of 1973 (Certo et al., 2008; Martinez et al., 2010; National Council on Disability, 2008). Hart, Zimbrich, and Whelley (2002) identified five major barriers to increased coordination: 1) partnerships are seldom effective at the state and local levels, 2) mechanisms for information sharing and shared service delivery are uncoordinated, 3) a lack of resource mapping exists at the state and local level, 4) gaps are present in service delivery, and 5) a lack of student– and family–professional partnerships exists.

Inadequate Emphasis on Community Employment Employment outcomes for individuals with intellectual and developmental disabilities are also grim within the adult service system. The number of overall vocational rehabilitation agency closures into employment for individuals with intellectual and developmental disabilities in the federal vocational rehabilitation system in fiscal year (FY) 2009 declined to the lowest figures since FY2002 (Butterworth et al., 2011). Only an estimated 20.3% of adults supported by state intellectual and developmental disabilities agencies nationally received integrated employment services, down from 25% in FY2001 (Butterworth et al., 2011). Data from the 2010 National Core Indicators Project suggested that only 14.4% of working age adults work in integrated employment (Human Services Research Institute & Institute for Community Inclusion, 2011). Participation in sheltered or facility-based employment and nonwork services has steadily grown, suggesting that employment services continue to be viewed as an add-on service rather than a systemic change (Mank, Cioffi, & Yovanoff, 2003).

Family Factors   Family engagement is a key component in successful transition planning, with a particular focus on building relationships and information sharing between families and professionals. Hetherington et al. (2010), however, found that parents lacked adequate knowledge to support their children in the transition process. Family factors found to influence transition outcomes include parents' lack of information about work incentives and fear of losing benefits (Luecking & Wittenburg, 2009; Winsor, Butterworth, Lugas, & Hall, 2010) and parents' expectations about work in general (Lindstrom, Doren, & Miesch, 2011; Timmons, Hall, et al., 2011). Carter, Austin, and Trainor (2011a) found that parental expectations was the family factor most predictive of paid work experiences in school.

Education System Factors   Carter et al. (2011a) found that many students with severe disabilities lack early vocational experiences. Additional education system factors include teacher expectations of students working (Carter et al., 2010), unmet needs for professional development of special education teachers (Winsor et al., 2010), lack of long-term follow-up of graduates following transition to employment (Rusch & Braddock, 2004), and limited diffusion of recommended practices such as person-centered planning in schools (Winsor et al., 2010).

Conceptualizing Transition at a Systems Level

Effective transition policy and strategy requires attention to school-based services, the relationship and partnerships between schools and adult service systems, and the policy and priorities of the adult service system that will provide adult supports.

Transition Services Models   The National Alliance for Secondary Education and Transition's (2005) research-based standards and quality indicators for successful transition outcomes for youth include schooling, career preparatory experiences, family involvement, and connecting activities. The National Collaborative on Workforce & Disability for Youth (NCWD/Y; 2005) produced the *Guideposts for Success* as a tool for practitioners. Certo et al.'s (2008) Transition Service Integration Model (TSIM) underscores the importance of early collaboration between the school and adult service systems and a direct focus on employment (Luecking & Certo, 2002). The TSIM emphasizes collaboration between the education, rehabilitation, and intellectual and developmental disabilities service systems and partnership between school and community rehabilitation provider staff, with a goal of establishing a paid integrated job and inclusive community activities during the last year of school services (Luecking & Certo, 2002).

High-Performing States Model   Hall, Butterworth, Winsor, Gilmore, and Metzel (2007) examined state intellectual and developmental disabilities agencies that support a high percentage of individuals in integrated employment. The model identifies seven characteristics of high-performing states that address contextual factors, system-level strategies, and interagency collaboration—leadership, strategic goals and operating policy, financing and contracting methods, training and technical assistance, interagency collaboration and partnerships, services and service innovation, and performance measurement and data management.

Factors that Influence Positive Transition Outcomes

Researchers have identified a wide range of factors that influence transition outcomes, including career preparation and work experiences, individual self-determination, family involvement, and connecting activities that link school and adult supports and experiences.

Career Preparatory Experiences   Career preparatory experiences such as work experience and employment preparation were the two most frequently substantiated correlates of positive post–high school employment status for youth with disabilities (Benz, Lindstrom, & Yovanoff, 2000; Doren & Benz, 1998; Landmark, Ju, & Zhang, 2010; Rabren, Dunn, & Chambers, 2002, as cited in Test et al., 2009). Research using the NLTS–2 yielded similar results. Postschool employment status of students with mild intellectual disability was positively related to the degree of participation in employment-related transition activities (e.g., job searching, training, counseling; assessment; job shadowing; community-based employment) while in school (Joshi, Bouck, & Maeda, 2012). Additional NLTS–2 research found that holding a paid community-based job while still in high school was strongly correlated with postschool employment success for students with severe disabilities (e.g., intellectual disability, multiple disabilities, autism) (Carter, Austin, & Trainor, 2012). Earlier research found that community-based on-the-job training in integrated settings with peers without disabilities was correlated with better integrated employment outcomes for youth with severe disabilities making the transition from school to work (Test et al., 2009; White & Weiner, 2004).

Work experiences for students with disabilities are classroom- or school-based nonpaid jobs, with only a small portion of students involved in career exploration, career counseling, or futures planning (Reynoso, Henry, Kwan, Sulewski, & Thomas, 2011). Limited opportunities for authentic work experience, career exploration, and futures planning can negatively affect posttransition employment success (Landmark et al., 2010; Reynoso et al., 2011).

Youth Development and Leadership   Research shows a correlation between transition outcomes and youth development characteristics, including self-advocacy and self-determination (Benz, Yovanoff, & Doren, 1997; Wehmeyer & Schwartz, 1997, as cited in Test et al., 2009). Student participation in IEP meetings has also been identified as a predictor of success (Wehmeyer et al., 2009; Wehmeyer, Palmer, Soukup, Garner, & Lawrence, 2007), and those involved in transition planning can benefit from opportunities for hands-on learning in ways that can improve employment outcomes (Cobb & Alwell, 2009; Flannery, Yovanoff, Benz, & McGrath-Kato, 2008).

Family Involvement   Research indicates the importance of family participation and expectations in the post–high school outcomes of students with disabilities. Students whose parents participated in more IEP meetings during 11th and 12th grades were more likely to have employment after exiting school (Fourqurean, Meisgeier, Swank, & Williams, 1991, as cited by Test et al., 2009). Other studies showed that parents are important influences in shaping the perceptions that youth themselves hold about their futures (Lindstrom, Doren, Metheny, Johnson, & Zane, 2007; Timmons, Hall, et al., 2011). Hall and Kramer (2009) found that the existence of social networks is positively related to increasing opportunities for employment for individuals with developmental disabilities. Higher parental expectations for their children's future work were associated with increased rates of employment after school for young adults with intellectual disabilities, autism, and multiple disabilities (Carter et al., 2012). Chiang, Cheung, Hickson, Xiang, and Tsai (2012) found a positive relationship between parental expectations and participation in postsecondary education for youth with autism.

Secondary data analysis of the NLTS-2 found lower parental expectations for students with intellectual disabilities and autism, despite the positive relationship between high parental expectations and outcomes (Timmons, Migliore, Lugas, & Butterworth, 2011). Hetherington et al. (2010) found that parents of youth with disabilities often lacked adequate knowledge to support their children in the transition process. Parental concerns about the potential loss of their young adult's SSI or Social Security Disability Insurance benefits as a result of competitive employment or concerns about the young adult's safety at work or while commuting often limit the acquisition of employment by young adults with intellectual disabilities (Luecking & Wittenburg, 2009; Winsor et al., 2010).

Connecting Activities   A strong relationship exists between comprehensive transition supports that include robust interagency collaboration and positive student outcomes in post–high school education and employment (Benz et al., 2000; Lindstrom et al., 2011; Repetto, Webb, Garvan, & Washington, 2002, as cited in Test et al., 2009). Interagency collaboration was also correlated with more positive post-school employment and postsecondary education outcomes (Repetto et al., 2002, as cited in Test et al., 2009). A study of Washington's Jobs by 21 Partnership Project showed that positive employment outcomes for youth with intellectual disabilities who were making the transition from school to work were supported by strengthened collaborative relationships among county developmental disabilities offices, school districts, state developmental disability and vocational rehabilitation agencies, employment providers, employers, participating young adults, and their families (Winsor, Butterworth, & Boone, 2011).

Additional Factors   Additional factors, including student, family, school, and community characteristics, may influence an outcome but are not under direct control from the education system. Research shows mixed findings about the relationships between moderating factors and transition outcomes. Several studies showed that gender, race, and other demographic variables are associated with transition outcomes (Carter et al., 2012; Flemming & Fairweather, 2012). Findings suggested that racially and ethnically diverse youth with disabilities experience lower employment rates compared with their White peers (Hasnain & Balcazar, 2009). Other studies, however, reported that gender and race/ethnicity are not always correlated with postsecondary education or employment (Newman et al., 2011; White & Weiner, 2004). Family wealth is also often found to be positively correlated with employment outcomes of young adults with disabilities (Chiang et al., 2012; Flemming & Fairweather, 2012; Newman et al., 2010).

Effect of Practice and Policy on Recommended Practices

Youth with intellectual, developmental, and other disabilities who remain in publicly supported education through the legally allowed age of 21 and exit school without a diploma face employment prospects that are among the lowest of any disability group receiving special education services (Wagner, Newman, Cameto, Garza, & Levine, 2005). These dim prospects exist despite multiple service systems charged with serving this group at various stages of their youth and young adult life. Public education, vocational rehabilitation, and the developmental disabilities service systems each have specific charges to provide services to these youth during their transition from school to work. These systems often operate in isolation from one another, however, or often participate in disjointed service and support (Certo et al., 2008). Consequently, there is a significantly low return on the public investment in the education of these youth, not to mention outcomes that counter the notion of presumed employability for all youth with disabilities that decades of legislation and advocacy have sought to promote (Wehman, 2006).

A growing body of literature fortunately has spotlighted research and practice that point to promising education and transition methodology that leads to desirable postschool outcomes for youth with disabilities. The NCWD/Y (2005) drew on a wide range of research and publications, as well as the expertise of well-informed leaders in the field, to identify optimal conditions and services that promote better school-to-work transition outcomes. Career preparatory/work experiences and youth empowerment were two key factors identified by NCWD/Y. The value of work experiences for youth during secondary education has long been identified, and continues to be identified, as clearly correlated with positive postschool outcomes (Carter, Austin, & Trainor, 2011a; Luecking & Fabian, 2000). Youth with disabilities who are empowered to make personal choices and assert individual preferences have been shown to exhibit better education and job performance (Wehmeyer & Palmer, 2003). A systematic review of the transition literature conducted by Test et al. (2009) analyzed selected correlational studies to determine to what degree distinct variables predicted improved postschool outcomes. Their review found that work experience and paid jobs as components of secondary education were among the strongest predictors of successful adult employment.

In addition, schools and their transition partners (e.g., vocational rehabilitation, developmental disabilities services) have respective and complementary charges to serve youth in transition, and there are indications that illustrate the value of their mutual collaboration toward the goal of adult employment for youth receiving special education. Specific models of transition service that include such collaboration have been reported to yield successful postschool outcomes for youth with disabilities who require ongoing support to find and maintain employment. The TSIM (Certo et al., 2008) features specific components of person-centered planning for the job search, paid employment in place in the final year in school, coordinated service integration prior to school exit by schools, vocational rehabilitation, developmental disabilities agencies, and community supported employment providers (Certo et al., 2008; Luecking & Certo, 2003). The intent of this model is to have employment and the support necessary to maintain this employment in place before exiting school so that youth have a seamless transition to their postschool adult lives. Certo et al. (2008) reported that model implementation in school districts in California and Maryland has resulted in employment rates as high as 65% at the point of transition for participating youth. These outcomes are significantly higher than those reported in the NLTS–2 (Wagner et al., 2005) for this group of special education service recipients.

Youth need early exposure to work in order to develop career and job preferences, build their repertoire of specific employment tasks and general work skills, and learn about optimal environments and supports that will contribute to well-matched, paid jobs as adults. Numerous factors mitigate against this circumstance, however. Gaps in and coordination of school-based services are reported by youth and families who often profess inadequate knowledge of services, especially educational services and accommodations that are also related to later workplace success (U.S. Government Accountability Office, 2006). The opportunities for work experiences and jobs are widely variable based on whether the student is on track to receive a diploma or other certificate of school completion, whether the school system embraces work-based experiences as essential adjuncts to the course of study, and whether there is strong collaboration with youth and adult employment entities that can assist in helping procure work experience, despite the strong research support for work-based educational services for youth making the transition from school to work (Luecking, 2009). These barriers must be mitigated in order to minimize the effect of disjointed service delivery as schools and postschool service providers prepare youth for employment and careers.

Challenges, Concerns, and Controversy

There is a long history of respectful debate and disagreement within TASH. Although it might seem that there would be relatively little controversy within a value-driven organization such as TASH regarding the strategies involving transition to employment, there has been tension between those who advocate for full inclusion, including access to the general curriculum, and those who advocate for students to have employment experiences while in high school. Students participating in employment experiences traditionally have left school during the regular school day to go to work experiences or jobs. The concern is that these students are pulled from opportunities for inclusion and access to the general curriculum. The obvious answer is that it must be possible to address both issues without having to shortchange either. There is a need to resolve any tension that may exist, however, considering both the dismal rates of inclusion in high schools and of employment for individuals with intellectual and developmental disabilities. Most researchers do not believe that inclusion alone is sufficient to ensure a working life for youth with disabilities (Ryndak, Ward, Alper, Montgomery, & Storch, 2010). There is ample evidence from traditional, self-contained special education services that teaching hard and soft component employment skills has not ensured access to employment. The key then is for educators to strive for the greatest degree of inclusion that is possible within their local schools and to provide an array of individually determined employment experiences that lead to a paid job in the community prior to graduation for all youth with intellectual and developmental disabilities.

We primarily want to address the issue of preparing for employment while students are in school, regardless of whether they are currently in inclusive settings and are gaining access to the general curriculum. The latest report by the Office of Special Education and Rehabilitation Services (2009) indicated that only 15.9% of all students with intellectual and developmental disabilities ages 6–21 are in general education classes 80% or more of their school day. The rate of inclusion of students ages 14–21, which are the transition years, is almost certainly lower, although reliable national data are not available. Educators need to consider that all students of transition age with intellectual and developmental disabilities need an array of work experiences, regardless of their current physical placements and academic focus.

Resolving the Dilemma of Full-Time School Inclusion versus Providing Access to Individual Community-Based Work Experiences During the School Day

We strongly believe that all students with intellectual and developmental disabilities should have full inclusion with their same-age peers and access to the general curriculum to the greatest degree possible while in the standard years of high school. We suggest that it is possible to accomplish full education inclusion and provide these students with school- and community-based employment experiences that will lead to securing a transition job prior to graduation. Compromises will be necessary, but only to a small degree. If preparation for employment as an educational goal is raised to a level of importance equal to meeting academic requirements for graduation and classroom inclusion, then the relatively small amount of time students may spend preparing for employment will be worth the loss of academic focus and classroom inclusion. If any student, regardless of disability, intends to work after graduation from high school, then it is critical that there be a shift from a fully academic focus to a balanced approach that involves both inclusive academics and employment preparation. Many students without disabilities engage in a similar balanced approach involving internships, service learning, volunteering, and other experiences aimed at ensuring preparation for employment.

A focus on employment planning needs to begin in school as early as possible, even into elementary school (Mississippi Youth Transition Innovation [MYTI], 2009), and individualized work experiences need to be offered throughout the high school years when so many typically developing students are working in part-time jobs and beginning to determine their interests regarding a working life. Yet, the burden shifts to the family for transportation and support when relying solely on after-school and weekend time frames for work experiences because most schools are strongly reluctant to provide staff after regular hours.

A balanced approach between gaining access to the general curriculum in inclusive school settings and time spent in individual work experiences emphasizes the fact that employment is an *expected outcome* of the educational process, whereas inclusion and access to the general curriculum are *valued characteristics* of the educational process. Establishing a clear educational goal of preparing for a working life demands that educators and families allow for the individual school time necessary for students to engage in work experiences while maximizing inclusion for time spent in classroom activities.

An inevitable loss of inclusion and access to the general curriculum occurs for students who are in self-contained classrooms or segregated educational settings. The debate over preserving classroom and curriculum inclusion or facilitating community-based work experience during school hours becomes moot because there is no argument that can be made against the value of community-based work experiences for students in these noninclusive educational situations.

Ensuring Students with Intellectual and Developmental Disabilities Are Not Devalued While Performing Work Experiences Another potential controversy involves the tasks to be performed by students with intellectual and developmental disabilities, particularly as a part of in-school work experiences. Some educators and advocates have voiced a concern that students with intellectual and developmental disabilities should not be assigned tasks that are different from those performed by students without disabilities, particularly janitorial and other service tasks that are basically custodial in nature. It is feared that students with intellectual and developmental disabilities will be perceived as only able to perform such tasks as opposed to more sophisticated ones and that they could be viewed as servants to students without disabilities (Tashie & Schuh, 1993). We suggest blending the best dimensions of each student's performance and interests with tasks typically performed by students without disabilities. The students' interests and skills should guide the selection of tasks to be performed in community workplaces, making sure that new experiences are gained, new skills are developed, and the opportunity for enhanced status is available.

Recommended Work Experiences in Making the Transition to Employment

The Social Security Administration funded a National Youth Transition Demonstration (YTD) in 2003 (MYTI, 2009). These seven sites combined to study factors that would serve to enhance making the transition from school to adult employment for individuals receiving SSI payments. The MYTI developed a sequence of experiences designed to offer students the necessary information for determining work interests, identifying conditions of success for each student, and developing skills to be offered to potential employers. Following are eight types of experiences that have been used in the MYTI project (Shumpert, Callahan, & Condon, 2009).

1. Volunteering or service learning

2. Job shadowing

3. General work experience

4. Matched work experience

5. Customized work experience

6. Part-time paid job

7. Customized job

8. Self-employment business ownership

Volunteering or service learning involves supporting students to participate in existing school and community service or volunteer efforts. Volunteering should start as young as 10 years old (or younger) and may continue throughout the school experience. Student outcomes for volunteering include participating in community and school activities, learning to perform a variety of tasks, completing work responsibilities, and developing new skills. Outcomes for school staff include having a different context in which to observe student performance and assess learning styles, work behaviors, motivators, and skills.

Job shadowing involves short-term observations of various types of job tasks and employment settings in the community. Job shadowing can start with students as young as 10 years old and continue throughout the school experience. The time spent on shadowing experiences may range from 1 to 2 hours per experience for younger students to as much as 2 days per experience for older adolescents. Students should not perform work tasks during shadowing. The intended outcome for youth and school staff is to gather additional information about the type of work that is performed in specific employment settings and provide students with a firsthand look at an employment location to determine if this is really what they want to pursue for employment.

General work experiences involve having students perform specific job duties in school and in workplaces in the community without pay. These experiences start at about age 14 and may continue until 16 or older. General work experiences give students a broad sense of the types of employment in their community. General experiences expose students to a variety of settings and tasks, enable them to gather information about their interests and preferred working conditions, and build a list of tasks that they have experience performing. School staff are able to observe students in a variety of settings and gather information about what features work and do not work for each student and then begin to foster some theories of the ideal working conditions for each student.

Matched work experiences refer to unpaid work experiences in community workplaces that are matched to the student's interests regarding employment as determined through the more general experiences. These matched experiences serve to clarify and affirm interests, test the theories about the work conditions necessary for success for that particular student, and provide an opportunity for specific skill and task development in their interest area.

Customized work experiences refer to unpaid work experiences in community workplaces that are matched in terms of the student's interests and for which either the conditions for success or the tasks offered to the employer are negotiated. These experiences are suitable for older students for whom additional information is needed prior to paid employment. For example, a customized experience is appropriate if one has developed a clear list of discreet tasks and skills a student has to offer an employer but is not yet clear on all of the conditions for success. The customized experience is also appropriate when one is clear on the conditions needed for success but wants to expand the list of the tasks the student can offer an employer. Due to the time involved in planning for and negotiating a customized experience, if there are no questions left to answer, then time might be better spent negotiating a paid job.

Part-time jobs involve assisting and encouraging students to obtain short-term, part-time employment paid by an employer. The jobs may be matched to student interests or used to assist in clarifying interests and general work behaviors. These jobs should ideally be after school or during the summer so they do not interfere with the student's opportunities to benefit from inclusion in his or her school. Part-time jobs are appropriate for students of employable age who have the skills to meet general expectations of employers without negotiation.

Customized employment refers to paid employment that is matched and negotiated to meet students' conditions for success, their interests, and their specific contributions as determined by discovery, prior work experiences, and a customized plan. Customized jobs may be short term and part time in nature for younger students of employable age. A transition job (i.e., a job that the students make the transition into as they leave school) should be developed prior to graduation using customized strategies. Customized jobs may be performed during school hours when students reach age 18.

Self-employment refers to a set of experiences and small business development activities that teachers can offer to students. The flow mirrors the experiences for wage employment, evolving from a more generic experience to a more individualized experience as the student's ideal conditions for employment become clearer and the student gets closer to high school graduation. Regardless, self-employment relates to a business owned by the student or small group of students, not by the school. Business types should reflect those typically engaged in by young people as well as the student's interests. For example, using self-employment for a general work experience might mean that a student develops a business of buying microwave popcorn by the case, redistributing it into individual size portions, and selling them to teachers and other students. This would be a short-term activity to provide students with the experience of self-employment to determine their interests and to expand the list of tasks they can perform. Using self-employment as a customized transition job might include having students purchase a small popcorn cart and develop a business that they run at school events with the future plan of running the business in the community.

FUTURE RESEARCH AND POLICY DEVELOPMENT

Although the research seems to clearly indicate that individualized work experiences positively correlate with employment for adults with intellectual and developmental disabilities, little is known about the strategic use of work experiences within inclusive school settings and with students who are gaining access to the general curriculum. We suggest that it is possible to have both inclusion and work experiences through a reasonable balance of the two issues as long as employment is viewed as a fundamental outcome of the educational process for students with intellectual and developmental disabilities.

It is inherent in the nature of schools to compare students through comparative assessments. Even alternate assessments are based on comparisons of students with disabilities in relation to the competitive aspect of successful performance (Rabinowitz, Sato, Case, Benitez, & Jordan, 2008). The discovery process is a qualitative strategy that focuses on strengths, interests, and conditions for successful performance and provides an alternative for educators of students making the transition to employment to use to guide work experiences and obtain jobs (Callahan et al., 2009). There has been a lack of research regarding the effectiveness of discovery within educational settings. There needs to be a study related to issues such as the willingness of school districts to embrace an expectation of employment as an outcome of education and the willingness of families to accept a balanced approach to inclusion as well as the presumption of the feasibility of employment for all students by educators and families.

We suggest that schools and educators need to adopt a policy of targeting employment as an expected outcome of the transition process for students to graduate from school with a paid job. This shift will require significant negotiation and explanation to accomplish. Implicit in this effort is the need to establish the expectancy and feasibility of employment for all students, including students with the most significant intellectual and developmental disabilities, by all parties, schools, vocational rehabilitation services, long-term supports, and families.

Many students with intellectual and developmental disabilities continue to be rejected by vocational rehabilitation services due to the presumption that they are not likely to benefit in terms of a rehabilitation outcome (National Council on Disability, 2008). Advocates, educators, and families need to push for policy changes that require vocational rehabilitation services to implement employment services for all students with intellectual and developmental disabilities who are making the transition from school to work prior to any closure based on a negative presumption of benefit.

CONCLUSION

The issue of making the transition from school to adult employment for students with intellectual and developmental disabilities is more important today than ever. After decades of effort to improve employment outcomes of transition services that primarily focused on preparation, it is time to narrow the intent of educational services during this time frame to include employment as an outcome. Research has shown that providing work experiences during transition correlates highly with adult employment. We suggest that transition services for students with intellectual and developmental disabilities include a balance of work experiences and inclusive educational opportunities. We also suggest that schools assist all students with intellectual and developmental disabilities to leave school with a paid job in the community. Teachers and educators should understand and embrace the newly conceived concept of customized employment, which allows increased access to employment for individuals with the most severe intellectual and developmental disabilities. Using customized employment and noncomparative approaches such as discovery provides a door to employment by avoiding the demands and comparisons implicit in competitive employment. We recommend the following for educational transition to employment for students with intellectual and developmental disabilities.

- Educators should send the message of the importance of a working lifestyle to students, families, and the community.

- Educators must embrace the feasibility of employment for all students and implement strategies that allow this to occur.

- Students should be provided with information and skills that address employment as early as possible in the educational experience.

- High school students should have access to all the experiences typically offered to students without disabilities to prepare for employment, such as service learning, volunteering, entrepreneurship, employment-focused clubs, and other extracurricular activities.

- High school students should have individualized work experiences during school time that reflect the student's interests and conditions for success and skills as an aspect of their IEPs and delivered in such a manner as to decrease the effect on school inclusion and access to the general curriculum.

- Educators should work with students and families to maximize as much time for work experiences as possible after school hours, in the summer, and during the 18- to 21-year-old time period.

- Curricular content should reflect and connect with the needs identified during individualized work experiences.

- Students should be assisted and supported to have a paid job in the community or a self-owned business prior to graduating from school.

Questions for Study and Reflection

1. What are the most critical features of successful transition to employment for students with intellectual and developmental disabilities?

2. What are the most relevant aspects of federal legislation regarding making the transition to employment for students with disabilities?

3. What factors contribute to the fact that students with intellectual and developmental disabilities are less likely to have competitive employment goals and outcomes as compared with other students with disabilities?

4. List and briefly discuss the factors that contribute to positive transition outcomes for students with disabilities.

5. How do the relationships among the major funders of services for individuals with intellectual and developmental disabilities—schools, vocational rehabilitation, and developmental disabilities service systems—tend to enhance or inhibit successful transition to employment?

6. What single factor has emerged from research to most closely correlate with successful transition from school to adult employment for students with disabilities?

7. What is a balanced approach to the tension experienced between the demand for the fullest inclusion/access to the general curriculum and the need for work experiences for students with intellectual and developmental disabilities?

8. List and briefly describe the array of work experiences that might be used to prepare students with intellectual and developmental disabilities for adult employment.

9. What additional research needs to be conducted to further enhance the successful transition from school to adult employment for students with intellectual and developmental disabilities?

RESOURCES

Center on Transition to Employment (*http://transitiontoemployment.org/*)—The center is designed to research and spotlight the strategies and circumstances that produce optimal employment and career achievement for youth with disabilities.

Condon, E., & Callahan, M. (2008). Individualized career planning for students with significant support needs utilizing the discovery and vocational profile process, cross-agency collaborative funding and Social Security work incentives. *Journal of Vocational Rehabilitation, 28,* 85–96.

Employment First Resource List *(http://www.selnmembers.org/components/ com_wordpress/wp-content/uploads/2012/08/emp_first_resources_2012. pdf)*—A continuously updated listing of state policies, legislation, and reports that support employment first organized by state.

Freeman, L., Jordan, M., & Van Gelder, M. (2010). *School days to pay days: An employment planning guide for families of young adults with intellectual disabilities.* Boston: Massachusetts Department of Developmental Services. Retrieved from http://www.communityinclusion.org/schooldays/

Integrated Employment Toolkit (*http://www.dol.gov/odep/ietoolkit/*)—Offers a collection of resources, reports, papers, policies, fact sheets, case studies, and discussion guides from a variety of sources to accommodate the full range of users and increase capacity and understanding about the value and potential of integrated employment.

Marc Gold & Associates (*http://marcgold.com*)—Transition resources include *Discovery: Charting the Course to Employment; Profiles: Capturing the Information of Discovery; A Journey to Discovery—Career Journey; Family Transition Guide; Finding a Career Direction: A Guide to Job Shadowing and Work Experiences;* and *Self-Employment Guide.* Additional materials include TIP Cards—Transition in Progress Cards and World of Employment Transition School to Work Poster.

Real People, Real Jobs (*http://www.realworkstories.org*)—Highlights the employment successes of people with intellectual and developmental disabilities who are working in paid jobs in their communities.

Rural Institute Transition Projects (*http://ruralinstitute.umt.edu/transition*)— Transition materials from the Rural Institute, University of Montana, include *Choosing Self-Employment* (Cordon & Brown, 2007) and *Work Experiences and Paid Employment: Proposing an Organized Progression of Distinct Experiences that lead to Employment for Youth with Disabilities* (Shumpert, Callahan, & Condon, 2009).

StateData.info (*http://www.StateData.info*)—On-demand data on employment outcomes and services. Includes data from state intellectual/developmental disability agencies, the Rehabilitation Services Administration, the Social Security Administration, the U.S. Department of Labor, state demographic data, and the American Community Survey.

Washington Initiative for Supported Employment (*http://www.gowise.org/*)— Transition information from Washington State.

REFERENCES

Benz, M.R., Lindstrom, L., & Yovanoff, P. (2000). Improving graduation and employment outcomes of students with disabilities: Predictive factors and student perspectives. *Exceptional Children, 66,* 509–541.

Benz, M.R., Yovanoff, P., & Doren, B. (1997). School-to-work components that predict post-school success for students with and without disabilities. *Exceptional Children, 63,* 151–165.

Butterworth, J., Hall, A., Smith, F., Migliore, A., Winsor, J., Timmons, J., & Domin, D. (2011). *StateData: The National Report on Employment Services and Outcomes (2010 data).* Boston: University of Massachusetts, Institute for Community Inclusion.

Callahan, M., Shumpert, N., & Condon, E. (2009). *Discovery: Charting the course to employment* [Monograph]. Gautier, MS: Marc Gold and Associates.

Cameto, R., Levine, P., & Wagner, M. (2004). *Transition planning for students with disabilities: A special topic report of findings from the National Longitudinal Transition Study–2.* Menlo Park, CA: SRI International.

Carter, E., Austin, D., & Trainor, A. (2011a). Factors associated with the early work experiences of adolescents with severe disabilities. *Intellectual and Developmental Disabilities, 49,* 233–247.

Carter, E.W., Austin, D, & Trainor, A.A. (2011b). Predictors of postschool employment outcomes for young adults with severe disabilities. *Journal of Disability Policy Studies, 20,* 1–14.

Carter, E.W., Austin, D., & Trainor, A.A. (2012). Predictors of postschool employment outcomes for young adults with severe disabilities. *Journal of Disability Policy Studies, 23,* 50–63.

Carter, E., Ditchman, N., Sun, Y., Trainor, A., Sweeden, B., & Owens, L. (2010). Summer employment and community experiences of transition-age youth with severe disabilities. *Exceptional Children, 76,* 194–212.

Certo, N.J., Luecking, R.G., Murphy, S., Brown, L., Courey, S., & Belanger, D. (2008). Seamless transition and long-term support for individuals with severe intellectual disabilities. *Research and Practice for Persons with Severe Disabilities, 33,* 85–95.

Certo, N.J., Mautz, D., Pumpian, I., Sax, C., Smalley, T., Wade, H., & Batterman, N. (2003). A review and discussion of a model for seamless transition to adulthood. *Education and Training in Developmental Disabilities, 38,* 3–17.

Chiang, H., Cheung, Y., Hickson, L., Xiang, R., & Tsai, L.Y. (2012). Predictive factors of participation in postsecondary education for high school leavers with autism. *Journal of Autism and Developmental Disorders, 42,* 685–696.

Cobb, R.B., & Alwell, M. (2009). Transition planning/coordinating interventions for youth with disabilities: A systematic review. *Career Development for Exceptional Individuals, 32,* 70–81.

Doren, B., & Benz, M.R. (1998). Employment inequality revisited: Predictors of better employment outcomes for young women with disabilities in transition. *Journal of Special Education, 31,* 425–442.

Fabian, E. (2007). Urban youth with disabilities: Factors affecting transition employment. *Rehabilitation Counseling Bulletin, 50,* 130–138.

Flannery, K.B., Yovanoff, P., Benz, M., & McGrath-Kato, M. (2008). Improving employment outcomes of individuals with disabilities through short term training. *Career Development for Exceptional Individuals, 31,* 26–36.

Flemming, A.R., & Fairweather, J.S. (2012). The role of postsecondary education in the path from high school to work for youth with disabilities. *Rehabilitation Counseling Bulletin, 55,* 71–81.

Fourqurean, J.M., Meisgeier, C., Swank, P.R., & Williams, R.E. (1991). Correlates of postsecondary employment outcomes for young adults with learning disabilities. *Journal of Learning Disabilities, 24,* 400–405.

Grigal, M., Hart, D., & Migliore, A. (2011). Comparing the transition planning, postsecondary education, and employment outcomes of students with intellectual and other disabilities. *Career Development for Exceptional Individuals, 34,* 4–17.

Grigal, M., Neubert, D.A., Moon, M.S., & Graham, S. (2003). Parents' and teachers' views of self-determination for secondary students with disabilities. *Exceptional Children, 70,* 97–112.

Hall, A.C., Butterworth, J., Winsor, J., Gilmore, D.S., & Metzel, D. (2007). Pushing the employment agenda: Case study research of high performing states in integrated employment. *Intellectual and Developmental Disabilities, 45,* 182–198.

Hall, A.C., & Kramer, J. (2009). Social capital through workplace connections: Opportunities for workers with intellectual disabilities. *Journal of Social Work in Disability and Rehabilitation, 8,* 146–170.

Hart, D., Zimbrich, K., & Whelley, T. (2002). *Challenges in coordinating and managing services and supports in secondary and postsecondary options.* Minneapolis: University of Minnesota, Institute on Community Integration, National Center on Secondary Education and Transition.

Hasnain, R., & Balcazar, F. (2009). Predicting community- versus facility-based employment for transition-aged young adults with disabilities: The role of race, ethnicity, and support systems. *Journal of Vocational Rehabilitation, 31,* 175–188.

Hetherington, S.A., Durant-Jones, L., Johnson, K., Nolan, K., Smith, E., Taylor-Brown, S., & Tuttle, J. (2010). The lived experiences of adolescents with disabilities and their parents in transition planning. *Focus on Autism and Other Developmental Disabilities, 25,* 163–172.

Human Services Research Institute & Institute for Community Inclusion. (2011). *Participation in integrated employment: National Core Indicators Project, 2009–2010.* Unpublished data.

Individuals with Disabilities Education Improvement Act (IDEA) of 2004, PL 108-446, 20 U.S.C. §§ 1400 *et seq.*

Joshi, G.S., Bouck, E.C., & Maeda, Y. (2012). Exploring employment preparation and post-school outcomes for students with mild intellectual disabilities. *Career Development for Exceptional Individuals.* Manuscript submitted for publication.

Landmark, L.J., Ju, S., & Zhang, D. (2010). Substantiated best practices in transition: Fifteen plus years later. *Career Development for Exceptional Individuals, 33,* 165–176.

Lindstrom, L., Doren, B., Metheny, J., Johnson, P., & Zane, C. (2007). Transition to employment: Role of the family in career development. *Exceptional Children, 73,* 348–366.

Lindstrom, L., Doren, B., & Miesch, J. (2011). Waging a living: Career development and long-term employment outcomes for young adults with disabilities. *Exceptional Children, 77,* 423–434.

Luecking, R. (2009). *The way to work: How to facilitate work experiences for youth in transition.* Baltimore, MD: Paul H. Brookes Publishing Co.

Luecking, R.G., & Certo, N.J. (2002). Integrating service systems at the point of transition for youth with significant disabilities: A model that works. *National Center on Secondary Education and Transition, 1.*

Luecking, R., & Certo, N.J. (2003). Service integration at the point of transition for youth with significant disabilities: A model that works. *American Rehabilitation, 27,* 2–9.

Luecking, R., & Fabian, E. (2000). Paid internships and employment success for youth in transition. *Career Development for Exceptional Individuals, 23,* 205–221.

Luecking, R.G., & Wittenburg, M. (2009). Providing supports to youth with disabilities transitioning to adulthood: Case descriptions from the Youth Transition Demonstration. *Journal of Vocational Rehabilitation, 30,* 241–251.

Mank, D., Cioffi, A., & Yovanoff, P. (2003). Supported employment outcomes across a decade: Is there evidence of improvement in the quality of implementation? *Mental Retardation, 41,* 188–197.

Martinez, J., Fraker, T., Manno, M., Baird, P., Mamun, A., O'Day, B., ... Wittenburg, D. (2010). *The Social Security Administration's Youth Transition Demonstration Projects: Implementation lessons from the original projects.* Washington, DC: Mathematical Policy Research.

Migliore, A., Mank, D., Grossi, T., & Rogan, P. (2007). Integrated employment or sheltered workshops: Preferences of adults with intellectual disabilities, their families, and staff. *Journal of Vocational Rehabilitation, 26,* 5–19.

Migliore, A., & Zalewska, A. (2012). *What are the employment experiences of youth with autism after high school? DataNote Series, DataNote 40.* Boston: University of Massachusetts Boston, Institute for Community Inclusion.

Mississippi Youth Transition Innovation. (2009). *Project description.* Retrieved from http://myti.org

National Alliance for Secondary Education and Transition. (2005). *National standards and quality indicators: Transition toolkit for systems improvement.* Minneapolis: University of Minnesota, Institute on Community Integration.

National Collaborative on Workforce and Disability for Youth. (2005). *Guideposts for success.* Washington, DC: Institute on Educational Leadership.

National Council on Disability. (2008). *The Rehabilitation Act: Outcomes for transition age youth.* Washington, DC: Author.

National Disability Rights Network. (2011). *Segregated and exploited: A call to action.* Washington, DC: Author.

National Longitudinal Transition Study–2. (n.d.). *Data tables.* Retrieved from http://www.nlts2.org/data_tables/index.html

Newman, L. (2005). *Family involvement in the educational development of youth with disabilities: A special topic report of findings from the National Longitudinal Transition Study–2.* Menlo Park, CA: SRI International.

Newman, L., Wagner, M., Cameto, R., & Knokey, A.M. (2009). *The post-high school outcomes of youth with disabilities up to 4 years after high school: A report of findings from the National Longitudinal Transition Study–2* (NCSER 2009-3017). Menlo Park, CA: SRI International.

Newman, L., Wagner, M., Cameto, R., Knokey, A.M., & Shaver, D. (2010). *Comparisons across time of the outcomes of youth with disabilities up to 4 years after high school: A report of findings from the National Longitudinal Transition Study–2.* Menlo Park, CA: SRI International.

Newman, L., Wagner, M., Knokey, A., Marder, C., Nagle, K., Shaver, D., & Wei, X. (2011). *The post-high school outcomes of young adults with disabilities up to 8 years after high school: A report from the National Longitudinal Transition Study–2.* Menlo Park, CA: SRI International.

Office of Special Education & Rehabilitation Services. (2009). *The FY2009 summary of performance and financial information.* Washington, DC: Author.

Rabinowitz, S., Sato, E., Case, B.J., Benitez, D., & Jordan, K. (2008). *Alternate assessments for special education students in the southwest region states.* Washington, DC: Institute for Educational Sciences.

Rabren, K., Dunn, C., & Chambers, D. (2002). Predictors of post–high school employment among young adults with disabilities. *Career Development for Exceptional Individuals, 25,* 25–40.

Rehabilitation Act of 1973, PL 93-112, 29 U.S.C. §§ 701 *et seq.*

Repetto, J.B., Webb, K.W., Garvan, C.W., & Washington, T. (2002). Connecting student outcomes with transition practices in Florida. *Career Development for Exceptional Individuals, 25,* 123–139.

Reynoso, M., Henry, K., Kwan, N., Sulewski, J., & Thomas, C. (2011). *Summary report: Massachusetts transitions practices survey.* Unpublished manuscript, Institute for Community Inclusion, University of Massachusetts, Boston.

Roberts, K.D. (2010). Topic areas to consider when planning transition from high school to postsecondary education for students with autism spectrum disorders. *Focus on Autism and Other Developmental Disabilities, 20,* 158–247.

Rusch, F.R., & Braddock, D. (2004). Adult day programs versus supported employment (1988–2002): Spending and service practices of mental retardation and developmental disabilities state agencies. *Research and Practice for Persons with Severe Disabilities, 29,* 237–242.

Ryndak, D.L., Ward, T., Alper, S., Montgomery, J.W., & Storch, J.F. (2010). Long-term outcomes of services of two persons with significant disabilities served in differing educational experiences: A qualititative consideration of the impact of educational experiences. *Education and Training in Autism and Developmental Disabilities, 45,* 323–338.

Self Advocates Becoming Empowered. (2009). *SABE policy statement on employment: SABE calls for ending sub-minimum wage in 2012.* Retrieved from http://sabeusa.org/?catid=179

Shumpert, N., Callahan, M., & Condon, E. (2009). Work experiences and paid employment: Proposing an organized progression of distinct experiences that lead to employment for youth with disabilities. *University of Montana Rural Institute Transition Projects E-News, 6,* 1–5.

Snyder, T.D., & Dillow, S.A. (2011). *Digest of education statistics 2010.* Washington, DC: U.S. Department of Education.

Sulewski, J.S., Zalewska, A., & Butterworth, J. (2012). *Indicators for improving educational, employment, and economic outcomes for youth and young adults with intellectual and developmental disabilities: A national report on existing data sources.* Boston: University of Massachusetts Boston, Institute for Community Inclusion.

TASH. (2009). *TASH resolution on integrated employment.* Retrieved from http://tash.org/advocacy-issues/employment

Tashie, C., & Schuh, M. (1993, Spring). Why not community-based instruction?: High school students with disabilities belong with their peers. *Equity and Excellence Newsletter,* 15–21.

Test, D.W., Mazzotti, V.L., Mustian, A.L., Fowler, C.H., Kortering, L., & Kohler, P. (2009). Evidence-based secondary transition predictors for improving post-school outcomes for students with disabilities. *Career Development for Exceptional Individuals, 32,* 160–181.

Timmons, J.C., Hall, A.C., Bose, J., Wolfe, A., & Winsor, J. (2011) Choosing employment: Factors that impact employment decisions for individuals with intellectual disability. *Intellectual and Developmental Disabilities, 49,* 285–299.

Timmons, J.C., Migliore, A., Lugas, J., & Butterworth, J. (2011). *Transition experiences of youth with ASD as compared to their peers: How do they relate to an employment outcome?* Manuscript submitted for publication.

U.S. Government Accountability Office. (2006). *Summary of a GAO Conference: Helping California youths with disabilities transition to work or postsecondary education.* Washington, DC: Author.

Wagner, M., Newman, L., Cameto, R., Garza, N., & Levine, P. (2005). *After high school: A first look at the post-school experiences of youth with disabilities. A report from the National Longitudinal Transition Study–2.* Menlo Park, CA: SRI International.

Wehman, P. (2006). Integrated employment: If not now, when? If not us, who? *Research and Practice for Persons with Severe Disabilities, 31,* 122–126.

Wehman, P. (2013). *Life beyond the classroom: Transition strategies for young people with disabilities* (5th ed.). Baltimore, MD: Paul Brookes Publishing Co.

Wehmeyer, M.L., & Palmer, S.B. (2003). Adult outcomes for students with cognitive disabilities three years after high school: The impact of self-determination. *Education and Training in Developmental Disabilities, 38,* 131–144.

Wehmeyer, M.L., Palmer, S., Soukup, J.H., Garner, N., & Lawrence, M. (2007). Self-determination and student transition-planning knowledge and skills: Predicting involvement. *Exceptionality, 15,* 31–44.

Wehmeyer, M.L., Parent, W., Lattimore, J., Obremski, S., Poston, D., & Rousso, H. (2009). Promoting self-determination and self-directed employment planning for people with disabilities. *Journal of Social Work in Disability and Rehabilitation, 8,* 117–131.

Wehmeyer, M.L., & Schwartz, M. (1997). Self-determination and positive adult outcomes: A follow-up study of youth with mental retardation or learning disabilities. *Exceptional Children, 63,* 245–255.

Whelley, T., Hart, D., & Zaft, C. (2004). *Coordination and management of services and supports for individuals with disabilities from secondary to postsecondary education and employment.* Manoa: University of Hawaii.

White, J., & Weiner, J.S. (2004). Influence of least restrictive environment and community based training on integrated employment outcomes for transitioning students with severe disabilities. *Journal of Vocational Rehabilitation, 21,* 149–156.

Winsor, J., Butterworth, J., & Boone, J. (2011). Jobs by 21 Partnership Project:

Impact of cross-system collaboration on employment outcomes of young adults with developmental disabilities. *Intellectual and Developmental Disabilities, 49,* 274–284.

Winsor, J., Butterworth, J., Lugas, J., & Hall, A. (2010). *Washington State Division of Developmental Disabilities Jobs by 21 Partnership Project Report for FY2009.* Boston, MA: Institute for Community Inclusion.

Workforce Investment Act (WIA) of 1998, PL 105-220, 29 U.S.C. §§ 2801 *et seq.*

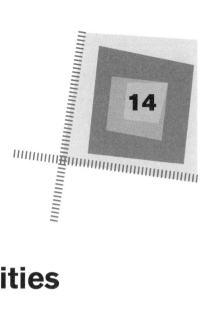

14

Postsecondary Education for Students with Intellectual Disabilities

Meg Grigal, Debra Hart, and Cate Weir

ostsecondary education has historically been unattainable for people with intellectual disability. The rigorous academic environment of colleges and universities seemed to put continuing education after high school out of reach for those with intellectual disability. Due to a number of factors, such as the inclusive education movement, there is clear growing interest in and opportunities for students with intellectual disability to participate in higher education. This change is evidenced by the significant growth in the number and types of postsecondary education options for students with intellectual disability. Although there were a handful of postsecondary education programs for students with intellectual disability in the 1990s, today there are well more than 200. The number of students with disabilities, including intellectual disability, who continue their education after high school is also increasing. A survey (2008–2009) of Title IV 2- and 4-year institutes of higher education found that 88% enrolled students with disabilities (Raue & Lewis, 2011). The same survey found that 41% of the institutes of higher education reported the enrollment of students with cognitive difficulties or intellectual disability.

This chapter provides an overview of current policy and legislation related to the development of postsecondary education options and describes current practices as well as the challenges that exist and the effect that postsecondary education for students with intellectual disability can have on related areas such as K–12 education and employment services. Future directions for policy development and research also are discussed. Finally, resources on postsecondary education for students with intellectual disability are shared.

RELEVANT LEGISLATION, MANDATES, AND POLICY

Various legislation as well as federal and state policies have affected the current status of postsecondary education for students with intellectual disability. The Higher Education Opportunity Act (HEOA) of 2008 (PL 110- 315), which is a reauthorization of the Higher Education Act of 1965 (PL 89-329), likely has had the most effect on the growth of opportunities for students with intellectual disability. The HEOA contains a number of new provisions that affect access to postsecondary education for students with intellectual disability (see Figure 14.1).

The HEOA defined for the first time the components that should be present in postsecondary education programs serving students with intellectual disability. The HEOA clearly indicated that a prevailing tenet of the programs was inclusive academic access and that these educational options should result in gainful employment. Funds were appropriated under the HEOA legislation to support program development and expansion in the form of model demonstration projects. The Office of Postsecondary Education awarded grants in 2010 to 27 institutes of higher education to fund model demonstration projects, referred to as Transition and Postsecondary Education Programs for Students with Intellectual Disabilities (TPSID), and to create a National Coordinating Center (see Figure 14.2). The intent of these funds was to promote the successful transition of students with intellectual disability into higher education and to enable institutes of higher education to create or expand high-quality inclusive model comprehensive transition and postsecondary programs for students with intellectual disabilities. Approximately 6,000 students with intel-

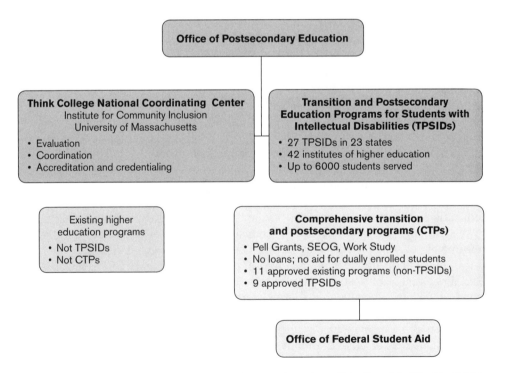

Figure 14.1. The Higher Education Opportunity Act and programs for students with intellectual disability. (*Key:* SEOG, Supplemental Educational Opportunity Grants.) (From Grigal, M., Hart, D., & Lee, S.S. [2012, May]. *A national snapshot of the postsecondary education landscape for students with intellectual disabilities.* Presented at the National Transition Conference, Washington, DC.)

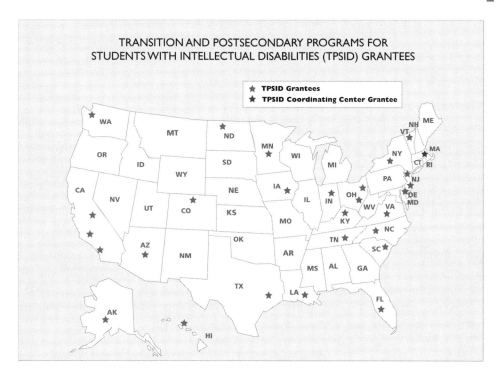

Figure 14.2. Transition and postsecondary programs for students with intellectual disabilities. (*Note:* One darker star representing the TPSID National Coordinating Center is in Massachusetts.) (From Grigal, M., Hart, D., Smith, F.A., Domin, D., & Sulewski, J. [2013]. *Think College National Coordinating Center: Annual report on the transition and postsecondary programs for students with intellectual disabilities.* Boston: University of Massachusetts Boston, Institute for Community Inclusion.)

lectual disability will be served on 42 college campuses in 23 states over the 5-year funding period. The National Coordinating Center is charged with developing model accreditation standards and credentialing options, providing technical assistance and training, and conducting an ongoing evaluation of all of the projects.

Comprehensive Transition Programs

The HEOA also created a new type of postsecondary education program that allows eligible students with intellectual disability to gain access to certain forms of federal student aid. Comprehensive transition and postsecondary programs (CTPs) support students with intellectual disability who are seeking to continue academic, career and technical, and independent living instruction at an institution of higher education in order to prepare for gainful employment and require at least half of the program consist of coursework and other activities with students without disabilities (§§ 1091, 1140).

The HEOA also waived some previous requirements to qualify for federal student aid for students with intellectual disability attending CTPs, including the need to have a high school diploma or general equivalency diploma and the intent to matriculate and earn a standard degree or certificate. Students with intellectual disability who document financial need and are out of high school are eligible to receive Federal Pell Grants, Federal Supplemental Educational Opportunity Grants, and Federal Work-Study funds but are not eligible to receive student loans. Federal Student Aid had approved 15 institutions of higher education as CTPs as of December

2012 (see http://studentaid.ed.gov/eligibility/intellectual-disabilities for a listing of approved CTPs). The HEOA raised the bar by providing guidelines about program requirements for students with intellectual disability, and it also raised questions about the practices that were established before this guidance was available.

The Americans with Disabilities Act Amendments and Section 504 of the Rehabilitation Act

Section 504 of the Rehabilitation Act of 1973 (PL 93-112) and the Americans with Disabilities Act (ADA) of 1990 (PL 101-336) prohibit discrimination on the basis of disability and require institutes of higher education to provide appropriate academic adjustments as necessary to ensure nondiscrimination on the basis of disability. Section 504 has required equal access since 1976 at all entities receiving federal funding, and the ADA expanded those requirements when it was passed in 1990 and reauthorized in 2008 (PL 110-325). These laws ensure equal access for students with disabilities, including those with intellectual disability. Since the passage of the ADA, most colleges in the United States have created a Disability Services Office to respond to requests for reasonable accommodations and have designated an ADA compliance officer to ensure equity of access to all campus facilities. The disability services that are available to students with other disabilities are also available to students with intellectual disability, although sometimes these reasonable accommodations may not prove sufficient for students with intellectual disability.

When Accommodations Are Necessary but Not Sufficient   Although students with intellectual disability may use academic accommodations in college, these accommodations may not be sufficient to allow the students to succeed in their desired course of study. Institutes of higher education are not required to lower or modify essential course requirements or make alterations that would fundamentally alter the nature of a service, program, or activity or would result in undue financial or administrative burdens. In addition, institutes of higher education do not have to provide personal attendants, individually prescribed devices, readers for personal use or study, or other devices or services of a personal nature. Institutes of higher education have implemented additional support structures to address the individualized support needs of some students with intellectual disability, including peer mentors and education coaches to provide additional scaffolding (Griffin, Summer, McMillan, Day, & Hodapp, 2012; Paiewonsky et al., 2010).

The Individuals with Disabilities Education Improvement Act

The Individuals with Disabilities Education Improvement Act (IDEA) of 2004 (PL 108-446) ensures that all children with disabilities have a free appropriate public education that emphasizes special education and related services designed to meet their unique needs and prepare them for further education, employment, and independent living. Congress stated, "As the graduation rates for children with disabilities continue to climb, providing effective transition services to promote successful post-school employment or education is an important measure of accountability for children with disabilities" (§ 2651 [14]).

Significant growth has occurred in providing college-based transition services to students with intellectual disability between the ages of 18 and 21. These transition programs are governed by IDEA 2004, and future authorizations of this law should directly address these types of programs and services and offer guidance regarding the desired program components and student outcomes. In addition, this guidance should be aligned with HEOA requirements. Also, there is no specific regulatory language in IDEA 2004 that supports using funds to support students with intellectual disability in going to college-based transition programs. School systems often struggle with translating meaningful, socially integrated transition experiences on a college campus for young adults with intellectual disability into the standard individualized education program (IEP) framework used to guide the delivery of secondary special education services in high school settings (Grigal, Hart, & Lewis, 2012).

National and State Vocational Rehabilitation Policies and Practices

The Rehabilitation Services Administration provides funds to state vocational rehabilitation agencies to provide employment-related services for individuals with disabilities, giving priority to individuals who have significant disabilities. Transition services are an allowable activity and are often provided through cooperative agreements between state systems (e.g., vocational rehabilitation agencies), local schools, and colleges. Although vocational rehabilitation provides resources and supports for students to attend college as a means of securing employment, vocational rehabilitation historically has not supported large-scale access to college for individuals with intellectual disability because these individuals were generally viewed as unable to benefit from a college education (Hart, Grigal, & Weir, 2010). A study by Grigal, Migliore, and Hart (in press), however, showed that state vocational rehabilitation agencies are playing a role in assisting youth with disabilities, and to a lesser extent youth with intellectual disability, to participate in postsecondary education. State vocational rehabilitation programs reported that up to 20% of youth with intellectual disability were in postsecondary education while receiving vocational rehabilitation services compared with 60% of youth with other disabilities.

Growing vocational rehabilitation support of postsecondary education for students with intellectual disability is also reflected in the initiatives in a number of states, including South Carolina, Kentucky, California, Ohio, and Hawaii, where pilot programs and articulation agreements related to providing vocational rehabilitation services to support access to higher education for students with intellectual disability have been initiated (Bailey, 2012; Thacker & Sheppard-Jones, 2011). The Florida state vocational rehabilitation program sought and received guidance from the Rehabilitation Services Administration indicating the appropriate use of vocational rehabilitation funds to support students with intellectual disability in college-based dual enrollment programs in that state (L. M. Ruttledge, personal communication, March 21, 2011). Such agreements and policies may affect practices in other states as well.

Current Status of Postsecondary
Education for Students with Intellectual Disability

National surveys illustrated significant variations in college experiences for students with intellectual disability (Grigal, Hart, & Weir, 2012a; Papay & Bambara, 2011). Postsecondary education options vary in their structure, academic and program focal areas, funding structures, age range and academic skills of students, length of program, type of available services and supports, access to residential options, level of inclusivity and campus membership, entrance criteria, and outcomes (Grigal & Hart, 2012).

Findings from one national survey of institutes of higher education that provided access to students with intellectual disability depicted the array of postsecondary education services and the spectrum of their differences (Grigal et al., 2012a). In this survey, 149 respondents from 37 states shared information about their program characteristics, referral and application process, college course access and supports, employment supports, and student outcomes.

Types of Colleges and Students Served   Four-year colleges or universities accounted for half of the responding programs, followed by 2-year colleges (40%; Grigal et al., 2012a). Trade or technical schools accounted for the smallest percent of respondents (10%, $n = 135$). Forty-five percent of respondents indicated that they served only adults with intellectual disability, 26% served dually enrolled students ages 18–22 years who were still being served by their school district, and 29% served both groups.

Focus of Programs and Level of Integration   When asked about the primary focus of their program, respondents surprisingly selected the category of independent living/life skills most frequently (34%). Employment was the next most frequent response (32%), whereas only 18% of the institutions of higher education reported that academic course access was the program's primary goal. Three quarters of the respondents indicated that they offered some level of segregated instruction or social events specifically designed for students with intellectual disability and that students may participate in group instruction or activities only with other students with intellectual disability.

Access to College Courses   Access to college courses, including credit and noncredit college classes, was offered by a slight majority of responding institutions of higher education. Some postsecondary education initiatives support students to enroll in typical college courses that relate to a career goal and other areas of personal interest as well as to participate in all aspects of campus life, whereas others offer only specially designed classes for students with intellectual disability and often focus on teaching life or independent living skills. Many postsecondary education programs support students with intellectual disability to take some college courses but also offer specially designed classes only for students with intellectual disability.

Campus Membership and Support   Postsecondary education programs also vary on the degree to which they foster campus membership. This is demonstrated in the range of supports they offer and policies they have established so that students can participate in all aspects of campus life (e.g., convocation, student government, clubs, student union, gaming, athletic center, cafeteria, library). Postsecondary education programs frequently provide support to students with intellectual disability (e.g., educational coaches, mentors, tutors) in addition to those typically available on a college campus.

Funding   Funding for the programs surveyed was provided via a wide variety of sources, including school district (IDEA 2004) funding (for dually enrolled students), family and student funds, developmental disability funding, scholarships, federal financial aid, Medicaid waiver or day habilitation dollars, National Service Segal Education Award, Social Security Administration Plans for Achieving Self Support (PASS) and Impairment Related Work Expense (IRWE) Plans, and public and private grant funding. Most respondents reported using a combination of funding strategies.

Completion and Credentials   Most students with intellectual disability who attend postsecondary education programs are not degree seeking, matriculating students and often enroll in courses using an audit or special student status. Institutes of higher education may offer the student a credential or certificate when leaving the program, but host institutions seldom formally recognize these credentials.

CHALLENGES, CONCERNS, AND CONTROVERSY REGARDING POSTSECONDARY EDUCATION FOR INDIVIDUALS WITH INTELLECTUAL DISABILITY

The emerging availability of higher education opportunities for people with intellectual disabilities has raised the bar for disability research, policy, and practice. It also places a spotlight on the current inconsistencies in program availability, professional know-how, and expectations about who is and is not considered "college material" in the world of special education.

Lack of Postsecondary Education Options

The need for college initiatives still far exceeds the availability of programs, even though interest and funding have emerged and created numerous new postsecondary education options for people with intellectual disability. Think College at the Institute for Community Inclusion at the University of Massachusetts updated its online college search database of postsecondary education programs that serve students with intellectual disability in 2012. This database lists 209 programs in the United States and Canada and provides an overview of each program, its primary focus, and details about its host college, including type of college or university, length of program, and costs. Forty-three states report having one or more programs. Only a handful of states (California, Maryland, New York, Massachusetts, and Illinois) have 10 or more programs (see Figure 14.3). More than half of the states that listed programs had one or two (see Figure 14.4). Seven states (Idaho, Mississippi, Montana, Nevada, Oklahoma, West Virginia, and Wyoming) as well as the District of Columbia have no programs listed. Although the Think College database represents the best available knowledge about postsecondary education options for people with intellectual disability, it also reflects that many programs are not available for youth with intellectual disability as compared with postsecondary education programs available to students without and with other disabilities.

Lack of Professional, Student, and Family Knowledge

Given the paucity of postsecondary options, it is not surprising that there is a parallel lack of professional, student, and family knowledge about the option of postsecondary education for youth with intellectual disability and other severe disabilities. Parents often determine what is possible for their children based on guidance from the

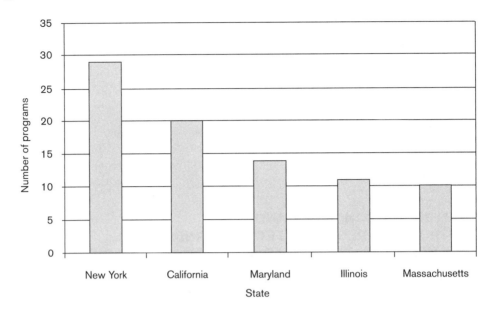

Figure 14.3. States with 10 or more programs in the Think College database. (*Source*: Think College, n.d.)

professionals in their lives (Grigal & Hart, 2012), and, therefore, the range of possibilities for their child's future, including college, can rely heavily on how informed the transition and educational personnel serving those families are about current options and practices. High school transition personnel, who are often the gate keepers to what is available to facilitate transition to postsecondary education and employment, are often unaware of these new and innovative postsecondary education options for students with intellectual disability (Griffin, McMillan, & Hodapp, 2010).

This lack of knowledge of what currently is available, coupled with a relative lack of postsecondary education options, leads students with intellectual disability to remain as one of the least likely groups of youth to have college listed as a goal on their IEP (Grigal, Hart, & Migliore, 2011) or to be enrolled in postsecondary education 4 years after high school (Newman, Wagner, Cameto, Knokey, & Shaver, 2010). Data from the National Longitudinal Transition Study–2 (NLTS–2; 2009) indicated that only 2.3% of youth with intellectual disability were enrolled in any kind of postsecondary education institution in 2009. Too often, college is still not a viable option for the majority of students with intellectual disability due in part to the adults in their lives lacking knowledge of postsecondary education options (Martinez, Conroy, & Cerreto, 2012).

Low Expectations

College expectations permeate the academic and social experiences of college-bound youth throughout their secondary education experiences (Grigal & Hart, 2012). Students who are of transition age base their desired future plans to a large extent on what they have been told is and is not possible by their family and teachers. The power of parent expectations was documented by Doren, Gau, and Lindstrom (2012), who conducted a secondary analysis of the NLTS–2 dataset and determined that parents' expectations about their child graduating with a diploma, getting a

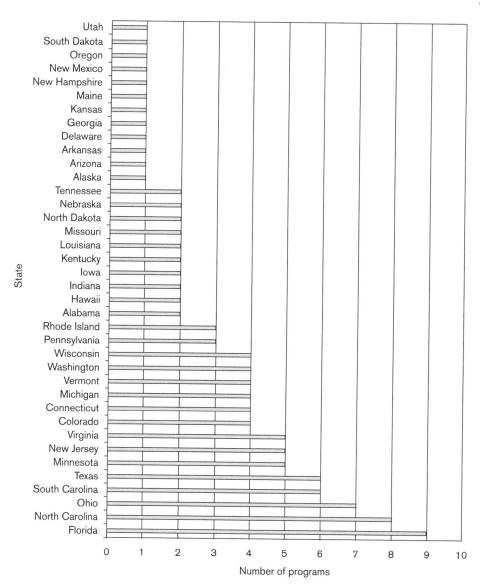

Figure 14.4. States with less than 10 programs in the Think College database. (*Source*: Think College, n.d.)

paid job, and/or attending postsecondary education were associated with student outcomes that reflected those expectations. Higher expectations for academic and career success have been found to relate to better high school completion rates and higher postsecondary school attendance rates (Wagner, Newman, Cameto, Levine, & Marder, 2007).

The lack of professional awareness of current postsecondary education options leads many professionals to provide families and students with little expectation that they will do anything other than what students like them have done in the past—exit high school and participate in a sheltered workshop or adult day habilitation center. Therefore, parents' hope that their child will go to college is often dismissed as unrealistic (Dwyre, Grigal, & Fialka, 2010).

In addition, assumptions are made based on the student's academic abilities because college historically has been deemed only for those with the most advanced academic skills. Griffin et al. (2010) found that parents of students with lower reading levels were less likely to think that postsecondary education would help their children make the transition to adulthood, were less often encouraged by school staff to pursue postsecondary education, and were less likely to enroll their child in postsecondary education. These low expectations are also reflected in transition goals for students with intellectual disability (Grigal et al., 2011; Migliore & Domin, 2011; Papay, 2011), which rarely include preparing for any level of postsecondary education.

Segregated versus Inclusive Higher Education

The issue of separate versus inclusive postsecondary education is a controversial element of college program design for people with intellectual disability (Grigal & Hart, 2010; Katovich, 2010). Access to inclusive college classes and experiences depends on the program location and perceived academic ability of the student (Papay & Bambara, 2011). It may also depend on the emphasis placed by those implementing the college program on creating, maintaining, and expanding such inclusive access. The inclusive nature of college for people with intellectual disability may differ due to preconceptions about what these students are viewed as capable of and what they need from postsecondary education. Although inclusion in K–12 education has been a strong movement since the 1990s and therefore has a clearer definition, simply being on campus is sometimes described as inclusion in the new environment of postsecondary education, even if academics are provided through a separate course of study specially designed only for individuals with intellectual disability.

Although many programs support inclusive college course access and social opportunities, they may also create specialized courses to address the needs of incoming students who were ill-prepared to navigate the college community and/or to respond to administration and parental concerns of vulnerability for students with intellectual disability (Hafner, Moffat, & Kisa, 2011).

Inclusion was directly addressed by the amendments in the HEOA, stating that programs seeking to provide students with access to federal student aid must provide academic and employment experiences with students without disabilities. This new guidance requires a substantial portion of a student's academic time be comprised of inclusive instruction and work-based training. It is clear that Congress attempted to emphasize the importance of access to inclusive college coursework and experiences. Uditsky and Hughson suggested,

> The degree of inclusion embraced by any postsecondary initiative is often a function of the values and knowledge of the architects of these efforts. There is a risk in the fast-paced growth of new postsecondary education options for people with ID that implementers may repeat some of the errors evident in past efforts by creating less than fully inclusive practices that succeeding generations will then have to struggle to alter. Postsecondary environments are highly valued, and many individuals and their families are thrilled to simply be allowed on campus. This leads to a further risk of their accepting being segregated at college, which may override the need for critical appraisal and advancement of authentic inclusion. (2012, p. 82)

It will become increasingly important to document students' access to coursework and the outcomes associated with all kinds of college experiences as postsecondary education options continue to develop and mature. Students, professionals, and families should consider to what extent the experiences being created in college for people with an intellectual disability are the same or different from the experiences of other college students.

IMPACT OF POSTSECONDARY EDUCATION FOR STUDENTS WITH INTELLECTUAL DISABILITY ON POLICY AND PRACTICE

Going to college in the 21st century has become a minimum requirement for getting a good job and succeeding in the work force. Almost two thirds of all jobs require skills associated with at least some education beyond high school (Carnevale & Desrochers, 2003). Research consistently has demonstrated that postsecondary education experiences lead to better outcomes, such as increased employment opportunities and higher wages (Schultz & Higbee, 2007). These gains in employment are also seen for people with disabilities who have experienced postsecondary education (Gilmore, Bose, & Hart, 2001; Madaus, 2006; Schley, 2010). Early research into the outcomes for students with intellectual disability who have attended college showed a similar relationship between college education and better employment outcomes, including higher wages (Migliore, Butterworth, & Hart, 2009).

Postsecondary education for youth with intellectual disability can be an ideal environment for the transition experience, providing opportunities for personal growth and development, interesting learning options, higher responsibility levels, access to adult learning and working environments, increased career opportunities, and new and expanded social networks (Grigal & Hart, 2010). Creating a path to and through higher education for students with intellectual disability clearly has the potential to affect those students who are given the opportunity to attend. In addition, opportunities for positive effect on educational practices at both the K–12 and higher education levels are also possible.

Effect on K–12 Education

The emergence of postsecondary education for youth with intellectual disability has been met with some resistance in the field of special education. This may be due to beliefs or assumptions about what constitutes people prepared for and worthy of a college education. As the population of college-educated youth with intellectual disability grows and is witnessed by the next generation of youth with intellectual disability, these students and their families may better see and believe in their own college potential. Greater numbers of students seeking postsecondary education may lead to significant changes in federal and state IEP standards, transition services, and partnerships on a local level. General and special education teachers, transition coordinators, administrators, and paraeducators will need to become better informed about the existing postsecondary education options and the skills students need to gain access to those options. Instead of relying primarily on transition personnel to guide parents toward adult rehabilitation systems as the only option for their children's future, high school guidance counselors must be involved in learning about new postsecondary options, including the existence of CTPs, and assisting families to apply for financial aid as they would with other college-bound students. In addition, K–12 personnel may begin to hold higher expectations for students with intellectual disability and ensure their access to inclusive academic classes while still in high school. The mindset that all academic learning stops at age 18 for students with an intellectual disability must be eradicated. Many educators shift from academic instruction to life skills or independent living instruction when students turn 18 years old, especially students with intellectual disability. Individuals with intellectual disability will be seen as having lifelong learning potential when post-secondary education is a viable option.

Effect on Higher Education

Higher education has its own challenges related to mission, funding, quality assessment, accountability, and outcomes. A wide array of nontraditional students has gained access to higher education for many years, seeking to learn desired skills and create a better future for themselves. Colleges have committed to being responsive to learners from diverse cultural, financial, and academic backgrounds. The infusion of people with intellectual disability into these learning environments has and will continue to help institutions of higher learning meet their vision of being responsive to diversity. The positive effect that students with intellectual disability have on faculty (Folk, Yamamoto, & Stodden, 2012; O'Connor, Kubiak, Espiner, & O'Brien 2012) and peers (Griffin et al., 2012; May, 2012) is starting to be documented. Peers of college students with intellectual disability tend to become more open minded about diversity and more accepting of people with disabilities (Griffin et al., 2012). Interactions with students with intellectual disability in college have influenced peers' career paths in some cases.

As program growth continues, higher education may benefit from increased collaboration between secondary and higher education, as well as collaboration with employers and adult service entities. These connections will strengthen the college and derive benefits for other college students facing diverse challenges. For example, some disability support coordinators indicated that they had virtually no interactions or involvement with high schools prior to being involved with these initiatives on their campus. Now these college staff are meeting with high school staff and becoming more aware of strategies to assist with the transition of students with a variety of disabilities. The focus on employment outcomes in these programs also adds external resources to the college—closer relationships with area employers can assist all of the college's graduates to find employment.

The emergence of students with intellectual disability on college campuses will also provide college faculty with the opportunity to develop teaching strategies reflecting universal design for learning (UDL), which is likely to benefit all students. The emergence of program options on college campuses affords faculty a wide array of opportunities for research and evaluation of new and emerging practices, which could lead to external funding opportunities to support this research.

Effect on Services and Supports for People from Culturally Diverse Backgrounds

Low socioeconomic status and poverty has lasting lifelong effects on individuals across all major life domains (Amelga, 2012; Greene, 2011). Having a disability or family member with a disability compounds the impact that poverty can have, given the multiple educational and human services systems that one has to navigate to receive services and supports (Amelga, 2012; Greene, 2011). Youth and families who have a low socioeconomic status and are from culturally and linguistically diverse backgrounds face even more challenges as they work their way through K–12 education into adult services. Greene identified numerous obstacles faced by families who are culturally and linguistically diverse, including a lack of professional understanding of family culture, differences in values and practices, and an overall lack of English language fluency and understanding of the transition requirements under IDEA 2004. Finally, immigration status of the student and other family members further contribute to a lack of trust on the part of the family and a desire to keep a distance from and limit communication with individuals who are perceived to be in a position of authority.

All of these factors contribute to a lower participation rate in higher education for individuals from culturally and linguistically diverse populations. Individuals who are culturally and linguistically diverse and individuals with disabilities lack preparation to gain access to and succeed in higher education. In 2010, 70% of White high school graduates entered college after graduating high school, but only 66% of Black and 60% of Hispanic graduates did the same (Aud et al., 2012).

Unfortunately, initial TPSID data revealed findings that are aligned with the previous data. Fewer students from culturally and linguistically diverse populations with intellectual disability enter postsecondary education. The early data from the 27 TPSID model demonstration projects indicated that most student participants (71.3%) were White. The following data is the breakout of students from culturally and linguistically diverse backgrounds (Grigal, Hart, & Smith, 2012).

- 21.4% were Black

- 9.4% were Hispanic/Latino

- 4.9% were Asian

- 0.9% were Native Hawaiian or Other Pacific Islander

- 0.2% were American Indian or Alaska Native

It will be critical to research and identify and/or develop strategies and practices to ameliorate these disparities, given the low participation rates of individuals from culturally and linguistically diverse populations with intellectual disability.

Culturally Responsive Strategies

The literature on individuals from culturally and linguistically diverse populations identified strategies that are better preparing students from culturally and linguistically diverse backgrounds for college and/or competitive employment (Greene, 2011). Educators of students with intellectual disability from culturally and linguistically diverse backgrounds can and should learn from these strategies (Greene, 2011).

- Obtain knowledge of a family's culture and how to frame transition planning that is inclusive of a family's beliefs.

- Respect family perspectives related to their family member with intellectual disability.

- Provide families and students with information on transition, why it is important, and their rights under the law; have material translated into the family's language when needed.

- Take the time to establish a trusting relationship with families and demonstrate sensitivity to their schedules (e.g., schedule meetings when they are not working).

Numerous federal initiatives are trying to address the needs of students from low socioeconomic and culturally and linguistically diverse populations (e.g., Gear Up and Trio grants, the American Association of Colleges and Universities, National College Access Network, Institute for Higher Education Policy, College and Career Readiness). The strategies that they have developed and continue to develop have relevance to students with intellectual disability who are from culturally and linguistically diverse populations.

- Use noncognitive measures/assessment to determine college career readiness.

- Teach noncognitive or soft skills (e.g., problem solving, communication, self-advocacy).

- Provide peer mentoring supports.

- Foster parental support and encouragement.

- Apply college and career readiness standards.

RECOMMENDED PRACTICES TO SUPPORT ACCESS TO POSTSECONDARY EDUCATION FOR YOUTH AND ADULTS WITH INTELLECTUAL DISABILITY

To ensure that higher education and its associated benefits continue to become more available to people with intellectual disability, it will be vital that future investments of attention and resources focus on critical areas. These include building an evidence base around standards of practice, improving and capturing education and employment outcomes associated with higher education, and ensuring that higher education is seen as part of all transition and life span frameworks for people with intellectual disability.

Use of Standards to Guide Planning Implementation and Evaluation

The Think College Standards, Quality Indicators, and Benchmarks provide a philosophical and structural framework for planning, implementing, and assessing practice as well as designing and conducting research (Grigal, Hart, & Weir, 2012b). They also provide a basis on which students and their families, as well as transition professionals, can discuss and prioritize the types of experiences they would value in a future college experience. The Think College standards-based conceptual framework for inclusive higher education depicts four standards as cornerstones of practice—academic access, career development, campus membership, and self-determination. These standards and associated quality indicators and benchmarks comprise what experts in the field have indicated are essential elements of quality practice.

An additional four standards—integration with college systems and practices, coordination and collaboration, sustainability, and ongoing evaluation—represent the interdependent elements of service, or programmatic infrastructure, necessary for the four cornerstones of practice to occur, be sustained over time, and result in desired outcomes. These eight key elements, along with 18 quality indicators and 87 corresponding benchmarks, represent a cohesive framework that supports the tenets of the HEOA while simultaneously acknowledging the individualized services that may be required by students with intellectual disability in postsecondary education (see Figure 14.5).

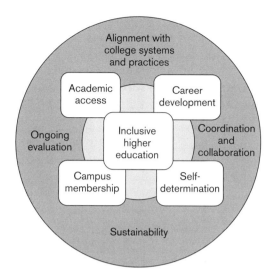

Figure 14.5. The Think College Standards for inclusive higher education conceptual framework. (From Grigal, M., Hart, D., & Weir, C. [2013]. Postsecondary education for people with intellectual disability: Current issues and critical challenges. *Inclusion, 1*[1], 50–63; reprinted by permission.)

The Think College Standards reflect an applied perspective and supports innovation while maintaining a call for feedback mechanisms on the effectiveness of the partnerships, services, and structures supporting students with intellectual disability in higher education. Using the Think College Standards will help future program developers and evaluators ensure that services are aligned with the definition of a comprehensive postsecondary and transition program for students with intellectual disability and reflect institutional and instructional practices that support a UDL framework.

Document and Evaluate Outcomes of Postsecondary Education

There is emerging research on promising practices or interventions for students with intellectual disability in higher education (Grigal & Hart, 2010). However the most critical questions have yet to be asked or answered. What effect does a college education, in its many iterations, have on the postcollege outcomes of people with intellectual disability? This question will be difficult to answer for a variety of reasons. First, implementing high-quality, evidence-based practices in postsecondary education programs is not consistent across programs or institutions. Therefore, not all postsecondary education experiences afford students the same opportunities for learning and working. Second, the purpose and intent of students with intellectual disability gaining access to college are varied, much like those of their counterparts with other disabilities and those without disabilities. Thus, what constitutes completion and achievement of a goal may depend on the student. Some students may want to take a few classes that lead to a desired job change, whereas others may seek to obtain a credential in a particular field of study. Determining a method to capture the student's attainment of desired goals will be challenging.

Funding is the final challenge. Previous research conducted on postsecondary education for people with intellectual disability was funded by different federal agencies with diverse foci. Funding for longitudinal data collection focused on students who have benefited from comparable postsecondary education experiences may be difficult to attain.

Expansion of and Dissemination About Current Postsecondary Education Options

Students without disabilities have an immense array of higher education choices of schools and programs nationwide. This is not true for students with intellectual disability. There remains a need to increase the number of postsecondary education options so that students and families have the choice of attending college in their community or going away to school. The field needs to disseminate information that clearly describes the different pathways into higher education for students with intellectual disability. Families most often get information about what is possible for their child with a disability from professionals in the medical, education, and disability systems. It is not uncommon for doctors, rehabilitation counselors, or therapists to influence parents' attitudes toward and understanding of their child's potential. These important influencers may inadvertently temper or derail parents' exploration of higher education as a possible future path because they do not have current knowledge of existing college options. Therefore, it is crucial that individuals guiding families all have up-to-date information about what is possible for all youth with disabilities. If professionals only offer the same sad stale options of congregate living, no further education, and sheltered work that reflect the lowest of expectations, then how are families to know that there are alternatives? Public awareness of inclusive education and work options has begun to emerge (see http://www.think beyondthelabel.com). Continued and sustained efforts must be made to get the best information about higher education and employment policies and options into the hands of those who support and guide family members so that youth with disabilities have the best chance of attaining their best possible future.

Information about the potential for youth with intellectual disability to go to college should be embedded in the preservice and in-service training of all special and general educators and guidance and rehabilitation counselors. Families must have access to professionals who understand the viability and legitimacy of college as a true transition option because the path to college often begins early in a student's life.

Improved Practices to Support Paid Employment

One little-known aspect of the new CTPs is that they are considered gainful employment programs by the U.S. Department of Education. This means that the programs must help students attain employment in a recognized occupation. Although this requirement brings with it an array of complications because not all CTPs are designed to support a single career path, it does establish the expectation that college programs for people with intellectual disability can and should result in employment. Many of the postsecondary education programs that existed prior to the passage of the HEOA purported to focus on employment (Grigal et al., 2012a); however, many of these programs implemented the same dated and ineffective practices widely used in secondary education (Grigal & Hart, 2010). Students and families approaching colleges and universities should ask about the employment component of programs they are considering, the rate of employed enrolled students, and those employed after graduation. Colleges that support students with intellectual disability must work with their partners in both K–12 transition and with adult services and rehabilitation agencies to ensure that college personnel are aware of the most relevant and effective customized employment strategies as part of their career services (Dwyre & Deschamps, 2013).

CURRENT AND EMERGING RESEARCH

Fortunately there has been growth in qualitative and quantitative research in the field of higher education for students with intellectual disability since the mid-2000s. Several researchers have conducted secondary data analysis using existing large national databases such as the NLTS–2, Rehabilitation Services Administration 911 Database, and the American Community Services Census data to examine different aspects of transition and higher education for students with intellectual disability (Grigal et al., 2011; Migliore et al., 2009; Newman et al., 2010; Papay, 2011; Smith, Grigal, & Sulewski, 2012). Researchers examined the effect of having students with intellectual disability in typical inclusive college courses on students without disabilities and faculty or instructors (Griffin et al., 2012; May, 2012; O'Connor et al., 2012). Other researchers looked at the student and family perspective on postsecondary education for students with intellectual disability (Dwyre et al., 2010; Martinez et al., 2012). Descriptive research detailed postsecondary education program profiles, descriptions of specific support strategies such as mentoring and educational coaches, historical perspectives, and editorials on higher education for students with intellectual disability (Folk et al., 2012; Grigal & Hart, 2010; Hafner et al., 2011; Jones & Goble, 2012; Katovich, 2010; Paiewonsky et al., 2010; Uditsky & Hughson, 2012). In addition, several researchers conducted national surveys that looked at the characteristics of postsecondary education programs that revealed their immense variability (Grigal et al., 2012a; Papay & Bambara, 2011).

Need for Connecting Access and Participation to Outcomes

No researchers have looked at the causal relationship between program structures, policies, and practices and their potential relationships to student outcomes. Current research has been primarily descriptive and qualitative in nature mainly due to the novice status of the field of postsecondary education for students with intellectual disability. The field now has a common language emanating from the development and implementation of the Think College Standards, however. In addition, a growing knowledge base has examined qualitative aspects of program attributes and the effect of participation of students with intellectual disability in college on students without disabilities, faculty perspectives, and campus life. It is now time to begin to research the different model approaches and practices on student outcomes and to compare and contrast these different approaches.

FUTURE POLICY DEVELOPMENT AND RESEARCH

The quality and consistency of higher education degrees, credentials, and certificates is the topic of much debate with the field of accreditation policy. This important issue is one that has just begun to emerge for higher education programs serving students with intellectual disability.

Accreditation

The goal of accreditation is to ensure that education provided by institutes of higher education meets acceptable levels of quality. Accrediting agencies, which are private educational associations of regional or national scope, develop evaluation criteria and conduct peer evaluations to assess whether those criteria are met. Institutions and/or programs that request an agency's evaluation and that meet an agency's criteria are then accredited by that agency. Programs that are serving students with intellectual disability currently fall under the existing institutional accreditation of their host institution. No programmatic accreditation standards for such programs currently exist.

Think College in its role as the National Coordinating Center is charged with developing model standards that could be used as accreditation standards. This work is being conducted by an accrediting workgroup who will create a report to be submitted to the U.S. Secretary of Education. Although there are questions about which agencies might use the model standards developed by the accreditation workgroup, the model standards will be important for a number of reasons. Having model standards will create a quality benchmark for programs that will be useful to institutions, students, and parents. It will also provide legitimacy for programs that meet the standards and guidelines for colleges and universities considering establishing high-quality programs.

Credentialing

The TPSID model demonstration projects were charged with creating and offering a meaningful credential for students with intellectual disability when they completed the model program. A credential awarded by a postsecondary provider signifies that an individual has mastered or achieved a specified body of knowledge or acquired a specific skill set—it raises expectations by others, such as employers, that individuals who have exited a program have attained or mastered a certain level of competence (Ganzglass, Bird, & Prince, 2011).

A survey conducted by the National Coordinating Center of the TPSID model demonstration projects indicated that there was little consistency across programs regarding the name or types of credentials being offered. Some credential titles were general in nature, such as career readiness credential, work force credential, and certificate (a sequential program in learning and life skills), whereas others were more specific to the content of the TPSID program, such as child development assistant teacher and office skills training certificate. Few of the TPSIDs had conducted any kind of labor market analysis to ensure that the credential would lead to future employment, and about one third indicated that they solicited feedback from business leaders.

Future efforts will need to be focused on helping all programs (TPSIDs, CTPs, and other existing postsecondary education programs that fall into neither of these categories) to consider what kind of culminating documentation their program affords to students and how that documentation will be perceived by employers and other institutions of higher education. The wide array of credential options that will be developed by the TPSIDs may provide guidance for future programs.

FUTURE RESEARCH

The field of postsecondary education has grown enormously since the mid-2000s, and the increased research on programs, students, peers, faculty, and institutions reflects that growth. Researchers should continue to explore both the quantitative as well as the qualitative aspects of providing people with intellectual disability access to higher education.

Much of the current research has been funded by disability-focused entities, and little current research on postsecondary education initiatives has been conducted as part of existing research initiatives related to higher education. The large-scale datasets on higher education do include people with disabilities (e.g., American Community Survey, National Postsecondary Student Aid Study). Most do not include or reflect students with intellectual disability, however. The 2011–2012 Common Data Set, which is used as a guiding framework for higher education data collection by entities such as Carnegie Mellon University, the College Board, Peterson's, and *U.S. News & World Report*, does not mention students with intellectual disability. The need for representation of youth and adults with intellectual disability in the large-scale datasets for higher education will increase as program development and practice increase.

Need for Blended Federal Investments in Research and Technical Assistance

The TPSIDs and the National Coordinating Center represent an important step toward deepening the understanding of the structures necessary to implement postsecondary education services for students with intellectual disabilities; sole reliance on these projects to build a knowledge base around this topic would be shortsighted. A coordinated effort between the federal agencies that have a stake in improved postsecondary and employment outcomes for youth and adults with intellectual disability is needed to secure funding to support the next generation of program development and evaluation. The National Council on Disability (2012) applauded the U.S. Department of Education and the U.S. Department of Health and Human Services for supporting the work of Think College because it used a braided funding approach to expand research, training and technical assistance, and information dissemination in the area of postsecondary education for students with intellectual disability. The National Council on Disability recommended that not only should the U.S. Department of Education and the Office of Civil Rights expand enforcement, guidance, and technical assistance activities aimed at securing the rights of students with disabilities in higher education, but also that Congress and the U.S. Department of Education should maintain and expand funding for inclusive higher education programs for students with intellectual disability. Collaborative investments by the U.S. Department of Education, the U.S. Department of Labor, and the U.S. Department of Health and Human Services could provide a braided funding stream that could potentially support continued national technical assistance as well as the collection and evaluation of longitudinal data on postsecondary education attainment and outcomes of people with intellectual disability.

CONCLUSION

Significant progress has been made since the mid-1990s in providing youth and adults with intellectual disability access to postsecondary education. The changes in legislation, policy, and practice described in this chapter will ideally lead to new, more inclusive higher education options, better informed transition personnel, and increased partnerships between secondary and higher education entities. The off-spring of these changes has been the creation of a new field—one that straddles both special education and higher education. These two systems now must face the challenge of learning how to work together to best meet the needs of people with intellectual disability who see postsecondary education as a path to a better future.

Questions for Study and Reflection

1. What are some of the benefits of postsecondary education for people with intellectual disability?

2. What are the different types of postsecondary education programs? How do they differ? How are they the same?

3. What could be done to change the systemic low expectations professionals have for youth with intellectual disability?

4. Name three positive outcomes that could result from creating more post-secondary education options for youth with intellectual disability.

5. What changes for students with intellectual disability have occurred as a result of the reauthorization of the HEOA?

6. How will the new disability documentation guidance change the experiences of college students with intellectual disability?

7. What strategies could professionals use in working with students from culturally and linguistically diverse families to better support their child's access to college?

8. How can access to federal student aid affect enrollment of students with intellectual disability? Do you see any challenges that these new regulations might create?

9. What kind of information should be included about postsecondary education options for students with intellectual disability in personnel preparation programs for general and special education, rehabilitation, and guidance counselors?

10. How will the Think College Standards, Quality Indicators, and Benchmarks for inclusive higher education influence future practice, evaluation, and research?

RESOURCES

Association on Higher Education and Disability Documentation (*http://www.ahead .org/resources/documentation_guidance*)—Conceptual framework to support appropriate practices in providing seamless access through equal treatment and accommodations. This revised guidance is necessitated by changes in society's understanding of disability—ADA 2008 and the updated regulations and guidance to Titles II and III of the ADA 2008. Although the amendments and regulatory revisions occurred through separate federal processes, together they reflect a more mature understanding of disability that is essential for fostering a positive campus perspective on disability. This framework is consistent with the letter and spirit of the law, reflective of legal and judicial thinking, and responsive to scholarly understandings of disability and its role in higher education and society.

Federal Student Aid (*http://studentaid.ed.gov/eligibility/intellectual-disabilities*) —Provides information on financial aid for students with intellectual disability.

Grigal, M., & Hart, D. (2010). *Think college: Postsecondary education options for students with intellectual disabilities.* Baltimore, MD: Paul H. Brookes Publishing Co. This comprehensive resource provides an overview of the history, legislation, and policy issues that affect higher education access for people with intellectual disability. Practical resources and strategies as well as first person accounts are provided from the perspectives of college personnel, transition personnel, and families.

Impact: Feature Issue on Postsecondary Education and Students with Intellectual, Developmental, and Other Disabilities—Explores what we know and what we still need to know about what works to support increased participation of students with disabilities, especially those with intellectual disabilities, in postsecondary education and why that participation is important. It includes stories about students with disabilities succeeding in higher education, strategies for families and school personnel to use in supporting planning for postsecondary education during high school, research findings, and historical overviews on the national journey to support full participation in all areas of life for individuals with intellectual and other disabilities.

Insight Brief 1: Overview of the Federal Higher Education Opportunity Act Reauthorization *http://www.thinkcollege.net/images/stories/HEAC_Overview.pdf*

Insight Brief 6: Impact on Teacher Education Programs of Students with Intellectual Disabilities Attending College *http://www.thinkcollege.net/images/stories/ Insight6_F.pdf*

Insight Brief 10: Framing the Future: A Standards-Based Conceptual Framework for Research and Practice in Inclusive Higher Education *http://www.think college.net/images/stories/Insight10new_D3.pdf*

Katovich, D. (2010). *The power to spring up: Postsecondary education opportunities for students with significant disabilities.* Bethesda, MD: Woodbine House. This guide to postsecondary education options is designed for students ages 14 and up with a variety of disabilities, including autism spectrum disorder, Down syndrome, and cerebral palsy; their families; advocates; and secondary school professionals.

Think College (*http://www.thinkcollege.net*)—Includes a searchable database of resources, a college search feature to locate college programs for students with intellectual disability, related publications, and information on what is happening related to postsecondary education for students with intellectual disability on the state level.

REFERENCES

Amelga, M. (2012). *College and career readiness: A quick stats fact sheet.* Washington, DC: National High School Center, American Institutes for Research.

Americans with Disabilities Act (ADA) of 1990, PL 101-336, 42 U.S.C. §§ 12101 *et seq.*

Americans with Disabilities Amendments Act (ADA) of 2008, PL 110-325, 42 U.S.C. §§ 12101 *et seq.*

Aud, S., Hussar, W., Johnson, F., Kena, G., Roth, E., Manning, E., ... Zhang, J. (2012). *The condition of education 2012* (NCES 2012-045). Washington, DC: U.S. Department of Education, Institute of Education Sciences, National Center for Education Statistics.

Bailey, D. (2012). *Life learning is for everyone: The true story of how South Carolina came to be a leader in providing opportunities for postsecondary education to young adults with intellectual disabilities*: IUniverse. Available at http://www.amazon.com/Life-Learning-Everyone-Opportunities-Postsecondary/dp/1469779285

Carnevale, A.P., & Desrochers, D.M. (2003). *Standards for what? The economic roots of K–16 reform.* Princeton, NJ: Educational Testing Service.

Doren, B., Gau, J.M., & Lindstrom, L.E. (2012). The relationship between parent expectations and postschool outcomes of adolescents with disabilities. *Exceptional Children, 79,* 7–23.

Dwyre, A., & Deschamps, A. (2013). *Changing the way we do business: A job development case study. Improving staff skills and paid job outcomes for students with disabilities.* Boston: University of Massachusetts, Institute for Community Inclusion.

Dwyre, A., Grigal, M., & Fialka, J. (2010). Student and family perspectives. In M. Grigal & D. Hart (Eds.), *Think college: Postsecondary education options for students with intellectual disabilities* (pp. 189–227). Baltimore, MD: Paul H. Brookes Publishing Co.

Folk, E.D., Yamamoto, K.K., & Stodden, R.A. (2012). Implementing inclusion and collaborative teaming in a model program of postsecondary education for young adults with intellectual disabilities. *Journal of Policy and Practice in Intellectual Disabilities, 9,* 257–269.

Ganzglass, E., Bird, K., & Prince, H. (2011). *Giving credit where credit is due: Creating a competency-based qualification framework for postsecondary education and training.* Washington, DC: Center for Postsecondary and Economic Success.

Gilmore, S., Bose, J., & Hart, D. (2001). Postsecondary education as a critical step toward meaningful employment: Vocational rehabilitation's role. *Research to Practice, 7,* 1–4.

Greene, G. (2011). *Transition planning for culturally and linguistically diverse youth.* Baltimore, MD: Paul H. Brookes Publishing Co.

Griffin, M.M., McMillan, E.D., & Hodapp, R.M. (2010). Family perspectives on postsecondary education for students with intellectual disabilities. *Education and Training in Developmental Disabilities, 45,* 339–346.

Griffin, M.M., Summer, A.H., McMillan, E.D., Day, T.L., & Hodapp, R.M. (2012). Attitudes toward including students with intellectual disabilities at college. *Journal of Policy and Practice in Intellectual Disabilities, 9,* 234–239.

Grigal, M. & Hart, D. (2010). *Think college: Postsecondary education options for students with intellectual disabilities.* Baltimore, MD: Paul H. Brookes Publishing Co.

Grigal, M., & Hart, D. (2012). The power of expectations. *Journal of Policy and Practice in Intellectual Disabilities, 9,* 221–222.

Grigal, M., Hart, D., & Lee, S.S. (2012, May). *A national snapshot of the postsecondary education landscape for students with intellectual disabilities.* Presented at the National Transition Conference, Washington, DC.

Grigal, M., Hart, D., & Lewis, C. (2012). *A prelude to progress: The evolution of postsecondary education for students with intellectual disabilities*. Boston: University of Massachusetts, Institute for Community Inclusion.

Grigal M., Hart, D., & Migliore, A. (2011). Comparing the transition planning, postsecondary education, and employment outcomes of students with intellectual and other disabilities. *Career Development for Exceptional Individuals, 34*, 4–17.

Grigal, M., Hart, D., & Paiewonsky, M. (2010). Postsecondary education: The next frontier for individuals with intellectual disabilities. In M. Grigal & D. Hart (Eds.), *Think college: Postsecondary education options for students with intellectual disabilities* (pp. 1–28). Baltimore, MD: Paul H. Brookes Publishing Co.

Grigal, M., Hart, D., & Smith, F. (2012). *Findings from the TPSID model demonstration project: Year I annual performance report*. Boston: University of Massachusetts, Institute for Community Inclusion.

Grigal, M., Hart, D., Smith, F.A., Domin, D., & Sulewski, J. (2013). *Think College National Coordinating Center: Annual report on the transition and postsecondary programs for students with intellectual disabilities*. Boston: University of Massachusetts Boston, Institute for Community Inclusion.

Grigal, M., Hart, D., & Weir, C. (2012a). A survey of postsecondary education programs for students with intellectual disabilities in the United States. *Journal of Policy and Practice in Intellectual Disabilities, 9*, 223–233.

Grigal, M., Hart, D., & Weir, C. (2012b). *Framing the future: A standards-based conceptual framework for research and practice in inclusive higher education*. Boston: University of Massachusetts, Institute for Community Inclusion.

Grigal, M., Hart, D., & Weir, C. (2013). Postsecondary education for people with intellectual disability: Current issues and critical challenges. *Inclusion, 1*(1), 50–63. doi:10.1352/2326-6988-1.1.050

Grigal, M., Migliore, A., & Hart, D. (in press). A state comparison of vocational rehabilitation support of youth with intellectual disabilities' participation in postsecondary education. *Journal of Vocational Rehabilitation.*

Hafner, D., Moffat, C., & Kisa, N. (2011). Cutting-edge: Integrating students with intellectual and developmental disabilities into a 4-year liberal arts college. *Career Development for Exceptional Individuals, 34*, 18–30.

Hart, D., Grigal, M., & Weir, C. (2010). Expanding the paradigm: Postsecondary education options for individuals with autism spectrum disorder and intellectual disabilities. *Focus on Autism and other Developmental Disabilities, 25*, 134–150.

Hart, D., Grigal, M., & Weir, C. (2012). A national survey of findings of a national survey of postsecondary education programs for students with intellectual disabilities. *Journal of Policy and Practice in Intellectual Disabilities.*

Higher Education Act of 1965, PL 89-329, 79 Stat. 1219.

Higher Education Opportunity Act of 2008, PL 110–315, 122 Stat. 3078.

Individuals with Disabilities Education Improvement Act (IDEA) of 2004, PL 108–446, 20 U.S.C. §§1400 *et seq.*

Jones, M., & Goble, Z. (2012). Creating effective mentoring partnerships for students with intellectual disabilities on campus. *Journal of Policy and Practice in Intellectual Disabilities, 9*, 270–278.

Katovich, D.M. (2010). *The power to spring up: Postsecondary education opportunities for students with significant disabilities*. Bethesda, MD: Woodbine House.

Madaus, J.W. (2006). Employment outcomes of university graduates with learning disabilities. *Learning Disability Quarterly, 29*, 19–31.

Martinez, D.C., Conroy, J.W., & Cerreto, M.C. (2012). Parent involvement in the transition process of children with intellectual disabilities: The influence of inclusion on parent desires and expectations for postsecondary education. *Journal of Policy and Practice in Intellectual Disabilities, 9*, 279–288.

May, C. (2012). An investigation of attitude change in inclusive college classes including young adults with an intellectual disability. *Journal of Policy and Practice in Intellectual Disabilities, 9*, 240–246.

Migliore, A., Butterworth, J., & Hart, D. (2009). *Postsecondary education and employment outcomes for youth with intellectual disabilities*. Boston: University of Massachusetts, Institute for Community Inclusion.

_298_

Migliore, A., & Domin, D. (2011). *Setting higher employment expectations for youth with intellectual disabilities.* Boston: University of Massachusetts, Institute for Community Inclusion.

National Council on Disability. (2012). *National disability policy: A progress report.* Washington, DC. Author.

National Longitudinal Transition Study–2. (2009). *NLTS–2 Wave 5 (2009) parent/young adult survey, Table 97.* Retrieved from http://www.nlts2.org/data_tables/tables/14/np5S3c_S4c_S5c_A3c_A3g_A3kfrm.html

Newman, L., Wagner, M., Cameto, R., Knokey, A.M., & Shaver, D. (2010). *Comparisons across time of the outcomes of youth with disabilities up to 4 years after high school. A Report of Findings From the National Longitudinal Transition Study (NLTS) and the National Longitudinal Transition Study–2 (NLTS–2).* Menlo Park, CA: SRI International.

O'Connor, B., Kubiak, J., Espiner, D., & O'Brien, P. (2012). Lecturer responses to the inclusion of students with intellectual disabilities auditing undergraduate classes. *Journal of Policy and Practice in Intellectual Disabilities, 9,* 247–256.

Paiewonsky, M., Mecca, K., Daniels, T., Katz, C., Nash, J., Hanson, T., & Gragoudas, S. (2010). *Students and educational coaches: Developing a support plan for college.* Boston: University of Massachusetts, Institute for Community Inclusion.

Papay, C. (2011). *Best practices in transition to adult life for youth with intellectual disabilities: A national perspective using the National Longitudinal Transition Study–2* (Unpublished doctoral dissertation). Lehigh University, Bethlehem, PA.

Papay, C., & Bambara, L. (2011). Postsecondary education for transition-age students with intellectual and other developmental disabilities: A national survey. *Education and Training in Autism and Developmental Disabilities, 46,* 78–93.

Raue, K., & Lewis, L. (2011). *Students with disabilities at degree-granting postsecondary institutions.* Washington, DC: U.S. Government Printing Office.

Rehabilitation Act of 1973, PL 93-112, 29 U.S.C. §§ 701 *et seq.*

Schley, S. (2010). *Effect of postsecondary education on the economic status of persons who are deaf or hard of hearing.* Retrieved from http://www.rit.edu/ntid/edr/sites/default/files/Fall%20'10%20Res%20Bull.pdf

Schultz, J.L., & Higbee, J.L. (2007). Reasons for attending college: The student point of view. *Research and Teaching in Developmental Education, 23,* 69–76.

Smith, F., Grigal, M., & Sulewski, J. (2012). *The impact of postsecondary education on employment outcomes for transition-age age youth with and without disabilities: A secondary analysis of American Community Survey Data.* Boston: University of Massachusetts, Institute for Community Inclusion.

Thacker, J., & Sheppard-Jones, K. (2011). *Research brief: Higher education for students with intellectual disabilities: A Study of KY OVR counselors.* Lexington: University of Kentucky, Human Development Institute.

Think College, Institute for Community Inclusion. (n.d.). Boston: University of Massachusetts Boston. Retrieved from http://www.thinkcollege.net/component/programsdatabase/?view=programsdatabase&Itemid=339

Uditsky, B., & Hughson, E. (2012). Inclusive postsecondary education: An evidence-based moral imperative. *Journal of Policy and Practice in Intellectual Disabilities, 9,* 298–302.

Wagner, M., Newman, L., Cameto, R., Levine, P., & Marder, C. (2007). *Perceptions and expectations of youth with disabilities. A special topic report of findings from the National Longitudinal Transition Study–2 (NLTS–2).* Menlo Park, CA: SRI International.

Evolving Narratives in Community Living

Lyle T. Romer and Pamela Walker

An emergence of a large, complex system of supports intended to make life in communities accessible to people with severe disabilities has occurred since the 1970s. This development of a full system of supports in which none previously existed and the decreasing reliance on large, state-operated institutions constituted one of the dominant narratives in the field of social services over the past half century. Almost no community supports were available prior to the late 1960s, with the exception of those organized and delivered by family members of people with disabilities. Community services and supports evolved during the subsequent 50 years, first from an emphasis on institutional care toward an eventual shift to support for people with disabilities to live in communities throughout the United States and other Western countries.

This chapter begins with a review of the history of community living services. From the late 1960s, the focus was on deinstitutionalization and then on promoting community integration. More recently, due to shortcomings of these approaches, there has been an emphasis on an individualized, person-centered approach to community living. First, an overview of this approach is provided, followed by a section discussing key elements of this approach. The chapter then includes discussion of the essential organizational commitments needed to provide person-centered supports. Finally, a discussion about organizational and systems strategies to promote further person-centered supports is provided, followed by a brief conclusion.

Preparation of this chapter was supported, in part, by a subcontract with the Research and Training Center on Community Living and Employment, University of Minnesota, supported by the U.S. Department of Education, Office of Special Education and Rehabilitation Services, National Institute on Disability and Rehabilitation Research, through Contract No. H133B080005.

THE POSTINSTITUTIONALIZATION NARRATIVE: DEINSTITUTIONALIZATION AND COMMUNITY INTEGRATION

The predominant narrative in the field of developmental disabilities since the late 1960s focused on deinstitutionalization and community integration. This section provides a brief description of these trends.

Deinstitutionalization

The approach to care for people with disabilities was custodial throughout the first half of the 20th century, and the population of institutions grew "exponentially" (Sheerenberger, 1987, p. 240). The number of people with intellectual disabilities in institutions reached a peak of 194,659 in 1967 (Prouty, Smith, & Lakin, 2005). The late 1960s and early 1970s brought about the beginning of a shift away from institutions, spurred in large part by exposés of the inhumane conditions in institutions (Blatt & Kaplan, 1966; Rivera, 1972). This deinstitutionalization movement was also prompted by introduction of the principle of normalization (Wolfensberger, 1971) and by federal policy (Bradley, 1994). Although the Intermediate Care Facilities for Persons with Mental Retardation (ICF-MR) program (Title XIX of the Social Security Amendments of 1965 [PL 89-97]) prompted federal funding for institutions, the expansion of the ICF-MR program to privately operated services in the late 1970s and early 1980s facilitated the development of group homes (Larson, Ryan, Salmi, Smith, & Wuorio, 2012).

Deinstitutionalization resulted in a steady decline in institutional populations. The number of people living in institutions (for 16 or more people) had declined to 131,345 by 1980 (Larson et al., 2012). This trend was accompanied by a shift away from a custodial focus to a developmental approach in which those who gained the requisite skills could attain community living (Bradley, 1994). This development, however, meant that individuals with more significant disabilities and, therefore, with needs for greater levels of support, were more likely to remain in state institutions or be transferred to private institutions or nursing homes (Lakin, Hayden, & Abery, 1994; Sheerenberger, 1987). Lakin et al. noted,

> The early years of state efforts to reduce the populations of large public institutions involved the development of many large private institutions and the transfer of tens of thousands of persons with mental retardation and other developmental disabilities to nursing homes. (1994, p. 5)

Community Integration

Beginning in the 1980s, the state of the art or narrative in residential services became the promotion of community integration (Lakin & Bruininks, 1985). This shift was accompanied by the enactment of the Medicaid Home and Community-Based Services waiver in 1981, which facilitated the development of noninstitutional services (Larson et al., 2012). Since this time, there has been a continual decline in the populations of state institutions and a continued rise in the number of people in group homes and community support arrangements. There were 30,602 individuals with intellectual and developmental disabilities living in large state institutions by 2010, a decline of approximately 77% from 1980 (Larson et al., 2012). In contrast, the number of people living in smaller residential settings (from 1–6 people) increased from 20,400 in 1977 to 353,195 in 2010 (Larson et al., 2012).

A growing recognition of the problems inherent in this model of services, even in the smallest size group homes (e.g., two to three individuals), began amid the continued growth of group homes in the late 1980s and early 1990s. Such services were based on a continuum model, which still incorporated many institutional features, and focused on training and treatment (Bradley, 1994; O'Brien, 1994; O'Brien & Mount, 1991; Smull & Bellamy, 1991; Taylor, 1988). Furthermore, while living in the community, residents were often not really part of the community (Bogdan & Taylor, 1987).

Although the expansion of community supports has undoubtedly resulted in improved services for many people with developmental disabilities, an underlying assumption exists that community programs offer their services in a manner fundamentally different from institutions. The fact that community programs are physically located in different places (i.e., in the community), however, does not warrant any conclusions about the support practices employed in these settings. Warning about this assumption came early when developing community programs. Wolfensberger (1967) provided the clearest and earliest of those warnings. Control of choices and attitudes toward the humanity of people with disabilities—not physical location—defines institutional practices. Some community programs employ practices just as controlling as large state-operated institutions. They may employ these practices in smaller scale settings, but similar control still exists. Brown (1991) issued a similar warning concerning the willingness to negotiate the size of institutions, which implies that serving people in smaller scale settings constitutes progress.

At a time when states are planning to close more of their institutions (Larson et al., 2012), let's consider what the new narrative should be for the continued evolution of the community support system. Because institutions are based on control of choices and people with disabilities, including severe intellectual disability, still have the right to self-determination, the new narrative should be one that empowers people to direct their own supports and be the authors of their own lives. Person-centered planning and person-centered supports fortunately have emerged since the 1990s.

THE NEW NARRATIVE: INDIVIDUALIZED, PERSON-CENTERED SUPPORTS FOR COMMUNITY LIVING

Beginning in the late 1980s, increasing calls were made for a radically new approach to supporting people in the community. This approach was called by many names, including supported living, individualized supports, and person-centered planning and supports (Bradley, Ashbaugh, & Blaney, 1994; Mount, 1992; O'Brien, 1993, 1994; Racino, Walker, O'Connor, & Taylor, 1993; Smull, 2002; Smull & Bellamy, 1991; Taylor, Biklen, & Knoll, 1987). Bradley called for a "new service paradigm" (1994, p. 11), whereas Smull and Bellamy argued that a "fundamental change in service design is required" (1991, p. 528). O'Brien (1993) articulated the difference that a supported living approach represented in contrast to traditional community services. Attention was focused on the need for a separation of housing and supports, the need to promote home ownership and control, and the need for individualized and flexible supports in the community (Klein, 1992; Racino et al., 1993; Taylor et al., 1987).

The number of people who receive supports in their own homes is one indicator of the expansion of this type of individualized support. In 2000, 73,147 people were supported in their own homes (Prouty et al., 2005), and in 2010, 127,455 individuals were supported at home (Larson et al., 2012). Research demonstrated the benefit of living in the community versus an institution (Horner, Stoner, & Ferguson, 1988; Lakin & Stancliffe, 2007). Lakin and Stancliffe stated, "The research establishes clearly and consistently that individuals with ID/DD [intellectual and developmental disabilities] experience greater personal freedom, more participation in social activities, more frequent associations with family and friends when living in the community rather than institutional settings" (p. 152).

In addition, research demonstrated that smaller settings are associated with more positive outcomes (Howe, Horner, & Newton, 1998; Lakin et al., 2006; Stancliffe, Abery, & Smith, 2000). Finally, studies indicated that people in supported living arrangements compared with those living in group homes experience better outcomes in relation to "choice, self-determination, autonomy, satisfaction, independence, lifestyle normalization, physical and social integration, domestic participation, community participation, and personal well being" (Lakin & Stancliffe, 2007, p. 155). Further research is needed to examine which features of supported living are more specifically related to better outcomes, particularly for people with the most significant support needs.

Impact of Policy and Legislation

The new narrative has been supported by shifts in policy spurred on by long-term advocacy by people with disabilities, family members, and other allies through organizations such as Self Advocates Becoming Empowered (SABE), TASH, and ADAPT as they worked for passage of the Americans with Disabilities Act (ADA) of 1990 (PL 101-336). They have continued to advocate for policies that promote community living characterized by inclusion, choice, and control. In 1995, SABE issued a *Position Statement on Closing Institutions,* and People First of New Hampshire is conducting a national campaign directed at institutional closure. TASH issued a *Resolution on Life in the Community* (2000a), a *Resolution on Choice and Community* (2011), and a Resolution on Supports in the Community (2000b), all calling for individuals with disabilities to have choice and control related to community living and supports for community living.

The Olmstead decision (*Olmstead v L.C.,* 1999) "called on states to offer services to individuals with disabilities, including persons who have intellectual and developmental disabilities, in the most integrated setting feasible" (Smith, Lakin, Larson, & Salmi, 2011, p. 53). Smith et al. contended that the Olmstead decision played a role in continued moves to smaller, more individualized residential service settings, and continued enforcement of Olmstead by the U.S. Department of Justice will play a role in this continuing trend. Further efforts are needed because there is still an institutional bias in services and funding. In order to help address this, advocates are pushing for the Community Choice Act, which would provide for real choice regarding community services as opposed to institutional services.

This new service paradigm called for starting with individuals and designing supports based on the individual's needs and desires. An emerging way to approach this was through person-centered planning and person-centered supports (Lyle O'Brien & O'Brien, 2002).

Emerging Practice

Person-centered planning was introduced as part of a "conscious search for new categories through which to understand the experience of people with developmental disabilities and work with them and their allies to change that experience for the better" (O'Brien & Lyle O'Brien, 1998, p. 20). This development emerged in the late 1970s and 1980s based on the work of people who were deeply embedded in the normalization "community of practice" (Lyle O'Brien & O'Brien, 2002, p. 27). Numerous approaches to person-centered planning were developed (Lyle O'Brien & O'Brien, 2002); however, they shared some common themes.

> Seeing people first rather than relating to diagnostic labels; using ordinary language and images rather than professional jargon; actively searching for a person's gifts and capacities in the context of community life; [and] strengthening the voice of the person and those who know the person best. (Mount, 1992, cited in Lyle O'Brien & O'Brien, 2002, p. 29)

A small body of research indicated that person-centered planning is associated with various positive outcomes for individuals (e.g., increased inclusion, relationships, life satisfaction) (Holburn, Jacobson, Schwartz, Flory, & Vietze, 2004; Malette, 2002). There is also debate as to the applicability of research to a concept such as person-centered planning (Evans, 2002; Halle & Lowrey, 2002; Holburn, 2002a, 2002b; O'Brien, 2002).

WHEN SUPPORT COMES TO A PERSON: FOCUS ON HOME, PERSONAL IDENTITY, AND BELONGING

Supported living initially was conceived of as a system of supports that changed as a person changed (Lakin et al., 1994; O'Brien, 1993). Individuals who gained certain competencies might require less support or they could remain where they were with less support. Support could be adjusted to the person's need without moving to a different place (e.g., from a group home to supported living). The problem lies in how this approach has often been applied, however. People have been required to move to a place that is not their own and live with people they did not choose in order to receive supports, rather than being supported in their own homes, neighborhoods, and communities.

Individualized and person-centered supports emphasize fitting supports into the places where a person chooses to spend his or her time and within the relationships that person develops with others. In short, the supports come to the person, rather than the older system whereby people had to move to a place where supports were provided.

Challenges and Concerns

The flawed method in which services are developed is a fundamental problem in the service systems for people with disabilities, especially those with more severe disabilities. People are assumed to be in need and be ready and willing to accept services created for them without their direct and personal input. Services are created for people but rarely with people. It is astonishing to realize how accepting systems have become of services that end up supporting people with disabilities in lives that are so different from those of other Americans. Person-centered and individualized supports seamlessly weave supports into the fabric of a life. Supports fit themselves to a life as opposed to life being altered or otherwise made different by the acceptance of services.

People with disabilities and their families and allies dream based on the limitations of a service system. Systems work from a premise that people with disabilities are flawed and need someone competent to make decisions, removing the essence of self-identity (i.e., the ability to shape one's life through personal choices). Person-centered and individualized supports seek to make the visions of people with disabilities the driving factor in building supports into individual lives, including their vision of home as the cornerstone of community living and their vision of a meaningful identity.

Home as the Cornerstone

Where do you live? If you are like most in a community, then you live in a home of your own. You chose the place where this home is located, and you also chose the people who share that home with you. How important is that home to you? Would it be as important if the location were chosen for you and you had housemates you did not know assigned to live with you? This is the reality for the majority of people with intellectual disability who participate in community living.

Most Americans live in a home of their own. They choose where home is in order to be close to friends and family, work, or school. The only limits on that choice are the financial ones we all deal with in our lives. We strive to find and keep a place of our own, a place that becomes sacred in our lives, the place where our children learn their most important lessons and we eat most of our meals, celebrate and create personal traditions, heal from illness, and touch the hearts of our family and loved ones. This place becomes central to our lives and is inseparable from our truest self-identities.

Home is a place of hospitality where friends and family visit, meals are prepared, stories are told, and dreams are conceived and shared (Bachelard, 1994). Some acquaintances visit our homes and become our friends. We dream of our futures in this place, maybe pray for loved ones lost. What completes this place as a home are the people we invite to share it with us. We make people feel welcome. This makes the place home. Consider the value of home described by Emerson, Jones, Romer, and Romer.

> What we have learned is to think of home as a set of relationships deeply rooted in a place. This place consists of walls that both include certain people and possessions and exclude, temporarily or permanently, certain other people or things. The physical location of this place and how it appears are important aspects but nothing defines home like the sense of self it provides us. We define who comes into our home, how long they stay and what they do while they are there. It is the one place where we have the most influence over our lives. We often refer to this as being the keeper of the threshold. This, to us, is the central defining point of home. From this flow other, important aspects: the sense of refuge and renewal provided by home; the ability to relax and be ourselves more completely than anywhere else; the ability to engage in intimate relationships with others of our choice; the simple opportunity to be alone and cherish our privacy; and, the ability, by our invitation to offer hospitality to others in our home. (2007)

The new narrative of community living has to have the concept of home and a life of belonging to that place and the people with whom we share it as envisioned by the person seeking supports. Person-centered supports are ideally suited to assist people to achieve their dreams of a home and a life of belonging.

Personal Identity and Belonging

Mount (1987, 1992), O'Brien (1987), and O'Brien and Lyle O'Brien (2000) were among the first to offer another way to achieve the dream of home. Their early work (i.e., personal futures planning) offered the collected wisdom of people thinking about supports based on a coherent vision of how a person with disabilities wants to live. This approach contrasted with the version of services that structured the lives of people with disabilities based on expert opinions with no place for a person's individual statement of a desirable future. Person-centered and individualized supports meant discovering the gifts and talents of people with disabilities and finding people and places where those personal gifts would be valued and welcomed. This approach is motivated by the belief that everyone has gifts to offer and communities are places where everyone's gifts are needed.

Whereas the traditional service system emphasizes independence and skill development, person-centered supports are associated with a different set of outcomes, including making choices about all aspects of one's life; developing a rich and extensive set of personal relationships based on mutual interest and commitments, not on the fact that one person is paid to be in support of the other; becoming a valued citizen who shares as an equal in the public life of a community; and being afforded dignity and respect from fellow citizens (O'Brien, Pearpoint, & Kahn, 2009). Choices are defining elements in a self-identity (e.g., where to live and with whom, what type of work/career to pursue, whom to invite in to social network, where to spend time in the community). Self-identity is not limited to one of client in a service system, but rather one based on an individual's purpose in life. Discerning the choices of people with severe disabilities means carefully and deeply listening. It also means listening by observing the preferences of people who communicate nonsymbolically. Building service systems based on preconceived and categorical ideas about people with disabilities has proven ineffective if the intent is to support people in valued roles as citizens, neighbors, co-workers, and friends. Working from a personal vision underscores an individual's value by creating supports in direct service to those personal visions.

ESSENTIAL ORGANIZATIONAL COMMITMENTS FOR PERSON-CENTERED SUPPORTS IN COMMUNITY LIVING

An increasing number of agencies are making efforts to develop truly individualized, person-centered supports (Walker, 2012). Kendrick (2009) described the emergence of person-centered and individualized home and community supports in eight agencies in the United States and Ireland, which was corroborated by an independent analysis of these agencies by Broderick (2007). This section is based on those analyses plus our extensive experience working in and with agencies in the United States that are doing person-centered work.

Kendrick (2009) found that not one of the eight agencies he studied had any form of special project funding or exceptions from current rules and regulations to do person-centered work. Every one of the eight agencies found ways to make person-centered supports available in their communities under the same conditions and circumstances existing for all community services. This finding is affirming and at the same time frustrating. How do we begin to understand why certain agencies were able to transform themselves while the vast majority continues to provide services with less freedom to make critical choices?

Kendrick summarized agencies' commitments thusly, "So, for those agencies, the concern was not whether a response was individualized, but rather whether this response was relevant, effective, and beneficial" (2009, p. 50). The fundamental commitment was to place the entire agency at the disposal of individuals' dreams for their lives. Underlying that one commitment, however, lies continuity in how agencies align themselves with values and practices that result in person-centered supports. Figure 15.1 represents one way of categorizing the commitments of person-centered agencies, which are described next.

Basic Agency Values

All other commitments start and flow from the basic agency commitment to social justice, equality, and fidelity. The agencies that offer person-centered supports fully embrace the moral position set forth by Blatt that "each of these individuals is equally human" (1969, p. 47). Everyone who seeks support from a person-centered agency is respected as an equal member of a community—a member with just as much to offer as anyone working in the agency or living in a local community. This commitment forms the base from which the other sides of Figure 15.1 emerge.

Commitment to the Person Seeking Support

These agencies listen to people and help them reach the goals that they want for their lives (Kendrick, 2009). They judge their effectiveness based on how well this

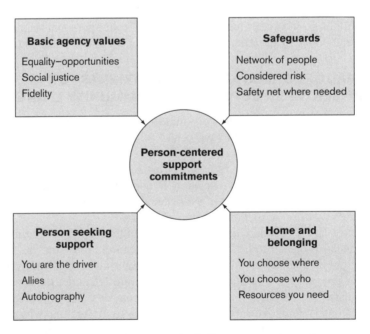

Figure 15.1. Organizational values associated with person-centered supports.

goal is accomplished, which is determined by the person for whom they organize supports. Listening and understanding take a lifetime. Listening consists of an ongoing dialogue that is referenced in Figure 15.1 as an autobiography—a personal story that does not end until the end of that person's life and may have a continued influence over others. Listening only matters when action is based on that listening, represented by the commitments to people as the director of their lives and the agency as a valued ally in seeking the fulfillment in that life.

Commitment to Home and a Sense of Belonging

Supported living emerged as an alternative to residential services and initially was conceived to provide a safe, secure home to people with disabilities (O'Brien, 1993). Common usage through the intervening years, however, has defined supported living as the types of residential services for which it was intended to be an alternative. It is still considered a defining characteristic of person-centered supports to adhere to the outcome of people living in homes of their choosing, living with whom they choose, and living in the place they choose. This choice also extends to decisions about who supports a person and when and how those supports are provided.

Agencies doing person-centered work recognize that committing to following people's choices often creates conflict and confusion. Living with the confusion and ambiguity of listening to choices is at the heart of person-centered work. Seeking harmony among all of the possible choices and the repercussions of other choices is the ultimate goal of a well-lived life. This goal requires ongoing commitment to a series of negotiations between people with disabilities and their support workers. The negotiation entails listening and then reflecting back on the choices and wondering about and asking questions with respect to possible outcomes of a choice and its alternatives.

Commitment to Safeguards

A disregard for guarding against unpleasant or damaging events can ruin the good efforts toward a life well lived. Negative events cannot be completely eliminated, but vigilance with regard to safeguards is a crucial element in ensuring against negative events. Relationships with others are important in mitigating against physical illness and ensuring mental and emotional well-being and a sense of security (Sarason, Sarason, & Pierce, 1990). Agencies doing person-centered work recognize the crucial role of having enough of the right people in an individual's life to achieve this sense of belonging. Doing so marks an area of significant overlap in agencies' commitments—the commitment to supporting people to achieve a sense of belonging also is a major element in supporting people to have adequate safeguards in their lives.

What constitutes safeguards for one person is an abridgement in the freedom of another person. Knowing what makes for an acceptable safeguard means understanding the relationship between risk and need. How much risk is acceptable to achieve what outcome? Is the risk reasonable with respect to the need met by taking the risk? Residential agencies typically err on the side of limiting risk and trading a person's needs for their presumed safety. Person-centered work recognizes the need to balance the consideration of risk with the need to define one's life through choices, some of which may carry the potential for negative outcomes.

For example, Harley is in his 40s and lives in a home of his own without any daily presence in his home. His daily support providers spend time with him throughout the day, but Harley did not want anyone in his house overnight—staff or housemate. This is a perfectly reasonable desire. Most residential agencies, however, would view Harley as a man with a severe intellectual disability and come to the conclusion that he would not be safe at home overnight without someone being physically present. How does an agency provide for a margin of safety while still respecting Harley's desire to live alone? Harley's agency developed several strategies to accomplish this. They helped Harley to ask his apartment complex managers (with whom he already had a friendly relationship) if Harley's smoke detectors and fire alarms could be wired to also sound inside the manager's apartment to ensure he could exit if needed; they and Harley also installed a door sensor to alert if the door was opened in the night and had it wired into the manager's apartment; Harley and his support providers devised a way for him to know when it was bedtime by setting the sleep alarm on his television—Harley goes to bed when the television goes off (at 11:00 p.m.). These were all simple devices employed by Harley's agency to respect his desire for privacy while also addressing safeguards. Harley's alarms have gone off twice in the 9 years he has lived in his apartment, and they were both system malfunctions.

The commitments made by an agency doing person-centered work to human rights, personal direction, home and belonging, and safety are the essence of continuity; the daily strategies employed to fulfill these commitments are how person-centered work is done. Any attempt to replicate person-centered work in more agencies without a primary focus on these commitments runs the risk of sounding good on paper but lacking in the strong value foundation required for the work to be done.

RECOMMENDED STRATEGIES TO PROMOTE PERSON-CENTERED SUPPORTS

Organizational provision of person-centered supports is not simply offering a specific program or specific types of person-centered services. Some organizations fall into the trap of attempting to use person-centered planning and doing so in routinized and bureaucratic ways (Lyle O'Brien, O'Brien, & Mount, 1997). Rather, person-centered supports require an entire organizational culture that is person-centered (O'Brien, 2008, 2010; O'Brien & Lyle O'Brien, 1994b). O'Brien and Lyle O'Brien described a person-centered organizational culture as one that fosters the abilities of "forming and sustaining relationships, listening and looking and thinking carefully, and inventing solutions to everyday problems" (p. 140). It is essential that planning entail deep listening and is undertaken without preconceived notions in mind (Fratangelo, Olney, & Lehr, 2001). Finally, it is critical to draw in community members so that planning is not only done with those paid to organize and/or provide daily support (Scott, Hasbury, & Wykowski, 2010).

Person-centered supports are not made up of a series of discrete tasks to be performed but rather are defined by the relationships among those seeking support, their allies, those working in organizations coordinating supports, and members of the local communities in which supports are offered. Attempting to break person-centered supports down into their constituent parts is likely to yield unsatisfactory results.

Person-centered supports are currently far from common in service systems. They are mostly found in smaller organizations. In addition to being somewhat scarce, person-centered supports are still frequently characterized as a series of tasks to be performed rather then relationships to be developed and nurtured. Therefore, it is unwise to rush too quickly to questions of technical assistance to teach person-centered supports and how to disseminate the components to more organizations. Both of these actions will at some point be laudable objectives. A more thorough and respectful approach, however, should be designed to achieve a better and fuller understanding of how people with disabilities and organizations work together in relationship. What conditions are most associated with developing these relationships? How do organizations best align themselves to support the development of these relationships? How do relationships among the members of an organization adapt to being in a person-centered milieu? How is management affected by a commitment to person-centered work?

Doing person-centered work is deeply rooted in specific knowledge of a person's dreams and how relationships with that person affect those dreams. This local knowledge is the autobiography of a person. Berry described local knowledge thusly, "Local knowledge, however, is difficult to control, since it is by definition dispersed and relatively autonomous. Nor can it be appropriated from without; [it] can be learned only from inside the community" (2011, p. 52).

The key to understanding person-centered supports is to know the concept in its entirety from within the relationships formed between people seeking support and those offering it on a day-to-day basis. Do not become lost in a futile, reductionist search for its essential parts. Appreciative inquiry is one method that seems to be particularly well suited for pursuing an understanding of person centered supports (Whitney & Trosten-Bloom, 2010).

Appreciative Inquiry

Appreciative inquiry was originally designed as a tool to study organizational development and is based on four steps—discovery, dream, design, and destiny. Discovery describes the best of what already is, focuses inquiry on the strengths of person-centered supports at their best, and describes current best practice. The discovery step focuses inquiry on people receiving supports, those who deliver those daily supports, and the family and allies of the person receiving support. Appreciative inquiry asks those interviewed to describe times when supports were at their very best in helping a person achieve highly valued outcomes.

The second step asks those interviewed to dream about a better future or imagine what could be in their lives. This step allows participants to describe crucial elements that would enhance the utilization of person-centered supports. The second step focuses inquiry with the same people in step one, but also includes those people whose responsibility includes managing an agency. The dream step identifies those practices that would strengthen person-centered supports by incorporating additional relationships both from within an agency and from its community.

Design describes what should be based on the results from the first two steps. This step identifies the most critical aspects related to expanding the availability of person-centered supports. The focus on inquiry begins to shift to include the perspectives of people charged with the oversight of agencies offering community living services, including state agency managers and federal agency staff such as the Center for Medicare & Medicaid Services and the Administration on Developmental Disabilities.

Finally, destiny implements the design from the third step. Implementation is guided by all of the participants contributing to the information gathered in the first three steps. This step articulates those strategies found to be most effective in making person-centered supports a viable option for people seeking greater autonomy in directing their supports to achieve a home of their own.

Positive Change Consortium

The process previously described constitutes an appreciative inquiry group referred to as a positive change consortium. (Whitney & Trosten-Bloom, 2010). Table 15.1 summarizes sample questions in appreciative inquiry used in the four steps of inquiry. The membership of the positive change consortium consists of 1) two to three people supported by each of the 8–10 agencies currently providing person-centered supports, 2) the people providing direct, daily supports to those people from the agencies, 3) family members and allies of the person receiving supports, 4) managers of the agencies, 5) community representatives from the communities where the agencies offer supports, 6) representatives from the state agencies responsible for the management and oversight of the agencies, 7) representatives of the federal agencies responsible for funding and/or monitoring service delivery and evaluation, and 8) organizations such as the National Association of State Directors of Developmental Disabilities Services, SABE, and TASH. This group would represent a wide variety of organizations and daily person-centered support practices as well as other organizations with a vested interest in supports for people with disabilities.

Engaging these individuals and organizations in appreciative inquiry would provide information about how people with disabilities and organizations engage in relationships to foster person-centered supports and how those supports are designed by organizations in collaboration with people with disabilities and their allies. This engagement would lead to a better understanding of how individual agencies align themselves with the values underlying person-centered supports and how those values influence the basis of relationship with people seeking supports (Bradley, Smith, Taub, & Heaviland, 2002; Smull, Bourne, & Sanderson, 2009). Including state and federal managers and advocacy organizations further explains how best to partner with governmental agencies to advance person-centered supports while maintaining the integrity of the work. Inquiry into person-centered supports with these individuals and groups reveals major strategies that would benefit people with disabilities and foster the development of new opportunities to disseminate person-centered supports.

The process of appreciative inquiry would yield a rich source of information that would touch on topics integral to person-centered supports at both the organizational and systems levels. Topics at the organizational level include the following.

- Implementing strategies that promote maximum control and choice for people who receive support

- Devoting organizational resources to promoting relationships and community connections

- Incorporating authentic person-centered planning

- Aligning organizational values and practice

Table 15.1. Appreciative inquiry questions on person-centered supports

Appreciative inquiry steps	Questions	Focal group(s)	Purpose
Discovery (what is now)	Could you tell me a story from your experience that best illustrates person-centered supports working at their best? Could you describe a time and situation in which you saw person-centered supports being done really well? What could your agency do to more effectively support the practice of person-centered supports?	People using person-centered supports Daily support providers Family members and allies of person using supports	Articulation through collected stories of the current best practice in person-centered supports
Dream (what could be)	If you could change anything about how person-centered supports are provided on a daily basis and toward a future of possibilities, what would that look like? What would you include as the obligations and responsibilities of people and agencies offering person-centered supports?	Same as Step 1	What would improve and expand the effectiveness of person-centered supports?
Design (what should be)	What other practices and resources beyond the daily delivery of person-centered supports would enhance the availability and effectiveness of person-centered supports? How could those additional resources and practices be integrated into what was learned from information gathered in Steps 1 and 2?	Same as Steps 1 and 2 Managers of agencies practicing person-centered supports Members of the community where people using person-centered supports live	Determine what elements of person-centered supports, agency practices, and community resources could be incorporated into enhancing the effectiveness and availability of person-centered supports, based on information gathered in Steps 1 and 2.
Destiny (what will be)	Could you describe a time when state, federal, and/or local community policies or practices positively affected access to and/or valuable outcomes in person-centered supports? How could those additional elements be best deployed to offer access to the process and outcomes of person-centered supports as described in Steps 1 and 2?	Same as Steps 1, 2, and 3 State and federal disability system managers	Guide, modify, and evaluate the practices developed and implemented in Step 3.

- Developing organizational mentoring strategies

- Promoting values-based leadership working to align values and practice

- Fostering flexible, streamlined budget mechanisms

- Maximizing resources and incentives that support organizational transformation as well as the creation of new organizations

- Developing partnerships and collaboration across organizations to address systems barriers and gaps to community living

CONCLUSION

Person-centered work focuses on who a person is and the life that person chooses to live. Such a statement may seem an insufficient or simplistic foundation on which to build a system of supports. Yet, living a life of personal satisfaction encompasses a great deal—holding oneself in high esteem; having confidence in one's abilities, gifts, talents, and uniqueness; loving and forgiving oneself and others; carrying compassion, understanding, and tolerance for others who share our world; knowing that one has a unique place in the world; being fully present with those one loves and is loved by; holding true to one's values and standing up for those values and deepest beliefs even when it may not be easy. The opportunity to live a personally satisfying life is available when an agency commits to the people for whom it organizes supports.

There is no guarantee of success. Lives are unpredictable, sometimes subject to forces beyond our control. Sometimes the best and only option is to steadfastly renew our commitment to stand beside one another. Making a commitment to individuals' freedom in directing their own lives is the source of the creativity, flexibility, and sensitivity that is essential to person-centered supports.

Questions for Study and Reflection

1. What tells you that institutional practices have crept into community places?

2. What is the difference between living in a community place and having a home of your own?

3. How do appreciative inquiry and person-centered planning help organize supports for people that honor the reality of change and fluidity in the many relationships that inform the life of people with disabilities, from the person and his or her allies to state and federal agencies?

4. How is continual making or renewing of commitments to people important in designing person-centered supports as opposed to counting outcomes or designing models that are one size fits all?

5. Can models of service delivery integrate multiple perspectives suggested in an appreciative inquiry approach?

 6. How does the human need for simplicity and certainty get in the way of organizing person-centered supports?

 7. How is appreciative inquiry different from problem identification and remediation?

 8. What are the assumptions about the value of people with disabilities, where they should live, and how they should be treated in the institutions of the past? When institutional practices are carried into community places, what assumptions lend themselves to justification of such practices?

9. How does storytelling in appreciative inquiry and person-centered planning shift assumptions about service delivery?

RESOURCES

Web Sites of Selected Agencies Offering Person-Centered Supports

Avenues Supported Living Services *http://www.avenuessls.org*

Community Housing Options: Integrated Community, Employment, and Social Services *http://www.choicess.com*

Community Vision *http://www.cvision.org*

Creative Support Alternatives *http://www.creativesupport.org*

Jay Nolan Community Services *http://www.jaynolan.org*

KFI, Inc. *http://www.kfimaine.org*

Neighbours, Inc. *http://www.neighbours-inc.com*

Onondaga Community Living *http://www.oclinc.org*

Spectrum Society for Community Living *http://www.spectrumsociety.org*

Total Living Concept *http://www.totallivingconcept.org*

Web Sites for Self-Advocacy Organizations

Autistic Self Advocacy Network *http://www.autisticadvocacy.org*

Self Advocates Becoming Empowered *http://www.sabeusa.org*

Self Advocates in Leadership *http://www.sailcoalition.org*

Community Inclusion Web Sites

Association of University Centers on Disabilities *http://www.aucd.org*

The Center on Human Policy *http://thechp.syr.edu*

REFERENCES

Americans with Disabilities Act (ADA) of 1990, PL 101-336, 42 U.S.C. §§ 12101 *et seq.*

Bachelard, G. (1994). *The poetics of space.* Boston, MA: Beacon Press.

Berry, W. (2011). *The poetry of William Carlos Williams of Rutherford.* Berkeley, CA: Counterpoint.

Blatt, B. (1969). Purgatory. In R. Kugel & W. Wolfsenberger (Eds.), *Changing patterns in residential services for the mentally retarded* (pp. 34–49). Washington, DC: President's Committee on Mental Retardation.

Blatt, B., & Kaplan, F. (1966). *Christmas in purgatory: A photographic essay on mental retardation.* Boston, MA: Allyn & Bacon.

Bogdan, R., & Taylor, S.J. (1987). Conclusion: The next wave. In S.J. Taylor, D. Biklen, & J. Knoll (Eds.), *Community integration for people with severe disabilities* (pp. 209–220). New York, NY: Teachers College Press.

Bradley, V. (1994). Evolution of a new service paradigm. In V.J. Bradley, J.W. Ashbaugh, & B.C. Blaney (Eds.), *Creating individual supports for people with developmental disabilities: A mandate for change at many levels* (pp. 11–32). Baltimore, MD: Paul H. Brookes Publishing Co.

Bradley, V.J., Ashbaugh, J.W., & Blaney, B.C. (1994). *Creating individual supports for people with developmental disabilities: A mandate for change at many levels.* Baltimore, MD: Paul H. Brookes Publishing Co.

Bradley, V.J., Smith, G., Taub, S., & Heaviland, M. (2002). *Person-centered supports: How do states make them work?* Boston, MA: Human Services Research Institute in collaboration with the National Association of State Directors of Developmental Disabilities Services and the Research and Training Center on Community Living, Institute on Community Integration, University of Minnesota.

Broderick, B. (2007). *Report on person-centered event.* Brussels, Belgium: The Generalate of the Sisters of Charity of Jesus and Mary.

Brown, L. (1991). Who are they and what do they want? An essay on TASH. In L.H. Meyer, C.A. Peck, & L. Brown (Eds.), *Critical issues in the lives of people with severe disabilities.* Baltimore, MD: Paul H. Brookes Publishing Co.

Emerson, D., Jones, B., Romer, L.T., & Romer, M.A. (2007). A place of our own. *TASH Connections, 12*(11/12).

Evans, I.M. (2002). Trying to make apple pie an independent variable. Commentary on "How science can evaluate and enhance person-centered planning." *Research and Practice for Persons with Severe Disabilities, 27,* 265–267.

Fratangelo, P., Olney, M., & Lehr, S. (2001). *One person at a time: How one agency changed from group to individualized services for people with disabilities.* St. Augustine, FL: Training Resource Network.

Halle, J.W., & Lowrey, K.A. (2002). Can person-centered planning be empirically analyzed to the satisfaction of all stakeholders? *Research and Practice for Persons with Severe Disabilities, 27,* 268–271.

Holburn, S. (2002a). How science can evaluate and enhance person-centered planning. *Research and Practice for Persons with Severe Disabilities, 27,* 250–260.

Holburn, S. (2002b). Person-centered planning must evolve: Rejoinder to O'Brien, Evans, Halle, & Lowrey. *Research and Practice for Persons with Severe Disabilities, 27,* 272–275.

Holburn, S., Jacobson, J.W., Schwartz, A.A., Flory, M.J., & Vietze, P.M. (2004). The Willowbrook Futures Project: A longitudinal analysis of person-centered planning. *American Journal on Mental Retardation, 109,* 63–76.

Horner, R.H., Stoner, S., & Ferguson, D.L. (1988). *An activity-based analysis of deinstitutionalization: The effects of community re-entry on the lives of residents leaving Oregon's Fairview Training Center.* Eugene: University of Oregon,

Specialized Training Program, Center on Human Development.

Howe, J., Horner, R.H., & Newton, J.S. (1998). Comparison of supported living and traditional residential services in the state of Oregon. *Mental Retardation, 36,* 1–11.

Kendrick, M.J. (2009). Some lessons concerning agency transformation towards personalized services. *International Journal of Leadership in Public Services, 5,* 47–54.

Klein, J. (1992). Get me the hell out of here: Supporting people with disabilities to live in their own homes. In J. Nisbet (Ed.), *Natural supports in school, at work, and in the community for people with severe disabilities* (pp. 277–339). Baltimore, MD: Paul H. Brookes Publishing Co.

Lakin, K.C., & Bruininks, R.H. (Eds.). (1985). *Strategies for achieving community integration of developmentally disabled citizens.* Baltimore, MD: Paul H. Brookes Publishing Co.

Lakin, K.C., Hayden, M.F., & Abery, B.H. (1994). An overview of the community living concept. In M.F. Hayden & B.H. Abery (Eds.), *Challenges for a service system in transition: Ensuring quality community experiences for persons with developmental disabilities* (pp. 3–22). Baltimore, MD: Paul H. Brookes Publishing Co.

Lakin, K.C., & Stancliffe, R.J. (2007). Residential supports for persons with intellectual and developmental disabilities. *Mental Retardation and Developmental Disabilities Research Reviews, 13,* 151–159.

Lakin, K.C., Taub, S., Doljanac, R., et al. (2006). *Self-determination among Medicaid ICF/MR and HCBS recipients in six states.* Minneapolis: University of Minnesota, Research and Training Center on Community Living.

Larson, S.A., Ryan, A., Salmi, P., Smith, D., & Wuorio, A. (2012). *Residential services for persons with developmental disabilities: Status and trends through 2010.* Minneapolis: University of Minnesota, Research and Training Center on Community Living, Institute on Community Integration.

Lyle O'Brien, C., & O'Brien, J. (2002). The origins of person-centered planning: A community of practice perspective. In J. O'Brien & C. Lyle O'Brien (Eds.), *Implementing person-centered planning: Voices of experience* (pp. 25–58). Toronto, Canada: Inclusion Press.

Lyle O'Brien, C., O'Brien, J., & Mount, B. (1997). Person-centered planning has arrived...or has it? *Mental Retardation, 35,* 480–484.

Malette, P. (2002). Lifestyle quality and person-centered support: Jeff, Janet, Stephanie, and the Microboard Project. In S. Holburn & P.M. Vietze (Eds.), *Person-centered planning: Research, practice, and future directions* (pp. 291–314). Baltimore, MD: Paul H. Brookes Publishing Co.

Mount, B. (1987). *Creating futures together: A workbook for people interested in creating desirable futures for people with handicaps.* Atlanta: Georgia Advocacy Office.

Mount, B. (1992). *Person-centered planning: A sourcebook of values, ideas, and methods to encourage person-centered development.* New York, NY: Graphic Futures.

Mount, B., O'Brien, J., & Lyle O'Brien, C. (2002). *Increasing the chances for deeper change through person-centered planning.* Lithonia, GA: Responsive Systems Associates.

O'Brien, J. (1987). A guide to lifestyle planning: Using the activity catalog to integrate services and natural supports systems. In B. Wilcox & G.T. Bellamy (Eds.), *A comprehensive guide to the activities catalog: An alternative curriculum for youth and adults with severe disabilities* (pp. 175–190). Baltimore, MD: Paul H. Brookes Publishing Co.

O'Brien, J. (1993). *Supported living: What's the difference?* Lithonia, GA: Responsive Systems Associates.

O'Brien, J. (1994). Down stairs that are never your own. *Mental Retardation, 32,* 1–6.

O'Brien, J. (2002). Person-centered planning as a contributing factor in organizational and social change. *Research and Practice for Persons with Severe Disabilities, 27,* 261–264.

O'Brien, J. (2008). *NYSACRA Learning Institute on Innovation in Individualized Supports: A learning history: Phase 1.* Albany: New York State Association of Community and Residential Agencies.

O'Brien, J. (2010). *NYSACRA Learning Institute on Innovation in Individualized Supports: A learning history: Part II.* Albany: New York State Association of Community and Residential Agencies.

O'Brien, J., & Lyle O'Brien, C. (1994a). *Assistance with integrity: A search for accountability and the lives of people with developmental disabilities.* Lithonia, GA: Responsive Systems Associates.

O'Brien, J., & Lyle O'Brien, C. (1994b). More than just a new address: Images of organization for supported living agencies. In V.J. Bradley, J.W. Ashbaugh, & B.C. Blaney (Eds.), *Creating individual supports for people with developmental disabilities: A mandate for change at many levels* (pp. 109–140). Baltimore, MD: Paul H. Brookes Publishing Co.

O'Brien, J., & Lyle O'Brien, C. (Eds.). (1998). *A little book about person-centered planning.* Toronto, Canada: Inclusion Press.

O'Brien, J., & Lyle O'Brien, C. (2000). *The origins of person-centered planning: A community of practice perspective.* Lithonia, GA: Responsive Systems Associates.

O'Brien, J., & Mount, B. (1991). Telling new stories: The search for capacity among people with severe handicaps. In L.H. Meyer, C.A. Peck, & L. Brown (Eds.), *Critical issues in the lives of people with severe disabilities* (pp. 89–92). Baltimore, MD: Paul H. Brookes Publishing Co.

O'Brien, J., Pearpoint, J., & Kahn, L. (2009). *The PATH and MAPS handbook: Person-centered ways to build community.* Toronto, Canada: Inclusion Press.

Olmstead vs. L.C., United States Supreme Court (1999).

Prouty, R.W., Smith, G., & Lakin, K.C. (Eds.). (2005). *Residential services for people with developmental disabilities: Status and trends through 2003.* Minneapolis: University of Minnesota, Institute on Community Integration.

Racino, J.A., Walker, P., O'Connor, S., & Taylor, S.J. (Eds.). (1993). *Housing, support, and community: Choices and strategies for adults with disabilities.* Baltimore, MD: Paul H. Brookes Publishing Co.

Rivera, G. (1972). *Willowbrook: A report on how it is and why it doesn't have to be that way.* New York, NY: Vintage.

Sarason, B.R., Sarason, I.G., & Pierce, G.R. (Eds.). (1990). *Social support: An interactional view.* New York, NY: Wiley.

Scott, P., Hasbury, D., & Wykowski, J. (2010). *Maryland's community of practice.* Highland Park, NJ: Neighbours International.

Self Advocates Becoming Empowered. (1995, April). *Position statement on closing institutions.* Kansas City, MO: Author.

Sheerenberger, R.C. *A history of mental retardation: A quarter century of promise.* Baltimore, MD: Paul H. Brookes Publishing Co.

Smith, D., Lakin, K.C., Larson, S.H., & Salmi, P. (2011). Changes in residential arrangements of persons with intellectual and developmental disabilities in the decade following the Olmstead Decision of 1999. *Intellectual and Developmental Disabilities, 49,* 53–56.

Smull, M. (2002). After the plan. In J. O'Brien & C. Lyle O'Brien (Eds.), *A little book about person-centered planning* (pp. 75–81). Toronto, Canada: Inclusion Press.

Smull, M., & Bellamy, G. (1991). Community services for adults with disabilities: Policy challenges in the emerging support paradigm. In L.H. Meyer, C.A. Peck, & L. Brown (Eds.), *Critical issues in the lives of people with severe disabilities* (pp. 527–536). Baltimore, MD: Paul H. Brookes Publishing Co.

Smull, M.W., Bourne, M.L., & Sanderson, H. (2009). *Becoming a person-centered system.* Washington, DC: Department of Health and Human Services, Centers for Medicare & Medicaid Services.

Social Security Amendments of 1965, PL 89-97, 42 U.S.C. §§ 401 *et seq.*

Stancliffe, R.J., Abery, B.H., & Smith, J. (2000). Personal control and the ecology of community living settings: Beyond living unit size and type. *American Journal on Mental Retardation, 105,* 431–454.

TASH. (2000a, July). *TASH resolution on life in the community.* Washington, DC: Author.

TASH. (2000b, July). *TASH resolution on supports in the community.* Washington, DC: Author.

TASH. (2011, Sept.). *TASH resolution on choice and community.* Washington, DC: Author.

Taylor, S.J. (1988). Caught in the continuum: A critical analysis of the principle of the least restrictive environment. *Journal of The Association for Persons with Severe Handicaps, 13,* 41–53.

Taylor, S.J., Biklen, D., & Knoll, J. (Eds.). (1987). *Community integration for people with severe disabilities.* New York, NY: Teachers College Press.

Walker, P. (2012). Strategies for organizational change from group homes to individualized supports. *Intellectual and Developmental Disabilities, 50,* 403–414.

Whitney, D., & Trosten-Bloom, A. (2010). *The power of appreciative inquiry: A practical guide to positive change* (2nd ed.). San Francisco, CA: Berrett-Koehler Publishers.

Wolfensberger, W. (1967). *The origin and nature of our institutional models.* Syracuse, NY: Human Policy Press.

Wolfensberger, W. (1971). *The principle of normalization in human services.* Toronto, Canada: G. Allan Roeher Institute.

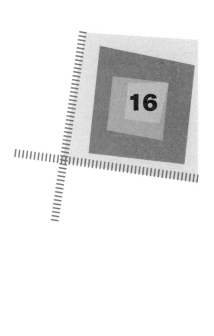

16

Serving an
Elderly Population

Christine Bigby, Philip McCallion, and Mary McCarron

ew people with intellectual and developmental disabilities survived past their
early 20s at the beginning of the 20th century. The gap between these individuals' life span and population norms has been progressively reduced since that
time, due primarily to improved health care and the effect of deinstitutionalization
(Patja, Iivanainen, Vesala, Oksanen, & Ruoppila, 2000). For example, the life span
of people with Down syndrome more than tripled from an average of 15 years in
1960 to 50 years in 1995 (Haveman, 2004). Aging is no longer a new phenomenon
for the field of severe disabilities. Since the mid-1980s, significantly improved life
expectancy has been evident, and researchers have consequently flagged the need
to reconfigure service systems to take into account the projected increase in numbers, changing needs, and social circumstances of middle-age and older people with
intellectual and developmental disabilities (Janicki & Wisniewski, 1985; McCarron
& Lawlor, 2003; Moss, 1993). Major challenges have been the translation of first
principles, such as normalization, rights and inclusion into provision of services, and
finding ways to bridge aging, long-term care, and intellectual and developmental
disability service systems to accommodate a changing balance between the need
for support and care as health issues begin to overshadow support for continued
development as people age.

Although considerable research has been conducted since the 1980s with
respect to experiences of aging, the adaptation of policy and service systems has
lagged behind (Bigby, 2010). This chapter provides an overview of current knowledge about the life circumstances of people with intellectual and developmental
disabilities who are aging. We consider the key issues that confront service systems
and debates about the policies and programs to deliver the types of support and

health care necessary to ensure a quality of life comparable to that of other older people. The issues of retirement and support for people with dementia will be used to exemplify some of these debates and the challenges posed to both disability and mainstream service systems in adapting to older people with intellectual and developmental disabilities. Drawing on the authors' contemporary research from Australia, Ireland, and the United States, some of the contrasting policy responses to these challenges will be exemplified, illustrating the varying and often context-specific strategies required to interpret and implement overarching principles.

OVERVIEW: CHARACTERISTICS OF OLDER PEOPLE WITH INTELLECTUAL AND DEVELOPMENTAL DISABILITIES

Although people with mild intellectual and developmental disabilities now have a life expectancy comparable with that of the general population, differences still exist for those with more extensive support needs or specific genetic syndromes. For example, people in Australia who have mild, moderate, and severe levels of disability can expect to live for 74.0, 67.6, and 58.6 years, respectively, compared with a population median of 78.6 years (Bittles et al., 2002). Increases in the population of older people with intellectual and developmental disabilities that have occurred since the 1980s will continue as improved life expectancy combines with the demographic of the aging baby boom generation. The number of people in Australia who are older than 60 years with intellectual and developmental disabilities known to the State of Victoria's disability system almost doubled from 321 (3%) in 1982 to 559 (4%) in 1990 and had increased to 1,327 (6.7%) by 2000 (Bigby, Fyffe, Balandin, Gordon, & McCubbery, 2001). Similar growth is expected in the United States, although on a different scale. Factor, Heller, and Janicki (2012) estimated that between 2010 and 2030 the number of people older than 60 years with intellectual and developmental disabilities will almost double from 850,6000 to 1.4 million. The National Intellectual Disability Database in Ireland documented a 60% growth from 1996 to 2010 for those older than 55 years (Kelly & Kelly, 2011). Nevertheless, people with intellectual and developmental disabilities will remain a very small proportion of all older people (between 0.13% and 0.4%; Bigby, 2004).

People aging with intellectual and developmental disabilities represent a diverse group, some of whom have distinctive patterns of aging. Some experience age-related health conditions relatively early. For example, people with Down syndrome have higher prevalence and earlier onset of age-related sensory and musculoskeletal disorders, resulting in additional disability (Bittles, Bower, Hussain, & Glasson, 2007; Holland, Hon, Huppert, & Stevens, 2000). They also have an exceptional risk of developing dementia in the sixth decade (Torr, Strydom, Patti, & Jokinen, 2010). It is estimated these individuals experience dementia at rates of 2% between 30–39 years, 9.4% between 40–49 years, 36.1% between 50–59 years, and 54.5% between 60–69 years (Prasher, 1995). These rates compare with estimated rates of 6% at age 65 to more than 50% for those age 85 years and older in the general population (Alzheimer's Association, 2012).

Some people will experience additional health needs that stem from the interaction of aging and secondary conditions associated with the progression of their impairments or as the consequences of long-term, poor quality health care and chronic conditions (Haveman et al., 2010). For example, people with cerebral palsy report reduced mobility, increased pain, and bowel and bladder problems beginning in their 40s and originating from the long-term effects of muscle tone abnormalities, overuse of some joints, and immobility of others (Balandin & Morgan 1997; Overeynder, Turk, Dalton, & Janicki, 1992). In addition, other related conditions such as small body size, poor diet, and prolonged use of anticonvulsant drugs may contribute to early and increased risk of osteoporosis, falls, and fractures. Diversity increases with age, however, and "older individuals with developmental disabilities probably encompass an even greater heterogeneity than is found in the general aging population" (Adlin, 1993, p. 51). Different patterns of aging highlight the importance of taking account of both chronological age and the nature of the disabling condition when planning service responses. It is also important to avoid making potentially discriminatory assumptions about the age of onset or effect of aging by ensuring that every older person is "evaluated individually in the context of his or her unique history and special concerns" (Adlin, 1993, p. 51). Reported differences may be related to varying patterns of chronic illness, disability type, and other conditions (Kirchberger et al., 2012; McCarron et al., 2013) as well as the effect of poor access and inadequate health care, rather than greater heterogeneity (Schoeni, Freedman, & Wallace, 2001). Differences in need for support, early onset of some conditions, and limited access to services for some subpopulations of older adults warrant policy and programmatic responses.

Premature Aging

The unique pattern of aging evident in people with Down syndrome has contributed to the assumption that premature aging is characteristic of people with intellectual and developmental disabilities. To some extent, researchers have reinforced this by including people as young as 40 years old in studies in order to ensure the inclusion of participants who have experienced symptoms of premature aging (Bigby & Balandin, 2004; McCarron et al., 2011). Understanding unique issues of premature aging in people with intellectual and developmental disabilities is important, given the tendency for old-age services to use 60 or 65 years as cutoffs for service eligibility. Doing so, however, can lead to a tendency to obscure middle age for people with intellectual and developmental disabilities and regard people in their 40s or 50s as old. This neglect of middle age as a stage in the life course has curtailed consideration of its normative challenges and the significant potential it could hold for further personal development and community participation (Bigby, 2012).

The tendency to regard adulthood as an undifferentiated period is evident in the literature (see Brown & Percy, 2007) and in retirement programs that include middle-age people as well as older people in their target group (Bigby, 2005; Bigby, Wilson, Balandin, & Stancliffe, 2011). Such practices are likely to be self-fulfilling by compounding the effect of low expectations held by staff in the intellectual and developmental disabilities system and wider discriminatory practices often associated with aging found in the community. In a similar vein, unlike the notions of "young old" and "old old" that exist in the general population, old age has seldom been conceptualized as a differentiated period in the lives of people with intellectual and developmental disabilities. The higher age-specific mortality rates of people with more severe or multiple disabilities compounds this concern because it means that older people with intellectual and developmental disabilities are predominantly the "young old" in their 60s and 70s, and as "healthy survivors," have milder impairment levels than their younger peers (Bigby, 2004).

Premature Aging versus Preventable Aging

The work of Evenhuis, Hermans, Hilgenkamp, Bastiaanse, and Echteld (2012) in the Netherlands is providing evidence to counter the notion of premature aging. Their findings demonstrated that, although people with intellectual and developmental disabilities have a pattern of age-related health vulnerabilities that differ from the general population, these vulnerabilities are of a different nature to that of an early onset of the aging process. Using the concept of frailty (i.e., high vulnerability to adverse health conditions) and the five criteria of frailty of the Cardiovascular Health Study (i.e., weight loss, poor grip strength, slow walking speed, low physical activity, poor endurance or exhaustion), they found people with intellectual and developmental disabilities at ages 50–64 years had a prevalence of frailty (11%) that was similar to that of the general population at 65 years and older (7%–9%). Although age, Down syndrome, dementia, motor disability, and severe intellectual disability were associated with frailty, these factors statistically explained only 25% of the variance. Using an alternative Frailty Index, Schoufour, Echteld, and Evenhuis (2012) found that people with intellectual and developmental disabilities who were older than age 50 years had frailty scores similar to most elderly people older than 75 years. The index comprised 50 health-related impairments, including physical, social, and medical problems. The study suggested that high levels of frailty in people with intellectual and developmental disabilities are associated with potentially preventable and reversible aging factors, including very low levels of physical activity, social relationships, and community participation rather than premature aging (Hilgenkamp, Reis, Wijck, & Evenhuis, 2012).

Aging from a Disadvantageous Position

People with intellectual and developmental disabilities, therefore, embark on the aging process from a particularly disadvantaged position with respect to their health and consequent risk of adverse outcomes. During both childhood and adulthood, they are more likely to have lived in poverty, have poorer physical and mental health, and have lived a more unhealthy and sedentary lifestyle than the general population, as well as being less likely to have benefited from preventative health screenings or other health promotion measures (Emerson, 2007; Emerson, Hatton, Felce, & Murphy, 2001; Haveman et al., 2010; McCarron et al., 2011). Their higher rates of obesity, nutritional problems and cholesterol, and lower rates of physical activity alone all potentially increase the chances of diseases such as diabetes, hypertension, heart disease, and arthritis (Bigby, 2004; Evenhuis, Theunissen, Denkers, Verschuure, & Kemme, 2001; McCarron et al., 2011).

Adults with intellectual and developmental disabilities also characteristically face social and economic exclusion, limiting their opportunity to exercise choice, participate in the community, and gain access to advocacy and informal support. Their low rates of employment and heavy reliance on government income support schemes that are close to or below poverty lines provide limited opportunities to accumulate wealth. As a consequence, people with intellectual and developmental disabilities generally do not have the funds to secure access to private health care and primarily are dependent on public health and welfare systems (Bigby, 2004). Limited informal social support often experienced by adults with intellectual and developmental disabilities restricts opportunities for social participation, emotional well-being, individual advocacy, and negotiation with formal services (Bigby, 1997a, 2003; McCarron et al., 2011). Compared with the general population, these individuals are less likely to have married or had children. For example, in a nationally representative sample of an older population with intellectual and developmental disabilities in Ireland, only 7 of 753 people reported they had ever been married or partnered, and only 16 were parents (McCarron et al., 2011).

The social networks of adults with intellectual and developmental disabilities are generally small and made up of family members, paid staff, or friends with intellectual disability. Their lack of a spouse or children suggests they may not have relatives, who typically provide the bulk of care for older people, and they may not have a compensatory robust network of close friends (Bigby, 2000; McCarron et al., 2011). Siblings or more distant relatives such as nephews, nieces, or cousins may be their closest family members after their parents die. Australian research suggested that relatives typically did not extend their role to the primary caregiving role played by parents, despite having a "caring about" stance that included advocacy and service coordination (Bigby, 1997b). Fujiura (1998) reported that in the United States, the high reliance on parents as primary caregivers of their adult children with intellectual and developmental disabilities well into adulthood foreshadowed substantial vulnerability in middle age as parents die, which may include a move from their long-time home and dislocation from a familiar locality. However, more recent longitudinal follow-up and secondary data analyses confirmed interview data from siblings in other studies that siblings have stepped in and assumed such care in large numbers (Fujiura, 2012; Zendell, 2010). Although there are still abrupt changes associated with the death of a parent, there is a greater likelihood of transition of caregiving roles within families than was previously thought. The long-term ability of siblings to continue such roles in the face of declining birth rates, geographic mobility, and multiple caregiving demands remains to be established, however (McCallion & Kolomer, 2003).

Effect of Context on Support Provision

The living situation of people aging with intellectual and developmental disabilities reflects their national or state context, the nature of disability service provision during their lifetime, and the historic cohort to which they belong. Adjustment of shared living environments and staff support is likely to be more challenging than support that is individualized or informal. For example, changes to the intensity and nature of the support required or daily pattern of activity as a result of retirement from employment or a vocational program has resource implications in terms of both cost and skills of staff and must also be sensitive to the needs of coresidents in a living situation whose needs may be changing at a different rate (Janicki, Dalton, McCallion, Baxley, & Zendell, 2005). People who are already living in some form of shared supported accommodation, such as group homes or larger residential facilities, are often faced with negotiating inflexible staffing and funding arrangements. There are anecdotal reports that they are particularly susceptible to having to move home as they age when their support needs diverge too far from the original model of services or those of coresidents (Janicki et al., 2005; Wilkinson, Kerr, Cunningham, & Rae, 2004). There are some indications, too, that it is the degree of change that makes people most vulnerable to moving, which places those whose support needs earlier in life are fairly low particularly at risk (Bigby, Bowers, & Webber, 2011). Alternatively, for those who have lived with parents for most of their lives or remained outside the intellectual and developmental disabilities service system, gaining entry into the system in later life is likely to be difficult in terms of proving eligibility and simply gaining access to community-based support or supported accommodation due to the high level of unmet demand in the form of waiting lists. Some people in Australia are diverted away from the disability service system and may be inappropriately referred to residential age care facilities at a relatively young age in the absence of other alternatives when parents are no longer able to provide primary care (Bigby, Webber, McKenzie-Green, & Bowers, 2008).

Adopting a Life Span Perspective to Aging

Preparing for aging is a lifelong task. The foregoing discussion of the challenges faced by people with intellectual and developmental disabilities as they age highlights the importance of a life span perspective to understanding issues associated with aging and support needs. This perspective recognizes the influence of earlier stages of the life course on aging by asking "how problems, needs, and patterns of adaptations of older people are shaped by their earlier life experiences and historical conditions" (Hareven, 2001, p. 142). Opportunities earlier in the life course for personal development, quality health care, a healthy lifestyle, formation of social networks, and employment all affect issues likely to confront people as they age. The historic time through which people have lived shapes their individual life experiences and creates a broader generational effect that may pose unique challenges for service systems. Ireland is a good example of this historic effect in which a high proportion of the current cohort of older people were institutionalized early in their lives. The effect was that most older individuals with intellectual and developmental disabilities were dislocated from their families. Thus, high concentrations of older people in particular localities are supported by the charitable organizations that ran the large institutions (McCarron et al., 2011). Addressing the unique needs of cohorts of people who have spent extended periods in out-of-home care is an important concern for public policy. Considering that 65% of people with intellectual and developmental disabilities in Ireland live independently or with family (Kelly & Kelly, 2011), as do 87% in the United States (Braddock, Hemp, Parish, & Westrich, 2011), life span policy approaches must also support people with intellectual and developmental disabilities who live and want to live in genuine community settings and may have family and neighborhood networks.

Aspirations held by practitioners and policy makers regarding the type of life possible for people with intellectual and developmental disabilities typically are similar across adulthood rather than age specific. The quest for social inclusion, meaningful occupation, choice, self-direction, family support, avoidance of institutionalization, and quality health care is equally as applicable to younger and older people with intellectual and developmental disabilities. The United Nations Convention on the Rights of Persons with Disabilities established a number of key principles relevant to quality of life, socialization, and supports for all people with disabilities.

- Respect for inherent dignity, individual autonomy including the freedom to make one's own choices, and independence of persons
- Non-discrimination
- Full and effective participation and inclusion in society
- Respect for difference and acceptance of persons with disabilities as part of human diversity and humanity
- Equality of opportunity
- Accessibility
- Equality between men and women (United Nations, 2006)

These principles are not dissimilar to the policy directions implicit in the question posed by the U.S. Administration on Developmental Disabilities:

What can we do to empower older individuals with developmental disabilities to remain in their own homes with high quality of life, to maintain independence and good health for as long as possible and to enjoy community and family relationships through to the end of life? (Factor & Janicki, 2012, p. 112)

Greater attention to issues such as quality health care, physical activity, and social connections earlier in the life span could substantially change the nature and severity of some issues to be addressed in later life for individuals with intellectual and developmental disabilities. If person-centered and flexible individualized support were available during adulthood, then the challenge of adapting support to meet changing needs as people age may not be as great. Finally, if the focus of remaining in the community were less on group homes and intellectual and developmental disabilities programs and more on supporting people where they have always lived, then a greater range of alternatives and greater integration with other aging-related resources may be possible.

POLICY CHALLENGES: BRIDGING THE AGE CARE AND INTELLECTUAL AND DEVELOPMENTAL DISABILITIES SUPPORT SYSTEMS

The interface between age care and intellectual and developmental disabilities service systems has been an enduring theme in debates about how best to respond to the support needs of people who are aging. The focus of much of the early literature on aging was the double jeopardy faced by older people in the form of discrimination based on their dual characteristics of being older and having a disability (McDonald & Tyson, 1988; Walker, Walker, & Ryan, 1996). The risk of a poorer quality of life was considered to be particularly high if the norms of lower status and expectations accorded to older people in the general population were applied to people aging with intellectual and developmental disability. They would be compounded if reliance for support were placed on the age care system that was thought to compare unfavorably with the intellectual and developmental disabilities system, in terms of its less progressive underlying philosophy, poorer quality, and more congregated institutionalized service models (Bigby, 2002; Hogg, 1993; Wolfensberger, 1985). Hogg asserted the following regarding the United Kingdom.

Clearly the marginalised state of many older people could hardly be taken as a model. Decline in income maintenance, or still worse poverty, social isolation, and inadequate provision for physical or mental health, all typify the lives of a substantial number in our aged and elderly population. (1993, p. 206)

In an early piece that discussed the difficulties of applying normalization to this part of the life course, Wolfsenberger (1985) suggested that the lifestyle of afflu-ent individuals who continue to flourish into old age should be the standard of care rather than that of ordinary older people for whom old age holds so many hazards. The two systems (i.e., supports for the general population and those for individuals with intellectual and developmental disabilities) were seen to run on parallel tracks, each with little knowledge or interest in the other; staff in the intellectual and devel-opmental disabilities system knew little about aging, and staff in the age care system knew little about intellectual and developmental disabilities. Negative perception of the age care system, outright agism, and a desire for a "rich and famous" aging lifestyle may all account for the often protective attitudes of intellectual and devel-opmental disabilities staff toward their aging clients and the enduring desire found among them to continue to serve them within the intellectual and developmental disabilities services (Bigby, 2004). A better and fairer understanding of each other's system and a more shared view of the attributes of successful aging have the poten-tial to support improved cross-system action (Rowe & Kahn, 1998).

The United States led the way in the 1980s to try to bridge the two systems by sharing knowledge, expertise, and relevant services and mandating joint planning (Janicki, 1992; see Factor et al., 2012, for a broad overview). An enduring legacy of these early attempts were programs within University-Affiliated Programs for Developmental Disabilities and the Rehabilitation Research and Training Center Consortium on Aging and Developmental Disabilities that disseminated briefs to develop public education, provided training and technical assistance to the field, and conducted demonstration programs. Some states funded projects to pilot bridg-ing initiatives, such as supporting the inclusion of older people with developmental disabilities in mainstream senior centers (LePore & Janicki, 1997) and collaborating with area agencies on aging to reach out to support elderly parental caregivers so they can begin to plan for the future care of their son or daughter with intellectual and developmental disabilities (Janicki, McCallion, Force, Bishop, & LePore, 1998). Notable, too, was the Nursing Home Reform Act of 1987 (part of the Omnibus Budget Reconciliation Act, PL 100-203) that addressed inappropriate placements through procedures to restrict admission of people with intellectual and developmental dis-abilities (Snowden, Piacitelli, & Koepsell, 1998).

Analysis of these initiatives suggests they lost momentum and failed to embed collaboration between systems (Ansello, 2004; Bigby, 2010; Factor et al., 2012). How-ever, court rulings and resulting legislation may have revived interest. Most signifi-cant have been the emerging ramifications of the Supreme Court's Olmstead Decision (*Olmstead v. L.C.*, 1999) that ruled that "unjustified isolation is properly regarded as discrimination based on disability" (28 CFR 35.130[d]). The decision stated that

(a) institutional placement of persons who can handle and benefit from community settings perpetuates unwarranted assumptions that persons so isolated are incapable or unworthy of participating in community life, and (b) confinement in an institu-tion severely diminishes the everyday life activities of individuals, including family relations, social contacts, work options, economic independence, educational advance-ment, and cultural enrichment. (28 CFR 35.130[d])

States are required to provide community-based services for people with disabili-ties who would otherwise be entitled to institutional services when 1) the state's treatment professionals reasonably determine that such placement is appropriate;

2) the affected people do not oppose such treatment; and 3) the placement can be reasonably accommodated, taking into account the resources available to the state and the needs of others who are receiving state-supported disability services. The ruling was not absolute in terms of requiring no institutional placements, and it did not support unlimited costs for community supports; however, the concept of the most integrated setting appropriate applies to all people with disabilities needing support (including the elderly), and it is encouraging that there is a development of cross-system solutions. An accumulation of related litigation of both public and private provision of services established the concept of the most integrated setting and successfully targeted unnecessary segregation in the full range of settings requiring opportunities 1) to live life like people without disabilities; 2) for integration, independence, choice, and self-determination where people live, spend their days, work, and participate in their community; and 3) for quality services that meet the individual needs of people with disabilities (Perez, 2012).

Continuing Support Services Challenges

Since the 1980s, the philosophical gap between the two support systems in various countries has narrowed. Notions such as successful aging (Rowe & Khan, 1998) and the World Health Organization's Active Aging framework (2002) changed the perceptions of aging and age care services. Policy goals for people who are aging are now more closely aligned with those for adults with intellectual and developmental disabilities, and both service systems have more fully embraced principles of community care, person centeredness, choice, autonomy, and consumer-directed care (Factor et al., 2012). As the balance of care has shifted to the community, both systems have better recognized their reliance on families and informal caregivers and have instigated family support and respite programs. Resource shortfalls and significant lags between policy and its implementation indicate that differences between the systems still exist on the ground. A continuing difference between the two systems is the much lower average per capita cost of support for clients receiving age care services compared with those in the developmental disability system. For example, the per capita cost of residential age care in 2005 in Australia was estimated to be $44,000 compared with $84,000 for supported housing for a person with disability (Senate Community Affairs Reference Committee, 2005), and the average per capita expenditure for home and community-based services under the 1915(c) Medicaid waiver in 2008 in the United States was $42,896 for people with intellectual and developmental disabilities and $9,510 for older people (Factor et al., 2012). The United States figures, however, reflect the average costs of people with intellectual and developmental disabilities of all ages and a pattern of greater use of assistive technology among people with intellectual and developmental disabilities as compared with older adults (Kitchener, Ng, Lee, & Harrington, 2008). This cost differential raises equity issues among populations. There are also concerns in Australia that people with intellectual and developmental disabilities and their advocates are seen as "double dipping" when they seek to gain access to age care to enable them to age in place in a specialist intellectual and developmental service, such as a group home (Bigby et al., 2008).

There is continuing debate about the relative merits and quality of these two systems and the part each should play in supporting older people with intellectual and developmental disabilities. The newer rights-based disability policy regards people with disability as citizens first and foremost and supports inclusion in the form of access to services available to other members of the community—whether the services are generally available, such as community centers, or targeted at specific groups of the population, such as older people (United Nations Economic and Social Council, 2007). This stance suggests that inclusive services should always be the first option and positions disability services as compensatory, serving to complement or increase accessibility of, rather than replace, inclusive supports. For example, specialist assessment or health services might provide consultative support or assist in providing accommodations to generic services.

Older people with intellectual and developmental disabilities are likely to continue to require some of the specialist disability services they have used earlier in their lifetime, which are not replicated by mainstream services, such as aids and equipment, support with participation in purposeful activities or tasks of everyday living (sometimes in the form of shared accommodation), and support with decision making and advocacy. Age-related changes will mean the nature and intensity of disability-specific support may change, for example, home modifications to reflect reduced mobility, increased escort and transportation support, more intensive health monitoring, or nighttime support. The need for some types of support, such as vocational support, may diminish and be replaced by new needs, such as access to geriatric health care, dementia assessments, support to gain access to leisure, or volunteering programs. Some of the needs of older people with intellectual and developmental disabilities are similar to those of the general population and may be met relatively easily by mainstream services. Some needs, however, will be quite different, occur at an earlier age than that of other older people, or may have to be met in a different manner or with unique expertise that is not applicable to other older people (Janicki, Otis, Puccio, Rettig, & Jacobson, 1985).

People who are aging are likely to need continuing access to disability services, an adaptable supports system, and access to responsive mainstream health, age care, and community-based services. Relevant questions regarding these supports and services include the following.

- What needs of people aging with intellectual and developmental disabilities can and should be met by mainstream aging and health care systems?

- How can the capacity of mainstream aging and health care systems to meet the needs of older people with intellectual and developmental disabilities be developed and supported?

- What needs do older people with intellectual and developmental disabilities have that are met with difficulty or cannot be met by mainstream services and, therefore, require additional, specialist, or compensatory services from the intellectual and developmental disabilities system?

- What should the associated cross-system training requirements for staff be to ensure that developed capacity in both service systems is effectively used?

- How should services—whether mainstream or disability specific—be resourced and delivered in a way that takes into account 1) equity between people with intellectual and developmental disabilities with age-related needs who have differential access to disability services and 2) equity between older people in general and people aging with intellectual and developmental disabilities?

The way these questions are addressed will differ across nations, states, provinces, and localities, depending on the unique combination of welfare and long-term care policies and the nature of the age care and intellectual and developmental disabilities service systems. Service system responses to the issues of retirement and care for people with dementia illustrate the different ways in which service systems have accommodated or adjusted to the needs of people aging with intellectual and developmental disabilities.

Retirement

The question of retirement illustrates several of the issues that have been raised in the previous discussion. First, the relevance of wider context—imperatives for change as people age—derives from the types of services used by younger and middle-age people with intellectual and developmental disabilities. The notion of "retirement from what" has been important in framing the question of "retirement to what?" One of the main early imperatives to develop retirement programs in the United States has been the strong training and developmental focus of day programs and the constraints imposed by funding models for this type of program. Early service development in the United States occurred in the context of a clear policy framework whereby the Older Americans Act Amendments of 1987 (PL 100-175) and the Developmental Disabilities Assistance and Bill of Rights Act Amendments of 1987 (PL 100-146) mandated access to generic-age services for older people with disabilities and collaboration between the two service systems. However, these changes were about ensuring that there was no denial of services to people with intellectual and developmental disabilities that were available to everyone else; there was no mandate that there was a sufficient number of senior centers or other post-retirement programs available to all older adults. A similar legal framework has not been present in Australia, where less vocational approaches to day programs meant more scope existed for flexibility and adaptation to occur within existing programs, reducing the imperative for new program developments (Moss, 1993).

The approach regarding retirement taken in the United States has been to foster integration of people with intellectual and developmental disabilities into mainstream day programs for older people, such as luncheon clubs or senior citizen centers, with some provision of specialist support and resources. Seltzer (1988) found that more than half of the generic programs she surveyed in Massachusetts were serving an older person with intellectual and developmental disabilities and that a sense of shared responsibility for this group existed between disability and age care service providers. One third of all older people with intellectual and developmental disabilities surveyed in Massachusetts were provided with services by the aging network. A survey by Lakin et al. (1991) found that specialist day programs were available to less than 10% of older people with intellectual and developmental disabilities and most attended a generic program. Considerable effort was put into strategies for integrating people with intellectual and developmental disabilities into mainstream seniors' programs as a result of this finding (see Janicki, 1992; LePore & Janicki, 1997). Considerable variation exists, however, across the United States and more segregated program models are also found that "replicate senior citizens group activities normally found in the community" (Seltzer & Krauss, 1987, p. 84), specifically for people with intellectual and developmental disabilities. There also is a network of social day and medical day programs for older adults with specific assessed needs that people with intellectual and developmental disabilities are also able to access (see Janicki, 1991, 1992; LePore & Janicki, 1997; Seltzer & Krauss, 1987).

In contrast, until recently in both Australia and England, center-based nonvocational day programs formed a backbone of services for people with intellectual and developmental disabilities. Many programs have internally reconfigured to create retirement programs more attuned to the activities thought to be desired by their aging participants since attention first turned to issues of aging. Although there is variation in model and organizational arrangements in Australia, these retirement programs most commonly aim to enable choice and flexible support to enable participation in social activities and formation or maintenance of social relationships (Bigby, Balandin, Fyffe, McCubbery, & Gordon, 2004). Much less importance is accorded to maintaining skills, independence, or health or physical fitness, and most programs are dominated by group and center-based activities. No model stands out as achieving better outcomes than others, and many reflect entrenched discriminatory attitudes toward older people exemplified by lower expectations, stereotypical views of their preferred activities, and provision of fewer opportunities compared with their younger peers (Bigby, 2005). Despite being formulated as programs for older people, few programs have staff with any expertise about issues of aging, and some include much younger people with complex needs as a means of offering more flexible programs to this group. Many programs are simply a continuation of the segregated group-based approach older people have experienced for much of their lives, albeit with less ambitious goals as a result of their age. The essence of service providers' views, which were canvassed in a national survey of retirement programs, were summed up by the comment, "Older people are less active, more passive, require more harmony, more physical assistance, need more support and their individual fixed behaviour becomes magnified" (Bigby et al., 2004, p. 247).

In both Australia and the United States, the shift away from block funding to day support programs to individual self-directed funding holds possibilities for less segregated and more flexible daytime support for older people with intellectual and developmental disabilities to pursue options more tailored to their lifetime interests and to purchase services and supports from a variety of providers to meet needs and wishes for social relationships, a sense of purpose, and activities to maintain health and well-being. The capacity of self-directed funding to deliver more person-centered outcomes will depend on the level of funding, quality of support purchased, openness of ability to purchase supports from different providers, and staff attitudes and their knowledge of the aging process and the individuals they support (Caldwell & Heller, 2007; Craig, 2013; Shanks & Young, 2010). More individualized options should not mean, however, asking service users to do everything on their own. For instance, in the absence of routine attendance at a day center program, explicit strategies will be required to promote the lifelong relationships older people may have, regardless of jurisdiction they have had with coparticipants in segregated day programs.

The advent of self-directed funding and the issue of retirement illustrate the point that although people aging with intellectual and developmental disabilities have similar overarching needs to those of other older people in retirement, their needs may have to be met in a different way. Only a small proportion of older people in the general community in Australia use the comprehensive network of senior citizens services that provide opportunities for activities and socialization at a local level. Many older people meet this type of need independently through their own family and social networks, participating in informal and formal social activities and taking advantage of opportunities offered by age-specific programs as well as generic community organizations. Older people are the largest group who volunteer their time across a wide array of cultural, philanthropic, environmental, sporting, and educational activities (Warburton & Cordingley, 2004). The more meager informal support networks of many older people with intellectual and developmental disabilities increase their need for formal support as they lack friends without intellectual and developmental disabilities to act as informal avenues to participation in community organizations or with whom to share activities. The type of support they require to participate is different from that of older people without intellectual and developmental disabilities and includes support to identify opportunities, exercise choice, negotiate entry, participate in activities, and obtain transport. This type of support is not available in mainstream aging and community care systems (Bigby, 1992; Bigby, Stancliffe, Balandin, Wilson, & Craig, 2012). This should be an area, however, where additional supports may be accessed through the intellectual and developmental disabilities network rather than be a justification for the maintenance or creation of segregated services.

Research from Australia and Norway shows that mainstream organizations that rely on volunteers (e.g., community gardens, museums, activities, organizations) frequented by older people include few people with disabilities, although their inclusion is supported in principle (Bigby & Balandin, 2005; Ingvaldsen & Balandin, 2011). Staff and members of these organizations lack confidence in their capacity to be inclusive, and their support for inclusion is often conditional on providing additional resources such as expertise, knowledge, and personnel to facilitate access. However, there are also examples of people with intellectual and developmental disabilities who, with supports, have meaningful volunteer roles in food pantry, companionship, delivery, and small chore support programs for their communities in general and for other older adults in particular. This speaks to a role for specialist disability programs assisting mainstream community organizations in building their capacity to include those with intellectual and developmental disabilities—not as a group but as individual members or volunteers. Case management "access and linkage" programs that work at individual and system levels to identify, locate, negotiate access, and provide orientation or mentoring to other participants to enable older people with intellectual and developmental disabilities to be included in mainstream activities have been repeatedly identified as an effective program model to help achieve this outcome (see Bigby, 1992; LePore & Janicki, 1997; Stancliffe, Wilson, Bigby, & Balandin, 2011; Wilson, Stancliffe, Bigby, Balandin, & Craig, 2010).

An Australian study identified the variable challenges that arise in supporting people with differing support needs to be included in community-based programs. The necessity for collaboration with all the sources of informal and formal support a person may receive, understanding the orientation and core focus of the group activities, and the potential failure rate and absence of capacity in some groups to be inclusive are among the challenges of long-term but episodic nature of support that is required (Craig, 2013; Stancliffe et al., 2011). The friendly interactions and acquaintances developed within a group, however, were not found to become stronger, be transferred to other settings, or provide a catalyst for a wider range of social activities.

The almost exclusive development of retirement programs from within the day support system for existing clients in Australia illustrates the importance of context and its implications for the small proportion of people with intellectual and developmental disabilities in paid open or supported employment (which resembles traditional sheltered workshops) (Australian Institute of Health and Welfare, 2008). For this group, retirement has become a major issue, not only because some older workers want to work less hours or retire, but also the financial viability of their employers (who are not-for-profit organizations) is threatened by the foreshadowed reduced productivity of an aging work force (McDermott, Edwards, Abello, & Katz, 2010). A split of funding responsibility between state governments, which are responsible for community-support programs, and the federal government, which is responsible for employment programs, has created a major obstacle to enabling older workers with disabilities to retire. Despite many years of debate, lobbying, and piloting program models, questions remain regarding which level of government should bear responsibility of continuing support for retired workers to be engaged in purposeful or meaningful activity and social relationships (Bigby, 2005; Bigby et al., 2001). The split of funding between levels of government and unresolved responsibility for retired workers, combined with the demand for day support programs among younger age groups, means that if workers retire they cannot easily gain access to self-directed funding packages to support continued social engagement or the retirement programs that have developed as part of day support services (which are targeted at people who have not worked). There are no firm alternatives to support older workers, and it is not surprising many perceive retirement as risky and fear it may lead to loss of identity, social relationships, and a sense of purpose (McDermott, Edwards, Abello, & Katz, 2009; Wilson et al., 2010).

There is a clear concern that retirement years in the absence of adequate pensions, other resources, and spouses/partners and children are likely to be more isolating and lonely for people with intellectual and developmental disabilities. Whereas participation in senior centers and other group programs is an optional support for the general population, it is more necessary for people with intellectual and developmental disabilities. At a minimum there is a need for increased access for people with intellectual and developmental disabilities to mainstream options; there may also be a need for more specialized programming supports and strategies for people with intellectual and developmental disabilities to continue to connect with the social networks formed during their work or day program career.

CARE FOR PEOPLE WITH DEMENTIA

The unique aging pattern of people with Down syndrome represents one of the most significant challenges associated with aging. This group not only has a higher risk of developing dementia than the general population but also developing it at a much earlier age (Prasher, 1995). The situation for people with intellectual and developmental disabilities from other etiologies is less clear, although reports suggest there is equal risk—in all, there is as much as five times greater risk of dementia for people with intellectual and developmental disabilities compared with the general population (Cooper, 1997; Janicki & Dalton, 2000). In addition to health care, the experience of dementia poses behavioral and care concerns such as wandering, sleep disturbance, incontinence, and auditory and visual hallucinations (Cooper & Prasher, 1998; Cosgrave et al., 1998; Holland et al., 2000; Tyrrell et al., 2001). Data suggest that the course of dementia may be different for people with Down syndrome with an early and precipitous decline in cognitive functions and skills (Visser, Aldenkamp, van Huffelen, & Kuilman, 1997). Another study that used survival analysis, however, reported a median survival of 7 years and dementia as likely to be for an extended period similar to the general population (McCarron et al., 2011).

Evidence about the increasing longevity of people with intellectual disability, and that by age 50 years 9.4% and age 60 years 54.5% of people with Down syndrome will develop dementia, provides a strong imperative for service systems to plan, at least for the relatively predictable number of people with Down syndrome. The effect of dementia must be considered from the perspective of family care providers as well as providers of day support programs and supported or shared accommodation services (Carling-Jenkins, Torr, Iacono, & Bigby, 2012; McCallion, Nickle, & McCarron, 2005). (*Note:* Increasingly fewer people in the United States will be living in resource- and support-intensive group homes as they age.) Applying an inclusive approach that utilizes dementia services available to other older people with dementia poses a number of key issues for people with intellectual and developmental disabilities, including the issue that current mainstream dementia care policies do not take sufficient account of this group, diagnosis is likely to be more complex because standard tools are not applicable, clinicians in dementia care are unlikely to have experience in working with people with intellectual and developmental disabilities, and people are likely to need to gain access to memory clinics and other specialized dementia services at a younger age, which means they may fall outside age-related eligibility criteria (McCallion et al., 2012).

Despite the potential to forecast the scale and nature of the problem, intellectual and developmental disabilities service systems in the United States, Australia, and Ireland have failed to be proactive and undertake population-based planning for this group. Although much policy development has occurred in response to the foreshadowed increase in dementia among the general population, there has not been a sufficient account of the unique needs of people with intellectual and developmental disabilities (McCarron & Lawlor, 2003; National Task Group on Intellectual Disabilities and Dementia Practice, 2012; Torr et al., 2010). Families and aging and disability service providers continue to face unanswered questions regarding how their resources and skills may best be pooled, as well as what service models should be developed and by whom (Bigby, 2002). Questions remain as to what care setting is most useful in addressing and responding to dementia care needs of people with intellectual and developmental disabilities in terms of both cost effectiveness and quality-of-life outcomes (McCallion, McCarron, Fahey-McCarthy, & Connaire, 2012). There is a need for evidence-based models for care if institutionalization and reinstitutionalization are to be avoided to ensure that quality of life is maintained and costs are contained. Researchers are responding to these challenges, and much is already known about effective diagnosis and maintaining quality of life as dementia progresses. For example, the International Association for the Scientific Study of Intellectual Disabilities outlined a model of recommended practice for dementia recognition, diagnosis, and care in people with intellectual disabilities that suggested the following (Burt & Alyward, 2000):

- Baseline assessment and annual follow-up of people with Down syndrome who are older than 35 years and people with intellectual disability who are older than 50 years

- Comprehensive diagnostic workup

- Person-centered approaches to care, including the need for staff training and service and policy redesign

Maintaining quality of life for people with dementia requires maintenance of function, management of co-morbid conditions and pain, and access to relationships and community participation, which can be summarized as requiring attention to the following (McCallion & McCarron, 2004b):

- Absence of pain

- Maintenance of health

- Psychosocial well-being

- Skills maintenance and support

- Absence of and supportive responses to problem behaviors

- Leisure and community participation

- Family and friends

- Dementia-focused programming

- Supportive environments

- Alleviation of caregiver burden

The generic dementia care literature argues for relationships and communication as critical to meaningful lives (McCallion, 2009), the centrality of relationships to good dementia care (Allan & Killick, 2008), and the desire by most individuals to live out their years in their home and community, regardless of their disability (Pynoos, Caraviello, & Cicero, 2009). Applications of concepts of relationship-based care (Koloroutis, 2004) to people with intellectual and developmental disabilities is complex, given the different constellations of family relationships and the length of time many in the current generation of older people have spent in out-of-home care. Maintaining valued and long-established relationships in the lives of people with intellectual disability and dementia (including long-standing relationships with staff) is a critical concern that requires purposeful actions to redress its previous absence from care strategies (McCallion & McCarron, 2004b; McCarron et al., 2011). Delivering quality dementia care at the system level requires strategic planning, staff training, environmental modification, care planning, and preparing for end-of-life care (McCarron & Reilly, 2010).

    Research suggests that the underlying policy issues in delivering quality dementia care have not been sorted out (Putnam, 2004). Across jurisdictions it appears that staff in the intellectual and developmental disabilities system are committed to enabling older residents, including those with dementia, to age in place but also accept the inevitability of a tipping point when they will be unable to do so (Janicki et al., 2005; Wilkinson et al., 2004). In the absence of clear policies to ensure access and responsiveness of mainstream dementia services and/or additional complementary resourcing from within the intellectual and developmental disabilities system to take account of increased support needs, the most common practices have been to place demands on existing providers and families that are increasingly overwhelming or transfer people with dementia to more restrictive environments, such as dementia units specifically for intellectual and developmental disabilities and/or mainstream long-term care (Bigby, 2010; Janicki & Dalton, 2000; Janicki et al., 2005). Existing living environments may simply not be suitable, however. Caring for a person with dementia and meeting the needs of others living in the home (family or formal placement) can be challenging, and those who do provide care (staff or families) may genuinely be overwhelmed; a different living situation may be needed in such circumstances.

Australian Responses

A national pilot project in Australia that funded intellectual and developmental disabilities service providers to purchase specialist or additional support for residents assessed as eligible for residential age care successfully demonstrated the benefits of blending expertise from age care and intellectual and developmental disabilities systems to enable aging individuals to stay in place and shift, if not remove, the tipping point at which a resident would have to move (Australian Institute of Health and Welfare, 2006). The additional funding was much less than the cost of residential age care, but the total cost well exceeded it; the additional cost may account for the reluctance of the Australian government to continue this program past the pilot phase. There are anecdotal suggestions that the additional cost of adapting accommodation services to older residents is absorbed by nongovernment service providers, or funding is negotiated on a one-by-one basis in the absence of policy. Staff in supported accommodation programs do not generally have health care expertise or easy access to nurses or other health professionals experienced with people with intellectual and developmental disabilities. An unpublished survey in the State of Victoria showed that less than half of group home staff felt confident to support a resident with dementia. Staff members are reliant on mainstream health, allied health, and dementia care services for advice and management of residents with dementia. Such services lack access to specialists in intellectual and developmental disabilities and dementia to provide consultation. Aging in place past the point at which a resident requires skilled nursing care and delaying a move to a dementia care unit or residential age care may be detrimental rather than beneficial to an individual's well-being. For example, one study found that, although such facilities struggled to include people with intellectual and developmental disabilities in social aspects of care, they did provide residents with superior health care compared with the group home (e.g., quickly addressing long-standing problems such as constipation) (Webber, Bowers, & Bigby, in press).

The policy vacuum in Australia leaves open the challenge of finding ways to improve the responsiveness of mainstream services to people with dementia and intellectual and developmental disabilities, equip staff and families with knowledge and skills to be advocates within mainstream systems, and understand the basics of providing care to people with dementia. It is also important to ensure clear and transparent decision-making procedures to weigh the individual risks and benefits of a move to a nursing facility and put strategies in place to reduce risks such as severing of long-term relationships, which may be associated with a move.

People with intellectual and developmental disabilities and dementia who are residents in supported accommodations, as well as those still living with their families or more independently in the community, are faced with navigating a system of dementia assessment and care that lacks specific knowledge or expertise about their particular needs or circumstances with often serendipitous and unsatisfactory outcomes (Carling-Jenkins, Torr, Iacono, & Bigby, 2012). There is, however, a glimmer of hope on the horizon in the form of the Australian Productivity Commission (2011) report on Disability Support and Care, which provided a blueprint for a National Disability Insurance Scheme. If the scheme is implemented as planned, then people with severe disabilities would have the right to an individual budget to purchase reasonable and necessary supports, and funds would be adjusted to take changed needs into account. As people age they would remain in the scheme and be able to purchase the mix of age-related or disability-specific supports that meet their needs. Trials conducted in 2013 will test this notion, but it has the potential to facilitate adaptation of support as people's needs change and remove many of the issues that arise from inflexibility of the intellectual and developmental disabilities service system that face people as they age. This solution leaves it up to the market to determine how to respond to consumer demand, which may generate innovative options and provide much needed consultancy or expertise in the mainstream and intellectual and developmental disabilities systems. The scheme will have a monetary tipping point, however, in which it will be determined that age care needs outweigh disability needs and a person should move from the scheme to the age care system. At what point and how this will be determined will be key issues.

Irish Responses

The context in Ireland is quite different, and there is less reliance on gaining access to mainstream services. The Irish population of people with intellectual and developmental disabilities is much smaller and less scattered than in Australia or the United States, and many of the cohorts of aging people are concentrated in particular geographic locations. It is important to note that a significant proportion of staff in intellectual and developmental disabilities services have nursing qualifications. All of these factors help explain the trend toward developing specialist dementia services within the intellectual and developmental disabilities service system. For example, large organizations such as the Daughters of Charity and St. Michaels House have commissioned research and developed their own services to respond to residents who are aging (McCarron & Reilly, 2010). For example, McCarron and Reilly worked with the Daughters of Charity to develop a specialist mobile memory service to provide diagnosis and ongoing support and consultancy to staff in the various types of supported accommodations provided by the organization. The service has not been developed in isolation, but it draws on the high-level expertise of the mainstream if necessary to back up specific knowledge of dementia for people who have intellectual and developmental disabilities. Dementia-capable cluster housing has been developed to enable residents to age in place and avoid further moves or reinstitutionalization in the age care system.

These developments have facilitated an understanding of the necessary components within the intellectual and developmental disabilities system needed to support community care and address the pressures and stresses on staff and families that may encourage placement of people with intellectual and developmental disabilities and dementia in more restrictive settings (Janicki & Dalton, 2000; McCallion et al., 2005). Service redesign for dementia is needed at individual, staff, family, residential/programming unit, and organizational levels and should include the following (McCallion & McCarron, 2004a).

- Specialist memory clinics

- Multidisciplinary and clinical support

- A mix of services able to respond to changing needs, including day, respite, and specialist residential and family support services

- Services located where needed and not where available

- Clear person-centered understanding on what each service offered is intended to achieve

- Sustainable services

- Education programs for staff, family, and generic health care professionals

The particular needs of people aging within the intellectual and developmental disabilities system have been recognized in Ireland by large charitable organizations responsible for service delivery that have a strong sense of commitment to aging people for whom they have provided support for much of their lives. One of the challenges in the future will be how these specialist services can also respond to the next generation of older people who are likely to be more geographically dispersed and who have lived in the community with family support for a much greater proportion of their lives.

American Responses

An emphasis on specialist response for people with dementia within the intellectual and developmental disabilities service system found in Ireland occurs in the United States, but is less likely to be sustainable in a post-Olmstead world because it is contrary to policy directions that favor using mainstream service options and maintaining family and community settings over developing new residential options. An increasing number of people are aging in their own homes in the community, either with family or in some form of supported community living, rather than more traditional group home facilities (Braddock et al., 2011). General and rapidly occurring long-term services and supports systems integration will mean that people with intellectual and developmental disabilities will be included in new community-based service constellations such as expanded Medicaid Waivers, Money Follows the Person, Participant Directed, and Medicaid Rebalancing changes. Consistent with these initiatives and the tenets of person-centered care, resources will increasingly be tied to the individual and his or her needs and desires and less focused on provider-defined packages of care. The challenge for advocacy groups will be to ensure the needs of people with intellectual and developmental disabilities and dementia and their families are included in the electronic data systems guiding person-centered care and the emerging range of methods of delivering support.

A mainstream approach with bridging disability-specific knowledge and resources recognizes that people aging with intellectual and developmental disabilities who are affected by dementia already live in a wide variety of community-based settings and will require varying levels and types of support depending on their situation. Such an approach aims to prepare all systems to respond well to this group, ensuring that specialist backup is available to families and staff in either system and facilitating greater sharing of expertise.

EMBEDDING KNOWLEDGE OF PEOPLE WITH INTELLECTUAL AND DEVELOPMENTAL DISABILITIES IN SERVICE SYSTEMS

Aging and disability resource centers, Alzheimer's Association chapters, memory clinics, Alzheimer research centers, and a range of Alzheimer and dementia-specific support centers and living units represent the referral, assessment, and care infrastructure of society's response to Alzheimer's disease and other dementias. If such facilities are to adequately respond to people with intellectual and developmental disabilities, then knowledge of dementia in people with intellectual and developmental disabilities will need to be embedded in each of these resources. One way of achieving this is to mandate that all federal and state-funded training of health care and age care services' professionals in dementia and dementia care include content specific to the unique presentation of dementia in people with intellectual and developmental disabilities. In addition, the centers responsible for intellectual and developmental disabilities dementia research, assessment, and care planning need to have virtual, telemedicine, and online training capacity so that generic dementia resources may easily access specialist knowledge.

Proactive Environmental Modifications

All intellectual and developmental disabilities out-of-home care real estate (residential and day) should be surveyed and their suitability assessed for continued community living if dementia symptoms occur for one or more participants. Low cost, unobtrusive environmental modifications should be initiated and gradually implemented with the purpose of increasing the likelihood that individuals with intellectual and developmental disabilities and dementia will be able to remain in their homes. For those who live independently and/or with family, suitability of their own homes for continued community living may necessitate providing resources to support such modifications to the greatest extent possible. Such strategies can benefit from the lessons learned in demonstrated community and home maintenance successes of low-cost, one-time environmental modifications for older adults with significant care needs (including dementia) who are identified at high risk for nursing home placement (McCallion & Ferretti, 2011). Indeed, many of the low-cost strategies now being advocated for the general aging population have also been successfully piloted in a federal demonstration with people with intellectual and developmental disabilities and dementia (McCallion & Harazin, 2005). Additional public policy and societal benefits occur when these measures are utilized for people with intellectual and developmental disabilities and dementia as these measures will probably ensure that other family members who are in need will also remain longer in the community.

Dementia Prevention Strategies

Demonstrated dementia preventive strategies such as obesity management and stroke prevention should be a feature of education and care for people with intellectual and developmental disabilities. Evidence-based or supported strategies for slowing the progression of symptoms of dementia should also be available for people with intellectual and developmental disabilities.

Preparation for End-of-Life Care

End-of-life care is most poorly decided when the end of life is imminent. There needs to be the encouragement of advanced planning to the greatest extent possible, the designation of decision makers, and an earnest assessment of what the individual would have wished. People with intellectual and developmental disabilities and dementia unfortunately are not provided the same opportunity to do this as others. In addition, greater collaboration needs to be fostered between intellectual and developmental disabilities services, families, and hospice/palliative care in effectively supporting those last days and offering education and preparation for the many decisions that need to be made (McCallion et al., 2012).

CONCLUSION

The discussion of retirement helps illustrate that there are needs that must be addressed for people with intellectual and developmental disabilities (a place to go and be engaged and be offered continued links to valued social relationships) that many other older adults are able to meet through family or monetary resources. Given extensive data that civic and social engagement play significant roles in quality of life and successful, healthy aging (Morrow-Howell, 2010; Rowe & Kahn, 1998), this may be an area where there are significant needs for additional services and provisions than are currently available for the general older population. Such provision must include opportunities for people with intellectual and developmental disabilities to connect with family, valued peers, and those they have shared their lives with to this time; to find new ways to engage with others in their communities; and to enjoy life rather than continue to meet goals. Developing policy and services frameworks to achieve this will offer solutions for other older adults who lack family and pension resources.

The experience of developing specialist dementia care in Ireland provides important understanding of the components required to deliver quality care, but, as with other aspects of support for aging, the way these are assembled and delivered will reflect differences between and within jurisdictions, in terms of philosophies, terminologies, fiscal arrangements, and priorities of service systems (McCallion & Kolomer, 2003; Wilkinson & Janicki, 2002). The most pressing issues are not to design uniform policy and service system responses but to further develop the components of support and care necessary to ensure a high quality of life for people with intellectual and developmental disabilities as they age and to use evidence-based models that can be translated and adapted to differing systems of intellectual and developmental disabilities, aging, and long-term care. There must also be greater consideration of the opportunities for improved collaboration between aging and intellectual and developmental disabilities service systems, including the following:

- Require that the needs of people with intellectual and developmental disabilities be specified in every policy and training program for mainstream services.

- Consider the needs of all people with intellectual and developmental disabilities who are aging, not only those who are in formal out-of-home services, and then support genuine aging in place.

- Explore the potential for intellectual and developmental disabilities resources to be used to purchase mainstream age care services for people with intellectual and developmental disabilities.

- Develop specialized services by the intellectual and developmental disabilities system that complement rather than duplicate mainstream options or further create dual systems, and ensure that age care systems recognize their need to gain access to those services.

An important realization for all stakeholders is that opportunities available to people with intellectual and developmental disabilities earlier in the life course will affect their experiences of aging. Well-accepted aims for younger people with intellectual and developmental disabilities, such as access to health care, meaningful employment, choice, and self-determination, may lay the foundation for successful aging in the form of a healthy lifestyle and social connection to friends, family, and other community members. The aging and intellectual and developmental disabilities networks must also reposition themselves to value, support, and compensate for these life course contributions.

Questions for Study and Reflection

1. Is healthy, successful aging something that is well understood and naturally attained, or may it be created and managed by policy makers and service providers?

2. What is the same and what is different about aging and aging resources for people with intellectual and developmental disabilities?

3. What are the advantages and what are the challenges in gaining access to mainstream services for people with intellectual and developmental disabilities?

4. After encouraging engagement in the community and using community resources throughout a person's lifetime, is old age and the experience of dementia a time when this strategy should be abandoned and intellectual and developmental disabilities services relied on because mainstream services will never be adequate?

RESOURCES

Australian Foundation for Disability. (2011). *Transition to retirement: Use of an active mentoring model to support participation of older people with intel-*

lectual disability in community groups. Available at http://www.afford.com .au/employment/transition-to-retirement

Baxley, D.L., Janicki, M.P., McCallion, P., & Zendell, A. (2003). *Aiding older caregivers of persons with intellectual and developmental disabilities: A tool kit for state and local aging agencies.* Albany, NY: Center on Intellectual Disabilities, University at Albany.

Bigby, C. (2000). *Moving on without parents: Planning, transitions and sources of support for older adults with intellectual disabilities.* New South Wales, Australia/Baltimore, MD: McLennan & Petty/Paul H. Brookes Publishing Co.

Bigby, C. (2004). *Aging with a lifelong disability: Policy, program and practice issues for professionals.* London, England: Jessica Kingsley.

Fahey-McCarthy, E., McCallion, P., Connaire, K., & McCarron, M. (2008). *Supporting persons with intellectual disability and advanced dementia: Fusing the horizons of care, an introductory education and training programme.* Dublin, Ireland: Trinity College.

McCallion, P. (2005, Winter). Maintaining communication in dementia. *The Frontline of Learning Disability, 64,* 20–21.

McCallion, P. (2006). *End of life care: Supporting older people with intellectual disabilities and their families.* Albany: NYSARC and New York State Developmental Disabilities Planning Council.

McCallion, P., & Janicki, M.P. (2002). *Intellectual disabilities and dementia.* Albany: New York State Developmental Disabilities Council.

McCallion, P., & McCarron, M. (2005, Winter). Environmental modification and dementia: Key recommendations. *The Frontline of Learning Disability, 64,* 28–29.

McCallion, P., & McCarron, M. (2005, Winter). Some resources on intellectual disability and dementia. *The Frontline of Learning Disability, 64,* 29.

McCallion, P., McCarron, M., & McLaughlin, M. (2005, Winter). Overview of dementia issues in intellectual disability. *The Frontline of Learning Disability, 64,* 14–15.

Nickle, T., & McCallion, P. (2005, Winter). Redesigning day programmes. *The Frontline of Learning Disability, 64,* 27–28.

Watchman, K., Kerr, D., & Wilkinson, H. (2010). *Supporting Derek: A practice development pack to support staff working with people who have learning disability and dementia* [DVD and book]. York, United Kingdom: Joseph Rowntree Foundation.

What is dementia? and *What is death?* Pamphlets created by the Scottish Down's Syndrome Association to use with adults with intellectual disabilities. Available at http://www.jrf.org.uk/publications/supporting-derek

World Health Organization Reports

Evenhuis, H., Henderson, C.M., Beange, H., Lennox, N., Chicoine, B., & Working Group. (2000). *Healthy ageing: Adults with intellectual disabilities: Physi-*

cal health issues. Geneva, Switzerland: World Health Organization (WHO/MSD/HPS/MDP/00.5).

Hogg, J., Lucchino, R., Wang, K., Janicki, M.P., & Working Group. (2000). *Healthy ageing: Adults with intellectual disabilities: Ageing and social policy.* Geneva, Switzerland: World Health Organization (WHO/MSD/HPS/MDP/00.7).

Thorpe, L., Davidson, P., Janicki, M.P., & Working Group. (2000). *Healthy ageing: Adults with intellectual disabilities: Biobehavioural issues.* Geneva, Switzerland: World Health Organization (WHO/MSD/HPS/MDP/00.4).

Walsh, P.N., Heller, T., Schupf, N., van Schrojenstein Lantman-de Valk, H., & Working Group. (2000). *Healthy ageing: Adults with intellectual disabilities: Women's health and related issues.* Geneva, Switzerland: World Health Organization (WHO/MSD/HPS/MDP/00.6).

World Health Organization. (2000). *Healthy ageing: Adults with intellectual disabilities: Summative report.* Geneva, Switzerland: World Health Organization (WHO/MSD/HPS/MDP/00.3).

REFERENCES

Adlin, M. (1993). Health care issues. In E. Sutton, A. Factor, B. Hawkins, T. Heller, & G. Seltzer (Eds.), *Older adults with developmental disabilities: Optimizing choice and change* (pp. 49–60). Baltimore, MD: Paul H. Brookes Publishing Co.

Allan, K., & Killick, J. (2008). Communication and relationships: An inclusive social world. In M. Downs & B. Bowers (Eds.), *Excellence in dementia care: Principles and practice.* Buckingham, United Kingdom: Open University Press.

Alzheimer's Association. (2012). Alzheimer's disease facts and figures. *Alzheimer's and Dementia: The Journal of the Alzheimer's Association, 8,* 131–168.

Aman, M.G., Burrow, W.H., & Wolford, P.L. (1995). The Aberrant Behavior Checklist—Community: Factor validity and effect of subject variables for adults in group homes. *American Journal on Mental Retardation, 100,* 283–292.

Ansello, E. (2004). Public policy writ small: Coalitions at the intersection of aging and lifelong disabilities. *Public Policy and Aging Report, 14,* 1–6.

Australian Institute of Health and Welfare. (2006). *National evaluation of the aged care innovative pool disability aged care interface pilot: Final report.* Canberra, Australia: Author.

Australian Institute of Health and Welfare. (2008). *Disability in Australia: Intellectual disability.* Canberra, Australia: Author.

Balandin, S., & Morgan, J. (1997). Adults with cerebral palsy: What's happening? *Journal of Intellectual and Developmental Disability, 22,* 109–124.

Bigby, C. (1992). Access and linkage: Two critical issues for older people with an intellectual disability. *Australia and New Zealand Journal of Developmental Disabilities, 18,* 95–110.

Bigby, C. (1997a). In place of parents? The sibling relationships of older people with intellectual disability. *Journal of Gerontological Social Work, 29,* 3–21.

Bigby, C. (1997b). When parents relinquish care. The informal support networks of older people with intellectual disability. *Journal of Applied Intellectual Disability Research, 10,* 333–344.

Bigby, C. (2000). *Moving on without parents: Planning, transitions and sources of support for older adults with intellectual disabilities.* New South Wales, Australia/Baltimore, MD: McLennan & Petty/Paul H. Brookes Publishing Co.

Bigby, C. (2002). Aging with a lifelong disability: Challenges for the aged care and disability sectors. *Journal of Intellectual and Developmental Disability, 24,* 231–241.

Bigby, C. (2003). The evolving informal support networks of older adults with intellectual disability. In M. Nolan, U. Lundh,

G. Grant, & J. Keady (Eds.), *Partnerships across the caregiving career* (pp. 167–182). Maidenhead, United Kingdom: Open University Press.

Bigby, C. (2004). *Aging with a lifelong disability: Policy, program and practice issues for professionals.* London, England: Jessica Kingsley.

Bigby, C. (2005). Comparative programs for older people with intellectual disabilities. *Journal of Policy and Practice in Intellectual Disabilities, 2,* 75–85.

Bigby, C. (2010). A five country comparative review of accommodation support policies for older people with intellectual disability. *Journal of Policy and Practice in Intellectual Disabilities, 7,* 3–15.

Bigby, C. (2012). I hope he dies before me. Unravelling debates about aging with intellectual disability. In N. Watson, A. Roulstone, & C. Thomas (Eds.), *Routledge companion to disability studies* (pp. 426–439). London, England: Routledge.

Bigby, C., & Balandin, S. (2004). Issues in researching the aging of people with intellectual disability. In E. Emerson, T. Thompson, T. Parmenter, & C. Hatton (Eds.), *International handbook of methods for research and evaluation in intellectual disabilities* (pp. 221–236). New York, NY: Wiley.

Bigby, C., & Balandin, S. (2005). Another minority group: Use of aged care day programs and community leisure services by older people with lifelong disability. *Australian Journal on Ageing, 24,* 14–18.

Bigby, C., Balandin, S., Fyffe, C., McCubbery, J., & Gordon, M. (2004) Retirement or just a change of pace: An Australian national survey of disability day services used by older people with disabilities. *Journal of Intellectual and Developmental Disability, 29,* 239–254.

Bigby, C., Bowers, B., & Webber, R. (2011). Planning and decision making about the future care of older group home residents and transition to residential aged care. *Journal of Intellectual Disability Research, 55,* 777–789.

Bigby, C., Fyffe, C., Balandin, S., Gordon, M., & McCubbery, J. (2001). *Day support services options for older adults with a disability.* Melbourne, Australia: National Disability Administrators Group.

Bigby, C., Stancliffe, R., Balandin, S., Wilson, N., & Craig, D. (2012). Active mentoring: A person-centred retirement support model. *Journal of Intellectual Disability Research, 56,* 660.

Bigby, C., Webber, R., McKenzie-Green, B., & Bowers, B. (2008). A survey of people with intellectual disabilities living in residential aged care facilities in Victoria. *Journal of Intellectual Disability Research, 52,* 404–414.

Bigby, C., Wilson, N., Balandin, S., & Stancliffe, R. (2011). Disconnected expectations: Staff, family and supported employee perspectives about retirement. *Journal of Intellectual and Developmental Disability, 36,* 167–174 .

Bittles, A.H., Bower, C., Hussain, R., & Glasson, E.J. (2007). The four ages of Down syndrome. *European Journal of Public Health, 17,* 221–225.

Bittles, A., Petterson, B., Sullivan, S., Hussain, R., Glasson, E., & Montgomery, P. (2002). The influence of intellectual disability on life expectancy. *Journal of Gerontology: Medical Sciences, 57A,* M470–M472.

Braddock, D., Hemp, R., Parish, S., & Westrich, J. (2011). *The state of the states in developmental disabilities: 2010.* Washington, DC: American Association on Intellectual and Developmental Disabilities.

Brown, I., & Percy, M. (Eds.). (2007). *A comprehensive guide to intellectual and developmental disabilities.* Baltimore, MD: Paul H. Brookes Publishing Co.

Burt, D.B., & Aylward, E.H. (2000). Test battery for the diagnosis of dementia in individuals with intellectual disability. *Journal of Intellectual Disability Research, 44,* 175–180.

Caldwell, J., & Heller, T. (2007). Longitudinal outcomes of a consumer-directed program supporting adults with developmental disabilities and their families. *Intellectual and Developmental Disabilities, 45,* 161–173.

Carling-Jenkins, R., Torr, J., Iacono, T., & Bigby, C. (2012). Supporting people with Down syndrome and Alzheimer's disease in aged care and family environments. *Journal of Intellectual and Developmental Disability, 37,* 1–23.

Cooper, S.A. (1997). High prevalence of dementia among people with learning disabilities not attributable to Down's syndrome. *Psychological Medicine, 27,* 609–616.

Cooper, S.A., & Prasher, V.P. (1998). Maladaptive behaviours and symptoms of dementia in adults with Down's syndrome compared with adults with intellectual disability of other aetiologies. *Journal of Intellectual Disability Research, 42,* 293–300.

Cosgrave, M.P., McCarron, M., Anderson, M., Tyrrell, J., Gill, M., & Lawlor, B.A. (1998). Cognitive decline in Down syndrome: A validity/reliability study of the Test for Severe Impairment. *American Journal on Mental Retardation, 103,* 193–197.

Craig, D. (2013). *Building participation: A socially connected retirement for people with intellectual disability.* Unpublished doctorial dissertion, LaTrobe University, Melbourne, Australia.

Developmental Disabilities Assistance and Bill of Rights Act Amendments of 1987, PL 100-146, 42 U.S.C. §§ 6000 *et seq.*

Emerson, E. (2007). Poverty and people with intellectual disabilities. *Mental Retardation and Developmental Disabilities Research Reviews, 13,* 107–113.

Emerson, E., Hatton, C., Felce, J., & Murphy, G. (2001). *Learning disabilities: The fundamental facts.* London, England: The Foundation for People with Learning Disabilities.

Evenhuis, H., Hermans, H., Hilgenkamp, M., Bastiaanse, L., & Echteld, M. (2012). Frailty and disability in older adults with intellectual disabilities: Results from the healthy ageing and intellectual disability study. *Journal of American Geriatric Society, 60,* 934–938.

Evenhuis, H.M., Theunissen, M., Denkers I., Verschuure H., & Kemme, H. (2001). Prevalence of visual and hearing impairment in a Dutch institutionalized population with intellectual disability. *Journal of Intellectual Disability Research, 45,* 457–464.

Factor, A., Heller, T., & Janicki, M. (2012). *Bridging the aging and developmental disabilities services networks: Challenges and best practices.* Chicago: Institute on Disability and Human Development, University of Illinois.

Factor, A., & Janicki, M. (2012). Bridging the aging and developmental disabilities service networks. In RRTC State of Science Conference (Ed.), *Lifespan health and function of adults with intellectual and developmental disabilities: Translating research into practice* (pp. 107–121). Chicago: Department of Disability and Human Development, University of Illinois.

Fujiura, G.T. (1998). Demography of family households. *American Journal on Mental Retardation, 103,* 225–235.

Fujiura, G.T. (2012). *Structure of I/DD households in the U.S.: The family in 2010.* Paper presented at the American Association on Intellectual and Developmental Disabilities, Charlotte, North Carolina.

Hareven, T. (2001). Historical perspectives on aging and family relations. In R. Binstock & L. George (Eds.), *Handbook of aging and the social sciences* (pp. 141–159). San Diego, CA: Academic Press.

Haveman, M.J. (2004). Disease epidemiology and aging people with intellectual disabilities. *Journal of Policy and Practice in Intellectual Disabilities, 1,* 16–23.

Haveman, M., Heller, T., Lee, L., Maaskant, M., Shooshtari, S., & Strydom, A. (2010). Major health risks in aging persons with intellectual disabilities: An overview of recent studies. *Journal of Policy and Practice in Intellectual Disabilities, 7,* 59–69.

Hilgenkamp, M., Reis, D., Wijck, R., & Evenhuis, H. (2012). Physical activity levels in older adults with intellectual disabilities are extremely low. *Research in Developmental Disabilities, 33,* 477–483.

Hogg, J. (1993). Creative, personal and social engagement in the later years: Realisation through leisure. *Irish Journal of Psychology, 14,* 204–218.

Holland, A.J., Hon, J., Huppert, F.A., & Stevens, F. (2000). Incidence and course of dementia in people with Down's syndrome: Findings from a population-based study. *Journal of Intellectual Disability Research, 44,* 138–146.

Ingvaldsen, A.K., & Balandin, S. (2011). If we are going to include them we have to do it before we die: Norwegian seniors' views of including seniors with intellectual disability in senior centres. *Journal of Applied Research in Intellectual Disabilities, 24,* 583–593. doi: 10.1111/j.1468-3148.2011 .00636.x

Janicki, M. (1991). *Building the future: Planning and community development in ageing and developmental disabilities:* Albany: New York State Office of Mental Retardation and Developmental Disabilities, Community Integration Project in Ageing and Developmental Disabilities.

Janicki, M. (1992). Lifelong disability and aging. In L. Rowitz (Ed.), *Mental retardation in the year 2000* (pp. 115–127). New York, NY: Springer.

Janicki, M., Ackerman, L., & Jacobson, J. (1985). State developmental disabilities/

aging plans and planning for the older developmentally disabled population. *Mental Retardation, 23,* 297–301.

Janicki, M.P., & Dalton, A.J. (2000). Prevalence of dementia and impact on disability services. *Mental Retardation, 29,* 276–288.

Janicki, M., Dalton, A., McCallion, P., Baxley, D., & Zendell, A. (2005). Group home care for adults with intellectual disabilities and Alzheimer's disease. *Dementia, 4,* 361–385.

Janicki, M., McCallion, P., Force, L., Bishop, K., & LePore, P. (1998). Area agency on aging and assistance for households with older carers of adults with a developmental disability. *Journal of Aging and Social Policy, 10,* 13–36.

Janicki, M., Otis, J., Puccio, P., Rettig, J., & Jacobson, J. (1985). Service needs among older developmentally disabled persons. In M. Janicki & H. Wisniewski (Eds.), *Aging and developmental disabilities: Issues and approaches.* Baltimore, MD: Paul H. Brookes Publishing Co.

Janicki, M., & Wisniewski, H. (1985). *Aging and developmental disabilities: Issues and approaches.* Baltimore, MD: Paul H. Brookes Publishing Co.

Kelly, F., & Kelly, C. (2011). *Annual report of the National Intellectual Disability Database Committee.* Dublin, Ireland: Health Research Board.

Kirchberger, I., Meisinger, C., Heier, M., Zimmermann, A.K., Thorand, B., Autenrieth, C. S., & Döring, A. (2012). Patterns of multimorbidity in the aged population: Results from the KORA-Age Study. *PloS One, 7,* e30556.

Kitchener, M., Ng, T., Lee, H.Y., & Harrington, H. (2008). Assistive technology in Medicaid home- and community-based waiver programs. *The Gerontologist, 48,* 181–189.

Koloroutis, M. (Ed.). (2004). *Relationship-based care: A model for transforming practice.* Minneapolis, MN: Creative Health Management.

Lakin, K., Anderson, S., Hill, B., Bruininks, R., & Wright, E. (1991). Programs and services received by older persons with mental retardation. *Mental Retardation, 29,* 65–74.

LePore, P., & Janicki, M. (1997). *The wit to win: How to integrate older persons with developmental disabilities into community aging programs* (2nd ed.) Albany: New York State Office of Aging.

McCallion, P. (2009). Social work research and ageing. In I. Shaw, K. Briar-Lawson, J. Orme, & R. Ruckdeschel (Eds.), *Sage handbook of social work research.* London: Sage.

McCallion, P., & Ferretti, L. (2011). *Nursing home diversion modernization program final evaluation report.* Albany: New York State Office of Aging.

McCallion, P., & Harazin, M. (2005). *Coordinated care demonstration project.* Albany: New York State Office of Aging.

McCallion, P., & Janicki, P. (1997). Area agencies on aging: Meeting the needs of persons with developmental disabilities and their aging families. *Journal of Applied Gerontology, 16,* 270–285.

McCallion, P., & Kolomer, S.R. (2003). Aging persons with developmental disabilities and their aging caregivers. In B. Berkman & L. Harootyan (Eds.), *Social work and health care in an aging world* (pp. 201–225). New York, NY: Springer.

McCallion, P., & McCarron, M. (2004a). Aging and intellectual disabilities: A review of recent literature. *Current Opinion in Psychiatry, 17,* 349–352.

McCallion, P., & McCarron, M. (2004b). Intellectual disabilities and dementia. In K. Doka (Ed.), *Living with grief: Alzheimer's disease* (pp. 67–84). Washington, DC: Hospice Foundation of America.

McCallion, P., McCarron, M., Fahey-McCarthy, E., & Connaire, K. (2012). Meeting the end of life needs of older adults with intellectual disabilities. In E. Chang & A. Johnson (Eds.), *Contemporary and innovative practice in palliative care* (pp. 255–267). Rijeka, Croatia: Intech.

McCallion, P., Nickle, T., & McCarron, M. (2005). A comparison of reports of caregiver burden between foster family care providers and staff caregivers of persons in other settings. *Dementia, 4,* 401–412.

McCarron, M., & Lawlor, B.A. (2003). Responding to the challenges of ageing and dementia in intellectual disability in Ireland. *Ageing and Mental Health, 7,* 413–417.

McCarron, M., & Reilly, E. (2010). *Supporting persons with intellectual disability and dementia: Quality dementia care standards, a guide to practice.* Dublin, Ireland: Daughters of Charity Service.

McCarron, M., Swinburne, J., Burke, E., McGlinchey, E., Carroll, R., & McCallion, P. (2013). Patterns of multimorbidity in an older population of persons with an intellectual disability: Results from the intellectual disability supplement to the Irish Longitudinal Study on Ageing (IDS-TILDA). *Research in Developmental Disabilities, 34,* 521–527.

McCarron, M., Swinburne, J., Burke, E., McGlinchey, E., Mulryan, N., Andrews, V. ... & McCallion, P. (2011). *Growing older with an intellectual disability in Ireland 2011: First results from the intellectual disability supplement of the Irish longitudinal study on ageing.* Dublin, Ireland: School of Nursing and Midwifery, Trinity College Dublin.

McDermott, S., Edwards, R., Abello, D., & Katz, I. (2009). *Ageing and Australian disability enterprises: Final report.* Sydney, Australia: University of New South Wales, Social Policy Research Centre.

McDermott, S., Edwards, R., Abello, D., & Katz, I. (2010). Community services and indigenous affairs. *Occasional Paper No. 27: Ageing and Australian Disability Enterprises.*

McDonald, M., & Tyson, P. (1988). Decajeopardy: The aging and aged developmentally disabled. In A. Marchetti (Ed.), *Developmental disabilities: A lifespan perspective* (pp. 256–291). San Diego, CA: Grune Stratton.

Morrow-Howell, N. (2010). Volunteering in later life: Research frontiers. *Journal of Gerontology: Social Sciences, 65B,* 461–469.

Moss, S. (1993). *Aging and developmental disabilities: Perspectives from nine countries.* Durham, NH: IEEIR.

National Task Group on Intellectual Disabilities and Dementia Practice. (2012). *My thinker's not working: A national strategy for enabling adults with intellectual disabilities affected by dementia to remain in their community and receive quality supports.* Retrieved from http://www.aadmd.org/ntg/thinker

Older Americans Act Amendments of 1987, PL 100-175, 42 U.S.C. §§ 3001 *et seq.*

Olmstead v. L.C., 527 U.S. 581, 119 S.Ct. 2176, 1999.

Omnibus Budget Reconciliation Act of 1987 (PL 100-203). Subtitle C: Nursing Home Reform. Signed by President Reagan, Washington, DC, December 22, 1987.

Overeynder, J., Turk, M., Dalton, A., & Janicki, M. (1992). *I'm worried about the future: The aging of adults with cerebral palsy.* Albany: New York State Developmental Disabilities Planning Council.

Patja, K., Iivanainen, M., Vesala, H., Oksanen, H., & Ruoppila, I. (2000). Life expectancy of people with intellectual disability: A 35 year follow up study. *Journal of Intellectual and Disability Research, 44,* 591–599.

Perez, T.E. (2012). *Testimony: The 13th anniversary of the Olmstead decision.* Washington, DC: U.S. Senate Committee on Health, Education, Labor, and Pensions.

Prasher, V. (1995). Age-specific prevalence, thyroid dysfunction and depressive symptomatology in adults with Down syndrome and dementia. *International Journal of Geriatric Psychiatry, 10,* 25–31.

Productivity Commission. (2011). *Inquiry report, disability care and support (Number 54).* Canberra, ACT: Australian Commonwealth Government.

Putnam, M. (2004). Issues in the further integration of aging and disability services. *Public Policy and Aging Report, 14,* 19–23.

Pynoos, J., Caraviello, R., & Cicero, C. (2009). Lifelong housing: The anchor in aging-friendly communities. *Generations, 33,* 26–32.

Rowe, J., & Kahn, R. (1998). *Successful aging.* New York, NY: Random House.

Schoeni, R.F., Freedman, V.A., & Wallace, R.B. (2001). Persistent, consistent, widespread, and robust? Another look at recent trends in old-age disability. *Journal of Gerontology: Social Sciences, 56B,* S206–S218.

Schoufour, J., Echteld, M., & Evenhuis, H. (2012). Frailty in elderly with intellectual disabilities. *Journal of Intellectual Disabilty Research, 56,* 661.

Seltzer, M. (1988). Structure and patterns of service utilisation by elderly persons with mental retardation. *Mental Retardation, 26,* 181–185.

Seltzer, M., & Krauss, M. (1987). *Ageing and mental retardation. Extending the continuum.* Washington DC: American Association on Mental Retardation.

Senate Community Affairs Reference Committee. (2005). *Access and equity in aged care.* Canberra: Commonwealth of Australia, Parliament of Australia.

Shanks, W., & Young, C. (2010). Creating pathways into the community: An evolutionary journey to community inclusion. In C. Bigby & C. Fyffe (Eds.), *More than community presence social inclusion for people with intellectual disability.*

Proceedings of the roundtable on intellectual disability (pp. 96–103). Melbourne, Australia: LaTrobe University.

Snowden, M., Piacitelli, J., & Koepsell, T. (1998). Compliance with PASARR recommendations for Medicaid recipients in nursing homes. *Journal of the American Geriatrics Society, 46,* 1132–1136.

Stancliffe, R., Wilson, N., Bigby, C., & Balandin, S. (2011). *Transition to retirement.* Retrieved from http://www.afford.com.au/ employment/transition-to-retirement

Torr, J., Strydom, A., Patti, P., & Jokinen, N. (2010). Ageing in Down syndrome: Morbidity and mortality. *Journal of Policy and Practice in Intellectual Disabilities, 7,* 70–81.

Tyrrell, J., Cosgrave, M., McCarron, M., McPherson, J., Clavert, J., Kelly, A.,...Lawlor, B.A. (2001). Dementia in people with Down's syndrome. *International Journal of Geriatric Psychiatry, 16,* 1168–1174.

United Nations. (2006). *Convention on the rights of persons with disabilities.* Retrieved from http://www.un.org/ disabilities

United Nations Economic and Social Council. (2007, 23 November). *Mainstreaming disability in the development agenda*: *Note by secretariat.*

Visser, F.E., Aldenkamp, A.P., van Huffelen, A.C., & Kuilman, M. (1997) Prospective study of the prevalence of Alzheimer-type dementia in institutionalized individuals with Down syndrome. *American Journal on Mental Retardation, 101,* 400–412.

Walker, A., Walker, C., & Ryan, T. (1996). Older people with learning difficulties leaving institutional care: A case of double jeopardy. *Ageing and Society, 16,* 125–150.

Warburton, J., & Cordingley, S. (2004). The contemporary challenges of volunteering in an ageing Australia. *Australian Journal of Volunteering, 9,* 67–74.

Webber, R., Bowers, B., & Bigby, C. (in press). Residential aged care: A good place to be for people with ID? *Australasian Journal of Aging.*

Wilkinson, H., & Janicki, M. (2002). The Edinburgh Principles with accompanying guidelines and recommendations. *Journal of Intellectual Disability Research, 46,* 279–284.

Wilkinson, H., Kerr, D., Cunningham, C., & Rae, C. (2004). *Home for good? Preparing to support people with a learning disability in a residential setting when they develop dementia.* Brighton, East Sussex, England: Joseph Rowntree Trust/ Pavillion.

Wilson, N.J., Stancliffe, R.J., Bigby, C., Balandin, S., & Craig, D. (2010). The potential for active mentoring to support a positive transition into retirement for older adults with a lifelong disability. *Journal of Intellectual and Developmental Disability, 35,* 211–214.

Wolfensberger, W. (1985). An overview of social role valorisation and some reflections on elderly mentally retarded persons. In M. Janicki & H. Wisniewski (Eds.), *Aging and developmental disabilities: Issues and approaches.* Baltimore, MD: Paul H. Brookes Publishing Co.

World Health Organization. (2002). *Active ageing: A policy framework.* Geneva, Switzerland: Author.

Zendell, A. (2010). *Decision-making among siblings of adults with intellectual or developmental disabilities* (Unpublished doctoral dissertation). University at Albany, New York.

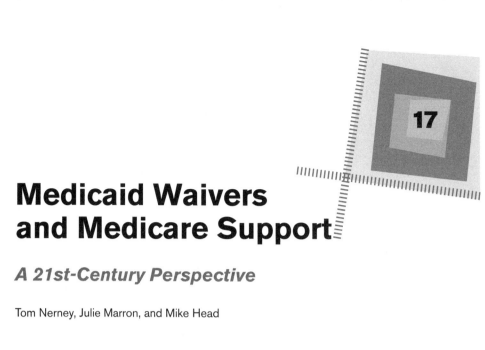

Medicaid Waivers and Medicare Support

A 21st-Century Perspective

Tom Nerney, Julie Marron, and Mike Head

More than half of the federal and state Medicaid long-term care budget—more than $123 billion in 2010—is spent on institutionalizing older Americans with disabilities and many younger individuals with disabilities in facilities where they are isolated from their communities. An individual must become impoverished to be eligible for the Medicaid program. Medicaid eligibility frequently means loss of control over where a person lives and who provides support. The program bias in favor of institutional placements reflects an ongoing, pervasive violation of civil rights for individuals with disabilities and aging Americans because many are forced into institutions in order to obtain services in spite of their preference for living at home (Bayer & Harper, 2000).

Although the Patient Protection and Affordable Care Act of 2010 (PL 111-148) provides some incentives for states to redouble efforts to expand home and community-based services, states have a long way to go toward utilizing these options. The infrastructure for supporting individuals with disabilities to success-fully live in the community is barely developed in most states, despite many years of advocacy on the part of disability advocates. Those served through the Social Security benefit programs and Medicaid reveal shocking rates of unemployment and underemployment, and nearly all working-age individuals covered by these two programs remain trapped in personal poverty. Only a fraction of those served to date enjoy the authority over public funds that enable them to craft meaningful lives within their chosen communities. Few are able to design individual budget plans that reflect the universal human aspirations for a place to call home, real community membership, ongoing long-term relationships, and the production of private income.

Individuals of all disabilities who require support from the federal/state Medicaid program, as well as from Supplemental Security Income (SSI) and Social Security Disability Insurance (SSDI), face a bleak future of limited public support as states target Medicaid expenditures for increased reductions, Social Security rules continue to trap working-age individuals in personal poverty, and nursing facilities and institutions consume billions of dollars for living arrangements that are less than desirable.

This chapter makes clear that Medicaid and Medicare programs are not only inordinately complex, but also the delivery of services among more than 300 waiver programs, state plan services, and institutional arrangements conceals the central fact that what happens with any one group of individuals profoundly affects every other disability group. The choices available to the exploding population of older Americans who will require public support in the near future will determine whether other individuals with disabilities who are eligible and worthy can even obtain support through the Medicaid program. Society can no longer afford to allow institutional programs to consume two to three times the resources that are required to serve individuals in the community. The time has come to work together across disabilities and ages to forge a new system of support that results in an end to the institutional bias in Medicaid, promotes real community and personal freedom, and addresses the forced impoverishment of so many.

This chapter's objectives are to 1) provide a brief history of Medicaid and Medicare and discuss how the two programs have evolved and how they currently function today, 2) discuss the primary challenges facing these two programs and the effect those challenges have or may have on individuals with disabilities, 3) identify deficiencies in services and supports available today, and 4) propose some of the changes that must take place in order to best serve individuals with disabilities.

AN OVERVIEW OF MEDICARE AND MEDICAID

Medicaid and Medicare were created by the Social Security Amendments of 1965 (PL 89-97) with much criticism for Medicare's socialized medicine but little commentary regarding Medicaid (Engel, 2006). One of the reasons for the difference in public response was that Medicaid was seen as a minor expansion of an existing welfare program that would be replaced within a short period of time by a national health insurance program (Engel, 2006). Both programs have not only survived but also have expanded and changed in ways that could not have been predicted at their inception.

Medicare serves nearly all Americans over the age of 65 (Klees, Wolfe, & Curtis, 2011), providing more comprehensive benefits today than originally envisioned. There are more than 50 Medicaid programs throughout the United States, all with different eligibility requirements, services, and regulations (Klees et al., 2011). Within these 50 state Medicaid programs are more than 300 waiver programs serving individuals with disabilities. Many individuals with disabilities who are considered dually eligible (Young, Garfield, Musumeci, Clemans-Cope, & Lawton, 2012) receive critical services from both Medicare and Medicaid and must navigate complex and often incomprehensible benefit requirements. Medicaid and Medicare have interesting histories and both have played, and continue to play, a disproportionate role in shaping the lives of individuals with disabilities.

History of Medicare

Medicare "is the largest health care insurance program—and the second-largest social insurance program—in the United States" (Klees et al., 2011, p. 20). Medicare provides health insurance benefits to individuals ages 65 and older, regardless of their income or health history, and to many people under the age of 65 with permanent disabilities. More than half of all Americans over the age of 65 lacked medical insurance prior to its inception. Medicare provided health insurance coverage to approximately 95% of older Americans by 2011, 8.3 million of whom were people with disabilities under the age of 65. Total 2011 expenditures of $549 billion represented approximately 12% of the total national budget and 3.6% of gross domestic product (Boards of Trustees, Federal Hospital Insurance and Federal Supplementary Medical Insurance Trust Funds, 2012).

Medicare provided Hospital Insurance and Supplemental Medical Insurance for most individuals over the age of 65 when it was initially implemented in 1966. These two programs are commonly referred to as Medicare Part A and Medicare Part B. Medicare Part A provides coverage for hospital, home health, skilled nursing facility, and hospice care, whereas Medicare Part B covers physician, outpatient hospital, home health, and other non–facility-based services (Klees et al., 2011). Medicare Part C was added in 1997 as an alternative to traditional Part A and Part B coverage, allowing beneficiaries to receive care from private Medicare Advantage and other health insurance plans that contract with Medicare. Part D was created by the Medicare Modernization Act of 2003 (PL 108-173) and provides subsidized access to drug insurance coverage and subsidies for premiums and other costs for low-income beneficiaries. Most U.S. citizens become eligible for Medicare when they reach age 65, regardless of income or health status, but they must have paid Medicare payroll taxes for a minimum period of time in order to be eligible. If an individual who is 65 is not Medicare eligible because payroll tax payments were insufficient, then he or she is eligible for enrollment in Medicaid.

Medicare plays an important role for younger people with disabilities, many of whom become eligible when a parent turns 65 or dies. Provider choices tend to be better than for Medicaid, which has historically provided lower reimbursement rates. Medicare is an acute care health care program; therefore, it does not provide coverage for many relatively expensive services such as institutional or community-based long-term care; extended specialty services (e.g., mental health services beyond the acute stage, habilitation services for individuals with developmental disabilities); or dental, vision, or hearing care. Medicare also has fairly high deductibles and cost-sharing requirements for covered benefits, which means that many individuals with disabilities also rely on Medicaid for many benefits (Young et al., 2012).

History of Medicaid

Medicaid was enacted in 1965 as an optional program for the states and was designed to be a partnership between the federal government and individual state governments (Young et al., 2012). Although the program is a state-operated health insurance program, the federal government provides incentives for state participation by financing the majority of the cost. In return, the state must meet the requirements of the program as stipulated in the Social Security Amendments of 1965 and regulations. Significant differences exist among states' eligibility requirements, however, and "the services provided in one state may differ considerably in amount duration, or scope from services provided in a similar or neighboring state" (Klees, Wolfe, & Curtis, 2012, p. 57). These significant differences across states have an enormous effect on the availability of services for individuals with developmental disabilities based on where they live.

Eligibility has been extended over time to many other groups, such as older Americans who have exhausted their ability to meet health care and long-term care costs, even though Medicaid was originally designed to assist specific groups of low-income individuals. Medicaid expenditures and enrollment have accelerated since the mid-2000s (see Figure 17.1). Enrollment in Medicaid is countercyclical, increasing during economic downturns and serving as an important social safety net for children and low-income individuals. Medicaid provided health care assistance for an estimated 54 million people in 2010, and approximately 20% of the population was enrolled in Medicaid for at least 1 month during the year, accounting for more than $400 billion in outlays (Truffer, Klemm, Wolfe, & Rennie, 2012). Medicaid pays for both health insurance and long-term care for those with disabilities who are truly poor, and every state has elected to participate in this program.

Eligibility in Medicaid

States must operate within a specific set of federal requirements to participate in the Medicaid program and receive the federal share of funding[1] for Medicaid services. These requirements are statutorily determined and include the populations that must be served, such as eligible children, adults in households with eligible children, and individuals 65 years of age or older who do not qualify for Medicare.

---

[1]The Federal Medical Assistance Percentage (FMAP) is statutorily determined. Title XIX specifies that the FMAP for each state cannot be lower than 50% or higher than 83%, although Title XIX permits the override of the normal formula to set specific FMAP levels for certain states. The Patient Protection and Affordable Care Act of 2010 (PL 111-148) also provides for 100% FMAP for new enrollees covered under the Patient Protection and Affordable Care Act for a set number of years.

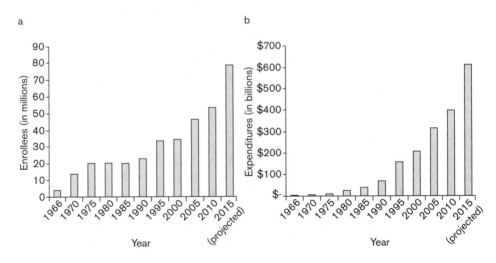

Figure 17.1. Medicaid enrollments in millions (a) and expenditures in billions (b). (*Source*: Truffer, Klemm, Wolfe, & Rennie, 2012.)

Mandatory populations also include people with disabilities who meet the Social Security disability determination that they cannot "engage in any other kind of substantial gainful work which exists in the national economy" (https://secure.ssa.gov/poms.nsf/lnx/0410105065). This concept of unemployability, however, is severely outdated since the passage of the Americans with Disabilities Act (ADA) of 1990 (PL 101-336), as societal expectations for individuals with disabilities have significantly changed since this legislation was enacted. Developments since the 1990s, including customized employment, assistive technology, workplace flexibility, and microenterprise development, have reflected these changes in expectations for community involvement and work force participation for individuals with developmental disabilities, and the term *unemployable* is no longer appropriate.

Enrollment eligibility for Medicaid is determined by a combination of federal and state law. Federal law specifies which groups of people must be eligible, but the states have considerable flexibility in extending coverage to additional groups. Eligibility typically is based on several factors, including income, assets, age, disability status, other government assistance, and health or medical conditions such as pregnancy.

Medicaid Long-Term Supports and Services

Medicaid is the single largest payer for long-term care in the United States, accounting for 43% of the $240 billion long-term care expenditures in 2009, according to one estimate (Ng, Harrington, Musumeci, & Reaves, 2012). Medicaid long-term supports and services (LTSS) are particularly important to individuals with disabilities because they are the primary source of funding for an independent life in the community.

Medicaid long-term care covers a variety of supports and services to assist individuals in activities of daily living and instrumental activities of daily living, including activities such as bathing, dressing, eating, assisting with home chores, and managing medication. The Medicaid LTSS program provides both institutional-based services and home and community-based services. Although users of long-term care supports and services represent only 6% of Medicaid beneficiaries (4 million individuals), they "accounted for nearly half of all Medicaid spending" in 2007 (O'Malley Watts, Lawton, & Young, 2011, p. 1). The 4% of Medicaid LTSS beneficiaries utilizing home and community-based services accounts for 22% of Medicaid spending, whereas the 2% of those in institutional settings consumes a full 26% of the total Medicaid budget (see Figure 17.2).

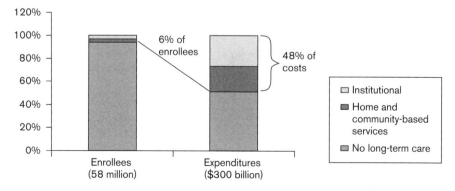

Figure 17.2. Medicaid enrollees and expenditures by long-term supports and services status. (From O'Malley Watts, M., Lawton, E., & Young, K., The Henry J. Kaiser Family Foundation. [2011, October]. *Medicaid's long-term care users: Spending patterns across institutional and community-based settings* [p. 1]. Menlo Park, CA: The Henry J. Kaiser Family Foundation; adapted by permission.)

Institutional Services   Two primary institutional alternatives under Medicaid are skilled nursing facilities and intermediate care facilities for developmentally disabled (ICF/DD; formerly referred to as intermediate care facilities for mentally retarded). How these services are accessed and funded depends on how the individual is labeled by the Centers for Medicare & Medicaid Services. Those labeled as having an intellectual or developmental disability are institutionalized in state centers that have been certified as ICF/DD. Those individuals identified as *aged/disabled,* consisting of older and younger people with physical disabilities, dementia, and other diagnoses not included in the individuals with developmental and intellectual disabilities label, are institutionalized in skilled nursing facilities. Skilled nursing facilities and ICF/DD are entitlements, meaning that they are mandatory Medicaid benefits for all individuals who qualify.

Home and Community-Based Services

A state can provide Medicaid home and community-based services through Medicaid waivers, via the mandatory home health benefit, and through the optional personal care services benefit. In 2009, 3.25 million individuals received Medicaid home and community-based services. Of those participants, 975,929 individuals received home health services through the mandatory state plan benefit, 912,076 individuals received personal care services through the optional state plan benefit, and 1,366,337 individuals were served through 1915(c) Home and Community-Based Services Waivers (Ng et al., 2012). Individuals receiving home and community-based services via 1915(c) waivers accounted for $33.7 billion, nearly 68% of the total expenditures; individuals utilizing the optional state plan benefit and mandatory home health benefit accounted for $11 billion and $5.3 billion, respectively (see Figure 17.3).

The Home and Community-Based Services Waiver programs can serve one or more distinct populations of individuals with disabilities and aging Americans who require assistance. Waiver programs tend to provide more robust services, but states may limit the number of services, specific disabilities served, and geographic area served. Expenditures on home and community-based services have steadily increased as demand has increased for noninstitutional services, despite state restrictions on home and community-based services. Home and community-based services accounted for 44% of Medicaid LTSS expenditures in 2009, increasing from 18% in 1999 (see Figure 17.4) (Eiken, Sredl, Burwell, & Gold, 2011).

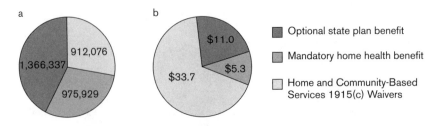

Figure 17.3.   2009 home and community-based services enrollees (a) and expenditures in billions (b) by program. Total enrollees equal 3.25 million. Total expenditures equal $50 billion. (From Ng, T., Harrington, C., Musumeci, M., & Reaves, E., The Henry J. Kaiser Family Foundation. [2012, December]. *Medicaid home and community-based services programs: 2009 data update* [pp. 5–6]. Menlo Park, CA: The Henry J. Kaiser Family Foundation; adapted by permission.)

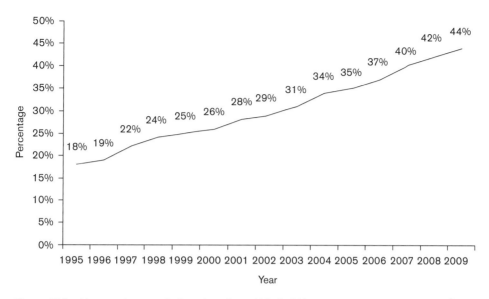

Figure 17.4. Home and community-based services of Medicaid long-term supports and services. (From Eiken, S., Sredl, K., Burwell, B., & Gold, L. [2011, October]. *Medicaid expenditures for long-term services and support: 2011 update.* Cambridge, MA: Thomson Reuters.)

Research demonstrated that effectively providing home and community-based services enables states to serve more individuals at a lower cost (Kaye, LaPlante, & Harrington, 2009). Effective rebalancing of Medicaid long-term care services and supports away from institutions and toward community-based care reduces growth in long-term care spending and can reduce overall spending while serving a greater number of individuals (Felix, Mays, Stewart, Cottoms, & Olson, 2011; Kaye et al., 2009). These programs more often experience restrictions during economic downturns, however, because home and community-based services are often provided under the Medicaid waiver programs, which allow states greater flexibility.

LONG-TERM CARE SUPPORT AND SERVICES AND THE BIRTH OF DEINSTITUTIONALIZATION

As the Medicaid program grew in the years after its implementation, the first serious revision to its long-term care provisions was enacted to serve older individuals in nursing facilities. Reagan administration officials concluded in 1981 that many of those who were elderly and living in nursing facilities did not require nursing care; they simply required some assistance in the activities of daily living (Engel, 2006). A waiver program was developed to allow these individuals to be served in their homes at a much lower cost. The term waiver was deliberately utilized to indicate that this was an exception to the guaranteed service provided at an institution. Although few older Americans with disabilities requested services under these waivers, individuals with intellectual and developmental disabilities began to take advantage of these new waiver possibilities. What followed was a major social transformation as individuals with developmental disabilities utilizing the new community-based services either left the institutions or avoided institutionalization altogether.

This transformation began decades ago and prevailing attitudes have significantly changed over that time. During the transition to community-based services, many critics claimed that institutions would always be a necessary option for those with disabilities and that efforts should be made to maintain and improve the institutions to improve quality rather than eradicate the large, state-run facilities. This is an argument that is frequently utilized to justify the continued existence of nursing facilities for aging Americans.

Medicaid Waivers

Federal law requires all states to provide Medicaid services on a comparable basis to any categorically eligible group. If a state elects to provide additional services, then these must also be provided to any group that is categorically eligible as previously described. Federal law also permits the Secretary of Health and Human Services to grant waivers to certain components of the Medicaid statutory provisions, however—a practice that enables states to receive federal funding for providing differentiated services or for serving groups in ways not ordinarily covered under Medicaid. The three primary types of waivers include Section 1115 waivers, 1915(b) waivers, and 1915(c) waivers. The 1915(c) waivers have been the most instrumental in the lives of individuals with disabilities by supporting independent life in the community as opposed to institutional settings. More than 1.2 million individuals currently receive home and community-based services through the 1915(c) waivers.

Home and Community-Based Services Waivers   The 1915(c) waivers were adopted by Congress in 1981 to reduce unnecessary institutional and hospital costs for aging Americans and permitted states to offer home and community-based services as an alternative for those individuals who were entitled to receive services in a nursing facility or other institutional setting. States were required to demonstrate that the average per-person costs for home and community-based services did not exceed the average per-person institutional costs.

Freedom of Choice Waivers   The 1915(b) waivers permit states to enroll Medicaid beneficiaries in managed care plans and limit the provider network based on the needs of recipients (providing freedom of choice to the states and not to the beneficiaries). These waivers were initially utilized by the states to implement managed care. The Balanced Budget Act of 1997 (PL 105-33), however, contained provisions that permitted the states to implement managed care measures for certain beneficiaries through state plan amendments.

Research and Demonstration Waivers   Section 1115 of the Social Security Act enables the U.S. Department of Health and Human Services to waive a broad range of statutory requirements in order for states to implement programs that provide additional services, expand coverage to additional groups, or demonstrate alternative means of providing services to existing beneficiaries. Three states (Arizona, Rhode Island, and Vermont) presently do not offer any 1915(c) waivers and instead use 1115 waivers to administer statewide Medicaid programs that include home and community-based services for all populations and services (Ng et al., 2012). Several other states have implemented home and community-based services programs under the 1115 waiver, and state applications for 1115 waivers have increased, notably requests to require "high need individuals to enroll in managed care" and "expand managed care to more services, including long-term services and supports"

(Artiga, 2012, p. 11). Although the goal of these programs is to reduce costs and provide better care coordination, disability advocates must remain vigilant because past attempts to provide managed care often have not resulted in lower costs but frequently have resulted in compromised care for individuals.

Wait Lists

Medicaid waivers, particularly the 1915(c) waivers, have played an important role in the movement to deinstitutionalize people with disabilities by providing access to necessary supports for active participation in the community. Waivers have also provided perverse incentives for states experiencing budgetary pressures, however, because the services provided under waivers are not entitlements, which has resulted in more restricted access to community-based services. The effect of this phenomenon is evidenced by the number of individuals with disabilities who have been wait-listed for necessary services, often for 3 or more years. Although the waiver programs have been a crucial factor in deinstitutionalization, they have not evolved quickly enough into standard services or been sufficiently integrated into the Medicaid system to adequately address the rights and ongoing needs of individuals with disabilities.

In 2011, 511,174 individuals were on waiver waiting lists, compared with 428,571 in 2010. The growth of waiting lists increased from 17% in 2010 to 19% in 2011. The average length of time an individual spent on a waiting list ranged from 2 months for mental health waivers to 40 months for individuals with developmental disabilities waivers (Ng et al., 2012). Of the 511,174 individuals on wait lists in 2011, 316,673 individuals (67%) had developmental disabilities (see Figure 17.5a). Although the average wait time for services was 25 months, individuals with developmental disabilities also experienced the longest average wait time at 40 months (see Figure 17.5b). These numbers underscore the fact that the current system fails to provide adequate services and supports to hundreds of thousands of individuals who qualify. The rate of growth in the numbers of individuals on wait lists and the year-over-year increase in wait times for individuals with disabilities also represents a disturbing trend in the wrong direction.

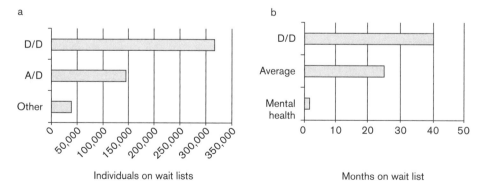

Figure 17.5. a) Individuals on home and community-based services wait list in 2011 ($n = 511,174$) and b) time on wait lists for home and community-based services in 2011 (in months). (*Key:* A/D, individuals identified as "aged/disabled"; D/D, individuals with developmental disabilities) (*Source*: Ng, Harrington, Musumeci, & Reaves, 2012.)

Waiver Cost Neutrality and Cost Containment

Federal regulations require cost neutrality for Home and Community-Based Services Waivers; that is, the total cost for individuals on Home and Community-Based Services Waivers cannot be greater than the institutional costs would be for the same number of individuals. States may apply this calculation on an aggregate basis or on an individual basis. The Medicaid waiver program, however, permits states to utilize a range of cost containment strategies for waiver programs that are not permitted with institutional care. All states reported utilizing some form of cost containment approaches in 2010 that exceed the federal requirements (Artiga, 2012), not only limiting the number of individuals who may obtain services and helping states control costs, but also resulting in waiting lists of eligible individuals. These typically are individuals who qualify for the institutional option but who are unwilling to leave home for care in an institution. In order to remain in their communities while they are awaiting a slot, they must gather an informal, unpaid network of individuals to provide those supports. A poll conducted by the Kaiser Commission on Medicaid Uninsured determined that all states utilize one or more of these measures to control the costs associated with home and community-based services (Artiga, 2012).

- *Financial eligibility:* 26% of waiver programs employ more restrictive financial eligibility standards for home and community-based services than for nursing facilities.

- *Functional eligibility:* 5% of states limit eligibility for Home and Community-Based Services Waivers through stricter functional eligibility criteria than those used to qualify for institutional care.

- *Cost controls:* More than 90% of states utilized some form of cost controls above the federal cost neutrality requirement (e.g., fixed expenditure caps, service provision and hourly caps, geographic limits within the state). More than one third of these states used two or more forms of cost controls.

- *Wait lists:* States frequently limit the number of slots available for waiver programs, and they use wait lists when funded program slots are filled.

Dual Eligibility

Although Medicare and Medicaid are distinct programs, 9 million individuals qualify for both programs and receive benefits under both. The majority of these dually eligible individuals are those with disabilities under the age of 65 and the "aged/disabled" individuals who qualify independently for each program. Dually eligible individuals are generally the poorest individuals, often have significant and chronic health needs, and typically account for a disproportionate amount of spending in each program. The CMS reported in 2011 that although 16% of Medicare beneficiaries are dually eligible, they accounted for 27% of expenditures, and the 15% of Medicaid beneficiaries with dual eligibility accounted for 39% of Medicaid expenditures. A significant overlap exists between individuals who are dually eligible and those in need of LTSS. "Almost three quarters (73%) of all Medicare beneficiaries living in a long-term care facility" (Jacobson, Neumann, & Damico, 2012, p. 3) are dually eligible individuals, and "dual eligible [individual]s accounted for more than two-thirds of Medicaid enrollees who used long-term services and supports" (O'Malley et al., 2011, p. 3). Although dually eligible individuals account for a very small percent of Medicare and Medicaid beneficiaries, they consume a disproportionate share of resources, and, as a result, this population is the target of frequent policy debate and public discussion (Adamy, 2011; Galewitz, 2011).

Comparison of Medicare and Medicaid Funding Sources

Medicare is a health insurance program entirely funded at the federal level through designated trust funds, payroll taxes, and federal general revenues, which recently became the largest source of Medicare funding (*Testimony before the House Committee on the Budget,* 2012). Beneficiaries are people age 65 or older who have contributed to the program through payroll deductions for a minimum number of quarters and some individuals with disabilities under the age 65. The program was initially funded primarily through payroll taxes during a time when retirement age more closely corresponded to life expectancy. Life expectancy has increased, health care costs have risen, and the economics of the program have changed considerably, however, as the baby boom generation has reached retirement age, resulting in greater reliance on contributions from the federal government's general revenues and more financial pressure on the system.

In contrast, Medicaid is a needs-based social welfare program that is funded at both the state and federal levels, which has significant implications for program structure and implementation. Eligibility for the program is largely determined by income, which plays no role in determining Medicare coverage. Medicaid also covers a wider range of health care and support services than Medicare and is a critical program for individuals with disabilities who require long-term care. States pay providers or managed care organizations for Medicaid costs, which are reported to the CMS. The federal government reimburses a percent of Medicaid costs according to the Federal Medical Assistance Percentage, which is calculated annually for each state based on a statutory formula. The federal share of Medicaid programs is never less than 50% and can range up to 83% for the poorest states; it depends upon the relative wealth of the state. Of the $404.1 billion in 2010 Medicaid payments, 68% ($272.8 billion) were paid by the federal government and 32% ($131.3 billion) were paid by the states. The distinction between the two programs is an important one for people with disabilities, many of whom obtain benefits from both programs.

Navigating the Programs

Medicare and Medicaid are two distinct programs that have evolved separately. Medicare is a federal insurance program; Medicaid is primarily a state insurance program. Each uses separate cost accounting requirements and billing systems, maintains different eligibility requirements, provides different benefits, utilizes a unique appeals process, and contracts with different providers. Understanding which benefits are covered within each program, how to gain access to the various service options, and how to coordinate services is a difficult task for the vast majority of individuals who utilize both programs. The high level of complexity associated with service delivery across the two programs and the lack of integration often has resulted in lower levels of service combined with higher associated costs. Dually eligible individuals have been a frequent topic of policy debate and a target for quality improvement and cost reductions because of their disproportionate utilization of resources.

CHALLENGES AND CONTROVERSIES

The Medicaid and Medicare programs face increasing pressures, both internal and external, which threaten their current structures. This section highlights some of the major challenges facing these two programs, including 1) a pervasive institutional bias that has led to a lack of adequate home and community-based services infrastructure and unnecessarily high costs of long-term care, 2) severe financial pressures that affect the availability of services and supports, and 3) demographic changes toward a rapidly increasing population of older Americans, a trend that will continue to affect availability of services and supports for all individuals.

Challenge 1: Institutional Bias

Sociey has an obligation under law to protect the rights of people with disabilities according to the ADA. The Supreme Court Olmstead Decision (*Olmstead v. L.C.*, 1999) affirmed that the isolation and segregation of individuals with disabilities in institutional settings is a serious and pervasive form of discrimination. Various disability populations, including older Americans, however, continue to be segregated by the Medicaid system, which promotes forced institutionalization for older Americans and poverty for people with all types of disabilities. Medicaid services and supports often are too inadequate to address the basic requirements of Olmstead and the ADA.

Few believe that institutions are either necessary or appropriate for people with developmental disabilities. Many critics today believe that nursing facilities will always be an important option for the elderly, however, just like proponents of institutionalization for those with developmental disabilities in the past. Although most people express strong personal preferences against nursing facilities as a long-term care option (Bayer & Harper, 2000), many do not question the pervasive bias toward confining the elderly in these institutions. This "systematic difference in the way older adults with disabilities are treated relative to younger individuals with disabilities constitutes ageism" (Kane, Priester, & Neumann, 2007, p. 1). Although 3% of the 8.8 million Medicaid enrollees with disabilities were institutionalized, a full 18% of the 5.9 million elderly Medicaid users were confined to institutions. Nearly 55% of Medicaid long-term care spending is for institutional care, despite purported commitment to community-based alternatives. Of $300 billion spending in 2007, 48%, or $144 billion, was for long-term care. Of that figure, $75 billion was spent on institutional care (O'Malley et al., 2011). States have responded to federal law and consumer preferences for community-based care over institutional care by expanding home and community-based services programs. Although enrollees in Home and Community-Based Services Waivers have increased, so have the numbers on waiting lists (exceeding 430,000 in 2010, with average wait times of 3 years for those with developmental disabilities). Individuals receiving community-based services meet the same eligibility requirements as those individuals served by an institution. Although institutional placements are guaranteed, community supports under waiver programs are not, making waiver programs vulnerable during periods of severe budget cuts.

Challenge 2: Fiscal Crisis Effect on Home and Community-Based Services and Dually Eligible Individuals

The Medicaid program has been described by the National Governor's Association as its biggest single budget worry (National Association of State Budget Officers, 2012). State budget concerns have meant that various cost containment measures have been applied to state Medicaid programs and have often resulted in short-sighted restrictions on home and community-based services, which defeats the goal of serving more individuals in community-based settings. A national recession was underway and state revenues were limited when home and community-based services were being added to Title XIX in the 1980s. Congress, therefore, permitted states to limit their commitment to home and community-based services to a number of individual slots that the state delineated in its plan for home and community-based services. This institutional bias—the fact that Title XIX mandates open entitlement for hospital and institutional services but allows states to limit the number of individuals who can obtain home and community-based services—has been the subject of much advocacy for change since the 1980s. States have been reluctant to expand entitlements due to budget and other concerns and have continued to limit the availability of home and community-based services, despite the fact that serving individuals in community settings is a staggering $44,000 lower than care in an institution (Kitchener, 2006) and effective rebalancing of long-term care toward home and community-based services reduces Medicaid spending and enables states to serve more individuals at a lower cost (Felix et al., 2011; Kaye et al., 2009). Spending appears to be affected by the way rebalancing is implemented, and shortsighted cuts to home and community-based services will almost certainly increase the costs of long-term care (Kaye, 2012). Furthermore, the lack of near-term investment in home and community-based services infrastructure also jeopardizes states' future ability to serve the growing number of elderly in less expensive community-based settings and affects availability of services to all disability groups.

A second major effect of this fiscal crisis is a new iteration of managed care that seeks to provide better service at lower cost. Managed long-term support and service (MLTSS) grew significantly between 2004 and 2012. The number of states with MLTSS programs doubled from 8 to 16, and the number of people receiving MLTSS through managed care programs increased from 105,000 to 389,000. The number of states projected to have MLTSS programs by 2014 is 26 (Saucier, Kasten, Burweel, & Gold, 2012). These attempts to provide managed care for those with developmental disabilities, including many who are dually eligible, vary widely by state. These programs must be carefully monitored; better care can and should be provided. Previous versions of managed care and the introduction of for-profit managed care entities, however, have resulted in cost cutting without predicted improvements in care, generally at the expense of those who are poor and have disabilities.

Challenge 3: Demographic Changes and the Effect of Aging Population

Nearly 89 million people, or 20% of the population, will be age 65 and older by 2050 (U.S. Census Bureau, 2008). The number of Americans with chronic conditions will increase by 37% between 2000 and 2030, an increase of 46 million people (Anderson, 2010), and a growing number of Americans with chronic conditions and functional impairments will require long-term care in the near future (Shugarman & Whitenhill, 2012). Little has been done to prepare for the long-term care needs of this population, despite the long-predicted demographic surge in the number of aging Americans. A large number of older Americans are predicted to outlive their savings due to increasing life expectancy and the high cost of their long-term care needs (annual nursing facility costs average $80,000); they likely will need to rely on Medicaid for their long-term care supports because their savings are exhausted. Medicaid long-term care is no longer reserved for the very poor, but increasingly will serve as an important safety net for aging Americans who were members of the middle class during their working years. Failure to develop the infrastructure and supports for the significantly less expensive home and community-based services for these aging individuals paves the way for a certain and easily predicted financial crisis within the Medicaid system.

Furthermore, the significant disparity in the institutionalization rates within the two populations has implications for the continued funding and availability of community-based Medicaid programs for individuals with developmental disabilities. Although 3% of the 8.8 million Medicaid enrollees with disabilities were institutionalized, a full 18% of the 5.9 million elderly Medicaid users were confined to institutions. The shockingly high numbers of elderly (as well as thousands of individuals with disabilities) in nursing facilities a full decade after the Olmstead decision indicates a troubling and pervasive bias toward institutionalizing aging Americans (Kane et al., 2007). The significant and disproportionate cost of this institutional care has also sapped resources from nearly all community-based programs and resulted in the severe rationing of the care provided to people with disabilities in their own communities.

The costs associated with institutionalizing aging Americans and the proliferation of for-profit nursing facilities will increasingly limit the options available to those with developmental disabilities. Advocates for the aging and those with developmental disabilities must coordinate their efforts and demand a more robust home and community-based services infrastructure, or the advances made in recent decades may begin to erode. An expanding for-profit nursing home industry, serving both elderly individuals and those with disabilities, is a real near-term possibility.

CURRENT SYSTEM VERSUS SYSTEM OF THE FUTURE

The pervasive impoverishment of individuals within the most costly system of care in the world is one of the great ironies of the current human services approach to long-term care for individuals with disabilities. Many more individuals with disabilities languish on waiting lists in order to obtain the most basic supports within their communities. The System of the Future is rooted in the principles of self-determination to enable individuals with disabilities to live a life of quality and purpose. This system serves a greater number of individuals at a lower cost because it eliminates the pervasive reliance on high-cost institutional services.

Current System

The high cost of the current human services system is partially a result of the focus on facilities, programs, and work activities. Those individuals with long-term care needs must choose from a predetermined set of services, typically offered by a predetermined group of service providers. Members of a large government bureaucracy and an entrenched group of service providers determine what services are available. Whether the services provided meet the needs or preferences of the individual is irrelevant in the current system. Little opportunity is available for the individual to exercise basic freedoms that most people take for granted.

The purpose of public funding is to assist citizens who need support because of long-term disability. The key question that must be addressed is, "Support for what?" Public dollars have historically funded facility care, segregated congregate settings, professionally driven programs that are clinically based, sequestered work environments that provide little or no income, and rules and regulations that require (and perpetuate) poverty for eligibility. The current system funds services without high expectations. It does not invest in lives of high quality and great purpose. These investments of public dollars should be in the arenas of community living that mirror the freedoms and goals that all Americans take for granted.

Self-Determination and the System of the Future

Self-determination posits that the way individuals are perceived and how they think about themselves does not emanate from the human services system or the efforts of human services programs. The outcomes are realized when free men and women engage in creating a home, getting involved in the community, establishing real relationships, and generating income. This is a direct, uncompromising approach that targets only a few spheres of life that are common to all individuals. Self-determination simply reflects the basic, everyday freedoms that most individuals enjoy. If individuals with disabilities do not have these basic freedoms, then they cannot be equal citizens.

Self-determination leads society to look closely at what the public tax dollars are purchasing in the name of human services and helping people. The poor use of public funds for programs that dehumanize individuals must be challenged by asking, "What is this support for?" and "What outcomes are we trying to achieve?" Even a cursory examination of the issue will make clear that public funds available through Medicare, and more important, through the Medicaid system of long-term services and support, are most often spent on promoting lives that individuals would not choose for themselves. Public funding should be used to promote a life well lived, which requires a fundamental change in policy and practice and a reorientation to the progress made by the individual. Only by adopting universal quality standards— those that the society takes for granted—can society ever live up to the rhetoric that people with disabilities are equal citizens. If individuals with disabilities are not entitled to the same basic freedoms as other citizens, then they are not equal citizens.

The System of the Future

The quality standards in a newly developed quality assurance system will be chosen from among those quality-of-life dimensions that all citizens can and do pursue (Nerney, Carver, & Kovach, 2005). Public funding is used as an investment in the lives of older Americans and individuals with disabilities to do the following.

- Help individuals stay in or create their own community home with supports, adaptations, and personnel when necessary.

- Enable individuals to keep and develop long-term relationships.

- Maintain or develop real community membership by supporting membership in various formal and informal community groups.

- Generate income, whether from employment, self-employment, other sources (e.g., rental income) or the preservation of assets.

Any set of quality standards that ignores these four dimensions immediately removes any hope of equality for individuals with disabilities. It becomes apparent looking at these four measures that the current human services system subjects individuals to second-class citizenship, rendering them incapable of reaching for common human aspirations.

CONCLUSION

Medicare and the Medicaid-funded long-term care system—the two systems that have the greatest effect on the lives of many individuals with disabilities—are under enormous strain that will only continue to increase as demographic and economic factors coalesce into the perfect storm. Waiting lists for home and community-based services are growing, and more than one third of individuals with disabilities who live at home are cared for by aging parents. The United States population will experience an unprecedented shift as the baby boom generation approaches retirement age, which no longer correlates with life expectancy, and many middle-class Americans will require long-term care. The cost of this long-term care will exhaust the resources of many individuals and force them to gain access to the Medicaid safety net, which previously had been reserved for the very poor.

The economic downturn means that states have been aggressively pursuing shortsighted budget cuts, which have already created barriers to adequate community services and supports for people with disabilities and aging Americans, just as the population of aging Americans is exploding. Other factors are also at work, including an institutional bias and a renewed focus on managed care. The institutional bias needs to be eliminated, and this will require disability advocates, who have largely ignored the institutionalization of aging Americans, to broaden their focus, coordinate their efforts, and demand a more robust home and community-based services infrastructure.

The attempts to provide better care at a lower cost using a new iteration of managed care must be carefully monitored. Better care can and should be provided. Previous versions of managed care and introducing for-profit managed care entities, however, have resulted in cost cutting without predicted improvements in care, generally at the expense of the poor and those with disabilities. The Center for Medicare & Medicaid Innovation (2012) is driving state efforts to create health homes, especially for those who are dually eligible. Although intentions may be good, the fact that medical nomenclature has replaced normal language portends a potential return to medical supervision for those with disabilities.

Even those community-based services and supports that are available are dominated by service providers, programs, and government bureaucracy. Measures of quality and performance are used to assess program or facility performance and bear little if any relation to outcomes for the individual beneficiaries. The individuals for whom the services are provided are an afterthought in the planning of their own lives, and no one is held accountable for the lack of real and meaningful outcomes.

The enormous challenges facing the programs today and in the near future mean that predictable and unpredictable changes will result from current political negotiations. Reevaluating the principles on which the programs are based and fashioning a future for the programs is of primary importance. There is little time before individuals with disabilities lose all hope for a meaningful life. Society needs to move quickly and responsibly to eliminate a system allowing lives to be lost to regulation, bureaucracy, and low expectations, instead replacing it with one that promotes lives of great expectations, filled with hope and meaning.

Questions for Study and Reflection

1. What are the essential differences between the Medicare and Medicaid programs?

2. Describe how each one supports individuals with disabilities.

3. What are some factors that are likely to affect the availability of services and supports for individuals with disabilities in the near future?

4. Which long-term supports and services are preferable? An institutional setting or a community setting? Explain why.

5. What is a Medicaid waiver? How have waivers played a role in the lives of individuals with disabilities?

6. Describe the purposes of the following Medicaid waivers: 1915(c), 1915(b), and 1115.

7. What are the elements of a good quality assurance system?

8. What constitutes quality in the lives of individuals with disabilities?

9. Why do you think this system is so complex?

10. What are your recommendations for the future?

RESOURCES

ArcLink *http://www.thearclink.org*

Center for Self-Determination *http://www.centerforself-determination.com*

Center on Aging and Disabilities *http://www.cad.med.miami.edu*

Center on Human Policy *http://thechp.syr.edu*

Centers for Medicare & Medicaid Services *http://www.cms.gov*

Children's Defense Fund *http://www.childrensdefense.org*

Consortium for Citizens with Disabilities *http://www.c-c-d.org*

Council of Parent Attorneys and Advocates *http://www.copaa.net*

Family Voices *http://www.familyvoices.org*

The Henry J. Kaiser Family Foundation *http://www.kff.org*

Inclusion BC *http://www.bcacl.org*

National Association of Councils on Developmental Disabilities *http://www.nacdd
    .org*

National Association of State Directors of Developmental Disabilities Services *http://
    www.nasddds.org/TeleconferenceSeries-Advocacy.shtml*

National Down Syndrome Society *http://www.ndss.org*

National Information Center for Children and Youth with Disabilities *http://www
    .nichcy.org*

National Organization on Disability *http://www.nod.org*

Partners in Policymaking *http://www.partnersinpolicymaking.com*

Robert Wood Johnson Foundation *http://www.rwjf.org*

U.S. Justice Department, Civil Rights Division *http://www.justice.gov/crt/*

REFERENCES

Adamy, J. (2011, June 27). *Overlapping health plans are double trouble for taxpayers.* Retrieved from http://online.wsj.com/article/SB10001424052702304453304576392194143220356.html

Americans with Disabilities Act (ADA) of 1990, PL 101-336, 42 U.S.C. §§ 12101 *et seq.*

Anderson, G. (2010). *Chronic care: Making the case for ongoing care.* Retrieved from http://www.rwjf.org/content/dam/web-assets/2010/01/chronic-care

Artiga, S. (2012). *An overview of recent section 1115 Medicaid waiver demonstration activity.* Menlo Park, CA: Kaiser Family Foundation, The Kaiser Commission on Medicaid and the Uninsured.

Balanced Budget Act of 1997, PL 105-33, 111 Stat. 251.

Bayer, A., & Harper, L. (2000). *Fixing to stay: A national survey of housing and some modification issues.* Washington, DC: American Association of Retired Persons.

Boards of Trustees, Federal Hospital Insurance and Federal Supplementary Medical Insurance Trust Funds. (2012). Retrieved from http://www.cms.gov/Research-Statistics-Data-and-Systems/Statistics-Trends-and-Reports/ReportsTrustFunds/downloads/tr2012.pdf

Center for Medicare & Medicaid Innovation. (2012). *Report to Congress.* Retrieved from http://innovation.cms.gov/Files/reports/RTC-12-2012.pdf

Eiken, S., Sredl, K., Burwell, B., & Gold, L. (2011, October). *Medicaid expenditures for long-term services and support: 2011 update*. Cambridge, MA: Thomson Reuters. Retrieved from http://www.hcbs.org/fi les /208/10395/2011LTSSExpenditures-final .pdf

Engel, J. (2006). *Poor people's medicine: Medicaid and American charity care since 1965*. Durham, NC: Duke University Press.

Felix, H., Mays, G., Stewart, M., Cottoms, N., & Olson, M. (2011). Medicaid savings resulted when community health workers matched those with needs to home and community care. *Health Affairs, 30,* 1366–1374.

Galewitz, P. (2011, November 17). Medicare medicaid "dual eligibles" under scrutiny. *USA Today*. Retrieved from http://usa today30.usatoday.com/news/health/ healthcare/health/healthcare/story/2011-11-17/Medicare-Medicaid-dual-eligibles-under-scrutiny/51271250/1

The Henry J. Kaiser Family Foundation. (2012, June). *Medicaid and long-term care services and supports*. Menlo Park, CA: Author. Retrieved from http://kaiser familyfoundation.files.wordpress.com/ 2013/01/2186-09.pdf

Jacobson, G., Neumann, T., & Damico, A. (2012). *Medicare's role for dual eligible beneficiaries*. Retrieved from http://www .kff.org/medicare/upload/8138-02.pdf

Kane, R., Priester, R., & Neumann, D. (2007). Does disparity in the way disabled older adults are treated imply ageism? *The Gerontologist, 47,* 271–279.

Kaye, H.S. (2012). *Gradual rebalancing of Medicaid long term care services and supports saves money and serves more people, statistical model shows*. Retrieved from http://content.healthaffairs .org/content/31/6/1195

Kaye, H.S., LaPlante, M.P., & Harrington, C. (2009). Do noninstitutional long-term care services reduce Medicaid spending? *Health Affairs, 28,* 262–272. doi:10.1377/ hlthaff.28.1.262

Kitchener, M. (2006). Institutional and community-based long term care: A comparative estimate of public costs. *Journal of Health and Social Policy, 22,* 31–50.

Klees, B., Wolfe, C., & Curtis, C. (2011). *Brief summaries of Medicare and Medicaid: Title XVIII and Title XIX of the Social Security Act*. Retrieved from http://www .cms.gov/Research-Statistics-Data-and-Systems/Statistics-Trends-and-Reports/ MedicareProgramRatesStats/downloads/ MedicareMedicaidSummaries2011.pdf

Klees, B., Wolfe, C., & Curtis, C. (2012). *Annual statistical supplement, 2012*. Washington, DC: U.S. Social Security Administration, Office of Retirement and Disability Policy. Retrieved from http:// www.ssa.gov/policy/docs/statcomps/sup plement/2012/medicaid.pdf

Medicare Modernization Act (Medicare Prescription Drug, Improvement, and Modernization Act) of 2003, PL 108-173, 117 Stat. 2066.

National Association of State Budget Officers and the National Governors Association. (2012). *The fiscal survey of states*. Retrieved from http://www.nasbo.org/ sites/default/files/Spring%202012%20 Fiscal%20Survey_1.pdf

Nerney, T., Carver, P., & Kovach, K. (2005). *Real life quality standards* (Vol. 4). Wayne, MI, Center for Self-Determination.

Ng, T., Harrington, C., Musumeci, M., & Reaves, E., The Henry J. Kaiser Family Foundation. (2012, December). *Medicaid home and community-based services programs: 2009 data update* (pp. 5–6). Menlo Park, CA: The Henry J. Kaiser Family Foundation. Retrieved from http://kff .org/medicaid/report/medicaid-home-and-community-based-service-programs/

Olmstead v. L.C. (98-536) 527 U.S. 581 (1999).

O'Malley Watts, M., Lawton, E., & Young, K., The Henry J. Kaiser Family Foundation. (2011, October). *Medicaid's long-term care users: Spending patterns across institutional and community-based settings* (p. 1). Menlo Park, CA: The Henry J. Kaiser Family Foundation. Retrieved from http:// kff.org/medicaid/issue-brief/medicaids-long-term-care-users-spending -patterns/

Patient Protection and Affordable Care Act of 2010, PL 111-148, 124 Stat. 119.

Saucier, P., Kasten, J., Burweel, B., & Gold, L. (2012). *The growth of managed long-term services and supports*. Ann Arbor, MI: Truven Health Analytics. Retrieved from http://www.medicaid.gov/Medicaid-CHIP-Program-Information/By-Topics/ Delivery-Systems/Downloads/MLTSSP_ White_paper_combined.pdf

Shugarman, L. & Whitenhill, K. (2012). *Growing demand for long-term care in the U.S.* Retrieved from http://www.thes canfoundation.org/sites/thescanfounda tion.org/files/us_growing_demand_for_ ltc_june_2012_fs.pdf

Social Security Amendments of 1965, PL 89-97, 42 U.S.C., §§ 401 *et seq.*

Testimony before the House Committee on the Budget (2012). (Testimony of Richard S. Foster, Chief Actuary, Centers for Medicare & Medicaid Services).

Truffer, C., Klemm, J., Wolfe, C., & Rennie, K. (2012). *2011 actuarial report on the financial outlook for Medicaid.* Baltimore, MD: Center for Medicare & Medicaid Services.

U.S. Census Bureau. (2008). *Projections of the population by selected age groups and sex for the United States: 2010 to 2050.* Retrieved from http://www.census .gov

Young, K., Garfield, R., Musumeci, M., Clemans-Cope, L., & Lawton, E. (2012). *Medicaid's role for dual-eligible beneficiaries.* Retrieved from http://www.kff.org/medi caid/upload/7846-03.pdf

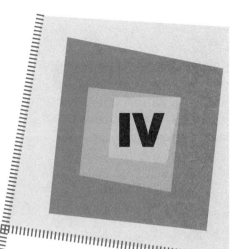

A Look
Around
and Ahead

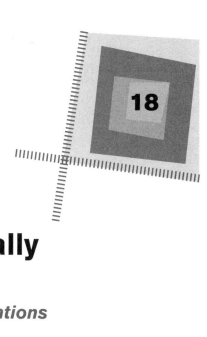

Societal Inclusion and Equity Internationally

Initiatives, Illustrations, Challenges, and Recommendations

Diane Ryndak, Deborah S. Reed, Grzegorz Szumski,
Ann-Marie Orlando, Joanna Smogorzewska, and Wei Gao

It has become more evident in this era of globalization that people with severe disabilities frequently are devalued and marginalized within their societies, denied access to and benefits derived from membership and participation in services (e.g., regular education) and opportunities (e.g., employment) readily available to others in their societies, and not awarded the same rights and respect as people without disabilities in their society. The reality is that social inclusion and equity remain elusive to various groups of people (e.g., people from diverse sociocultural backgrounds, social classes, genders, and socioeconomic statuses) in every culture, depending on its values, history, politics, and use of available resources. These and other variables shape the manner in which a society perceives and serves its most marginalized members. Understanding them provides insight on how a society's systems (e.g., educational system, supports for living in the community) have developed and either how they are evolving or why they are not evolving.

This chapter discusses the state of societal inclusion and international equity for people with severe disabilities. The chapter first describes international initiatives that address the rights and needs of people with disabilities. Second, it discusses how the cultural values, history, politics, and use of available resources in a country or region are interrelated and shape the supports and services provided, or not provided, for people with severe disabilities. Third, the chapter provides two illustrations of how services for people with disabilities have been shaped by the cultural values, history, politics, and use of available resources in two countries—Poland and Mainland China. These countries were selected because they exemplify two types of contexts: 1) countries previously under Communist control with newly formed democracies and 2) countries with a Confucian cultural heritage. Fourth, it summarizes some of the challenges, concerns, and controversies faced in these countries, and it provides recommendations for future research, policy development, and collaboration with TASH. The chapter does not address the challenges, concerns, and controversies faced in well-established European and Commonwealth countries; rather, it focuses on countries that represent sets of countries with challenges that are distinctive and divergent from those faced in the United States because of their unique history and heritage.

INTERNATIONAL INITIATIVES RELATED TO PEOPLE WITH DISABILITIES AND INCLUSION IN SOCIETY

Societal inclusion and equity for all individuals is a challenge in every country. An international disability rights movement has advocated for all countries to commit to meeting goals put forth in agreements that call for basic human rights, gender equity, and inclusive practices in education, employment, and living options for all people (Artiles, Kozleski, & Waitoller, 2011). Although international agreements are in place, comparisons of the lives of people with and without disabilities globally are discouraging. Children with disabilities fare poorly in established educational systems in many countries throughout the world. In developing countries with limited resources few children with disabilities receive a basic public education, complete school, gain access to inclusive community contexts, and experience a quality of life commensurate with that of their neighbors without disabilities (Turnbull, Brown, & Turnbull, 2004). In developed countries that have adequate resources children with disabilities often are segregated from other children, have limited participation in inclusive community contexts, and experience poor educational outcomes (Artiles et al., 2011).

International initiatives provide a framework for and summary of overall global intentions for providing all children and adults equitable, high-quality inclusive opportunities for education, employment, and living (see Table 18.1). Ongoing global inequalities exist for several marginalized and excluded groups, even though these agreements were established to ensure equal rights for all people (Kozleski, Artiles, & Waitoller, 2011). For instance, the Convention on the Rights of the Child (United Nations, 1989) called for protection of children from discrimination, neglect, and abuse. It purported the importance of international cooperation and assistance and called for each country to take positive steps to protect each of its children. Two optional protocols to the convention were established in 2000; one limited using children in armed conflict, and the other set forth standards for preventing and protecting victims related to the sale of children, child prostitution, and child pornography.

The World Declaration on Education for All (United Nations Educational, Scientific and Cultural Organization [UNESCO], 1994b) established a global commitment to providing all children, youth, and adults with equitable quality education. It specifically established an alliance among government agencies, society, and the private sector to work collaboratively toward the achievement of six goals by the year 2015. These goals collectively 1) focused on improving access to and quality of early childhood care and education and primary and secondary education; 2) highlighted literacy, numeracy, and life skills; and 3) targeted equity for girls and children with disabilities, both in difficult circumstances and from ethnic minorities.

Table 18.1. International legislation and agreements

Date	Legislation and agreements	Initiative
1989	Convention on the Rights of the Child	Protect the civil, cultural, economic, political, and social rights of children. Four core principles: 1. Nondiscrimination 2. Devotion to the best interests of the child 3. Right to life, survival, and development 4. Respect for the views of the child
1990	World Declaration on Education for All	Started as an alliance of national governments, civil society groups, and development agencies. Describes education as a human right. Six basic goals: 1. Expand and improve early childhood care and education; specifically mentions the most vulnerable and disadvantaged children. 2. All children have access to good quality education by 2015 that is complete, is free, and includes compulsory primary education; specifically mentions access for girls, children in difficult circumstances, and children from ethnic minorities. 3. Achieve equitable access to learning and life skills for young people and adults. 4. Improve adult literacy by 50% by 2015. Specifically mentions improvement for women; equitable access to basic and continuing education for all adults by 2015. 5. Eliminate gender disparities in primary and secondary education access and achieve gender equality by 2015. Specifically mentions complete and equal access to quality education for girls. 6. Improve quality education and excellence through recognition and measurable learning outcomes achieved by all. Specifically mentions literacy, numeracy, and essential life skills.
1993	Standard Rules on the Equalization of Opportunities for Persons with Disabilities	Delineates quality of life and equality principles. Describes the need for collaborative partnerships. Specifically mentions equalization of opportunities for women, children, elderly, poor, migrant workers, people with dual or multiple disabilities, indigenous people, and ethnic minorities.
1994	Salamanca Statement	Specifically attends to the need for education of children with disabilities. Addresses the need for the inclusion of children with disabilities in regular education contexts and systems. Two major points 1. Children with special needs must have access to regular schools that will accommodate for their needs by using child-centered pedagogy that is capable of meeting those needs. 2. Regular schools that are inclusive are effective in addressing discriminatory attitudes, which lead to an inclusive society and education for all.
1998	World Declaration on Higher Education	Education is the foundation of human rights, democracy, sustainable development, and peace. Addresses equity of access to higher education. States that no discrimination can occur on the grounds of race; gender; language; religion; economic, cultural, or social distinctions; or physical disabilities.
2000	Dakar Framework for Action	Reaffirms the previous agreements about education for all due to limited progress over the 10 years. Outlines a framework for the six education-for-all goals to ensure achievement.
2007	United Nations Convention on the Rights of Persons with Disabilities	Promotes protection of human rights for people with disabilities; specifically mentions people with disabilities that require more intensive support. Affirms the right to individual choice. Confirms that children with disabilities should have full human rights and freedoms equal to that of children without disabilities. Recognizes the importance of accessibility (i.e., physical, social, economic, cultural, health, education, information, communication).

Source: Gabel and Danforth (2008).

373

The Standard Rules on the Equalization of Opportunities for Persons with Disabilities (United Nations, 1993) offered a moral and political commitment of governments to take action that would result in opportunities for people with disabilities equal to those provided for people without disabilities. The rules were applied beyond issues related to people with disabilities; specifically, issues related to age (i.e., children, elderly), gender (i.e., women), and socioeconomic and sociocultural roles (i.e., poor, migrant, indigenous, and ethnic minorities). It delineated 22 rules that serve as a foundation for policy making and act as a basis for technical and economic cooperation.

The Salamanca Statement (UNESCO, 1994a) set forth a challenge to ensure that schools fulfill the goals of education for all for children with special needs, including those with severe disabilities, regardless of their physical, intellectual, emotional, social, or linguistic state. It also stipulated that schools provide those services in inclusive regular education contexts with accommodations required to meet each student's needs.

The World Declaration on Higher Education (UNESCO, 1998) called for equity of access to higher education so that no discrimination occurs on the grounds of race, gender, language, religion, or physical disabilities, as well as economic, cultural, or social distinctions. It also called for access to higher education for specific groups, including indigenous people, cultural and linguistic minorities, disadvantaged groups, people living under occupation, and people who have disabilities, although it made no reference to intellectual or severe disabilities. It stated that the experience and talents of people in these groups might have value to societal development, and their access to higher education might be accomplished with special assistance.

The Dakar Framework for Action (UNESCO, 2000) was developed as a joint commitment to action that would ensure the education-for-all goals would be reached and sustained. The intent was to accomplish this through partnerships within countries, with the support of agencies and institutions at the regional and international levels.

Finally, the Convention on the Rights of Persons with Disabilities (United Nations, 2007) was developed to ensure that all people with disabilities, including those with severe disabilities, experience full and equal human rights and freedoms. This convention also promoted the respect and dignity of people with disabilities who struggle to reach full and effective participation in society.

EFFECT OF CULTURAL VALUES, HISTORY, POLITICS, AND RESOURCES ON PERCEPTIONS AND SERVICES

Although numerous countries have officially committed to meeting the intent of one or more international agreements that called for human rights, equality, equity of access, and inclusion for all people across the life span, the cultural values, history, politics, and use of available resources shape each country's interpretation and implementation of these agreements. Differences in interpretation and implementation have led to disparities in how the agreements affect a society's perceptions of various sets of people (e.g., those with disabilities, women, indigenous peoples). This is evident when differentiated services (e.g., education) are delivered to various sets of people in a country, particularly those most marginalized based on sociocultural diversity, social class, gender, socioeconomic status, and disability.

The conditions for Roma children (i.e., children of nomads living in the European Union) are an example of marginalization related to cultural diversity and social class. Ringold, Orenstein, and Wilkens stated in their report for the World Bank that "in some cases, Roma poverty rates are more than 10 times that of non-Roma" (2005, p. xiv), and Roma children often are educated in segregated settings (Greenberg, 2010; Ringold et al., 2005). The Roma have origins in northwest India, speak a language known as Romani, and comprise the largest ethnic minority in the European Union (Murray, 2012). Their lifestyle, which is similar to other nomadic groups (e.g., Irish Travellers, Manush, Sinti), is not valued by the dominant societies in which they live, resulting in limited access to services such as education (White, 2012).

Marginalization based on gender also is evident to varying degrees across countries. Cooray and Potrafke (2011) examined gender equality in education and found that both the culture and dominant religious practices in a region had greater influence on gender equality in education than the political model of their country. For instance, their analysis showed that society has made progress toward gender equality in some Latin American countries (e.g., Argentina) where women have had an important role in the democratization of the country. In contrast, the authors described high rates of gender inequality in both education and the work force for countries while part of the Communist bloc; however, no significant changes related to gender equality occurred once they gained independence from the Communist bloc and began to develop a democratic political model. The authors made a similar comparison in relation to autocratic countries. For instance, gender equality in educational opportunity in some autocratic countries (e.g., Qatar) is promoted in the absence of a prominent role for women in society, whereas gender equality is not promoted in other autocratic countries (e.g., Afghanistan), and females are denied access to education. Cooray and Potrafke argued that the same conclusion can be reached in relation to the effect of religion on gender equality; that is, religion has a greater effect than a political model on the extent to which gender equality is demonstrated.

The United Nations (2012) uses the Human Development Index (HDI) as a measure of a country's social and economic development to rank 187 countries on three factors—health, education, and income. These indicators are considered to be interdependent and jointly provide one perspective on the quality of life experienced by the citizens of a country. The rankings then are divided into four levels of development (i.e., very high, high, medium, and low human development). For instance, countries ranked 1–47 comprise the very high human development level (i.e., the highest level). Norway is ranked first with 1) an average life expectancy of 81.3 years, 2) a mean number of years in school of 12.6, and 3) a mean gross national income of approximately $49,000 annually. In contrast, Cameroon is ranked 150, considered a low human development level, with 1) an average life expectancy of 52.1 years, 2) a mean number of years in school of 5.9, and 3) a mean gross national income of approximately $2,000 annually. Thus, the lower a country's HDI, the less likely it is that people with and without disabilities have equitable access to and benefits of high-quality education.

Beyond the perspective provided by using HDI scores and levels, the influence of socioeconomic status alone on education can be seen in the outcomes of children living in countries with low gross national incomes (GNIs). The negative effects of poverty on children's health and education are well documented in the United States and European countries with high GNIs. The negative effects of poverty are even greater, however, for children living in countries with low to middle GNIs. Researchers examined the development and growth of children living in four countries with low and middle GNIs (i.e., India, Indonesia, Peru, Senegal) and found that children from families with lower incomes had both lower developmental scores and less growth than children from families with higher incomes (Fernald, Kariger, Hidrobo, & Gertler, 2012). In addition, these researchers found the combination of a family's socioeconomic status and the mother's education level becomes more pronounced with a child's age in countries with low and middle GNIs; that is, a child from a low-income family that included a mother with a low level of education was negatively affected, and the impact was more pronounced as the child got older (Fernald et al., 2012). Thus, the lower a country's GNI, the less likely people with and without disabilities are to have equitable access to and benefits of high-quality education.

Disability remains a significant factor in children's access to education. Even with multiple international agreements (see Table 18.1), 61 million children across the globe do not attend primary school (UNESCO, 2012), and one third of these children have disabilities (World Vision, 2007). Policies relating to the education of children with disabilities historically have been based on charity, rights, or equity (Bines & Lei, 2011). Although less preferred, charity has been the most traditional basis for providing these services. For example, the basis for policies related to the education of children with disabilities in Poland has been equity of access to services, although not equity of curriculum or contexts in which services are provided. Parents in Mainland China historically have relied on the benevolence of the providers of education to gain access for their children with disabilities.

Each of these variables (i.e., sociocultural diversity, social class, gender, socioeconomic status, disability) is used in some countries to marginalize groups of people and limit their access to services. The following section describes various perceptions of people with disabilities, especially those with severe disabilities, and services provided in two countries with differing cultural values, history, politics, and use of available resources.

EXAMPLES OF INTERNATIONAL CONTEXTS

Two examples are provided to illustrate societal inclusion and equity in various international contexts. Many of the issues described in the first example (i.e., Poland) exemplify issues evident in countries that recently secured their independence from the Communist bloc. In contrast, many of the issues in the second example (i.e., Mainland China) exemplify issues evident in countries with cultures based on Confucian beliefs. These two examples do not address all of the cultural contexts in which societal inclusion and equity are being sought for people across types of diversity (e.g., sociocultural, social class, gender, socioeconomic status, disability). Rather, they focus on the status of and efforts toward societal inclusion and equity for individuals with severe disabilities across the life span within countries representing two types of contexts.

Social Inclusion and Equity for
People with Severe Disabilities in Poland

Poland has a long history of being militarily conquered by other countries, groups of countries, and ideologically motivated groups (History of Nations, 2013). Poland has a very high HDI level, with a rank of 39 (see Figure 18.1), based on scores for health, education, and income (see Figure 18.2). This combination of political his-

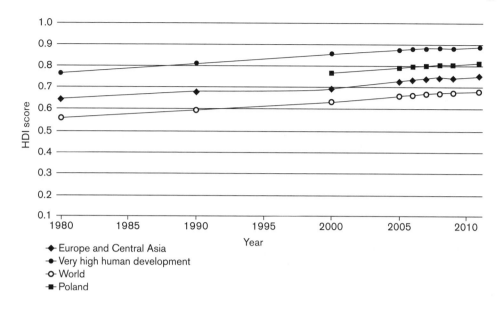

Figure 18.1. Comparative human development level in Poland. (*Key:* HDI, Human Development Index.) (From *2012 Human Development Report*, United Nations Development Programme; reprinted by permission.)

tory and use of available resources has resulted in a context that reflects both rigid adherence to societal rules that initially were dictated and passionate exploration of societal rules elsewhere and how those might affect societal rules in Poland.

Culture and Use of Available Resources The manner in which people with severe disabilities are perceived and served in Poland is influenced by two views of society and citizenship. First, it is influenced by the legacy of years during which Poland was under Communist rule and the concepts related to disabilities and people with disabilities developed during those years. For instance, people with disabilities were regarded through a prism of defects (i.e., defectology) while under

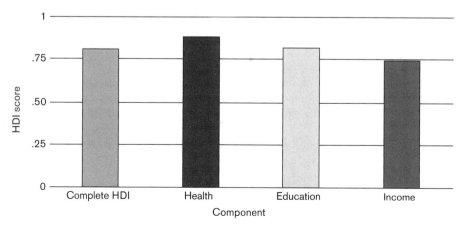

Figure 18.2. Component scores for Human Development Index (HDI) in Poland. (From *2012 Human Development Report*, United Nations Development Programme; reprinted by permission.)

the Communist socialist ideology, which influenced the system of services (e.g., education, rehabilitation, vocational and day activities, living options) for people with disabilities developed and administered by the state. This system mainly focused on people with mild disabilities because the prevailing perception was that they would be able to achieve independence, be employed, and be useful to society. The assumption that drove policy was that people with mild disabilities would lead independent lives and not require ongoing support from the state when they became adults. In contrast, support for people with severe disabilities was very limited and mostly focused on residential institutions. If an individual with severe disabilities was not living in an institution, then the prevailing perception was that his or her existence and the responsibility for his or her life were private issues to be addressed by their parents. In short, the guiding assumption was that these individuals can contribute little or nothing to society.

Second, current perceptions and services also are influenced by democratic ideals based on civil rights, equal rights, and nondiscrimination. Much attention has been given to the rights of all of Poland's citizens and the development of services to meet the needs of all citizens since Poland became an independent democratic country in 1989.

Both of these ideologies, as well as the services and practices that reflect them, are strongly rooted in Polish society and culture. A democratic, nondiscrimination ideology has been gaining presence throughout Poland, however, since the mid-1990s. There is more public discussion of and interest in the lives of people with disabilities; there are legislation, policies, and procedures that articulate the rights of people with disabilities and their families; and there are more financial resources allocated for services and practices that enhance the possibility that people with all types of disabilities will benefit from the rights to which they are entitled.

The Concept of Severe Disabilities in Poland and the Scope of the Population   The term *severe disabilities* is not particularly prevalent in Poland. Very few publications attempt to define the term or evaluate its scientific and practical usefulness. Nevertheless, the concept exists in education and other fields as evidenced by distinctions between people with mild, moderate, and "serious" (i.e., heavy) disabilities. Legal regulations and guidelines for services exist that consider the level of disability experienced by people; however, the criteria for defining such levels differ. For example, a system with three levels of disability is used for purposes that are not related to educational services. These levels are similar to the approach of the American Association on Intellectual and Developmental Disabilities (Wolfe, Tarnai, & Ostryn, 2009) and are defined by a combination of 1) the level of damage to the organism, per se (i.e., level of disability experienced anatomically); 2) the person's need for support in daily functioning; and 3) the person's ability to engage in employment (The Directive of the Ministry of Labour and Social Policy, 2002).

It appears that the combination of the moderate and "serious" levels of disability used for purposes that are not related to educational services in Poland most closely match the concept of severe disabilities. Both of these levels are applied to people who require assistance, at least some of the time or in some manner, to participate and have a valued role in society, including employment with customized support or adaptation of the environment. These combined groups represent 60% of the people with disabilities older than 16 years of age in Poland (Olszewski, Parys, & Trojańska, 2012). When considering the general population in Poland, 3.3% are considered to have "serious" disabilities, and 3.9% are considered to have moderate disabilities (Główny Urząd Statystyczny [Government Central Statistical Office; GUS], 2011).

Polish students with disabilities are not labeled with a level of disability during their educational years. They are divided, however, based on their type of disability, and varying access to the regular education program is provided based on students' IQ scores. Polish law assumes that students with moderate or "serious" intellectual disability (i.e., IQ score below 50) should receive services in an educational program that is separate from the regular education program and which has a functional (e.g., life skills) curriculum. This group of students can be considered to have severe disabilities and comprises about 1% of the student population (GUS, 2010a).

Societal Attitude Toward and Expectations of People with Disabilities

Polish society's attitude toward people with disabilities has undergone a radical improvement since the collapse of the Communist bloc and the Communist ideological hold on Poland's government. The shift from a Communist ideology to a more democratic ideology has led to a societal view that more strongly values individuals' contributions to society. This new societal view appears to have created favorable conditions for major changes related to each person's rights, including equal rights and the right to self-realization (i.e., self-determination). These changes have resulted in an increase in the diversification of people in Poland's society and a culture that is more tolerant of variation and diversity.

This increased tolerance has created a cultural basis for the acceptance and emancipation of people with disabilities. People with disabilities in Poland increasingly are viewed through the prism of their rights to participate in the life experienced by the rest of society, gain access to establishments (e.g., cultural, governmental, sporting, businesses), and engage in self-determination. The Rights of Persons with Disabilities Charter adopted by the Polish Parliament in 1997 strengthened the national policy of nondiscrimination. This document directly refers to human and civil rights expressed in international documents (e.g., United Nations Convention on the Rights of Persons with Disabilities). It obligates Poland's government to undertake activities to improve the degree to which services reflect the rights of people with disabilities and to submit a public annual report of these activities to Parliament. Numerous social campaigns have used the Polish media in recent years to increase society's knowledge about disability and disability issues and to increase society's tolerance toward people with disabilities. Studies indicate that these social campaigns are effective at improving the attitude of various social and professional groups toward people with disabilities (Wojtyńska & Fijałkowska, 2008).

Rights, Advocacy, and Roles in Developing Services

Although nongovernmental organizations (NGOs) in Poland have played a major role in advocating and offering services for people with disabilities even when it was under Communist rule, their influence mainly has been felt since the mid-1990s. Research on 430 NGOs in Poland indicates that approximately 40% of NGO members are people with disabilities, and another 40% are family members or friends of people with disabilities (Państwowy Fundusz Rehabilitacji Osób Niepełnosprawnych [State Fund for Rehabilitation of People with Disability; PFRON], 2010). People with disabilities are in positions of authority in 46% of these NGOs. Although all of these NGOs provide services to meet the needs of people with disabilities, 60% also engage in lobbying activities for legal and political change, 35% provide legal assistance for people with disabilities, and 24% represent the interests of people with disabilities and NGOs at large (PFRON, 2010).

These data support the idea that a citizen's society is developing in Poland and that challenges faced by people with disabilities are an integral part of this democratic movement. Some NGOs are well established and have significant influence with the government and other entities in Poland. For instance, the Polish Association for People with Intellectual Disabilities (PSOUU) is one of the most influential organizations related to people with severe disabilities. This association actively lobbies for new legislation and systemic solutions to identified problems. For example, the PSOUU fought to limit the practice of depriving people with intellectual disabilities of their legal rights (Firkowska-Mankiewicz & Seroczyńska, 2009). The PSOUU publishes a monthly magazine with easy-to-read text inserts, operates schools that serve 3,000 students with "serious" intellectual disabilities, has secured living accommodation for about 500 people with intellectual disabilities, develops and administers early intervention centers that serve about 11,000 children with disabilities, and initiates an active self-advocacy movement.

Educational Services   There are two sets of students for whom extensive educational reform is occurring in Poland—students with disabilities and students who do not have disabilities but have other special educational needs, such as homelessness, poverty, and mental illness. This reform was initiated after the collapse of Communism, and legislation was passed in 1997 that mandated education for all students, including those with "serious" intellectual disabilities. Furthermore, their education would be free of charge to families and include the option for parents to find a regular education school that would accept their child (Ministry of National Education, 1999). Although this legislation neither required regular schools to accept children with "serious" intellectual disabilities nor provided parents with due process rights or procedures, it did mandate that all children would have access to education. It also laid the groundwork for inclusive education by delineating an integrative education model of services. This model is most similar to coteaching models in the United States, with one regular education teacher and one special education teacher providing services in the same classroom for a combination of students with and without disabilities. In essence, if a school director is willing to serve students with severe disabilities in an integrative class because of his or her own beliefs about equal access, political motivations, experiences with friends or family members who have disabilities, or other factors, then the legislation allows the addition of one or more students with disabilities to a regular education class with fewer regular education students, all served by two teachers.

Three additional changes occurred in Polish legislation as of 2010. First, it continued to lay the foundation for inclusive education by allowing a second model of service known as inclusion. Instead of reflecting quality indicators of inclusive education supported in other countries (Barnitt et al., 2007; Booth, Ainscow, & Kingston, 2006), this model allowed one student with "serious" intellectual disabilities to be enrolled in any regular education class without adding a special education teacher or other support. Second, this legislation required schools to have an education team for each student with special educational needs, including those with "serious" intellectual disabilities. Third, it required the education team to develop an *individualized education plan* that is based roughly on the individualized education program mandated in the United States. Although these mandates were added, legislative changes were not made related to 1) a lack of a regular school's requirement to enroll students with "serious" intellectual disabilities, 2) a lack of parental due process rights and procedures, 3) use of a life skills curriculum for students with "serious" intellectual disabilities, or 4) clarification regarding the needs of students with other types of severe disabilities (e.g., multiple disabilities). Education reform efforts still are needed, therefore, to address these issues and ensure that students with severe disabilities have equal access to the regular curriculum, contexts, and peers.

In addition, students with various types of disabilities have much more limited access to primary schools (i.e., ages 7–13), and students with "serious" intellectual disabilities are still routinely educated in segregated special schools (i.e., separate day schools, residential schools). Although students with moderate and "serious" intellectual disabilities, severe/multiple disabilities, and autism may attend regular primary schools if a school director allows, this happens much more rarely than in the case of students with mild disabilities. For example, 42% of students with mild intellectual disabilities attend special schools, compared with more than 70% of students with moderate and "serious" intellectual disabilities (GUS, 2010a). Many parents want their children with severe disabilities to attend regular schools but are aware of the low level of support provided in these schools and the unwillingness of parents of children who do not have disabilities to be enrolled in integrative education or inclusion classes (Żyta, 2003). Antoszewska, Ćwirynkało, and Wójcik (2004) indicated that the majority of special education teachers and pedagogues in Poland are opposed to students with severe disabilities being served in regular classes. It is unlikely that this situation will change in the near future because local educational authorities do not consider this a priority.

Employment and Employment Services   The Polish system for supporting employment for people with disabilities has not been effective, despite a relatively large investment by the government. International data indicate that only 17.6% of working-age people with disabilities in Poland were employed in 2004, compared with 39.9% in the United States (Institute on Disability, 2011). Polish government data indicate that 22% of working-age people with disabilities are employed, as compared with 69% of people without disabilities (GUS, 2010b). In addition, the majority of those employed represent people with mild disabilities, with only 15% of people with moderate disabilities and less than 5% of people with "serious" disabilities employed (Olszewski et al., 2012). Many factors might affect this low rate of employment for people with disabilities. For instance, the overall rate of employment generally has remained high since the collapse of the Communist bloc, and many special enterprises for individuals with disabilities (i.e., segregated vocational settings such as sheltered workshops) were unable to compete in the new market economy and closed. Employing people with disabilities in competitive community-based positions, however, has been set as a priority. Legislation regarding the number of hours that an employer is allowed to pay an individual worker is a second factor. Although one employer may pay a worker without disabilities or with mild disabilities for working up to 8 hours per day or 40 hours per week, an employer may pay workers with moderate and "serious" disabilities no more than 7 hours a day or 35 hours per week unless they have a certificate from a physician indicating additional work time will not be harmful to their health (Towalski, 2003). Employers could infer that people with severe disabilities are less likely to be successful workers and will refrain from hiring them.

Many forms of support (e.g., personal assistant, on-the-job training) are available to encourage competitive employment in Poland, although their use is not very common. Almost 80% of employed people with severe disabilities are working in special enterprises (i.e., sheltered workshops) (PFRON, 2008). No attempts at reform have occurred, even though many government, research, and advocacy reports have criticized the system (PFRON, 2008). It appears that increasing access to competitive employment for people with severe disabilities currently is not a priority for the state authorities. Instead, they are focused on reducing the unemployment of people without disabilities.

Poland also provides services in work activity centers, which are similar to day activity centers in the United States. It has been assumed that people with disabilities who would not be able to find competitive employment after attending technical school would be prepared for work activity centers. These centers serve adults with severe disabilities and were developed to teach social, household, community, and employment skills. Although a large number of such centers were created (e.g., 539 for nearly 20,000 people with disabilities in 2008), they have not achieved their goal (Olszewski et al., 2012). Many families and guardians in Poland believe that people with severe disabilities are unable to cope with employment and they support work activity centers.

Living Options and Services   There is a large-scale problem in Poland related to enabling people with severe disabilities to live independently. Although pressure is placed by parents, advocacy organizations, service providers, and the state on social integration in the community, this pressure does not extend to independent living options. The majority of adults with severe disabilities currently live with their parents or other family members or in institutions in which the quality of life does not significantly differ from that in institutions in other countries (Included in Society, 2004). The government has invested in modernizing these institutions and improving the quality of their services in recent years, rather than developing other living options. Regardless, alternative living options (e.g., group homes, apartment living) are developing very slowly. Data are not available, however, on the number of people with disabilities living in or the types of supports and services provided by these alternative living options.

Research and Outcomes   Most data available related to services for people with severe disabilities in Poland are restricted to demographic information. Little information is available or being collected across the life span on either the quality of supports and services, the relative outcomes achieved through different supports and services, the effectiveness of specific interventions, or the quality of life for individuals and their families (Turnbull, Brown, & Turnbull, 2004).

Social Inclusion and Equity for People with Severe Disabilities in China

The People's Republic of China is composed of a vast geographic area that has several regions that reflect unique combinations of cultural values, history, beliefs, and availability of resources. These regions also have a long history of cultural isolation. The People's Republic of China has a medium HDI level, with a rank of 101 (see Figure 18.3) based on scores related to health, education, and income (see Figure 18.4). The following section highlights only one of the regions of the People's Republic of China—Mainland China—to illustrate societal inclusion and equity in a second type of international context.

Culture and Use of Available Resources Gao, Orlando, Ryndak, and Johnson (in press) described the manner in which people with disabilities in China are perceived and the influence of the Confucian heritage culture (CHC) on the services provided. CHC is based on an ideology that encourages social and educational stratification and discrimination between individuals based on their characteristics (Mcloughlin, Zhou, & Clark, 2005). The concept of disability within the CHC bears a negative connotation of abnormality, shame, misfortune, and retribution for people with disabilities and their families (Mcloughlin et al., 2005).

CHC places societal decision making in the hands of community elders, a practice that has attenuated cultural reform (Mcloughlin et al., 2005). The focus on people as a collective body, rather than as individuals, continues to dictate how services for people with disabilities are developed and implemented in Mainland China, even with the influence of economic reforms that began in 1978 and espoused the concept of individuals generating wealth based on personal effort. For example, families from Mainland China often consider the education of their children with disabilities to be solely their responsibility, relying on the benevolence of their governing party for access to services, rather than actively pursuing their right as individuals to obtain services.

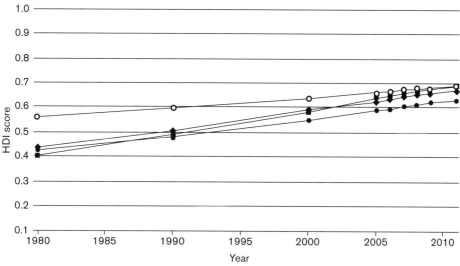

Figure 18.3. Comparative human development level in Mainland China. (*Key:* HDI, Human Development Index.) (From *2012 Human Development Report*, United Nations Development Programme; reprinted by permission.)

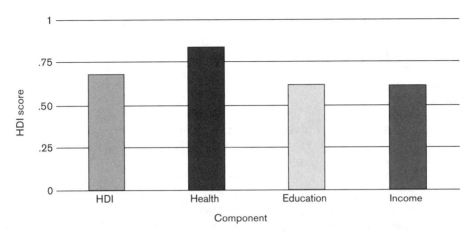

Figure 18.4. Component scores for Human Development Index (HDI) in Mainland China. (From *2012 Human Development Report*, United Nations Development Programme; reprinted by permission.)

Several challenges to meeting the educational needs of children with disabilities in Mainland China that stem from this ideology have been identified. For instance, Mcloughlin et al. (2005) noted the lack of a systematic evaluation process and intervention programs to meet the educational needs of children with disabilities, as well as the financial resources to support these aspects of services.

The Concept of Severe Disabilities in China and the Scope of the Population Although Mainland China has the largest population of children with disabilities in the world, their legislation defines fewer services than legislation in similar CHC areas (e.g., Taiwan, South Korea, Japan), each of which mandates a variety of special education and related services (Gao et al., in press). Specifically, Mainland China has 3.87 million children with disabilities (i.e., birth through 14 years of age), comprising 4.66% of the total population of people with disabilities (People's Republic of China National Bureau of Statistics, 2006). Only 63.19% of the school-age children with disabilities (i.e., 6–14 years of age) receive educational services, and the location of services depends on whether the child lives in an urban or rural community and on the severity of his or her disability. When children with severe disabilities receive educational services, most do so in segregated contexts, regardless of these factors.

There are eight disability categories in Mainland China under which children can become eligible for special education and related services: 1) hearing impairment, 2) speech-language impairment, 3) visual impairment, 4) physical disabilities, 5) mental illness, 6) mental retardation (i.e., intellectual disability), 7) other disabilities, and 8) multiple disabilities. These disability categories are defined by China's legislation on compulsory education, legislation on special education, or regulations related to special education. For example, the Compulsory Education Law (CEL; People's Republic of China National People's Congress, 2006) addresses four of the disability categories: hearing impairment; visual impairment; mental retardation (i.e., intellectual disability), and other disabilities. Other legislation (i.e., Law of the People's Republic of China on the Protection of Persons with Disabilities [LPPD]; People's Republic of China National People's Congress, 2008), however, addresses additional disability categories (i.e., speech-language impairment, physical disability, mental illness, multiple disabilities). Learning disabilities and behavior disorders are not identified in current legislation, and psychiatrists determine whether a person has a disability.

Societal Attitude Toward and Expectations of People with Disabilities

The societal attitude toward people with disabilities in Mainland China has undergone change during the 20th century and following World War II. For instance, the Constitution that supports protection of people with disabilities was enacted in 1982. In addition, China has ratified and signed the Convention on the Rights of the Child (United Nations, 1989) and Convention on the Rights of Persons with Disabilities (United Nations, 2007). Provisions for special education during the 9-year compulsory education period in Mainland China were embedded in the CEL first enacted in 1986 and reauthorized in 2006 to further support people with disabilities (People's Republic of China National People's Congress, 2006). In addition, specific educational rights of and services for children with disabilities were stipulated in regulations (i.e., Regulations on Education for Persons with Disabilities [REPD]) disseminated in 1994 by the State Council of the People's Republic of China).

Increasing social and economic changes have occurred as a consequence of China's entrance into the free market in the 1990s, leading to a shift in the structure of services provided by families and communities to support people with disabilities. Unlike Western societies, Mainland China does not have the governmental infrastructure of health and welfare to support people with disabilities and their families.

Rights, Advocacy, and Roles in Developing Services

The major provisions in Mainland China related to issues such as identifying disabilities and recommending services for children with disabilities, as well as regulations that guide providing and overseeing special education and related services, appear in the REPD (People's Republic of China State Council, 1994). The REPD advises that health care agencies, early childhood education agencies serving children with disabilities from birth through 5 years of age, and families should be attentive to indicators that might lead to early detection of a disability in young children. The REPD (People's Republic of China State Council, 1994) encourages educational and health care administrative departments of the local government to develop procedures for identifying children with disabilities during the years of compulsory education (i.e., 6–15 years of age). The procedures must include 1) screening and evaluating a child, 2) determining whether a child is eligible for special education and related services, and 3) recommending a location in which those services might be provided for eligible children. Thus, identification, eligibility determination, and service recommendation are aspects of the same process. None of these aspects, however, is clearly defined in the regulations.

Local governments in Mainland China are encouraged to develop multiple types of services for people with disabilities: 1) compulsory and vocational education, 2) early rehabilitation and early education, 3) vocational education, and 4) high school and postsecondary education (People's Republic of China State Council, 1994). Recommendations for location of these services are made based on the type and severity of the child's disability. CEL (People's Republic of China National People's Congress, 2006) mandates that the provision of compulsory education for children with hearing or speech-language impairment, visual impairment, or mental retardation (i.e., intellectual disability) occur in special schools or special classes. The location for service provision for children identified as having other disabilities, however, is not specifically mentioned in either CEL (People's Republic of China National People's Congress, 2006) or REPD (People's Republic of China State Council, 1994).

In contrast, CEL (People's Republic of China National People's Congress, 2006) mandates that regular schools accept children with disabilities who are deemed able to learn in regular education classes. CEL also suggests that appropriate supports be provided for students in resource rooms, if the schools can afford to do so. The law, however, does not define how children are deemed able, what constitutes appropriate supports, or grounds for affording services.

Although Mainland China's legislation mandating special education and related services calls for accommodating individual needs of children with disabilities, it does not delineate the types of accommodations that may be used. The accommodations that might be necessary for a student with disabilities are determined by individual schools and agencies.

Mainland China's legislation does not include a budget mandate for special education; rather, the funding of all special education and related services is the responsibility of local governments that have three levels, including a province, county, and city division. REPD (People's Republic of China State Council, 1994) stipulates that all three levels of government should increasingly provide funding for special education and related services, and these services should be provided either by local education, welfare, or rehabilitation agencies or by families. Finally, it mandates that local education agencies and relevant administrative departments at all levels of government are responsible for overseeing special education and related services.

Educational Services   China provides 9 years of compulsory education for all children 6–15 years of age (People's Republic of China National People's Congress, 2006; Republic of China Legislative Yuan, 2009). Compulsory education consists of 6 years of elementary and 3 years of lower secondary education. Stratification is evident in the overall structure of educational services in Mainland China, with structural segregation dominating services (Mcloughlin et al., 2005). Students must compete with all other students and achieve outstanding levels of performance in order to enter vocational, professional, or academic programs at institutions of higher education. Mcloughlin and colleagues stated that this "places heightened pressure on children with disabilities who are fundamentally incapable of mastering the entry requirements for Chinese higher education" (p. 275). They further stated that 80% of the 1.3 billion people in China live in rural areas that are under-resourced, yet are required to meet the same performance levels as those living in the highly resourced cities.

Only 63.19% of the 3.87 million children with disabilities (i.e., birth to 15 years of age) have access to educational services in Mainland China; however, only 0.18% of the student population is identified as having disabilities. In contrast, 2%–3% of the student population in other CHC areas is identified as having disabilities; that is, 11–17 times more children with disabilities in three other CHC areas have access to educational services than in Mainland China (Gao et al., in press).

Mainland China predominately relies on a segregated system to provide educational services for their children with disabilities; however, more than 60% of children with disabilities receiving educational services in Mainland China are learning in regular classrooms, which is their model of inclusive education (Deng & Harris, 2008). The ratio of special education teachers to children with disabilities in Mainland China is 1 special education teacher to 12 children with disabilities.

Employment and Employment Services The Chinese government created a social model of employment that encouraged state-owned enterprises (SOEs) during the prereformed period, leaving few privately owned enterprises. The intent of the SOEs was to stimulate economic growth, and workers took part in SOE production work both to earn a living and to contribute to the realization of Communism. Participating in SOE work opportunities was viewed as a way for people to be members of a socialist society. The Chinese government arranged opportunities to work in SOEs for many people in urban areas. Workers were provided with a nominal wage and welfare in lieu of higher wages (Chau, 2009).

People with disabilities were part of this social model of employment, with SOEs employing a certain number of workers with disabilities and providing them with on-the-job training and fringe benefits. Their production and the quality of their work often were not considered, although SOEs received financial support and tax exemptions from the government for hiring them (Chau, 2009). The increase of free market enterprises, however, created competition that led to a financial decline of the SOEs. Many SOEs have seen financial loss or bankruptcy since the 1980s (Saunders & Shang, 2001; Tang & Ngan, 2001), resulting in job loss or lower wages for workers with disabilities (Chau, 2009).

A law was passed in 1991 that protected people with disabilities and their right to work. In addition, it indicated that employment policies should encourage integrating workers with disabilities. A quota system set by the Chinese government ensures the right of people with disabilities to work, requiring both public and free market enterprises to guarantee that 1.5% of job opportunities per enterprise are filled by workers with disabilities. Employers who disregard the quota are fined, and proceeds are deposited in the Disabled Persons' Employment Security Fund. When at least 35% of its work force is composed of people with disabilities, companies receive corporate tax credits, and those with more than 50% receive many kinds of tax credits. Some remaining SOEs choose to pay fines rather than employ people with disabilities (Chau, 2009; Lu, 2009), and it is becoming commonplace for enterprises to employ people with disabilities in meaningless jobs in order to receive tax credits (Chau, 2009). Finally, self-employment of people with disabilities is encouraged (Disabled World News, 2010), and people with disabilities who operate their own business are eligible to receive tax credits (Chau, 2009).

Occupational therapy stations were set up in neighborhoods to assist with employment opportunities for people with disabilities and to provide rehabilitation and vocational services integrated in community settings. These and other employment initiatives, however, have offered little to ensure social inclusion and improved quality of life.

Data on the rate of employment for people with disabilities in Mainland China is difficult to ascertain for two reasons. First, several changes have occurred with the onset of the free market system, making it difficult to obtain accurate data. Second, reports from government agencies and independent researchers vary greatly, calling into question the validity of the limited data that are available.

Living Options and Services   People with disabilities have the same rights related to access to housing as people without disabilities because China ratified the Convention on the Rights of the Child and Convention on the Rights of Persons with Disabilities (United Nations, 1989, 2007). Fisher and Jing (2008), however, found few indications that ratifying these international conventions has resulted in national policies ensuring government support for people with disabilities to live either independently or with their families. Although there is evidence of policies that provide government-supported housing at a reduced rate for people with disabilities and their own families, such housing is limited, and people with and without disabilities are increasingly encouraged to seek housing in the private market (Fisher & Jing, 2008). As a result, most people with disabilities in China live with their familial relations (e.g., parents, siblings, relatives) (Weiss, 2010), and those who do not have living support provided by their familial relations often are homeless or live in institutions. Initiatives from residential committees, the smallest form of government in Mainland China, have provided social services (i.e., personal care, home-based care); however, these services are provided in few areas across Mainland China. Limited social inclusion for people with disabilities is the result of these combined living options.

Research and Outcomes   Little research exists on child psychopathology or the educational needs of students with disabilities prior to 1980 (Mcloughlin et al., 2005). The research that exists since then has used small-scale methodology and does not provide national information. Research, therefore, is needed on 1) national statistics on incidence and prevalence of disabilities; 2) the need for and services provided related to education, employment, and living options for people with disabilities, birth through adulthood; 3) interventions, contexts, and practices in service delivery; and 4) outcomes of services.

ALIGNMENT WITH TASH
MISSION, VISION, AND NATIONAL AGENDA

This chapter discussed issues of social inclusion and equity that are faced internationally by marginalized groups of people. These issues are consistent with the mission of TASH of promoting the "full inclusion and participation of children and adults with significant disabilities in every aspect of their community, and to eliminate the social injustices that diminish human rights" (2013). TASH calls for the following to realize this mission: 1) advocacy to achieve equity, opportunities, social justice, and human rights; 2) education of the public, government officials, community leaders, and service providers; 3) research that translates excellence to practice; 4) individualized, quality supports within the community, instead of services in congregate and segregated contexts; and 5) legislation, litigation, and public policy that are consistent with the mission and vision of TASH. Specifically, TASH focuses on

Supporting those people with significant disabilities and support needs who are most at risk for being excluded from society; most likely to have their rights abridged; most likely to be at risk for living, working, playing and learning in segregated environments. (2013)

Consistent with this mission, TASH has

A vision of a world in which people with disabilities are included and fully participating members of their communities, with no obstacles preventing equity, diversity and quality of life and communities in which no one is segregated and everyone belongs. (2013)

TASH established national agenda committees related to inclusive education, community living, employment, diversity and cultural competency, and human rights to work toward this vision. TASH also established a Board of Directors' Committee on International Issues that are consistent with its mission and vision.

Legislation, policies, and supports and services in many countries support the segregation of people with severe disabilities, as well as people marginalized due to other factors (e.g., gender), in major life areas (e.g., education, community living, employment). This suggests the need for further global initiatives that increasingly call for legislation and policies that ensure social inclusion and equity across the life span for people with severe disabilities and other people. Efforts to address this international need are consistent with TASH's mission, vision, and national agenda efforts. TASH needs to continue to expand their efforts related to issues of advocacy, training, and research within various international contexts. TASH's vision cannot be realized fully until such issues are globally rectified.

CONCLUSION

People with severe disabilities internationally contend with many issues that also are faced by other marginalized people. This chapter discussed the state of societal inclusion and equity, specifically for people with severe disabilities across the world, by 1) describing international initiatives that address the rights and needs of people with disabilities; 2) discussing how the cultural values, history, politics, and use of available resources in a country or region are interrelated and shape the supports and services provided for people with severe disabilities; and 3) providing illustrations of how services for people with disabilities have been shaped in two countries by their cultural values, history, politics, and use of available resources. Numerous challenges currently are being faced across countries, such as ethnic, racial, and religious persecution; poverty and hunger; and gender and class prejudice. Each of these would affect the daily lives of people with severe disabilities, as well as the long-term outcomes they might achieve.

These challenges must be addressed to achieve societal inclusion and equity for people with severe disabilities and other marginalized people. Each society must ensure human rights for every citizen and implement services accordingly. Although many countries with diverse ideologies and political frameworks might espouse equality for all, the equality enjoyed among a country's elite citizens does not necessarily trickle down to the country's marginalized populations. The way a country supports and its society treats people from the most marginalized groups reflects the degree to which human rights are valued and upheld. A country's respect for, civility toward, and inclusion of all members of its society is the final indicator of its development and stance on human rights, regardless of receiving a very high, high, medium, or low HDI score.

Achieving social inclusion and equity for people with severe disabilities internationally will require an extensive effort from numerous sources over an extended period. An international research agenda that is systematically implemented is needed to measure the effect of those efforts. Rigorous studies are needed on the current state of services, the outcomes from those services, and the quality of life experienced by people with severe disabilities across countries. In addition, there is a need for research related to the identification of evidence-based practices in services for people with severe disabilities, efficacy of systems change efforts, and efficacy of professional development efforts, as well as international dissemination of the findings of such research to develop and refine high-quality services across countries. These efforts, however, must reflect the idea that different practices might be effective in different countries because of contextual issues (e.g., cultural differences). This body of research then could be used to develop targeted policy at international, national, and local levels.

Questions for Study and Reflection

1. The international agreements that frame the disability rights movement call for basic human rights of all people. They call for societal inclusion and equity in gaining access to education, employment, and living options through inclusive practices. How might people with and without disabilities demonstrate acknowledgment of and support for these agreements in their own societies and communities, given that these agreements are implemented with varying levels of fidelity across countries?

2. This chapter includes examples of how a country's cultural values, history, politics, and use of available resources shape perceptions of people with disabilities and the services provided for them. How do your community's cultural values, history, politics, and use of available resources affect the status of and efforts toward societal inclusion and equity for individuals with severe disabilities across the life span? How could services in your community evolve to improve performance toward the international goals?

3. The cultural values, history, politics, and use of available resources of a country are projected on the human rights, equality, equity of access, and inclusion afforded its people. How might the cultural values, history, politics, and use of available resources of a community, employer, or classroom affect equality, equity of access, and inclusion? How might community leaders, employers, or educational personnel promote equality for all?

4. How might the cultural values, history, politics, and use of available resources of a family affect their access to and acquisition of services for their child with severe disabilities? How might community leaders, employers, and educational personnel support families in obtaining effective services for their children with severe disabilities?

RESOURCES

Artiles, B., Kozleski, E., & Waitoller, F. (2011). *Inclusive education: Examining equity on five continents.* Cambridge, MA: Harvard University Press.

Turnbull, A., Brown, I., & Turnbull, H.R. (2004). *Families and persons with mental retardation and quality of life: International perspectives.* Washington, DC: American Association on Mental Retardation.

United Nations Development Program (*http://hdr.undp.org/en/statistics/hdi/*)— An organization that is funded through voluntary contribution of United Nations members, its purpose is to help countries address challenges of poverty reduction and achievement of the millennium development goals, democratic governance, crisis prevention and recovery, and environment and energy for sustainable development.

REFERENCES

Antoszewska, B., Ćwirynkało, K., & Wójcik, M. (2004). Nauczyciele szkół specjalnych i masowych wobec integracji osób pełno- i niepełnosprawnych na gruncie szkoły [Teachers from special and regular schools collaborate for integration of people with and without disability on school grounds]. In G. Dryżałowska & H. Żuraw (Eds.), *Integracja społeczna osób niepełnosprawnych [Social integration of people with disability]* (pp. 255–265). Warsaw, Poland: Academic Publisher Żak.

Artiles, B., Kozleski, E., & Waitoller, F. (2011). *Inclusive education: Examining equity on five continents.* Cambridge, MA: Harvard University Press.

Barnitt, V., Benner, S., Hayes, E., Weser, S., Ryndak, D.L., & Reardon, R. (2007). *Best practices in inclusive education: An assessment and planning tool for systemic change.* Tallahassee: Florida Department of Education.

Bines, H., & Lei, P. (2011). Disability and education: The longest road to inclusion. *International Journal of Educational Development, 31,* 419–424.

Booth, T., Ainscow, M., & Kingston, D. (2006). *Index for inclusion: Developing play, learning and participation in schools.* Manchester, United Kingdom: Center for Studies on Inclusive Education.

Chau, R. (2009). Socialism and social dimension of work: Employment policies on disabled groups in China. *Hong Kong Journal of Social Work, 43,* 19–29.

Cooray, A., & Potrafke, N. (2011). Gender inequality in education: Political institutions or culture and religion? *European Journal of Political Economy, 27,* 268–280.

Deng, M., & Harris, K. (2008). Meeting the needs of students with disabilities in general education classrooms in China. *Teacher Education and Special Education, 31,* 195–207.

Directive of the Ministry of Labour and Social Policy. [*Rozp. Ministra Pracy i Polityki Społecznej z dn. 1 lutego 2002 r. w sprawie kryteriów oceny niepełnosprawności u osób w wieku do 16 roku życia. Dz. U. z 2002 r., Nr 17, poz. 162.*] (2002). Warsaw, Poland: Author.

Disabled World News. (2010). *Societal attitudes towards people with disabilities have gone through a gradual change in China.* Retrieved from http://www.disabled-world.com/news/asia/china/disability-china.php#ixzz2HPo8jbGl

Fernald, L.C.H., Kariger, P., Hidrobo, M., & Gertler, P.J. (2012). Socioeconomic gradients in child development in very young children: Evidence from India, Indonesia, Peru, and Senegal. *Proceedings of the National Academy of Sciences, 109,* 17273–17280.

Firkowska-Mankiewicz, A., & Seroczyńska, M. (2009). Impact of social advocacy on updating incapacity determination procedures for people with intellectual disabilities in Poland. *Journal of Policy and Practice in Intellectual Disabilities, 6,* 219–228.

Fisher, K., & Jing, L. (2008). Chinese disability independent living policy. *Disability and Society, 23,* 171–185

Gabel, S.L., & Danforth, S. (2008). *Disability and the politics of education: An international reader.* New York, NY: Peter Lang.

Gao, W., Orlando, A., Ryndak, D.L., & Johnson, B. (in press). *Legislative foundations for inclusive education: The case of four East-Asian Confucian heritage culture regions.*

Główny Urząd Statystyczny [Government Central Statistical Office]. (2010a).

Oświata i wychowanie w roku szkolnym 2009/2010 [*Education and upbringing during the school year 2009/2010*]. Warsaw, Poland: Zakład Wydawnictw Statystycznych.

Główny Urząd Statystyczny [Government Central Statistical Office]. (2010b). *Aktywność ekonomiczna ludności Polski, IV kwartał 2010* [*Economic activity of Polish population, the fourth quarter of 2010*]. Warsaw, Poland: Zakład Wydawnictw Statystycznych.

Główny Urząd Statystyczny [Government Central Statistical Office]. (2011). *Stan zdrowia ludności Polski w 2009r* [*The health condition of Polish population in 2009*]. Warsaw, Poland: Zakład Wydawnictw Statystycznych.

Greenberg, J. (2010). Report on Roma education today: From slavery to segregation and beyond. *Columbia Law Review, 110,* 919–1001.

History of Nations. (2013). *History of Poland.* Retrieved from http://www.histo ryofnations.net/europe/poland.html

Included in Society: Results and Recommendations of the European Research Initiative on Community-Based Residential Alternatives for Disabled People. (2004). Retrieved from http://www .community-living.info/contentpics/226/ Included_in_Society.pdf

Institute on Disability. (2011). *2011 annual disability statistics compendium.* Durham: University of New Hampshire.

Kozleski, E.B., Artiles, A.J., & Waitoller, F.R. (2011). Equity in inclusive education: Historical trajectories and theoretical commitments. In A.J. Artiles, E.B. Kozleski, & F.R. Waitoller (Eds.), *Inclusive education: Examining equity on five continents* (pp. 1–14). Cambridge, MA: Harvard University Press.

Lu, J. (2009). Employment discrimination in China: The current situation and principle challenges. *Hamline Law Review, 1.*

Ministry of National Education. (1999). Reforma ksztalcenia uczniow ze specjalnymi potrzebami edukacylnymi [The reform to the education of pupils with special educational needs]. In R. Ossowski (Ed.), *Ksztalcenie specjalne I integracyjne* [*Special and integration education*] (pp. 65–75). Warsaw, Poland: Author.

Mcloughlin, C.S., Zhou, Z., & Clark, E. (2005). Reflections on the development and status of contemporary special education services in China. *Psychology in the Schools, 42,* 273–283. doi: 10.1002/pits.20078

Murray, C. (2012). A minority within a minority? Social justice for Traveler and Roma children in ECEC. *European Journal of Education, 47,* 569–583.

Olszewski, S., Parys, K., & Trojańska, M. (2012). *Przestrzeń życia osób z niepełnosprawnością* [*The living space of people with disability*]. Krakow, Poland: Wydawnictwo Naukowe Uniwersytetu Pedagogicznego.

Państwowy Fundusz Rehabilitacji Osób Niepełnosprawnych (PFRON) [State Fund for Rehabilitation of People with Disability]. (2008). *Raport z badania Warsztatów Terapii Zajęciowej. Analiza porównawcza badań zrealizowanych w latach 2003–2005* [*The study report about occupational therapy workshops during the years 2003–2005*]. Warsaw, Poland: Author.

Państwowy Fundusz Rehabilitacji Osób Niepełnosprawnych (PFRON) [State Fund for Rehabilitation of People with Disability]. (2010). *Działalność organizacji pozarządowych w zakresie integracji, rehabilitacji społecznej i zawodowej osób niepełnosprawnych* [*The activity of non-government organizations within the scope of integration, social and professional rehabilitation of people with disability*]. Warsaw, Poland: Author.

People's Republic of China Ministry of Education. (1994). Guanyu kai-zhan canji ertong shaonian sui ban jiu du gongzuo de shixing banfa [*Trial measures of implementing learning in regular classrooms for children and adolescents with disabilities.*] Unpublished official document of the Ministry of Education in China, Beijing.

People's Republic of China National Bureau of Statistics. (2006). *The 2006 population census of the handicapped.* Retrieved from http://www.cdpf.org.cn/sjcx/ node_50872.htm

People's Republic of China National People's Congress. (2006). *Compulsory Education Law.* Retrieved from http://www.gov .cn/flfg/2006-06/30/content_323302.htm

People's Republic of China National People's Congress. (2008). *The law of the People's Republic of China on the protection of persons with disabilities.* Retrieved from http://www.chinanews.com/gj/kong/ news/2008/04-24/1231112.shtml

People's Republic of China State Council. (1994). *Regulations on Education for Persons with Disabilities*. Retrieved from http://www.cdpf.org.cn/zcfg/content/2001-11/06/content_50522.htm

Republic of China Legislative Yuan. (2009). *Special Education Act*. Retrieved from http://law.moj.gov.tw/LawClass/LawContent.aspx?pcode=H0080027

Ringold, D., Orenstein, M.A., & Wilkens, E. (2005). *Roma in an expanding Europe: Breaking the poverty cycle*. Washington, DC: The World Bank.

Saunders, P., & Shang, X.Y. (2001). Social security reform in China's transition to a market economy. *Social Policy and Administration, 35,* 274–289.

Shang, X.Y. (2001). Moving towards a multi-level and multi-pillar system: Changes in institutional care in two Chinese cities. *Journal of Social Policy, 30,* 259–282.

Tang, K., & Ngan, R. (2001). China: Developmentalism and social security. *International Journal of Social Welfare, 10,* 253–259.

TASH. (2013). *TASH mission and vision*. Retrieved from http://tash.org/about/mission

Towalski, R. (2003). *Kształtowanie sie wynagrodzeń w sektorze publicznym [The changing regulation of normal working time]*. Retrieved from www.eurofound.europa.eu/eiro/2003/11/feature/pl0311107fpl.doc

Turnbull, A., Brown, I., & Turnbull, H.R. (2004). *Families and people with mental retardation and quality of life: International perspectives*. Washington, DC: American Association on Mental Retardation.

United Nations. (1975). *Declaration of the Rights of Disabled People*. New York, NY: Author.

United Nations. (1989). *Convention on the Rights of the Child*. Retrieved from http://www.ohchr.org/EN/ProfessionalInterest/Pages/CRC.aspx

United Nations. (1993). *The standard rules on the equalization of opportunities for persons with disabilities*. New York, NY: Author.

United Nations. (2007). *Convention on the Rights of Persons with Disabilities*. Retrieved from http://www.un.org/disabilities/convention/conventionfull.shtml

United Nations Development Programme. (2011). *Human development report: Sustainability and equity: A better future for all*. New York, NY: Author.

United Nations Development Programme. (2012). *2012 Human development report*. New York, NY: Author. Retrieved from http://hdrstats.undp.org/en/countries/profiles/POL.html

United Nations Educational, Scientific and Cultural Organization (UNESCO). (1994a). *The Salamanca statement and framework for action on special needs education*. Paris, France: Author.

United Nations Educational, Scientific and Cultural Organization (UNESCO). (1994b). *World declaration on education for all*. Paris, France: Author.

United Nations Educational, Scientific and Cultural Organization (UNESCO). (1998). *World declaration on higher education for the twenty-first century: Vision and action*. Retrieved from http://www.unesco.org/education/educprog/wche/declaration_eng.htm#world%20declaration

United Nations Educational, Scientific and Cultural Organization (UNESCO). (2000). *Dakar framework for action*. Retrieved from http://unesdoc.unesco.org/images/0012/001211/121147e.pdf

United Nations Educational, Scientific and Cultural Organization (UNESCO). (2011). The hidden crisis: Armed conflict and education. *EFA global monitoring report*.

United Nations Educational, Scientific and Cultural Organization (UNESCO). (2012). *Opportunities lost: The impact of grade repetition and early school leaving*. Montreal, Quebec, Canada: UNESCO Institute for Statistics.

Weiss, T.C. (2010). *Overview of disability in China*. Retrieved from http://www.disabled-world.com/news/asia/china/disability-china.php

White, J. (2012). *Pitfalls and bias: Entry testing and the overrepresentation of Romani children in special education*. Budapest, Hungary: Roma Education Fund.

Wojtyńska, J., & Fijałkowska, A. (2008). *Ewaluacja projektów – kampanii informacyjno-promocyjnych przełamujących negatywne stereotypy osób niepełnosprawnych [The evaluation of projects and information-promotional campaigns, which break down the negative stereotypes about people with disability]*. Warsaw, Poland: Centrum Badania Opinii Społecznej.

Wolfe, P.S., Tarnai, B., & Ostryn, C. (2009). Defining severe disabilities: Implication for research and practice. *International Journal of Special Education, 24,* 19–28.

World Vision. (2007). *Education's missing millions: Including disabled children in education through EFA.* Retrieved from http://www.psouu.org.pl

Żyta, A. (2003). Szanse i zagrożenia integracyjnego kształcenia i bytowania osób z głębszą niepełnosprawnością intelektualną [The chances and threats of integrative education and living of people with severe intellectual disability]. In Z. Kazanowski & D. Osik-Chudowolska (Eds.), *Integracja osób w edukacji i interakcjach społecznych* [*Integration of people in education and in social interactions*] (pp. 27–35). Lublin, Poland: Maria Curie-Skłodowska University (UMCS).

Future Directions and Possibilities

Martha E. Snell and Virginia L. Walker

This chapter focuses on TASH national agenda items of 2010—inclusive education, community living, employment, diversity and cultural competency, and human rights. It starts by summarizing each of the five agenda items, then sketches out needed steps or the target future directions the country must take with the possibilities that lie ahead. The latter sections address the directions to take in research and policy and legal matters. Finally, the chapter describes the key players involved in taking these directions. Although the chapter limits its coverage to the United States, Chapter 18 addresses international initiatives. The United States shares a commonality in its current status and in the future directions it must pursue with many countries, but there are vast differences in status and priorities globally and more pressing agendas for nations with poorer economies (Emerson, Fujiura, & Hatton, 2007).

INCLUSIVE EDUCATION

TASH (2010) called for transforming school communities based on social justice principles in which all students 1) are presumed competent, 2) are welcomed as valued members of all general education classes and extracurricular activities in their local schools, 3) fully participate and learn alongside their same-age peers in general education instruction based on the general education curriculum, and 4) experience reciprocal social relationships.

Current Status

These goals on inclusion are not easily measured, and current data sources do not directly address their status. State data gathered by the U.S. Department of Education under the Individuals with Disabilities Education Improvement Act (IDEA) of 2004 (PL 108-446) for the annual report to Congress, however, provide a partially relevant but slippery metric. For example, 94.8% of all students with disabilities ages 6–21 served under IDEA 2004 spent some of their school day in a regular education class (averaged across all states) (U.S. Department of Education, 2010c). The proportion of the school day that students spend in general education classrooms is a more revealing statistic that denotes less inclusion: > 80% of day = 60% of students with disabilities; 40%–79% of day = 20% of students with disabilities; < 40% of day = 14% of students with disabilities (U.S. Department of Education, 2010c). Most of the remaining students (5%) spent no school time with peers and attended separate schools (2.96%), whereas others attended residential schools, correctional facilities, private schools, or hospitals (U.S. Department of Education, 2010c). Other data indicate that race makes a difference, with numbers of Black and Hispanic students with disabilities increasing in less inclusive environments and numbers of White students increasing in more inclusive environments (U.S. Department of Education, 2010a, 2010b). It is difficult to know the number or percentage of students with severe disabilities who are educated in general education for different proportions of the school day or in other settings (e.g., separate school) because states do not report data on students with severe disabilities (Ryndak, Alper, Hughes, & McDonnell, 2012).

These and other reports indicate that improvement since the mid-2000s has been almost stationary, with an annual increase of about 1% overall in terms of the numbers of students with disabilities who are attending general education classrooms (Giangreco, Hurley, & Suter, 2009). There is "inconsistent access to inclusive classrooms" across communities for students with severe disabilities, with inclusion primarily depending on where one lives (Giangreco, Broer, & Suter, 2011, p. 28). Additional problems include continued debate among educators about its appropriateness, a lack of skills among many professionals on how to provide quality services and supports in inclusive settings, and significant discrepancies in inclusive environments relative to quality.

Future Directions

Adequate dependent measures are lacking in terms of research. "Researchers tend to study what we can measure, even if it is not what we really want to study" (Stoneman, 2007, p. 41). One simple illustration is the absence of a measurable definition and an accurate count of students with severe disabilities. The U.S. Department of Education reports student numbers in traditional categories (e.g., mental retardation, autism), but these numbers cannot be added together to yield an estimate of students with severe disabilities because such extrapolations are inaccurate (Ryndak et al., 2012). Students having severe disabilities are heterogeneous and draw from several categories, including intellectual disabilities, multiple disabilities, autism, deaf-blindness, and developmental delay. Each category, however, includes students who are not regarded as having severe disabilities. For example, a fraction of those in the autism category have Asperger syndrome, whereas many students with intellectual disability do not have extensive support needs. More serious is the absence of acceptable ways for measuring 1) characteristics of school services (e.g., time in general education, number of classes taken, mastery of adapted objectives, intensity of educational support), 2) social interaction or connectedness, 3) peer attitudes, and 4) quality of life (Ryndak et al., 2012; Stoneman, 2007). For example, although there appears to be no good way to measure time spent in general education, the U.S. Department of Education questionably counts noninstructional time spent during lunch, recess, and study periods "as time spent inside the regular classroom" (2012, p. 1). Vignes, Coley, Grandjean, Godeau, and Arnaud (2008) identified 19 psychometrically sound measures of peer attitudes but found that only two assessed affective, behavioral, and cognitive dimensions; all instruments were old and somewhat deficient in their coverage of current cultural characteristics. Because of communication difficulties, quality of life is challenging to assess with direct report, whereas using parental reports as a substitute for child report (even when the child is typically developing) appears to produce dissimilar responses due to differences in reasoning and response styles (Davis et al., 2007).

A second research need relates to narrow schools of methodological practice. Because of the low incidence of students with severe disabilities, intervention effects are almost always assessed with single-case research design, whose interpretation may be challenging to laypeople accustomed to large number comparison group findings. Some researchers have made a case for longitudinal studies of the effects of inclusive schooling on student learning, social appropriateness, and postschool outcomes, with the reasoning that such findings could affect educational policy (Cornish, Roberts, & Scerif, 2012; Ryndak et al., 2012). Funders will need to be convinced of the value of longitudinal research in the current economy due to the expense and delay of research findings. Dependent measures that combine qualitative and quantitative features may be most able to capture TASH's difficult-to-quantify inclusion goals (Stoneman, 2007). Mixed-method designs are associated with such measures (Johnson & Onwuegbuzie, 2004), including using effect size metrics and time series analyses with single-case research. Integrated approaches depend on having teams of broadly minded and skilled researchers.

The future foundation of policy and laws contributing to inclusion builds on the core concept of integration that "recognizes that people with disabilities have been subjected to various types of segregation, and that although the core concepts of anti-discrimination and liberty will blunt unjustified confinement, they do not drive a policy toward integration" (Turnbull, Stowe, Turnbull, & Schrandt, 2007, p. 29). Several laws (e.g., IDEA 2004, the Developmental Disabilities Assistance and Bill of Rights Act Amendments of 2000 [PL 106-402]) have driven the policy toward integration by favoring inclusion over exclusion and by relying on the rationale that all individuals should be served in the least restrictive environment. These laws have been applied to support court decisions about educational inclusion, to craft state regulations, and to shape school administrative procedures, all of which have gradually influenced public opinion and school practices. Tracking U.S. Department of Education educational environment statistics since the 1980s reveals slow but certain improvements overall, but with large discrepancies across disabilities and across and within states. When a child with a significant intellectual disability lives within a southern state, for example, he or she is far more likely to be educated in a separate classroom most or all of the day than if he or she lives in Vermont. Legal strategies that consistently enforce existing laws are crucial for promoting uniform change but so are 1) the human stories that describe successes and motivate change (e.g., Habib, 2009), 2) the research that identifies relevant strategies and informs change (e.g., Carter, Moss, Hoffman, Chung, & Sisco, 2011; Fisher & Meyer, 2002; Odom et al., 2004), and 3) preservice and professional development programs that educate teachers and administrators on creating and sustaining successful inclusive schools (e.g, Hunt, Soto, Maier, & Doering, 2003).

The players in inclusive education are many; they involve those in schools (all teachers and students, paraprofessionals, related services professionals, and administrators) along with parents, state and national school administrators, and the lay public. Horizontal interaction is an old strategy that has only informal support but has been applied by some of these players; this strategy suggests that greater success for understanding and conversion will result when resistant players hear reports of successful inclusion from experienced and knowledgeable peers (Snell & Eichner, 1989). For example, principals prefer to hear from their experienced peers about practices they need to implement. Horizontal interactions may yield more success than the traditional expert informant because the messenger is more credible to the listeners, shares routines and terminology, and experiences similar role expectations and tasks; however, the interactions still must provide sound advice and evidence-based strategies.

COMMUNITY LIVING

TASH (2010) called for expanding the provision of person-centered, long-term supports and individualized choice for community living for people with intellectual and developmental disabilities in every state.

Current Status

Individuals with severe disabilities can successfully live in the community when they receive extensive and individualized support from or associated with service agencies (Felce & Perry, 2007). With deinstitutionalization and court decisions have come the expansion of community-based and supported living options, but researchers report great variability in the outcomes for individuals who live in the community and in the quality of supports they receive (Felce & Perry, 2007). The U.S. Supreme Court ruling in *Olmstead v. L.C.* (1999) requested that states make available to people with disabilities the most integrated living setting feasible. Smith, Lakin, Larson, and Salmi (2011) analyzed the effect this ruling has had on current residential arrangements for people with disabilities between 1999 and 2009. They found that six states have eliminated institutions, whereas almost all states have significantly reduced the number and population of large public and private facilities, resulting in a 27.9% reduction of individuals living in these settings (Smith et al., 2011). There has been an increase during this period in 1) community group homes by 17%, 2) giving support to individuals in their own home by 90%, and 3) host or foster care homes by 28%. There are still 59,604 individuals with intellectual disability residing in public/private institutions, however. The number of people with intellectual and developmental disabilities living in small residential settings of six or fewer increased by 311% between 1998 and 2008, with growth reported in every state and growth exceeding 100% in all but one state (Salmi, Scott, Webster,

Larson, & Lakin, 2010). In addition, the data from 1998 to 2008 indicated a 60% growth rate in the number of people living in places with three or less residents. Finally, a large decrease was reflected in the proportion of individuals with intellectual and developmental disabilities living in large residential facilities (with 16 or more residents) between 1998 and 2008, "from a majority (51%) in 1988 to 14% in 2008" (Salmi et al., 2010, p. 168).

Older individuals with chronic health conditions are more likely to remain in institutions based on the belief that their care is more easily provided in that setting (Allen, 2001). A review of research on chronic health conditions in children and adolescents with intellectual disability found that prevalence rates for a number of chronic conditions were much higher than exists in the general population (Oeseburg, Dijkstra, Goothoff, Reijneveld, & Jansen, 2011). The six most frequent conditions included epilepsy (22%), cerebral palsy (20%), anxiety disorders (17%), oppositional defiant disorder (12%), Down syndrome (11%), and autism spectrum disorder (10%). People with chronic health conditions require supports that are more intense and long lasting than people without such conditions. This is consistent with the fact that most researchers in the Oeseburg et al. review who studied this population recruited individuals from residential settings.

"Homes are central to the way people live" and are "likely to have a significant influence on their overall quality of life" (Felce & Perry, 2007, p. 410). The U.S. Department of Health and Human Services (2000) agreed with this position and set numerous national objectives within the Healthy People 2010 initiative; one goal relevant to this discussion was to "[r]educe to zero the number of children aged 17 years and younger living in congregate care facilities" (Larson et al., 2011, p. 209). Larson and her colleagues evaluated this objective by surveying state developmental disability directors and reported on the progress made across and within states between 1977 and 2009. Congregate care facilities were defined as a "non-family residential setting of any size that provides housing for children and youth with intellectual or developmental disabilities in which rotating (or shift) staff members provide care" (p. 209); this definition would include group homes and Medicaid intermediate care facilities. Results indicated an overall decline in the proportion of individuals in congregate care facilities who were children and youth—a 0.7% decline between two time spans: 1987–1997 and 1997–2005, and a larger decline (1.3%) between 2005 and 2009. Concerning children ages 0—14, 6 states achieved this goal, 7 states reduced the number to less than 20 individuals, and 11 states indicated that less than 2% of the state's population of young people (0–21 years) with intellectual disabilities lived in congregate facilities. This analysis also revealed that the overall objective was not met—22 states found increases for the 15- to 21-year age group, and the total number of youth overall living in such settings increased by 24% between 1997 and 2009. It will be important to understand the reasons for failing to meet the objective. It is possible that the consistent use of person-centered planning, as demonstrated on a small scale by Holburn, Jacobson, Schwartz, Flory, and Vietze (2004), will promote greater success in the complex process of deinstitutionalization.

Future Directions

These data show that the United States is on the right track for replacing large living settings (16 or more people) with small living settings (six or fewer). It is crucial to continue basic research to monitor progress and allow for objective goal setting that accelerates the trajectory. The statistical research conducted by University of Minnesota's Research and Training Center on Community Living has enabled an objective evaluation of progress on the Olmstead decision and other legislated targets; its funding must continue. Second, the demographic research of Stancliffe et al. (2012) with adults having Down syndrome illustrated the value that statistical analyses can have in understanding the connections between demographic characteristics, health conditions, and use of residential services. The field would benefit if similar studies were conducted of groups of individuals with intellectual disability and high-support conditions (e.g., epilepsy, cerebral palsy, anxiety disorders); such studies can establish specific baselines to assess progress as well as tease out the factors that may be inhibiting the inclusion of those with high-support conditions in small community settings (Felce & Perry, 2007). Third, researchers need to get beyond simply knowing where individuals live and identify factors that influence social well-being in supported living (e.g., staff–client ratio, number of residents, home-likeness, location, staff attitudes, technology); research has produced some conflicting findings (Felce & Perry, 2007). Future researchers would benefit from having more sophisticated tools such as outcome measures to evaluate adult services (e.g., Personal Outcome Measure; cited in Stoneman, 2007) and statistical analyses (e.g., path analysis) to help understand the relationships between the many operating factors, while controlling for adaptive behavior and other client characteristics (Felce & Perry, 2007).

Other researchers reported that individuals moving from institutions to community homes do not continue their improvements in adaptive behavior but instead show a plateau effect; these data could be misused to slow down deinstitutionalization of some groups (Felce & Perry, 2007). It is crucial to demonstrate whether this negative effect can be replicated by other researchers and, if so, to understand what supported living conditions (e.g., types of places and support) are related to growth or decline in adaptive behavior. For example, factors such as the amount of choice residents with intellectual disability have and the attractiveness of the home both have been shown to be associated with higher adaptive behavior scores during follow-up assessment (Heller, Miller, & Hsieh, 2002). Research has not addressed the influence that community neighborhoods have on such residences and also should identify which social and operational processes in community residences have positive influences (Felce & Perry, 2007).

Person-centered planning is the approach widely used to plan individualized transition plans, specifically goals for work, leisure, and living. For example, Flannery et al. (2000) found that training in person-centered planning resulted in improvements for students with disabilities who were transition age (e.g., more written goals supported outside school hours, higher numbers of unpaid support people, and improved satisfaction with the transition planning). A review by Claes, Van Hove, Vandevelde, van Loon, and Schalock (2010), however, found several problems with person-centered planning (e.g., no universal definition of person-centered planning for people with intellectual disability, limited research examining the effectiveness of this approach), but moderate support for its effect on clients' personal outcomes. These authors concluded that the person-centered planning process 1) reaches only a small fraction of people who use public services, 2) "might be a paper exercise that is not related to the real lives of individuals" (p. 448), 3) requires flexible supports that often are incompatible with traditional service systems, and 4) depends on a high level of optimism that may produce goals and expectations that are not suitable or practical for individuals. These conclusions point out both discouraging characteristics of service systems and limitations of the process. Future research should develop and test more functional person-centered planning processes, perhaps using a quality-of-life conceptual framework suggested by Claes et al. so that relevant indicators (e.g., personal development, self-determination, rights, interpersonal relations, social inclusion, physical well-being) can be considered and assessed. Development of more functional person-centered planning methods must also address the communication challenges of many people with severe disabilities.

Future developers of policy on community dwellings for people with disabilities will want to explore smart house technology in order to make supported home living more accessible, safe, and efficient (Storey, 2010). Smart technology has been applied to promote safety (e.g., taking medications, installing cameras to see who is at the door, having wireless transceivers to report emergencies), accessibility (e.g., automated lifts with ceiling tracks, remote control of appliances and lights), and efficiency (e.g., prompts doing maintenance tasks and video guide steps, staff and resource management). Residents will require less attendant care and achieve greater self-sufficiency while potentially reducing the cost of support when smart houses are more ordinary and less costly.

Future policy and laws will continue to set the bar for community living options and drive change. The Olmstead decision is primarily responsible for reducing large congregate facilities and creating small living options in U.S. communities. The ongoing monitoring of these changes by government and advocacy groups will continue to steer future legal actions and determine continued progress. It will be of value to expand monitoring beyond residential statistics (where people reside) and keep track of these influential factors (e.g., opportunity for choice, home-likeness, social interactions, activities outside the home) as more is learned about the association between the characteristics of living settings and individual outcomes. A second issue concerns the influence of the economy on the availability of community-based services (residential and family support). For example, Larson and Lakin (2010) examined the expenditure patterns between 2004 and 2009 for Medicaid-supported living programs (e.g., home and community-based services). The stimulus package of 2009 resulted in large average increases in community supports but also wide variations across states. "Total expenditures for Medicaid long-term supports for people with disabilities grew by 37%" during this period (p. 481); their predictions about declines in these same expenditure patterns from 2009 to 2012 unfortunately appear to be accurate. Advocacy groups will play a crucial role when bad economic indicators cause negative fluctuations in the progress of replacing congregate care with community homes.

Individuals with significant disabilities and their families are centermost as players in the community living realm. Funding, licensing, and monitoring by federal, state, and local officials are also key to the availability and quality of the residences. Alongside this central group are the employees of large and small living settings and their administrators who influence the atmosphere and set and enforce the rules that directly determine the quality of life possible in such places. Felce and Perry (2007) reviewed research on the operational culture of living settings and concluded that it had significant influence on client outcomes. All players will need to be tapped for their knowledge and viewpoints in order to address the priority research questions and identify future policy in residential services.

EMPLOYMENT

TASH (2010) called for increasing the employment rate for people with intellectual and developmental disabilities and eliminating federally sanctioned subminimum wages.

Current Status

Several significant pieces of legislation (e.g., Individuals with Disabilities Education Act [IDEA] of 1990 [PL 101-476], Workforce Investment Act [WIA] of 1998 [PL 105-220]) have been enacted with the intent to improve employment outcomes for individuals with disabilities (Rogan & Rinne, 2011). Such efforts to promote positive employment outcomes are indicative of a shared value and mission among various stakeholders and of the high priority placed on employment opportunities for individuals with disabilities. Although these efforts are encouraging and have been made with the intent to effectively change the state of employment for individuals with disabilities, examination of data collected since the mid-1990s reveals a disappointing reality—individuals with disabilities continue to experience economic and employment disparities (Butterworth et al., 2012; Inge et al., 2009).

The StateData employment report (Butterworth et al., 2012) provided 20 years of data from several national datasets that address the status of employment for individuals with intellectual and developmental disabilities. Summarized next are several notable national trends from the StateData employment report that allow us to address the current status. The overall data indicate that individuals with disabilities experience low rates of employment and low or subminimum wages and tend to work in segregated employment settings. Employment rates of individuals with disabilities are quite disproportional to those of individuals without disabilities. Individuals with disabilities were employed at much lower rates (32.9%) in 2010 than those without disabilities (70.3%). Individuals with cognitive disabilities who received Supplemental Security Income experienced even lower levels of employment (8.3%).

Disparities in income continue to exist. For instance, individuals with disabilities receive substantially lower wages in the vocational rehabilitation system than those without disabilities, whereas individuals with intellectual disability earn the least. Individuals tend to earn subminimum wages when they receive services in facility-based employment settings, such as sheltered workshops. Inge et al.'s (2009) survey of community rehabilitation programs illustrated this problem with its finding that a staggering 73.7% of individuals receiving supports in facility-based settings earned less than minimum wage, while 2% earned no wages.

Data on employment settings highlights the continued tendency to provide employment services in segregated environments. Individuals with disabilities who receive employment support from state agencies are more likely to receive services in segregated settings (79.9%) than in integrated employment settings (20.1%). Although these statistics reflect an overall decrease in the number of individuals receiving employment support in segregated settings, there was not a corresponding increase in integrated employment services. This overall decrease may be attributed to the recent recession and lack of necessary funding. Rusch and Braddock (2004) found similar trends in their evaluation of spending and service practices of state agencies. That is, individuals with intellectual and developmental disabilities typically receive services in segregated settings, even though the rate at which individuals receive services in supportive or competitive employment settings has increased since the mid-1990s, suggesting that transition programs have not produced desirable outcomes for individuals with severe disabilities. Moreover, states providing services through facility-based employment tend to allocate more funds (85% in 2010) to support such services than do states providing services through integrated employment (10.6% in 2010). An increasing number of individuals with disabilities receive support through community-based nonwork services, an emerging service model characterized by activities that do not involve paid employment and take place in integrated community settings; community-based nonwork services increased from 18.7% of individuals in 1999 to 47% in 2010. Butterworth et al. (2012) suggested these data reflect a growing emphasis on community presence; however, community-based nonwork program characteristics and outcomes remain unclear.

Although these data generally offer a grim account of the current status, postsecondary education is one employment area that offers promising data. Education is linked to positive employment outcomes for individuals with disabilities in that higher rates of employment coincide with higher levels of education attainment. Furthermore, postsecondary education has a positive relationship to employment for youth with disabilities who are transition age, thus suggesting that college placement may be a viable option for individuals with disabilities. Individuals with severe disabilities participate in postsecondary education less often than individuals with disabilities who have fewer support needs, so it will be important to identify barriers to and effective inclusion strategies for their involvement in postsecondary education opportunities.

Future Directions

Several research needs emerge from the current state of employment for individuals with disabilities. A need exists to translate research into practice so that stakeholders understand strategies that are effective in promoting positive employment outcomes for individuals with disabilities (e.g., Mank, 2007). Postsecondary education is one growing area that warrants additional research. Although limited, data lend support to the idea that postsecondary education may encourage positive employment outcomes for youth who are transition age (e.g., Butterworth et al., 2012; Hughson, Moodie, & Uditsky, 2006; Zafft, Hart, & Zimbrich, 2004). Several additional areas need to be addressed in future research to allow for research-based decision making regarding postsecondary options, including 1) documenting the perceptions and satisfaction of various stakeholders involved in postsecondary education; 2) providing in-depth analyses of program characteristics; 3) comparing large samples of programs at different settings and with different program emphases; 4) evaluating relationships between program characteristics, participant characteristics, and outcomes; and 5) collecting longitudinal data to document long-term outcomes.

It becomes imperative to identify characteristics of community-based nonwork services and determine whether they lead to integrated, gainful employment outcomes as the number of individuals with disabilities participating in services increases. A variety of methods (e.g., qualitative research, mixed-methods research) may be of value in exploring these issues. If community-based nonwork services are found to prevent or limit community inclusion or participation in vocational opportunities, then strategies must be developed to transition individuals out of such programs and into programs that are associated with positive outcomes. Furthermore, the overall public cost and pay benefits of individuals supported in segregated employment settings should be addressed in future research in order to raise awareness of potential discrepancies between community investment and community outcomes, such as sufficient wages for workers with disabilities (e.g., Cimera, Wehman, West, & Burgess, 2012). The lack of longitudinal data in the current body of literature that lend support to nondiscriminatory employment practices is also a concern. Although the movement to improve human rights alone should be the catalyst for systems change, longitudinal research documenting cost effectiveness of employment practices may provide additional (and necessary) evidence to support shifts in policy.

Policy and laws continue to govern the employment opportunities that are available to individuals with disabilities; thus, their role in future efforts to establish a system that promotes nondiscriminatory employment practices is significant. It becomes crucial to align policies and laws with the expectation that all individuals with disabilities have the right to participate in integrated, gainful employment. TASH's national agenda goal to eliminate federally sanctioned subminimum wages serves as a central step toward realignment. The Fair Labor Standards Act (FLSA; PL 106-151) of 1938 authorized employers to pay special (reduced) minimum wages to workers who have disabilities, a wage that is "based on the worker's individual productivity, no matter how limited, in proportion to the wage and productivity of experienced workers who do not have disabilities" (U.S. Department of Labor, 2008). The policies set forth by the FLSA promote discrimination and subject workers with disabilities to severely diminished wages. Educators must continue to encourage an amendment to the FLSA through advocacy efforts and collaboration among national organizations to discontinue policies that permit individuals with disabilities to be paid at lower than minimum wage (e.g., Fair Wages for Workers with Disabilities Act of 2011 [H.R. 3086]).

A second future goal relates to funding. Various employment systems that promote equality and inclusion (e.g., customized employment, supported employment, Employment First) are supported to different degrees at the state and national level. These systems, however, are competing against an existing system (one that appears to place little value on inclusion and equality) that is controlled by federal and state dollars. In fact, a majority of state funding is allocated to programs that are segregated (Butterworth et al., 2012). Policies need to be established that favor expanding funding opportunities for programs that offer employment services in integrated environments and set forth clear guidelines for doing so.

Finally, if postsecondary education is to become a viable option for all individuals with disabilities, then work must be done 1) to advocate for such programs to increase availability of postsecondary education options and 2) to develop financial support strategies that sustain postsecondary education programs and allow for participation by individuals with varying financial support needs. Barriers to program availability, funding, and student financial aid continue to exist and need to be addressed in the future, even with recent legislation (i.e., Higher Education Opportunity Act of 2008 [H.R. 4137]) that expands program development, research, and financial support (Lee, 2009).

Education and advocacy are two primary themes that apply to the various players involved in employment opportunities for individuals with disabilities. Families and individuals with disabilities need access to information about employment options, including relevant research-based practices. In addition, person-centered planning and self-determination practices should be incorporated into a lifelong education process (starting during the school years) to allow individuals with disabilities to make informed, independent decisions about their employment. Practitioners (e.g., teachers, transition specialists) also need access to current information on employment opportunities for individuals with disabilities; teacher preparation programs, professional learning opportunities, and collaboration among local organizations, postsecondary programs, and school systems may serve as mechanisms through which dissemination of information occurs. Employer education also plays a critical role in efforts to improve employment opportunities because negative perceptions of individuals with disabilities often create barriers to positive employment opportunities (e.g., Inge et al., 2009). Employer education should focus on adapting new business models in which all employees are valued and presumed competent, despite their varying support needs. Finally, advocacy must continue to be embraced as a powerful tool through which change can occur. Involvement as advocates and encouragement of others to become advocates will contribute to the movement toward equitable employment.

DIVERSITY AND CULTURAL COMPETENCY

TASH (2010) called for expanding the participation rates of people of diverse backgrounds who have disabilities in advocacy efforts and every aspect of life.

Current Status

The inclusion of individuals with disabilities has been a primary focus of many research, advocacy, and political efforts since the mid-1990s. The role of ethnic, racial, and cultural diversity among individuals with disabilities, however, is one aspect of inclusion that typically has been overlooked. Individuals of diverse backgrounds with disabilities still face multiple barriers to inclusive opportunities, despite strong documentation and recognition of significant disparities in education, employment, independent living, and health (Hasnain et al., 2009). Overall rates of inclusion in schools have increased for individuals with disabilities; yet, many individuals of diverse backgrounds with disabilities, largely Blacks and Hispanics, continue to receive education in segregated school settings at disproportional rates (U.S. Department of Education, 2010c). Also, students of color with severe disabilities, particularly those from high-poverty areas, receive educational services in settings that lack recommended practices and provide few opportunities for self-determination (Hughes, Cosgriff, Agran, & Washington, 2013; Washington, Hughes, & Cosgriff, 2012).

Furthermore, individuals of diverse backgrounds with disabilities disproportionately experience poor adult outcomes (e.g., limited access to postsecondary education, unemployment, incarceration, poor health). These people are less likely to receive rehabilitation services or obtain gainful employment, and they earn less than their White counterparts when they are employed (Butterworth et al., 2012; Taylor-Ritzler et al., 2010). Although adults with disabilities are more likely to report poor health than adults without disabilities, reports of poor health are most common among adults with diverse backgrounds and disabilities (Wolf, Armour, & Campbell, 2008).

These and other data emphasize the significant inequalities faced by individuals of diverse backgrounds who have disabilities. Diversity has become widely recognized as a contributing factor to the ways in which individuals with disabilities engage in inclusive opportunities. Many programs that serve individuals with disabilities are encouraging the provision of culturally competent services. By definition, *culturally competent services* apply knowledge of individuals' traditional, ethnic, and linguistic backgrounds to inform pedagogical and service delivery practices (e.g., instructional strategies, communication strategies, assessment tools, service delivery models) (Klingner, Blanchett, & Harry, 2007). Although only a few researchers have addressed the efficacy of culturally competent service delivery interventions (see Hasnain et al., 2009), such data lend support to the notion that these services reduce disparities and improve adult outcomes for diverse individuals with a wide variety of disabilities. Furthermore, disability and human rights organizations have promoted culturally competent services and initiated advocacy efforts to empower individuals of diverse backgrounds with disabilities and their families (e.g., TASH, 2010). The movement to address diversity among individuals with disabilities is slowly gaining momentum, as evidenced by increased awareness of and response to the alarming inequities. Thus TASH's goal to expand the participation of people of diverse backgrounds who have disabilities in advocacy efforts and every aspect of life is both timely and necessary to promote inclusion across various life activities.

Future Directions

Expanding current knowledge regarding diversity among individuals with disabilities through various research endeavors is the most influential future direction. Relying on "static proxy measures" of diversity (e.g., using race and ethnic classification systems) (Taylor-Ritzler et al., 2010, p. 4) is a major limitation of the current body of research. Understanding the complexities of diversity consequently has been limited to identifying differences among individuals with various racial and ethnic backgrounds (Taylor-Ritzler et al., 2010). A need exists to develop a comprehensive understanding of how various aspects of diversity, above and beyond simple categories of race and ethnicity, affect the inclusive opportunities experienced by people with disabilities. These aspects of diversity might include gender, language, socioeconomic status, religion, and so forth. Furthermore, continued assessment of access issues and barriers and the identification of variables contributing to such issues is warranted. A general awareness of the barriers that may contribute to discrepancies in inclusive experiences exists (e.g., differing cultural perspectives of disability, limited access to and unfamiliarity with available service delivery options, service providers' misunderstanding the effect of families' race, social class, cultural values, and beliefs) (Klingner et al., 2007). Professionals need to understand the conditions under which individuals from diverse backgrounds experience successful inclusion. Qualitative research may serve as a useful tool for this task because these research methods allow for in-depth exploration of people's experiences.

The application of culturally competent service delivery has gained popularity; yet, data supporting this approach are limited in two notable ways: 1) only a small number of research studies have assessed the efficacy of culturally competent service delivery and 2) the characteristics of such interventions that yield positive results generally remain unclear (Hasnain et al., 2009). Research is needed to replicate documented intervention effects (e.g., reduced disparity, increased positive adult outcomes) in order to validate the use of culturally competent service delivery. The factors that contribute to the efficacy of such interventions need to be known. Having clear descriptions of these procedures not only will provide service providers with unambiguous guidelines for implementing culturally competent services but also will provide opportunities to assess fidelity of implementation by service providers, including teachers, employers, and so forth.

Identifying evidence-based practices can lead to developing policies and laws that govern how service delivery systems respect cultural diversity among individuals with disabilities. Several immediate actions, however, can serve to 1) improve how systems address cultural diversity in individuals with disabilities and 2) facilitate preparation for future shifts in policy. First, policy makers must be educated about the barriers faced by people with disabilities who come from diverse backgrounds. Second, individuals of diverse groups with disabilities and their families need to become politically active regarding the diversity barriers they face because their voices lend weight. Finally, capacity must be built by appointing more people from diverse groups to positions at the state and national level who are responsible for tackling issues of diversity.

Several key players are affected by the challenges that face individuals of diverse backgrounds with disabilities. The inclusive opportunities afforded to those with diverse backgrounds clearly are limited. Their voices and their self-advocacy are key to any resolution of these problems. Various disability advocates and human rights organizations also can contribute by holding annual symposiums, web-based educational series, and local programs to raise awareness and provide education to those affected by diversity-related barriers. Furthermore, service providers can facilitate self-advocacy by using person-centered planning as a primary tool. Service providers, including administrators, teachers, employers, and vocational coaches, are centrally involved as are their abilities to understand and provide culturally competent and responsive services to a diverse population. These individuals must be equipped with the tools necessary to understand and provide services for individuals with severe disabilities from diverse backgrounds (e.g., Rogers-Adkinson, Ochoa, & Delgado, 2003).

HUMAN RIGHTS

TASH (2010) called for eliminating the use of aversive interventions as an acceptable strategy for behavior modification or control and promoting positive and proactive strategies to prevent dangerous situations.

Current Status

The goal to limit or eliminate aversive interventions remains at the forefront of the human rights movement for individuals with severe disabilities as the public's awareness continues to grow regarding 1) the use of aversive interventions to address challenging behavior and 2) the negative outcomes associated with such interventions. Several significant advances have been made since the mid-1990s that are indicative of progress. First, advances in understanding trauma and development have made it possible to identify the adverse outcomes associated with aversive interventions; among these outcomes are elevated risk of injury or death, short- and long-term effects similar to that of posttraumatic stress disorder, and imbalances in cortisol levels that lead to negative physical and emotional consequences (e.g., anxiety, inability to control emotional outbursts, elevated resting heart rates and blood pressure) (Kennedy & Mohr, 2001). Having access to this science-based evidence has prompted many to reconsider using aversive practices.

The empirical validation of positive behavior interventions and supports (PBIS) is another important advancement toward eliminating aversive interventions. More than two decades of research provide strong evidence for using positive and proactive strategies to address challenging behavior (e.g., Goh & Bambara, 2010; Marquis et al., 2000). The underlying principles of PBIS are characterized as educative, proactive, and respectful (Bambara & Kern, 2005); thus, PBIS provides an ethical, person-centered alternative to using aversive strategies that typically are viewed as noneducational, reactive, and disrespectful. Finally, efforts have been made to 1) monitor the use and document the prevalence of aversive interventions, 2) inform stakeholders of the known dangers of aversive strategies, and 3) shift policy at the state and federal level (e.g., Keeping All Students Safe Act of 2013 [H.R. 1893]).

Clear efforts have been made to identify the extent to which aversive interventions are employed (e.g., Butler, 2009; National Disability Rights Network, 2009), but several barriers limit the ability to gauge the current state of aversive interventions used with individuals with severe disabilities. The limited monitoring of aversive intervention application, both their incidence and prevalence, is of primary concern (Kennedy & Mohr, 2001). The Government Accountability Office reviewed federal and state laws pertaining to aversive practices and found no mandated system in place to collect or report information on using such practices, whereas only five states gathered this information (Kutz, 2009). Most cases of death and abuse likely are undocumented, even though reports exposed hundreds of death or abuse cases attributed to aversive interventions (Kutz, 2009), thus clouding the extent to which individuals with severe disabilities are subjected to harmful behavioral practices. A second concern involves the divergent policies governing the application of aversive interventions at the state level and the absence of such at the federal level. Although only 30 states have protections against restraint and seclusion (Butler, 2012), these policies differ state to state (Kutz, 2009). The absence of federal regulations that protect individuals with disabilities from aversive practices is perhaps most disappointing. The Children's Health Care Act of 2000 (PL 106-310) protects children from these practices in certain facilities that receive government funding (e.g., hospitals, group homes); yet, these protections do not extend to public or private schools. Furthermore, IDEA 2004 includes language that emphasizes using positive and proactive practices to address challenging behavior but still does not contain explicit language that limits aversive interventions.

Future Directions

Several key areas of research need to be addressed so that the goal of limiting or eliminating the use of aversive practices as behavioral interventions can be achieved. It is clear that available data reflecting the prevalence of aversive intervention use are severely limited; thus, research efforts are needed to document the frequency of occurrence, and these data will provide a quantitative description from which decisions can be made. Qualitative data that describe such cases will show the extent to which and the conditions under which certain aversive practices are used (e.g., diagnoses of recipients, language of existing behavioral support plan). Although several reports have exemplified this research approach (e.g., National Disability Rights Network, 2009), qualitative data are limited to a presumably unrepresentative sample of documented cases; thus, data collection must occur on a larger scale to account for this limitation. Research directed toward the following are also of value: 1) identifying barriers to implementing PBIS interventions in schools and other settings (e.g., administrative supports needed to initiate and sustain PBIS) and 2) identifying factors contributing to using aversive interventions in these settings (e.g., lack of education, perceptions, attitudes, and beliefs regarding punishment). Research directed toward these issues can provide an evidence base that will inform the development of teaching programs (e.g., teacher preparation programs, professional development) and promote positive systems change within school and residential settings.

Implementing policies and laws either at the federal or state level that eliminate or restrict using aversive practices and set forth clear guidelines regarding their highly restricted potential use under special conditions, such as emergency situations, is a necessary future direction (see Keeping All Students Safe Act of 2013). The efficacy of aversive techniques as a behavioral intervention has limited support; yet, programs serving individuals with disabilities continue to use these techniques to address challenging behavior. A staggering 71% of schools apply behavioral support plans that do not contain research-based interventions (Butler, 2009). It is critical to enforce existing laws that govern the programs in which individuals with disabilities participate and require use of scientifically based practices (i.e., IDEA 2004); individuals with disabilities will be more likely to receive respectful, effective behavioral supports with this enforcement. Furthermore, a mandatory reporting system must be in place to ensure that programs serving individuals with disabilities comply with such policies. Mandatory reporting systems also may serve a research purpose whereby trends in prevalence rates and other reported variables may be examined.

Finally, the need for policy reform is illustrated further by the fact that many individuals who implement aversive interventions do not have training in PBIS or in the design of safety plans or crisis management strategies. It seems logical that an individual's lack of education ultimately affects the extent to which an individual uses such interventions. Policies must be established that require the obligatory training of all personnel, ranging from paraprofessionals to school administrators, in the use of research-validated behavioral interventions. All personnel must be equipped with the necessary skills to keep children and adults safe because safety often is a schoolwide or programwide priority. Mandatory education of all personnel with regard to a program's legal obligations related to various aspects of behavioral interventions also is important.

The education and advocacy efforts of various players fill an important role in both the disuse of aversive interventions and the use of positive, proactive interventions to address challenging behavior. A parent or guardian is one of the most powerful advocates for an individual with a disability. Parents and guardians must be informed of their rights and their children's rights. Although it is expected that programs assisting individuals with disabilities will take on this responsibility, this may not necessarily be the case. For example, almost three quarters of parents do not consent to using aversive practices (Butler, 2009). Thus, schools violate the informed consent requirement of IDEA 2004 and the requirement that all members of an individualized education program team, including parents and guardians, must participate in decision making when they do not include families in planning or inform them of planned aversive interventions. This indicates that those who are working with individuals with disabilities must receive education, including parents and guardians. They must specifically understand their legal obligations under the requirements of IDEA 2004 and the importance of parental consent and involvement, as well as comprehend the technology of PBIS. Webinars and dissemination of information packets may serve as viable methods to educate a large number of players in a cost-effective manner (e.g., Alliance to Prevent Restraint, Averisive Interventions, and Seclusion, 2005). Finally, advocacy efforts to educate policy makers about the importance of enforcing policies to protect all individuals who experience challenging behavior must continue. This is especially critical at a time when no federal policies or laws exist that serve to prevent or limit using potentially harmful behavioral interventions.

CONCLUSION

TASH's (2010) national agenda items spelled out bold but relevant goals on inclusive education, community living, employment, diversity and cultural competency, and human rights. This review, along with earlier chapters in this book, reveal some similarities across the current status of and the future directions for these five agenda items. Furthermore, areas of overlap occurring in pertinent policies and legal history and in the key players involved in each agenda item were identified. Current status of these goals indicate that people with severe disabilities consistently fall behind those without disabilities or with less serious disabilities in their being included with peers in schools, living normalized lives in the community, being employed, having services equally available across diverse subgroups, and having their human rights respected. Our recommendations on future directions reveal several common yet critical themes—better dependent measures, the need for continued monitoring, and research that goes beyond monitoring to understand influential factors and their effects on people. Improvements in most of the five areas affect one or more of the other areas in positive ways. Yet, vast discrepancies for people with severe disabilities in all these areas exist, despite a network of supportive laws put in place since the mid-1970s, along with court cases that relate to each agenda item.

The many discrepancies between typical citizens' lives and the lives of those with severe disabilities raise several questions. Why are these laws not enforced and the disparities rectified? Why do typical citizens seem unmotivated to treat people with disabilities in the same way as those without disabilities? Does it take personal involvement with someone who has a disability (e.g., daughter, brother, cousin, friend) to see the discrepancies and be motivated to resolve them? History has shown the positive influence that family members with disabilities can have— Rosemary Kennedy was a force on her brother John F. Kennedy, and thus on the nation, in initiating legal protections and in shifting attitudes from shame to caring. Trends tell us that things are better now in all these five areas than they were in the 1960s; these improvements appear to have been accompanied by a gradual positive shift in public attitudes during this period, made possible through parental action and societal familiarity based on positive examples of inclusion. Although fluctuations in economic well-being may pose the biggest threat to this current progress, examples of the fiscal savings that may come with meaningful improvement in services and supports were reviewed.

It will take organizations such as TASH to act as the bellwether and influence these trends and foretell future progress. To do so will require a range of powerful tools that affect public opinion and create supportive societal conditions, including 1) relevant research findings translated and disseminated through public media and technology venues, 2) informative personal histories of individuals with severe disabilities and their families portrayed in the media, 3) political advocacy for improvements in policy and laws, 4) strategic court cases to oppose legal and ethical violations, and 5) masterful use of technology to educate the lay public and decision makers about the optimistic possibilities for people with severe disabilities.

REFERENCES

Allen, K.G. (2001). *Long-term care: Implications of Supreme Court's Olmstead decision are still unfolding.* Retrieved from http://www.gao.gov/new.items/d011167t.pdf

Alliance to Prevent Restraint, Aversive Interventions, and Seclusion. (2005). *In the name of treatment: A parent's guide to protecting your child from the use of restraint, aversive interventions, and seclusion.* Retrieved from http://66.147.244.209/~tashorg/wp-content/uploads/2011/01/APRAIS_In-the-Name-of-Treatmentfinal.pdf

Americans with Disabilities Act (ADA) of 1990, PL 101-336, 42 U.S.C. §§ 12101 et seq.

Americans with Disabilities Amendments Act (ADA) of 2008, PL 110-325, 42 U.S.C. §§ 12101 et seq.

Bambara, L.M., & Kern, L. (2005). *Individualized supports for students with problem behaviors: Designing positive behavior plans.* New York, NY: Guilford Press.

Butler, J. (2009). *Unsafe in the schoolhouse: Abuse of children with disabilities.* Retrieved from http://www.copaa.org/pdf/UnsafeCOPAAMay_27_2009.pdf

Butler, J. (2012). *How safe is the schoolhouse? An analysis of state seclusion and restraint laws and policies.* Retrieved from http://www.autcom.org/pdf/HowSafeSchoolhouse.pdf

Butterworth, J., Smith, F.A., Hall, A.C., Migliore, A., Winsor, J., Domin, D., & Timmons, J.C. (2012). *StateData: The national report on employment services and outcomes.* Boston: Institute for Community Inclusion, University of Massachusetts.

Carter, E.W., Moss, C.K., Hoffman, A., Chung, Y., & Sisco, L. (2011). Efficacy and social validity of peer support arrangements for adolescents with disabilities. *Exceptional Children, 78,* 107–125.

Children's Health Care Act of 2000, PL 106-310, 114 Stat. 1101.

Cimera, R.E., Wehman, P., West, M., & Burgess, S. (2012). Do sheltered workshops enhance employment outcomes for adults with autism spectrum disorder? *Autism, 16,* 87–94.

Claes, C., Van Hove, G., Vandevelde, S., van Loon, J., & Schalock, R.L. (2010). Person-centered planning: Analysis of research and effectiveness. *Intellectual and Developmental Disabilities, 48,* 432–453.

Cornish, K., Roberts, J.E., & Scerif, G. (2012). Editorial: Capturing developmental trajectories of change in persons with intellectual and developmental disability. *American Journal on Intellectual and Developmental Disabilities, 117,* 83–86.

Davis, E., Nicolas, C., Waters, E., Cook, K., Gibbs, L., Gosch, A., & Ravens-Sieberer, U. (2007). Parent-proxy and child self-reported health-related quality of life: Using qualitative methods to explain the discordance. *Quality of Life Research, 16,* 863–871.

Developmental Disabilities Assistance and Bill of Rights Act Amendments of 2000, PL 106-402, 42 U.S.C. §§ 6000 et seq.

Emerson, E., Fujiura, G.T., & Hatton, C. (2007). International perspectives. In S.L. Odom, R.H. Horner, M.E. Snell, & J. Blacher (Eds.), *Handbook of developmental disabilities* (pp. 593–613). New York, NY: Guilford Press.

Fair Labor Standards Act of 1938, PL 106-151, 29 U.S.C. §§ 201 *et seq.*

Fair Wages for Workers with Disabilities Act of 2011, H.R. 3086.

Felce, D., & Perry, J. (2007). Living with support in the community. In S.L. Odom, R.H. Horner, M.E. Snell, & J. Blacher (Eds.), *Handbook of developmental disabilities* (pp. 410–428). New York, NY: Guilford Press.

Fisher, M., & Meyer, L.H. (2002). Development and social competence after two years for students enrolled in inclusive and self-contained educational programs. *Research and Practice for Persons with Severe Disabilities, 27,* 165–174.

Flannery, K.B., Newton, S., Horner, R.H., Slovic, R., Blumberg, R., & Ard, W.R. (2000). The impact of person centered planning on the content and organization of individual supports. *Career Development for Exceptional Individuals, 23,* 123–137.

Giangreco, M.F. (2011). Educating students with severe disabilities: Foundational concepts and practices. In M.E. Snell & F. Brown (Eds.), *Instruction of students with severe disabilities* (7th ed., pp. 1–30). Upper Saddle River, NJ: Pearson.

Giangreco, M.F., Broer, S.M., & Suter, J.C. (2011). Guidelines for selecting alternatives to overreliance on paraprofessionals: Field-testing in inclusion-oriented schools. *Remedial and Special Education, 32,* 22–38.

Giangreco, M.F., Hurley, S.M., & Suter, J.C. (2009). Personnel utilization and general class placement of students with disabilities: Ranges and ratios. *Intellectual and Developmental Disabilities, 47,* 53–56.

Goh, A.E., & Bambara, L.M. (2010). Individualized positive behavior support in school settings: A meta-analysis. *Remedial and Special Education.* Advance online publication. doi: 10.1177/0741932510383990

Habib, D. (2009). *Including Samuel: A documentary.* Durham: Institute on Disability/University Center for Excellence on Disability, University of New Hampshire.

Hasnain, R., Kondratowicz, D.M., Portillo, N., Balcazar, F., Johnson, T., Gould, R., ... Hanz, K. (2009). *The use of culturally adapted competency interventions to improve rehabilitation service outcomes for culturally diverse individuals with disabilities.* Retrieved from http://www.ncddr.org/partners/subgroup/resources/hasnain_competency_interventions_review_2010.pdf

Heller, T., Miller, A., & Hsieh, K. (2002). Eight-year follow-up of the impact of environmental characteristics on the well-being of adults with developmental disabilities. *Mental Retardation, 40,* 366–378.

Higher Education Opportunity Act of 2008, H.R. 4137.

Holburn, S., Jacobson, J.W., Schwartz, A. A., Flory, M.J., & Vietze, P.M. (2004). The Willowbrook Futures Project: A longitudinal analysis of person-centered planning. *American Journal of Mental Retardation, 109,* 63–76.

Hughes, C., Cosgriff, J., Agran, M., & Washington, B.H. (2013). Student self-determination: A preliminary investigation of the role of participation in inclusive settings. *Education and Training in Autism and Developmental Disabilities, 48,* 3–17.

Hughson, E.A., Moodie, S., & Uditsky, B. (2006). *The story of inclusive post secondary education in Alberta: Final research report 2004–2005.* Alberta, Canada: Alberta Association for Community Living.

Hunt, P., Soto, G., Maier, J., & Doering, K. (2003). Collaborative teaming to support students at risk and students with severe disabilities in general education classrooms. *Exceptional Children, 69,* 315–332.

Individuals with Disabilities Education Act (IDEA) of 1990, PL 101-476, 20 U.S.C. §§ 1400 *et seq.*

Individuals with Disabilities Education Improvement Act (IDEA) of 2004, PL 108-446, 20 U.S.C. §§ 1400 *et seq.*

Inge, K.J., Wehman, P., Revell, G., Erickson, D., Butterworth, J., & Gilmore, D.S. (2009). Survey results from a national survey of community rehabilitation providers holding special wage certificates. *Journal of Vocational Rehabilitation 30,* 67–85.

Johnson, R.B., & Onwuegbuzie, A.J. (2004). Mixed methods research: A research paradigm whose time has come. *Educational Researcher, 33,* 14–26.

Keeping All Students Safe Act of 2013, H.R. 1893.

Kennedy, S.S., & Mohr, W.K. (2001). A prolegomenon on restraint of children: Implicating constitutional rights. *American Journal of Orthopsychiatry, 77,* 26–37.

Klingner, J.K., Blanchett, W.J., & Harry, B. (2007). Race, culture, and developmental disabilities. In S.L. Odom, R.H. Horner, M.E. Snell, & J. Blacher (Eds.), *Handbook of developmental disabilities* (pp. 55–75). New York, NY: Guilford Press.

Kutz, G.D. (2009). *Seclusions and restraints: Selected cases of death and abuse at public and private schools and treatment centers.* Retrieved from http://www.gao.gov/assets/130/122526.pdf

Larson, S.A., & Lakin, K.C. (2010). Expenditure patterns for ICF/MR and HCBS long-term supports for persons with intellectual or developmental disabilities: Fiscal years 2004–2009, with projections to fiscal year 2012. *Intellectual and Developmental Disabilities, 48,* 480–484.

Larson, S.A., Lakin, K.C., Salmi, P., Smith, D., Scott, N., & Webster, A. (2011). Children and youth with intellectual or developmental disabilities living in congregate care settings (1977–2009): Healthy People 2010 Objective 6.7b outcomes (Revised). *Intellectual and Developmental Disabilities, 49,* 209–213.

Lee, S.S. (2009). *Overview of the Federal Higher Education Opportunity Act Reauthorization.* http://www.thinkcollege.net/images/stories/HEAC_Overview.pdf

Mank, D. (2007). Employment. In S.L. Odom, R.H. Horner, M.E., Snell, & J. Bacher (Eds.), *Handbook of developmental disabilities* (pp. 390–409). New York, NY: Guilford Press.

Marquis, J.G., Horner, R.H., Carr, E.G., Turnbull, A.P., Thompson, M., Behrens, G.A., ... Doolabh, A. (2000). A meta-analysis of positive behavior support. In R. Gersten, E.P. Schiller, & S. Vaughn (Eds.), *Contemporary special education research: Syntheses of the knowledge base on critical instructional issues* (pp. 125–161). Mahwah, NJ: Lawrence Erlbaum Associates.

National Disability Rights Network. (2009). *School is not supposed to hurt: Investigative report on abusive restraint and seclusion in schools.* Retrieved from http://www.disabilityrightsohio.org/sites/default/.../NDRNAbuseNeglectReport.pdf

Odom, S.L., Bitztum, J., Wolery, R., Lieber, J., Sandall, S., Hanson, M.J. ... Horn, E. (2004). Preschool inclusion in the United States: A review of research from an ecological systems perspective. *Journal of Research in Special Education Needs, 4,* 17–49.

Oeseburg, B., Dijkstra, G.J., Goothoff, J.W., Reijneveld, S.A., & Jansen, E. (2011). Prevalence of chronic health conditions in children with intellectual disability: A systematic literature review. *Intellectual and Developmental Disabilities, 49,* 59–85.

Olmstead v. L.C. (98-536) 527 U.S. 581 (1999).

Rogan, P., & Rinne, S. (2011). National call for organizational change from sheltered to integrated employment. *Intellectual and Developmental Disabilities, 49,* 248–260.

Rogers-Adkinson, D.L., Ochoa, T.A., & Delgado, B. (2003). Developing cross-cultural competence: Serving families of children with significant developmental needs. *Focus on Autism and Other Developmental Disabilities, 18,* 4–8.

Rusch, F.R., & Braddock, D. (2004). Adult day programs versus supported employment (1988–2002): Spending and service practices of mental retardation and developmental disabilities state agencies. *Research and Practice for Persons with Severe Disabilities, 29,* 237–242.

Ryndak, D.L., Alper, S., Hughes, C., & McDonnell, J. (2012). Documenting impact of educational contexts on long-term outcomes for students with significant disabilities. *Education and Training in Autism and Developmental Disabilities, 47,* 127–138.

Salmi, P., Scott, N., Webster, A., Larson, S.A., & Lakin, K.C. (2010). Residential services for people with intellectual or developmental disabilities at the 20th anniversary of the Americans with Disabilities Act, the 10th anniversary of Olmstead, and in the year of community living. *Intellectual and Developmental Disabilities, 48,* 168–171.

Smith, D., Lakin, K.C., Larson, S., & Salmi, P. (2011). Changes in residential arrangements of persons with intellectual and developmental disabilities in the decade following the Olmstead decision of 1999. *Intellectual and Developmental Disabilities, 49,* 53–56.

Snell, M.E., & Eichner, S.J. (1989). Integration for students with profound disabilities. In F. Brown & D. Lehr (Eds.), *Persons with profound disabilities: Issues and practices* (pp. 109–138). Baltimore, MD: Paul H. Brookes Publishing Co.

Stancliffe, R.J., Lakin, K.C., Larson, S.A. Engler, J., Taub, S., Fortune, J., & Bershadsky, J. (2012). Demographic characteristics, health conditions, and residential service use in adults with Down syndrome in 25 U.S. states. *Intellectual and Developmental Disabilities, 50,* 92–108.

Stoneman, Z. (2007). Disability research methodology: Current issues and future challenges. In S.L. Odom, R.H. Horner, M.E. Snell, & J. Blacher (Eds.), *Handbook of developmental disabilities* (pp. 35–54). New York, NY: Guilford Press.

Storey, K. (2010). Smart houses and smart technology: Overview and implications for independent living and supported living services. *Intellectual and Developmental Disabilities, 48,* 464–469.

TASH. (2010). *Diversity and cultural competency in disability advocacy initiative: Working to empower persons of diverse backgrounds with disabilities and their families in disability rights.* Retrieved from http://66.147.244.209/~tashorg/wp-content/uploads/2010/10/TASH_Diversity-Cultural-Competency-Initiative.pdf

Taylor-Ritzler, T., Balcazar, F.E., Suarez-Balcazar, Y., Kilbury, R., Francisco, A., & James, M. (2010). Engaging ethnically diverse individuals with disabilities in the vocational rehabilitation system: Themes of empowerment and oppression. *Journal of Vocational Rehabilitation, 33,* 3–14.

Turnbull, H.R., Stowe, M.J., Turnbull, A.P., & Schrandt, M.S. (2007). Public policy and developmental disabilities. In S.L. Odom, R.H. Horner, M.E., Snell, & J. Blacher (Eds.), *Handbook of developmental disabilities* (pp. 15–34). New York, NY: Guilford Press.

U.S. Department of Education. (2010a). *Percent of children ages 6 through 21 receiving education services inside a regular class 40% to 79% of the day and by the race/ethnic categories and state.* Retrieved from http://www.ideadata.org/arc_toc12.asp#partbCC

U.S. Department of Education. (2010b). *Percent of children ages 6 through 21 receiving education services inside a regular class less than 40% of the day and by the race/ethnic categories and state.* Retrieved from http://www.ideadata .org/arc_toc12.asp#partbCC

U.S. Department of Education. (2010c). *Percent of students ages 6 through 21 served under IDEA, Part B, by educational environment and state.* Retrieved from http://www.ideadata.org/arc_toc12 .asp#partbCC

U.S. Department of Education. (2012). *Part B educational environments data collection for students ages 6–21.* Retrieved from https://www.ideadata.org/docs/6-21 EdEnvironsPtBQA.pdf

U.S. Department of Health and Human Services. (2000). *Focus Area 6: Disability and secondary conditions.* Retrieved from http://www.cdc.gov/nchs/data/hpdata2010/ hp2010_final_review_focus_area_06.pdf

U.S. Department of Labor. (2008). *Fact Sheet #39: The employment of workers with disabilities at special minimum wages under section 14(c) of the Fair Labor Standards Act.* Retrieved from http://www.dol.gov/whd/regs/compliance/ whdfs39.pdf

Vignes, C., Coley, N., Grandjean, H., Godeau, E., & Arnaud, C. (2008). Measuring children's attitudes toward peers with disabilities: A review of instruments. *Developmental Medicine and Child Neurology, 50,* 182–189.

Washington, B.H., Hughes, C., & Cosgriff, J.C. (2012). High-poverty youth: Self-determination and involvement in educational planning. *Career Development and Transition for Exceptional Individuals, 35,* 14–28.

Wolf, L.A., Armour, B.S., & Campbell, V.A. (2008). Racial and ethnic disparities in self-rated health status amount adults with and without disabilities: United States, 2004–2006. *Morbidity and Mortality Weekly Report, 57,* 1069–1073.

Workforce Investment Act (WIA) of 1998, PL 105-220, 29 U.S.C. §§ 2801 *et seq.*

Zafft, C., Hart, D., & Zimbrich, K. (2004). College career connection: A study of youth with intellectual disabilities and the impact of postsecondary education. *Education and Training in Developmental Disabilities, 39,* 45–53.

Index

Page numbers followed by *f* indicate figures; those followed by *t* indicate tables.